Improving E-Commerce Web Applications Through Business Intelligence Techniques

G. Sreedhar
Rashtriya Sanskrit Vidyapeetha (Deemed University), India

A volume in the Advances in E-Business Research (AEBR) Book Series

IGI Global
DISSEMINATOR OF KNOWLEDGE

Published in the United States of America by
IGI Global
Business Science Reference (an imprint of IGI Global)
701 E. Chocolate Avenue
Hershey PA, USA 17033
Tel: 717-533-8845
Fax: 717-533-8661
E-mail: cust@igi-global.com
Web site: http://www.igi-global.com

Library of Congress Cataloging-in-Publication Data

Names: Sreedhar, G., 1974- editor.
Title: Improving e-commerce web applications through business intelligence techniques / G. Sreedhar, editor.
Description: Hershey : Business Science Reference, [2017]
Identifiers: LCCN 2017019853| ISBN 9781522536468 (hardcover) | ISBN 9781522536475 (ebook)
Subjects: LCSH: Electronic commerce--Computer programs. | Data mining.
Classification: LCC HF5548.32 .I49 2017 | DDC 658.8/72028553--dc23 LC record available at https://lccn.loc.gov/2017019853

This book is published in the IGI Global book series Advances in E-Business Research (AEBR) (ISSN: 1935-2700; eISSN: 1935-2719)

British Cataloguing in Publication Data
A Cataloguing in Publication record for this book is available from the British Library.

Advances in E-Business Research (AEBR) Book Series

In Lee
Western Illinois University, USA

ISSN:1935-2700
EISSN:1935-2719

Mission

Technology has played a vital role in the emergence of e-business and its applications incorporate strategies. These processes have aided in the use of electronic transactions via telecommunications networks for collaborating with business partners, buying and selling of goods and services, and customer service. Research in this field continues to develop into a wide range of topics, including marketing, psychology, information systems, accounting, economics, and computer science.

The **Advances in E-Business Research (AEBR) Book Series** provides multidisciplinary references for researchers and practitioners in this area. Instructors, researchers, and professionals interested in the most up-to-date research on the concepts, issues, applications, and trends in the e-business field will find this collection, or individual books, extremely useful. This collection contains the highest quality academic books that advance understanding of e-business and addresses the challenges faced by researchers and practitioners.

Coverage

- Interorganizational information systems
- E-marketing
- E-business technology investment strategies
- Web 2.0
- Web advertising
- E-CRM
- Virtual organization
- Trends in e-business models and technologies
- B2B e-marketplaces
- E-business standardizations

The Advances in E-Business Research (AEBR) Book Series (ISSN 1935-2700) is published by IGI Global, 701 E. Chocolate Avenue, Hershey, PA 17033-1240, USA, www.igi-global.com. This series is composed of titles available for purchase individually; each title is edited to be contextually exclusive from any other title within the series. For pricing and ordering information please visit http://www.igi-global.com/book-series/advances-business-research/37144. Postmaster: Send all address changes to above address.

Titles in this Series

For a list of additional titles in this series, please visit: www.igi-global.com/book-series

Mobile Platforms, Design, and Apps for Social Commerce
Jean-Éric Pelet (ESCE International Business School, Paris, France)
Business Science Reference • copyright 2017 • 411pp • H/C (ISBN: 9781522524694) • US $215.00 (our price)

The Internet of Things in the Modern Business Environment
In Lee (Western Illinois University, USA)
Business Science Reference • copyright 2017 • 340pp • H/C (ISBN: 9781522521044) • US $205.00 (our price)

Key Challenges and Opportunities in Web Entrepreneurship
Alexandru Capatina (Dunarea de Jos University of Galati, Romania) and Elisa Rancati (University of Milan – Bicocca, Italy & Beta Consulting, Italy)
Business Science Reference • copyright 2017 • 291pp • H/C (ISBN: 9781522524663) • US $205.00 (our price)

Apps Management and E-Commerce Transactions in Real-Time
Sajad Rezaei (Taylor's University, Malaysia)
Business Science Reference • copyright 2017 • 379pp • H/C (ISBN: 9781522524496) • US $210.00 (our price)

Driving Innovation and Business Success in the Digital Economy
Ionica Oncioiu (Titu Maiorescu University, Romania)
Business Science Reference • copyright 2017 • 321pp • H/C (ISBN: 9781522517795) • US $200.00 (our price)

Social Media Listening and Monitoring for Business Applications
N. Raghavendra Rao (FINAIT Consultancy Services, India)
Business Science Reference • copyright 2017 • 470pp • H/C (ISBN: 9781522508465) • US $205.00 (our price)

Analyzing the Strategic Role of Social Networking in Firm Growth and Productivity
Vladlena Benson (Kingston University, UK) Ronald Tuninga (Kingston Business School, UK) and George Saridakis (Kingston University, UK)
Business Science Reference • copyright 2017 • 525pp • H/C (ISBN: 9781522505594) • US $220.00 (our price)

Securing Transactions and Payment Systems for M-Commerce
Sushila Madan (University of Delhi, India) and Jyoti Batra Arora (Banasthali Vidyapeeth University, India)
Business Science Reference • copyright 2016 • 349pp • H/C (ISBN: 9781522502364) • US $205.00 (our price)

IGI Global
DISSEMINATOR OF KNOWLEDGE

701 East Chocolate Avenue, Hershey, PA 17033, USA
Tel: 717-533-8845 x100 • Fax: 717-533-8661
E-Mail: cust@igi-global.com • www.igi-global.com

Table of Contents

Preface xiii

Acknowledgment xvi

Chapter 1
A Framework to Improve Performance of E-Commerce Websites 1
G. Sreedhar, Rashtriya Sanskrit Vidyapeetha (Deemed University), India

Chapter 2
Identification of User Preference for Multi-Criteria Reporting in Business Intelligence: A Case Study on Banking Business 16
Martin Aruldoss, Central University of Tamil Nadu, India
Miranda Lakshmi Travis, Bharathiyar University, India
Prasanna Venkatesan Venkatasamy, Pondicherry University, India

Chapter 3
Botnet Threats to E-Commerce Web Applications and Their Detection 48
Rizwan Ur Rahman, Maulana Azad National Institute of Technology, India
Deepak Singh Tomar, Maulana Azad National Institute of Technology, India

Chapter 4
Secure Framework for E-Commerce Applications in Cloud Environment 82
Sonika Shrivastava, Maulana Azad National Institute of Technology, India
R. K. Pateriya, Maulana Azad National Institute of Technology, India

Chapter 5
E-Commerce Business Model 110
Durga Patel, University Institute of Technology, India
Sachin Goyal, University Institute of Technology, India
Ratish Agarwal, University Institute of Technology, India

Chapter 6
Search Optimization to Select an Item Across E-Commerce Platforms: App Development – QuickCompare 130
Sridevi M., Anurag Group of Institutions, India
Rajeshwara Rao R., JNTU Kakinada, India
Varaprasad Rao M., CMR Technical Campus, India

Chapter 7
E-Commerce and Its Software 148
Rebika Rai, Sikkim University, India
Prashant Chettri, HRDD Sikkim, India
Lekhika Chettri, Sikkim University, India

Chapter 8
Security Issues in E-Commerce 179
Arram Sriram, Anurag Group of Institutions, India
Adiraju Prashanth Rao, Anurag Group of Institutions, India

Chapter 9
Secure Payment Modes Technology for E-Commerce Applications 208
Niteesha Sharma, Anurag Group of Institutions, India
Adiraju Rao Prashanth, Anurag Group of Institutions, India

Chapter 10
Design Methodology for Effective User Interface Design for E-Commerce Applications 223
Namratha Birudaraju, Anurag Group of Institutions, India
Adiraju Prasanth Rao, Anurag Group of Institutions, India

Chapter 11
Electronic Commerce and Decision Support Systems: Theories and Applications 251
Kijpokin Kasemsap, Suan Sunandha Rajabhat University, Thailand

Chapter 12
Application of Opinion Mining in E-Commerce 271
Brojo Kishore Mishra, C. V. Raman College of Engineering, India
Rekhanjali Sahoo, BPUT Rourkela, India

Chapter 13
Applications of Social Graphs: Author, Email, Telephone Using Graph Mining Techniques 297
Bapuji Rao, Indira Gandhi Institute of Technology, India
Sasmita Mishra, Indira Gandhi Institute of Technology, India
Sarojananda Mishra, Indira Gandhi Institute of Technology, India

Compilation of References 332

About the Contributors 357

Index 362

Detailed Table of Contents

Preface xiii

Acknowledgment xvi

Chapter 1
A Framework to Improve Performance of E-Commerce Websites 1
G. Sreedhar, Rashtriya Sanskrit Vidyapeetha (Deemed University), India

The growth of the world wide web has made business functions fast and easier. E-commerce has provided cost effective ways of doing business. E-commerce websites have the advantage of reaching a large number of customers regardless of distance and time limitations. The advantage of e-commerce over traditional businesses is faster speed and lower expenses for both businessmen and customers. The main objective of the chapter is to provide an efficient framework to analyse the performance of e-commerce websites and suggest the factors that need to be incorporated in e-commerce websites for better business intelligence. The purpose of business intelligence is to support better business decision making. In this chapter, a detailed description of business intelligence enables the web developer and end user to know the insights of e-commerce web applications. The methodology is comprehensive and it elaborates all aspects of the performance of a website.

Chapter 2
Identification of User Preference for Multi-Criteria Reporting in Business Intelligence: A Case Study on Banking Business 16
Martin Aruldoss, Central University of Tamil Nadu, India
Miranda Lakshmi Travis, Bharathiyar University, India
Prasanna Venkatesan Venkatasamy, Pondicherry University, India

Business intelligence (BI) is an integrated set of tools used to support the transformation of data into information in order to support decision making. Among different functionalities, reporting plays a significant role that provides information to its readers to make better decisions. BI lacks user-specific reporting to the different levels of users of an organization. Different users require different kinds of reporting with respect to different requirement (criteria) in an organization. A multi-criteria reporting (MCR) finds the suitable information to suitable user based on the multiple conflicting preferences of a user. Technique for order preference by similarity to ideal solution (TOPSIS) is the most popularly applied multi-criteria decision-making (MCDM) technique selected to identify different levels of user preference for MCR. Banking business is considered as a case study to identify user preference for MCR. This research also designs evaluation metrics for TOPSIS.

Chapter 3
Botnet Threats to E-Commerce Web Applications and Their Detection 48
Rizwan Ur Rahman, Maulana Azad National Institute of Technology, India
Deepak Singh Tomar, Maulana Azad National Institute of Technology, India

Security issues in e-commerce web applications are still exploratory, and in spite of an increase in e-commerce application research and development, lots of security challenges remain unanswered. Botnets are the most malicious threats to web applications, especially the e-commerce applications. Botnet is a network of BOTs. It executes automated scripts to launch different types of attack on web applications. Botnets are typically controlled by one or more hackers known as Bot masters and are exploited for different types of attacks including Dos (denial of service), DDos (distributed denial of service), phishing, spreading of malware, adware, Spyware, identity fraud, and logic bombs. The aim of this chapter is to scrutinize to what degree botnets can cause a threat to e-commerce security. In the first section, an adequate overview of botnets in the context of e-commerce security is presented in order to provide the reader with an understanding of the background for the remaining sections.

Chapter 4
Secure Framework for E-Commerce Applications in Cloud Environment 82
Sonika Shrivastava, Maulana Azad National Institute of Technology, India
R. K. Pateriya, Maulana Azad National Institute of Technology, India

There has been a massive increase in the use of the internet for shopping and payment. The ease and availability of the internet has accelerated the growth of online applications. E-commerce applications handle many sensitive pieces of data like financial or personal data, which are used for critical tasks like banking, socializing, shopping, and tax filling. Online financial service and shopping sites are an attractive target for fraudsters because money transactions are done through these sites. Credit card fraud, identity theft, and account hijack are key concerns for these organizations. These frauds cause financial loss and hurt the reputation of e-commerce sites. The use of the cloud platform has made these sites more productive, but at the same time, it has opened them to a variety of threats. This chapter describes a framework for credit card and identity fraud detection using big data analytics and machine learning techniques to make e-commerce sites more secure and efficient.

Chapter 5
E-Commerce Business Model.. 110
Durga Patel, University Institute of Technology, India
Sachin Goyal, University Institute of Technology, India
Ratish Agarwal, University Institute of Technology, India

This chapter provides an overview of the e-commerce business model, the history of e-commerce, the scope of e-commerce, the difference between e-commerce and traditional commerce, issues related to e-commerce, electronic data interchange, value chain, and supply chain, and the pros and cons and limitations of e-commerce.

Chapter 6
Search Optimization to Select an Item Across E-Commerce Platforms: App Development – QuickCompare 130
Sridevi M., Anurag Group of Institutions, India
Rajeshwara Rao R., JNTU Kakinada, India
Varaprasad Rao M., CMR Technical Campus, India

E-commerce is a transaction of buying or selling online. These sites have made life simpler by delivering products to your doorstep. The entire idea of e-commerce is to save the user's time while purchasing goods. This massive expansion of e-commerce gave rise to many applications for the user to choose to buy from. Therefore, people now spend more time comparing the prices of products on various applications before purchasing. This price comparison turned out to be a tedious task for users. With many applications available in the market, it is difficult for the user to navigate between apps to compare specifications like cost, life time, on-time delivery, customer satisfaction, etc. of products or items. So, this chapter explores the "Quick Compare" search, a solution for this hassle that provides instantaneous recommendations based on the end user's input. An android application is developed for this problem and it focuses on efficiency and interoperability.

Chapter 7
E-Commerce and Its Software 148
Rebika Rai, Sikkim University, India
Prashant Chettri, HRDD Sikkim, India
Lekhika Chettri, Sikkim University, India

Today we are moving into an era of "intangible" business processes, where business communication and transactions can be conducted anywhere, anytime, and with a simple click of a mouse. With the speedy amplification and expansion of technology, information systems have become a normal component of our everyday life. The phenomenal growth of the internet has led to the emergence of a great number of new technologies and one of the most important ones is the ability to conduct business over the internet. E-commerce is currently changing the way business is conducted by assisting business progressions and transactions with very few organizations debating whether or not to participate in it. E-commerce software is the engine behind the scenes of an online store, making it possible to easily manage inventory, add or remove products, calculate taxes, and everything else required to manage a website and fulfill orders.

Chapter 8
Security Issues in E-Commerce 179
Arram Sriram, Anurag Group of Institutions, India
Adiraju Prashanth Rao, Anurag Group of Institutions, India

E-commerce is selling and buying products in online shopping through the internet. When purchasing the products using internet, many security issues arise. These issues are to be addressed effectively and to be resolved. The security issue is an essential part of any transaction that takes place over the internet. Security becomes paramount not only for retailers but for any business that operates via the internet as the popularity of online shopping grows. This chapter focuses security protocols and their achievements in providing effective communication between end-users and business people.

Chapter 9
Secure Payment Modes Technology for E-Commerce Applications 208
Niteesha Sharma, Anurag Group of Institutions, India
Adiraju Rao Prashanth, Anurag Group of Institutions, India

E-commerce refers to business and customers buying and selling products online. There are significant improvements in the areas of initiating sale of products, placing orders, making payments, and transfer of funds. This has led to a much better global economy and better living standards for all. While buying products online, it is essential to know the payment method that ensures authentication and also many other security issues. There are many payments modes available in market today. This chapter presents different protocols and its security issues that relate to a specific payment mode.

Chapter 10
Design Methodology for Effective User Interface Design for E-Commerce Applications 223
Namratha Birudaraju, Anurag Group of Institutions, India
Adiraju Prasanth Rao, Anurag Group of Institutions, India

There are many customers who shop online. Many of these users interact with the system using well-defined user interfaces only. So, there is a need to develop effective user interfaces that are more user friendly, minimize the keyboard operations, and maximize effective interaction with the system. This chapter focuses on designing effective user interfaces by considering human parameters for e-commerce applications.

Chapter 11
Electronic Commerce and Decision Support Systems: Theories and Applications 251
Kijpokin Kasemsap, Suan Sunandha Rajabhat University, Thailand

Electronic Commerce (e-commerce) is an advanced online business tool that allows many companies to launch their websites and helps customers search their specific products shown on the websites. Decision Support Systems (DSSs) are computerized tools designed to facilitate strategic decision making. With the support of data mining and business intelligence methods, DSSs can effectively increase the performance of decision making and can present a sophisticated method of managerial thinking in a timely and effective manner toward gaining competitive advantage. The chapter argues that utilizing e-commerce and DSSs has the potential to enhance business performance and reach strategic goals in modern business.

Chapter 12
Application of Opinion Mining in E-Commerce 271
Brojo Kishore Mishra, C. V. Raman College of Engineering, India
Rekhanjali Sahoo, BPUT Rourkela, India

Social media has become an increasingly important part of our daily lives in the last few years. An area of substantial research is that of predicting product sales, such as books, video games, and movie tickets. Customer opinions play a very crucial role in daily life. When we have to make decisions, opinions of other individuals are also considered. Business organizations and corporate organizations are always eager to find consumer or individual views regarding their products, support, and service. In e-commerce, online shopping, and online tourism, it is very crucial to analyze the social data present on the web automatically; therefore, it is very important to create methods that automatically classify them. In this chapter, the authors do future prediction of financial market by taking past observations so that they can maximize their profit and orders can be placed on time.

Chapter 13
Applications of Social Graphs: Author, Email, Telephone Using Graph Mining Techniques 297
Bapuji Rao, Indira Gandhi Institute of Technology, India
Sasmita Mishra, Indira Gandhi Institute of Technology, India
Sarojananda Mishra, Indira Gandhi Institute of Technology, India

The chapter focuses on the applications of three social graphs, namely author, email, and telephone. The important application of author graph is the real network communications among the authors publishing research papers. The authors have proposed an algorithm to extract sub-graphs of authors. Individual email sending is more frequently within a group rather than group sending. Such group entities can be detected and analyzed further for knowledge discovery. For this, the authors have proposed an algorithm for extraction of strong and weak communicator's sub-graph. The telephone graph with multiple distinct types of connectivity information can be derived as layers and considered an important application. Therefore, the information retrieval can be represented as multi-layer graphs. Each layer has its own set of edges over the same underlying nodes of base-layer. Therefore, the edges of different layers typically are related but unique in behavior. For this, the authors have proposed an algorithm for representation of telephone graph as a multi-layer graph.

Compilation of References 332

About the Contributors 357

Index 362

Preface

In the present day scenario, the World Wide Web (WWW) is an important and popular information search tool. It provides convenient access to almost all kinds of information from education to entertainment. The World Wide Web is the key source of information and it is growing rapidly. The growth of World Wide Web and technologies has made business functions to be executed fast and easier. E-commerce has provided a cost efficient and effective way of doing business. As large amount of transactions are performed through ecommerce sites and the huge amount of data is stored, valuable knowledge can be obtained by applying the Web Mining techniques. E-commerce websites have the advantage of reaching a large number of customers regardless of distance and time limitations. The advantage of e-commerce over traditional businesses is the faster speed and the lower expenses for both e-commerce website owners and customers in completing customer transactions and orders. The World Wide Web (WWW) has become an important channel for information retrieval, electronic commerce and entertainment. E-commerce websites have the advantage of reaching a large number of customers regardless of distance and time limitations. The advantage of e-commerce over traditional businesses is the faster speed and the lower expenses for both e-commerce website owners and customers in completing customer transactions and orders. Because of the above advantages of e-commerce over traditional businesses, a lot of industries in different fields such as retailing, banking, medical services, transportation, communication, and education are establishing their business in the web. But creating a successful online business can be a very difficult and costly task if not taking into account e-commerce website design principles, web engineering techniques, and what e-commerce is supposed to do for the online business. Unfortunately, to most companies, web is nothing more than a place where transactions take place. All the e-commerce sites have high traffic. People surf the sites very often but the income is not always very high. So, the web data mining appeared and also nowadays much attention is paid to it. It is very important to apply web data mining to e-commerce in order to gather knowledge about users and rank data accordingly. It is advance successful technology through which information is filtered easier. So, web data mining became a publicly accessible source that gives promising results. With the use of e-commerce through internet, companies find a new and better way to do business. After developing the web site thought companies get benefits, they have to implement Web mining systems to understand their customers' profiles and to identify their own strength and weakness of their E-marketing efforts on the web through continuous improvements. Internet is a gold mine, but only for those companies who realize the importance of Web mining and adopt a Web mining strategy now. Web mining technology has many important roles that should be mentioned. It can automatically find, extract information from the variety web resources. It also develops, improves and enhances the quality and the efficiency of search engines, determines web pages or files, makes classifications. The main objective of book is to develop E-Commerce

Web Applications in view of end user accessibility and comfortability. Identifying insights of web sites for improving Business Intelligence of E-Commerce Applications. To extract and analyze useful information from large amounts of web documents using various data mining techniques. The book is going to be useful for E-Commerce vendors, E-Commerce Website developers, online customers, online banking vendors, researchers in the field of e-commerce web applications. The book is divided into 13 chapters and each chapter explores the core area of e-commerce web applications. The main objective of the Chapter 1 is to provide efficient frame work to analyze the performance of e-commerce website and suggests the factors that need to be incorporated in the e-commerce websites for better business intelligence. The purpose of Business Intelligence is to support better business decision making. In Chapter 1, detailed description of business intelligence, enable the web developer and end user to know the insights of e-commerce web applications. The methodology is very much comprehensive and it elaborates all aspects of performance of website. The Chapter 2 emphasizes the necessary information for Business Intelligence in order to support decision making. Business Intelligence lacks user specific reporting to the different levels of users of an organization. Different users require different kinds of reporting with respect to different criteria in an organization. A Multi Criteria Reporting (MCR) finds the suitable information to suitable user based on multiple conflicting preference of a user. Technique for Order Preference by Similarity to Ideal Solution (TOPSIS) is most popularly applied Multi Criteria Decision Making (MCDM) technique selected to identify different levels of user preference for MCR. In Chapter 2, attempt is made to design metrics for TOPSIS applications and these metrics are validated with banking multi criteria application. These metrics are designed from the functionalities of the TOPSIS method. In most of the MCDM applications, the evaluation parameters such as time complexity, space complexity, sensitivity analysis and ranking reversal are applied for validation. Security issues in e-commerce web application are still exploratory and in spite of an increase in e-commerce application research and development, lots of security challenges remain unanswered. Botnets are the most malicious threats to the web application, especially the e-commerce applications. The aim of Chapter 3 is to scrutinize to what degree botnets can cause a threat to e-commerce security. E-commerce applications handle many sensitive data like financial or personal data which are used for critical task like banking, socializing, shopping and tax filling. Online financial service and shopping sites is most attractive target for fraudster because money transactions are done through these sites. The Chapter 4 describes framework for credit card and identity fraud detection using big data analytics and machine learning technique to make e-commerce site more secure and efficient. E-commerce used in different areas like Exchange of digitized information, Direct marketing, selling and service, Online banking and billing, Secure distribution of data, Shopping on the World Wide Web, Product sales and services on the web. The Chapter 5 briefly provides overview on E-commerce business Model, History of E-commerce, Scope of E-commerce, Difference between E-commerce and Traditional commerce, issue related to E-Commerce, electronic data interchange, value chain and supply chain, pros & cons of E-commerce, Limitation. The massive expansion of e-commerce gave rise to many applications for the user to choose to buy from. Therefore, people now spend more time comparing the prices of products on various applications before purchasing. This price comparison turned out to be a tedious task for users. With many applications, available in the market, it is difficult for the user to navigate between apps to compare between specifications like cost, life time, on-time delivery, customer satisfaction, etc., of products or items. In Chapter 6, Quick Compare search, a solution for this hassle is provided instantaneous recommendations based on the end user's input. An android application is developed to this problem and it mainly focuses on efficiency and interoperability. In Chapter 7, overview of e-commerce business models and related e-commerce software were presented by the author. The security becomes a paramount as the popularity of online shopping grows exponentially in the present days, not only for retailers but for any business that operates via internet. The Chapter 8 mainly focuses security protocols and its achievement for providing effective communication between end-user and Business people. While buying products online, it is very essential to know the payment method which ensures authentication and also many other security issues. There are many payments modes are available in market today. The Chapter 9 presents different protocols survey and its security issues which relates to the specific payment mode. There is a need to develop effective user interfaces which should be more user friendly, minimizing the keyboard operations and maximizing effective interaction with the system. The Chapter 10 mainly focuses on designing effective user interface by considering human parameters for E-commerce applications. Decision Support Systems are the computerized tools designed to facilitate the strategic decision making. With the support of data mining and business intelligence methods, Decision Support Systems can effectively increase the performance of decision making and can present the sophisticated method of managerial thinking in the timely and effective manner toward gaining competitive advantage. The Chapter 11 describes that utilizing e-commerce and Decision Support Systems has the potential to enhance business performance and reach strategic goals in modern business. In E-commerce, online shopping and online tourism, it's very crucial to analyze the good amount of social data present on the web automatically therefore it's very important to create methods that automatically classify them. In Chapter 12, authors describe how to improve the business intelligence by considering previous observations of the e-commerce web application. The Chapter 13 focuses on the applications of three social graphs namely Author, Email, and Telephone. The important application of author graph is the real network communications among the authors publishing research papers. The authors have proposed an algorithm to extract sub-graphs of authors. Individual email sending is more frequently within a group rather than group sending.

Acknowledgment

I am very much happy and thankful to IGI Global for giving opportunity to produce my third book, *Improving E-Commerce Web Applications Through Business Intelligence Techniques*. I express deep sense of gratitude to the Kayla Wolfe, Jan Travers, Marianne Caesar, and other members of IGI Global who are supported directly or indirectly during book project. I am thankful to all authors who contributed their valuable efforts and ideas in the form of chapters in the book.

I am thankful to Honorable Vice Chancellor Prof V. Muralidhara Sarma, for his continuous support and encouragement in academic and research activities. I also thankful to registrar and other faculty members of Rashtriya Sanskrit Vidyapeetha, Tirupati for their support and kindness in completing the book.

Finally, I am very much thankful my parents and family members for their support and encouragement in achieving target goal in my academic career.

Chapter 1
A Framework to Improve Performance of E-Commerce Websites

G. Sreedhar
Rashtriya Sanskrit Vidyapeetha (Deemed University), India

ABSTRACT

The growth of the world wide web has made business functions fast and easier. E-commerce has provided cost effective ways of doing business. E-commerce websites have the advantage of reaching a large number of customers regardless of distance and time limitations. The advantage of e-commerce over traditional businesses is faster speed and lower expenses for both businessmen and customers. The main objective of the chapter is to provide an efficient framework to analyse the performance of e-commerce websites and suggest the factors that need to be incorporated in e-commerce websites for better business intelligence. The purpose of business intelligence is to support better business decision making. In this chapter, a detailed description of business intelligence enables the web developer and end user to know the insights of e-commerce web applications. The methodology is comprehensive and it elaborates all aspects of the performance of a website.

INTRODUCTION

The World Wide Web (WWW) has become an important channel for information retrieval, electronic commerce and entertainment. However, long Web page download times have remained a major cause of frustration among Web users. According to the findings of the surveys conducted by Lightner et al, (1996) and the GVU (Graphic, Visualization and Usability) Centre at Georgia Institute of Technology (GVU, 1998), long download times have always been a major problem experienced by Web users. The survey by Pitkow et al, (1996) also indicates that the most widely cited problem using the WWW was that it took too long to download Web pages (i.e. 69% of respondents cited this problem). This problem is worsened by the exponential increase in the number of Web users over the years and the popularity of multimedia (e.g. video, voice) technology. This problem is so noticeable that Web users often equate

DOI: 10.4018/978-1-5225-3646-8.ch001

the "WWW" acronym with "World Wide Wait"! According to The long waiting time for downloading Web pages is often not tolerable even in the wired environment. Due to the increasing and excessive use of multimedia data (i.e. audio and video clips) on Web pages, this concern is continuously growing. The problem of 'long download time' is relevant not only to Web users but also to the authors and designers of websites, as websites that take a long time to download are rarely or less frequently visited (Reaux et al, 1997). The authors (G. Sreedhar et al, 2017) suggested in their research work slow Loading pages affects the sales and longer negative effect and 40% on line shoppers feel comfortable to revisit if the website load quickly.

Objectives

- To study and analyze the components of e-commerce application and relevance of web mining.
- To find insights of Business Intelligence.
- To incorporate the idea of Internet of Things.
- To provide a comprehensive frame work for analyzing the e-commerce website.
- To analyze the performance of e-commerce website through frame work.

BACKGROUND

E-Commerce Web Applications and Web Mining

E-commerce websites have the advantage of reaching a large number of customers regardless of distance and time limitations. The advantage of e-commerce over traditional businesses is the faster speed and the lower expenses for both e-commerce website owners and customers in completing customer transactions and orders. Because of the above advantages of e-commerce over traditional businesses, a lot of industries in different fields such as retailing, banking, medical services, transportation, communication, and education are establishing their business in the web. But creating a successful online business can be a very difficult and costly task if not taking into account e-commerce website design principles, web engineering techniques, and what e-commerce is supposed to do for the online business. Unfortunately, to most companies, web is nothing more than a place where transactions take place. All the e-commerce sites have high traffic. People surf the sites very often but the income is not always very high. So, the web data mining appeared and also nowadays much attention is paid to it. It is very important to apply web data mining to e-commerce in order to gather knowledge about users and rank data accordingly. It is advance successful technology through which information is filtered easier. So, web data mining became a publicly accessible source that gives promising results. With the use of e-commerce through internet, companies find a new and better way to do business. After developing the web site thought companies get benefits, they have to implement Web mining systems to understand their customers' profiles and to identify their own strength and weakness of their E-marketing efforts on the web through continuous improvements. Internet is a gold mine, but only for those companies who realize the importance of Web mining and adopt a Web mining strategy now. Web mining technology has many important roles that should be mentioned. It can automatically find, extract information from the variety web resources. The authors Etnoteam S. et al (2000) said that web mining develops, improves and enhances the quality and the efficiency of search engines, determines web pages or files, makes classifications. It can also generate large-scale real-time data. Web data mining discovers useful information from the Web hyperlink and page content. It has already changed the face of many business functions in a modern competitive enterprise. It is obviously easier to make right business decisions or understand the information that came from customers with the help of web data mining. It helps e-commerce to understand how to improve its services for special groups of customers and clients, and what tasks to realize. The e-commerce site can increase the exposure of its product pages and so average order size can be increased. Companies can save percentage of its budget per month owing to knowledge that was received from web mining analysis. Web data mining gathers implicit knowledge about clients and instructs e-commerce in every aspect. Then, it extracts valuable and comprehensible information from huge web resources to instruct e-commerce. It also gathers the information in an automated way and builds models used to predict customer purchasing decisions. Web mining is very precious to the company in the fields of understanding customer behaviour, improving customer services and relationship, launching target marketing campaigns, measuring the success of marketing efforts, and so on. Attractiveness of the site depends on its reasonable design of content and organizational structure. The author TIAN Meirong et al (2010) described that Web Mining can provide details of user behaviour, providing web site designers basis of decision making to improve the design of the site . E-Commerce generally refers to a new business model, where consumer makes online shopping, online transactions between merchants and online electronic payments and a variety of business activities, trading activities, financial activities and related integrated services activities, buyers and sellers are not met to conduct various business activities based on browser/server application mode.

Business Intelligence

The author Jayanthi Ranjan (2009) explained that the term Business Intelligence (BI) refers to technologies, applications and practices for the collection, integration, analysis, and presentation of business information. The purpose of Business Intelligence is to support better business decision making. Essentially, Business Intelligence systems are data-driven Decision Support Systems (DSS). Business Intelligence is sometimes used interchangeably with briefing books, report and query tools and executive information systems. Software elements support reporting, interactive "slice-and-dice" pivot-table analyses, visualization, and statistical data mining. Applications tackle sales, production, financial, and many other sources of business data for purposes that include business performance management. Information is often gathered about other companies in the same industry which is known as benchmarking. Common functions of business intelligence technologies include reporting, online analytical processing, analytics, data mining, process mining, complex event processing, business performance management, benchmarking, text mining, predictive analytics and prescriptive analytics. *Business intelligence* may be defined as a set of mathematical models and analysis methodologies that exploit the available data to generate information and knowledge useful for complex decision-making processes. Figure 1 illustrates the major benefits that a given organization may draw from the adoption of a business intelligence system. With the help of mathematical models and algorithms, it is actually possible to analyze a larger number of alternative actions, achieve more accurate conclusions and reach effective and timely decisions. The components of Business Intelligence are shown in Figure 2.

Figure 1. Benefits of business intelligence

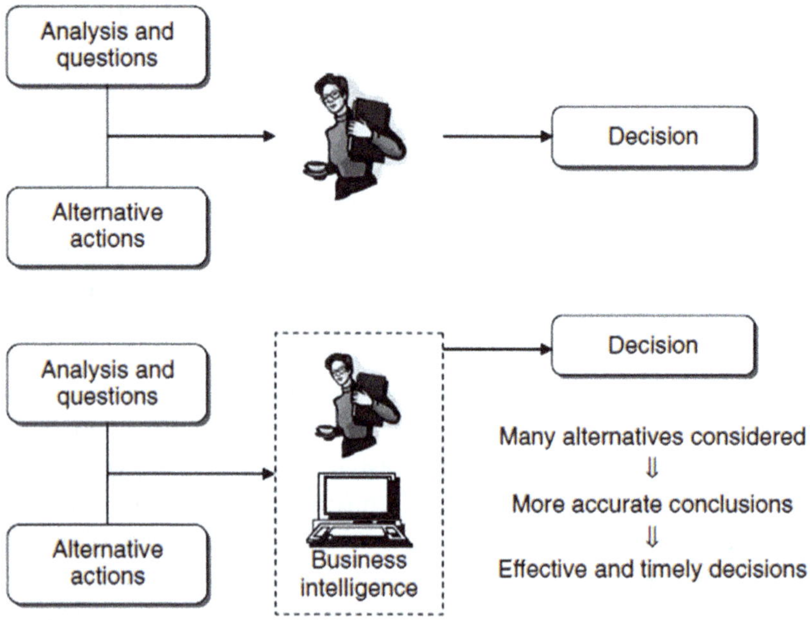

Figure 2. Business intelligence architecture

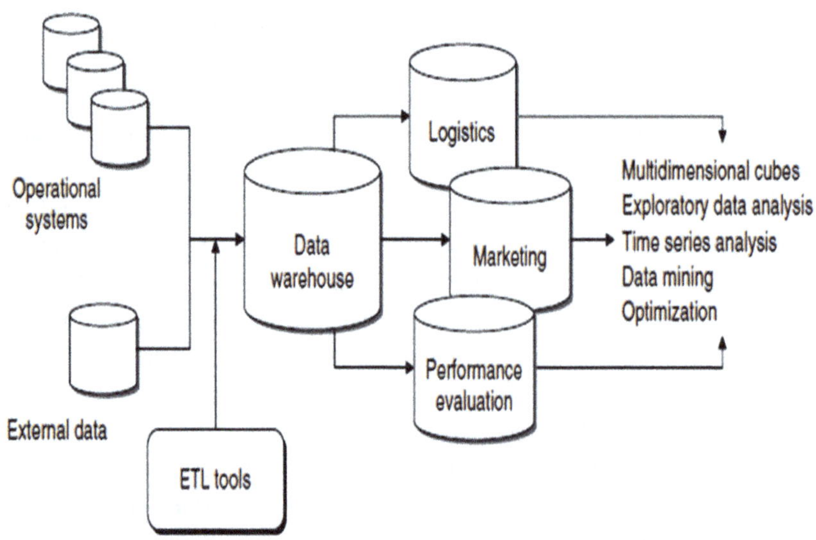

Data Warehouses and Data Marts

Using extraction and transformation tools known as *extract, transform, load* (ETL), the data originating from the different sources are stored in databases intended to support business intelligence analyses. These databases are usually referred to as *data warehouses* and *data marts*.

Business Intelligence Methodologies

Data are finally extracted and used to feed mathematical models and analysis methodologies intended to support decision makers. In a business intelligence system, several decision support applications may be implemented.

- Multidimensional cube analysis;
- Exploratory data analysis;
- Time series analysis;
- Inductive learning models for data mining;
- Optimization models.

The pyramid in Figure 3 shows the building blocks of a business intelligence system.

Figure 3. Pyramidical structure of business intelligence system

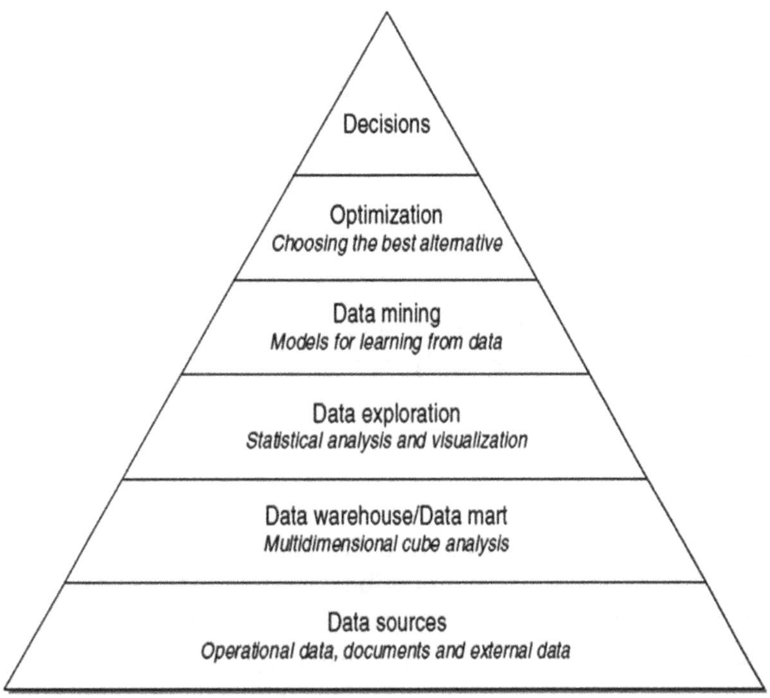

Data Exploration

At the third level of the pyramid includes the tools for performing a *passive* business intelligence analysis, which consist of query and reporting systems, as well as statistical methods. These are referred to as passive methodologies because decision makers are requested to generate prior hypotheses or define data extraction criteria, and then use the analysis tools to find answers and confirm their original insight.

Data Mining

The fourth level includes *active* business intelligence methodologies, whose purpose is the extraction of information and knowledge from data. These include mathematical models for pattern recognition, machine learning and data mining techniques. Unlike the tools described at the previous level of the pyramid, the models of an active kind do not require decision makers to formulate any prior hypothesis to be later verified. Their purpose is instead to expand the decision makers' knowledge.

Optimization

The optimization level in the pyramid allow the user to determine the best solution out of a set of alternative actions.

Decisions

Finally, the top of the pyramid corresponds to the choice and the actual adoption of a specific decision and in some way represents the natural conclusion of the decision-making process. Even when business intelligence methodologies are available and successfully adopted, the choice of a decision pertains to the decision makers, who may also take advantage of informal and unstructured information available to adapt and modify the recommendations and the conclusions achieved through the use of mathematical models. The top of the pyramid supports advanced support tools of an active type. At the bottom, the required competencies are provided for the most part by the information systems specialists within the organization, usually referred to as *database administrators*. Analysts and experts in mathematical and statistical models are responsible for the intermediate phases. Finally, the activities of decision makers responsible for the application domain appear dominant at the top. As described above, business intelligence systems address the needs of different types of complex organizations, including agencies of public administration and associations.

Internet of Things (IoT)

The author G. Sreedhar (2017) in his book specified that Internet of Things (IoT) is a network which is composed with Radio Frequency Identification (RFID), infrared sensors, global positioning systems, laser scanners, gas sensors and other information sensing device, according to the agreed protocol, any goods is connected with the Internet for information exchange, communication, IoT is used to make intelligent identification, positioning, tracking, monitoring and management. The schematic diagram IoT is shown in the following Figure 4.

Figure 4. Schematic structure of IoT

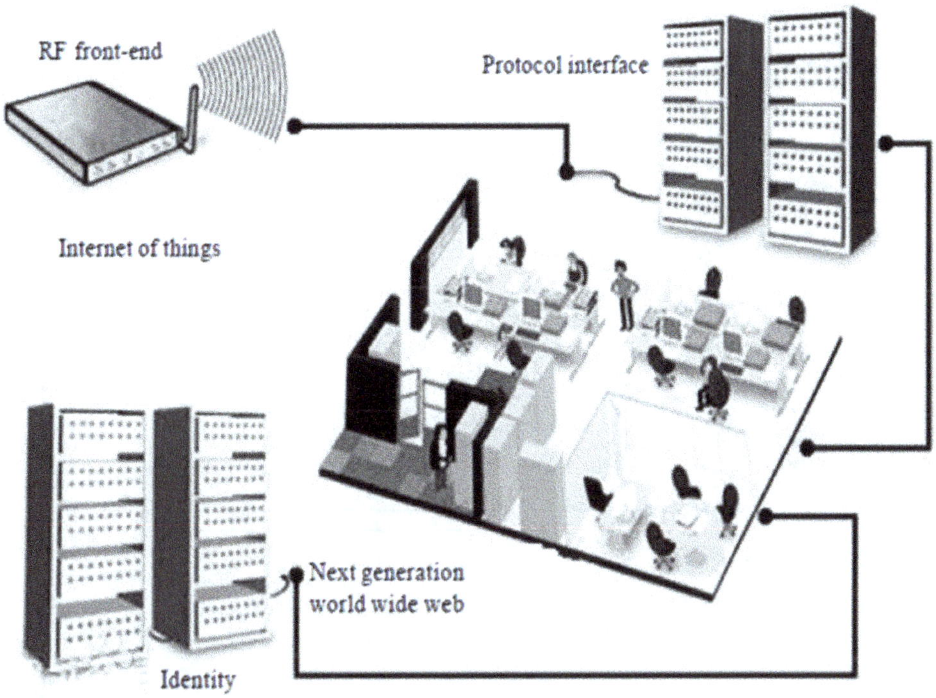

With the rapid development of e-commerce, its technology requirements will also increase on all aspects of future e-commerce. Firstly, the e-commerce applications are combined with IoT development and IoT technologies are applied in three important aspects of e-commerce, such as inventory, logistics and payment. An e-commerce system includes inventory, logistics, electronic payment and other important aspects, if IoT technology is used in various aspects of e-commerce, e-commerce will greatly improve the efficiency of the system. The diagram of E-Commerce with components of IoT is shown in the Figure 5.

ANALYZING THE PERFORMANCE OF THE E-COMMERCE WEB APPLICATIONS

In order to improve the performance of the E-Commerce Web Applications, a well defined framework is needed. Following are various modules considered in analysing the performance of E-Commerce Web Applications

1. W3C Validation
2. Search Engine Optimization
3. Security
4. HTTP Compression
5. SURBL Check

Figure 5: Various components of Internet of Things

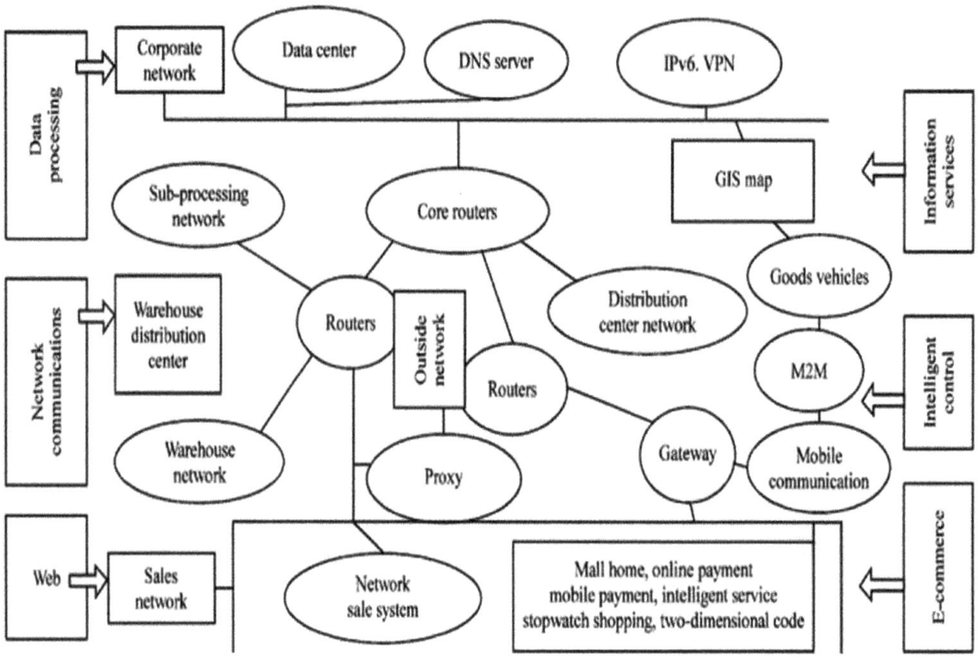

W3C Validation

Web standards are rules and guidelines established by the World Wide Web Consortium (W3C) developed to promote consistency in the design code which makes up a web page. Without getting technical, simply it's the guideline for the mark-up language which determines how a web page. Website Standards Association Inc. has been set up to identify the minimum website standards that websites should meet and educate internet users about how to get the most out of their websites. Web standards are the formal, non-proprietary standards and other technical specifications that define and describe aspects of the World Wide Web. The advantages in adhering to these standards are many:

- Web pages will display in a wide variety of browsers and computers, including new technology like iPhones, Droids, iPads, PDA devices, mobile phones, which greatly increases the viewing audience.
- W3C Standards promote the use of "Cascading Style Sheets" (CSS) or design code which is attached to the web page. rather than embedded in the page. The use of style sheets significantly reduces the page file size which means not only a faster page loading time but lower hosting costs for frequently visited sites due to using less bandwidth.
- Design features such as colors and fonts can be easily changed by just modifying one style sheet instead of editing every individual page in a web site, reducing the costs to modify your site.
- Search Engines are able to access and index pages designed to web standards with greater efficiency.

Search Engine Optimization

Search engine optimization (SEO) is the process of affecting the visibility of a website or a web page in a search engine's unpaid results, often referred to as natural, organic, or earned results. In general, the earlier (or higher ranked on the search results page), and more frequently a site appears in the search results list, the more visitors it will receive from the search engine's users. SEO may target different kinds of search, including image search, local search, video search, academic search, news search and industry-specific vertical search engines.

Security

Security is not an easy thing that you only need to implement or apply. The authors Steve Petite (2002) and Butler W. Lampson (2004) discussed in their research that the cost of securing small static web sites for some organizations could be larger than the organization could pay or think to pay. This high cost came from that you do not only need to protect the customer data but also you need to protect your systems from frequent attacks which may cause to Denial of service attack, that make your web site down. The author Sean-Philip Oriyano (2009) discussed in his research that attacks can prevent some organizations that depend on e-business or e-commerce from doing their Job. Therefore, most of the companies' web applications are likely to be under the risk of attacks. In order to protect these web applications, Sergey Gordeychik (2007) suggested that security experts must have the ability to detect the security threats and the back doors in their web application. After that, they can provide the solution starting with the urgent and highest priority problems such as Denial of service until covering all the security threats according to Caleb Sima (2004). Following protection techniques are suggested by majority authors like Craig Hinley et al (2015) to secure internet and web applications. They are as follows.

- **Intrusion Detection System (IDS):** The Intrusion Detection System (IDS) is used to detect many kinds of attacks behaviour that can compromise the security of the web application system. The author Fernando Esponda (2009) described in his research, these kinds of attacks that can be detected by the IDS include Worms, Viruses, unauthorized logins, access to sensitive files and folders, increase access privileges.
- **Intrusion Prevention System (IPS):** Another automated protection tools is called the Intrusion Prevention System (IPS). The authors Phurivit Sangkatsanee & Chalermpol Charnsripinyo (2011) explained in their research, IPS is usually a device that monitors the network in order to study the behaviour of the authorized user in the network. Therefore, the IPS will prevent unauthorized users from access the web application and the network resources.
- **Passwords:** The passwords strength of security is depending on the users who create them and the combination of characters, letters and numbers. Generally, the easiest method to access a password of web application defences is with inside knowledge. The authors Beate Grawemeyer & Hilary Johnson (2011) explained in their research, the attacker may track someone profile of social web site in order to get information about him to guess his organization web application password. Nowadays, most of the web application that server clients try to show the clients the complexity level of their password when creating their accounts or after that. Other web application also choose a default random password that is very complex and hard to remember from the users

themselves, which make them write it down anywhere cause another threat possibility. Password itself cannot be the only protection technique that a company uses.

- **SSL and Data Encryption:** The authors Xiaowei Li and Yuan Xue (2011) explains that Socket Secure Layer (SSL) protocol and data encryption may secure the customer data during the transmission of these data from the web server to the client machine. The authors Kyu Ho Park and Ki-Woong Park (2011) described in their research the server and the client system need to decrypt these data once they want to read it or modify it. Data encryption same as password cannot be work alone without other protection technique. Usually this encryption and decryption are based on shared key that both the client and the server need to know. Therefore, distribution of this shared key should be also run through a secure process.
- **Firewalls:** As shown in Figure 6 the firewall is like a barrier inside the network to allow only the people who have authorized access to pass through this gate. Firewall can be either hardware device or software tool that can be configured to allow and block certain users, packets, ports, or even Internet Addresses (IPs). The authors Peder Jungck and Simon S.Y Shim (2004) and Alex X. Liu (2012) discussed in their research, the attacker may make a huge process in order to convince the firewall that he is an authorized user to pass through it and this is what usually happens in the Trojan horse virus. In the computer networks, a firewall is working with a router. The firewall scans each network packet to decide whether to forward it toward its destination inside my company network or forbidden its pass. A firewall also includes or works with a proxy server that creates network requests on behalf of the users systems. A firewall is often installed in a specially designated computer separate from the rest of the network so that not any arrived packet can get directly at the servers system in the company network.
- **Standard Scanning Programs:** The known attacks and security threats are stored in automated tools to scan all the programs and packet sent or received on the clients system. Most of these automated scanners protect the organizations network from known attacks made before on hardware devices and software. Most of these scanners secure your systems from fixed list of threats. Therefore, there is no guarantee to protect your applications and systems from new expected kind of attacks that did not happen before. Sometimes they can alert them users that doing some actions or accessing some file will be vulnerable and security risk. Usually these applications require daily update for its libraries in order to update the list of threats to include the new threats according the authors Marjan Korosec & Joze Duhovnik (2010) that just happen to other computer systems.
- **Internet Service Provider:** Most of the protection techniques are mainly to guarantee securing the systems and data inside an organization. However, what about the internet service providers (ISPs). Most of the ISPs do not care about security same as the application productions companies. Security is not their business. Nevertheless, nowadays most of these third parties start looking for security improvements in order to enhance or keep their reputation in the IT markets as specified by authors Serguei Netessine and Nils Rudi (2006).
- **Code Implementation:** Programmers are not security experts that why they do not consider that much the security threats while developing an application. Some huge development companies apply security testing for their applications after the development phase. While the most of these companies only deals with security after their applications face an attack. However, in order to protect your system you should not only test the code but you need to implement all the validation

Figure 6. Schematic diagram of firewall

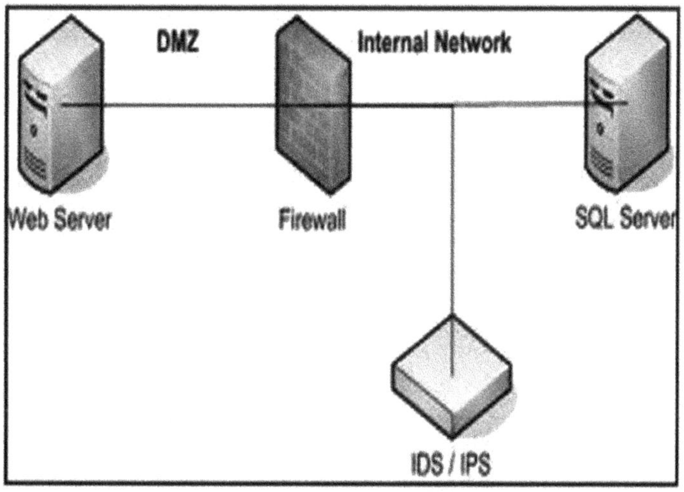

and verification required in the code development phase. In addition, to secure all the servers and databases that is worked in the background of these applications. Tester mainly are not attacker that why he cannot imagine the complete way of attacking the system. Therefore, the authors Lingli Zhang and Chandra Krintz (2005) and Mu-Woong Lee and Sunghun Kim (2011) suggested that companies should start looking for hiring attacker in their quality assurance departments.

HTTP Compression

HTTP compression is a capability that can be built into web servers and web clients to improve transfer speed and bandwidth utilization. HTTP data is compressed before it is sent from the server: compliant browsers will announce what methods are supported to the server before downloading the correct format; browsers that do not support compliant compression method will download uncompressed data. There are two different ways compression can be done in HTTP. At a lower level, a Transfer-Encoding header field may indicate the payload of a HTTP message is compressed. At a higher level, a Content-Encoding header field may indicate that a resource being transferred, cached, or otherwise referenced is compressed. Compression using Content-Encoding is more widely supported than Transfer-Encoding, and some browsers do not advertise support for Transfer-Encoding compression to avoid triggering bugs in servers.

SURBL Database Check

SURBLs are lists of *web sites* that have appeared in unsolicited messages. Sender lists can be used in a first stage filter to help identify 80% to 90% of unsolicited messages. SURBLs can help find about 75% of the otherwise difficult, remaining unsolicited messages in a second stage filter. Used together with sender lists, SURBLs have proven to be a highly-effective way to detect 95% of unsolicited messages. Using SURBLs requires a mail filter that can extract web sites from message bodies and check them against the lists.

IMPLEMENTATION

In order to suggest the status of e-commerce web applications for better business intelligence a web program is developed with the standard tool known as *webcheckme*. The web program accepts the URL of e-commerce website and verifies all the aspects of as mentioned in above section. The web program produces the status of e-commerce website in 10-point scale. The web developer of e-commerce website can improve the performance of website based on the value of 10-point scale and comments. A case study was conducted on some of the popular e-commerce websites and the following table lists these websites.

The analysis of web program is shown in Figure 7.

The results of web program on 10 e-commerce websites with 10-point score value are shown in Table 2 and snapshot of 10 e-commerce websites' scores are shown in Figure 8.

Table 1. List of e-commerce websites

S.No	E-Commerce Website
1	www.shopclues.com
2	www.paytm.com
3	www.snapdeal.com
4	www.shopbychoice.com
5	www.ebay.com
6	www.irctc.co.in
7	www.flipkart.com
8	www.amazon.com
9	www.zapstore.com
10	www.homeshop18.com

Table 2. E-commerce websites with 10-point score

S.No	E-Commerce Website	10-point Score
1	www.shopclues.com	3.73
2	www.paytm.com	3.73
3	www.snapdeal.com	3.73
4	www.shopbychoice.com	5.33
5	www.ebay.com	3.73
6	www.irctc.co.in	3.6
7	www.flipkart.com	6.71
8	www.amazon.com	3.73
9	www.zapstore.com	6.27
10	www.homeshop18.com	6.49

Figure 7. A sample website scan report of e-commerce website

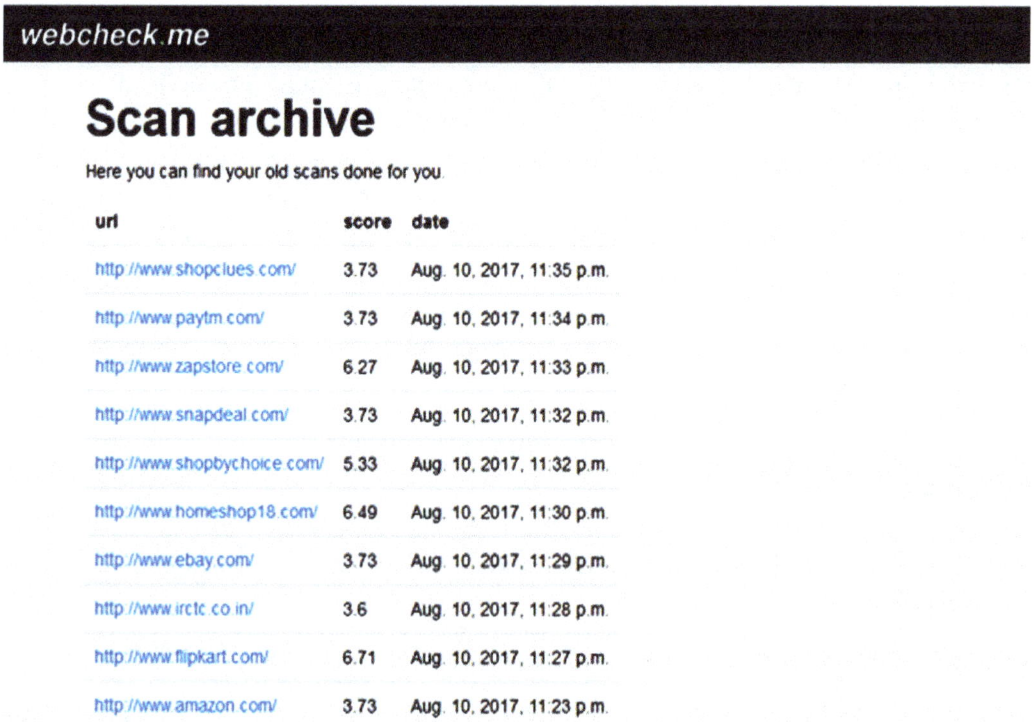

webcheck.me

Scan archive

Here you can find your old scans done for you

url	score	date
http://www.shopclues.com/	3.73	Aug. 10, 2017, 11:35 p.m.
http://www.paytm.com/	3.73	Aug. 10, 2017, 11:34 p.m.
http://www.zapstore.com/	6.27	Aug. 10, 2017, 11:33 p.m.
http://www.snapdeal.com/	3.73	Aug. 10, 2017, 11:32 p.m.
http://www.shopbychoice.com/	5.33	Aug. 10, 2017, 11:32 p.m.
http://www.homeshop18.com/	6.49	Aug. 10, 2017, 11:30 p.m.
http://www.ebay.com/	3.73	Aug. 10, 2017, 11:29 p.m.
http://www.irctc.co.in/	3.6	Aug. 10, 2017, 11:28 p.m.
http://www.flipkart.com/	6.71	Aug. 10, 2017, 11:27 p.m.
http://www.amazon.com/	3.73	Aug. 10, 2017, 11:23 p.m.

Figure 8. 10-Point Scores of various e-commerce websites

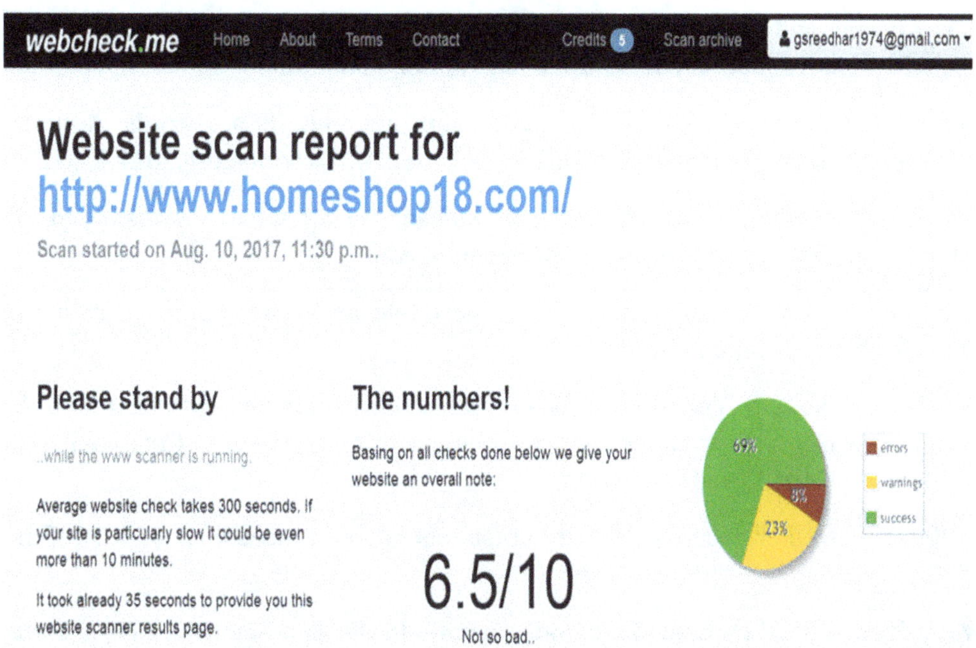

CONCLUSION

The chapter identifies the various factors that need to be consider the in analyzing the performance of e-commerce website. The methodology is very much comprehensive and well applicable to e-commerce web application product because web application is the integration of number of different components. In this chapter, a significant effort is made to evaluate status of e-commerce website. The chapter has shown the path and cautiousness to be adopted in web design process for the web designers for better service to the end users. The importance of the quality of Web Design is essential in the light of enormous growth of web applications. In this connection the theme of the chapter shows a direction to improve the web applications more viable to the need of common man and to achieve user friendly websites. Thus the presented information in the chapter is quite helpful to for e-commerce web developers in the context of today's business world.

REFERENCES

Esponda, F. (2009). *Immune System Inspired Digital Representations: Storing all but the valuable data.* VDM Verlag Saarbrucken.

EtnoteamS. P. A. (2000). Retrieved from http://ww.etnoteam.it/webquality

Etzioni, O. (1996). The World Wide Web: Quagmire or Gold Mine. Communications of the ACM, 39(11), 65-68.

Gordeychik, S. (2007). *Web Application Security Statistics.* Retrieved September 1, 2017, from http://projects.webappsec.org/w/page/13246989/webapplicationsecuritystatistics

Graphics, Visualization and Usability (GVU) Centre. (1998). *GVU's user surveys.* Georgia Tech Research Corporation. Retrieved from WWW.cc.gatech.edu/gvu/user_ surveys/

Grawemeyer, B., & Johnson, H. (2011). Using and managing multiple passwords: A week to a view. *Journal of Interacting with Computers*, *23*(3), 256–267. doi:10.1016/j.intcom.2011.03.007

Hinley, C., O'Leary, R., & Samdarshi, S. (2015). *WhiteHat website security statistic report 2015.* Retrieved September 1, 2017 from https://www.whitehatsec.com

Jungck, P., & Shim, S. S. Y. (2004). Issues in High Speed Internet Security. In *Proceedings of Computing Practices.* The IEEE Computer Society.

Korosec, M., Duhovnik, J., & Vukasinovic, N. (2010). Identification and optimization of key process parameters in noncontact laser scanning for reverse engineering. *Journal of Computer-Aided Design*, *42*(8), 744–748. doi:10.1016/j.cad.2010.02.003

Lampson. (2004). Computer Security Security in the real World. Proceedings of IEEE Computer, 37, 37-46.

Lee, M.-W., & Kim, S. (2011), Integrating code search into the development session. *Proceedings of the 27th International Conference on Data Engineering*, 1336-1339. doi:10.1109/ICDE.2011.5767948

Li & Xue. (2011). *A Survey on Web Application Security (Technical report)*. Vanderbilt University.

Liu, A. X. (2012, March). Firewall policy change-impact analysis. *Journal of ACM Transactions on Internet Technology*, *11*(4), 15.

Meirong, T., & Xuedong, C. (2010). Application of Agent-based Web Mining in E-business. *Second International Conference on Intelligent Human-Machine Systems and Cybernetics*.

Netessine, S., & Rudi, N. (2006). Supply Chain Choice on the Internet. *Journal of Management Science*, *52*(6), 844–864. doi:10.1287/mnsc.1060.0512

Oriyano. (2009). *Anatomy of a Web attack: Understanding the most common attack types*. IBM Corporation.

Park, K. H., & Park, K.-W. (2011). ACCENT: Cognitive cryptography plugged compression for SSL/TLS-based cloud computing services. *Journal of ACM Transactions on Internet Technology*, *11*(2), 7.

Petite, S. (2002). *Anatomy of a Web Application: Security Considerations*. White Paper. Sanctum Inc.

Pitkow, J. E., & Kehoe, C. M. (1996). Emerging trends in the WWW user population. *Communications of the ACM*, *39*(6), 106–108. doi:10.1145/228503.228525

Ranjan, J. (2009). Business Intelligence: Concepts, components, techniques and benefits. *Journal of Theoretical and Applied Information Technology*, *9*(1), 60–70.

Reaux, R. A., & Carroll, J. M. (1997). Human factors in information access of distributed systems. In G. Salvendy (Ed.), *Handbook of Human Factors and Ergonomics* (2nd ed.). New York: Wiley.

Sangkatsanee, P., & Charnsripinyo, C. (2011). Practical real-time intrusion detection using machine learning approaches. *Journal of Computer Communications*, *34*(18), 2227–2235. doi:10.1016/j.comcom.2011.07.001

Sima, C. (2004). *Security at Next Level. Whitepaper*. SPI Dynamic Inc.

Sreedhar, G. (2017). Development of Efficient Decision Support Systems using Web Data Mining. In G. Sreedhar (Ed.), *Web Data Mining and the Development of Knowledge based Decision Support Systems* (pp. 1–11). Hershey, PA: Information Science Publishing. doi:10.4018/978-1-5225-1877-8.ch001

Sreedhar, G., & Anandaraja Chari, A. (2017). First Look on Web Mining Techniques to Improve Business Intelligence of E-Commerce Web Applications. In *Hand Book of Research on Advanced Data Mining Techniques and Applications of Business Intelligence* (pp. 298–314). Hershey, PA: Information Science Publishing. doi:10.4018/978-1-5225-2031-3.ch018

Zhang, L., & Krintz, C. (2005). The design, implementation, and evaluation of adaptive code unloading for resource-constrained devices. *Journal of ACM Transactions on Architecture and Code Optimization*, *2*(2), 131–164. doi:10.1145/1071604.1071606

Chapter 2
Identification of User Preference for Multi-Criteria Reporting in Business Intelligence: A Case Study on Banking Business

Martin Aruldoss
Central University of Tamil Nadu, India

Miranda Lakshmi Travis
Bharathiyar University, India

Prasanna Venkatesan Venkatasamy
Pondicherry University, India

ABSTRACT

Business intelligence (BI) is an integrated set of tools used to support the transformation of data into information in order to support decision making. Among different functionalities, reporting plays a significant role that provides information to its readers to make better decisions. BI lacks user-specific reporting to the different levels of users of an organization. Different users require different kinds of reporting with respect to different requirement (criteria) in an organization. A multi-criteria reporting (MCR) finds the suitable information to suitable user based on the multiple conflicting preferences of a user. Technique for order preference by similarity to ideal solution (TOPSIS) is the most popularly applied multi-criteria decision-making (MCDM) technique selected to identify different levels of user preference for MCR. Banking business is considered as a case study to identify user preference for MCR. This research also designs evaluation metrics for TOPSIS.

DOI: 10.4018/978-1-5225-3646-8.ch002

1. INTRODUCTION

Report is methodical, well-organized document that defines and analyzes a certain issue or a problem and recommends solution. It also presents, the expected performance and future outcomes of an organization. There are different kinds of reporting methodologies such as informative report, interpretative report, summarized report and so on. In this modern business environment, business analysis and reporting are influenced by BI. It provides comprehensive solution to different business domains and it reports to different levels of users of an organization. To address the needs of today's innovative, rapid and dynamic business environment the role of BI is significantly very important.

BI is an integrated set of tools used to support the transformation of data into information in order to support decision making (George et al., 2015), (Rouhani et al., 2012). It analyses the performance of an organization, increases its revenue and competitiveness (Trumpy et al., 2015),(Hsieh, 2011). A Business Intelligence System (BIS) environment consists of data source, analytical techniques and reporting tools (Foster et al., 2015). The different functionalities of BIS are problem driven and comprehensive data collection strategies for information extraction process (Thiagarajan et al., 2011), (Chung& Tseng, 2012), providing a rapid analytics to make a better and quicker decisions (Genc et al., 2013), (Foster et al., 2015) and reporting (Larson&Chang, 2016).

Among different functionalities of BIS, reporting plays a significant role and it forecast the expected performance and future outcomes of an organization. BI provides better reporting with minimal training cost (Gounder et al., 2016). An organization has different levels of users and makes decisions from different kinds of information (Tobias & Trindade, 2011). Hence, customized report should be developed based on the requirements of the users of the organization. BI reporting lacks user specific reporting to the different levels of users of an organization according to the criteria (Miller et al., 2016). To address user specific reporting, Multi Criteria Reporting (MCR) is developed which can be customized according to criteria (Fairwarning.com, 2016), (Martin et al., 2014), (UNDP, 2011).

MCR is originated from business analysis process. It requires a reporting, which may be static report targeting all level of users (Hinze et al., 2009). The levels of users are from top management to customers and common users (Mohammad &Rosnah, 2011). Instead of a normal business reporting a customized business reporting finds suitable information to suitable user at right time (Martin et al., 2015). To customize the information, user preference should be identified according to various criteria (Moro et al., 2014). Multi Criteria Decision Making (MCDM) techniques have been applied to structure and solve decision making problems involving multiple criteria (Hemmati et al., 2016).In this research, most widely used MCDM technique,Technique for Order Preference by Similarity to Ideal Solution (TOPSIS) is applied to find the user preference for MCR (Obayiuwana, 2015).

The rest of the paper is organized as follows. Section 2 describes the literature review on BI functionalities, TOPSIS applications and its evaluation metrics. It also describes about different evaluation parameters developed for MCDM applications. Section 3 describes the metrics designed for TOPSIS and section 4 designs the MCR for banking application, section 5 describes the experimentation details for MCR, section 6 discuss the results and section 7 concludes the paper.

2. LITERATURE REVIEW

This literature reviews the functionalities of BI, different multi criteria applications which are solved using TOPSIS. It also describes various evaluation parameters applied in TOPSIS.

2.1 Business Intelligence (BI)

BI is a data driven decision support system that combines data gathering, data storage and analysis to provide input to the decision process (Ishaya & Musiliudeen, 2012), (Bajo et al., 2012). From the literature, it is understood that BI takes data from multiple sources, transforms these data into information through people, processes and analytical tools to make better decisions. It improves the performance of the business or an organization. Business Intelligence Systems (BIS) combines operational data with analytical tools and technologies to make quality decisions (Yeoh & Andy, 2010).

It has been applied in different business domains such as curriculum development (Gupta et al., 2015), technological adaption in banking (Moro et al., 2015), stock return volatility (Rubin & Amir, 2013), consumers' consideration probabilities (Zhao et al., 2012), targeted marketing (Cox & Margie, 2012), study at abroad recommendations (Hsieh, 2011), consumer heterogeneity for food choice (Hayashi et al., 2010), enhancement teaching-learning process (Piedade & Santos, 2009) and so on. The various developments in BIS has been categorized and described in Figure 1.

The recent developments in BI are classified into three categories such as building blocks of BI, functionalities of BI and realization of BI which are described as follows.

Figure 1. Classification of Recent Developments in BI

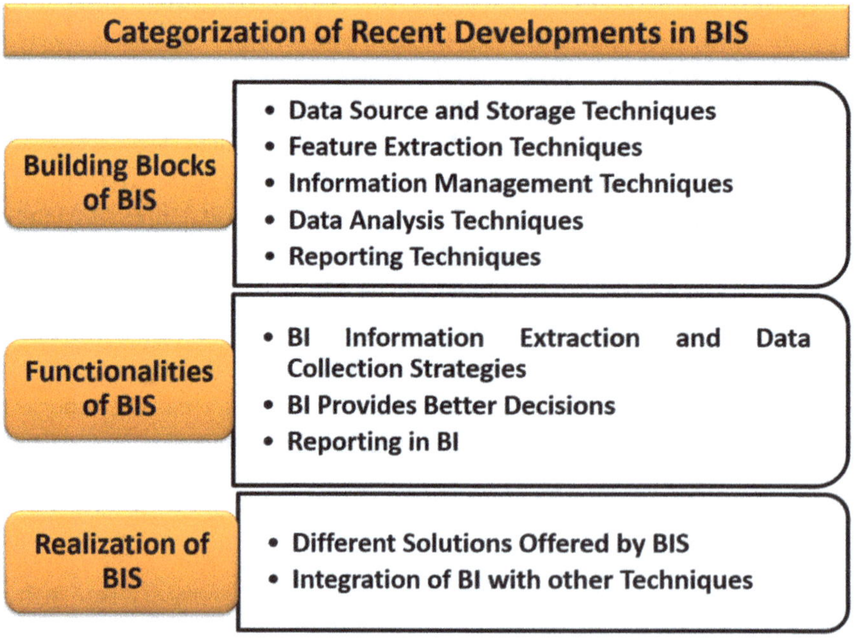

2.1.1 Building Blocks of BIS

Enterprise users need a technology to access integrated data, to store, to analyze and to make wiser decisions. BI satisfies these needs by applying its wiser building blocks (components). A typical BI application is made up of many numbers of components such as data warehouse, Extract, Transform and Load (ETL), data mining, analytical tools, data visualization and analysis, dashboard, score board, Customer Relationship Management (CRM), Enterprise Resource Planning (ERP), Online Analytical Process (OLAP) and any other related components. The widely applied components of BI (Martin et al., 2014) are depicted in Figure 2.

Figure 2 depicts the different components of BIS. According to the business requirement, the business intelligence components may vary from one application to another application. These components have been applied to carry out the different functionalities of BIS. The different functionalities of BIS have been described as follows.

2.1.2 Functionalities of BIS

BI has different functionalities according to the domain, commonly it provides a data driven decision support. BI has been applied in various domains to provide better solution such as inventory management, market management, education, consumer heterogeneity, pharmaceutical, etc.,. The web is an information repository which contains an enormous amount of data. To find exact or relevant information, business intelligence provides different number of information extraction techniques which are described in Table 1.

Figure 2. Business Intelligence System and its Components

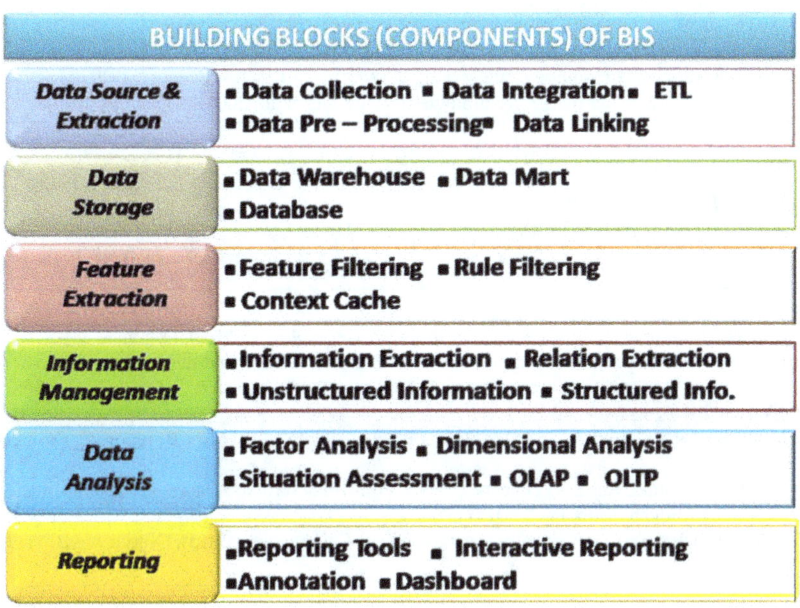

Table 1. BI Information extraction and data collection strategies

BI Information Extraction and Data Collection Strategies
▪ Improved market sentiment analysis (Wingyan & Tzu-Liang, 2012). ▪ Simplified and Enriched information extraction process (Cvitas, 2011) ▪ Enterprise risk management from review comments (Kaiquan, 2011).

From the different kinds of information extraction techniques, the required data is collected for analysis to make better decisions. The different kinds of better decisions taken in various domains using BI are described in Table 2.

An important functionality of BI is reporting and it is very essential for enterprise to make decisions. Report is the term used for a group of documents that inform, analyze or recommend. It is methodical, well-organized document that defines and analyzes a certain issue or a problem. The main purpose of a report is to provide information to its readers and it is very essential in the enterprise for decision making. From the different sources of BI reporting it is defined as,

BI reporting is a business analytical report which present results, analyses and interprets the results and draw conclusions.

A BI report attempts to describe the cause, impact and outcome of the problems (E.g.: A famous product which lost its highest sales target). There are different kinds of reporting methodologies are followed in BI which are described in Table 3.

Table 2. Better decisions by BI

BI Provides Better Decisions
▪ Market Management - Attaining their goals using BI (Mahdi, 2012). ▪ Product / Service - Quality of service improved (Kun-Lin, 2011). ▪ Education - Monitors and controls the resources (Sirawit et al., 2010). ▪ Consumer heterogeneity - Factors identified for changing behavior (Yoichi et al., 2010). ▪ Reduced cost by using open negotiable environment (Aciar et al., 2009). ▪ Internet Service Provider - Formulate proper marketing strategies (Sheng-Tun et al., 2008).

Table 3. BI Reporting Methodologies

Reporting in BI
▪ BI tools lacks in felt involvement (Miller et al., 2016) ▪ Effective reporting methods are required for BI to be used by different users (Morris, 2016), (Yasmine & peter, 2015) ▪ A comparative analysis on BI tools for dashboards based on ease of use, visualization and minimal training cost (Gounder et al., 2016) ▪ BI tools provides better reporting than traditional reporting tools (Al-Azmi, and Abdul-Aziz Rashid, 2013) (Source:Softwareadvice.com, 2016), (Deanne & Victor, 2016), ▪ At present a paradigm shift is taking place in BI from traditional BI reporting to self service BI reporting (Source:Timoelliott.com, 2014). ▪ BI Tools: IBM Cognos Analysis Studio, Business Objects, Cognos PowerPlay -provides more general information using dynamic drill-down, slicing, dicing and filtering (Source: Bitool.net, 2015) ▪ BI Tools: Calumo BI – Write back report - setting sales targets (Source: Calumo.com, 2015), Qlikview – BI analysis tool (Ayushi & Saru, 2016)

From the literature it has been found that BI reporting gives better analytical information for decision making compared to traditional reporting tools. For reporting, the methodologies like dashboards, visualization tools, text & table based reports and write back report are applied. The functionalities of BIS have been realized as different solutions for various kinds of problems which are described as follows.

2.1.3 Realization of BIS

BIS offers different solutions in which the widely applied solutions are algorithm based solutions, architecture based solutions and model based solutions, which are described in Table 4.

The different solution offered by BI has been integrated with different kinds of systems. At present, there are many researches which integrate BI with Service Oriented Architecture (SOA), CRM, ERP and Mobile BI. The outcome of integration is described in Table 5.

The BIS building blocks, different functionalities of BIS and its realization are described. Among its different functionalities the reporting is very important, which helps to analyze an issue or a problem, provides information to its readers and it is very essential in the enterprise for decision making (Miller et al., 2016). From the literature it is also evident that most of the BI tools are lacks in user specific reporting with respect to different levels of user requirement.

In an organization, decision making take place in different levels and each level of user requires different kinds of information for decision making. The levels of users are from top management to customers and common users. Instead of normal business reporting a customized business reporting which finds right information to right user at right time. For example consider an agricultural domain, in which different farmer requires different kinds of information for cultivation according to their pres-

Table 4. Different solutions offered by business intelligence

BI Solutions
Algorithm Based BI Solutions
▪ Semantic BI - Mobile BI service based on adaptive recognition of user intention and usage patterns (Kim et al., 2013), (Li Niu et al., 2013). ▪ Uncovering hidden sales patterns - Marketing Management (Cheung & Li, 2012).
Architecture Based BI Solutions
▪ BI architecture for the integration of business and technological domains (Ortega et al., 2014) ▪ BI architecture to capture knowledge of employees carrying out the interpretation (Givens et al., 2013), (Cheung, 2012)
Model Based BI Solutions
▪ BI framework to treat the chronic liver disease (Ayman & Khedr, 2013) ▪ BI model for SOA approach to find customer satisfaction in telecom domain (Tanko & Musiliudeen, 2012), (Yeoh et al., 2013).

Table 5. Integration of BI with other techniques

Integration of BI With Other Techniques
▪ BI + CRM = Customer relations and Customer satisfaction are improved (Dien & Douglas, 2010) ▪ BI + ERP = Time taken for decision making is minimized and the utilization rate of the resources is maximized (Long-Wen et al., 2008). ▪ BI + Socio-Environmental indicators = Managing sustainability with the support of BI (Maria & Marlei, 2009).

ent requirement. The criteria such as soil nature, atmospheric condition, present monsoon condition, ground water level and its availability, present requirement of market condition and nature of different kinds of seed has to be considered to develop a MCR for farmers. Moreover, each farmer may have different interest. By considering all these requirement suitable seed and cultivation information has to be delivered to the respective farmer. The same situation may exist in any business domain to find the suitable alternative user.

Hence a customized reporting is required to deliver the information according to user preference with respect to different criteria. In order to identify the user preference, MCDM techniques are applied. Among the different MCDM techniques, TOPSIS is widely applied for different multi criteria problems. The next section describes about the functionalities of TOPSIS and its applications.

2.2 Functionalities of TOPSIS

TOPSIS ranks the alternatives according to the distances to identify the better alternative (Hwang, 1981) and it solves simple and complex problems with conflicting criteria. The logic which is applied in TOPSIS is to identify a better alternative represents rationale of human choice (Shih et al., 2007). Among the different MCDM methods, TOPSIS has been applied widely to solve multi criteria problems. In the past fifteen years, TOPSIS has tremendous development (Zavadskas et al., 2016). In order to quantify its development, the various works (number of publications: 408) carried out in TOPSIS from 2000 to 2016 is grouped into three categories such as applications solved using TOPSIS (number of publications: 283), extension works carried out in TOPSIS (number of publications: 64) and modifications in TOPSIS (number of publications: 61). These works were referred from standard operations research and management sciences journals which are described in Figure 3.

It has been applied popularly, to solve different kinds of multi criteria problems such as green operations initiatives (Wang, 2015), decision analysis in emergency management (Chen & Du, 2009), Performance of Foreign and Turkish banks financial parameters of Serbian banks (Mandic et al., 2014), content management systems selection (Oztaysi, 2014), best biodiesel blend selection (Sakthivel et al., 2015), network selection process in heterogeneous wireless networks (Obayiuwana, 2015), managing arriving orders (Hemmati et al., 2012) and so on. From these applications, the best features of TOPSIS are described in Figure 4.

Figure 3. Research contributions in TOPSIS
** - These papers were taken from major reputed journals*

Figure 4. Best features of TOPSIS

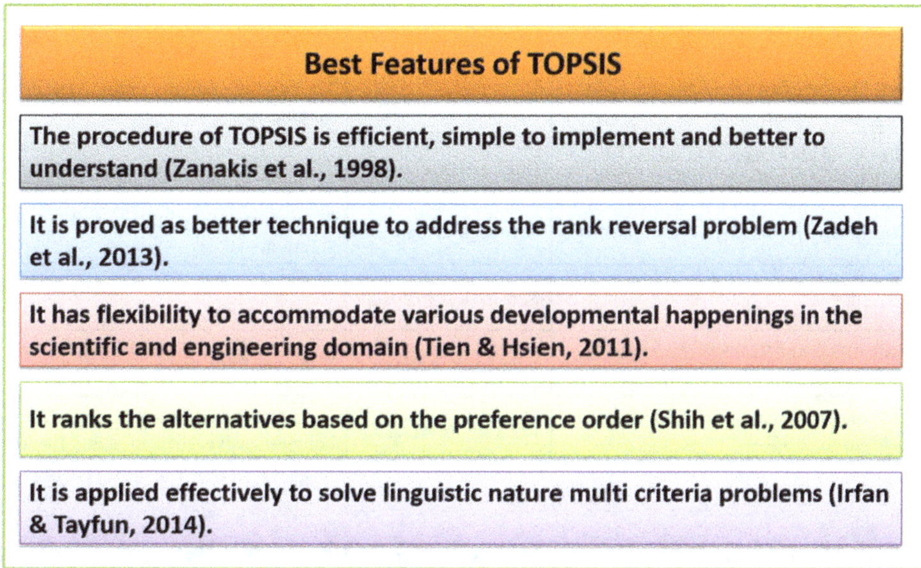

Though different kinds of MCDM techniques are developed, TOPSIS retain its popularity because of its unique features to solve multi criteria problems. Hence, in this research TOPSIS has been applied to find the suitable user for MCR in banking business.

In order to evaluate the TOPSIS applications, different evaluation parameters are required. From the literature study it has been found that there is no specific evaluation parameters are developed to evaluate the TOPSIS application (Mao et al., 2016), (Büyüközkan & Sezin, 2016). Most of the TOPSIS applications are evaluated by evaluation parameters developed for MCDM techniques. Hence a literature study is conducted to identify the evaluation parameters developed for MCDM techniques which is described as follows.

2.3 Evaluation Parameters in MCDM

The different kinds of evaluation parameters applied in MCDM are described in Table 6.

From Table 6 it has been found that, very limited evaluation parameters such as sensitivity analysis, rank reversal, time complexity and space complexity (Pedro, 2013), (Tavana & Hatami-Marbini, 2011), (Ishizaka & Labib, 2009) are found for MCDM applications. Among the different evaluation parameters, sensitivity analysis is a fundamental concept to check the effective implementation of quantitative decision models (Senthil et al., 2014). It examines the effect of the changes of a single parameter on the final rankings of the alternatives (Triantaphyllou & Lin, 1996), (Masuda, 1990). In the previous literature, the evaluation parameters are designed for MCDM applications have described the impact but they have not addressed quantification of the impact. From the literature it is also evident that to evaluate the MCDM applications metrics has not been designed for evaluation parameters to quantify its impact. Hence this research designs evaluation metrics for TOPSIS.

The next section describes the design of MCR for banking business and designs evaluation metrics for TOPSIS.

Table 6. Evaluation parameters applied in MCDM

MCDM Application	Evaluation Parameters	Outcome
A sensitivity analysis algorithm for hierarchical decision models (AHP) (Hongyi & Dundar, 2008)	Sensitivity Analysis	To reveal the ranking order of the decision alternatives
Review of the rank reversal phenomenon in the AHP (Maleki & Zahir, 2013)	Rank Reversal	To interpret AHP ranking using rank reversals
Comparative analysis of MCDM methods (Pedro, 2013)	Sensitivity Analysis	To understand the influence of criteria over the solution
AHP and Expert Choice: Benefits and limitations (Ishizaka & Labib, 2009)	Sensitivity Analysis	The impact of sensitivity analysis on the synthesis of criteria weights
A hybrid method using AHP and TOPSIS (Senthil et al., 2014)	Sensitivity Analysis	Improves Robustness
AHP-TOPSIS framework for human spaceflight mission (Tavana & Hatami-Marbini, 2011)	Ranking Reversal	Proposed model possess certain features: analytical, comprehensive, structured and flexible

3. DESIGN OF MULTI CRITERIA REPORTING FOR BANKING BUSINESS

In banking, huge amount information is available. In traditional Banking system, common information is given to many users which are irrelevant to their requirement. Moreover, banking sector has a wide scope for reporting activities. It has wide variety of stake holders and the required data need to be delivered to different users through different channels. Hence it is essential to find the suitable information to the suitable users according to their requirement. To provide more importance to customization for reporting, MCR is introduced. It finds the user preference based on criteria and generates the report. It provides the suitable information to suitable user according to various criteria. The different elements of MCR are described as follows.

Stakeholders

The users of an organization who are going to receive the MCR are called stakeholders. The different levels of stakeholders of banking business are described in Table 7.

Table 7 list outs the important stakeholders of banking and each stakeholders requires different kinds of reporting. The objective of MCR is to identify and present the required information to the stakeholders.

Table 7. Stakeholders of banking business

Stakeholders of Bankruptcy Prediction Analysis					
A1: General Manager	A2: Customers	A3: Manager	A4: Regional Manager	A5: Chief General Manager	A6: Chairman
A7: Deputy General Manager	A8: Shareholders	A9: Investment analysts	A10: Assistant Manager	A11: Deputy Managing Director	

Information

There are different kinds of information available in banking domain. The information which is considered in this case study is as follows.

- **New Loan Products (LP):** Many customers may have different type of loan like housing, educational, gold, etc. with different kinds of requirement.
- **Wealth Management (WM):** This is a type of financial service that combines personal investments, tax planning strategies, estate planning and legal counsel.
- **Investment Management (IM):** The process of managing money, including investments, budgeting, banking, and taxes are called money management.
- **Resource Management (RM):** Resource Management is the efficient and effective deployment of an organization's resources when they are needed. Such resources may include financial resources, inventory, human skills, production resources, or Information Technology (IT).
- **Trust Services (TS):** The Trust Services are the party, who manages the trust's assets in accordance with the terms of the trust agreement and holds legal title to the trust property.
- **New Initiatives (NI):** The power or ability to begin or to follow through energetically with a plan or task; enterprise and determination.
- **Bank Regulations (BR):** A form of government regulation is termed as Bank regulations which subject banks to certain restrictions, requirements and guidelines.
- **Other Information:** The other bank information such as security news, policy, laws, new training and so on.

Criteria

A criterion is a condition based on that information is customized for MCR. The different kinds of criteria applied for banking domain are described in Table 8.

- Interest of Information

Interest of information identifies the information according to the user interest. For example, customers like to get more information on new loan product whereas government may need information like trust services, so it varies, from one user to another user.

- Level of Information

The information obtained from interest of users decides the level of information. It may vary from one user to another user according to user interest.

Table 8. Criteria for banking to generate MCR

Criteria for Banking Business			
Interest of information	Level of information	Speed of delivery	Level of Security

- Speed of Delivery

Many users want the information to be delivered to them immediately. The period of time in which the information to be delivered is decided by speed of delivery.

- Level of Security

Based on the users and their requirement different level of security is provided.

To generate the MCR, the respective user preference on various information of the banking domain should be identified. It is identified according to the various criteria selected for that domain. In a typical business organization, there are different kinds of users are working and each user has different levels of responsibility (Martin et al., 2014). According to their responsibility, preference and interest the MCR should be generated. To generate the MCR, user preference with respect to different criteria (Table 8) should be identified.

For example, interest of information differs from one user to another user. Different users may have different kinds of requirements. Hence inconsistency arises due to conflicting needs of the users. Once the interest of information is obtained, the next process is examining the level of information. It may not be same for all users and it leads to uncertainty. Thus these decisions are independent to each other. The level of security is applied according to user profile. Hence, to develop the multi criteria reporting, user preference should be identified according to different criteria. To identify the user preference TOPSIS is applied.

The next section describes about design of metrics to evaluate the proposed banking application.

4. DESIGN OF METRICS FOR TOPSIS

This section designs the metrics for TOPSIS. In this section, the first part designs metrics for existing evaluation parameters and the second part designs metrics for new evaluation parameters.

Existing Evaluation Parameters

The existing evaluation parameters are described as follows.

- Time Complexity
- Space Complexity
- Sensitivity Analysis
- Ranking Reversal

New Evaluation Parameters

In addition to existing evaluation parameters, two new ranking evaluation parameters are designed for TOPSIS which are described as follows.

- Repeated Ranking
- Rank Occurrence

Metrics are units of measurement. A software metric is a quantitative measure of a degree to which a software system or process possesses some property. It is defined as follows.

METRIC DEFINED

A metric temple is designed to represent the metrics which is depicted in Figure 5. The template contains name, definition, formulating, value range (i.e. high, medium and low on ranking order of alternatives) and interpretation.

In Design template, the element metric definition describes the intent or purpose of metric, formulation addresses the different factors used to define the metric. Measures fall in percentage level scale and it stands between 0% and 100%. The result of each metric is interpreted based on the value.

4.1 Time Complexity

Time complexity measures the execution time taken by an algorithm.

- **Name:** Time Complexity metric
- **Definition:** Time complexity metric is denoted by R_{TC}. It measures the execution time.
- **Metric Formulation:** R_{TC} is calculated by the following equation

Let TOPSIS_Process be the total amount time taken by the algorithm for its execution and it is measured in seconds.

Figure 5. Metric Template

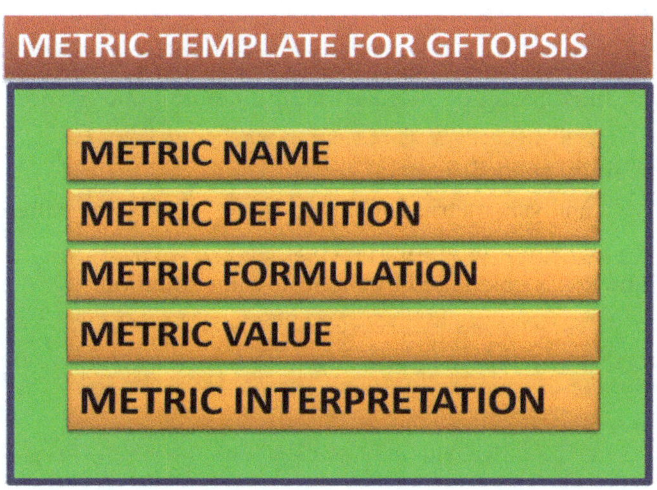

$$R_{TC} = \sum_{i=1}^{m} TOPSIS\_Process \ldots \quad (1)$$

- **Metric Value:** R_{TC} metric value lies from 0 to N.

where, N – maximum time taken by the algorithm

- **Interpretation:** Lower the value of R_{TC} indicates efficient performance of the algorithm.

4.2 Space Complexity

Space complexity measures the memory space required by an algorithm for its execution

- **Name:** Space Complexity metric
- **Definition:** Space complexity metric is denoted by R_{SC}. It measures the required storage space.
- **Metric Formulation:** R_{SC} is calculated by the following equation

Let TOPSIS_Process be the total amount memory space taken by the algorithm for its execution.

$$R_{SC} = \sum_{i=1}^{m} TOPSIS\_Process \ldots \quad (2)$$

- **Metric Value:** R_{SC} metric value lies from 0 to N.

where, N – maximum memory space taken by the algorithm

- **Interpretation:** Lower the value of R_{SC} indicates efficient performance of the algorithm.

4.3 Sensitivity Analysis

It measures the stability of the ranking of alternatives by changing one or more key input values.

- **Metric Name:** Sensitivity analysis metric
- **Definition:** Sensitivity analysis metric is denoted by R_{SA}. It is a measure of number of ranks that are altered when change in weight of alternatives.
- **Metric Formulation:** R_{SA} is calculated by the following equation

Let N_{SA} be the number of ranks that are altered and TNA be the total number of alternatives.

$$R_{SA} = \frac{N_{SA}}{TNA} * 100\%$$

- **Metric Value:** The Sensitivity analysis R_{SA} metric value lies from 0 to 100%.
- **Interpretation:** Lower the value of R_{SA} depicts robustness of the ranking.

4.4 Ranking Reversal

It measures the robustness of the ranking of alternatives by adding and removing of alternatives.

- **Metric Name:** Ranking reversal metric
- **Definition:** Ranking reversal metric is denoted by R_{RE}. It is a measure of number of ranks that are altered when number of alternatives is added or deleted.
- **Metric Formulation:** R_{RE} is calculated by the following equation
  Let N_{RE} be the number of ranks that are altered and TNA be the total number of alternatives.

$$R_{RE} = \frac{N_{RE}}{TNA} * 100\%$$

- **Metric Value:** R_{RE} metric value lies from 0 to 100%.
- **Interpretation:** Lower the value of R_{RE} depicts robustness of the ranking.

4.5 Repeated Ranking

Repeated Ranking is defined as number of ranks that are repeated.

- **Metric Name:** Repeated ranking metric
- **Definition:** Repeated ranking metric is denoted by R_{RR}. It is the ratio of number of ranks repeated to total number of items.
- **Metric Formulation:** Let ratio of Repeated ranking be denoted by R_{RR} and it is calculated by the following equation.

Let N_{RR} be the number of ranks repeated and TNA be the Total Number of Alternatives.

$$R_{RR} = \frac{N_{RR}}{TNA} * 100\%$$

- **Metric Value:** Repeated ranking metric value lies from 0 to 100%.
- **Interpretation:** Lower the value of this ratio depicts better performance in ranking.

4.6 Rank Occurrence

Rank Occurrence is defined as number of times the ranks occurred.

- **Metric Name:** Rank Occurrence metric
- **Definition:** Rank Occurrence metric is denoted by R_{RO}. It is the ratio of number of repeated rank occurrence to total number of items.
- **Metric Formulation:** Let ratio of rank occurrence be denoted by R_{RO} and it is calculated by the following equation.

Let N_O be the number of repeated rank occurrence and TNI is the Total Number of alternatives.

$$R_{RO} = \frac{N_O}{TNA} *100\%$$

- **Metric Value:** Rank Occurrence metric value lies from 0 to 100%.
- **Interpretation:** Lower the value of this ratio depicts efficient ranking.

These metrics are applied to evaluate the proposed banking application developed using TOPSIS to identify user preference. The next section describes about experimentation of TOPSIS to identify user preference required to develop MCR for banking business.

5. EXPERIMENTAL DESIGN

To develop the MCR, the user preference on different banking information should be identified. Moreover, each of these criteria applied in this reporting should be assigned weight (preference) based on either probability measure or necessary measure. To obtain user preference (weight of different criteria) a questionnaire is designed. The questionnaire is evaluated by different banking users who are in managerial positions. The weight that is assigned different criteria is described in Table 9.

In this questionnaire, each of the banking information is assigned weight according to the criteria and it starts from highest value (10) to lowest value (1). The highest value indicates that most preferred user to receive the particular information. The lowest value indicates that user is having lowest priority to receive the information. The different weight assigned by various bank users on New Loan Product has been described in Table 10.

Table 9. Weight assigned to different criteria

Criteria	Weight		
	W_1	W_2	W3
Interest of Information	0.4	0.5	0.6
Level of Information	0.5	0.6	0.7
Level of Security	0.6	0.7	0.8
Speed of Delivery	0.3	0.4	0.5

Table 10. Weights assigned to "new loan product" with respect to the criteria "interest of information"

Users/ Banks	Loan Products (Criteria: Interest of Information)																							
	HDFC Bank				KVB*				ICICI Bank			AXIS Bank			IOB*				INDIAN Bank					
Customer	9	8	9	8	9	8	8	8	4	7	8	6	6	5	4	9	9	9	1	8	5	1	7	7
Competitors	8	1	8	7	5	1	4	2	1	1	3	8	8	6	1	8	2	1	1	3	6	1	1	1
Government	5	2	2	4	1	3	2	1	4	5	2	2	2	6	5	1	8	5	1	2	6	1	2	2
Economist	4	8	5	4	5	2	6	6	8	7	7	8	8	7	8	9	7	9	1	7	7	1	7	7
Management	6	8	6	5	9	5	8	9	5	8	9	4	4	6	5	1	6	5	1	9	6	1	8	8
Investment Analysts	7	4	3	5	8	4	3	4	4	7	7	6	6	7	4	1	5	4	1	7	7	1	8	8
Employees	5	5	4	9	1	3	5	5	6	6	1	7	7	5	6	8	8	1	1	1	5	1	6	6

*IOB – Indian Overseas Bank, KVB – Karur Vysya Bank

The weight (preference on information) expressed by different banking users belongs to various banks, according to the criteria "interest of information" for the information "New Loan Product" is described in Table 10. The weight expressed by directors and managers to New Loan Product is higher and least weight is assigned to government. The economist and other lenders are assigned the weight in the range of 5-7. Similarly, for other bankruptcy prediction indicators such as investment management, resource management and bank regulation the weights are assigned. The weight expressed by different banking users for investment management according to the criteria "level of information" has been described in Table11.

The weights expressed by banking users are used form the decision matrix. The weights for each of the banking information according to the criteria such as Interest of Information, Level of Information, Level of Security and Speed of Delivery have been obtained from the banking users. The weight of various alternatives for the criteria "Interest to Information" has been described in Table 12.

Table 11. Weights assigned to "investment management" with respect to the criteria "level of information"

Users/ Banks	Investment Management (Criteria: Level of information)																				
	HDFC Bank				KVB*				ICICI Bank				AXIS Bank			IOB*			INDIAN Bank		
A1: General Manager	9	8	8	9	9	9	8	6	6	8	7	6	6	5	6	4	4	6	6	5	2
A2: Customers	9	6	6	1	8	7	4	5	5	1	5	4	1	1	1	7	7	5	1	5	8
A3: Manager	4	6	6	1	8	5	3	4	4	1	4	6	8	6	2	5	5	8	8	7	9
A4: Regional Manager	3	6	6	9	7	7	7	6	5	1	5	5	9	4	7	4	4	5	9	8	7
A5: Chief General Manager	2	6	6	5	8	6	6	6	6	1	7	8	6	3	6	5	5	8	6	1	6
A6: Chairman	1	2	2	4	9	3	3	8	8	1	9	6	7	5	2	4	4	4	7	1	5
A7: Deputy General Manager	1	2	2	7	1	2	2	6	6	1	6	5	5	7	1	3	3	5	5	7	6

Table 12. Weight of various alternatives for criteria "interest of information"

Criteria\ Alternatives	Loan Products	Investment Mgmt.	Other Services	Wealth Mgmt.	Resource Mgmt.	Trust Service	New Initiative	Bank Regulations
A1: General Manager	$\bar{9}$	$\bar{6}$	$\bar{7}$	$\bar{5}$	$\bar{5}$	$\bar{9}$	$\bar{8}$	$\bar{5}$
A2: Customer	$\bar{4}$	$\bar{3}$	$\bar{4}$	$\bar{2}$	$\bar{3}$	$\bar{4}$	$\bar{6}$	$\bar{4}$
A3: Manager	$\bar{7}$	$\bar{5}$	$\bar{6}$	$\bar{4}$	$\bar{8}$	$\bar{8}$	$\bar{5}$	$\bar{3}$
A4: Regional Manager	$\bar{6}$	$\bar{8}$	$\bar{7}$	$\bar{7}$	$\bar{6}$	$\bar{7}$	$\bar{7}$	$\bar{6}$
A5: Chief General Manager	$\bar{8}$	$\bar{2}$	$\bar{4}$	$\bar{3}$	$\bar{4}$	$\bar{3}$	$\bar{3}$	$\bar{2}$
A6: Chairman	7	$\bar{3}$	$\bar{2}$	$\bar{2}$	$\bar{2}$	$\bar{2}$	$\bar{4}$	$\bar{2}$
A7: Deputy General Manager	$\bar{8}$	$\bar{7}$	$\bar{8}$	$\bar{5}$	$\bar{5}$	$\bar{6}$	$\bar{9}$	$\bar{9}$

The alternatives and their interest in banking information are described in Table 12. For loan product customers is having more interest and they are given highest value of 9. The level of interest goes to employees and weight is assigned the value of 7. The least interest user on loan product is competitors with the value of 4. Similarly, for the information "new initiatives" the employees are most preferred users. Likewise all the banking information is given least and most preferred users with fuzzy weight value is assigned. The weights of the various alternatives are given for the criteria "Level of Information". The weighs are given based on the guidelines of the experts in the banking fields which are described in Table 13.

Table 13. Weight of various alternatives for criteria "level of information"

Criteria\ Alternatives	Loan Products	Investment Mgmt.	Other Services	Wealth Mgmt.	Resource Mgmt.	Trust Service	New Initiative	Bank Regulations
A1: General Manager	$\bar{9}$	$\bar{6}$	$\bar{6}$	$\bar{4}$	$\bar{5}$	$\bar{9}$	$\bar{8}$	$\bar{3}$
A2: Customers	$\bar{4}$	$\bar{4}$	$\bar{3}$	$\bar{4}$	$\bar{3}$	$\bar{5}$	$\bar{4}$	$\bar{2}$
A3: Manager	$\bar{3}$	$\bar{4}$	$\bar{4}$	$\bar{5}$	$\bar{5}$	$\bar{6}$	$\bar{7}$	$\bar{5}$
A4: Regional Manager	$\bar{7}$	$\bar{7}$	$\bar{6}$	$\bar{7}$	$\bar{7}$	$\bar{9}$	$\bar{5}$	$\bar{7}$
A5: Chief General Manager	$\bar{4}$	$\bar{3}$	$\bar{5}$	$\bar{2}$	$\bar{5}$	$\bar{4}$	$\bar{3}$	$\bar{4}$
A6: Chairman	$\bar{1}$	$\bar{3}$	$\bar{2}$	$\bar{3}$	$\bar{4}$	$\bar{3}$	$\bar{2}$	$\bar{3}$
A7: Deputy General Manager	$\bar{7}$	$\bar{7}$	$\bar{8}$	$\bar{6}$	$\bar{8}$	$\bar{8}$	$\bar{6}$	$\bar{8}$

Likewise the weight of alternative are calculated based on criteria such as "speed of delivery" and "level of security". These weights are applied in TOPSIS and RCC is calculated from which the alternatives are ranked to identify the user preference. The procedure of TOPSIS is implemented in MATLAB.

6. RESULTS AND DISCUSSION

The user preference on different banking information has been identified. This section also describes the results obtained for evaluation metrics designed to evaluate the TOPSIS. The user preference obtained for the banking information such as loan products, investment management and new initiatives are described in Table 14.

The RCC value of loan products for A11: deputy managing director is 0.7936 which is very closer to 1. Hence deputy managing director is most preferred user for loan products and the least preferred user is A9: Investment analysts (RCC: 113). The different user preference on various banking information is shown in a graph depicted in Figure 6.

According to preference shown in graph the information about loan products, investment management and new initiatives is customized to develop the MCR. The graph shows the preference of different users towards various banking information. The most preferred and least preferred users for various banking information is described in Table 15.

The most preferred user and least preferred user for different banking information is described in Table 15. To generate MCR for new loan products, customer is most preferred user and suppliers are least preferred user. These results are passed to reporting tools to generate the MCR.

This research also designed evaluation metrics to evaluate the proposed TOPSIS application. The proposed metrics are time complexity, space complexity, sensitivity analysis, ranking reversal, rank occurrence and repeated ranking. The results obtained for these metrics are described as follows.

Table 14.User Preference on Different Banking Information

Bank Information	Loan Products		Investment Mgmt.		New Initiatives	
Alternatives	***RCC**	**Rank**	***RCC**	**Rank**	***RCC**	**Rank**
A1: General Manager	0.6887	3	0.4528	8	0.7925	1
A2: Customers	0.4315	7	0.5248	6	0.6589	6
A3: Manager	0.5705	4	0.5102	7	0.5154	9
A4: Regional Manager	0.7705	2	0.6548	3	0.7125	3
A5: Chief General Manager	0.5666	6	0.4123	10	0.7113	4
A6: Chairman	0.5669	5	0.7978	1	0.6985	5
A7: Deputy General Manager	0.4266	8	0.3579	11	0.7456	2
A8: Shareholders	0.3747	9	0.7805	2	0.6187	7
A9: Investment analysts	0.1113	11	0.6402	4	0.5676	8
A10: Assistant Manager	0.2572	10	0.5666	5	0.4586	10
A11: Deputy Managing Director	0.7936	1	0.4266	9	0.4289	11

Figure 6. Different user preference on banking information

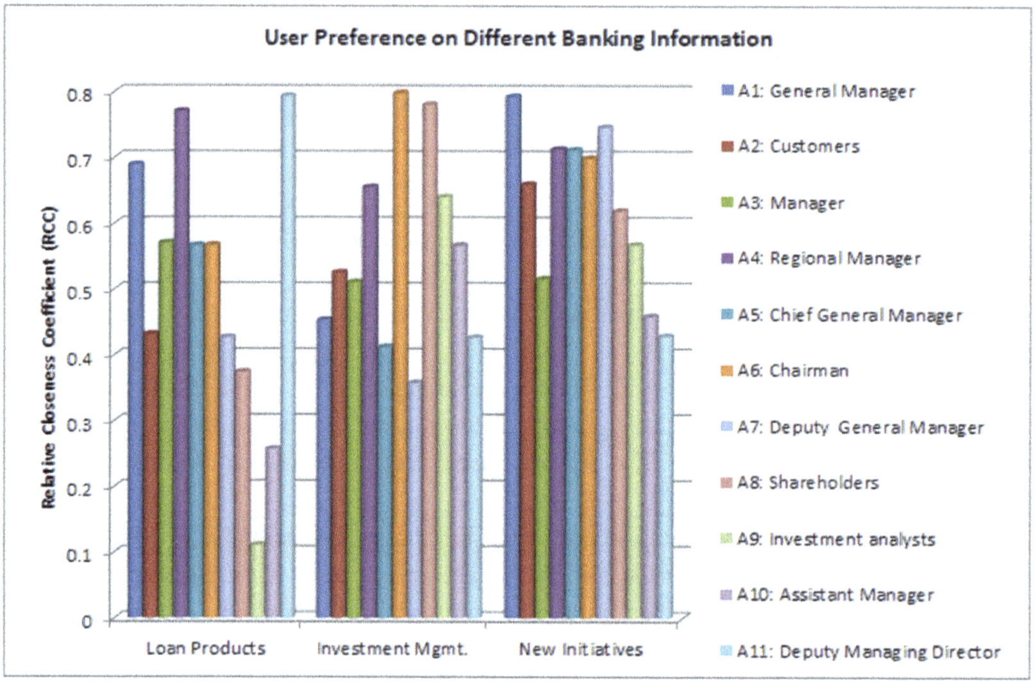

Table 15. Banking user preference on different banking information

Banking Information	Most Preferred user	Least Preferred user
New Loan products	Customer	Suppliers
Investment management	Management	Economist
Other information of Bank	Customer	Investment Analyst
Wealth Management	Management	Investment Analyst
Resource Management	Management	Competitor
Trust service	Customer	Competitor
New initiatives	Employee	Lenders
Bank Regulations	Government	Investment Analyst

6.1 Time and Space Complexity

The time and space complexity of banking application evaluated using TOPSIS is described in Table 16.

6.2 Sensitivity Analysis

Sensitivity analysis measures the impact on the outcome by changing one or more key input values. The sensitivity analysis operates on TOPSIS method and checks the stability of its outputs by modifying the input parameters. Hence, performing a sensitivity analysis on the results of a decision problem may

Table 16. Time and Space Complexity of Fuzzy TOPSIS

Metric	Time Complexity (Seconds)	Space Complexity (bytes)
TOPSIS	0.195191	2612

provide valuable information to the decision maker about the robustness of the solution. The weights are changed in two different ways and the efficiency is checked. In the first case, all the criteria are assigned equal weight. The impact of sensitivity analysis is described in Table 17.

In this analysis, the RCC value for the alternatives are differs whereas the ranking order alternatives has not been changed which is plotted as graph and depicted in Figure 7.

The sensitivity analysis metric R_{SA} iscomputed as

$$R_{SA} = \frac{N_{SA}}{TNA} * 100\% = (0/11) * 100 = 0\%$$

R_{SA} has 0% value which indicates robustness of the ranking. The sensitivity analysis on TOPSIS has been conducted on exchanging the criteria weight from one to another described in Table 18.

The result of sensitivity analysis on TOPSIS by exchanging weight is shown in Table 19.

In this analysis, the ranking order of the alternatives A4, A6 and A11 have been changed. The other alternatives have retained their rankings. The value of $R_{SA} = (3/11) * 100 = 27.27\%$. R_{SA} has minimum

Table 17. Sensitivity Analysis on TOPSIS by assigning equal weights to all criteria

*ALT	SENSITIVITY ANALYSIS			
	BEFORE		AFTER	
	#RCC	RANK	#RCC	RANK
A1	0.7705	2	0.7203	2
A2	0.7936	1	0.8174	1
A3	0.5666	4	0.5334	4
A4	0.3747	9	0.4079	9
A5	0.1113	11	0.0982	11
A6	0.4266	7	0.4083	7
A7	0.2572	10	0.2654	10
A8	0.6887	3	0.6401	3
A9	0.5666	4	0.5334	4
A10	0.5666	4	0.5334	4
A11	0.4266	7	0.4083	7

*ALT – Alternatives, # RCC - Relative Closeness Coefficient

Figure 7. Sensitivity analysis on changing weights to 1

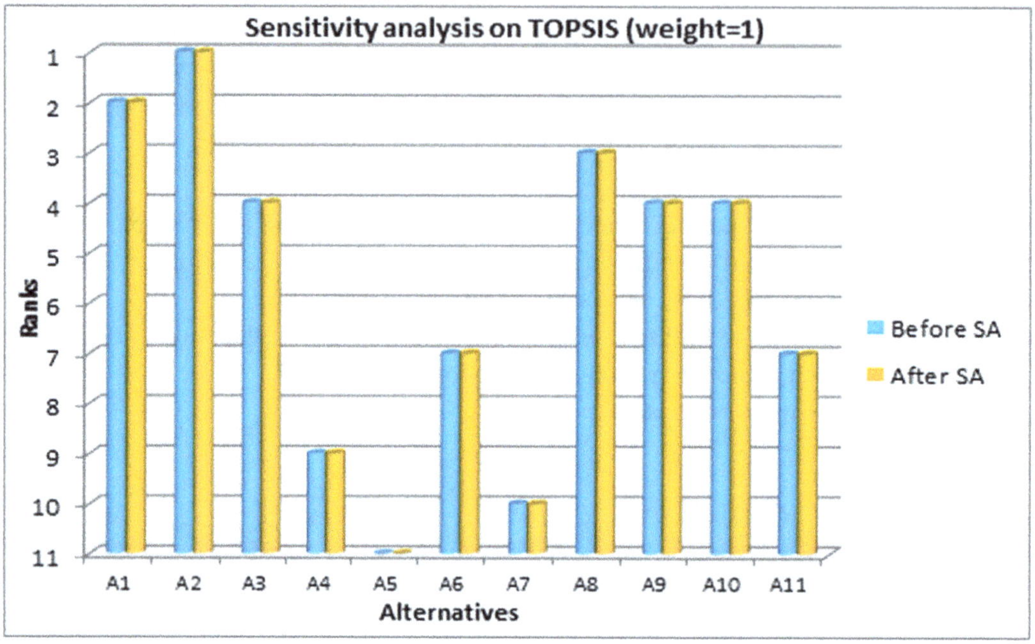

Table 18. Sensitivity analysis to exchange the criteria weight

Criteria	Original weight			Exchanging weight		
Interest of Information	0.4	0.5	0.6	0.5	0.6	0.7
Level of Information	0.5	0.6	0.7	0.4	0.5	0.6
Level of Security	0.6	0.7	0.8	0.3	0.4	0.5
Speed of Delivery	0.3	0.4	0.5	0.6	0.7	0.8

value which indicates that ranking obtained for the alternatives are highly robust. The next metric rank reversal is applied on this application and its results are described.

6.3 Rank Reversal

Adding an Alternative

An identical copy of a best alternative is introduced to validate the robustness of the best alternative (changes or not). To perform this, the new alternative A12 is introduced in the original data. The RCC and ranks obtain before and after rank reversal is shown in Table 20.

When rank reversal has been applied the ranking order of the first four alternatives has not been changed. The ranking order of the alternatives such as A5 and A7 are changed. The newly added alter-

Table 19. Sensitivity Analysis on TOPSIS by exchanging the criteria weight

*ALT	Sensitivity analysis			
	Before		After	
	#RCC	RANK	#RCC	RANK
A1	0.7705	2	0.6740	2
A2	0.7936	1	0.8396	1
A3	0.5666	4	0.5034	4
A4	**0.3747**	**9**	**0.4387**	**7**
A5	0.1113	11	0.0855	11
A6	**0.4266**	**7**	**0.3914**	**8**
A7	0.2572	10	0.2733	10
A8	0.6887	3	0.5946	3
A9	0.5666	4	0.5034	4
A10	0.5666	4	0.5034	4
A11	**0.4266**	**7**	**0.3914**	**8**

Table 20. Rank Reversal on TOPSIS for adding a new alternative

*ALT	RANK REVERSAL			
	BEFORE		AFTER	
	#RCC	RANK	#RCC	RANK
A1	0.7705	2	0.7709	2
A2	0.7936	1	0.7938	1
A3	0.5666	4	0.5662	4
A4	0.3747	9	0.3754	9
A5	**0.1113**	**11**	**0.1109**	**12**
A6	0.4266	7	0.4265	7
A7	**0.2572**	**10**	**0.2586**	**11**
A8	0.6887	3	0.6882	3
A9	0.5666	4	0.5662	4
A10	0.5666	4	0.5662	4
A11	0.4266	7	0.4265	7
A12	**-**	**-**	**0.3023**	**10**

native A12 has ranking order of 10. The rank reversal metric (R_{RE}) for this equation is calculated as $R_{RE} = \frac{N_{RE}}{TNA} * 100\%$ = (2/11)*100 = 18.18%. The number of ranking order change is very minimal and it is described in Figure 8.

Similarly, rank reversal is performed for TOPSIS to identify the robustness of ranking by removing lest alternative.

Figure 8. Rank Reversal on TOPSIS for adding a new alternative

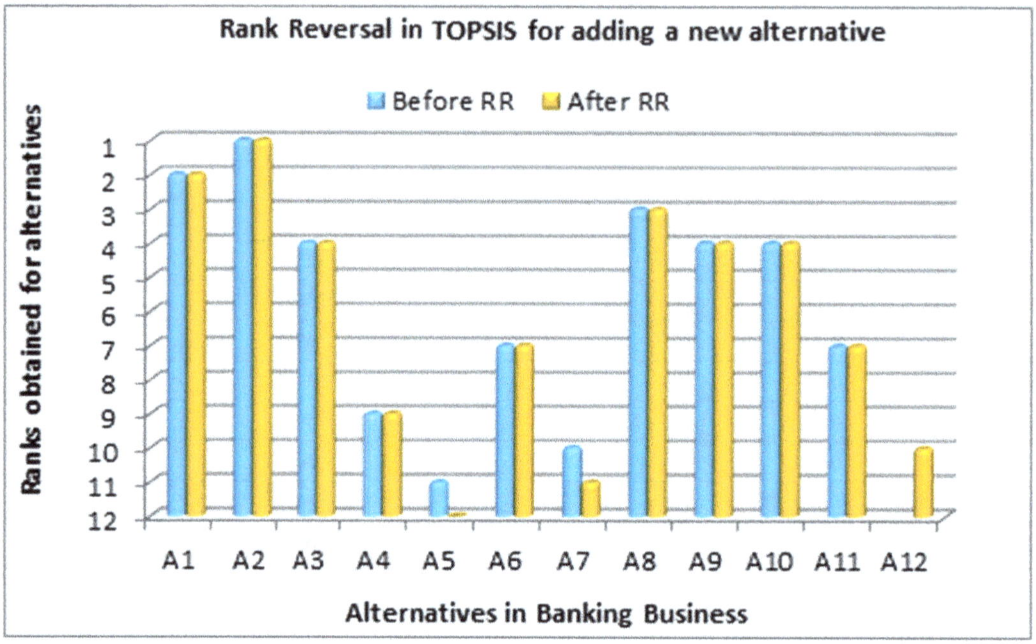

Removing an Alternative

A least alternative is removed in order to verify the change in the ranking order of alternatives. To perform this, the least alternative is found and removed from the original data. From Table 21, it has been found that alternative 5 is the least alternative and it is removed. The RCC and ranks obtained before and after rank reversal is shown in the Table 21.

Table 21. Rank Reversal in TOPSIS for removing a least alternative

*ALT	RANK REVERSAL			
	BEFORE		AFTER	
	#RCC	RANK	#RCC	RANK
A1	0.7705	2	0.7127	2
A2	0.7936	1	0.7550	1
A3	0.5666	4	0.4740	4
A4	0.3747	9	0.2489	9
A5	Removed			
A6	0.4266	7	0.3056	7
A7	0.2572	10	0.1000	10
A8	0.6887	3	0.6171	3
A9	0.5666	4	0.4740	4
A10	0.5666	4	0.4740	4
A11	0.4266	7	0.3056	7

In this case the ranking order of the alternatives has not been changed. The RCC value of the alternatives is differs when rank reversal is conducted but ranking order is retained which is depicted in Figure 9.

The value of ranking reversal metric is computed by the equation.

$$R_{RE} = \frac{N_{RE}}{TNA} * 100\% = (0/11) * 100\% = 0\%.$$

This value gives the confident that ranking order of alternatives obtained using ranking reversal does not have impact in ranking order of the alternatives.

6.4 Rank Occurrence and Repeated Ranking

The RCC value obtained for all the alternatives are described. From these RCC values the rank occurrence and repeated ranking are computed. Consider an example. The RCC obtained for an application is described in Figure 10.

6.4.1 Repeated Ranking (R_{RR})

Repeated Ranking is defined as number of ranks that are repeated. For this banking multi criteria reporting the ranks such as 0.2352 0.1725 0.2362 0.1720 0.2353 0.2349 0.2550 0.1717 0.2348 and other ranks are repeated. The total number of ranks that are repeated in this banking application is 27. From this information the repeated ranking is computed as follows.

Figure 9. Rank orders in TOPSIS by removing a least alternative

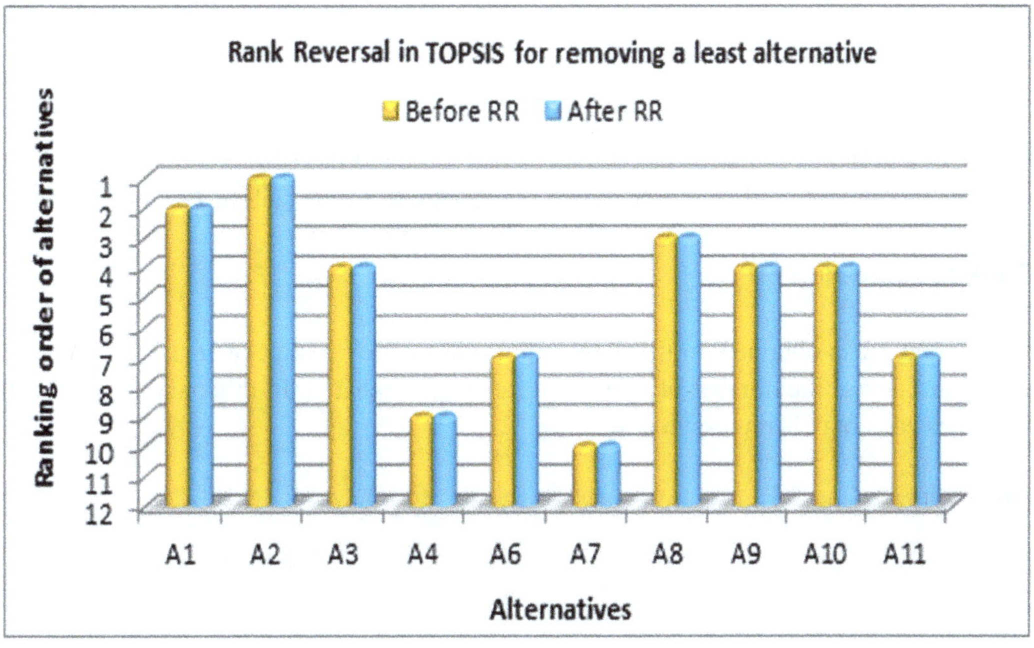

Figure 10. RCC value obtained for all the alternatives

0.2352 0.2534 0.17250.23620.1720 0.2557 0.2265 0.25370.2246 0.2261
0.3366 0.2368 0.3027 0.2533 0.2342 0.2752 0.2352 0.2350 0.1877 0.2352
0.3032 0.2046 0.23480.2537 0.2357 0.2343 0.23450.2348 0.2758 0.2337
0.23450.17210.23560.17250.1713 0.1888 0.2755 0.1068 0.2760 0.2763
0.1176 0.1732 0.18620.2533 0.1714 0.2030 0.23470.2353 0.1867 0.2347
0.3042 0.2781 0.23550.20530.23490.2352 0.1886 0.2355 0.1858 0.2341
0.2355 0.1180 0.17230.17310.17230.20620.2550 0.2765 0.1307 0.2046
0.2278 0.2370 0.2526 0.2535 0.2544 0.3020 0.23520.2353 0.2552 0.2352
0.2051 0.1063 0.2353 0.1164 0.17170.17150.23520.23530.25330.2347
0.1724 0.2067 0.3030 0.3367 0.2549 0.17250.1720 0.1722 0.1862 0.2363
0.1883 0.1719 0.1872 0.2360 0.17240.2354 0.1061 0.2351 0.2033 0.2362
0.23490.2353 0.2050 0.1713 0.0971 0.20620.1719 0.2049 0.17210.2356
0.23620.2353 0.1856 0.23470.1725 0.1734 0.2352 0.1085 0.2546 0.2053
0.3043 0.2767 0.1306 0.2370 0.3343 0.1717 0.2551 0.22460.17150.2535
0.1731 0.0983 0.2356 0.0995 0.1866 0.1874 0.2045 0.1871 0.2273 0.1735
0.1057 0.2520 0.2356 0.2247 0.17210.23520.25500.1720 0.1181 0.3040
0.2354 0.2044

$R_{RR} = 18.18\%$

Generally the repeated ranking (R_{RR}) should be minimal. In this application, the value of repeated ranking is 18.18%. The metric R_{RR} is used to find the steadiness of the ranking order of the alternatives.

6.4.2 Rank Occurrence ($\mathbf{R_{RO}}$)

From the different ranks obtained on this application the metric, rank occurrence is computed. Rank occurrence is defined as the number of times that ranks are repeated. In this banking application, the number of times each rank is represented in Table 22.

$R_{RO} = 45.4545$

Table 22. List of Repeated Ranks

RCC	No. of times rank repeated	RCC	No. of times rank repeated	RCC	No. of times rank repeated
0.2352	7	0.2537	2	0.2356	4
0.1725	4	0.2246	2	0.1713	2
0.2362	3	0.2533	3	0.1862	2
0.1720	3	0.2046	2	0.2347	3
0.2353	5	0.2355	3	0.2053	2
0.2349	2	0.1723	2	0.2062	2
0.2550	2	0.2370	2	0.2535	2
0.1717	2	0.1715	2	0.1721	2
0.2348	2	0.1731	2	0.2354	2

In this application, the ranks such as 0.2352, 0.1725 , 0.2356 0.2353 are repeated 7, 4, 4 and 5 numbers of times. The ranks such as 0.2362, 0.1720, 0.2533,0.2355 and 0.2347 are repeated three times. The other ranks are repeated only two times. From these repeated ranks, the rank occurrence is computed as follows.

The value of R_{RO} is 45.4545. In this banking application, the number of times the same rank is repeated many number of times. This metric is very useful to measure the stability of the ranking order of the alternatives. The values obtained for the metrics designed in this research for banking application is described in Table 23.

Table 23. Evaluation Metrics results for Banking Application

S.No	TOPSIS Evaluation Metrics	Value
1.	Time Complexity (R_{TC})	0.195191 seconds
2.	Space Complexity (R_{SC})	2612 bytes
3.	Sensitivity Analysis (R_{SA}) (Basic weight)	0%
4.	Sensitivity Analysis (R_{SA}) (Exchanging weight)	27.27%
5.	Ranking Reversal (R_{RE}) (Adding a new alternative)	18.18%
6.	Ranking Reversal (R_{RE}) (Removing an alternative)	0%
7.	Repeated Ranking (R_{RR})	18.18%
8.	Rank Occurrence (R_{RO})	45.45%
9.	Relative Closeness Efficiency (R_{RC})	0.7936

The metrics which are designed in this research has been applied for banking application and its values are described. These metrics are useful to evaluate the TOPSIS application. The same metrics can be applied to other applications of TOPSIS. The comparative analysis of these metrics on different TOPSIS applications will give an analysis on suitability of these metrics. These metrics also can be applied to other MCDM applications. For example these metrics should be applied to MCDM applications which are evaluated using Analytic Hierarchy Process (AHP), Simple Additive Weighting (SAW), Complex Proportional ASsessment (COPRAS) and other MCDM techniques. This kind of analysis will be useful to find the suitability of these metrics to different MCDM applications. In recent research, there are limited evaluations parameters are designed for MCDM applications. This research has taken effort to design metrics for TOPSIS applications. It can be extended other kinds of MCDM techniques to design the metrics.

7. CONCLUSION

This research made an attempt to design metrics for TOPSIS applications and these metrics are validated with banking multi criteria application. These metrics are designed from the functionalities of the TOPSIS method. In most of the MCDM applications, the evaluation parameters such as time complexity, space complexity, sensitivity analysis and ranking reversal are applied for validation. These evaluation parameters have not been considered as metrics in previous research. Along with these evaluation parameters this research has identified two evaluation parameters such repeated ranking and rank occurrence from relative closeness coefficient. These evaluation parameters are designed as metrics and applied in banking application to evaluate it.

The customization of the multi criteria reporting is depends upon the selected criteria such as interest of information, level of information, level of security and speed of delivery. The functionalities of the MCR can be improved by adding more number of criteria according to the user requirement.

REFERENCES

Aciar, S., Avesani, P., De la Rosa, J. L., Hormazabal, N., & Serra, A. (2009, June). Adaptive business intelligence for an open negotiation environment. In *Digital Ecosystems and Technologies, 2009. DEST'09. 3rd IEEE International Conference on* (pp. 517-522). IEEE. doi:10.1109/DEST.2009.5276732

Al-Azmi & Abdul-Aziz. (2013). *Data, text and web mining for business intelligence: A survey*. arXiv preprint arXiv:1304.3563

Bahrami, M., Arabzad, S. M., & Ghorbani, M. (2012). Innovation in market management by utilizing business intelligence: Introducing proposed framework. *Procedia: Social and Behavioral Sciences, 41*, 160–167. doi:10.1016/j.sbspro.2012.04.020

Bajo, J., Borrajo, M. L., De Paz, J. F., Corchado, J. M., & Pellicer, M. A. (2012). A multi-agent system for web-based risk management in small and medium business. *Expert Systems with Applications, 39*(8), 6921–6931. doi:10.1016/j.eswa.2012.01.001

Bitools.net. (n.d.). *Business Intelligence Tools and Software - Pentaho Analysis*. Retrieved October 03, 2016, from http://www.bitool.net/software/pentaho-analysis.html

Business Intelligent-Columo. (n.d.). *Business Intelligence for Finance People*. Retrieved December 23, 2016, from http://www.calumo.com/business-intelligence-for-finance/

Büyüközkan, G., & Güleryüz, S. (2016). Multi Criteria Group Decision Making Approach for Smart Phone Selection Using Intuitionistic Fuzzy TOPSIS. *International Journal of Computational Intelligence Systems*, *9*(4), 709–725. doi:10.1080/18756891.2016.1204119

Chen, W. S., & Du, Y. K. (2009). Using neural networks and data mining techniques for the financial distress prediction model. *Expert Systems with Applications*, *36*(2), 4075–4086. doi:10.1016/j.eswa.2008.03.020

Cheung, C. F., & Li, F. L. (2012). A quantitative correlation coefficient mining method for business intelligence in small and medium enterprises of trading business. *Expert Systems with Applications*, *39*(7), 6279–6291. doi:10.1016/j.eswa.2011.10.021

Chung, W., & Tseng, T. L. B. (2012). Discovering business intelligence from online product reviews: A rule-induction framework. *Expert Systems with Applications*, *39*(15), 11870–11879. doi:10.1016/j.eswa.2012.02.059

Cox, B. L., & Jantti, M. (2012). Capturing business intelligence required for targeted marketing, demonstrating value, and driving process improvement. *Library & Information Science Research*, *34*(4), 308–316. doi:10.1016/j.lisr.2012.06.002

Cvitaš, A. (2011, May). Relation extraction from text documents. In *MIPRO, 2011 Proceedings of the 34th International Convention* (pp. 1565-1570). IEEE.

ElliottTimo. (2014). *Digital Business & Business Analytics–Self-Service vs Traditional Business Intelligence*. Retrieved October 03, 2016, from http://timoelliott.com/blog/2014/04/qa-self-service-vs-traditional-business-intelligence.html

Fairwarning. (2016). *Salesforce Data Protection through User Activity Monitoring*. FairWarning, Inc.

Foster, K., Smith, G., Ariyachandra, T., & Frolick, M. N. (2015). Business intelligence competency center: Improving data and decisions. *Information Systems Management*, *32*(3), 229–233. doi:10.1080/10580530.2015.1044343

Genc, Y., Mason, W., & Nickerson, J. V. (2013). *Semantic transforms using collaborative knowledge bases*. Academic Press.

George, J., Kumar, V., & Kumar, S. (2015). Data Warehouse Design Considerations for a Healthcare Business Intelligence System. *World Congress on Engineering*.

Givens, Storey, & Sugumaran. (2013). A method for improving business intelligence interpretation through the use of semantic technology. In *International Conference on Application of Natural Language to Information Systems*. Springer.

Gounder, M. S., Iyer, V. V., & Al Mazyad, A. (2016, March). A survey on business intelligence tools for university dashboard development. In *Big Data and Smart City (ICBDSC), 2016 3rd MEC International Conference on* (pp. 1-7). IEEE. doi:10.1109/ICBDSC.2016.7460347

Gupta, B., Goul, M., & Dinter, B. (2015). Business Intelligence and Big Data in Higher Education: Status of a Multi-Year Model Curriculum Development Effort for Business School Undergraduates, MS Graduates, and MBAs. CAIS, 36, 23.

Hayashi, Y., Hsieh, M. H., & Setiono, R. (2010). Understanding consumer heterogeneity: A business intelligence application of neural networks. *Knowledge-Based Systems*, *23*(8), 856–863. doi:10.1016/j.knosys.2010.05.010

Hemmati, S., Ebadian, M., & Nahvi, A. (2012). A new decision making structure for managing arriving orders in MTO environments. *Expert Systems with Applications*, *39*(3), 2669–2676. doi:10.1016/j.eswa.2011.08.122

Hinze, A., Voisard, A., & Buchanan, G. (2009). Tip: Personalizing information delivery in a tourist information system. *Information Technology & Tourism*, *11*(3), 247–264. doi:10.3727/109830509X12596187864071

Hongyi, C., & Kocaoglu, D. F. (2008). A sensitivity analysis algorithm for hierarchical decision models. *European Journal of Operational Research*, *185*(1), 266–288. doi:10.1016/j.ejor.2006.12.029

Hsieh, K. L. (2011). Employing a recommendation expert system based on mental accounting and artificial neural networks into mining business intelligence for study abroad's P/S recommendations. *Expert Systems with Applications*, *38*(12), 14376–14381. doi:10.1016/j.eswa.2011.03.078

Hwang & Yoon. (1981). Multiple criteria decision making. *Lecture Notes in Economics and Mathematical Systems, 186.*

Ishaya, T., & Folarin, M. (2012). A service oriented approach to Business Intelligence in Telecoms industry. *Telematics and Informatics*, *29*(3), 273–285. doi:10.1016/j.tele.2012.01.004

Ishizaka, A., & Labib, A. (2009). Analytic hierarchy process and expert choice: Benefits and limitations. *Or Insight, 22*(4), 201-220.

Khedr, A. (2013). Business intelligence framework to support chronic liver disease treatment. *International Journal of Computers & Technology, 4*(2), 307-312.

Kim, H. D., Lee, I., & Lee, C. K. (2013). Building Web 2.0 enterprises: A study of small and medium enterprises in the United States. *International Small Business Journal*, *31*(2), 156–174. doi:10.1177/0266242611409785

Kleesuwan, S., Mitatha, S., Yupapin, P. P., & Piyatamrong, B. (2010). Business intelligence in Thailand's higher educational resources management. *Procedia: Social and Behavioral Sciences*, *2*(1), 84–87. doi:10.1016/j.sbspro.2010.01.018

Larson, D., & Chang, V. (2016). A review and future direction of agile, business intelligence, analytics and data science. *International Journal of Information Management*, *36*(5), 700–710. doi:10.1016/j.ijinfomgt.2016.04.013

Li, S. T., Shue, L. Y., & Lee, S. F. (2008). Business intelligence approach to supporting strategy-making of ISP service management. *Expert Systems with Applications*, *35*(3), 739–754. doi:10.1016/j.eswa.2007.07.049

Maleki, H., & Zahir, S. (2013). A comprehensive literature review of the rank reversal phenomenon in the analytic hierarchy process. *Journal of Multi-Criteria Decision Analysis*, *20*(3-4), 141–155. doi:10.1002/mcda.1479

Mandic, K., Delibasic, B., Knezevic, S., & Benkovic, S. (2014). Analysis of the financial parameters of Serbian banks through the application of the fuzzy AHP and TOPSIS methods. *Economic Modelling*, *43*, 30–37. doi:10.1016/j.econmod.2014.07.036

Mao, N., Song, M., & Deng, S. (2016). Application of TOPSIS method in evaluating the effects of supply vane angle of a task/ambient air conditioning system on energy utilization and thermal comfort. *Applied Energy*, *180*, 536–545. doi:10.1016/j.apenergy.2016.08.011

Martin, A., Lakshmi, T. M., & Venkatesan, V. P. (2014). An information delivery model for banking business. *International Journal of Information Management*, *34*(2), 139–150. doi:10.1016/j.ijinfomgt.2013.12.003

Masuda, T. (1990). Hierarchical sensitivity analysis of priority used in analytic hierarchy process. *International Journal of Systems Science*, *21*(2), 415–427. doi:10.1080/00207729008910371

Miller, S., McRobbie, G., & Begg, C. (2016, July). Business intelligence tools: Should they be 'gamified'? Project 'GamBIT': Evaluating user engagement. In *SAI Computing Conference (SAI)*, 2016 (pp. 758-763). IEEE. doi:10.1109/SAI.2016.7556065

Moro, S., Cortez, P., & Rita, P. (2015). Business intelligence in banking: A literature analysis from 2002 to 2013 using text mining and latent Dirichlet allocation. *Expert Systems with Applications*, *42*(3), 1314–1324. doi:10.1016/j.eswa.2014.09.024

Morris, L. V. (2016). The imperative for faculty: Understanding student success technologies and other analytics. *Innovative Higher Education*, *41*(4), 269–271. doi:10.1007/s10755-016-9369-4

Niu, L., Lu, J., Zhang, G., & Wu, D. (2013). FACETS: A cognitive business intelligence system. *Information Systems*, *38*(6), 835–862. doi:10.1016/j.is.2013.02.002

Obayiuwana, E., & Falowo, O. (2015, September). A multimoora approach to access network selection process in heterogeneous wireless networks. In *AFRICON, 2015* (pp. 1–5). IEEE. doi:10.1109/AFRCON.2015.7331973

Ortega, C. M., Lorences, C. P., & Marx-Gómez, H. J. (2014). Architecture for business intelligence design on the IT service management scope. In *Engineering and Management of IT-based Service Systems* (pp. 201–213). Springer Berlin Heidelberg. doi:10.1007/978-3-642-39928-2_10

Oztaysi, B. (2014). A decision model for information technology selection using AHP integrated TOPSIS-Grey: The case of content management systems. *Knowledge-Based Systems*, *70*, 44–54. doi:10.1016/j.knosys.2014.02.010

Phan, D. D., & Vogel, D. R. (2010). A model of customer relationship management and business intelligence systems for catalogue and online retailers. *Information & Management*, *47*(2), 69–77. doi:10.1016/j.im.2009.09.001

Piedade, M. B., & Santos, M. Y. (2009). *Business intelligence in higher education: managing the relationships with students*. Academic Press.

Ramakrishnan, T., Jones, M. C., & Sidorova, A. (2012). Factors influencing business intelligence (BI) data collection strategies: An empirical investigation. *Decision Support Systems*, *52*(2), 486–496. doi:10.1016/j.dss.2011.10.009

Rouhani, S., Ghazanfari, M., & Jafari, M. (2012). Evaluation model of business intelligence for enterprise systems using fuzzy TOPSIS. *Expert Systems with Applications*, *39*(3), 3764–3771. doi:10.1016/j.eswa.2011.09.074

Rubin, E., & Rubin, A. (2013). The impact of business intelligence systems on stock return volatility. *Information & Management*, *50*(2), 67–75. doi:10.1016/j.im.2013.01.002

Sakthivel, G., Ilangkumaran, M., & Gaikwad, A. (2015). A hybrid multi-criteria decision modeling approach for the best biodiesel blend selection based on ANP-TOPSIS analysis. *Ain Shams Engineering Journal*, *6*(1), 239–256. doi:10.1016/j.asej.2014.08.003

Senthil, S., Srirangacharyulu, B., & Ramesh, A. (2014). A robust hybrid multi-criteria decision making methodology for contractor evaluation and selection in third-party reverse logistics. *Expert Systems with Applications*, *41*(1), 50–58. doi:10.1016/j.eswa.2013.07.010

Shih, H. S., Shyur, H. J., & Lee, E. S. (2007). An extension of TOPSIS for group decision making. *Mathematical and Computer Modelling*, *45*(7), 801–813. doi:10.1016/j.mcm.2006.03.023

Shukla, A., & Dhir, S. (2016). Tools for Data Visualization in Business Intelligence: Case Study Using the Tool Qlikview. In *Information Systems Design and Intelligent Applications* (pp. 319–326). New Delhi: Springer. doi:10.1007/978-81-322-2752-6_31

Tavana, M., & Hatami-Marbini, A. (2011). A group AHP-TOPSIS framework for human spaceflight mission planning at NASA. *Expert Systems with Applications*, *38*(11), 13588–13603.

Tobias, P. A., & Trindade, D. (2011). *Applied reliability*. CRC Press.

Triantaphyllou, E., & Lin, C. T. (1996). Development and evaluation of five fuzzy multiattribute decision-making methods. *International Journal of Approximate Reasoning, 14*(4), 281-310.

Trumpy, E., Bertani, R., Manzella, A., & Sander, M. (2015). The web-oriented framework of the world geothermal production database: A business intelligence platform for wide data distribution and analysis. *Renewable Energy*, *74*, 379–389. doi:10.1016/j.renene.2014.08.036

UNDP. (2011). *Invitation to Bid - Version Control Software*. United Nations Development Programme Procurement Support Office.

Wang, X. (2015). A comprehensive decision making model for the evaluation of green operations initiatives. *Technological Forecasting and Social Change*, *95*, 191–207. doi:10.1016/j.techfore.2015.02.004

Xu, K., Liao, S. S., Li, J., & Song, Y. (2011). Mining comparative opinions from customer reviews for Competitive Intelligence. *Decision Support Systems*, *50*(4), 743–754. doi:10.1016/j.dss.2010.08.021

Yeoh, W., & Koronios, A. (2010). Critical success factors for business intelligence systems. *Journal of Computer Information Systems*, *50*(3), 23–32.

Zavadskas, E. K., Mardani, A., Turskis, Z., Jusoh, A., & Nor, K. M. (2016). Development of TOPSIS Method to Solve Complicated Decision-Making Problems—An Overview on Developments from 2000 to 2015. *International Journal of Information Technology & Decision Making*, *15*(03), 645–682. doi:10.1142/S0219622016300019

Zhao, L., Tian, P., & Li, X. (2012). Dynamic pricing in the presence of consumer inertia. *Omega*, *40*(2), 137–148. doi:10.1016/j.omega.2011.04.004

Zhao, L. W., & Zhang, W. (2008, October). A study on an integrative structure of business intelligence and ERP system based on multi-agent. In *Wireless Communications, Networking and Mobile Computing, 2008. WiCOM'08. 4th International Conference on* (pp. 1-4). IEEE. doi:10.1109/WiCom.2008.2828

Chapter 3
Botnet Threats to E-Commerce Web Applications and Their Detection

Rizwan Ur Rahman
Maulana Azad National Institute of Technology, India

Deepak Singh Tomar
Maulana Azad National Institute of Technology, India

ABSTRACT

Security issues in e-commerce web applications are still exploratory, and in spite of an increase in e-commerce application research and development, lots of security challenges remain unanswered. Botnets are the most malicious threats to web applications, especially the e-commerce applications. Botnet is a network of BOTs. It executes automated scripts to launch different types of attack on web applications. Botnets are typically controlled by one or more hackers known as Bot masters and are exploited for different types of attacks including Dos (denial of service), DDos (distributed denial of service), phishing, spreading of malware, adware, Spyware, identity fraud, and logic bombs. The aim of this chapter is to scrutinize to what degree botnets can cause a threat to e-commerce security. In the first section, an adequate overview of botnets in the context of e-commerce security is presented in order to provide the reader with an understanding of the background for the remaining sections.

INTRODUCTION

Electronic Commerce is a transaction of purchasing, selling and marketing online. E-commerce makes use of computer technologies such as Internet, World Wide Web, EFT (Electronic Funds Transfer), Internet marketing, and online transaction. Current electronic commerce usually uses the World Wide Web for one part of the life cycle of transaction even though it could also use e-mail systems (O'Leary, 2000).

E-Commerce uses different Business models such as B2B (Business - to - Business), C2C (Consumer - to - Consumer), C2B (Consumer - to - Business), B2C (Business - to - Consumer). The main objective of this chapter is to study the perception of security in different business models of e-commerce

DOI: 10.4018/978-1-5225-3646-8.ch003

such as B2B, B2C, C2B, and C2C web application from both organizational and consumer viewpoint (Combe, 2012).

Security is one of the principal and ongoing concerns that limit clients and organizations engaging with e-commerce. E-commerce Security is a part of the Computer Security and is particularly applied to the components that concern e-commerce applications including Information Security and Data security. This chapter addresses the vulnerabilities, threats, and detection methods in the context of e-commerce applications. This chapter explores the perception of security in e-commerce websites from Bot and Botnet attacks viewpoint.

E-Commerce applications have numerous components including web server, database server, and payment gateway for online transaction. In Cyber world each component of e-commerce application is targeted by different attacks. According to numbers of survey reports, almost ninety percent (90%) of the attack comes from either Bot or Botnet. The given figure (Figure 1) shows the typical components involved in simple life cycle of e-commerce with different attacks on each component (Wokosin, 2002). For instance, attacks particularly targets customers are account takeover and account lockout. Similarly, the attacks that target the application are price scraping, content scraping, and database scraping.

The first section introduces the overview of Bots including basic and advanced Bots, good and bad Bots, generalized and specialized Bots. Further, this section elaborates the attacks on different components of e-commerce application such as Price Scarping, Content Scrapping, and Man in the Browser attack on e-commerce transaction.

The next section presents the more malicious form of Bot known as Botnet i.e., network of Bots. In this section technologies related to Botnet are explored and different architecture of Botnet including centralized and decentralized architectures is presented. Additionally, this section explores the taxonomy of attacks which are executed by Botnets including, Malware, DoS, Phishing, Injection attacks.

Figure 1. E-commerce components and cycle

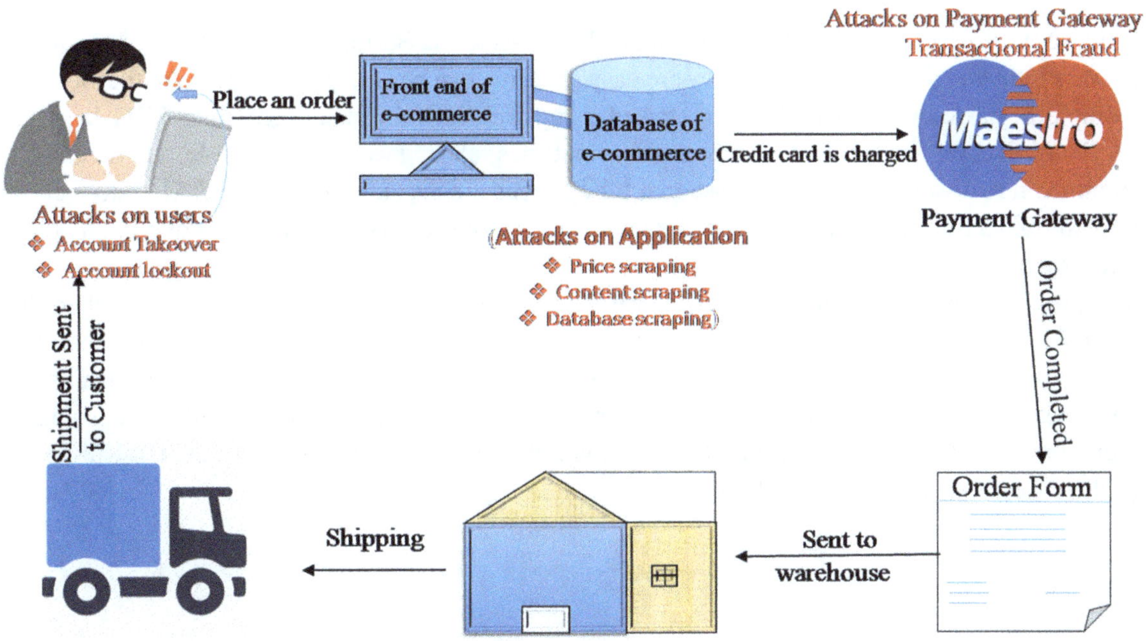

The last section presents the taxonomy of detection and prevention methods such as various forms of CAPTCHA, Honeypot, and Firewalls. It also explores the Data mining techniques including anomaly and rule base detection. Finally, it introduces briefly the Big Data Approach such as Security Analytics. At last conclusion of the chapter is presented.

OVERVIEW AND INTRODUCTION OF BOT

The term Bot has come from the word robot. Fundamentally, the Bot is a software program which is used to execute fully automated, well-defined, repetitive task over a network. Bots can interact with any web application that has an API (Application Programming Interface). The tasks usually performed by Bots could vary from making lunch reservation in a restaurant, booking a ticket, giving an email reply and, checking product's price on their e-commerce websites (Geer, 2005).

Taxonomy of Bots

There is huge number of Bots and every single day new Bots are coming with many different reasons. According to Global Bot Traffic Report (Bariso, 2016) more than fifty percent (50%) of the internet traffic is from the Bots. In literature, different categorizations are proposed by different scholars. In this section, taxonomy of Bots is presented in three different headings.

- Basic Bot vs. Advanced Bots.
- Good Bot vs. Bad Bots.
- Generalized Bot vs. Specialized Bot.

Basic Bot vs. Advanced Bots

Bot started with very simple scripting languages like w-get, VB Script, and Perl. These scripting languages are light weight languages and they are easy to script, can be easily uploaded on to the web server and simple to parse the HTML. Then, it started using web scripting languages like PHP, JavaScript, and ASP (Active Server Pages). These Bots are sometimes referred as a basic Bots. Fundamentally, it is different from real web browser in a sense that they are easy to execute, parse the HTML, store cookies and execute Java Script. Since, the basic Bots are very simple scripts they can be spotted and detected with no troubles.

The programmers then, started moving towards more advanced Bots. These Bots can embed themselves into a real web browser using open source languages like Ruby and Python and custom malwares. They can fully automate the web browsers can actually masquerade that; Bot is a real human user can do anything a real person can do. So, they can move the page, move the mouse, scroll down, submit the information on web server, and extract the information from server (Jeong et al., 2010). Unlike basic Bots, they are difficult to spot and detect.

Good Bots vs. Bad Bots

The purpose and the behavior categorized the Bot to be either good or bad bot. Good bots are useful for all e-commerce application. These Bots assist in making the required visibility of the e-commerce application on the internet, and in addition assist these businesses attain an online visibility. When customer searches for an e-commerce website or key-word related to the products in website, the result is the relevant list of products on the search page. This can be achieved only with the help of search engine Bots also known as spiders, or web crawler Bots.

On the other hand, bad Bots are created to execute a variety of malicious tasks. Their behavior and pattern are malicious and generally unregulated. Generally, they do not follow the rules. If huge number of web page requests are originating from a particular IP address in a very short duration. This type of malicious activity burden or exhaust e-commerce web application, and block the available network bandwidth. These malicious activities directly affect those legitimate users on e-commerce application, trying to search a product or doing a transaction (Dunham et al., 2008).

One more example of bad Bot is that, it can exploit third party web scrapers to take contents from website. The contents can be unique to website or e-commerce web application. For instance, the contents could be reviews of product, information related to dynamic pricing of products available on e-commerce website, product list, and so on.

The good Bot are further categorized as given below.

- Web Crawler
- Social Media Bot
- Chatbot
- Informational Bot

Web Crawler

This is specialized Internet Bot also known as a spider, which thoroughly browses the WWW (World Wide Web), usually for indexing the websites. These Bots run constantly mainly obtain data from websites, and are obedient in a sense that they follow directions define in (robots.txt) file.

For instance, the entire website or web service from search engine Bots can be hidden by stopping search engine Bots in (robots.txt) file of website. This will keep the contents of website out of search engines (Markov et al., 2007).

These Bots extract URLs (Hyperlinks) from HTML Pages, and fetch all the contents from each URL, and then it passes the contents to search engines system for building the searchable index. Googlebot from Google and Bingbot from Microsoft are the two most familiar examples of spiders or search engine Bots.

Social Media Bot

Social Media Bot also known as socialbot or social networking Bot is s a type of Bot that runs automatically accounts of social media websites. It has the capability to perform essential activities for instance, message posting, send a request for joining a group, and posting updated weather forecasts. Since social media Bot penetrates a targeted social media websites, additionally they are able to steal user data for instance, phone numbers, emails, and other private data that could have monetary value (Sharma et al., 2017). Facebook Bot and Twitter Bot are the two most common examples of social media Bots

Chatbot

A chatbot sometimes referred as a Chatterbot, Chatterbox, and Talkbot is an automated computer programs that can be used with users in natural communication. The first Chabot program was made in 1960s; the goal was to determine whether Chatbots could convince users that they are really human beings (Shawar et al., 2003). Chatbots are not only built to imitate human communication and to provide users an entertainment but also useful in education and e-commerce applications.

Chatterbot Assistants in E-Commerce Applications

Shopping assistant is the most useful things in conventional commerce. Shopping assistant supports in a store, by giving further information on products and make things easier for decision making process helping to find a best product that makes customer happy (Bog-danovych et al., 2005).

Happy Assistant is a natural language based system that assists users accessing e-commerce application to find appropriate information about products and services (Chai et al., 2000). The system is composed of three main modules: the Action Manager, the dialog Manager, and the presentation manager.

Informational Bot

Bots in this group assists in information related things; include breaking news and push notifications. A number of informational Bots transmit data as soon as it becomes available.

Similarly, the bad Bot are also further categorized as follows

- Web Scrapper
- Spammer
- Vulnerability Scanner
- Impersonator

Generalized Bot vs. Specialized Bot

The Bots can be categorized as “General Bot” and “Special Bot. The general Bots are created for general tasks. For instance, the attacker can create a Bot which searches for website vulnerabilities and loopholes. As soon as it finds any vulnerability it attacks the website by injecting malicious code. On the other hand, “Special Bot” is created by attacker to attack a particular website.

Bot Traffic

When examining website traffic, it is imperative to distinguish between human and Bot. Further, it is also required to make a distinction between good and bad Bots. According to global Bot traffic report (Figure 2) (2016) almost report fifty percent (50%) of the web traffic is coming from web Bots.

Figure 2. Bot traffic by type

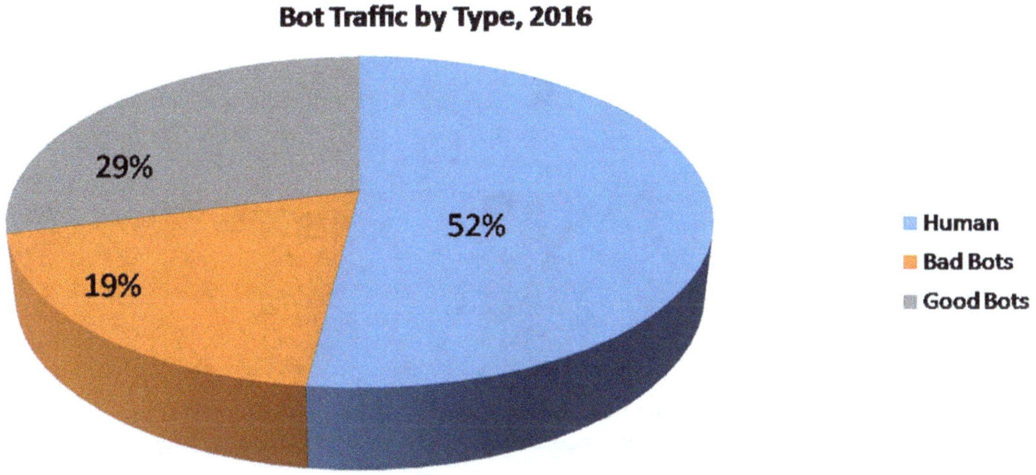

Out of fifty percent (50%) about thirty percent (30%) constitute good Bot traffic and rest of the twenty percent (20%) is from bad Bots. The year wise distribution of the Bot traffic from the year 2012 to 2014 is shown in figure (Figure 3). It shows that human traffic drops in year 2013 and then it increases to five percent (5%). The important point to be noticed is that, the bad Bot traffic is almost constant (30%).

Analyzing deeper, the report shows whether particular sized websites were further exposed to cyber attacks using Bots in the year 2014. As it comes up, bad Bots attacked categorically to all the websites, regardless of their size.

As shown in the next graph (Figure 4), the percentage of bad Bots traffic comparing to total visits is constantly thirty percent (30%), regardless of website popularity or size. The larger sites are attacked by a huge number of malicious Bots; on the whole, risk factor is the identical for every website administrator that is approximately one in three requests is a malicious Bots.

Figure 3. Year wise bot traffic

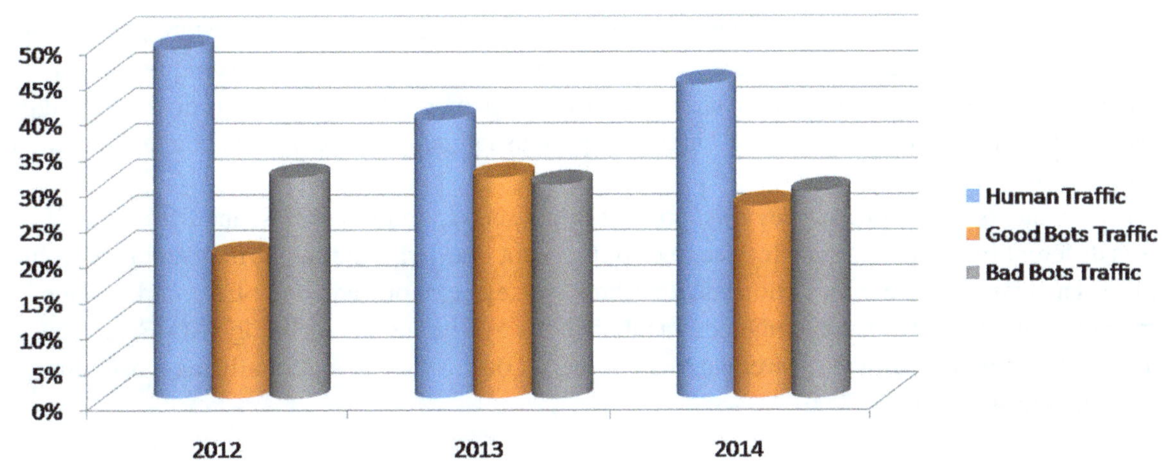

Figure 4. Bot traffic according to size of applications

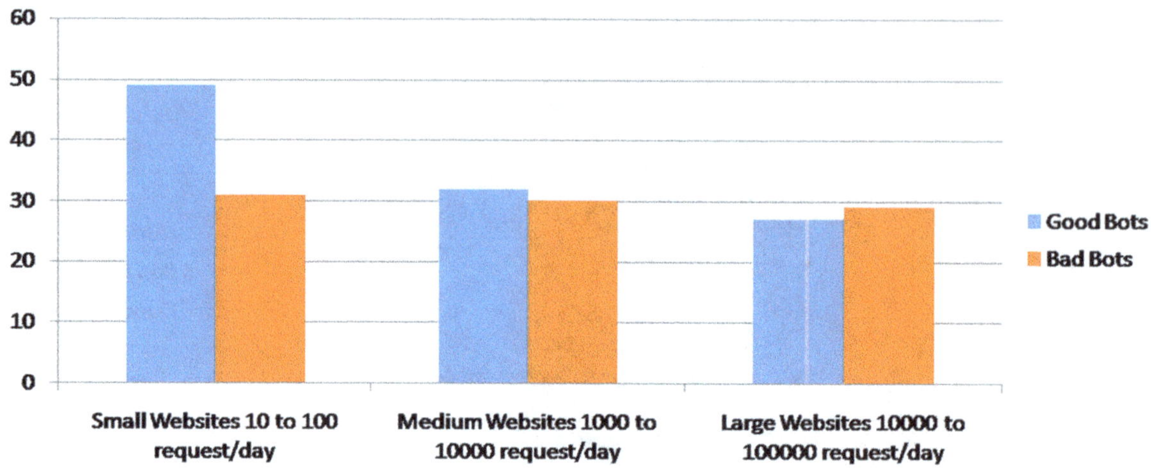

Threats of Bot to E-Commerce Applications

In this section, Bot threats to e-commerce application are explored in detail. As mention in the previous section, Bot traffic survey report from the year 2012 to 2014 bad Bot traffic is continuously about 30%. The bad Bots causes the majority of website attacks. These attacks are ranging from minor cyber crimes like spamming, click fraud to big crimes credential stuffing. These attacks can be classified into five major categories and their taxonomy is shown in figure (Figure 5).

- Web Scraping
- Transactional Fraud
- Accounts -linked Attacks (Semantic attacks)
- Security Breach
- Skewed Analytics

Web Scraping

Web Scrapping is further categorized into Content Scraping, Price Scarping, and Database Scraping.

Content scraping sometimes also known as data scraping is stealing original and unique content from websites and publishing or pasting it in another website. This method is illicit as it is done without permission of the original website owner. Content scraping usually copy the complete content and passed it to its own website.

These contents can be product reviews, product prices, news, opinion pieces, and list of classifieds. This is different from web crawler Bots, scraper Bots do not obey with the set of rules set in the (robots.txt) file. The aim is to take information and distribute it elsewhere, or trade it in black market. This sort of fraudulent scraping affects e-commerce in a number of ways, including declining SEO (Search engine optimization) rankings, growing server bandwidth, impact on customers, and finally the most important revenue loss (Salerno et al., 2006).

Figure 5. Taxonomy of bot attacks

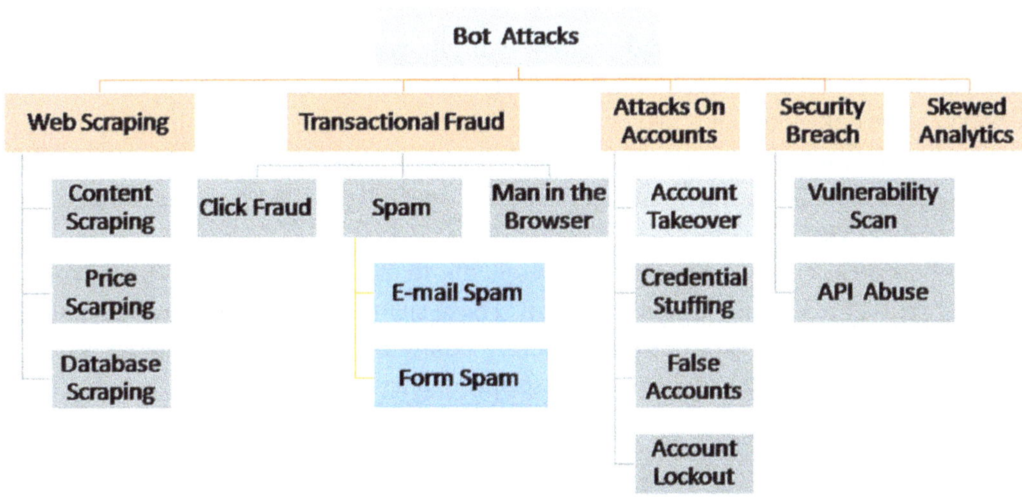

Price Scarping is when a competitor indexes an entire e-commerce website inventory and identifies what is in stock inventory, price of the products and all the details related to the cost of products. Then, it creates an automated strategy to adjust their pricing based on the inventory and prices this makes you less competitive and gives them a competitive advantage.

Competitors exploit this tactic to take over the dynamic price. Dynamic pricing is an important tactic used by e-commerce application to attract customer buying decisions and optimize profits in real-time, so that they can draw attention of customers by putting their prices lower than baseline prices in the e-commerce market.

Database Scraping, in this type of scraping in which the Bot master uses programming scripts to lift off the entire database of e-commerce portals.

Transactional Fraud

The transactional fraud or fraudulent transactions attacks specifically target transactional data on the e-commerce applications. These types of fraud include Click Fraud, E-Mail Spam, Form Spam, and Man in the browser attack.

Click Fraud

Click fraud is a type of cybercrime in which an attacker continuously clicks on the websites having advertisements of pay per click. This is special kind of digital advertising; where administrators of websites that publish the ads are remunerated a sum of money decided by how many website visitors click on the advertisements. Fraud takes place when an attacker, makes a Bot which mimics a genuine user of a web browser, clicking on an advertisement (Wilbur et al., 2009).

E-Mail Spamming

Email spamming sometimes also referred as, junk mailing, is a type of digital spam where unwanted email messages are sent by an attacker. A lot of email spam messages are viable in nature but may also contain masked hyperlinks that seem to be well-known websites but in reality, they redirect to phishing websites. An email spammer usually, sends an email to lacks of mailing addresses, with the probability that only a few numbers will answer. Spammers make use specialized Bot known as spambot to generate mass email list (Mijatovic, 2004).

These spambots steal e-mail addresses from contents found on the World Wide Web in order to construct mailing lists for sending unwanted e-mail. These spambots works as crawlers that can collect e-mail addresses from blogs, news-groups, and Social media sites. Since, e-mail addresses have a typical format; such Bots are easy to script using simple scripting languages.

Man in the Browser Attack

Most important category where Bots are used in transactional fraud is the Man in the browser attack. These types of attacks infects a browser by exploiting the vulnerabilities in web browser for instance, change the web pages, hijacking sessions, modify transactions, all in a entirely hidden way undetectable to both the end user and the hosting websites. It is also represented by MitB, MiB, MIB, and MITB.

A Man in the browser attack works by exploiting general services provided to increase the browser facilities for instance, browser extensions such as Flash, Browser Helper Objects only in Microsoft's Internet Explorer, and browser scripts such as JavaScript.

An associated, but simpler attack is the Boy in the browser attack sometimes represented by BITB, BitB. The mainstream banking service employees believed that Man in the browser attack is the biggest threat to banking systems (Weigold et al., 2008).

Security Breaches

A security breach is an event that results in illegal access of applications, network data, web services, network devices by bypassing their fundamental security mechanisms. Generally, security violation is used for the term security breach. These types of Bot attacks can be further classified as Vulnerability Scanning and API Abuse.

Vulnerability Scanning

The Vulnerability Scanning is an automated process of constantly identifying security weakness of websites in a network in order to exploit, threaten, and attack the websites. Vulnerability scanning makes use of Bots that search for security flaws and compare in a database with identified flaws (Fonseca et al., 2007).

API Abuse

The problem of API abuse is a growing one, as attackers are taking interest to the mobile application as a way of targeting APIs (Application Programming Interface) to steal sensitive information. An API Abuse is illegal or unauthorized access to the servers API through mobile applications or web applications. This may result in stealing of precious intellectual property application codes. Mobile application development is a vital area, where the applications are becoming a growing target for the attackers. It is important for both end users and application programmers to ensure that APIs are protected against attacks, and an important measure is ensuring that the application use to access the servers API is recognized and well-known (Tsipenyuk et al., 2005).

Skewed Analytics

Web behavior analytical systems are developed to assist traffic patterns analysis and end user behavior on a web site or web service. As discussed in the previous section about fifty percent (50%) of all the traffic on the website and web services are generated by Bots. An efficient web behavior analytical systems need to distinguish between the legitimate human traffic and the Bot the traffic and provide particulars of both categories of traffic individually.

OVERVIEW AND INTRODUCTION OF BOTNET

The word Botnet is used to define an interconnected network of infected (infected with viruses without the user's information) computers known as Bot, are under the command and control of a computer programmer usually known as the Bot-Master. The Botnet make use of vulnerable computers by using techniques such as Malware, Viruses Trojans, exploiting software vulnerabilities and social engineering to connect Bots to their Bot-Masters. The Bot-Master could control the Botnet using C&C (command and control) application. The term Botnet is a combination of the two words Bot and network (Rodríguez et al., 2013).

They are generally used to send spam emails, performing DDoS (Distributed Denial of Service) attack, transmit malwares and employed in other work of cybercrime. Botnet is also known as a zombie army and they are considered as the biggest threats on web security today. The given figure (Figure 6) shows the typical structure of Botnet.

The Bot-Master uses command and control servers, first to infect the computers and then, to form a network of infected computers (zombies). This network can be used launch an attack to target a system using a variety of attacks such as DDos.

Evolution of Botnet

The earliest Botnet were exclusively based on IRC (Internet Relay Chat) and during those days IRC was the most frequent protocol used for communication. IRC is a protocol that facilitates many users to communicate in real time via the internet. This protocol was developed by Jarkko Oikarinen in the year 1988. Oikarinen defines: "The key idea is to allow discussion on news and create groups on a Bulletin Board Service in real time discussions and other Bulletin Board Service associated stuff". IRC

Figure 6. Structure of botnet

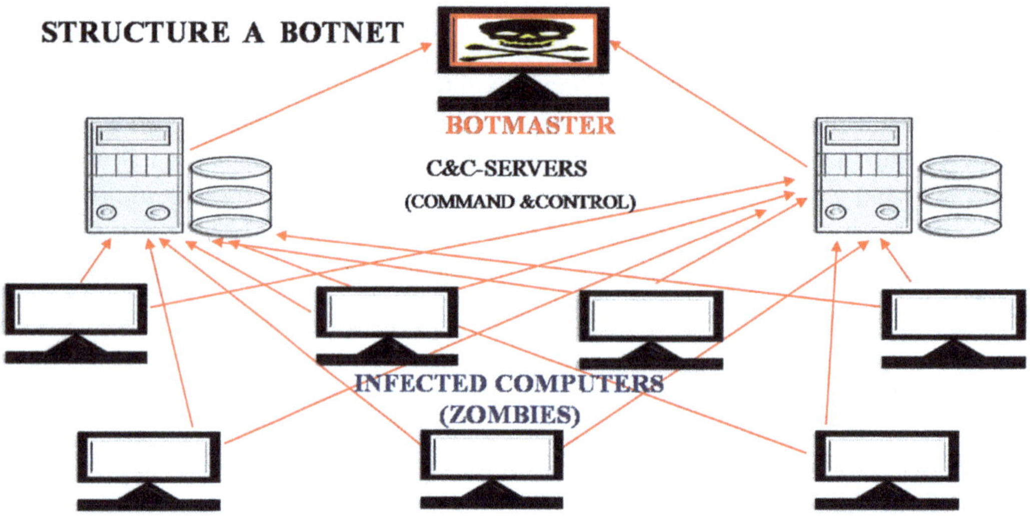

end users have an application client on their terminal that facilitates them to make a connection to an IRC server. Different users can make a connection to channels and converse to other users. The server of IRC makes connections simultaneously to all the IRC clients. Bots invented from the condition for automated administrative tasks on servers. The Bot can reside on an IRC channel and carry out tasks as set by an owner of channel (Tyagi et al., 2011).

Botnet Classification According to Their Architectures

Botnet can be classified according to their architectures into two categories namely, centralized Botnet and decentralized Botnet.

Centralized Botnet Architecture

In Centralized Bot network, all Bots are associated to a particular command and control center (C&C). The C&C keep on waiting for other Bots to join, list them in its Botnet database, monitor their status and sends them commands chosen by the Bot-Master from a list of commands in C&C. All the Bots (computers) in the Bot network are visible to the C&C. In a centralized architecture, the Botnet establishes their communication channel with one or more connection points mainly using IRC protocols and Hyper Text transfer protocol (HTTP), the latter being increasingly preferred because widely allowed in networks (Zeidanloo et al., 2010). The Centralized Botnet architecture is shown in figure (Figure 7).

Decentralized Botnet Architecture

In this type of Botnet architecture, infected computers are connected to a number of Bot on a Botnet (network) instead of command and control center. Instructions are move from one Bot to other Bot. Every Bot maintains a list of a number of neighboring Bots, and any instruction received by a Bot from

Figure 7. Centralized Botnet

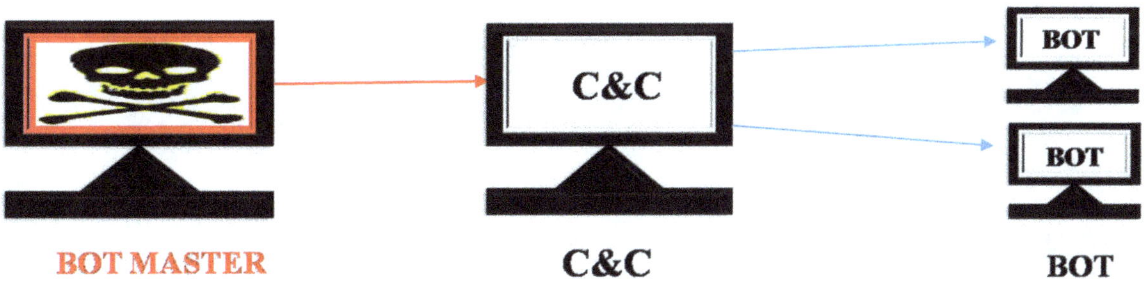

its neighboring Bot will be passed on to the other Bots, finally making the zombie network. In decentralized Botnet, an attacker must have an access to at least one Bot on the Bot network in order to control the entire Botnet (Studer et al., 2011).

A decentralized architecture enables the point of intrinsic failure of a centralized architecture. This is done to peer-to peer networks, each Bot contributing according to its capacities to the whole command and control systems. The Decentralized Botnet architecture is shown in figure (Figure 8).

It should be noted that the HTTP communication protocol can be used in centralized as well in decentralized architectures. In particular, it is often used because it allows communications to cross private networks protected by a firewall.

Taxonomy of Botnet Attacks

Once the network of infected computers that is Botnet is formed, then the Bot-master is used to launch numerous types of attacks on web applications. These attacks are classified into four categories including Malwares, Denial of Service, Injection Attacks, Phishing, and their taxonomy is shown in figure (Figure 9).

Figure 8. Decentralized Botnet

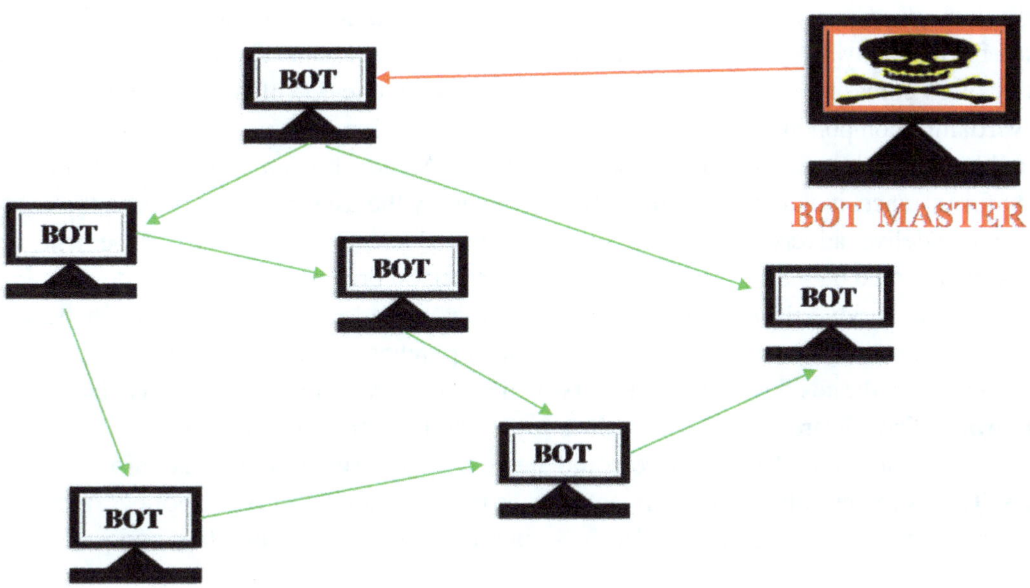

Figure 9. Taxonomy of Botnet attacks

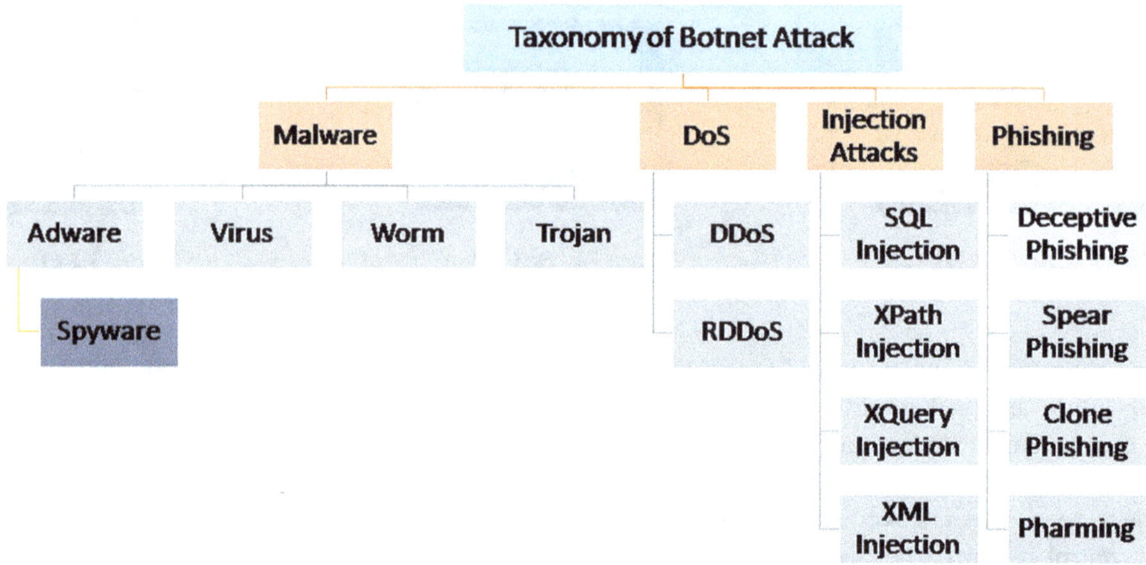

Malware

Malware is the broader term including all the types of threats to web application protection such as Adware, Spyware, Virus, Trojans, and Worms. Malware is short form of malicious software programs developed to penetrate and harm software without the users consent. Malicious software is software program either directly executable or in some interpreted language inserted in a system, usually in a discreet manner, with the intention of compromising Confidentiality, Integrity or Availability of the victim's Data, its Applications, Operating system and to try to annoy or disturb the victim.

- **Adware:** An Adware is ad-supported software or advertising-supported software that automatically put advertisements on websites to generate an income for its developer. These terms are used for any software program that downloads and displays unnecessary banner advertisements. They often comes bundled with some software that someone downloads, developers may include advertising- component in their software to recover development costs this way they are able to provide the product for free or in discounted price. An adware can be designed to collect user's data for instance, it can monitor the websites visited by the user then sent back to the company so that it can deliver advertisement based on the collected information. The advertisements produced by Adware could be seen as an interruption and attack on privacy. In return the developer receives profits from the advertisers he may use it to maintain upgrade and hence continue to develop more software. Generally users are given the option to purchase a registered or licensed version that would remove the ads the adware free version may also offer more functionality (Dai et al., 2007).
- **Spyware:** The adware may also contain a spying component; in this case the malware would be classified as spyware. The Spyware could steal user's information and may also corrupt system files. This is the reason the software companies usually state the privacy policy, saying no sensitive information will be collected. However, there is no way to be one hundred percent sure that

no spying is taking place. Therefore because of privacy concerns most antivirus software today detects and removes both the adware and spyware (Kirda et al., 2006).

- **Virus:** A virus is self replicating computer program that attaches itself to the host program and only exists in on the infected host computer. Computer Virus attacker use security vulnerabilities exploits and social engineering to gain access to their host computer and resources.
- **Worm:** A Worm is self replicating and stand alone software program that replicates itself over the network connections. Generally, it makes use of network to spread itself, rely on system weakness on the target machine to gain access in it. As a minimum Worms always cause harm to the network, albeit only by consuming network bandwidth, while viruses damage or modify the files on a targeted machine.
- **Trojan:** A Trojan is software program performing unidentified and unwanted actions for the user while posing as genuine program. Trojans are usually propagated by various types of social engineering, for instance where an end user is tricked into opening an e-mail attachment containing malicious files or by drive by download. Even though their payload could be anything, a lot of current type operates as a backdoor, having a controller which could then have illegal access to the affected machine.

Denial of Service

During Denial of Service a mostly single computer is used by the Bot to exploit the vulnerabilities of application. It could be done in number of ways for instance, flooding a network by redundant traffic their by preventing legitimate user request, twisting the connection information for instance, resetting a TCP session, blocking the access by disrupting the connection among the communicating systems. A typical DoS Attack is shown in figure (Figure 10).

Figure 10. Typical DoS attack

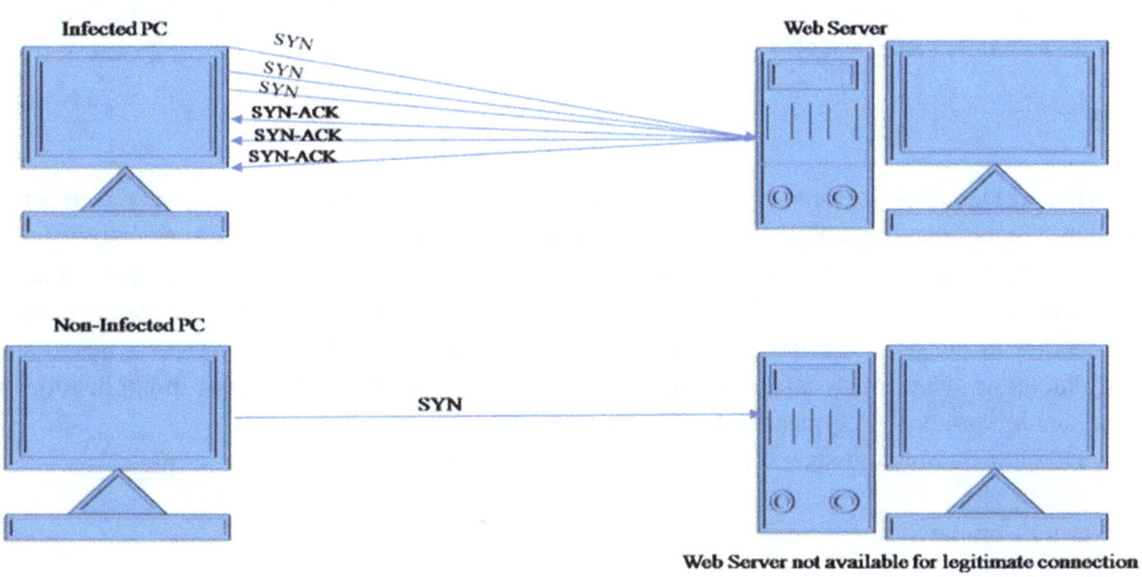

Flooding

In Flooding Denial of Services attack, continuous and particular types of data frames are sent into the computer network. In flood attack, Botnet floods victim with unbounded number of request but does not respond with Acknowledgment packet when a packet is received from the server their by making half open connection with the server. As the number of pending request increases the server resource get consumed and fails to provide service to other genuine clients. Flooding in networks can be of two types Authentication flooding and De-Authentication flooding.

Ping of Death Attack

Ping is used to check the reachability of a client on a network. Ping sends ICMP echo request packets and waits for ICMP echo reply. Ping of Death attack is performed by sending packets of size larger as large as 65535 bytes. A ping packet is of size 56 bytes if it is correctly formed. If a packet is of size larger than the allowed limit packet gets divided into multiple packets. Victim system crashes when it performs reassembling of these malformed packets.

Smurf Attack

Smurf attacks are those attacks caused because of misconfiguration of network devices. Spoofed packets are sent to the broadcast address of the network. Source IP is spoofed to victim IP address by the attacker. Each host receiving the broadcasted packet try to reply the spoofed IP address their by exhausting victim resources.

Teardrop Attack

If a packet is travelling from the source to the destination host, it may be broken up into smaller fragments, through the process of fragmentation. In Teardrop attack a stream of IP fragments are made with their offset field overloaded. If the destination machine tries to reassemble these malformed data fragments, it eventually gets crashed.

DDoS

A Distributed Denial of Service is type of Botnet attack where an effort is made to make web service unavailable by bombarding ample of requests from several sources. It interrupts the availability of resources to legitimate users. Bot masters mainly targets services provided by web servers of financial and ecommerce sites during attack. Financial websites for instance, HSBC UK hit by gigantic denial of service attack in January 29, 2016 (Bawany et al., 2017). Attack could come in various types as some directly targeting the primary infrastructure and the others that utilize weak spots in application and communication protocol. A typical DDoS attack is shown in Figure 11.

A DDoS attack army mostly consists of two types of systems

- Master Zombie System
- Slave Zombie System

Figure 11. Distributed Denial of Service attack

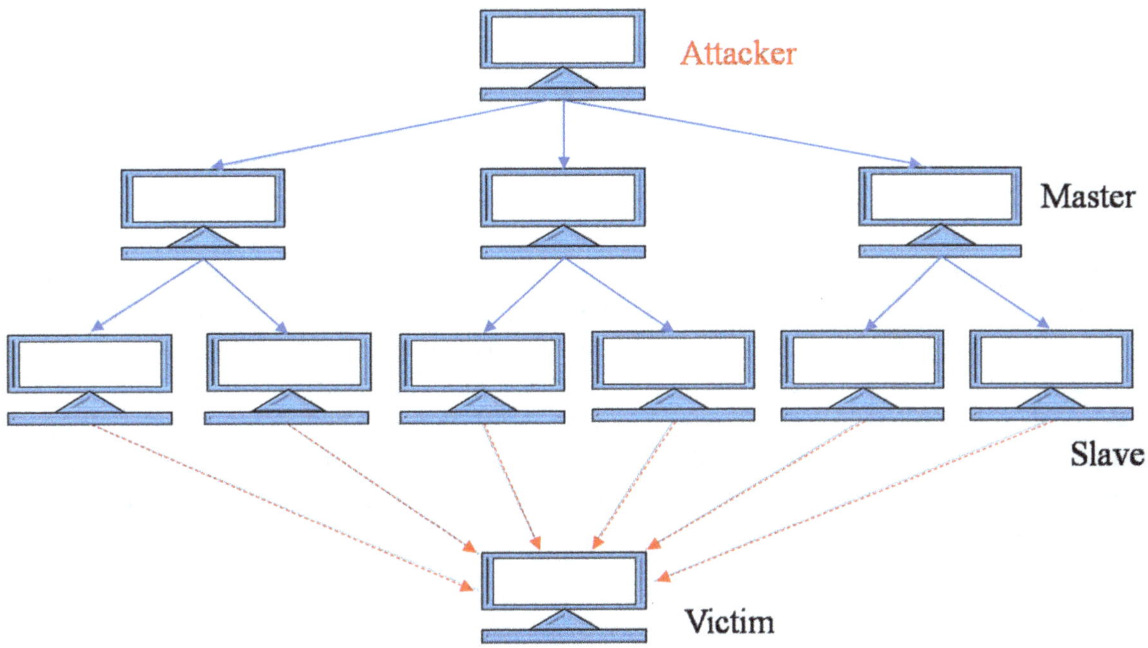

Systems of both these categories are compromised systems which are employed at the time of scanning process and are infected with malicious code. Various processes which happen during a typical DDoS attack include.

- The Bot master controls and coordinates master machine which then coordinates and starts slave systems.
- Bot master then commands master zombies to start all the attack commands present on that system.
- Bot master using those processes, launch attack instructions to slave systems, instructing them to initiate a DDoS attack against the victim system.
- Slave systems then start sending an enormous amount of traffic to the victim system, flooding it with bogus traffic and overwhelming its resources.

Phishing

Phishing is the technique to achieve confidential information such as credentials (username and password, and bank card details (debit card and credit card) regularly for malicious cause, by acting as an honest entity in network communication. The most common types of phishing are Deceptive Phishing, Spear Phishing, Clone Phishing, and Pharming.

Deceptive Phishing

The word "phishing" initially used for account credential theft using instant messaging services but today, the most common technique is a deceptive email message (spam). Emails which ask for verification of account information, system breakdown users need to re enter their username and password, false account charges, unwanted changes in account, fresh free services requiring rapid action, and a lot of other scams are send to a big group of recipients with the target that the unaware recipients (victims) will reply by clicking a hyperlink to or registering onto a fake website where their confidential data could be gathered (Huang et al., 2009).

Spear Phishing

The deceptive technique of sending emails apparently from a well-known or trustworthy sender in order to disclose confidential information of targeted individuals. For example, in spear phishing, an attacker customize their spam emails with the name of target, status, corporation, work cell number and other data in an effort to deceive the recipient into a trust that it has a link with the sender. The objective is the identical as deceptive phishing, trap the victim into clicking on a malicious hyperlink or open an email attachment, so that they will submit their personal data. Spear phishing is particularly common on social media web sites like Facebook, where an attacker could use numerous places of information to launch an attack (Parmar, 2012).

Clone Phishing

In this phishing attack the contents and recipient address of a genuine and earlier delivered email is stolen and used to make a cloned email or nearly identical email. The hyperlink or the attachment files inside the email is replaced with malicious files and contents and then resend from a spoofed email address; seems like it has come from the legitimate sender. The Clone Phishing email could ask to resend the updated information (Khan, 2013).

Pharming

This type of Pharming attack also known as DNS cache poisoning or DNS spoofing. In this attack a fraudulent Domain Name System data is inserted into the DNS cache resolver, as a result the domain name server returns a false IP address. At the end, the attackers are able to divert the HTTP traffic to their system or any other system. The World Wide Web naming system makes use of DNS servers to convert website URLs, such as "www.flipkart.com," to particular format of IP addresses used to locate computer devices. In DNS spoofing attack, a pharmer attacks a Domain Name Server and modifies the IP address related with URL of website. This means pharmer may redirect end users to a malicious website even though the users typed the correct URL of website (Karlof et al., 2007).

XML Injection

In XML Injection attack, the attacker attempt to alter or modify XML document, particularly SOAP message structure by placing parameters having XML tags such as "<" ">" characters. These attacks are only possible if the special characters are not escaped properly. This content is considered as an element of SOAP message and can cause damage at web service provider side.

Different security goals could be violated depending on the executed code. For example, modification of sensitive payment data, here the integrity of payment data has been violated. Another example is the unauthorized login; here the authentication has been violated. For instance, the following code (Figure 12) snippet is an XML injection attack.

This type of an XML message might result in xml injection attack because <y> 2 </y> is inserted without escaping the special characters “<”,”>”. The resultant variable values within the application for this particular service request were: x = 2, y = 0. As a result, the attacker is able to modify the value of y just by changing the content of x.

An important check in identification of XML injection attack is a strict validation of schema on the XML message, for instance, in given code data type validation should be applied. This validation will reject the message from the given attack.

XQuery Injection

The idea of XQuery Injection attack is borrowed from the SQL injection attack. In this attack, the attacker exploits the XML XQuery Language instead of structured query language through invalidated data that is given to XQuery commands.

XQuery injection could be used to inject XQuery commands to the service provider, enumerate XML elements of document on the victim’s end, or execute XQuery to remote servers and XML data sources. Very similar to SQL injection attacks, the attacker exploits the application entry point to attack the XML data resource. For instance, consider the following code snippet shown in figure (Figure 8).

The XQuery of this XML document for the User Aakash

```
doc(“XMLFile1.xml”)/UserList/user[UserName =”Manager”]
```

Figure 12. XML injection attack

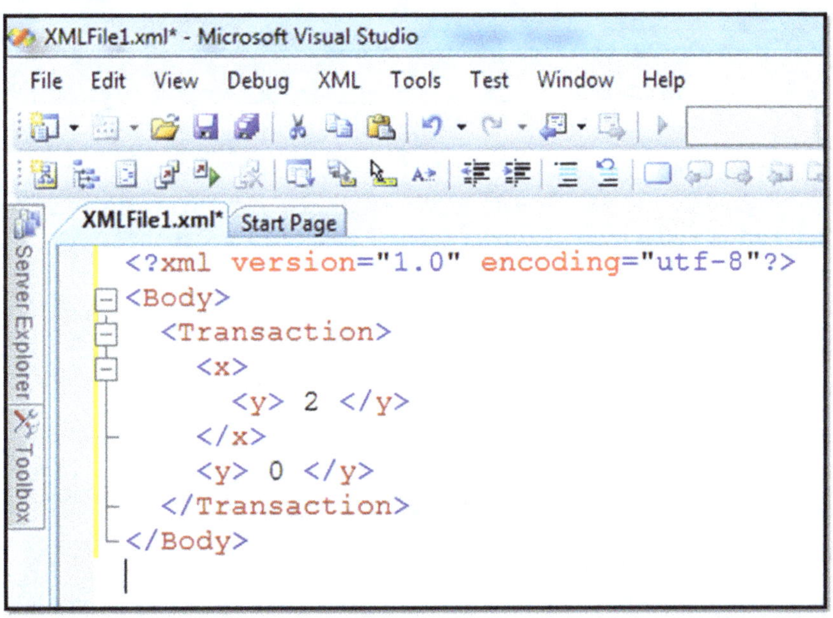

Would return:

```
<user level="Manager">
   <UserName>Manager</UserName>
   <FirstName>Aakash</FirstName>
   <LastName>Patel</LastName>
   <Status>good</Status>
 </user>
```

Now, the attacker may manipulate this typical query into returning the list of all users. By give the input command

```
Username or "1" = "1"
```

Now, the XQuery is:

```
doc("XMLFile1.xml ")/ UserList /user[UserName =" Username " or "1" = "1"]
```

This XQuery will return a set of all users. There are numerous variants of attack that are likely to be possible through XQuery and are difficult to identify. Appropriate validation of input before executing the XQuery can mitigate the XQuery injection attacks. XQuery injection attack is shown in Figure 13.

Figure 13. XQuery injection attack

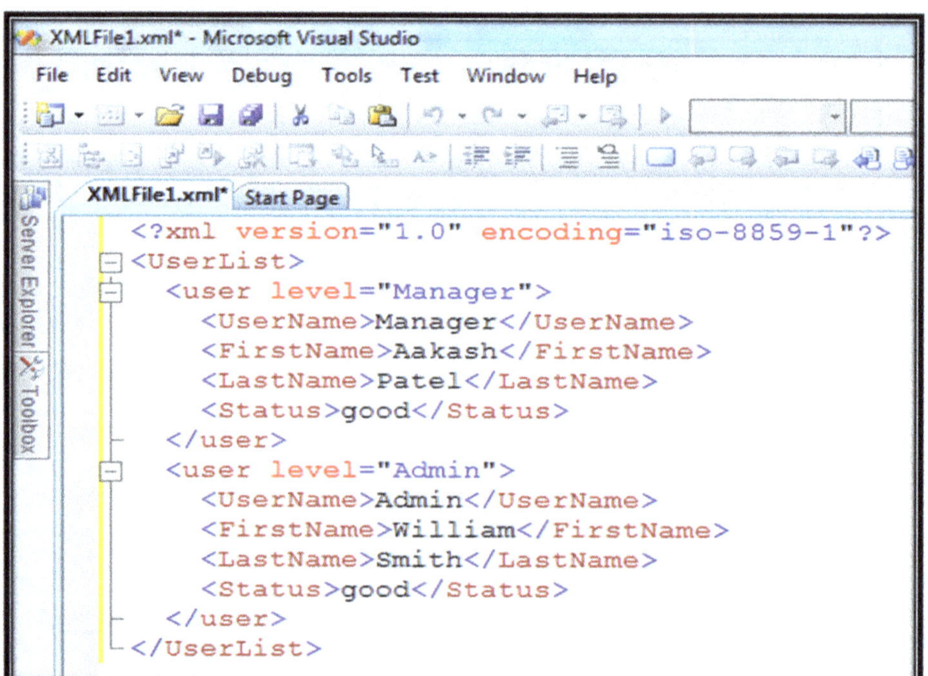

XPath Injection

XPath Injection is also related to XQuery Injection, XPath Injection attacks happen when a web application takes information supplied by user to construct an XPath query for XML document. By supplying deliberately twisted information into the web application, an attacker could expose how the XML document is made, or could gain the document access.

Coercive Parsing

The concept of Coercive Parsing is borrowed from denial of service attack (DoS). The very first step in processing a request of Web Service is to parse the SOAP message and converting the message content to make it available for the application. In particular while using XML namespaces, it may become complex and deadly in parsing, contrast to other message parsing. As a result, the XML parsing permits s possibilities for a particular type of Denial-of- Service attacks, which is known as Coercive Parsing attacks.

The goal of Coercive Parsing attacks is to exhaust the system resources of the victim web service. The attacker sends indefinite number of opening tags in the SOAP Body of SOAP message. That is the attacker sends an intensely nested XML document to the victim web service. Coercive Parsing attack might results in a hundred present utilization of CPU; when the SOAP message is processed. Typical Coercive Parsing attack is shown in Figure (Figure 14)

Figure 14. Coercive Parsing attack

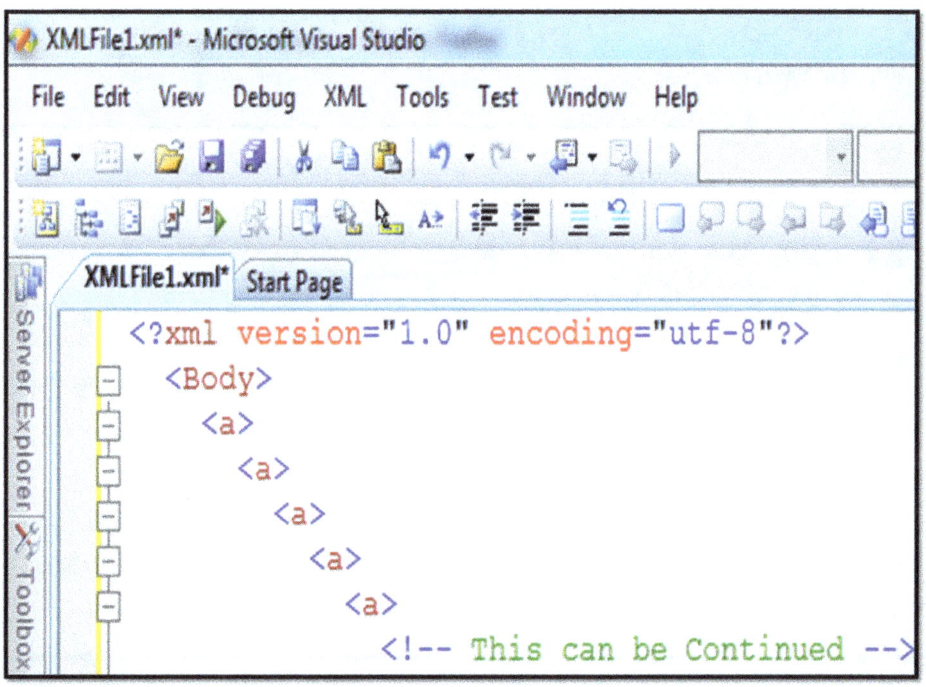

Oversized XML Attack

Typical SOAP message components inside an XML tag generally have a length of a small number of characters. The Namespace declarations can have hardly hundred characters but that generally doesn't cause any problem to XML parser.

On the other hand, if it is used in a malicious means the components inside an XML tag may be exploit to launch Oversized XML attack. For instance, by using excessively long names of attribute, a parser could break down due to memory exhaustion. Oversized XML attack is achievable since the standard of XML does not restrict the number of characters in XML tags. For instance the following code snippet shows the Oversized XML attack. Here, the name of element continued till it a size becomes in MBs. This attack is shown in Figure (Figure 15)

BOTNET DETECTION AND PREVENTION METHODS

In spite of the very long presence of Botnets, numerous researchers have put their efforts in Botnet detection and prevention techniques. Up till now, little is identified about the malicious behavior of Botnets. Nevertheless, research is in progress to counter the Botnet attacks, detection of Botnets, and defense mechanism against their attacks. Botnet detection and prevention is main research area in recent years. A number of techniques have been proposed in academia as well as in industries. The given figure (Figure 16) shows the taxonomy of Botnet detection and preventions methods. The classification detection and prevention methods include, CAPTCHA, HONEYPOT, Firewalls, Data Mining based Approaches, and Big Data Approaches.

Figure 15. Oversized XML attack

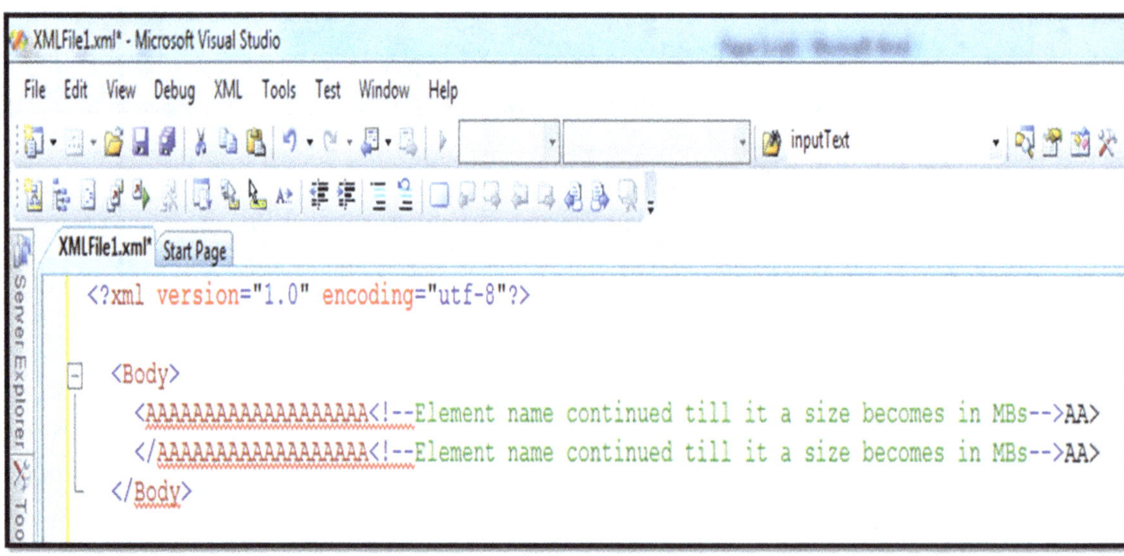

Figure 16. Taxonomy of Botnet detection and prevention methods

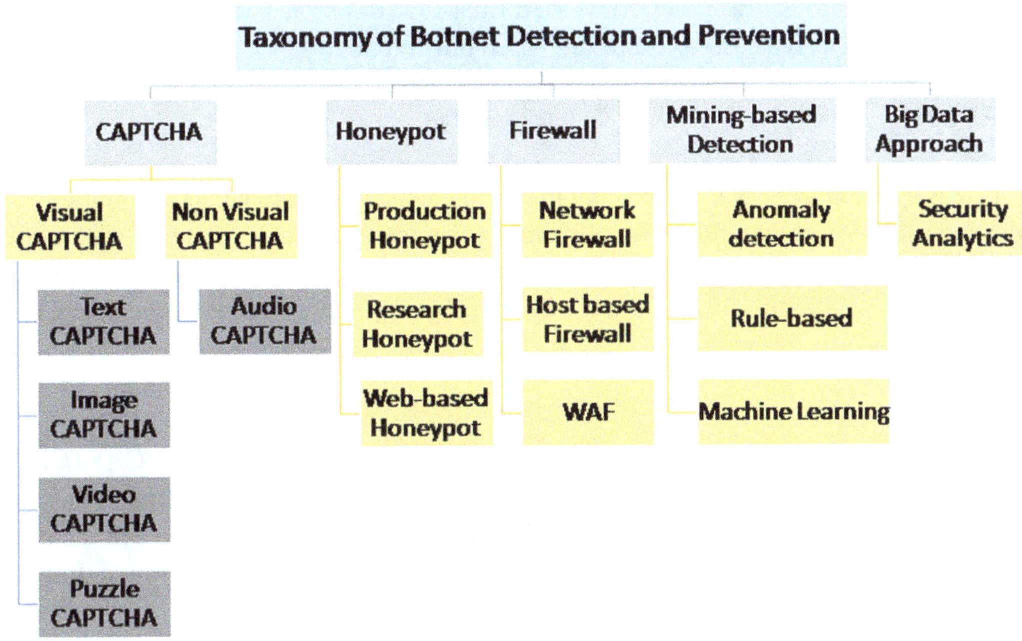

CAPTCHA

CAPTCHA is security mechanism against specialized Bot attacks known as Form Spamming. This system is developed a security mechanism to differentiate between legitimate human users and illegitimate Bots particularly in online registration. A typical security mechanism used at this time to address the problem is CAPTCHA Acronym of Completely Automated Public Turing Test to Tell Computers and Humans Apart. The notion of CAPTCHA is based on the capability of human beings to accomplish some tasks which software programs cannot accomplish for instance, asking end users to type alphabets in a distorted image of text or select a particular image from a number of displayed images. For instance, humans could read the distorted text shown in figure (Figure 17) however, present computer Bots cannot read (Von Ahn et al., 2003).

Figure 17. Text CAPTCHA

The CAPTCHA systems can be categorized into two types visual and non-visual. Visual CAPTCHA systems are further categorized as Text CAPTCHA, Image CAPTCHA, Video CAPTCHA, and Puzzle CAPTCHA. Non visual CAPTCHA systems are based only on audio.

Text CAPTCH

Text CAPTCHA systems are easy to implement in which a sequence of alphabets and numeric digits are given to the end user with adding a little alteration to the characters for instance, noise, rotation, drawing, or alphabets in 3D form. These alterations added to stop computer Bot programs from identifying the real characters. Humans can identify easily these characters. Figure (Figure 13) shows the Text CAPTCHA.

Image CAPTCHA

In this CAPTCHA system end user is ask to select an image. ESP Pix is an earliest CAPTCHA system based on images and it was first developed and tested at Carnegie Mellon University. A picture of ESP Pix is shown in Figure (Figure 18). In ESP Pix CAPTCHA four pictures are shown and in order to pass Turing test the end user has to choose word associated with those four pictures from a drop-down list having seventy two (72) choices.

Puzzle CAPTCHA

In puzzle CAPTCHA, a little mathematical puzzle is created according to a number of predefined rules. The puzzle then displayed by system is and user has to solved the puzzle. Answering of this puzzle requires an ability of comprehending text of puzzle, only a human user can solve it (Gao et al., 2010). Figure shows the puzzle CAPTCHA System. (Figure 19).

Figure 18. Image CAPTCHA

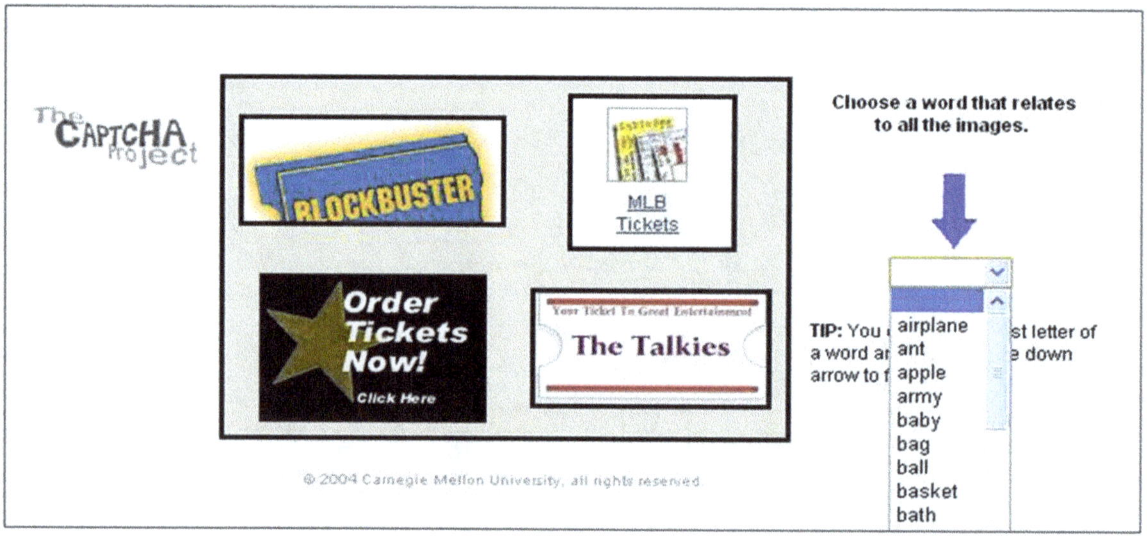

Figure 19. Puzzle CAPTCHA

Audio CAPTCHA

In Audio CAPTCHA system, am end user is ask to pass typical audio or voice recognition task. A particular audio CAPTCHA system is shown in Figure 20 (Gao et al., 2010).

HONEYPOT

In web environment, a Honeypot is a security method use to detect, repel, and counter attempts of illegal use of information systems. Honeypot are trap systems setup to collect the data of an intruder and attacker who are penetrating into the information system. Usually, a honeypot system having data for instance, in a website that seems to be a genuine data of the website, however it is in fact and isolated and under monitoring, and it gathers the information of an attackers, which are then blocked. It should be noted that Honeypots cannot substitute the other conventional computer security systems. They are installed as an additional security level to the system. Honeypots are categorized as production honeypots, research honeypots, web based honeypots.

Figure 20. Audio CAPTCHA

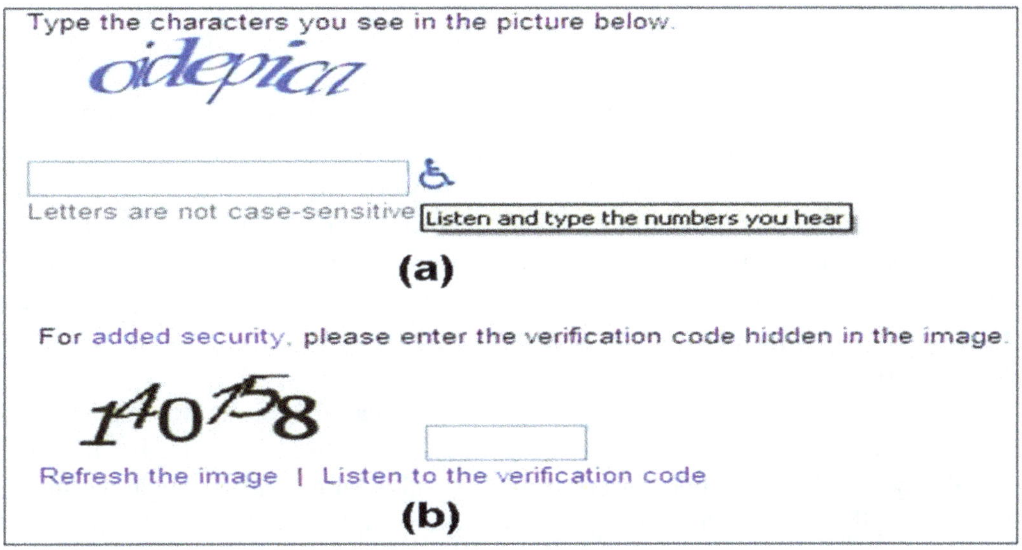

Production Honeypot

These types of honeypots are easy to developed, gather only limited amount of data, and are mainly used in IT companies. They are installed inside the network with other different servers such as web servers and Database servers by a software organization to attain the overall security. Generally, production honeypots are little interactive honeypots, which can simply be deployed. They provide a lesser amount of information about the intruders or attackers as compared to the research honeypots (Zhang et al., 2003).

Research Honeypots

These Types of honeypots are developed to collect massive information about the strategies and motives and of the attackers and intruders targeting different systems. These Research honeypots do not put the direct value to a particular user or network; rather, they are used to investigate and explore the attacks and threats that companies are facing and to examine how to better guard against those attacks and threats. Research honeypots are difficult to develop and their maintenance is high. They gather extensive amount of data, and mainly used in research and development, Intelligence Agencies, and government organizations (Abbasi et al., 2009).

Web-Based Honeypot

Web-based honeypots are based on HTML and Java Script. They use hidden links, hidden forms, and hidden elements of HTML. Legitimate user will not click on hidden link or hidden button. If a Bot clicks on hidden button or link it gets caught. The Key in web-based honeypot is its constant changing. For instance, Form honeypot is based on giving a fixed single or several invisible form fields rendering as a honeypot. If invisible form field is filled out, in case of Bots, they will typically fill in a value, and then the HTML form will give back an error. The fields are not visible to real users, so they will not fill it out (Watson et al., 2008).

FIREWALL

A firewall is a security mechanism in computer networks that constantly monitor and manage the network traffic both the incoming and outgoing based on predefined security policies. A firewall normally set up a boundary between a genuine, protected internal network and outside network, for instance, the Internet. Firewalls could be made in hardware as well as software or sometimes a mixture of both. Firewalls are often used to check illegal users from gain an access to private network of some organization linked to the Internet, particularly the Intranet. Every incoming or outgoing message of intranet goes through the firewall, which monitors a message and stops those that do not qualify the security criteria (Zaliva et al., 2008).

Firewalls are generally categorized as network firewalls, host based firewalls, web application firewall. Network firewalls set up a boundary between two networks. Host based firewalls give an extra layer of software on the system that monitors network incoming and outgoing of that single machine. A third category is specifically made for the web application is Web Application Firewall (WAF).

A web application firewall constantly monitors HTTP (Hyper Text Transfer Protocol) traffic and apply rules to communication using HTTP and HTTPs. Mostly, these rules used to check whether the HTTP traffic containing Injection attacks, DoS, DDOS, cross site scripting (XSS) or any other attack on web application. Proxy sites typically guard clients, while web application firewall guards application servers. A web application firewall can be installed to protect a particular website or web applications. A web application firewall can be thought as a reverse proxy (Rahimi, 2006).

The web application firewall secures the web server by examining every HTTP or HTTPS request. It inspects through the deep packet inspection and the web traffic analysis of patterns. If found any sort of security breach or threat not according to the security policy, then the web application firewall stops the attack by blocking the particular HTTP request or session or, user agent or by IP.

Mining-Based Detection

Numerous data mining and machine learning techniques, such as Supervised Learning, Unsupervised Learning, Rule based Classification, and Anomaly based Detection using clustering can be used effectively and efficiently to detect HTTP Botnet traffic and C&C Botnet traffic.

Anomaly Detection Methods

In Anomaly detection methods, they try to distinguish Botnet traffic from genuine traffic based on a number of network traffic variance i.e., anomalies for instance, large volume traffic, high latency of network, traffic of unusual ports, and abnormal behavior of system that may specify presence of system Botnet in the network. The effective method for Botnet detection is to find out the Botnet HTTP traffic and C&C traffic. Although, the Botnet HTTP traffic is not easy to detect, however, Botnet make use of normal HTTP traffic communications, the HTTP Bot traffic is similar to normal HTTP traffic. In addition to that, the HTTP traffic is not a large volume and not causes high latency of network. Consequently, anomaly based methods cannot be used to identify HTTP Botnet traffic (Bhuyan et al., 2014).

Rule-Based Detection

Information of patterns and behavior of existing Bots is useful for Bot detection and identification. For instance, SNORT is the most common IDS (Intrusion Detection System) that monitors traffic of network to identify the patterns of Bots and intrusions. Similar to all the Intrusion Detection System, Snort can be configured with signatures or patterns or a set of rules or to keep a record of traffic which is considered as suspicious. On the other hand, rule-based detection techniques mostly, could be used for identification and detection of known Bots. As a result, this technique is not helpful for detecting the unknown Bots.

Supervised Learning and Unsupervised Learning

Supervised Learning and Unsupervised Learning techniques are based on Machine Learning Algorithms such as Classification including Decision Trees, Random Forest, K-Nearest Neighbor, and Clustering Techniques including Flat and Hierarchical Clustering.

The well-known system based on supervised learning and unsupervised learning is Botminer approach which implements Hierarchical and K-Means Clustering algorithm for HTTP Botnet traffic and C&C traffic detection.

The Botminer (Perdisci et al., 2008) is an enhancement of Botsniffer. It groups the similar legitimate HTTP traffic in one group and similar malicious Bot traffic in other group. After that, it carries out cross correlation on different clusters to classify the users that has both similar normal communication patterns and similar abnormal communication patterns. The Botminer tool is a sophisticated Bot detection system which is not dependent on communication protocol and its structure. Botminer is able to detect actual Botnets including HTTP based Botnet, and Peer to Peer Botnets with quite high accuracy.

Big Data Approach

In a last decade, numerous researchers have proposed solutions for mitigating security threats through machine learning techniques. Lot of packet processing tools are used for web traffic analysis such as Wireshark, Nmap, netsniff-ng, tcpdump and wireshark, and snort. In general, these packet-processing tools have limitations that they run on a single machine with limited amount of storage and computing resources. Furthermore, with a single machine, it is hard to give fault tolerant analysis services against a node failure, which over and over again happens when read/write jobs are repeatedly performed on disks. Researchers have steadily shifting from SIEM based methods to Big Data approaches like in (Lee et al., 2011) developing DDoS attack detection system based on Hadoop using large network traffic for mitigation of security threats. In (Suryawanshi et al., 2014), authors devise the first packet processing technique for Hadoop that examines packet trace files using map reduce by analyzing packets across multiple HDFS blocks. Researchers (Lee et al., 2013) report their work on developing a novel traffic monitoring system that carry out flow analysis on terabytes of web traffic in a scalable manner. They developed Map Reduce algorithm with a new format able to handle libpcap files in parallel manner. But there is limitation associated with this method. They hardcode the features that are extracted from the libpcap files and thereby the user is not allow to decide the feature set based on the problem instance.

In (Yen et al., 2010) authors made a distinction based on certain features related to traffic volume and classify them as benign and malicious in network flow records. Authors in (Guntuku et al., 2013) developed Bayesian Regularized Neural Network based Botnet detection method which achieved high precision. Researchers in (Singh et al., 2010) build up scalable quasi-real-time intrusion detection system. It is used to detect Peer-to-Peer Bot net attacks using machine-learning approach. This is based on distributed framework using Hive and Mahout. Francois, et al., (2010) describes a scalable method for detecting P2P Bot net regarding the relationships between hosts and it based on a Hadoop cluster. Their evaluation illustrates reasonably high detection accuracy and a good efficiency.

Cheon et al., (2013) developed a distributed Snort system that assembles warning messages from numerous Snort processes, which execute warning messages on different machines in a parallel manner using MapReduce functionality by Hadoop. Their experiment shows that using two or more slave nodes has enhanced performance than a single node system, also system with eight slave nodes shows almost four times faster speed than that of a single node system. However, it is not capable of real-time analytics.

Kumar and Hanumanthappa (2013) proposed scalable NIDS (Network Intrusion Detection System) log analysis system based on cloud computing. The main purpose is to efficiently handle large volume of NIDS logs from server's machines using Mapreduce and cloud computing. Analysis is carried out on

Snort log report with file size of 4 GB. The running time for log analysis is found by evaluating with Hadoop based system and with a single node without Hadoop. As number of nodes increases, the system performance increases as compared to the single system. When number of nodes in the system is five, performance of the system is almost double than that of the single node.

Prathibha and Dileesh (2013) developed Hybrid intrusion detection system, analysis is performed using Hadoop Hive ecosystem. Hive is used as data warehousing tool, which efficiently analyses large size of data. Hadoop configured with Hive makes IDS very scalable by giving packet analysis with language HiveQL similar to SQL. Another Network Intrusion Detection System (Bandr et al., 2015) is able to perform analytics over the behavior of intrusion and their patterns on the network, which assists administrator to configure policies and settings for network security. Analytics over intrusion is performed by using a Score-Weight approach known as Pattern Frequency Inverse Cluster Frequency (PF-ICF).

Earlier most of the attempt from researcher was focused on detecting a specific activity and specific attack and their solutions were not described to be successful in identifying general malicious behavior and attacks, whose features were not used in the training data set. Indeed, it can be observed that using a machine learning techniques for the detection of malicious behavior is far better than conventional signature based approach as the attackers redesign the scripts frequently and the behavior and functionality of attacks varies quite extensively with each version release of the virus. Signature based techniques depends a lot upon the existing virus signatures to identify any activity.

In particular when handling zero-day attacks, signature based technique fall short completely as there is no account of prior activity for that attack. As a result, a machine learning technique is preferred to identify suspicious activity based on the anomalous behavior of the request.

On the other hand, SIEM (Security Information and Event Management) based tools provide real time analysis of security alerts generated by network hardware and applications (Miller et al., 2010).

SIEM has been a foundational tool for long time on the market place and it is the core data repository for security events about most organizations. However, it has number of limitations, which causes researches to move from SIEM based tools to Security analytics. Limitations of SIEM based tools are briefly given as follows.

- SIEM does the limited analysis mainly based on correlating and normalization of alerts.
- SIEM only understands those events inside of its defined rules or policies because it is primarily rules based, policy-based and trigger-based.
- SIEM does not understand application specific activity and behaviour or pattern (anomaly detection) to find out how a number of activities raise threat level.
- SIEM only understands log entries and network information to compare events at network level and find out network alerts.
- For advanced security notification, SIEM requires manual investigation.

Consequently, the existing correlation capabilities of SIEM tools, primarily based on a single machine in centralized servers, have confirmed to be inadequate to process large volume of events and data.

Due to these limitations, the scenario has been shifted from SIEM base approach to security analytics, which can analyze security intelligence in real time. It incorporates current data being generated and the massive volumes of event data and existing logs.

By applying this it is possible to stop and distinguish advanced threats as they occur, for that parallel processing is necessary; the tools should have the intelligence to evaluate anomalies and make a decision whether they are true threats or not, to keep away from troubles and damage to the productivity. Salient features of Security analytics are as follows (Cybenko & Landwehr, 2012).

- The ability to analyze and process huge volumes of security related data (offline and online) in real time.
- Reduce false positives and alert volumes.
- Provide better prioritization and enhanced visualization.
- Increased ability to easily aggregate and cross analyze data from non-security sources for instance web access logs and server logs.
- Sophisticated process engine for correlating the information from different sources.
- Advanced automated response capabilities.
- Ability to use of data from outside sources to give information on the new categories of threat that have been observed somewhere else.

CONCLUSION

As described in the chapter, although there are tremendous advantages of using e-commerce applications but there are lot of practical issues related to e-commerce security needs to be solved. Similar to any technology, several security issues confront e-commerce applications. In this chapter security mechanism of (Detection methods and prevention methods) e-commerce web applications from Bot and Botnets are reviewed, and the primary characteristics and elements of Botnets are also discussed. It is revealed that these attacks have a severe impact on e-commerce applications and the attacks may lead to the serious problem for e-commerce. Nearly all central attacks of Botnets in e-commerce along with the possible impacts and the available countermeasures have been described.

REFERENCES

Abbasi, F. H., & Harris, R. J. (2009, November). Experiences with a Generation III virtual Honeynet. In *Telecommunication Networks and Applications Conference (ATNAC), 2009 Australasian* (pp. 1-6). IEEE. doi:10.1109/ATNAC.2009.5464785

Ashley, P., Hinton, H., & Vandenwauver, M. (2001, December). Wired versus wireless security: The Internet, WAP and iMode for e-commerce. In *Computer Security Applications Conference, 2001. ACSAC 2001. Proceedings 17th Annual* (pp. 296-306). IEEE. doi:10.1109/ACSAC.2001.991545

Bandre, S. R., & Nandimath, J. N. (2015, January). Design consideration of network intrusion detection system using Hadoop and GPGPU. In *Pervasive Computing (ICPC), 2015 International Conference on* (pp. 1-6). IEEE. doi:10.1109/PERVASIVE.2015.7087201

Bariso, P. F., III. (2016). *No Need to Fear Robots: Online "Bot" Use under the Computer Fraud and Abuse Act.* Academic Press.

Bawany, N. Z., Shamsi, J. A., & Salah, K. (2017). DDoS Attack Detection and Mitigation Using SDN: Methods, Practices, and Solutions. *Arabian Journal for Science and Engineering*, *42*(2), 425–441. doi:10.1007/s13369-017-2414-5

Bherde, G. P., & Pund, M. A. (2016, September). Recent attack prevention techniques in web service applications. In *Automatic Control and Dynamic Optimization Techniques (ICACDOT), International Conference on* (pp. 1174-1180). IEEE. doi:10.1109/ICACDOT.2016.7877771

Bhuyan, M. H., Bhattacharyya, D. K., & Kalita, J. K. (2014). Network anomaly detection: Methods, systems and tools. *IEEE Communications Surveys and Tutorials*, *16*(1), 303–336. doi:10.1109/SURV.2013.052213.00046

Cheon, J., & Choe, T. Y. (2013). Distributed processing of snort alert log using hadoop. *IACSIT International Journal of Engineering and Technology*, *5*(3), 2685–2690.

Chonka, A., Xiang, Y., Zhou, W., & Bonti, A. (2011). Cloud security defence to protect cloud computing against HTTP-DoS and XML-DoS attacks. *Journal of Network and Computer Applications*, *34*(4), 1097–1107. doi:10.1016/j.jnca.2010.06.004

Combe, C. (2012). Introduction to *e*-business. Routledge. doi:10.1017/CBO9780511805936

Cybenko, G., & Landwehr, C. E. (2012). Security analytics and measurements. *IEEE Security and Privacy*, *3*(10), 5–8. doi:10.1109/MSP.2012.75

Dai, S. Y., & Kuo, S. Y. (2007, December). Mapmon: A host-based malware detection tool. In *Dependable Computing, 2007. PRDC 2007. 13th Pacific Rim International Symposium on* (pp. 349-356). IEEE. doi:10.1109/PRDC.2007.23

Dunham, K., & Melnick, J. (2008). *Malicious bots: an inside look into the cyber-criminal underground of the internet.* CRC Press. doi:10.1201/9781420069068

Fonseca, J., Vieira, M., & Madeira, H. (2007, December). Testing and comparing web vulnerability scanning tools for SQL injection and XSS attacks. In *Dependable Computing, 2007. PRDC 2007. 13th Pacific Rim International Symposium on* (pp. 365-372). IEEE. doi:10.1109/PRDC.2007.55

Francois, J., Wang, S., Bronzi, W., State, R., & Engel, T. (2014, November). Botcloud: Detecting botnets using mapreduce. In *2014 IEEE International Workshop on Information Forensics and Security* (pp. 1-6). IEEE.

Furnell, S. (2006). E-commerce security. In Enterprise Information Systems Assurance and System Security: Managerial and Technical Issues (pp. 131-149). IGI Global. doi:10.4018/978-1-59140-911-3.ch009

Gadge, J. (2008, December). Comprehensive test mechanism to detect attack on Web Services. In *Networks, 2008. ICON 2008. 16th IEEE International Conference on* (pp. 1-6). IEEE.

Gao, H., Liu, H., Yao, D., Liu, X., & Aickelin, U. (2010, July). An audio CAPTCHA to distinguish humans from computers. In *Electronic Commerce and Security (ISECS), 2010 Third International Symposium on* (pp. 265-269). IEEE. doi:10.1109/ISECS.2010.65

Gao, H., Yao, D., Liu, H., Liu, X., & Wang, L. (2010, December). A novel image based CAPTCHA using jigsaw puzzle. In *Computational Science and Engineering (CSE), 2010 IEEE 13th International Conference on* (pp. 351-356). IEEE. doi:10.1109/CSE.2010.53

Geer, D. (2005). Malicious bots threaten network security. *Computer*, *38*(1), 18–20. doi:10.1109/MC.2005.26

Gordeychik, S., Grossman, J., Khera, M., Lantinga, M., Wysopal, C., Eng, C., & Evteev, D. (2010). *Web application security statistics*. The Web Application Security Consortium.

Gu, G., Perdisci, R., Zhang, J., & Lee, W. (2008, July). BotMiner: Clustering Analysis of Network Traffic for Protocol-and Structure-Independent Botnet Detection. In *USENIX Security Symposium* (*Vol. 5*, No. 2, pp. 139-154). Academic Press.

Guntuku, S. C., Narang, P., & Hota, C. (2013). *Real-time Peer-to-Peer Botnet Detection Framework based on Bayesian Regularized Neural Network*. Academic Press.

Gupta, A. N., & Thilagam, P. S. (2013). Attacks on web services need to secure xml on web. *Computing in Science & Engineering*, *3*(5), 1.

Gupta, A. N., & Thilagam, P. S. (2013). Attacks on web services need to secure xml on web. *Computing in Science & Engineering*, *3*(5), 1.

Huang, H., Zhong, S., & Tan, J. (2009, August). Browser-side countermeasures for deceptive phishing attack. In *Information Assurance and Security, 2009. IAS'09. Fifth International Conference on* (Vol. 1, pp. 352-355). IEEE. doi:10.1109/IAS.2009.12

Karlof, C., Shankar, U., Tygar, J. D., & Wagner, D. (2007, October). Dynamic pharming attacks and locked same-origin policies for web browsers. In *Proceedings of the 14th ACM conference on Computer and communications security* (pp. 58-71). ACM. doi:10.1145/1315245.1315254

Khan, A. A. (2013). *Preventing phishing attacks using one time password and user machine identification*. arXiv preprint arXiv:1305.2704

Kirda, E., Kruegel, C., Banks, G., Vigna, G., & Kemmerer, R. (2006, August). Behavior-based Spyware Detection. *Usenix Security, 6*.

Kumar, M., & Hanumanthappa, M. (2013, December). Scalable intrusion detection systems log analysis using cloud computing infrastructure. In *Computational Intelligence and Computing Research (ICCIC), 2013 IEEE International Conference on* (pp. 1-4). IEEE. doi:10.1109/ICCIC.2013.6724158

Kumar, S. (2007, July). Smurf-based distributed denial of service (ddos) attack amplification in internet. In *Internet Monitoring and Protection, 2007. ICIMP 2007. Second International Conference on* (pp. 25-25). IEEE.

Lau, F., Rubin, S. H., Smith, M. H., & Trajkovic, L. (2000). Distributed denial of service attacks. In *Systems, Man, and Cybernetics, 2000 IEEE International Conference on* (Vol. 3, pp. 2275-2280). IEEE. doi:10.1109/ICSMC.2000.886455

Lee, Y., & Lee, Y. (2013). Toward scalable internet traffic measurement and analysis with hadoop. *Computer Communication Review*, *43*(1), 5–13. doi:10.1145/2427036.2427038

Markov, Z., & Larose, D. T. (2007). *Data Mining the Web: Uncovering Patterns in Web Content*. Academic Press.

Mijatovic, V. (2004). Mechanisms for Detection and Prevention of Email Spamming. P*eer to Peer and SPAM in the Internet, 135*.

Miller, D., Harris, S., Harper, A., VanDyke, S., & Blask, C. (2010). *Security information and event management (SIEM) implementation*. McGraw Hill Professional.

O'Leary, D. E. (2000). *Enterprise resource planning systems: Systems, life cycle, electronic commerce, and risk*. Cambridge University Press.

Oh, J., Im, C., & Jeong, H. (2010, March). A system for analyzing advance bot behavior. In *International Conference on Information Systems, Technology and Management* (pp. 56-63). Springer Berlin Heidelberg. doi:10.1007/978-3-642-12035-0_7

Orrin, S. (2007). The SOA/XML Threat Model and New XML/SOA/Web 2.0 Attacks & Threats. In Security conference DEFCON (Vol. 15). Academic Press.

Parmar, B. (2012). Protecting against spear-phishing. *Computer Fraud & Security*, *2012*(1), 8–11. doi:10.1016/S1361-3723(12)70007-6

Prathibha, P. G., & Dileesh, E. D. (2013). Design of a hybrid intrusion detection system using snort and hadoop. *International Journal of Computers and Applications*, *73*(10).

Rahimi, M. I. (2006). *Web application firewall*. University Technology, Mara.

Richards, K. (1999). Network based intrusion detection: A review of technologies. *Computers & Security*, *18*(8), 671–682. doi:10.1016/S0167-4048(99)80131-X

Rodríguez-Gómez, R. A., Maciá-Fernández, G., & García-Teodoro, P. (2013). Survey and taxonomy of botnet research through life-cycle. *ACM Computing Surveys*, *45*(4), 45. doi:10.1145/2501654.2501659

Salerno, J. J., & Boulware, D. M. (2006). *U.S. Patent No. 7,072,890*. Washington, DC: U.S. Patent and Trademark Office.

Sharma, M., Yadav, K., Yadav, N., & Ferdinand, K. C. (2017). Zika virus pandemic—analysis of Facebook as a social media health information platform. *American Journal of Infection Control*, *45*(3), 301–302. doi:10.1016/j.ajic.2016.08.022 PMID:27776823

Shawar, B. A., & Atwell, E. (2003). Using dialogue corpora to train a chatbot. *Proceedings of the Corpus Linguistics 2003 conference*, 681-690.

Shawar, B. A., & Atwell, E. (2007). Chatbots: are they really useful? In *LDV Forum* (Vol. 22, No. 1, pp. 29-49). Academic Press.

Singh, K., Guntuku, S. C., Thakur, A., & Hota, C. (2014). Big data analytics framework for peer-to-peer botnet detection using random forests. *Information Sciences*, *278*, 488–497. doi:10.1016/j.ins.2014.03.066

Studer, R. (2011). Economic and technical analysis of botnets and denial-of-service attacks. *Communication Systems, 4*, 19.

Su, Z., & Wassermann, G. (2006, January). The essence of command injection attacks in web applications. *ACM SIGPLAN Notices*, *41*(1), 372–382. doi:10.1145/1111320.1111070

Suryawanshi, D. J., & Mande, U. A (2014). *Parallel Processing of Internet Traffic Measurement and Analysis Using Hadoop*. Academic Press.

Tan, Z., Jamdagni, A., He, X., Nanda, P., & Liu, R. P. (2014). A system for denial-of-service attack detection based on multivariate correlation analysis. *IEEE Transactions on Parallel and Distributed Systems*, *25*(2), 447–456. doi:10.1109/TPDS.2013.146

Tao, Z. (2013, August). Detection and service security mechanism of xml injection attacks. In *International Conference on Information Computing and Applications* (pp. 67-75). Springer. doi:10.1007/978-3-642-53703-5_8

Tsipenyuk, K., Chess, B., & McGraw, G. (2005). Seven pernicious kingdoms: A taxonomy of software security errors. *IEEE Security and Privacy*, *3*(6), 81–84. doi:10.1109/MSP.2005.159

Tyagi, A. K., & Aghila, G. (2011). A wide scale survey on botnet. *International Journal of Computers and Applications*, *34*(9), 9–22.

Vargiu, E., & Urru, M. (2012). Exploiting web scraping in a collaborative filtering-based approach to web advertising. *Artificial Intelligence Review*, *2*(1), 44.

Vieira, M., Antunes, N., & Madeira, H. (2009, June). Using web security scanners to detect vulnerabilities in web services. In *Dependable Systems & Networks, 2009. DSN'09. IEEE/IFIP International Conference on* (pp. 566-571). IEEE. doi:10.1109/DSN.2009.5270294

Von Ahn, L., Blum, M., Hopper, N. J., & Langford, J. (2003, May). CAPTCHA: Using hard AI problems for security. In *International Conference on the Theory and Applications of Cryptographic Techniques* (pp. 294-311). Springer Berlin Heidelberg. doi:10.1007/3-540-39200-9_18

Wang, X., Kohno, T., & Blakley, B. (2014, June). Polymorphism as a defense for automated attack of websites. In *International Conference on Applied Cryptography and Network Security* (pp. 513-530). Springer International Publishing. doi:10.1007/978-3-319-07536-5_30

Watson, D., & Riden, J. (2008, April). The honeynet project: Data collection tools, infrastructure, archives and analysis. In *Information Security Threats Data Collection and Sharing, 2008. WISTDCS'08. WOMBAT Workshop on* (pp. 24-30). IEEE.

Weigold, T., Kramp, T., Hermann, R., Höring, F., Buhler, P., & Baentsch, M. (2008, March). The Zurich Trusted Information Channel–an efficient defence against man-in-the-middle and malicious software attacks. In *International Conference on Trusted Computing* (pp. 75-91). Springer Berlin Heidelberg. doi:10.1007/978-3-540-68979-9_6

Wilbur, K. C., & Zhu, Y. (2009). Click fraud. *Marketing Science*, *28*(2), 293–308. doi:10.1287/mksc.1080.0397

Wokosin, L. (2002). Components of E-Commerce. *Annual Conference-Society for Technical Communication*, *49*, 172–175.

Yee, C. G., Shin, W. H., & Rao, G. S. V. R. K. (2007, November). An adaptive intrusion detection and prevention (ID/IP) framework for web services. In *Convergence Information Technology, 2007. International Conference on* (pp. 528-534). IEEE.

Yee, C. G., Shin, W. H., & Rao, G. S. V. R. K. (2007, November). An adaptive intrusion detection and prevention (ID/IP) framework for web services. In *Convergence Information Technology, 2007. International Conference on* (pp. 528-534). IEEE.

Yen, T. F., & Reiter, M. K. (2010, June). Are your hosts trading or plotting? Telling P2P file-sharing and bots apart. In *Distributed Computing Systems (ICDCS), 2010 IEEE 30th International Conference on* (pp. 241-252). IEEE.

Zaliva, V. (2008). *Firewall policy modeling, analysis and simulation: a survey*. Source-Forge, Tech. Rep.

Zeidanloo, H. R., Shooshtari, M. J. Z., Amoli, P. V., Safari, M., & Zamani, M. (2010, July). A taxonomy of botnet detection techniques. In *Computer Science and Information Technology (ICCSIT), 2010 3rd IEEE International Conference on* (Vol. 2, pp. 158-162). IEEE. doi:10.1109/ICCSIT.2010.5563555

Zhang, F., Zhou, S., Qin, Z., & Liu, J. (2003, August). Honeypot: a supplemented active defense system for network security. In *Parallel and Distributed Computing, Applications and Technologies, 2003. PDCAT'2003. Proceedings of the Fourth International Conference on* (pp. 231-235). IEEE. doi:10.1109/PDCAT.2003.1236295

Chapter 4
Secure Framework for E-Commerce Applications in Cloud Environment

Sonika Shrivastava
Maulana Azad National Institute of Technology, India

R. K. Pateriya
Maulana Azad National Institute of Technology, India

ABSTRACT

There has been a massive increase in the use of the internet for shopping and payment. The ease and availability of the internet has accelerated the growth of online applications. E-commerce applications handle many sensitive pieces of data like financial or personal data, which are used for critical tasks like banking, socializing, shopping, and tax filling. Online financial service and shopping sites are an attractive target for fraudsters because money transactions are done through these sites. Credit card fraud, identity theft, and account hijack are key concerns for these organizations. These frauds cause financial loss and hurt the reputation of e-commerce sites. The use of the cloud platform has made these sites more productive, but at the same time, it has opened them to a variety of threats. This chapter describes a framework for credit card and identity fraud detection using big data analytics and machine learning techniques to make e-commerce sites more secure and efficient.

INTRODUCTION

With extensive use of internet number of fraudulent activities is also increasing. Fraud is defined as well considered, concealed, time evolving and well organized crime (Vlasselaer et al., 2015). Above definition clearly state that fraudster do well planning to commit crime, always try to hide its activities behind valid ones and updates its methodology with time. With ease and ubiquitous use of online e-commerce sites business opportunities are increasing but there is rise in various types of online frauds that can cause harm to the organization. Usage of various technologies for maintaining online e-commerce applications makes them prone to attacks and frauds. Fraud involves significant financial risks which may threaten

DOI: 10.4018/978-1-5225-3646-8.ch004

profitability and an image of an organization. Fraud benefitted the fraudster at the cost of victims. The Main driving force behind fraud is pressure, opportunity and rationalization. Incidence like credit card fraud, insurance fraud, identity fraud, social security fraud, money laundering etc is increasing day by day. Fraud control is necessary requirement for today's competitive business world. To check systems for any fraudster incidence, every transactions, data sources and internal control are tested against specified system parameters and rules. Fraudsters are applying new technologies like big data, cloud, mobile computing, machine learning to increase the magnitude and severity of frauds. So now organizations are investing more on new techniques to save guard against variety of frauds. To reduce the fraud losses, solution are such developed that are less time consuming, faster learning, adaptable and maintainable. Fraud detection and prevention are two methods for reducing financial losses. Fraud detection is process of detecting malicious activity or behavior using various pattern recognition and statistical techniques. Fraud prevention is process by which fraud are proactively avoided. Some of pre-fraud prevention practices are manual card inspection, payment authentication codes and internet protocols for secure information exchange. Fraud prevention technique applied for any business depends on organizational practices, legislative framework, technologies and government policies.

Business Intelligence (BI) is now used by an organization to tackle security problem. BI solutions are efficient in taking important decision regarding governance and security of business. BI is basically combination of data integration, storage and extraction to gain knowledge for efficiently operating and securing business. The aim of business intelligence will be helpful in taking appropriate sequence of actions at right time. Business Intelligence include Business Analytics which is the methods to gain useful information from historical data for describing fact, forecasting growth and risk.

E-commerce online transaction includes following line of control online merchants, customers, issuing and acquiring banks. Multi layered approach must be applied for securing businesses which include business intelligence, fraud detection and prevention layer. Techniques like encryption, tokenization, advanced multi authentication system, identity verification and device fingerprinting technology can combine to make system more secure. Monitoring the frequency and velocity of critical transaction, detecting financial fraud by analyzing user behavioral profile with the help of analytics tools is the best approach that an organization can apply to safe its online trade. Now businesses are adopting cloud for storage and computation. It is used as an attractive medium for organization to store huge data and apply various available analytics services. Cloud base BI tools provides scalable, efficient, on demand cost effective platform for securing online business.

Main objective behind this chapter is the study of different approaches of securing business against different fraud. Data mining, Machine Learning, Data Analytics and Business Intelligence techniques for fraud management is described here. A secure multilayered framework for e-commerce application is also covered here. Various data analysis tools and their usage is also explained in this chapter. It also covers details of service oriented architecture and cloud computing service model which is providing scalable and efficient platform for analyzing data to take appropriate action and hence enhances the overall security of e-commerce application against financial fraud with minimum time and cost.

E-COMMERCE FRAUD

Fraud is any wrong doing with the motive of obtaining any financial or personal gain. Higher the flow of money in the e-commerce market, incidence of online fraud is also increasing. Fraud can spread through various methods like wire, mail and internet, cloud, smart phones, social media that are causing huge losses etc. There are many types of frauds that are creating problems for e-commerce sites (Baesen et al.,2015; Jaccard & Nepal,2014; Levy, 2012).

Different types of frauds are listed below:

- **Credit Card Frauds:**
  - **Stolen Card Fraud:** As the name suggest if credit card is stolen and used by illegal person This type of fraud can be detected by observing the usage pattern any deviation from normal behavior can detect fraud.
  - **Cardholder-Not-Present Fraud**: In this fraud credit credential are used for committing crime, credit card is not stolen. It needs more attention because credit card owner itself unaware of crime. It is online fraud which do not need real credit card but require all its details
  - **Application Fraud**: Fake card with false personal information is used to commit crime. This is rare kind of fraud and can be easily detected by checking information.
  - **Buyer Fraud**: Exaggerate claim for property falsified medical history or claim for faked damages.
  - **Seller Fraud**: Like selling polices for nonexisting company.
- **Health Care Fraud:** Filling duplicate claim, obtaining subsidized medicine using other's insurance card, providing false information or selling prescription medicine.
- **Money Laundering:** Illegally obtaining funds from legitimate source and pretends it to be legal.
- **Click Fraud:** Abrupt clicking on advertisement to give advantages to the advertiser.
- **Identity Theft:** Using someone else personal and financial details for committing crime. Online platform provides safe and easy medium for fake purchasing.
- **Intellectual Property Theft:** Intellectual property means the rights on any created material. Easy availability of material via internet make them easily be stolen and copied, this type of crime is named as intellectual property theft.
- **Phishing:** It is one type of crime where a fake email is received by victim. This mail allure victim by informing about any bumper draw or any other fake news and demand about private information like account number, credit card number or password etc. If victim send information fraudster can use it unlawfully.
- **Page Jacking:** When a person click on a link and connected to unexpected site, it is known as page jacking. The fake site can force to steal information or may contain some offensive material which can harm in any way.
- **Botnet:** Infected devices are used to steal personal or payment information from online site.
- **Pharming:** In this form of fraud customer are redirected to fake sites and unknowingly enter their credential information.

Following are the reports that are revealing the truth about increasing fraud incident and their severity in present world: Report by Nilson (2013), has revealed one fact that global credit, debit, and prepaid card fraud losses reached $11.27 Billion in 2012 which is 14.6% over the year 2011.A survey done by Morgan (2015) has revealed some key facts about payment frauds that checks and credit/debit cards are the most-often targeted payment method for committing fraud as depicted in Figure 1 sixty-two percent of companies were subject to payments fraud in year 2014.

Figure 1. Percentage of fraud losses with different payment methods

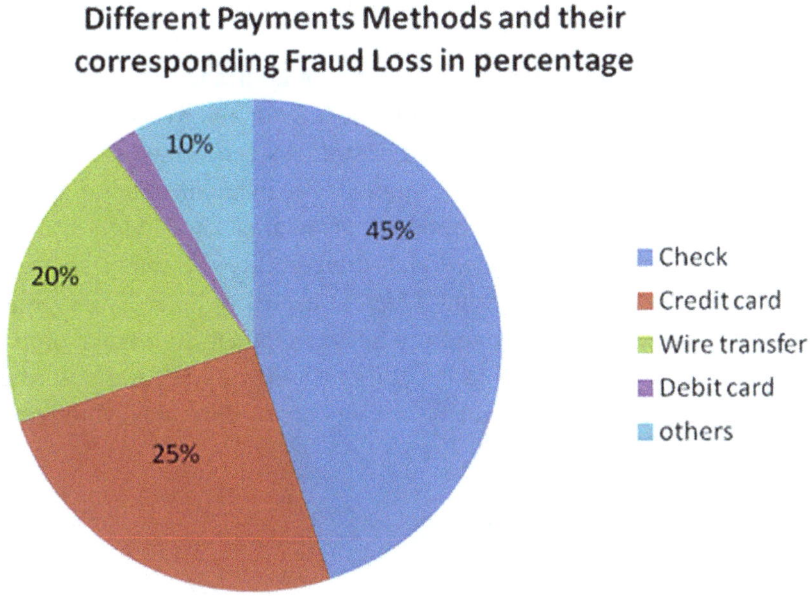

The report "True cost of fraud study" (2014) reveals one fact that fraudulent card transactions reaches around $11 billion in the year 2014. User's credential like name, address, account number, password etc are easily available through e-commerce sites and by using these credential fraudster can hijack account, change shipping address, password etc.

IMPACT OF FRAUD ON ORGANIZATION

Fraud can cause damage to any organization or any person, the impact of fraud can vary and are listed below:

- Financial loss due to theft of material or monetary asset.
- Reduces sales and profit.
- Decreases value of stock/services.
- Additional burden or cost incur due to transaction reversal.
- Decline in investment.
- Poor or damaged reputation.
- Loss of customer trust and confidence.
- Heavy decline in investor confidence.
- Extra costs of time/money to manage each fraud incident.
- Bring down staff morale and trust.
- Possible legal costs.

Credit card information are easily accessible, so tangible and digital goods can be resell easily through these sites, weak defensive layer make them prone to attack. So it is important fact to consider security issues while application development so as to effectively prevent and detect frauds. According to the ACFE report (2014),that proactive data monitoring for antifraud control helps in reducing 59.7% losses in the business as compared to the organization that has not opted this method given in (Banaresc, 2015*)*. Fraudulent activity affect the profitability of business, so anti fraud measure are to be taken by continuous monitoring and analysis of behavioral pattern for maintain growth and productivity of an e-commerce organization. Data analysis is the means of gaining knowledge from the business data. By carefully analyzing the data gaps, weakness and vulnerability are easily identified. Strategic and operational data analysis is helpful in analyzing different aspect of data. Every organization are now investing more and more on gaining knowledge from business data to strengthen their decision making, organizational competitiveness and governing capability. Following section describes the techniques applied by e-commerce organization to be capable to combat fraud in this fast moving world.

FRAUD DETECTION TECHNIQUES

To combat frauds all online shopping sites record every information about their customer either personal or sales data in their database. Careful examination of stored data identifies data gaps, strengths, weaknesses, vulnerabilities and risk factors that may constitute threats and finally suggests guiding lines for securing their application (Banarescu, 2015).

Data Mining

Data mining techniques are then applied to extract and identify customer interest, shopping pattern and other details, so that they can recommend useful product to customers, promote their sales and above all increase their profit.

Data mining includes following steps:

- **Data Gathering:** It includes collection of consumer behavior, personal details and transaction details.
- Data Extraction and analysis.
- Automated reaction and information visualization.

Various tools and techniques of data mining are helpful to analyze data in accordance with different parameter like finding relationship, identify valid patterns, Association, classification, sequence or path analysis, clustering and forecasting are also identified, which will be helpful in detection of fraudulent transaction like credit card fraud.

Machine Learning Technique

The process of acquiring knowledge by identifying pattern hidden in the data.Machine learning technique (ML) are closely related to the fields of statistics, pattern recognition and data mining . It provides cost effective processing for fraud detection and prevention in lesser time (Pozzolo, 2015). Machine Learning

(ML) techniques can efficiently discover fraudulent patterns and predict transactions that are most likely to be fraudulent, it can also infer a prediction model on the basis of set of examples.

The use of ML techniques in the domain of fraud detection is attractive for a number of reasons.

- High dimensional data streams can be handled by this technique.
- Fraudulent behavior are repetitive i.e, fraudsters typically try to commit similar type of frauds.
- Predictive model for fraud detection will enhance accuracy of model by regularly updated with new identified strategies of fraud detection.

Two approaches of learning are: Supervised Machine learning and Unsupervised Machine learning. Supervised learning is the one where the response variable is available but in unsupervised learning response variable is not available. In Supervised Machine learning algorithms training is done using some annotated data (the training set) to build predictive models or the learning process is done under the supervision of an output variables as shown in Figure 2. Input random vector x include both quantitative and qualitative features in the input domain X and helpful in predicting the value of output response y, which can take its value in the output domain Y. The generator will generate input vectors x according to the probability distribution function. The supervisor assigns to every input x to an output value y according to the conditional probability. The training samples are independent and identically distributed samples from joint distribution. The learning machine that are given with some training samples returns a class of hypothesis for defining a mapping between the input domain, output domain and predict response variable for new observation (Pozzolo, 2015).

Figure 2. Supervised learning approach

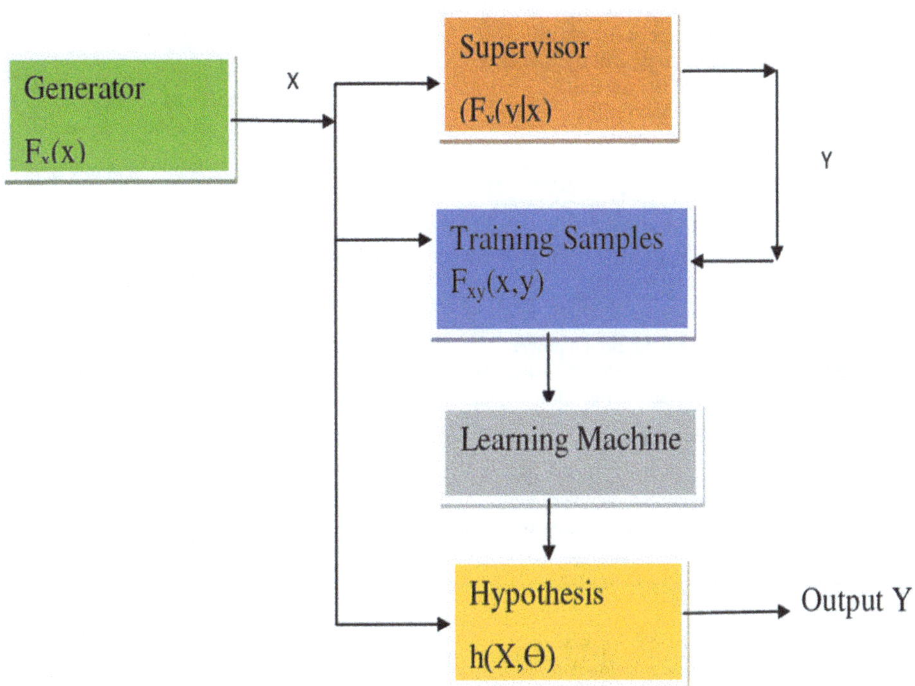

Supervised learning is categorized in two type based on response variable:

- **Classification Technique:** Response output is categorical like fraud detection belongs the transaction is either genuine or fraudulent.
- **Regression Technique:** When Output is continuous like stock price predictions where response is a continuous variable.

Various classification method can be used to build fraud detection model. There are number of Machine Learning algorithm but the best algorithm is the only selected based on size and type of problems. In following Table, some of ML algorithm are listed with their advantages and disadvantages.

Machine learning technique for fraud detection is very cumbersome and time taking approach. As it has steep learning curve which requires knowledge of tools like WEKA etc Model creation process is also complex with frequently changing data. ML is suitable for fraud prevention because of its fast processing capacity and real time decision making capability lower down the fraud rates and can be applied in preventing payment fraud and abuse.

The Expert Driven Technique

In this approach fraud investigators apply domain knowledge to define rules, only deviation from normal behaviour is detected. New updates on rules are not possible because there is no training process applied

Table 1. Advantages and disadvantages of ML algorithm

ML Algorithm	Advantages	Disadvantages
Decision Tree (Random Forest)	o Pattern are easily identified o Robust to type of file and error o Provide fast training o Require less tuning o Output is probabilistic o Good prediction capability	o Complexity increases with the size of problem o Labeled data are required
Deep learning	o Labeled data is not necessary o Highly parallel o Prediction power is strong in area of text and image classification	o Slow and need tuning o Require scaling of inputs o Poor Interpretability
Support Vector Machine(SVM)	o Excellent prediction power o Complex pattern are easily identified o Can applied in high dimensional space	o Require labeled data o Slow and need tuning o Require scaling of inputs o Cannot process different types of data o Poor Interpretability
Neural Network	o Good Prediction power o Complex pattern are easily identified	o Require labeled data o Slow and need tuning o Require scaling of inputs o Cannot process different types of data o Poor Interpretability
K-Nearest Neighbors	o Good Prediction power o Robust to missing data	o Require labeled data o Slow and need tuning o Require scaling of inputs o Cannot process different types of data o Poor Interpretability

here, that can be used to predict the probability of a new transaction to be fraudulent. It is also known as descriptive analytics with unsupervised learning approach. (Baesens et. al., 2015; Pozzolo et al., 2015). In expert system rules engine extract knowledge from the data .Rules are derived using principal of fuzzy logic to design smooth classifier. Expert system develops a knowledge base for detection.

Advantages of Expert Driven Approach are:

- Easy to develop, understand and provide explanation of any alert that is generated.
- Easily detect correlations between variables and frauds.

Drawbacks of Expert Driven Approach are:

- They require human monitoring/supervision.
- Impossible to explore all possible pattern combinations.
- Able to detect only known fraudulent strategies and become obsolete soon due to evolution of new fraud.
- Limited Controllability.
- Lack of adaptive capability.

Data Analytics

Analytics facilitates realization of business objectives through reporting of data to analyze trends, creating predictive models to foresee future problems, opportunities and optimizing business processes to enhance organizational performance. More or more data required more automatic management is required, for automated handling of fraud detection data analysis is required. The objective of fraud detection is to identify transaction having high probability of being fraudster. Mostly frauds are detected using pattern matching algorithm. Credit card frauds are identified as the type of fraud which are creating maximum losses to organization, if it is physically stolen or its credential are used for doing fake transaction over the internet. credit card fraud are detected easily by searching abnormal behavior in the database (Banarescu, 2015).

Advantage of Data Analysis for Fraud Detection

- **Improved Efficiency:** Automatic data collection, fast access to all data through data indexing software, easy elimination of double records and errors, improving quality of data, help in easy detection and monitoring of fraudulent behavior.
- **Repeatable Tests:** Fraud testing can be done on any data at any time.
- **Wider Coverage:** More chances of finding exceptional items through full coverage of testing population rather than spot checking on transactions.
- **Early Warning System:** Early fraud detection and recovery is possible through data analysis.
- **Reduction in False Positive Rate:** False rate of detection is minimized.
- **Precision:** Use of statistical analysis tool will provide with high degree of accuracy.
- **Cost Effective:** Data analysis will increased rate for fraud detection and reducing fraudulent claims.

Challenges Associated With Data Analysis

- **Data Quality:** For better results from analytics tests are only as good as the input data. Before performing tests data should be cleaned and validated.
- **Data Volumes:** With heavy increase in the business data volume, data analytics testing infrastructure must be capable of handling these volumes.
- **Data Security:** It is essential that appropriate security protocols are considered throughout the extraction and analysis to protect confidentiality and integrity of source data.
- **Skill Sets:** To provide meaningful value from result proper skill are required for analyzing and interpreting the Data Analytics skill is combination of business and technical skills.

Data analytics bring dramatic changes on the way of doing business. It enhances the capability of fraud detection and works from underneath the business process to expertise in investigation. Signature-based and anomaly-based approaches to identify fraud are applied with combination of data analytics and various techniques like decision tree, rule-based technique, fuzzy logic with association rules and frequent episodes, genetic algorithm, neural network, Bayesian network, support vector machine and so on. To analyze data for detecting fraud every transaction has to be scanned which is not manually possible without any analytical tool. Web analytics is also used for knowledge discovery. It includes following methods web server logfile analysis and page tagging, conversion paths (funnel) analyses, click path analyses. Some classification and regression methods for web analyses are clickmap, heatmap, motion player, attention map, visibility map, and visitor feedback prediction. Clustering, mining association rules, and visualization are also used used. Most recently, sentiment analysis have become very popular to provide induced information about customer's opinion.

Big Data Analytics

There is continuous flow of data from various sources like phones, e-mails, faxes and others sources. Data is analyzed for various purposes like developing strategies, opportunities identification, goodwill development, preventing and detecting fraud etc. With the increasing volume velocity and variety of traditional data analysis are failing. Need of large scale information management and analysis of technology came into existence, named as big data analytics which analyses and mine large dataset to identify trends and gain business intelligence. Big data analytics uses elastic ad scalable cloud computing technology for storage. Development of New HADOOP framework help in storage of large voluminous data and apply parallel processing for analysis and extracting useful knowledge from it (Sun et al., 2015). Big Data technologies can be divided into two groups: Batch processing in which data at rest is analyzed and Stream processing in which data in motion is analyzed.

Now organization are using big data analytics for analyzing their financial transactions, log files and network traffic to identify suspicious behavior and helps in fraud detection. Big Data analysis tool are hard to configured but are given too much attention because it is efficient in detection of anomalies in various sector like healthcare, insurance, and other fields. Any abnormal behavior or pattern in the data is identified for various purposes like fraud investigation, recommendation system. Different area where big data analysis is actively used is shown in Figure 3.

Earlier Big data analytics are used in creating Intrusion Detection System (IDS) and Security information and event management (SIEM) by analyzing financial transactions, log files, and network traf-

Figure 3. Application areas for big data analytics

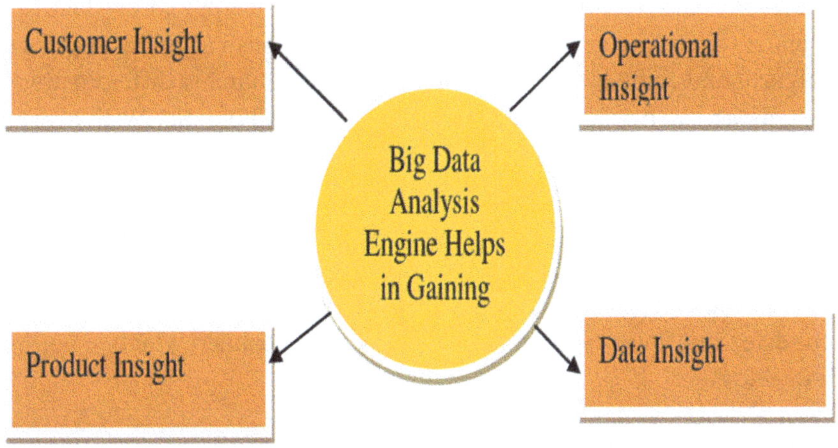

fic to identify anomalies suspicious activities and issue alarm. This technique is used to correlate and consolidate security event information and historical data set to be used for forensic purpose. It is more advantageous than data analytics because it can analyze large volume apply more techniques and can analyze unstructured data and also effectively operational in new service oriented paradigm.

Social Network Analysis

Social Network Analysis (SNA) is a data mining technique which represents set of linked object. It is used in detection of variety of fraud like Anti money laundering, network fraud and denial of services attacks (Chan & Leibowitz, 2006). It is an efficient data mining method that can apply graph mining algorithm on data sources for successfully identifying suspicious individual, groups and relationship. It is a powerful tool as it analyses the relationship between entities to detect fraud. When user post their details on social sites fraudster take their name, address, phone number, account number etc. Some of the common methods of network analysis that can be used in fraud detection are network visualization, entity link analysis, graph walking, snowball method, peer graph analysis etc. SNA visual and analytics capability is helpful in combat dynamic nature of fraud but it also has some limitation, like slow data processing, regulation etc. For fraud prevention SNA can be used in following ways: First social network is built using expert knowledge, so that proper visibility is provided. Networks are build recursively until no new nodes are identified. Then visualize network and calculate measure that can be used for fraud prevention (Chan & Leibowitz, 2006). SAS fraud framework is a good example in which SNA technique is used for fraud prevention.

Business Analytics

Business analytics (BA) is a process of applying various tool and techniques on organizational data to gain business intelligence (BI). Business analytics help to extract valuable knowledge and hidden pattern. It provides a fast easy, efficient and cost effective medium to access and process the data. Statistical and quantitative techniques, explanatory and predictive models, data warehouses, on-line analytical processing (OLAP), visualization and data mining are some of the tools applied on data to extract business value. With exponential increase in data, usage of big data analytics is gaining popularity for enhancing organizational analytical and competitive capability. BA is used in many different areas like to generate query, reports, alert, data visualization, analysis and decision making etc. With ever increasing online transaction the scrutiny of such large dataset to detect for fraud, penetration and abusive incident is very cumbersome and complex task. Now a days to monitor and test each and every internal controls of any e-commerce application BA is mostly applied (Delen and Demirkan, 2013). Till now Business Analytics are used to increase their sales promotion activities as well as to develop recommendation system now combining with big data analytics to detect fraud like Botnet and Advanced Persistent Threat (APT) . To analyze data for detecting fraud every transaction has to be scanned which is not manually possible without any analytical tool.

Classification of Business Analytics

- **Descriptive Analytics:** It is used to identify opportunities and problems in business by periodic and interactive reporting for e.g. reporting (OLAP slice/dice, drill-down/roll-up, etc.)
- **Predictive Analytics:** As the name suggest it is used to effective forecast for business needs and happenings using data mining, text mining, web/media mining and statistical time series forecasting techniques. Predictive analysis empower business, open flexible platform, it help business by provides various services like detection of fraud and abuse, credit scoring, risk modeling and revenue and loss analysis. It includes following steps: Data Preparation, Model Creation and Model Management, model interpretation, scoring and validation
- **Prescriptive Analytics:** It provides facts and information for taking decision effective decisions to enhance business performance. It uses various techniques like optimization modeling, simulation modeling, multi-criteria decision modeling, expert systems and group support systems to solve tackle complex set of objectives, requirements, and constraints. It helps in providing best action regarding specific condition. All these classification is shown in Figure 4.

Business Intelligence

Business intelligence (BI) is combination of tool that integrate data from various sources process them and extract useful knowledge. The method and tools employed for gaining BI is dependent upon type of business. Proper data warehouse is to be maintained and proper analysis tool is to be used specific to business needs. Business intelligence infrastructure consists of data layer, logic layer and access layer. Data layer store all structured and unstructured business related data, like user profile, transaction detail in well organized manner. Proper data ware house is maintained and with the help of tool useful information are extracted. Its first layer is logic layer whose main function is to analyze data and properly distribute information to the relevant user. Tools used in this layer are reporting tools and data mining tool .The third layer is access layer provides necessary interface to access all analyzed information. BI can be used in analysis of many problems like financial, marketing and logistic. To analyze data for detecting fraud every transaction has to be scanned which is not manually possible without any analytical tool

Figure 4. Different classification of business analytics

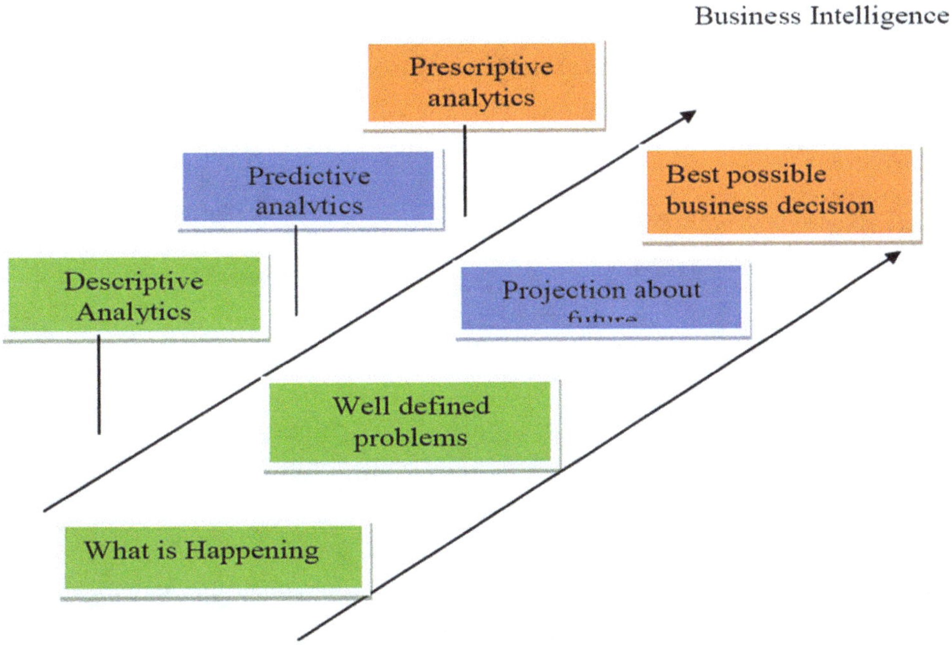

Cloud Based Business Intelligence/Analytics

The concept of cloud computing came into existence after number of transitions, from grid and utility computing, According to the National institute of Standards and Technology(NIST), cloud computing is defined as follows: "Cloud computing is model for enabling convenient, on-demand network access to a shared pool of configurable and reliable computing resources (e.g. Networks, servers, storage, applications, services) that can be rapidly provisioned and released with minimal consumer management effort or service provider interaction." (Mell & Grance,2011). Cloud provide various service model: Software as Service (SaaS), Platform as Service (PaaS) and Infrastructure as a Service (IaaS), main services model provided by cloud is shown in Figure 5.

Cloud have the many favorable feature that are useful in this big data world. Cloud provides the facility of robustness, scalability, cost effective and on demand services. Cloud provides efficient medium to develop or operate on data for extracting knowledge. To cope in this competitive world ecommerce application have to be deployed on cloud which is supporting service oriented architecture. Service Oriented Architecture (SOA) is not a product but is an architectural style which is independent of any technology platform and web services. A service-oriented architecture is essentially a collection of services. These services communicate with each other. For making SOA effective there is a need of clear understanding of the term service which refers as self contained process. Interconnection between services is also required to make it more effective. This approach helps in flourishing your business. The key concept behind SOA is service composition. This refers to putting together several different services to create a new service.

Benefits gained by organizations because of cloud usage are as follows (Erl, 2009):

Figure 5. Service models of cloud computing

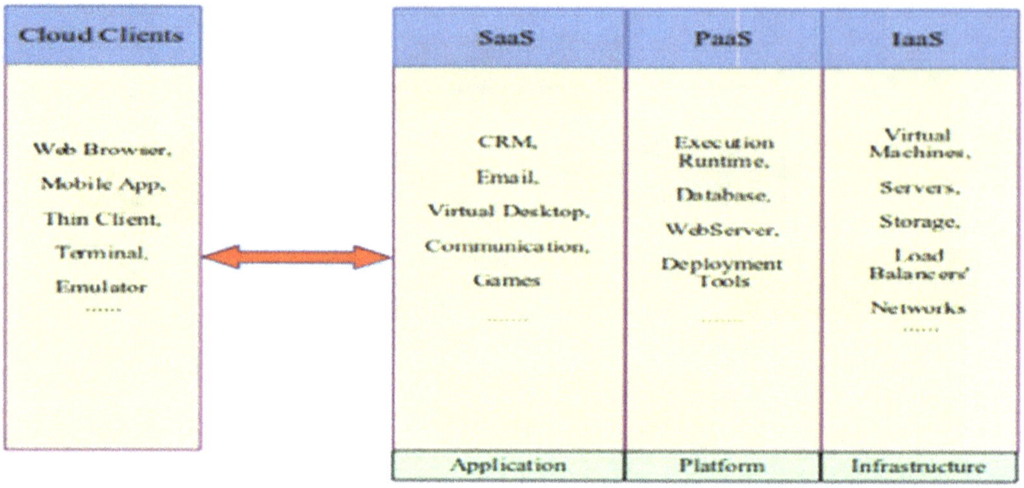

- **Business Agility and Extensibility:** To cope in this rapidly changing business environment is. How fast an enterprise system is able to react to these changes has important consequences to an organization. Service composition plays an important part in this aspect. The agility of enterprise system is demonstrated say when the requirements of a composite service changes, all that needs to be done is to replace relevant constituent services in order to update the composite service. Extensibility comes in when a totally new business service needs to be implemented, all that needs to be done is to assemble relevant services that already exists.
- **Lower Total Cost of Ownership:** All the above benefits results in lowering cost of ownership of IT infrastructure. This logically follows from reusability of services. Not only the service is reused, the IT infrastructure supporting these services is also being reused. Another cost savings comes from the fact that the shorter time-to-market of business applications also translates to better returns on the investment of IT infrastructure.
- **Build Business Applications Faster and More Easily:** It will identify all the business services correctly and help the application to consume correct service.SOA reduces the application code that helps easy and early development and testing of any application.
- **Simple and Easier Maintenance / Update:** Reducing code requires less maintenance operations. For example if a new database is added to the data, the web service will just include information from the new database in its response without the developer having to do a single thing.

These models can be helpful for e-commerce organization to deploy their application based on their requirement and optimize their profit.

Cloud have many deployment model:

- **Private Cloud:** Enterprise owned.
- **Public Cloud:** Mega scale infrastructure.
- **Hybrid Cloud:** Integration of two or more cloud deployment models.
- **Community Cloud:** Shared infrastructure for specific community.

Cloud is providing support for e-commerce site in many ways like efficiency, elasticity, scalability, fault tolerance and encryption. At present there are handful of cloud service providers like Openstack, Cloudify, Microsoft Azure, Amazon and many more.As faster adoption of cloud for providing DaaS, there is need to improve stored data efficiency and security. Rise of cloud based services, security was one of the mind piercing issue. The biggest threat is from the cloud service provider, because they know what type of data is being stored by which particular user. Even if user uploads encrypted data cloud service provider may try to decrypt it for getting information. Apart from cloud service provider, unauthorised users also breach the security and access other user data for personal or professional use. In order to stop all these security breakdown, researchers built up cryptographic concept of functional encryption. It not even stops cloud service provider from accessing authorized user data but also prohibits unauthorised users from getting access to other users data. Security is provided in terms of data, user's identity, virtual machines, transaction etc. Cloud security solution providers implement security features they are earning billions of dollars by providing secure framework for applications. Security providers apply strong cryptographic encryption and decryption algorithms with appreciably efficient implementation methods.

As data is now voluminous, so fraud detection and other security measure are now beyond the manual control, automated management is needed. Cloud service provider like Amazon or Azure provides various online tools that can be used to analyze data efficiently with minimum cost. For example Mapreduce Software, Pig project, ACL software program and SAS software etc. Cloud BI solution allow user to use analytics as a service in cost effective way. User can access data through browser and create reports. For the organization that are maintaining their ERP and CRM in cloud, using BI tool available in cloud platform they can effectively and efficiently analyze data to take necessary decision in various areas. Through connectors available in cloud, data from various sources can be integrated appropriately. Software as a service based BI is used by most of the organization. Security and privacy of business data are concern of every organization, private cloud is most appropriate option to secure data as well as avail cloud services. Managing and analyzing data in the cloud can reduce IT costs and simplify technology deployments and upgrades. But adoption levels remain relatively low, despite the potential benefits.

DATA ANALYSIS TOOLS

Most of the organization now a day's uses data analysis tools so as to efficiently handle the large data and to identify fraud easily and in less time. To analyze large voluminous data new big data technology like Hadoop, Mapreduce exist that can apply parallel algorithms on large data set. Forensic analysis software like Access Control List (ACL) can easily manage authorized access. Data mining tools like WEKA and R are also available for statistical analysis of data. In Banrescu (2015) usage percentage of different tools by an organization is given in Figure 6. Data analysis tools can be efficiently used for proper detection and prediction of fraud from large volume of data.

These tools can be helpful for applying periodic checks and policy renewal. On an average use of these tool helps in reducing the cost of fraud detection in an organization by almost 50% as given by ACFE 2014 report. MATLAB tool can be used for efficient data analysis, it can access data from various data store like excel, HDFS,S3 etc.

Fraud detection system is benefited with the use of data analysis tools in following ways:

Figure 6. Usage percentage of Data Analysis Tool in an organization

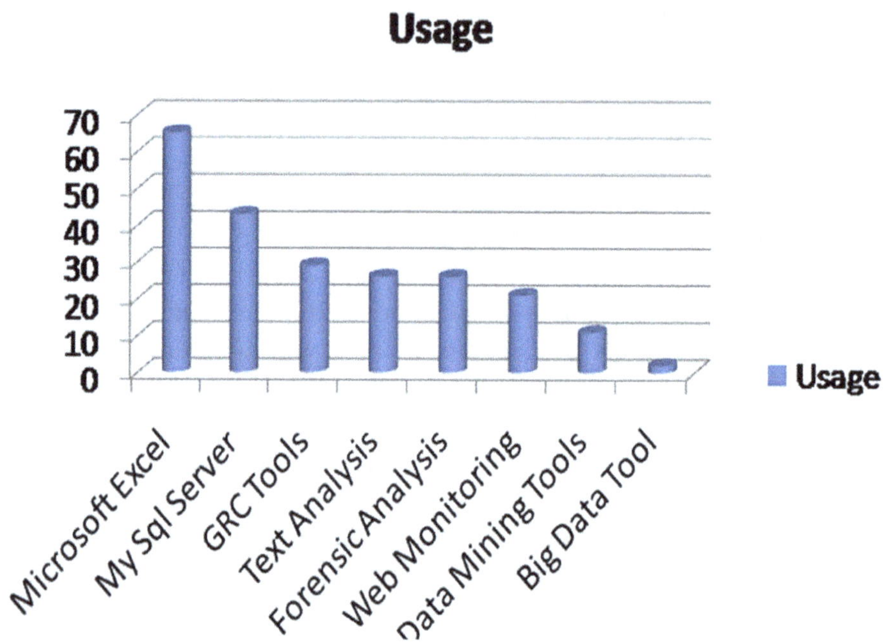

- Automated data collection.
- Real time fraud detection.
- Fast data access and analysis.
- Easy in eliminating duplicate data.
- High Accuracy.
- Low false rate.

With all these advantage, these are not cheap alternative but complex and still time optimization is needed for fraud detection.

Business Intelligence Tools

For taking better decision more data source are to be integrated and analyzed like data from third-party systems, social media channels, emails, or even macroeconomic . So following are some business intelligent software that are capable of extracting knowledge for creating better business solution in cost effective manner .They are differentiated based on their ease of use, price and services.

Following are the list of some BI tools /software available today:

- **Microsoft Proclarity BI:** For securing e-commerce application from attack an automate approach is applied that create a scorecard defining relevance of various risk and vulnerability of the based on priority set by owner of business. This is type of business intelligence decision taken in an organization. This tool helpful in securing business decision by in analyzing data, ad-hoc reporting, dashboards, and scorecards with an extremely powerful GUI.

- **Sisense:** Effectively simplify complex data analyses, make big data insights and integrate multiple data sources.
- **Actuate Business Intelligence and Reporting Tools (BIRT):** It is java reporting tool, integrate multiple data sources and easily incorporate with java application.
- **Domo:** Provide customizable and visual platform for data analyses.
- **Board Management Intelligence Toolkit (BOARD):** It provides BI and CPM functionalities with graphical platform which includes some more facilities like multi-dimensional analysis, ad hoc querying, dash boarding and reporting.
- **Clear Analytics:** It consolidates data from various sources to better analyze and visualize. It provide Excel-based automated business intelligence solution.
- **Ducen:** It analyze historical data with operational data to take appropriate decision at right time.
- **Gooddata:** This tool provides solution for protected, managed and secured business solution based on data analytics.
- **IBM Cognos Intelligence:** It integrates data from various data sources and analyze them with different angle and extract knowledge for better decision.
- **Microsoft BI:** It provides various services including Analysis Services, Integration Services, Master Data Services, Reporting Services, it analyses data for various perspective.
- **Oracle BI and Oracle Enterprise BI Server:** It provides various services including dashboards, full adhoc, proactive intelligence, alerts, scorecard strategy management and so on for reducing total cost of ownership.
- **QlikView:** It provides BI solution for developing, enhancing and maintaining applications. It helps in making various business decision and reporting solutions.
- **SAP Business Intelligence:** It explore data for taking BI decision. This solution help to develop model to plan for future and forecasting growth .It also help in governing risk and compliance of business by controlling access. it is easier in use and create good data visualization. It can be integrated with many other services like SAP NetWeaver BW and SAP HANA. It is scalable and efficient BI solution. It is used for predictive analysis which describes the historical data for prediction. Automated Predictive Library (APL) is used for applying statistical analysis and data-mining for predictive modeling. It provides efficient, automated, operational support to businesses. R script and PAL script are the languages used with SAP HANA ("Unleash the Power of Predictive Analytics with the SAP HANA",2016.). Cloud-based SAP Analytics help user to work directly from browser no need for any installation. Data connection allow to work directly to apply data visualization, exploration and real-time business intelligence on your data. Data volume is not an issue it gives effective reporting in less time. It is SaaS based Business Intelligence tool.
- **IBM SPSS Modeler**: It provides various data analysis diversity with various integrated techniques like neural network and has enhanced visualization capability.
- **Amazon Analysis Product**: It provides various product with different capability like Amazon Athena analyses data stored in S3 using SQL query. It is server less service. Amazon EMR distribute and process data on Hadoop platform in cost effective manner. Kinesis and Quicksights are some of its more product.
- **Google Analytics Tool:** Used to analyze and visualize relevant metrics for controlling e-shop activities.

FRAUD DETECTION SYSTEM: CASE STUDY

Fraud detection System (FDS) system can detect fraud manually using discovery or sampling method and automatically using data mining technique like classification, clustering, regression, detection, visualization, and prediction (Abdallah, 2016). Anomaly based detection technique is basically based on behavior profiling approach to identify novel fraud. They are further categorized as supervised unsupervised and semi supervised techniques. In supervised learning techniques labeled data set is necessary and the data set must be small and this approach gives high false rate, where in unsupervised learning technique unlabelled data are used where the third category of detection technique called semi supervised can utilize both labeled and unlabeled data. Misuse based detection technique can only detect known fraud. So Hybrid FDS now uses combination of anomaly based and misuse based detection technique to enhance its ability. Fraud detection system analyzes customer profile and transaction record to identify fraud score and take necessary action. Modern FDS are typically categorized in three groups: expert systems, supervised learning techniques and anomaly detection methods and inference engine.

Credit Card Fraud Detection Techniques

Sherly and Nedunchezhian, (2010) has discussed various fraud prevention technique like signature credit card number, identification number one time password etc but these are not sufficient for preventing fraud so need of FDS exist, so they uses both misuse based and anomaly based fraud detection method. Use of Boot strapped Optimistic Algorithm (Boat) which will minimize training time for reducing.

Malekian and Hashemi (2013) discussed the anomaly based detection system based on behavior profiling approach for identifying any abnormal behavior. They make use of two profile temporal and behavioral profile.

Chandola et. al. (2009) discussed two approaches for behavioral profiling, first is owner approach based on analyzing spending behavior and another operational approach that create a profile while keeping eye on the location of transaction. Minegishi and Niimi (2011) explained about online fraud detection using very Fast Decision Tree (VFDT).

Dal Poz-zolo et al. (2014) discussed the adaptive learning approach for FDS which constantly adapt to the changing behavior of cardholder and apply evolving learning based technique called Adaptive ensemble and base model. They utilize user buying details, non-parametric method for creating model to identify fraud. Pozzolo et al. (2013) proposes a racing method for enhancing fraud detection rate even in the presence of unbalance input data. Seeja and Zareapoor (2014) has developed a classifier model called FraudMiner Model that can handle unbalanced data set and transfer better result

Sahin and Duman (2011), discussed various Decision Tree classification algorithm for detection credit card fraud. Classifier is built to flagged or label the credit card transaction as legitimate or normal. Based on this training data set classifier model is developed that will predict about future transaction. Training and test data for credit card fraud detection system is formed by certain percentage of normal and fraudulent. Historical data about credit card usage is used to form data mart and creating a card usage profile which is the base to check the authenticity of transaction .In this classifier model each records is recursively split into mutually exclusive subgroups based on the selected variable till there is no record is available. There are number of decision tree algorithms, ID3, C5.0 and C&RT, main difference among them is splitting attribute it is considering. ID3 uses information gain while C5.0 uses gain ratio, C&RT uses gini coefficient and CHAID uses chi-square or F statistic. For incoming records tree is traversed if reached to leaf node the record is classified and labelled to that particular class.

Sahin and Duman (2011) also describe Support Vector Machine (SVM) techniques for defining classes that are separated via hyperplane. Main accuracy lies in obtaining optimal hyperplane that minimizes the classification error and maximizes the margin between the classes main function that are used polynomial, sigmoid, radial basis or a linear kernel function. There are many classification algorithms: Bayes Net, Naive Bayes, K Star, Classification via Clustering, Filtered Classifiers, END, JRIP, used for credit card fraud detection Ridor, Decision Table, J48, Simple Cart. These algorithm are compared according to different performance measure and time to build the model.

Bhattacharyya et al. (2011) and Jha et al. (2012) explain use of the logistic regression for monitoring of credit card fraud.

Steps involved in building classifier for

- Pre-processing the data before modelling.
- Most important attribute is distinguished or found.
- Then arrange records based on these attribute to form stratified samples.
- Then stratified samples combines with legitimate records to form training samples.

Following Figure 7 describe the credit card fraud detection framework

Figure 7. Credit card fraud detection framework

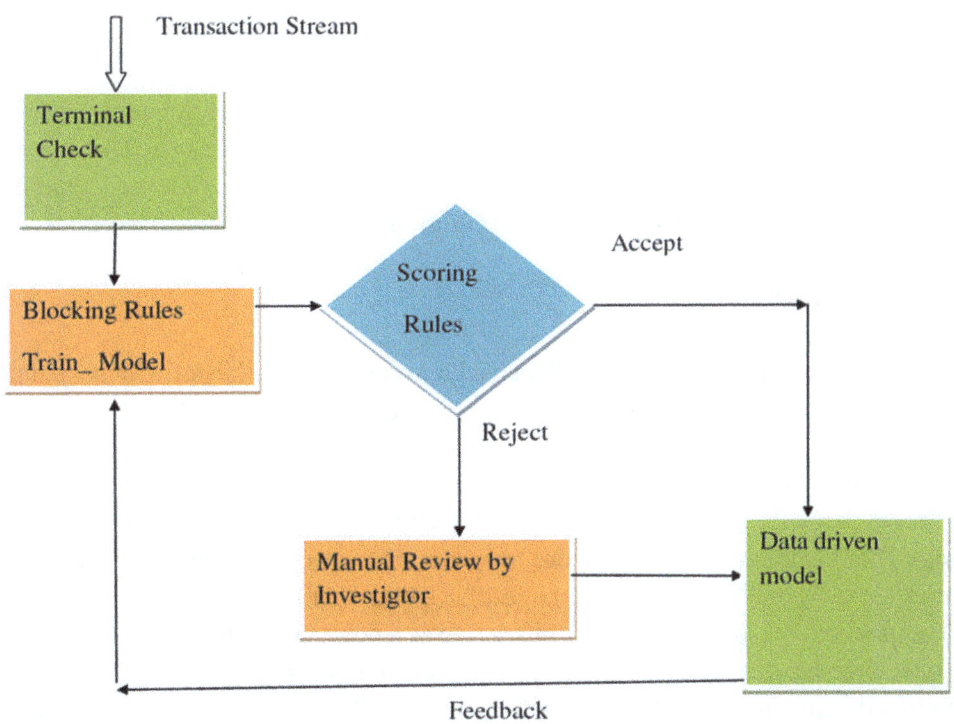

Phases of Credit Card Fraud Detection Framework

Phase One: Terminal Check Stage

To get through this stage real time evaluation is done so one have valid PIN code, password, status of the card (active or blocked), sufficient balance and expenditure, if any of them is not satisfied, the transaction is denied. a number of fraud detection and authentication tools can be used here.

Phase Two: Transaction Blocking Rule

These rules are common fraud schemes clearly defining fraud definition so as to identify fraud easily. It is based upon investigator experience and are very precise. Denial of any transaction request is done when specific conditions are met or denial of any of the static rule .Behavioral rules can be applied to differentiate the customers and identify any of their anomalous behavior to detect fraud.

Phase Three: Scoring Rule

The data is then compared against 'normal' attributes using behavioral rules/Static rules that can be applied to identify any of anomalous behavior to detect fraudIt assign fraud score and act like a rule-based classifier. These rules are made by investigator experience, they are easy to understand and fast to deploy, but require manual revision when their performance drops which makes these rules more e expensive to maintain.These rules can be updated using expert experience. They assign a score to each authorized transaction: the larger the score, the more likely the transaction is to be a fraud

Phase Four: Data Driven Model (DDM)

Machine learning algorithm is used in this phase that gives the probability of transaction to be fraudulent. It identifies Complex correlation in large volume and high dimensional data. The DDMs require a large set of samples to train an accurate model, so is usually updated every day at midnight and the detection model is then applied to all the transactions occurring in the next days.

Phase Five: Investigator

Investigation expert check the transaction and labeled them and sent as feedback which will update DDM.

Modules involved in Credit Card Fraud Detection Process:

- **Model Training:** With the help of samples and delayed transaction this module will provide training to model that will predict the probability of new transaction to be fraudulent.
- **Scoring:** This module will provide score to incoming continuous transaction stream at day one. Each transaction is first scored by both the feedback classifier and the delayed classifier. This module is the most critical because transactions arrive as a continuous stream and have to be scored in Near Real Time i.e. the Prediction function receives in input transactions.
- **Review:** In this module, investigator verifies score of all transactions, label them and feedback. These are named as delayed samples. If transition is not labelled they are termed as genuine.

Identity Fraud Detection

Big data approach combine with profile-based digital identity management to develop social fingerprinting, an IT-enabled capability to combat identity fraud. (Tana et al. (2016).The use of other's personal information for obtaining financial or other benefits is named as Identity fraud. With growth in e-commerce identity fraud is also emerged as challenge for these organization .So there is need of framework which will be helpful in fraud detection. Organizations are taking advantages of their Business Analytics capability for organization, standardization, and manipulation of data to combat identity fraud. They can adopt interpretive structural modeling (ISM) technique and the Means–End Chain (MEC) theory to develop a framework that can efficiently handle identity fraud.

The means–end chain (MEC) theory is used to find relationship or connection among attribute, consequence and goal for a specific organization. Attributes are features of any products or services consequence means reflected benefits of these attributes and goal is the objective or deriving force related to an aorganization.MEC theory is applied in any organizational context for providing goal-directed decision making. Gutman, (1982) uses this theory first for finding relationship between product or service attributes for performing marketing and advertising research. Now the means–end chain (MEC) theory is applied with a goal of performing identity fraud detection as shown in Figure 8, attributes in figure refers to preconditions necessary for developing analytic capability of an organization, consequence refers to is organization business analytically capability. Interpretive structural modeling (ISM) technique is widely used to create systematic model using interrelated variables belongs to an organization context to solve complex issues. Social–Finger printing for detection to identity theft by the use of digital identity and dynamic verification technology. Now a days availability of huge volume of digital information

Figure 8. Framework for identity fraud detection

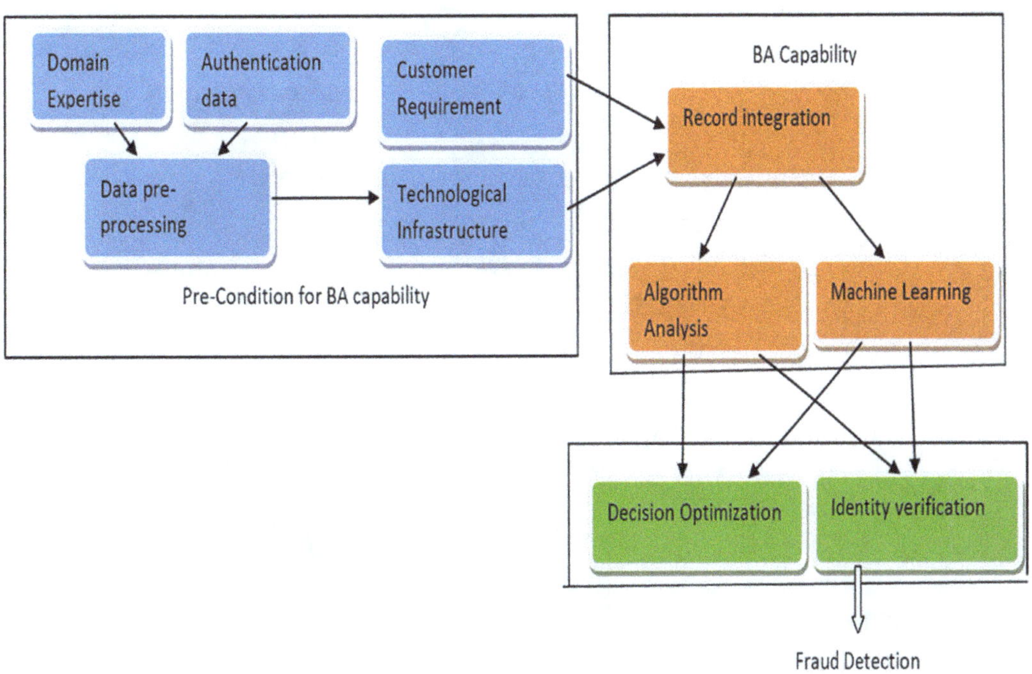

from various sources like sensors, mobile phones, e-commerce websites, GPS, and social media, are providing base for organization to analyze these data for fulfilling different kinds of business objectives. Framework as shown below in Figure 8 is used for detection of identity fraud using Big Data Analytics in combination with Machine Learning technique

It uses a type of authentication system which combine social fingerprinting technique with other system to formulate score out of 100 to retailers and customer to distinguished them as authentic one. Merchant/Retailer/customer who get low score are suspected for doing fraudulent activities. Various kind of data like behavioral, transactional, and social data is collected for the analysis purpose, like in the social data category user's face book account is checked, transaction history and operational log data are also be used, .These data combines with domain knowledge like reporting, and discovery for the data pre processing. Data preprocessing involves creation of tables or classification metrics that creates rich data set for further processing and to extract meaningful information from data and to formulate score. Low score for any person indicates it is fraudster. Then machine learning and analysis algorithm are applied on extracted data to optimized the solution for better accuracy and speed and detect identify fraud. This technique is better that rule based decision making because it uses dynamic data source like authentication data is collected from various source and it apply ML algorithm to extract knowledge.

Baesens et. al., (2015) has discussed about various steps involved in developing fraud protection model for any specific organization as shown in Figure 9.

Step One: Identifying business problem and collection of relevant data.
Step Two: Preprocessing and data cleansing for filling the gaps and inconsistency.
Step Three: Transforming and analyzing data.
Step Four: Interpreting, Evaluating and Model deployment.

Figure 9. Fraud analytical process model

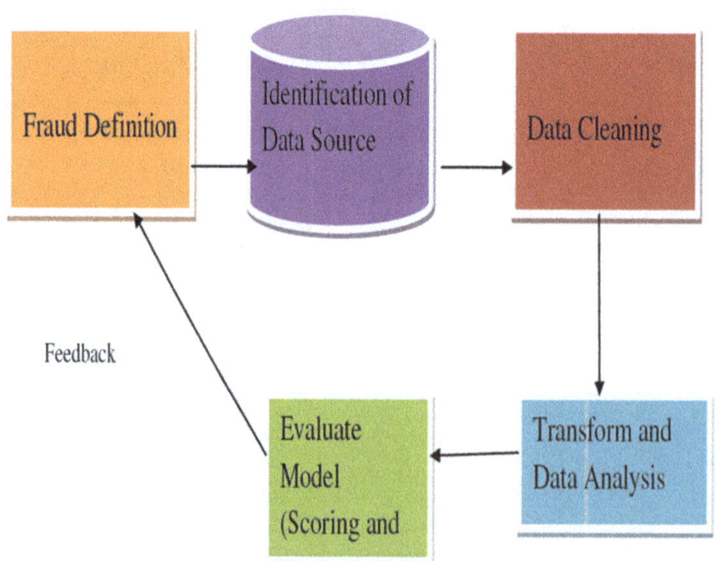

Main problem facing data analytics for fraud detection are detection of fraudulent activity mainly depend upon statistical accuracy, interpretability means how effectively mathematical formulation are done so that fraud can be detected easily. Operational efficiency is criteria based on which detection model is tested, means how effectively and timely fraud is detected with less false alarm. Training and testing set should be properly selected so that proper model is created which is abiding by regulatory compliance.

SECURE FRAMEWORK FOR E-COMMERCE

Online business plays significant role increasing revenue, attracting customer in achieving the growth and profitability goals. E-commerce online transaction follow this line of control online merchants, customers, issuing and acquiring banks. For securing e-commerce application multilayered model is to be develop that can detect, investigate and discover fraud efficiently (Henderson & Hammersburg, 2016). FEEIC has given guideline to all organization performing financial transaction to adopt layered and integrated approach to fight against fraud and attacks (Sahin & Duman, 2011). This multilayer approach enhances the capability of fraud detection because if one layer misses the fraud detection, it will likely be picked up by another layer. At least 2 to 3 layers must be present. Main motive of this layered architecture is minimizing false positive and false negative with minimum cost (Levy, 2012). Fraud detection and prevention system can together used for securing electronics commerce system. Following Figure 10 shows secure framework for e-commerce.

Description of Framework

The foundation layer is provided by Business analytics. Business analytics includes collection of quality data from various sources and their integration is a necessary in fraud protection methods because

Figure 10. Secure framework for e-commerce application

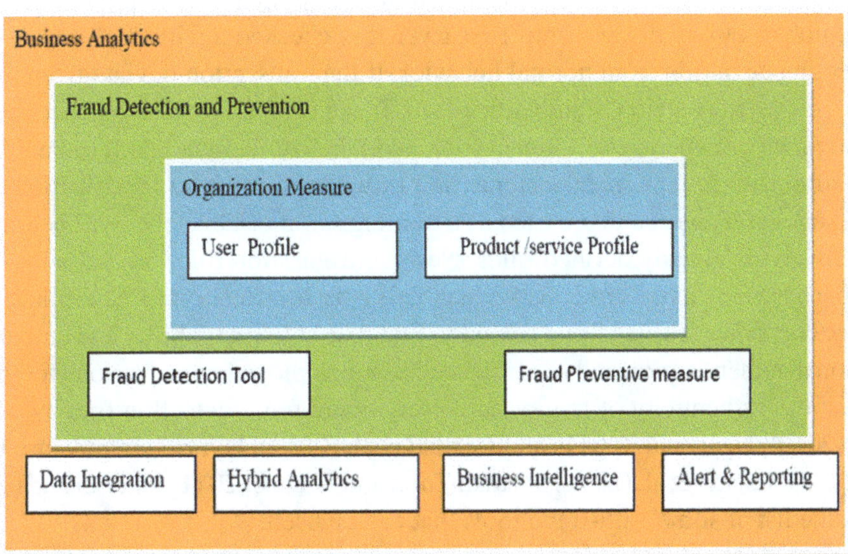

fraudster try to hide some necessary details which can be easily detected. Identifying fraud patterns is the next step based on organization defined modules. Hybrid analytics techniques can be applied for enhancing fraud protection capability like database searching, text mining, anomaly based detection or social network analysis for identifying unknown and complex pattern. Application of business intelligence and proper reporting is also a necessary step in fraud detection. Special investigation unit is created above this analytics layer using various fraud detection tools.

FPS system tries to stop, suppress, control or prevent occurrence of fault.FPS systems generally define policies for organization to remove faults. Encryption algorithms are applied for preventing fault. Some more preventive methods like Address Verification Systems (AVS), Card Verification Method (CVM)

Personal Identification Number (PIN), Captha code and (OTP) one-time password are mostly used. Fraud detection system tries to detect and recognize fraud. Data Driven approaches with Machine learning algorithm is advantageous for setting up a FDS as it increases its ability to learn, identify, predict and take real time decision. This combination can easily handle technical or business challenges and can be applied in many areas like Spam detection, Content recommendation, Image recognition and fraud management. It is also known as predictive analytics and supervised learning approach. They apply many data mining and statistical techniques like pair wise matching, decision tree, clustering or neural network or genetic algorithm for detection. Fraud detection systems collect the transaction, evaluate and assign score. These score are then compared with predefined threshold value to check the transaction is normal or fraudulent .Combining multi factor authentication and biometric based identification like fingerprint, iris and facial recognition techniques can work effectively or behavior profile integrated with advanced device profile technologies is also very effective. Device fingerprinting where authentic device can be recognized with the help of token. Tokenization approach help device not to store any credit card information but generates a single-use, sixteen digit number for each transaction. For fraudster obtaining the digit is merely of no use so fraud incidence can be minimized and used to identify authentic user (Baesens et. al., 2015; Pozzolo et al., 2015). Feedback path is also there which will do necessary updates

Final layer is organizational dependent layer that design various modules to identify fraud. This layer is designed based on organization requirement, like what type of product it is handling, how the user profile is created, this module will be helpful in detection of known and unknown pattern. New Transactions/observations are collected and detection algorithm are applied based on model.

If Transaction/observation cleared from first layer it is checked against defined rules set, fraud is detected by detecting deviation from normal behavior. If the transaction deviate from normal behavior then score distinguishes transaction is authentic or not. It can be done by manual checking or automated checking. Investigators or experts check transaction and labelled them as fraud or genuine and provide alert.Manual or automated review are taken for review on authentication and verification. Labelled transactions are then sent as feedback and are used as a training sample. This layer will help in defining new rules and to optimize the already defined rules. New Configuration rules are added in historical data. It is important because new cases are added which will help in detection of new fraud. The update on frequency depends upon factors like: fraud behavior, Fraud detection capability and amount of confirmed cases. Conventional authentication and security checks are employed here. Various tools and model are acquired to check the authenticity of transactions. Automatic fraud detection framework is covered in Sudjianto et al. (2010), Ngai et al. (2011) and Behdad et al. (2012). Hybrid architecture for fraud detection is discussed in Robinson et al. (2011), Ryman-Tubb and Krause (2011) and Lei and Ghorbani (2012)

Following is the list of some Anti-fraud tools that can be used:

- Automated identity verification by out-of-wallet challenge/response questions.
- Monitor website to detect abnormal behavior in purchasing and usage via Tools.
- Screening transaction according to some defined parameters and identify them.
- Geolocation tracking for identifying shopper's IP address.
- Device "fingerprinting" tools to identify the PC or mobile device used in placing or order

Merchant can employs some analytics tools like Dashboard reporting, Key Performance Indicator (KPI) reporting, Transaction query, Chargeback analysis, Return analysis, Interchange analysis and Payment method analysis. The proactive approach for antifraud control it involves continuous monitoring and analyzing data. It is better in reducing financial losses then detection technique because it check and prevent the fraudulent activities. Based on organization need the rule and pattern for fraud detection and prevention can be changed in this framework.

Secure Framework Objectives

Main objective of fraud detection is covered in "E-Commerce Proficient Analytics in Security and Sales for SMEs", (2014) is defined below:

- Extracting common fraudulent behaviors.
- Disseminating novel patterns of cybercriminal activity.
- Developing hybrid system architectures
- Improving the readability of the automated fraud detection process.
- Creating an adaptive fraud-detection framework.
- Improving the cost-efficiency of the overall fraud detection process.
- Exploitation of cross-sectoral data and global information sources.

Key Challenges in Implementing Secure Framework

- **Concept Drift:** There is problem with supervised learning approach if there is the changes in the relationship between input and output variable with time, there is increase in the false rate, so traditional approach for detection fail here, so constant updates required.
- **Skewed Class Distribution:** It is the problem associated with unbalanced number of fraudster cases as compared to normal one, so model training set is very small.
- **Large Amount of Data:** For detection, large volume of data is collected, analysis of such huge data is also a major issue, so reduction of data is necessary so that irrelevant data are removed.
- **Real Time Detection:** To optimize the online and offline detection of fraud is very much needed to reduce the complexity of detection algorithm and also minimize the resource consumption.
- **Organized Criminal Networks:** New technology strengthen the knowledge of criminals so information gain from one channel is utilized to commit fraud in another channel.
- **Awareness:** There is need of enhancing awareness about FDP solutions, because most of the vendors do not know about new techniques of fraud detection.
- **Investment in FDP Solutions:** As fraud losses are increasing so organization has to increase the percentage of investment in fraud detection solutions.

- **Privacy Concerns:** There is law that obstruct the collection of personal information as it comes under the attack on privacy but this rule is an obstacle in providing security by means of monitoring and analysis of collected data.

Some more challenges include: Regulatory barrier, Cultural and technology barrier. Some of the other challenges includes overlapping class, noisy data challenge and misclassification cost-challenge .The Report("*True Cost*",2014) on Fraud revealed one fact that Multilayered approach for fraud mitigation is an effective solution. It combines various techniques of verification, authentication for tracking fraud. Some more advanced tool can be used for fraud tracking like automated transaction scoring/rules and logic filtering, real-time transaction tracking, transaction / customer verification and authentication, geo location and/or device identification. This paper study different framework for fraud detection and prevention that apply hybrid approach by combining Big data analytics and Machine Learning Technique. Credit card fraud detection and identity fraud detection framework provides a pathway for organization to combat fraud. As most of the organization are using cloud for storage of huge data set, cloud analytics services can efficiently be applied on these data set and hence protection against fraud is achieved with minimum resource utilization and cost. This multi-layered approach can reduce the amount of successful fraud attempts, reduces false positive and use of new tools make it more cost effective and fast.

CONCLUSION AND FUTURE WORK

Online business plays significant role increasing revenue, attracting customer in achieving the growth and profitability goals. Online market an ample amount of money flows through wired channel which makes online fraud one of the biggest challenge. To fight against online fraud like identity theft or Credit Card Fraud organization are strengthening their business analytics capabilities. Although traditional strategies for controlling online fraud like data mining are effective but continuing growth of e-commerce across geographies and vertical markets needs innovative ideas for securing online business. Hybrid framework which employ combination of fraud detection, prevention and business intelligence techniques like Big data analytics and Machine Learning Technique will be helpful in developing and securing online business successfully. As most of the organization are using cloud for storage of huge data set, cloud analytics services can efficiently be applied on these data set and hence protection against fraud is achieved with minimum resource utilization and cost. This multi-layered approach can reduce the amount of successful fraud attempts, reduces false positive and use of new tools make it more cost effective and fast. Analytics and BI tools are very useful for automated and fast fraud control .Proper combination of techniques and tools based on your business goal is effective area of research. How data visualization and analytics tool automatically handle fraud management with ease and optimum cost.

REFERENCES

Abdallah, A., Maarof, M. A., & Zainal, A. (2016). Fraud detection system: A survey. *Journal of Network and Computer Applications*, *68*, 90–113. doi:10.1016/j.jnca.2016.04.007

Baesens, B. (2015). APATE: A novel approach for automated credit card transaction fraud detection using network-based extensions. *Decision Support Systems*, 38–48.

Baesens, B., Van Vlasslaer, V., & Verbeke, W. (2015). Fraud:Detection, Prevention and Analystics. In *Fraud Analytics using Discriptive, Predictive and Social Network Techniques, A Guide To Data Science for Fraud Detection* (pp. 1–25). Wiley & Sons.

Banrescu, A. (2015). Detecting and Preventing Fraud with Data Analytics. *Procedia Economics and Finance*, *32*, 1827–1836. doi:10.1016/S2212-5671(15)01485-9

Behdad, M., Barone, L., Bennamoun, M., & French, T. (2012). Nature-Inspired Techniques in the Context of Fraud Detection. *IEEE Transactions on Systems, Man and Cybernetics. Part C, Applications and Reviews*, *42*(6), 1273–1290. doi:10.1109/TSMCC.2012.2215851

Bhattacharyya, S., Jha, S., Tharakunnel, K., & Westland, J. Ch. (2011). Data mining for credit card fraud: A comparative study. *Decision Support Systems*, *3*(50), 602–613. doi:10.1016/j.dss.2010.08.008

Bolton, R. J., & Hand, D. J. (2002). Statistical fraud detection: A review. *Statistical Science*, *28*(3), 235–255.

Chan, K., & Leibowitz, J. (2006). The synergy of social network analysis and knowledge mapping: A case study. *Int. J. Management and Decision Making*, *7*(1), 19. doi:10.1504/IJMDM.2006.008169

Chandola, V., Banerjee, A., & Kumar, V. (2009). Anomalydetection:a urveyrvey. *ACM Computing Surveys*, *41*(3), 1–58. doi:10.1145/1541880.1541882

Coderre, D. G. (2009). *Fraud Analysis Techniques Using ACL*. John Wiley & Sons.

Dal Pozzolo, A., Caelen, O., Borgne, Y., Waterschoot, S., & Bontempi, G. (2014). Learned lessons in credit card fraud detection from a practitioner perspective. *Expert Systems with Applications*, *41*(10), 4915–4928. doi:10.1016/j.eswa.2014.02.026

Delen, D., & Demirkan, H. (2013). Data, information and analytics as services. *Decision Support Systems*, *55*(1), 359–363. doi:10.1016/j.dss.2012.05.044

Erl, T. (2009).I ntroducing SOA. In Service Oriented Architecture Concept, Technologies and Design (pp. 1-42). Pearson Education Inc.

Ghosh, S., & Reilly, D. L. (1994). Credit card fraud detection with a neural network. *Proceedings of the 27th Hawaii International Conference on system Sciences*, 3. doi:10.1109/HICSS.1994.323314

Henderson, G., & Hammersburg, C. (2016). *An Enterprise Approach to Fraud Detection and Prevention in Government Programs*. White paper by SAS Institute Inc.

Jang-Jaccard, J., & Nepal, S. (2014). A survey of emerging threats in cyber security. *Journal of Computer and System Sciences*, *80*(5), 973–993. doi:10.1016/j.jcss.2014.02.005

Jha, S., Guillen, M., & Westland, J. C. (2012). Employing transaction aggregation strategy to detect credit card fraud. *Expert Systems with Applications*, *16*(39), 12650–12657. doi:10.1016/j.eswa.2012.05.018

Lei, J., & Ghorbani, A. (2012). Improved competitive learning neural networks for network intrusion and fraud detection. *Neurocomputing*, *1*(75), 135–145. doi:10.1016/j.neucom.2011.02.021

Leonard, K. J. (1993). Detecting credit card fraud using expert systems. *Computers & Industrial Engineering*, 25.

Levy, P. (2012). *Simple Strategies for Enhancing eCommerce Profitability*. First Data Corporation.

Lexis Nexis. (2014). *True cost of fraud study*. Retrieved from http://www.lexisnexis.com/risk/insights/true-cost-fraud.aspx

Malekian, D., & Hashemi, M. R. (2013). *An Adaptive Profile based Fraud Detection Framework For Handling Concept Drift*. Academic Press.

Manadhata, P. K., Horne, W., & Rao, P. (Forthcoming). Big Data for Security: Processing Very Large Enterprise Event Datasets. In B. Furht & A. Escalante (Eds.), *Handbook of Big Data Analytics. s.l.* Springer. doi:10.1145/2382416.2382420

Mell, P., & Grance, T. (2011). *The NIST definition of cloud*. Recommendations of the National Institute of Standards and Technology.

Minegishi, T., & Niimi, A. (2011). Proposal of credit card fraudulent use detection by online- type decision tree construction and verification of generality. *Int. J. Inf. Secur. Res.*, *1*(4), 229–235.

Modi, T. (2011). *The cloud SOA ecosystem, ebiZ the insider's guide to next generation BPM, 2011.* Available at http://www.ebizq.net/topics/soa_management/features/11787.html?page=2

Morgan, J. P. (2015). *Payments Fraud and Control Survey report*. Retrieved from www.AFPonline.org

Nahorney, B. (2014). *Internet Security Threat Report 2014*. Retrived from www.threatmetrix.com

Ngai, E. W. T., Hu, Y., Wong, Y. H., Chen, Y., & Sun, X. (2011). The application of data mining techniques in financial fraud detection: A classification framework and an academic review of literature. *Decision Support Systems*, *50*(3), 559–569. doi:10.1016/j.dss.2010.08.006

Pozzolo, A. D., Caelen, O., & Bontempi, G. (2015). When is under sampling effective in unbalanced classification tasks. *European Conference on Machine Learning(ECML-KDD).*

Pozzolo, A. D., Caelen, O., Johnson, R. A., & Bontempi, G. (2015). Calibrating Probability with Undersampling for Unbalanced Classification. *IEEE Symposium on Computational Intelligence and Data Mining (CIDM)*. doi:10.1109/SSCI.2015.33

Pozzolo, A. D., Caelen, O., Waterschoot, S., & Bontempi, G. (2013).Racing for unbalanced methods selection. *Proceedings of the IEEE 14th International Conference on Intelligent Data Engineering and Automated Learning (IDEAL)*. doi:10.1007/978-3-642-41278-3_4

Robinson, N., Graux, H., Parrilli, D., Klautzer, L., & Lorenzo, V. (2011). *Comparative study on legislative and non-legislative measures to combat identity theft and identity related crime*. Technical Report TR-982-EC, RAND Europe and Time-lex.

Ryman-Tubb, N., & Krause, P. (2011). Neural Network Rule Extraction to Detect Credit Card Fraud. In L. Iliadis & C. Jayne (Eds.), *Engineering Applications of Neural Networks, IFIP Advances in Information and Communication Technology 363* (pp. 101–110). Springer Berlin Heidelberg. doi:10.1007/978-3-642-23957-1_12

Sahin, Y., & Duman, E. (2011). Detecting Credit Card Fraud by Decision Trees and Support Vector Machines. *Proceeding of International MultiConference of Engineers and Computer Scientist.*

Sherly, K.K., & Nedunchezhian, R. (2010). *Boat adaptive credit card fraud detection system.* Academic Press.

Singh, M., & Huhns, M. (2004). *Service-Oriented Computing: Semantics, Processes, Agents.* Wiley. doi:10.1002/0470091509

Sudjianto, A., Nair, S., Yuan, M., Zhang, A. J., Kern, D., & Cela-Diaz, F. (2010). Statistical Methods for Fighting Financial Crimes. *Technometrics, 52*(1), 5–19. doi:10.1198/TECH.2010.07032

Sun, Z., Zou, H., & Strang, K. (2015). *Big Data Analytics as a service for Business Intelligence.* International Federation for Information Processing.

Chian Tan, F.T., Guo, Z., Cahalaneb, M., & Cheng, D. (n.d.). *Developing business analytic capabilities for combating e-commerce identity fraud: A study of Trustev's digital verification solution.* Academic Press.

Unleash the Power of Predictive Analytics with the SAP HANA. (2016). Retrieved from www.sap.com/trypredictive

Van Vlasselaer, V., Bravo, C., Caelen, O., Eliassi-Rad, T., Akoglu, L., Snoeck, M., & Baesens, B. (2015). APATE: a novel approach for automated credit card transaction fraud detection using network-based extensions. In Decis. Support Syst. (pp. 38– 48). Academic Press.

Verizon Inc. (2010). *2010 Data Breach Investigation Report.* Retrieved July 15th, 2013, from http://www.verizonenterprise.com/resources/reports/rp_2010-data-breach-report_en_xg.pdf

Vlasselaer, V., Eliassi-Rad, T., Akoglu, L., Snoeck, M., & Basens, B. (2015). Gotchal Network Based fraud Detection for Social Security Fraud. *Management Science.*

Chapter 5
E-Commerce Business Model

Durga Patel
University Institute of Technology, India

Sachin Goyal
University Institute of Technology, India

Ratish Agarwal
University Institute of Technology, India

ABSTRACT

This chapter provides an overview of the e-commerce business model, the history of e-commerce, the scope of e-commerce, the difference between e-commerce and traditional commerce, issues related to e-commerce, electronic data interchange, value chain, and supply chain, and the pros and cons and limitations of e-commerce.

INTRODUCTION: E-COMMERCE

E-commerce is made of two word electronic and commerce:

- **Electronic:** Means of electronic in term of e-commerce is doing any activity (related to business, marketing, payment, communication) online.
- **Commerce:** Commerce is a branch of business. it is concerned to buying or selling of products and goods. It includes all those activities, which directly or indirectly related to business. An interchange of goods or commodities between different nations or between areas of the same nation (Hanson & Kalyanam,2009).

In this way we can say E-commerce is shifting or changing the way of doing business. It is a dot com revolution. It transfers all the business activity over the internet. so, today e-commerce is changing the way of human life. E-commerce takes place between organization, between organization and customers, or between organization and public administrative. This concept shown in Figure 1.

There are several definition of electronic commerce. Some of them are.

DOI: 10.4018/978-1-5225-3646-8.ch005

Figure 1. A transaction (a) Between organization (b) Between organization and company (c) Between organization and public administrator

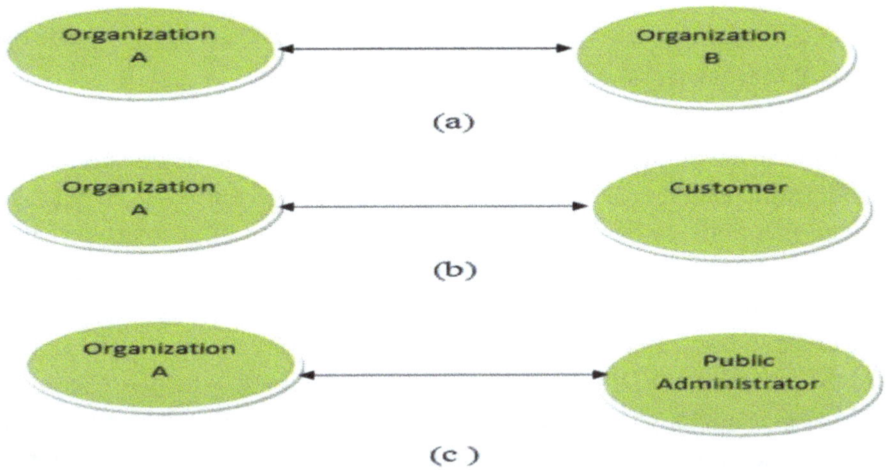

According to world trade organization – " The Production, distribution, marketing, sales or delivery of goods and services by electronics means".

Kalakota and Whintons defined the term E-commerce from different perspectives. These perspectives are:

- Communication
- Business Process
- Service
- Online

- **Communication Perspective:** According to this perspective, E-commerce is the delivery of information, product/services or payments over tele-communication channels, computer networks or any other electronic mode of communication.
- **Business Process Perspective:** This says that E-commerce is the application of technology towards the automation of business transactions and work flow.
- **Service Perspective:** E-commerce is defines as a tool that addresses the desire of firms, consumers and management to cut service cost while improving the quality of goods/services and increasing the speed of service delivery.
- **Online Perspective:** Electronic commerce provide opportunity of buying and selling products and information on the internet and other online services.

According to Lou Gerstner, IBM's CEO, "E-commerce is all about time cycle, speed, globalization, enhanced productivity, reaching new customers, and sharing knowledge across institutions for competitive advantage." Zwass (1996) defines e-commerce as:

The sharing of business information, maintaining business relationships, and the conducting business transactions by means of telecommunications networks.

HISTORY OF E-COMMERCE

In 1970 introduce a term electronic fund transfer, whereby funds could be transfer or routed electronically from one company to another company. Generally these application was used only few organization like banks, large corporations. In banks are electronic transmission of account exchange information over private networks. After some year electronic data interchange occur when one business transmit computer readable data in standard format to another business. It means sending business documents such as purchase order and invoice electronically (Schneide P.G.,2007).

The standard formats used in EDI contain the same information that business have always included in their standard paper invoices, purchase order and shipping documents. Some farms such as general electric(GE) and wal-mart have been pioneer in using EDI to improve their purchasing process and their suppliers. One major problem with EDI faced is the high cost of implementation because it used private or value added network. A VAN is an independent firm that after connection and transaction forwarding services to buyers and seller engaged in EDI. When the internet become commercialized and users began to participate in the world wide web. In early 1990, the term electronic commerce was introduced. A large number of dot coms or internet based business started rapidly. One reason for this rapid expansion was the development of new networks, protocol and electronic commerce software. The other reason was increase in competition and other business pressures (Dennis P.,2004).

In starting year of 1995, most of medium and large size organization in world has a web site. Many of these web sites contain thousand of page and links. In 1999, the emphasis of electronic commerce shifted from B2C to B2B and in 2001 from B2B to B2E, e-government, e-learning, M-commerce.

Scope of Electronic Commerce

There are some main areas where scope of E-commerce. These are:

- EDI on the Internet
- Exchange of digitized information
- Direct marketing, selling and service.
- Online banking and billing.
- Secure distribution of data.
- Shopping on the World Wide Web.
- Product sales and services on the web.

In E -Commerce there are some steps for purchasing the products and take some services from the e- commerce, starting from the requirement identification, searching the web sites for purchasing, and then analyzing that product then place it for payment and complete this cycle of purchasing by receiving the product shown in Figure 2.

Figure 2. Process flow in e-commerce

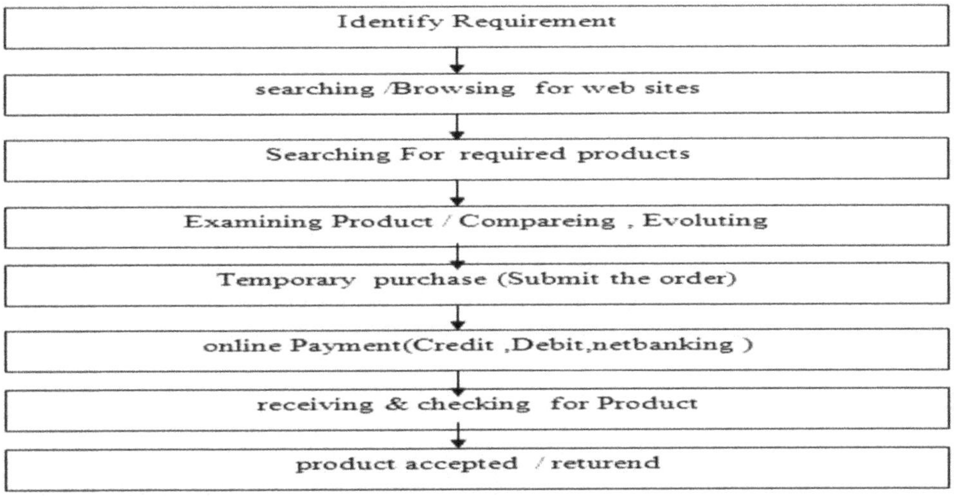

Differences Between Electronic Commerce and Traditional Commerce

Face to Face Interaction

Traditional commerce based on face to face interaction. the consumer has a chance to ask questions frequently and satisfy before purchasing a product. On the other hand, E-commerce doesn't based on face to face interaction.

Real Estate Cost

Traditional commerce relies on physical store space that needs to be rented. It is too much costly while e-commerce there is no cost for real estate.

Reach

With an online shop you can do business with anybody living on a country you are able and willing to send mail to, unlike traditional commerce where you are restricted to people who actually come to your shop. This also opens the door to many other forms of marketing that can be done entirely online, which often results in a much larger volume of sales and even foot traffic to the store. An online store has no capability limits, and you can have as many clients as your stock can serve.

Returns Rate

In a traditional store, the customer will be purchasing the product in person, which has some benefits for both the him and the store. The customer will be able to touch and check the items, to make sure they are suitable, and even try them on, which reduces the number of returned items or complaints due to an item not being as advertised on a catalogue. or promotional leaflet. Expect a significantly higher rate of returns if you start trading online, as many will just order and try the items at home, and won't hesitate to return them as they can do it by post without having to talk with anybody in person (Greenstein & Feinman, 2001).

Credit Card Fraud

The remote nature of E-commerce makes much more difficult to detect fraud, which means stores can lose money due to fraud. While traditional commerce is not totally secure, it's easier for a sales attendant to verify that the person buying something is actually the owner of the credit card, by asking for photographic ID. However, the fight against card fraud is well underway and banks and responsible e-Commerce owners work together to verify that all card use is legitimate.

Availability

E-commerce based online store available for purchasing any item every time. It means you can do business 24/7. In Traditional commerce do not provide such type of facility.

E-COMMERCE ARCHİTECTURE

E-commerce is based on the client –server architecture. A client can act as an application, which follows a Graphical User Interface (GUI) for sending request to server for certain services. The server is used to provide the services upon the request of client. In E-commerce, a client refers to a customer that sends a requests to a server for a service then that request is further transferred to business applications which helps in providing the service. The business application is mainly dependent on Web Server. Web server is a program that deliver services to other computer programs and serves the Hyper Text Mark-up Language pages or files. In client server architecture, a machine behave like client and a server. There are two types of client-server architecture: Two – Tier and Three-Tier.

Two –Tier Architecture

In two tier architecture there is two level that is presentation layer and data layer.

The client handles the user interface part and provide an interface for the customer that gather and present the data on the computer of customer. This part of application is known as presentation layer. The application logic can be run on the client or the server. It allows the separation of client processes from server processes on different computer. The database is stored on the server. This part of application is known as data layer. The data validation, monitors security permissions and performs other business rules done by business logic can be kept on the client or the server.

Three-Tier Architecture

This architecture emerged in 1990's to overcome the limitation of two tier .In three tier there is an independent module for user interface and business application logic. The three tier include the three tier: top tier, middle tier and third tier.

Figure 3. Two –tier architecture

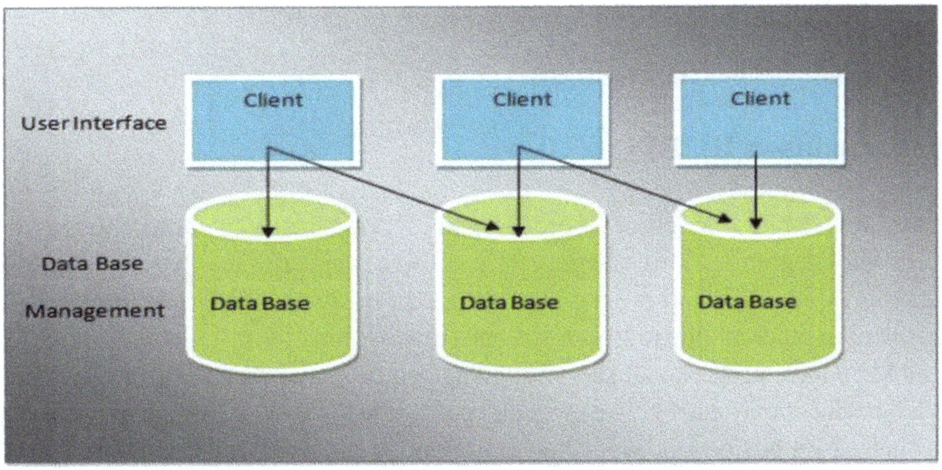

The top tier acts as a presentation layer which provides services as session, text input, dialog and display management reside.

The middle tier provides services of process management such as process development, process resourcing and process monitoring that are shared by multiple applications. It also has centralized process logic which makes administration easier by localizing the system functionality.

The third tier provides database management functionality. The component ensures that data is consistent throughout the environment.

TYPES OF E-COMMERCE MODEL

There are four major segments under the category of e-commerce model. These are:

Figure 4. Three –tier architecture

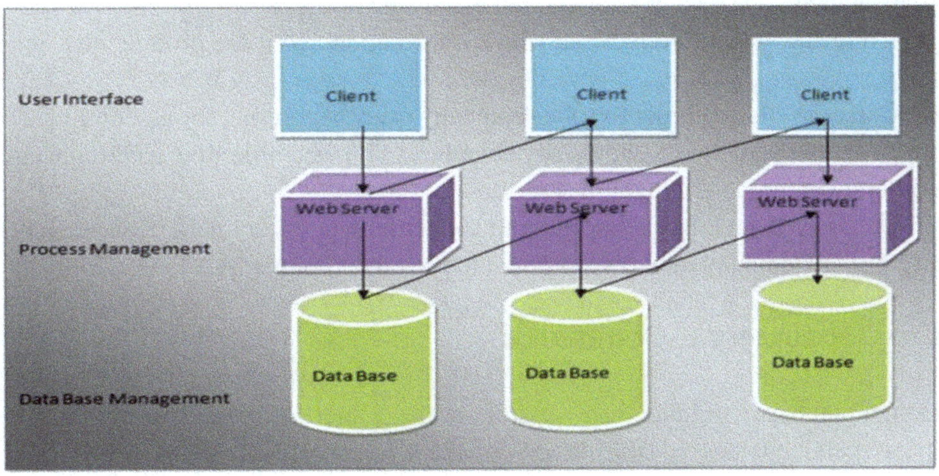

- Business to business e-commerce (B2B).
- Business to consumers e-commerce (B2C).
- Consumers to consumers e-commerce (C2C).
- Consumer to business e-commerce (C2B).

Business to Business (B2B)

Business-to-business implies the selling of products and services between corporations and the automation of systems via integration. This category of commerce typically involves suppliers, distributors, manufacturers, stores, etc. On the other hand The B2B model involves electronic transactions for ordering, purchasing, as well as other administrative tasks between organizations. It includes trading goods, such as business subscriptions, professional services, manufacturing, and wholesale dealings. Sometimes in the B2B model, business may exist between virtual companies, neither of which may have any physical existence. In such cases, business is conducted only through the Internet (Rajaraman V.2009).

Let us look at the same example of amazon.com . As you know, amazon.com is an online bookstore that sells books form various publishers including TMH, PHI, O'Reilly, Wrox, and so on. In this case, the publishers have the option of either developing their own site or displaying their books on the amazon site, or both. The publishers mainly choose to display their books on amazon at it gives them a larger audience. Now, to do this, the publishers need to transact with amazon, involving business houses on both the ends, is the B2B model.

Consider a hypothetical example. ABC company sells electronic parts and XYZ company assembles these part and then sells the electronic item to customers. XYZ company comes across the web site of ABC and finds it suitable. XYZ company, requests for more information about ABC and finally, decides to purchase electronic parts from ABC. To do this, XYZ places an order on the web site of ABC. After ABC receives the order details, it validates the information. As soon as the order is confirmed, the payment procedures are settled. Finally, ABC sends an acknowledgement of payment to XYZ and delivers the goods as per the shipment details decided between the two organizations. Figure 5 show Business to Business Model.

Majorly there are four step involve when one business communicate to another Business. These are:

Step 1: Seller Company make a website and display all the product detail. For example electronic company give detail all the product related to all electronic product.

Step 2: Buyer Company view a product and find a information about the product on a seller company website.

Step 3: Buyer Company place a order to seller company over the internet for assembling a product. For example buyer company make Laptop or computer, so it place order like electronic circuit, SMPS, Fan, motherboard, processor, hard disk etc.

Step 4: Receive a order from buyer company and the settlement of payment between seller and buyer company. Seller Company delivers a product to the buyer company.

Business to Consumers E-Commerce

When a consumer purchase a product form a e-store over the internet and fully transaction is carried out electronically, we call it business to consumer e-commerce or business to consumer e-commerce. Busi-

Figure 5. Business to Business Model

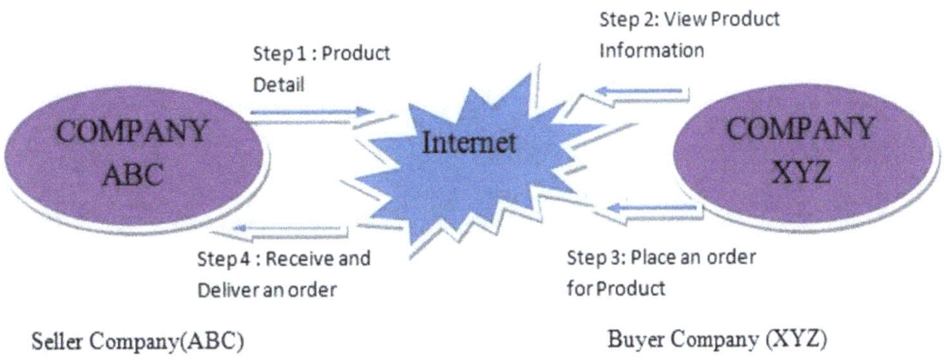

ness to consumer involves interaction and transaction between a business and its end consumer and so it create electronic storefronts that offer information, services, product between business and consumer in a retailing transaction. It applies to any business organization that sells its products or services to consumers over the Internet. These sites display product information in an online catalog and store it in a database. The B2C model also includes services online banking, travel services, and health information. Business to consumer model include virtual malls, which are website, host may placed order online virtual malls (Joseph P.T. & S.J.,2009).

Consider a hypothetical example in which a transaction is conducted between a business Company and a consumer. A Company, XYZ Department Store, displays and sells a range of products on their Web site, www.xyz.com. The details information of all their products is contained in the huge catalogs maintained by xyz Department Stores. Now, a consumer, ABC wants to buy a gift for his wife. He therefore, logs on to the site of XYZ Department Stores and selects a gift from the catalog. He also gets the detailed information about the gift such as, the price, availability, discounts, and so on from their catalog. Finally, when he decides to buy the gift, he places an order for the gift on their Web site. To place an order, he needs to specify his personal and credit card information on xyz company. This information is then validated by XYZ Department Store and stored in their database. On verification of the information the order is processed. Therefore, as you can see, the B2C model involves transactions between a consumer an done or more business organizations. Figure 6 show Business to consumer model.

Majorly there are four step involve between business and customer transaction. These are:

Step 1: Seller Company make a website and display all the product detail. Details information of all their products is contained in the huge catalogs maintained by Company Store. For example electronic company give detail all the product related to all electronic product i.e cost, availability, discount, technical feature of product .

Step 2: Customer view a product and find and analysis a information about the product on a seller company website.

Step 3: Customer place a order to seller company over the internet. For example purchase Laptop or computer, so it place order to seller company.

Step 4: Receive a order and payment from customer. Seller Company delivers a product to customer.

Figure 6. Business to Consumer Model

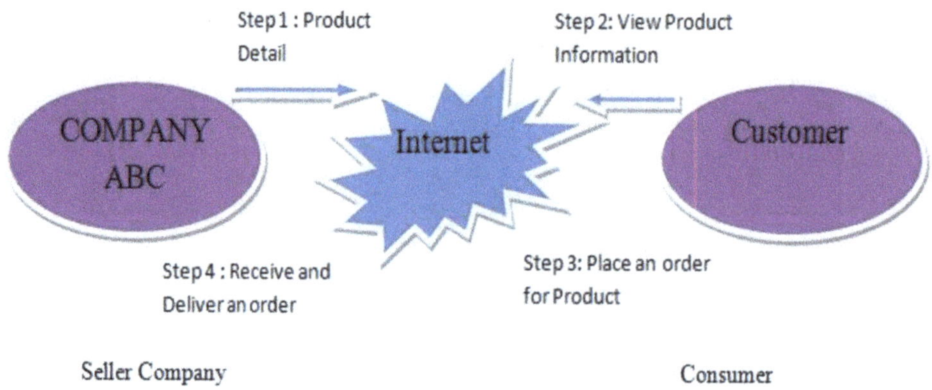

The example of the amazon site also involves the B2C model in which the consumer searches for a book on their site and places an order, if required. This implies that a complete business solution might be an integration solution of more than one business model. For example, amazon includes the B2B model in which the publishers transact with amazon and the B2C model in which an individual consumer transact with the business organization.

The B2C model of e-commerce is more prone to the security threats because individual consumers provide their credit card and personal information on the web site of a business organization. In addition, the consumer might doubt that his information is secured and used effectively by the business organization. This is the main reason why the B2C model is not very widely accepted. Therefore, it becomes very essential for the business organizations to provide robust security mechanisms that can guarantee a consumer for securing his information.

Table 1. Difference between B2B and B2C model

Subject	B2B	B2C
Commerce Activity	Transaction between Organization	Transaction between organization and company
Business Models	The business models in B2B are much more defensible than in B2C. In B2B, buyers and suppliers are made more efficient, competitive and profitable.	The B2C models are based on optimizing the ability to directly attract, manage and support the individual customer, thus eliminating the traditional middleman.
Order size	Order size is large	Order size is small
Customer Relationships	Relationships are much more complex, long-term, often contractual and involve bigger dollar amount. They involve intricate procurement models, supply chain automation, engineering and planning collaboration.	B2C relationships are usually one-sided, where businesses define and control the relationship with the consumer.
Example	SalesForce,Ripple,Replyup	Apple, Microsoft, Ebay, Walmart, Disney, Coca-Cola,

Customer to Business Model (C2B)

The C2B model involves a transaction that is conducted between a consumer and a business organization. It is similar to the B2C model, however, the difference is that in this case the consumer is the seller and the business organization is the buyer. In this kind of a transaction, the consumers decide the price of a particular product rather than the supplier. This category includes individuals who sell products and services to organizations (Wbiteley D.,2005). For example, monster.com, naukari.com is a job related Web site on which a consumer can post his bio-data for the services he can offer. Any business organization that is interested in deploying the services of the consumer can contact him and then employ him, if suitable .

Majorly there are five step involve between customer and business transaction. These are:

Step 1: Post the product or information on the portal. This portal manages by third company not related to seller and buyer. This company provide a facility to seller consumer and Buyer Company make a business.
Step 2: Buyer company view a product or information from the portal.
Step 3: After analysis a product or information, buyer company place a order on portal.
Step 4: Facilator or mediator Company give a information to seller, buyer company purchase your product or information.
Step 5: Consumer give a confirmation to Facilator or mediator company. This company sell a product or information to the buyer company.

Let us look at another example of the C2B model. Rohan needs to buy an airline ticket for his journey from New Delhi to Bombay. Rohan needs to travel immediately. Therefore, he searches a Web site for a ticket. The Web site offers bidding facility to people who want to buy tickets immediately. On the Web site, Rohan quotes the highest price and gets the ticket.

Figure 7. Consumer to Business Model

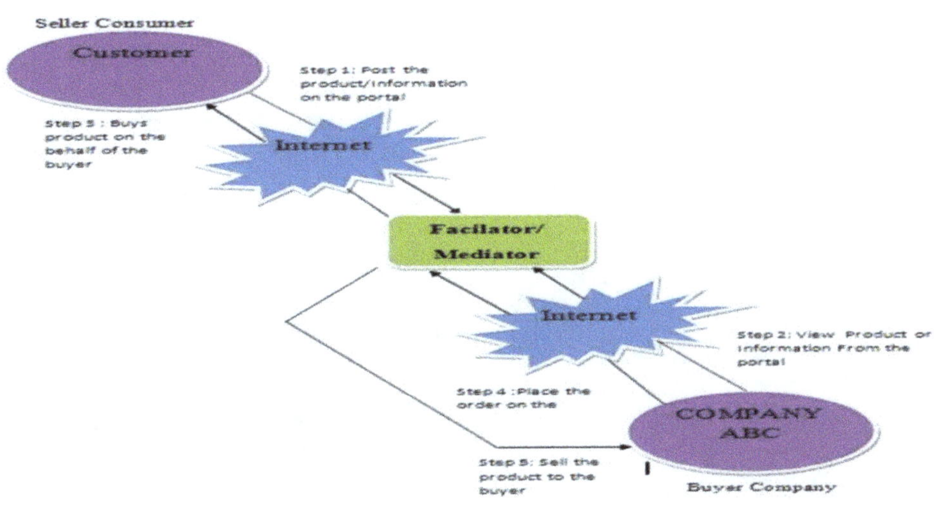

Customer to Customer Model

The C2C model involves transaction between consumers. Here, a consumer sells directly to another consumer. eBay, QUCKIER and OLX, are common examples of online auction Web sites that provide a consumer to advertise and sell their products online to another consumer. However, it is essential that both the seller and the buyer must register with the auction site. While the seller needs to pay a fixed fee to the online auction house to sell their products, the buyer can bid without paying any fee. The site brings the buyer and seller together to conduct deals (Chan H. et al, 2008).

Let us now look at the previous figure with respect to eBay. When a customer plans to sell his products to other customers on the Web site of eBay, he first needs to interact with an eBay site, which in this case acts as a facilitator of the overall transaction. Then, the seller can host his product on www.ebay.com, which in turn charges him for this. Any buyer can now browse the site of eBay to search for the product he interested in. If the buyer comes across such a product, he places an order for the same on the Web site of eBay. eBay now purchase the product from the seller and then, sells it to the buyer. In this way, though the transaction is between two customers, an organization acts as an interface between the two organizations. Figure 8 shows a Consumer to Consumer Model.

Majorly there are five step involve between customer and customer transaction. These are:

Step 1: Post the product or information on the portal. This portal manages by third company not related to seller consumer and buyer consumer. This company provide a facility to seller consumer and Buyer consumer make a business.

Step 2: Buyer Consumer view a product or information from the portal.

Step 3: After analysis a product or information, buyer consumer place a order on portal.

Step 4: Facilator or mediator Company give a information to seller Consumer, a buyer consumer purchase your product or information.

Step 5: Seller consumer give a confirmation to Facilator or mediator company. This company sell a product or information to the buyer consumer.

Figure 8. Consumer to Consumer Model

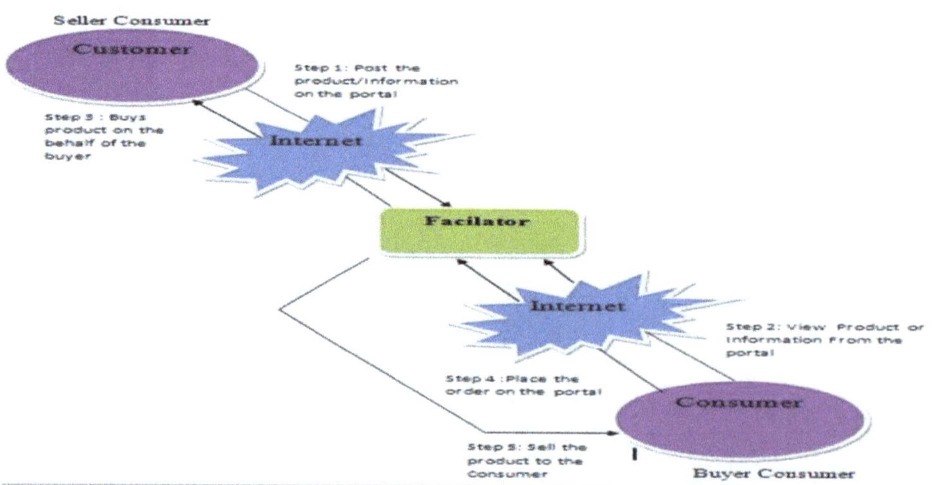

Table 2. Difference between C2B and C2C

Subject	C2B	C2C
Commerce Activity	transaction between consumer and business organization	transaction between consumers
Business Models	In this case the consumer is the seller and the business organization is the buyer. consumers decide the price of a particular product rather than the supplier	a consumer sells directly to another consumer
Example	monster.com, naukari.com	eBay, QUCKIER and OLX

ADVANTAGES AND DISADVANTAGES

Proper implementation of E-commerce can increase the sell of business. Every technology have own advantage or disadvantage. Some of them are.

Advantages

Business is Open 24 x 7 x 364 7/8

We can also sell any time, night or day, 365 days a year. Even while we are resting, it works while you play or sleep. They are open for business every hour of the day, every day of the week, every week of the year.

Choice of Product

Electronic commerce provides buyers with a wider range of choices than traditional commerce.

Tax Benefit for Government

Electronic payments can be easier to monitor than payments are made by cheques/cash. All the transaction online so it is benefit for government and there are no chances of stealing a tax.

Worldwide Market Space

Advertising on the web can make a big or small firm's promotional message reach out to potential customers all over the world quickly and small cost as an online marketing strategy.

Decrease Transaction Costs

If we buy from online store, we spend low operational cost, we have better quality of service, and we can cut the many unnecessary costs. For example, if our goods or services downloadable, we will have transport costs completely cancel.

Conduct a Business Easily

In electronic commerce, we do not need to physical company setups or there are not any crowds to deal with. We can buy from our house comfortable; users can easily choose goods from various procedures without moving around physically.

Comparison in Prices

Everyone can easily compare fees among the various web sites. We can usually earn discounts on fees when compared with normal shop fees.

The Decrease of the Functioning Costs

These costs may be drastically diminished by the automatics of the orders process. There is also the possibility of a total automatics by the integration with the administration system thus leading to the increase of the general productivity of the company.

International Markets Penetration Facilities

The world network is not limited by borders, it does not belong to anyone and the access and publication costs are extremely low. The communication with a customer positioned to the opposite pole of the world is as easy as the communication with someone in the next room. Any producer now can sell his products in any country by the means of the web site and no contacts with local companies or large investments are necessary anymore(Lawrence E., 2000).

Disadvantages

The Security

Security is a main problem in electronic commerce. Everyone good or bad can easily open a web site, and there are many bad sites, which their aim is fool user's and earn money (Kalakota R. & Andrew B. Whinston,1997).

Guarantee

There is no guarantee for product quality. Our orders might be damage in the post or things may look different online to what you actually receive for example, slightly different colours and feel of clothes or the freshness of vegetables and fruits.

Social Relationships

Electronic commerce allows to users that buying and selling goods and services without geographic limitations but in this method we have not any contacts and relationships with other persons and loss our social contacts.

Inability to Feel the Physical

It is nearly impossible to sell things like furniture and tires online. Furniture is something people like to sit on and know the feel. Tires need to be installed once purchased. The old tires also need to be disposed of. In both instances, there is a need for real actions to fulfil the reason for the purchase. That's why things like food, jewellery, antiques etc. can never turn to E-commerce.

Economics

In industry world, managers must encourage and conduct employees to devise plans to take advantages of new economic opportunities. Electronic commerce is creating new opportunities to the global economic, for example in global travel and tourism industry. Transforming from traditional business method to electronic commerce method is hard and there were many different factors for companies to adapt them with electronic commerce factors. For this work, they must used Internet and many other online networks, because for grow and use from new economic opportunities in each industry it is necessary to be match with new technologies.

FINANCE AND ACCOUNTING

Two decades of progress in information technology and development of its applications in the field of economic and social to form a new chapter of relations between people, institutions, companies and governments and new concepts are emerging on literature of economic and trade. Internet as a global network, as well as prerequisite of electronic commerce, for reason flexibility, attractive, ease for use, low cost access and ubiquity, is changing the traditional business moreover, electronic commerce had a significant impact on finance and accounting that include saving time, disinflation, increase productivity, reduce the demand for money (reduce the cost of publishing) and etc.

Limitations

There are some barriers for electronic commerce setup, which include:

- Lack of knowledge and necessary information for use of electronic commerce and Internet network.
- Protection of consumer rights in electronic commerce.
- Lack of legal infrastructures in electronic commerce such documents that are not acceptable and electronic signature.
- Low security of electronic funds transfer in some countries.
- Lower speed and limitations on the use of Internet.
- Lack of information intermediary institutions and manufacturing companies of the benefits of Internet business.
- The security and confidentiality of information exchanged.

Case Study on Online Marketing (Amazon)

In 1994 when Amazon was launched it just a small book store and now that become a big name in e-commerce world. In USA, it is the top online retailer, helps for distribution of all products and services. Its popularity has aroused a question as how it has become popular and the answer is its effective business policies and marketing plans.

So the purpose of this case study is to discuss the ideas that lies behind the successful business of the Amazon. So the ideas are:

1. **Name Selection:** At initial stages the name of the company was "Cadabra" which is more similar to abracadabra. The owner of the company "Jeff Bezos" changed its name to "Amazon" to make it unique. The reason behind that was as "A" is the first alphabetical letter among other 26 letters. Secondly, The name depicts a biggest river "Amazon" like that he wants to make his store a bigger store. In an interview "Jeff Bezos" said, "There's nothing about our model that can't be copied over time. But you know, McDonald's got copied. And it still built a huge, multibillion-dollar company. A lot of it comes down to the brand name. Brand names are more important online than they are in the physical world."
2. **Product Planning Should be Best:** In a report it has been stated that in future e commerce will develop upto 2300%. Jeff Bezos at that time selected a list of product to be put online for sell. He narrowed these upto 20 products and later upto 5 books, videos, computer software, hardware, and compact discs and then at last selected Books. Their result of good planning and innovative thinking was achieved in first two months with sales rise upto $20,000/week.
3. **Logo Name:** After 2000, Amazon has changed his logo with a curve showing a smile sign and an arrow from A to Z, it means that Amazon has all a to z products in its store. This make its logo unique(Amazon Web Services, n.d.).
4. **Initial Growth:** During earlier phases of Amazon was bit slow and its stockholders thought that this will bring less profit in the future .In 2001, it has started gaining profit. The strong business plan that helped in survival from dot-com bubble.
5. **Partnerships:** The company has done different partnerships with types of companies like ToysRus, Borders bookstores, Marks & Spencer, Mothercare, and Lacoste etc. which helped in the stability.
6. **Expansion of Business:** The company is now focused on the expansion of services. In this respect, Amazon has started its store in 2014 in India. Along with it it is also focused on the festival season by giving their services like Diwali Dhamaka Week sale that helped in its popularity.
7. **Membership:** The membership program has started in which the members are paying $79 per month .The features provided is the purchased product will be delivered within two days with some discount. Another membership benefits are free access to instant videos streaming and TV shows, Kindle Owners' Lending Library.
8. **Consumer Services and Use of Technology:** The main focus is on providing best services to their customers. In regards to that for e book readers, the Amazon Kindle was introduced in 2007, for book download and then reading through proper display. Amazon has introduced its tablet computer series followed by second generation tablet in 2011 along with other products such as Fire TV and smart phone.
9. **Separate Website for Each Country:** Each country has different preference and prospective so Amazon has a separate website for each country like:

a. amazon.in for India
b. amazon.fr for France
c. amazon.de for Germany
d. amazon.it for Italy

10. **Third Party Selling:** Along with the items that are available in store, Amazon provides an opportunity to other store to sell their products. The product must be unique. This also provides opportunity for other businesses and the biggest source of profit for the Amazon. There are about 900,000 members' with their product available on Amazon.

What Amazon Is Doing Right That Others Are Not?

E-commerce website involve many element. Even the smaller detail can make a huge impact. With the increase in competition user experience has been playing an important role. If user experience has not good then they will switch on to other site. Digital user experience is the experience a user undergoes, while he is searching for company product until making a payment. For any website to stand in the competition the focus will be on user experience and maximization of information about the product. The Amazon focuses heavily on the points such a s Customer Delight & Experience, Technology, Metrics and Analytics, Complete focus on customer experience even at a low cost of margins. Amazon has innovated a lot in terms of technology, products, services and marketing. Here are some live case examples:

1. **Amazon's Login Page:** Sign in -If you see closely Amazon uses "Sign in using our secure server" button for Login rather than just using "sign in" text on the button. They are reinforcing that sign in process is secure and safe to grab a user's attention.
2. **Product Pages:** In the product pages, they provide maximum details by using same product name as that of title and same name in the meta description along with product code.
3. **FAQ's Section:** has been started where customers can put up their queries for their response. Users can also search if his question has already been asked and answered; if not then the user can post a question for the response. There also an option of up vote and down vote the answer to signify that whether you were satisfied with the response. Almost all products has FAQs this helps the users in a great way as their doubts are answered which increases the chances of a purchase from consumer.
4. **Mail Tracking:** Track package details in Email: Amazon is one of the few E-Commerce companies which uses email schema markup to the fullest. So when user orders something, an email is sent to the customer telling about the details about the order and the delivery stage along with a link to see the status of delivery. The email schema is also provided in which they do not have to open the email.
5. **Amazon Customer Care:** Amazon does have significant customer base and sometimes these customers wants to connect with the customer care of Amazon. Many customer search google so as to reduce the effort of the customer, Amazon uses schema markup to let search engines know what their customer care number is. The searching for customer care for service oriented company has lot of search traffic.
6. **Amazon Device Adaptability:** Amazon.in site has device adaptability for all most browsers. It supports right from IE6 to latest IE, Chrome, Mozilla. if you see flipkart.com, it doesn't support any browsers less than IE7.

Figure 9. FAQ's section

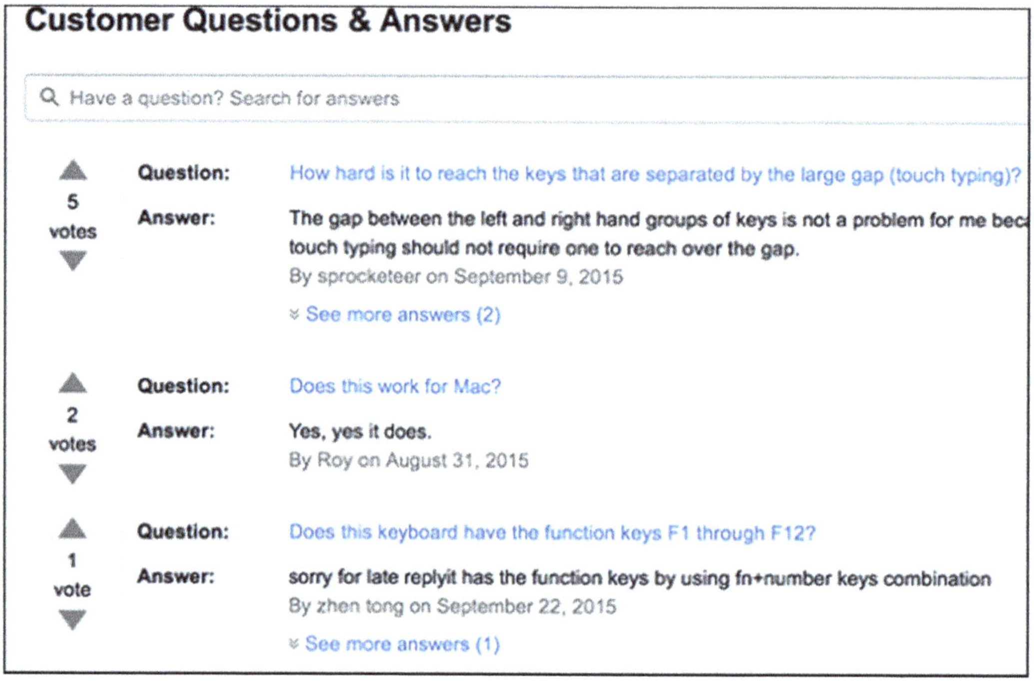

Figure 10. Mail tracking

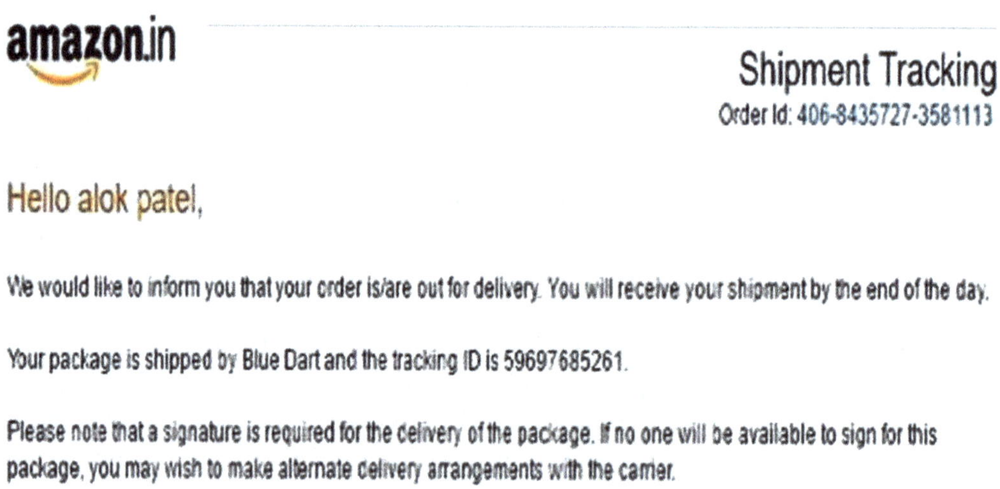

What to Learn?

Every person who want to make their business successful can adapt the following things:

- Unique and Planned selection of name .

- Planning of product should be long term. The products which are frequent should be sold which is a long term planning.
- A logo with a small graphic through which whole business can be explained .
- Don't be afraid of failures, work hard till success.
- Partnerships helps in popularity so on share basis do partnership.
- Focus the expansion in one country then take it to another slowly.

Table 3. Different types of web sites on web for transaction

Type of Product	Web Sites for Search	Services by Web Sites
Finance	1. Money Control.com 2. Rediff Money.com 3. Yahoo Finance.com 1. Jagoinvestor.com 2. Subramoney .com 3. The Financial Literates .com 4. Basu Nivesh.com 5. One Mint.com 1. Safal Niveshak .com 2. Fundoo Professor.com 1. www.screener.in 2.MoneyWorks4Me.com 3. ResearchBytes.com	News/Updates News/Updates News/Updates Personal Finance Blogs Personal Finance Blogs Personal Finance Blogs Personal Finance Blogs Personal Finance Blogs Value Investing Value Investing Stock Analysis Stock Analysis Stock Analysis
Automobiles	1.team-bhp.com 2.automartindia.com 3.overdrive.in 4. autoportal.com	New & Used Auto Mobiles in India New & Used Auto Mobiles in India Cars Prices in India New & Used *Auto* Mobiles in *India*
General Shopping	Paytm.com ebay.in Myntra.com Shopclues.com Pepperfry.com Homeshop18.com	All type of Goods All type of Goods Clothing All type of Goods All type of Goods
Job Searching	www.naukri.com www.indeed.co.in www.shine.com	Jo Placement
Books/Music	Open Library Google Books Smashwords Blurb Scribd Hungama.com Youtube.com	Books Songs
Art	Artstall.com Art.com	Buying and selling painting
Ticket Booking	Irctc.co.in Yatra.com	Seats Reservation
Eduction	Nptl.ac.in Edx.org Shiksha.com	On-Line Tuitions
Free Services	Way2sms Gmail.com Yahoo.com	SMS Mailing

- Offer various services like membership packages for the customers and give them promising advantage so that they start trusting you.
- High speed technology to add latest features will help in gaining popularity.
- Depending on the places make separate websites so that preference should be clear. Personalization of Website should be done according to the preferences.
- Give opportunity to others after you have become stable.

SUMMARY

All the above ideas are implemented by Amazon. So, you can adopt these ideas without any worry.

There are different types of web sites on the World Wide Web for various types of services or transaction.

CONCLUSION

E-commerce has now become a key component for many organizations for daily running their business. In actually E-commerce is buying and selling of goods on the internet known as E-Business, making a lot of opportunities for profit and advancements for businesses, whereas making a lot of choices for shoppers. However, similar to anything, e-commerce has its disadvantages as well as client uncertainties, however, nothing which will not be resolved or avoided by smart decision-making and business practices.

There are many factors associated variables that require to be thought of and set upon once beginning an e-commerce business. A number of these include: kinds of e-commerce, selling ways, and myriad a lot of. If the right strategies and practices are followed, a business can prosper in associate e-commerce setting with abundant success and profit.

REFERENCES

Amazon Web Services. (n.d.). *Customer Success*. Reterieved from https://aws.amazon.com/solutions/case-studies/

Chan, H., Lee, R., Dillon, T., & Chang, E. (2008). *E-Commerce Fundamental and Applications*. New Delhi: WILEY.

Colin, J. (2001). *The Amazon Case Study Analysis*. Retrieved from http://www.ecommerce-digest.com/amazon-case-study.html

Dennis, P. (2004). *E-Commerce Principles and Introduction Technology*. New Delhi: Tata McGraw Hill Publication.

Greenstein, M., Feinman, T., & Vasarhelyi, M. (2001). *Electronic Commerce: Security, Risk management, and Control with Powerweb Passcode Card (E-Commerce)*. New Delhi: Tata McGraw Hill Publications.

Hanson, W., & Kalyanam, K. (2009). *E-Commerce Web Marketing*. New Delhi: Cengage Learning.

Joseph, P. T., & S. J. (2009). E-Commerce: An Indian Perspective. New Delhi: PHI.

Kalakota, R., & Whinston, A. B. (1997). *Electronic Commerce: A Manager's Guide.* Addison-Wesley.

Lawrence, E. (2000). *Internet Commerce: Digital Models for Business.* New Delhi: Wiley.

Minoli, D., & Minoli, E. (1997). *Web Commerce Technology Handbook.* McGraw Hill.

Rajaraman, V. (2009). *Essentials of E-Commerce Techonology.* New Delhi: PHI.

Schneide, P. G. (2007). *E-Commerce: Strategy, Technology and Implementation.* New Delhi: Cengage Learning.

Whiteley, D. (2005). *E-Commerce: Strategy, Technologies and Application,Information System Series.* New Delhi: TMH.

Chapter 6
Search Optimization to Select an Item Across E-Commerce Platforms:
App Development – QuickCompare

Sridevi M.
Anurag Group of Institutions, India

Rajeshwara Rao R.
JNTU Kakinada, India

Varaprasad Rao M.
CMR Technical Campus, India

ABSTRACT

E-commerce is a transaction of buying or selling online. These sites have made life simpler by delivering products to your doorstep. The entire idea of e-commerce is to save the user's time while purchasing goods. This massive expansion of e-commerce gave rise to many applications for the user to choose to buy from. Therefore, people now spend more time comparing the prices of products on various applications before purchasing. This price comparison turned out to be a tedious task for users. With many applications available in the market, it is difficult for the user to navigate between apps to compare specifications like cost, life time, on-time delivery, customer satisfaction, etc. of products or items. So, this chapter explores the "Quick Compare" search, a solution for this hassle that provides instantaneous recommendations based on the end user's input. An android application is developed for this problem and it focuses on efficiency and interoperability.

DOI: 10.4018/978-1-5225-3646-8.ch006

INTRODUCTION

QuickCompare, as the name suggests, is an Android application that is designed and developed to save both money and time which people spend, on comparing product prices. Users can search for mobile phones online and find the best deal online. The interface is pretty simple and elegant in which the user just needs to enter the product name, and click search. The application searches for the product on various sites and displays the corresponding information. Hence, the user gets to compare prices from multiple sites in one go. Besides the prices, the application also presents reviews of previous buyers. So, the user also gets to know the actual quality and performance of the product searched, along with basic information about the product.

Motivation

The entire idea of e-commerce is to save the user's time while purchasing goods. This massive expansion of e-commerce gave rise to many applications for the user to choose to buy from. Therefore, people now spend more time comparing the prices of products on various applications before purchasing. This price comparison turned out to be a hectic task for users. With so many applications in the market, it is difficult for the user to navigate between apps to compare prices of products. So, QuickCompare is a solution for this hassle.

Problem Definition

People who regularly use E-commerce to purchase products make a lot of comparisons of products on different applications. Even for the unseasoned, it is quite a dreary task. This situation is being worsened by increase in the number of applications in the market.

Objective of the Project

The main objective of the project is to make the process of price comparison of mobile phones on multiple e-commerce a lot easier to any user. The specifications of the product are also displayed which helps the user better understand the item under comparison. The user reviews of the product are shown which help the user decide on a particular product.

Literature Survey

MV Rao et al., (2017), discussed Web-enabled DSS, Web mining, related to knowledge repositories, and Repository Management Systems that facilitate the problem solving and learning. This approach to the knowledge representation allows considering contemporary DSS as integrated parts of the corresponding Repository Management Systems.

Sridevi et al., (2016) provides the landscape of different recommendation methods and their basic approaches.

Viharika Padma et al. (2016), focuses mainly on user to item based filtering technique. Here, a comparative study is conducted between TOPSIS and AHP for selecting a mobile based on filtering

SYSTEM ARCHITECTURE

Modules

The proposed model has 4 modules as Module 1: Price List of an Item, which displays the prices from multiple e-commerce platforms in a single fragment. Module 2: Collecting Reviews, it conveys the user reviews relevant to the product. Module 3: Specifications, it displays the specifications relevant to the product and final Module 4: Recommendation, the resultant is Recommendation the product based on the user rating.

DESIGN

According to Booch, Jacobson and Rumbaugh (1999), the Unified Modeling Language (UML), is a standard language for writing software blue prints. The UML is a language for Visualizing, Specifying, Constructing and Documenting the artifacts of a software intensive system.

The UML is a language which provides vocabulary and the rules for combining words in that vocabulary for the purpose of communication. A modeling language is a language whose vocabulary and the rules focus on the conceptual and physical representation of a system. Modeling yields an understanding of a system.

Figure 1. System architecture

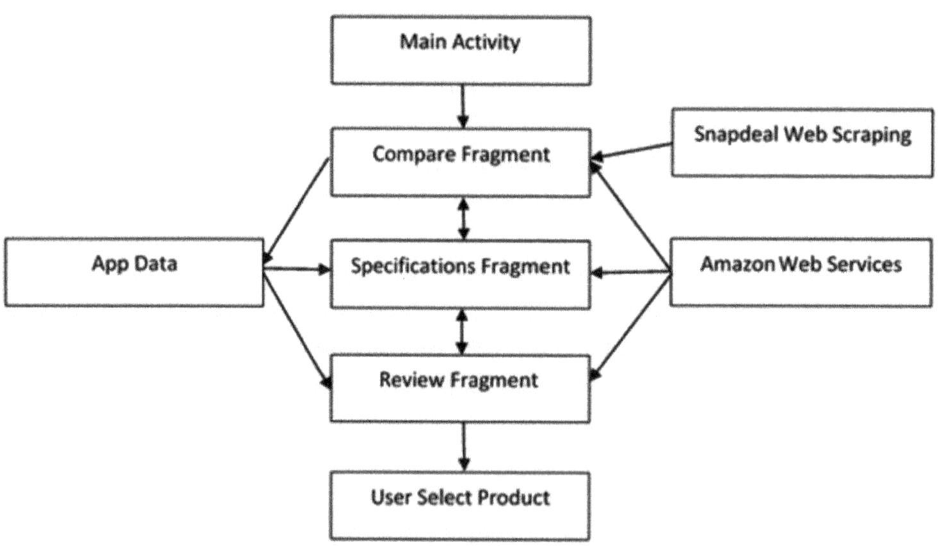

Use Case Diagram

The use case model defines the outside (actors) and inside (use case) of the system's behaviour. Use case diagram is quite simple in nature and depicts two types of elements: one representing the business roles and the other representing the business processes.

Class Diagram

Classes are typically modeled as rectangles with three sections: the top section for the name of the class, the middle section for the attributes of the class, the bottom section for the methods of the class. Attributes are the information stored about an object, while methods are the things an object or class do. The authors have used five (5) classes as 'Main Activity' deals with the main activity of the application, 'Signed Request Helper' discusses user request's information will be handled, 'Reviews Fragment' specifies user reviews are obtained only if the item has at least 3 stars, 'Comparing Fragment' deals with comparing an item from two websites and 'Specification Fragment' discusses about recommendation of an item to be accepted or rejected.

Sequence Diagram

The sequence diagram gives the sequence operations among the actors and the service and their interactions with other services. Here the user is interacting with the application and other services behind the application.

Amazon Web Services API

Overview of Product Advertising API

Amazon (Amazon API, 2017) has developed a world-class web service that millions of customers use every day. As a developer, you can build Product Advertising API applications that leverage this robust, scalable, and reliable technology. You get access to a lot of the data used by Amazon including the items for sale, customer reviews, seller reviews, as well as most of the functionality you see on Amazon.com, such as finding items, displaying customer reviews, and product promotions. Product Advertising API operations open the doors to Amazon's databases so that you can take advantage of Amazon's sophisticated e-commerce data and functionality. Build your own web store to sell Amazon items or your own items.

Best of all, Product Advertising API is free. By signing up to become a Product Advertising API developer, you join the tens of thousands of developers who are already realizing financial gains by creating Product Advertising API-driven applications and web stores.

How Product Advertising API Works

Your application uses the Product Advertising API to display item descriptions, images, and reviews to your customers. Customers shop and add items to their shopping cart. When the customer is ready to purchase the items, your application sends an HTML form to Product Advertising API and Amazon

Figure 2. Sequence diagram

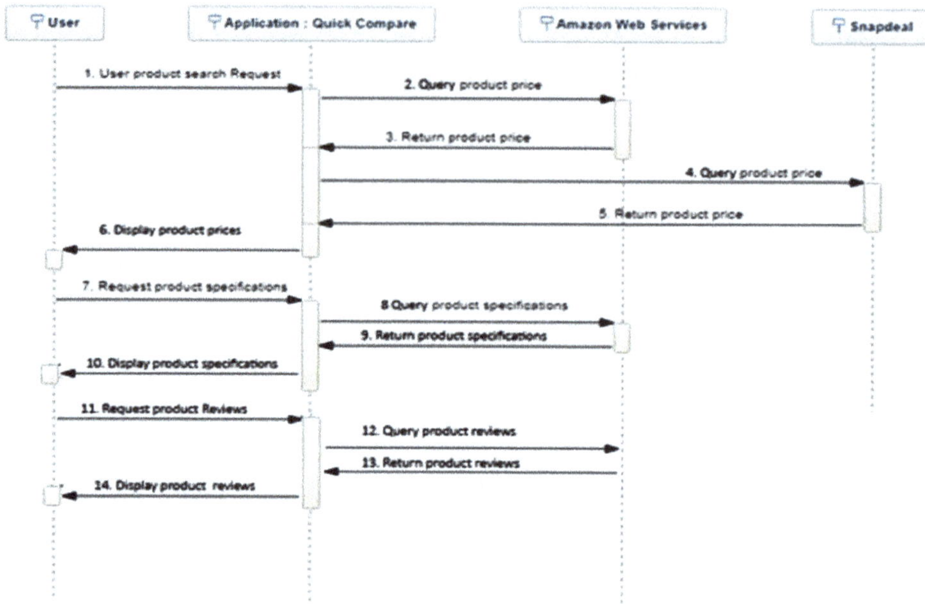

completes the purchase by getting purchase information, such as payment method and shipping address. Amazon then fulfills the order by shipping the items.

The Process of Collecting/Requesting API From Amazon

Product Advertising API REST requests are URLs. The following example is an ItemSearchrequest.

http://webservices.amazon.com/onca/xml?
Service=AWSECommerceService&
Operation=ItemSearch&
AWSAccessKeyId=[Access Key ID]&
AssociateTag=[Associate ID]&
SearchIndex=Apparel&
Keywords=Shirt&
Timestamp=[YYYY-MM-DDThh:mm:ssZ] &
Signature=[Request Signature]

- **Endpoint:** When you register for Product Advertising API in your locale, use the locale-specific endpoint for each request (for example, http://webservices.amazon.com/onca/xml is the endpoint for the US).
- **Service:** This term identifies the service in the request. The value is AWSECommerceService for all requests and locales.
- **Operation:** The operation parameter determines the type of request (for example, ItemSearch, ItemLookup).

- **AWSAccessKeyId:** The AWS access key ID. When registering as a Product Advertising API developer, an AWS account is created for you.
- **AssociateTag:** The Amazon Associates account ID. This value must be included in each request to be eligible to receive a referral fee for customer purchases.
- **Parameter:** Parameters help you customize your request. For example, the SearchIndexparameter limits a request to a specific category. The Sort parameter can be used to return items by price. Requests can have up to ten parameters.
- **ResponseGroup:** Response groups filter the type of information returned by the request. For example, the Images response group returns item images.
- **Timestamp:** The date and time the request was sent.
- **Signature:** The signature authenticates your request.
- **Response Groups:** The ResponseGroup parameter is optional for all Product Advertising API operations. Response groups filter the type of information returned by the request. For example, if you want to return images, the Image response group is used in the request. If price information is required, use the Offer response group. All Product Advertising API operations share some response groups. For example, all operations use the Request response group, which returns the operation name and input parameters sent in the request.

Flipkart

Flipkart (Flipkart, 2015) is an electronic commerce company for providing online shopping by various APIs like product, offers, reports and change logs, with the following functions.

- **productId:** A unique SKU ID assigned by Flipkart to a particular product.
- **codAvailable:** This column mentions whether COD (Cash On Delivery) is available for this product. The value would be true or false.
- **availability:** Availability of products with offer as LIVE (In-stock) or OOS (Out-of-stock)
- **customerType:** Whether the order was the customer's first purchase or not
- **API Access:** Access the APIs by passing the following headers as an HTTPS request. Without the headers, the APIs respond with an authentication error has explained in the website https://affiliate.flipkart.com/api-docs as shown in Box 1.

Sample HTTPS Request

curl -H "Fk-Affiliate-Id:<your Affiliate Tracking ID>" -H "Fk-Affiliate-Token:<your Affiliate API Token>" "<API URL>"

Box 1.

Header	Value
Fk-Affiliate-Id	<your Affiliate Tracking ID>
Fk-Affiliate-Token	<your Affiliate API Token>

Once the token is generated, your Affiliate Tracking ID automatically becomes eligible to access the API via HTTPS request. All the URLs returned by the API feeds are appended with your tracking ID, by default.

To Verify the API Response

Go to API > API Status (URL: https://affiliate.flipkart.com/api/status-check).
Paste the API URL in the text box.
Click Check Status, this displays the relevant success or error response code.

IMPLEMENTATION

Introduction

Android is a mobile operating system developed by Google, based on the Linux kernel and designed primarily for touchscreen mobile devices such as smart phones and tablets. Android's user interface is mainly based on direct manipulation, using touch gestures that loosely correspond to real-world actions, such as swiping, tapping and pinching, to manipulate on-screen objects, along with a virtual keyboard for text input. In addition to touch screen devices, Google has further developed Android TV for televisions, Android Auto for cars, and Android Wear for wrist watches, each with a specialized user interface. Variants of Android are also used on game consoles, digital cameras, PCs and other electronics.

The History of Google Android

The fact that hitherto dedicated devices such as mobile phones can now count themselves among the venerable general-computing platforms is great news for programmers. This new trend makes mobile devices accessible through general-purpose computing languages, which increases the range and share for mobile applications. The Android Platform (Android Operating System, 2017) embraces the idea of general-purpose computing for handheld devices. It is a comprehensive platform that features a Linux-based operating system stack for managing devices, memory, and processes. Android's libraries cover telephony, video, graphics, UI programming, and a number of other aspects of the device.

The Android SDK (Android operating system 2017) supports most of the Java Platform Standard Edition (Java SE) except for the Abstract Window Toolkit (AWT) and Swing. In place of AWT and Swing, Android SDK has its own extensive modern UI framework. Because you're programming your applications in Java, you could expect that you need a Java Virtual Machine (JVM) that is responsible for interpreting the runtime Java byte code. A JVM typically provides the necessary optimization to help Java reach performance levels comparable to compiled languages such as C and C++. Android offers its own optimized JVM to run the compiled Java class files in order to counter the handheld device limitations such as memory, processor speed, and power. This virtual machine is called the Dalvik virtual machine.

The familiarity and simplicity of the Java programming language coupled with Android's extensive class library makes Android a compelling platform to write programs for.Let us look at how Android arrived on the Mobile OS landscape. Mobile phones use a variety of operating systems such as Symbian OS, Microsoft's Windows Mobile, Mobile Linux, iPhone operating system (based on Mac OS X),

Moblin (from Intel), and many other proprietary operating systems. So far no single operating system has become the de facto standard. The available APIs and environments for developing mobile applications are too restrictive and seem to fall behind when compared to desktop frameworks. This is where Google comes in. The Android platform promised openness, affordability, open source code, and a high-end development framework.

Google acquired the startup company Android Inc. (in 2005) to start the development of the Android Platform The key players at Android Inc. included Andy Rubin, Rich Miner, Nick Sears, and Chris White. In late 2007, a group of industry leaders came together around the Android Platform to form the Open Handset Alliance some of the alliance's prominent members are as, Sprint Nextel, T-Mobile, Motorola, Samsung, Sony Ericsson, Toshiba, Vodafone, Google, Intel, and Texas Instruments.

Part of the alliance's goal is to innovate rapidly and respond better to consumer needs, and its first key outcome was the Android Platform. Android was designed to serve the needs of mobile operators, handset manufacturers, and application developers. The members have committed to release significant intellectual property through the open source Apache License, Version 2.0.

The Android SDK was first issued (Android operating system, 2017) as an "early look" release in November 2007. In September 2008, T-Mobile announced the availability of T-Mobile G1, the first Smartphone based on the Android platform. A few days after that, Google announced the availability of Android SDK Release Candidate 1.0. In October 2008, Google made the source code of the Android platform available under Apache's open source license. When Android was released, one of its key architectural goals was to allow applications to interact with one another and reuse components from one another. This reuse not only applies to services, but also to data and the user interface (UI). As a result, the Android platform has a number of architectural features that keep this openness a reality.

Android has also attracted an early following because of its fully developed features to exploit the cloud-computing model offered by web resources and to enhance that experience with local data stores on the handset itself. Android's support for a relational database on the handset also played a part in early adoption.

In late 2008 Google released a handheld device called AndroidDevPhone1 that was capable of running Android applications without being tied to any cell phone provider network. The goal of this device (at an approximate cost of $400.00) was to allow developers to experiment with a real device that could run the Android OS without any contracts. At around the same time, Google also released a bug fix, version 1.1 of the OS that is solely based on version 1.0. In releases 1.0 and 1.1 Android did not support soft keyboards, requiring the devices to carry physical keys. Android fixed this issue by releasing the 1.5 SDK in April 2009, along with a number of other features, such as advanced media-recording capabilities, widgets, and live folders.

Technologies Used

Android

Android is a mobile operating system initially developed by Android Inc. Android was purchased by Google in 2005. Android is based upon a modified version of the Linux kernel. Google and other members of the Open Handset Alliance collaborated to develop and release Android to the world. The Android Open Source Project (AOSP) is tasked with the maintenance and further development of Android. Unit sales for Android OS Smartphone ranked first among all Smartphone OS handsets sold in the US in the second and third quarters of 2010, with a third quarter market share of 43.6%.

Android has a large community of developers writing application programs ("apps") that extend the functionality of the devices. There are currently over 100,000 apps available for Android. Android Market is the online app store run by Google, though apps can be downloaded from third party sites (except on AT&T, which disallows this). Developers write in the Java language, controlling the device via Google-developed Java libraries.

The unveiling of the Android distribution on 5 November 2007 was announced with the founding of the Open Handset Alliance, a consortium of 79 hardware, software, and telecom companies devoted to advancing open standards for mobile devices. Google released most of the Android code under the Apache License, a free software and open source license.

The Android operating system software stack consists of Java applications running on a Java based object oriented application framework on top of Java core libraries running on a Dalvik virtual machine featuring JIT compilation. Libraries written in C include the surface manager, Open Coremedia framework, SQLite relational database management system, OpenGL ES 2.03D graphics API, Web Kit layout engine, SGL graphics engine, SSL, and Bionic libc. The Android operating system consists of 12 million lines of code including 3 million lines of XML, 2.8 million lines of C, 2.1 million lines of Java, and 1.75 million lines of C++.

Android SDK

The Android Software Development Kit (SDK) includes a comprehensive set of development tools. These include a debugger, libraries, a handset emulator (based on QEMU), documentation, sample code, and tutorials. Currently supported development platforms include computers running Linux (any modern desktop Linux distribution), Mac OS X 10.4.9 or later, Windows XP or later. The officially supported integrated development environment (IDE) is Eclipse (currently 3.4 or 3.5) using the Android Development Tools (ADT) Plugin, though developers may use any text editor to edit Java and XML files then use command line tools (Java Development Kit and Apache Ant are required) to create, build and debug Android applications as well as control attached Android devices (e.g., triggering a reboot, installing software package(s) remotely).

A preview release of the Android SDK (Android operating system, 2017;thenewboston, 2017) was released on 12 November 2007. On 15 July 2008, the Android Developer Challenge Team accidentally sent an email to all entrants in the Android Developer Challenge announcing that a new release of the SDK was available in a "private" download area. The email was intended for winners of the first round of the Android Developer Challenge. The revelation that Google was supplying new SDK releases to some developers and not others (and keeping this arrangement private) led to widely reported frustration within the Android developer community at the time.

On 18 August 2008 the Android 0.9 SDK (Android operating system, 2017) beta was released. This release provided an updated and extended API, improved development tools and an updated design for the home screen. Detailed instructions for upgrading are available to those already working with an earlier release. On 23 September 2008 the Android 1.0 SDK (Release 1) was released. According to the release notes, it included "mainly bug fixes, although some smaller features were added". It also included several API changes from the 0.9 version. Multiple versions have been released since.

Enhancements to Android's SDK go hand in hand with the overall Android platform development. The SDK also supports older versions of the Android platform in case developers wish to target their applications at older devices. Development tools are downloadable components, so after one has downloaded the latest version and platform, older platforms and tools can also be downloaded for compatibility testing.

Android applications are packaged in .apk format and stored under /data/app folder on the Android OS (the folder is accessible to root user only for security reasons). APK package contains .dexfiles (compiled byte code files called Dalvik executable), resource files, etc.

Amazon Web Services

Amazon Web Services (AWS) is a subsidiary of Amazon.com (Amazon Web Services, 2017), offers a suite of cloud-computing services that make up an on-demand computing platform. These services operate from 16 geographical regions across the world. They include Amazon Elastic Compute Cloud, also known as "EC2", and Amazon Simple Storage Service, also known as "S3". As of 2016 AWS has more than 70 services, spanning a wide range, including compute, storage, networking, database, analytics, application services, deployment, management, mobile, developer tools and tools for the Internet of things. Amazon markets AWS as a service to provide large computing capacity quicker and cheaper than a client company building an actual physical server farm.

We chose Amazon Web Services since it is known for its reliability, robustness and ease of use. AWS offers a variety of EC2 instances for different workloads divided into different families. AWS is geographically more widespread and has about its presence in 10 regions spanning US, Europe, South America and Asia. AWS offers a lot more flexibility to the customers to configure their instances according to their computing requirements.

History of AWS

Officially launched in 2006, Amazon Web Services (2017) provides online services for other web sites or client-side applications. Most of these services are not exposed directly to end users, but instead offer functionality that other developers can use in their applications. Amazon Web Services' offerings are accessed over HTTP, using the REST architectural style and SOAP protocol. All services are billed based on usage, but how usage is measured for billing varies from service to service.

In late 2003, Chris Pinkham and Benjamin Black presented a paper describing a vision for Amazon's retail computing infrastructure that was completely standardized, completely automated, and would rely extensively on web services for services such as storage, drawing on internal work already underway. Near the end they mentioned the possibility of selling virtual servers as a service, proposing the company could generate revenue from the new infrastructure investment. The first AWS service launched for public usage was Simple Queue Service in November 2004. Amazon EC2 was built by a team in Cape Town, South Africa, under Pinkham and lead developer Chris Brown.

In June 2007, Amazon claimed that more than 180,000 developers had signed up to use Amazon Web Services. In November 2010, it was reported that all of Amazon.com retail web services had been moved to AWS. On April 20, 2011, some parts of Amazon Web Services suffered a major outage. A portion of volumes using the Elastic Block Store (EBS) service became "stuck" and were unable to fulfill read/write requests. It took at least two days for service to be fully restored. On June 29, 2012, several websites that rely on Amazon Web Services were taken offline due to a severe storm of historic proportions in Northern Virginia, where AWS' largest datacenter cluster is located.

On October 22, 2012, a major outage occurred, affecting many sites such as Reddit, Foursquare, Pinterest, and others. The cause was a latent memory leak bug in an operational data collection agent. On December 24, 2012, AWS suffered another outage, causing websites such as Netflix instant video to be unavailable for customers in the Northeastern United States. AWS later issued a statement detailing the issues with the Elastic Load Balancing service that led up to the outage.

In November 2012, AWS hosted its first customer event in Las Vegas. On April 30, 2013, AWS began offering a certification program for computer engineers with expertise in cloud computing.AWS revenue was not stated separately in the past, but in 2012 it was estimated by industry watchers at over $1.5 billion. On May 13, 2013, AWS was awarded an Agency Authority to Operate (ATO) from the U.S. Department of Health and Human Services under the Federal Risk and Authorization Management Program. In October 2013, it was revealed that AWS was awarded a $600M contract with the CIA. During August 2014, AWS received Department of Defense-Wide provisional authorization for all U.S. Regions.

In April 2015, AWS was reported to be profitable, with sales of $1.57 billion in the first quarter of the year, and $265 million of operating income. Founder Jeff Bezos described it as a fast-growing $5 billion business; analysts described it as "surprisingly more profitable than forecast". In October 2015, Amazon.com said in its Q3 earnings report that AWS's operating income was $521 million, with operating margins at 25 percent. AWS's Q3 2015 revenue was $2.1 billion, a 78% increase from Q3 2014's revenue of $1.17 billion. Q4 2015 revenue for the AWS segment increased 69.5% y/y to $2.4 billion with 28.5% operating margin, making AWS a $9.6 billion run rate. In Q1 2016, revenue was $2.57 billion with net income of $604 million, a 64% increase over Q1 2015 that resulted in AWS being more profitable than Amazon's North American retail business for the first time.

In 2015, Gartner "estimated that AWS customers are deploying 10x more infrastructure on AWS than the combined adoption of the next 14 providers. During the 2015 re:Invent keynote, AWS disclosed that they have more than a million active customers every month in 190 countries, including nearly 2,000 government agencies, 5,000 education institutions and more than 17,500 nonprofits." (CREST Infotech2016), AWS adoption has increased since launch in 2006. Notable customers include NASA, the Obama presidential campaign 2012, Kempinski Hotels, and Netflix. In 2016, AWS engineer James Hamilton created a ten-year timeline of the online service. In 2016, AWS founder Andy Jassy was named CEO of the division.

In the first quarter of 2016, Amazon experienced a 42% rise in stock value as a result of increased earnings, of which AWS contributed 56% to company's profit. With a 50% increase in revenues the past few years, it is predicted AWS will have $13 billion in revenue in 2017.

Flipkart

Started in the year 2007 with online book shopping, in 2008 launched 24X7 customer care support. Subsequently they also developed in other categories like music, movies and electronic gadgets like mobiles and accessories by 2010. In the year 2011, delivery of goods is also introduced electronic transactions for purchases and also goods delivery status has improved. Subsequently, they also introduced replacement policy up to 50 days. Another category on fashion and cloths has been introduced in 2012. In 2013 reached one lakh book sales on single day on-line and delivery of the goods on same day or 24 hours. They also acquired some companies in 2014, and also introduced lite version of website in 2015. The first Indian app crossed 50 million users in 2016.

Android Studio(IDE)

Android Studio is the official Integrated Development Environment (IDE) for the Android platform. It was announced on May 16, 2013 at the Google I/O conference. Android Studio is freely available under the Apache License 2.0. Android Studio was in early access preview stage starting from version 0.1 in May 2013, then entered beta stage starting from version 0.8 which was released in June 2014. The first stable build was released in December 2014, starting from version 1.0. Based on JetBrains' IntelliJ IDEA software, Android Studio is designed specifically for Android development. It is available for download on Windows, Macintosh OS and Linux, and replaced Eclipse Android Development Tools (ADT) as Google's primary IDE for native Android application development.

Jsoup

Jsoup is Java HTML Parser (Herdley, 2017) and Java library for working with real-world HTML. It provides a very convenient API for extracting and manipulating data, using the best of DOM, CSS, and jquery-like methods. JSOUP allows you to scrape and parse HTML from a URL, file, or string and many more.

Jsoup implements the WHATWG HTML5 specification, and parses HTML to the same DOM as modern browsers do.

- Scrape and parse HTML from a URL, file, or string
- Find and extract data, using DOM traversal or CSS selectors
- Manipulate the HTML elements, attributes, and text
- Clean user-submitted content against a safe white-list, to prevent XSS attacks
- Output tidy HTML

Jsoup is designed to deal with all varieties of HTML found in the wild; from pristine and validating, to invalid tag-soup; jsoup will create a sensible parse tree.

- Jsoup functionalities
    - **Multiple Read Support:** It reads and parses HTML using URL, file, or string.
    - **CSS Selectors:** It can find and extract data, using DOM traversal or CSS selectors.
    - **DOM Manipulation:** It can manipulate the HTML elements, attributes, and text.
    - **Prevent XSS Attacks:** It can clean user-submitted content against a given safe white-list, to prevent XSS attacks.
    - **Tidy:** It outputs tidy HTML.
    - **Handles Invalid Data:** jsoup can handle unclosed tags, implicit tags and can reliably create the document structure.

JSON

Douglas Crockford has specified a format of JSON (JavaScript Object Notation) is a lightweight data-interchange format (Douglas Crockford, 2017; Introducing JSON, 2017). It is easy for humans to read and write. It is easy for machines to parse and generate. It is based on a subset of the JavaScript Programming Language, Standard ECMA-262 3rd Edition - December 1999. JSON is a text format that is completely language independent but uses conventions that are familiar to programmers of the C-family of languages, including C, C++, C#, Java, JavaScript, Perl, Python, and many others. These properties make JSON an ideal data-interchange language.

JSON Is Built on Two Structures

A collection of name/value pairs. In various languages, this is realized as an object, record, struct, dictionary, hash table, keyed list, or associative array. An ordered list of values. In most languages, this is realized as an array, vector, list, or sequence.These are universal data structures. Virtually all modern programming languages support them in one form or another. It makes sense that a data format that is interchangeable with programming languages also be based on these structures.

In JSON, they take on these forms:

An object is an unordered set of name/value pairs. An object begins with
{ (left brace) and
ends with } (right brace).
Each name is followed by: (colon) and
the name/value pairs are separated by, (comma).

The Uses of JSON

- It is used while writing JavaScript based applications that includes browser extensions and websites.
- JSON format is used for serializing and transmitting structured data over network connection.
- It is primarily used to transmit data between a server and web applications.
- Web services and APIs use JSON format to provide public data.
- It can be used with modern programming languages.

Screenshots

See Figures 3 and 4.

TEST CASES

Introduction

The purpose of testing is to discover errors. Testing is the process of trying to discover every conceivable fault or weakness in a work product. It provides a way to check the functionality of components, sub-assemblies, assemblies and/or a finished product (Types of Software testing and definitions of testing terms, 2017). It is the process of exercising software with the intent of ensuring that the software system meets its requirements and user expectations and does not fail in an unacceptable manner. There are various types of test. Each test type addresses a specific testing requirement.

Figure 3. Show product prices from multiple e-commerce sites and Display specifications of product

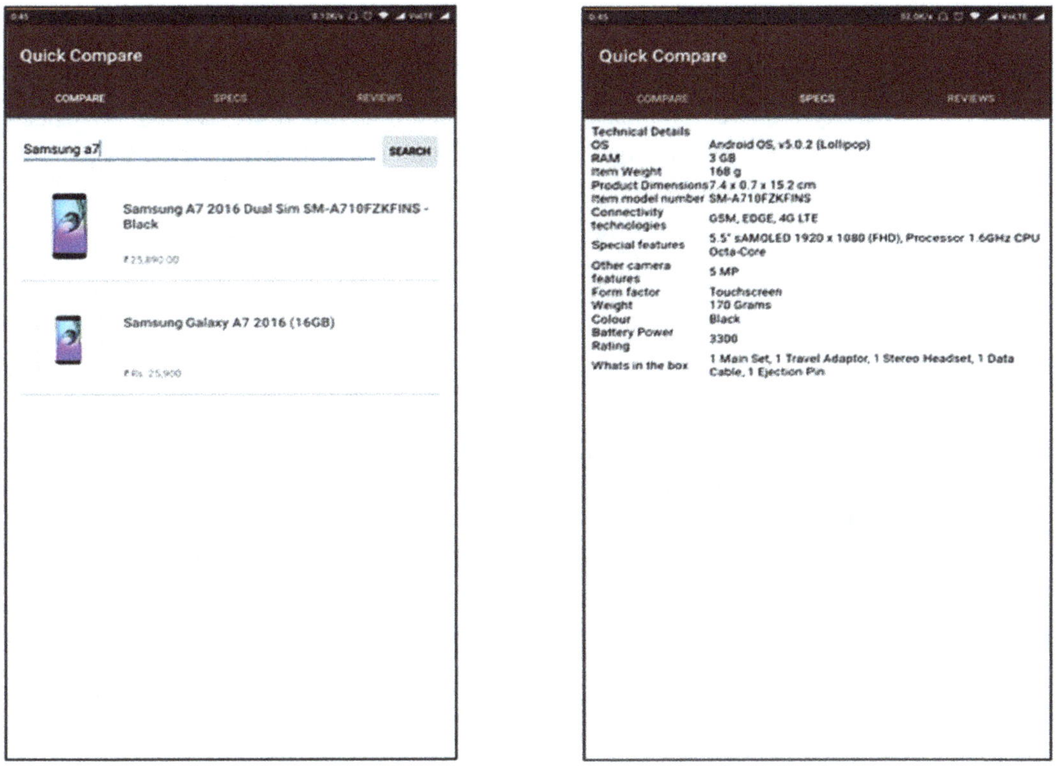

Figure 4. Displaying user reviews and recommending a product

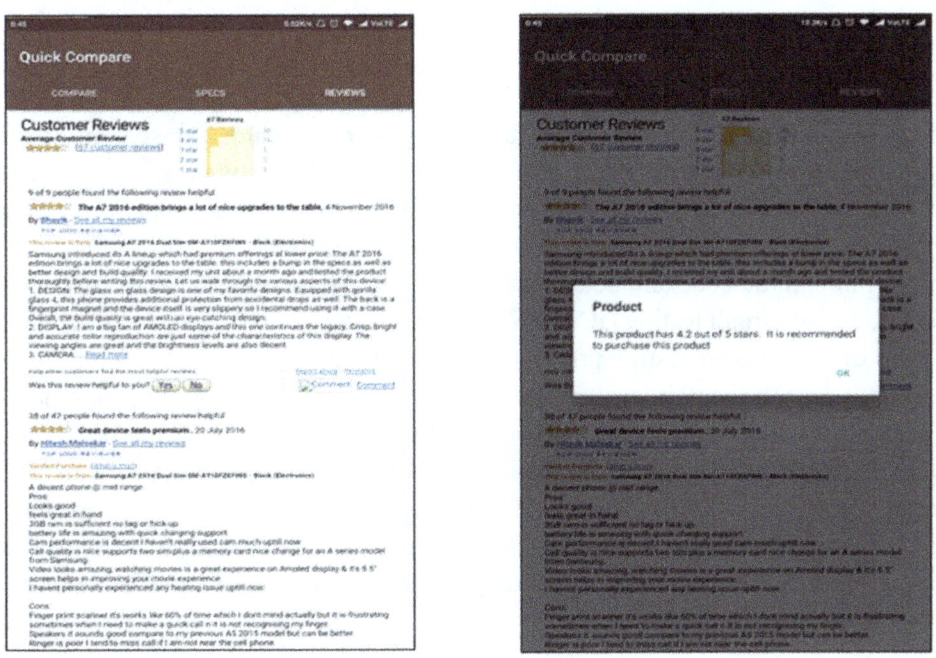

Types of Tests

1. Functional Testing

Functional tests provide systematic demonstrations that functions tested are available as specified by the business and technical requirements, system documentation and user manuals. Organization and preparation of functional tests is focused on requirements, key functions or special test cases. In addition, systematic coverage pertaining to identify Business process flows, data fields, predefined processes and successive processes must be considered for testing. Before functional testing is complete, additional tests are identified and the effective value of current tests is determined.

2. Unit Testing

Unit testing is essentially for the verification of the code produced during the coding phase and the goal is test the internal logic of the module/program. In the Generic code project, the unit testing is done during coding phase of data entry forms whether the functions are working properly or not. In this phase, all the drivers are tested they are rightly connected or not. Unit testing is usually conducted as part of a combined code and unit test phase of the software lifecycle, although it is not uncommon for coding and unit testing to be conducted as two different phases.

3. Black-Box Testing

Black-box testing is a method of software testing that examines the functionality of an application without peering into its internal structures or workings. This method of test can be applied virtually to every level of software testing: unit, integration, system and acceptance. It typically comprises most if not all higher level testing, but can also dominate unit testing as well.

4. White-Box Testing

White-box testing (also known as clear box testing, glass box testing, transparent box testing, and structural testing) is a method of testing software that tests internal structures or workings of an application, as opposed to its functionality (i.e. black-box testing). In white-box testing an internal perspective of the system, as well as programming skills, are used to design test cases. The tester chooses inputs to exercise paths through the code and determine the appropriate outputs. This is analogous to testing nodes in a circuit, e.g. in-circuit testing (ICT). White-box testing can be applied at the unit, integration and system levels of the software testing process. Although traditional testers tended to think of white-box testing as being done at the unit level, it is used for integration and system testing more frequently today. It can test paths within a unit, paths between units during integration, and between subsystems during a system–level test. Though this method of test design can uncover many errors or problems, it has the potential to miss unimplemented parts of the specification or missing requirements.

White-box test design techniques include the following code coverage criteria: Control flow testing, Data flow testing, Branch testing, Statement coverage, Decision coverage, Modified condition/decision coverage, Prime path testing, Path testing.

Table 1. Test cases

ID	Description	Conditions	Test Input	Steps	Expected Result	Actual Result	Pass/Fail
1	Retrieve Details	Internet connection	User query	Click Search	Details Shown	Details Shown	Pass
2	Retrieve Details	No internet connection	User Query	Click Search	No Details Shown	Cards Shown	Pass
3	Retrieve Details	No User Query	-	Click Search	Ask to search for product	Ask to search for product	Pass
4	Specifications & User Reviews	Internet Connection	-	Swipe Tabs	Details shown	Details shown	Pass
5	Specifications & User Reviews	No internet Connection	-	Swipe Tabs	Ask for internet connection	Empty Details	Pass

The authors have tested for information retrieval from Amazon Web Services and Flipkart under multiple test conditions. Information retrieval contains data related to product price, specifications and reviews.

CONCLUSION

QuickCompareApp for android helps the e-commerce users to find the products in minimum time and effectively. The app retrieves the data from Amazon and Flipkart websites, for the requested search keyword. The authors have compared mobile phones in Amazon and Flipkart by considering user reviews helping us to make a quick decision. Itgets the required information if the item has at least 3 stars out of 5 stars user reviews, by which the users can save the search time. This gives a result in achieving comparative study of an item based on selection criteria. A limitation of this application can only display the price, specifications and reviews of a product already available in the catalog of the e-commerce platforms.

FUTURE ENHANCEMENTS

The authors have tried only two E-Commerce portals of Amazon and Flipkart. There is a scope for the comparison of items from more than three e-commerce portals to collect fastest reviews and recommend the item or product to the user.

ACKNOWLEDGMENT

Words cannot express my gratitude to Editor Prof. G Sreedhar for his assistance in polishing this manuscript. Thanks to all the technical reviewers who reviewed this chapter and made me in strengthen the chapter not only by catching mistakes but also by suggesting those additions. I thank to one and all, who directly or indirectly, have lent their hand in this completion of the chapter. I would like to express my sincere gratitude to my advisor Prof. B Vishnu Vardhan for the continuous support to complete this chapter, for his patience, motivation, and immense knowledge. I'd like to thank my parents for allowing me to follow my ambitions throughout my childhood. This chapter would not have been possible without the support, motivation and encouragement of my wife, Mrs. PV Prajwala. For understanding my long nights at the computer, I'd like to thank my children, Karthikeya and Harshith. Finally, my sincere thanks to IGI Publisher to publish the chapter/book.

REFERENCES

Amazon Web Services (AWS). (2017). Retrieved from https://aws.amazon.com/

Android. (2017). Retrieved in February, 2017, from www.developer.android.com

Android Operating System. (2017). Retrieved from http://en.wikipedia.org/wiki/Android

API Amazon Document. (2017, 12 February), Retrieved from http://docs.2017.aws.amazon.com/api-gateway/api-reference/

AWS. (2017). *AWS History and Benefits*. Retrieved January 29, 2017, from http://www.crestinfotech.com/aws-history-benefits/

Booch, G., Jacobson, I., & Rumbaugh, J. (1999). *Unified Modeling Language User Guide* (2nd ed.). Addison-Wesley.

Douglas Crockford. (2017). In *Wikipedia.* Retrieved on February 21, 2017 from https://en.wikipedia.org/wiki/Douglas_Crockford

Flipkart. (2015). *Product APIs Reference.* Retrieved from https://affiliate.flipkart.com/api-docs/af_prod_ref.html

Herdley, J. (2017). *Jsoup Java HTML Parser, with best of DOM, CSS, and jquery*. Retrieved February 2017, from https://jsoup.org/

Introducing, J. S. O. N. (2017). Retrieved February 2017, from http://www.json.org/

Java Virtual Machine. (2017). Retrieved February 15, 2017 from. from https://en.wikipedia.org/wiki/Java_virtual_machine

M., R. V., & G., V. M. (2017). DSS for web mining using recommendation system. In G. Sreedhar (Ed.), *Web data mining and development of knowledge-based decision support systems* (pp. 22-34). Hershey, PA: IGI Global.

Padma, V., Sanjana, B. L., & Rao, M. V. (2017). Comparative study for selection of an item based on multi-criteria DSS. *International Journal of Computer Science and Information Security, 15*(2).

Sridevi, M., Rao, R. R., & Rao, M. V. (2016). A survey on Recommender Systems. *International Journal of Computer Science and Information Security, 14*(5).

The New Boston. (n.d.). *Featured Tutorial - Android App Development for Beginners.* Retrieved in February 2017, from http://www.thenewboston.com/

Types of software testing and definitions of testing terms. (2017, April 17). Retrieved from http://www.softwaretestinghelp.com/types-of-software-testing/

Chapter 7
E-Commerce and Its Software

Rebika Rai
Sikkim University, India

Prashant Chettri
HRDD Sikkim, India

Lekhika Chettri
Sikkim University, India

ABSTRACT

Today we are moving into an era of "intangible" business processes, where business communication and transactions can be conducted anywhere, anytime, and with a simple click of a mouse. With the speedy amplification and expansion of technology, information systems have become a normal component of our everyday life. The phenomenal growth of the internet has led to the emergence of a great number of new technologies and one of the most important ones is the ability to conduct business over the internet. E-commerce is currently changing the way business is conducted by assisting business progressions and transactions with very few organizations debating whether or not to participate in it. E-commerce software is the engine behind the scenes of an online store, making it possible to easily manage inventory, add or remove products, calculate taxes, and everything else required to manage a website and fulfill orders.

1. E- COMMERCE OVERVIEW

The internet has transpired as the foremost worldwide dissemination channel for goods, services, managerial and professional jobs thereby intensely altering economics, industry structure, products, services, consumer behavior, jobs, and markets. The phenomenal growth of the internet has led to the emergence of a great number of new technologies and one of the most important ones is the ability to conduct business over the internet. Businesses have progressively clinched Electronic Commerce or E-Commerce to revolutionize their procedures nowadays. E-Commerce can be said to be a policy of contemporary business that basically addresses the requirements of business associations, vendors and customers to lessen cost and improve the quality of goods and services while increasing the speed of delivery by procuring and vending goods and services, or transmitting funds or data, over an electronic network,

DOI: 10.4018/978-1-5225-3646-8.ch007

predominantly the internet. The E-Commerce can be significantly explained using several perspectives such as Communication, Service, Business process and Commercial as shown in Figure 1.

Good communication plays a vital role in business not just for the daily basis functioning of the company, but also influences the sales and turnover in an organization. Communication could be in terms of delivery of goods, payment over networks or other electronic medium that is involved in E-Commerce. Service on the other hand addresses to cater the need of organization, government sectors as well as consumers to improve the quality of different types of services to be rendered. Commercial (Advertising) for buying and selling products using online services available such as email campaigns, ads, affiliate programs, pay-per-click ads etc. Business process enhances E-Commerce as a means to totally substitute physical business and perform business electronically. However, E-Commerce is not just about buying and selling products but it is a mechanism of electronically communicating, determining information and collaborating that has a significant impact on business, organization, profession and customer.

E-Commerce deals with several ways of exchanging business information *viz.* Electronic Document Interchange, Electronic Publishing, Electronic Messaging and other Network- based technologies as depicted in Figure 2.

Figure 1. Different perspective of e-commerce

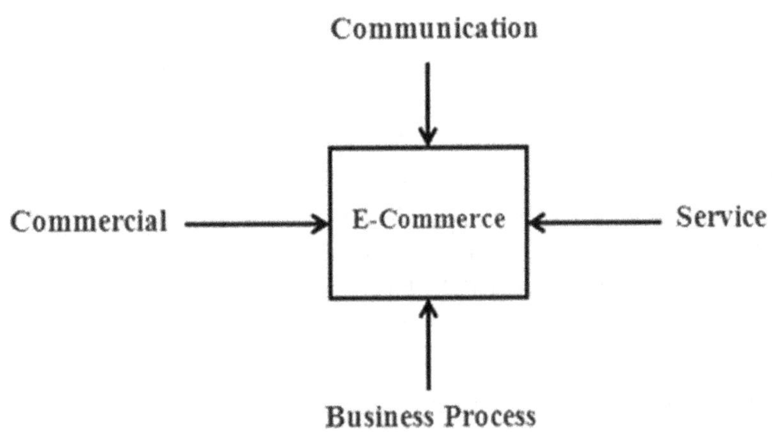

Figure 2. Several ways of business information exchange in E-Commerce

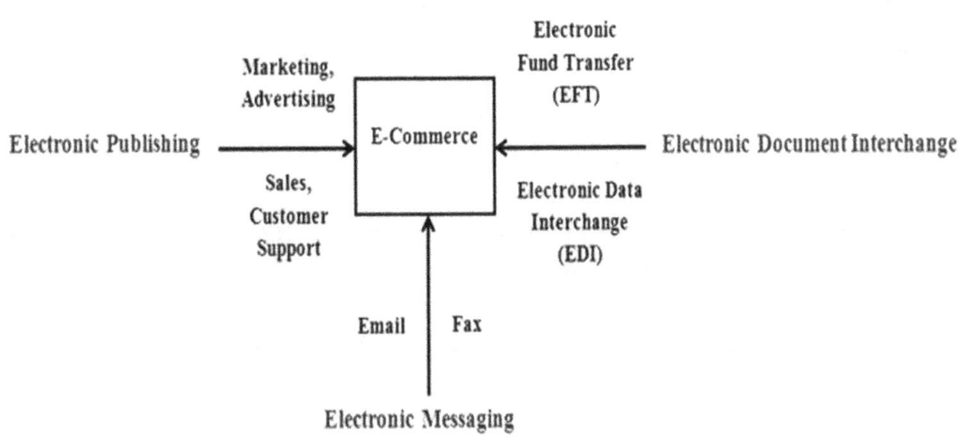

Electronic Data Interchange or EDI is an electronic way of transferring business documents from one computer system to another in an organization internally or externally without the human intervention as internet as a medium for data exchange. EDI permits the exchange internally among the various departments of an organization or externally with suppliers, customers or any subsidiaries possibly located remotely in different countries. The most common business documents transferred using EDI are Invoices, Purchase orders, Shipping requests, Acknowledgement, Business correspondence letters, Financial information letters and many more. Electronic Funds Transfer or EFT refereed as paperless monetary transactions is a mechanism of transferring money from one bank account directly to another through an electronic terminal using Automated Teller Machine (ATM) or computer system for both credit transfers, such as payroll payments, and for debit transfers, such as mortgage payments. E-Commerce employs other ways to exchange business information's: Electronic messaging either using Email or Fax and Electronic Publishing by marketing, advertising, sales and customer support.

1.1 History of E-Commerce

Ecommerce has continued to grow with latest technologies, novelty, and several numbers of businesses entering the online marketplace every year. The expediency, safety, and experience of user's and customers of E-Commerce have improved exponentially since its commencement in the year 1970's with the development of Electronic Funds Transfer (EFT). The development of E-Commerce applications began its journey using the concept of EFT but was confined to financial institutes, restricted business and huge organizations. In the late 1970's Electronic Data Interchange (EDI) came into picture that enhanced the limited collection organizations and allowed participation from retailers, manufacturers, services and others enabling the concept of IOS i.e. Inter Organizational System. IOS facilitated the automated information to traversal among the organizations without human intervention replacing the traditional mailing and faxing of documents (Lim Xin Yin, 2008).

Enterprise Resource Planning Systems (ERP), data mining and data warehousing were incorporated to the existing E-Commerce from 1990 onwards wherein the term E-Commerce was coined when internet was gaining its popularity and user began to participate in World Wide Web (WWW). This resulted in the rapid expansion of several applications in E-Commerce.

In the mid 1990's to 2000, major advancement was witnesses making the widespread usage of internet with Amazon, the largest online retailer in the world launched an online bookstore in the year 1995 without any physical limitations on the number of books. Today apart from just books, Amazon offers many products such as CDs, DVDs, computer software, electronics, apparel, furniture, toys and list is unending. In the same year i.e. 1995, Ebay followed by Zappos and Victoria Secret introduced their online shopping sites.

The inception of Yahoo followed by Google, two leading search engines, in the year 1998 came out with their successful web directories that turned out to be their E-Commerce subsidiaries as Google Shopping and Yahoo! Auction thereafter. In the same year, PayPal, a global E-Commerce company began delivering its services as online payment system for online money transfer that serves as an electronic alternative to traditional paper methods like money orders, cheque etc. It allowed customers world-wide to send, receive and hold funds in 24 different currencies. Currently, PayPal manages more than 232 million accounts, more than 100 million of them active. This was the turning point in the E-Commerce business as more and more people was attracted towards carrying out their business online, this led to the need of more secure communication and transaction systems and protocols.

In the year 2004, Payment Card Industry (PCI) security standard council was created in order to check out the growth, propagation accomplishment, enrichment and storage of security standard requirements to be met by different business that starts up basically focusing on account data protection.

The drastic growth in the technology and usage of smart phones coupled with huge consumer confidence and social media added to it, the association of business and consumer has turned out to be more promising making online purchase and transaction easier and reliable (Rajendra Madhukar Sarode, 2015). Thereby, E-Commerce market is growing and shall evolve in days to come.

1.2 Features of E-Commerce

1.2.1 Features of E-Commerce

Hundreds of E-Commerce solutions and vendors are running and constantly developing the finest features to make it functional, responsive and ideal for their customers taking into account their requirements and going through the feedbacks provided (Pappas, 2015). The important features provided by E-Commerce Technology (Zhao Huang & Morad Benyoucef, 2013) in regard to Technology and Business implication has been summarised in Table 1.

1.3 Traditional Commerce vs. E-Commerce

In contrast to E-Commerce that totally depends on online sales, drop shipments and 24 hour access for consumers using electronic medium, traditional commerce relies more on local consumers interacting with sales executives, managers and customer service personnel personally. Traditional commerce does not typically share information with competitors whereas E-Commerce prices, specials and inventory are ready available online for consumers and competitors (Christopher Pappas, 2015). The major differences between traditional Commerce and E-Commerce has been listed based on features such as information exchange, transaction and communication mechanism, platform, cost effectiveness, time, geographical accessibility, introduction of new products, physical inspection, product suitability, cybercrime and human resource in Table 2.

1.4 E-Commerce Business Models

The Business models of E-Commerce can be divided into following categories and the same has been projected in Figure 3.

1.4.1 Business-to-Business (B2B)

In B2B E-Commerce environment, all electronic transaction of products or services is conducted between Business organizations. Business organization / Manufacturer tend to sell their products online to other organization without getting engaged to the procedure of selling products to the customers. For instance, Manufacturer might sell their products to wholesalers or distributors who in turn might sale its product to the retailers / customers with pricing of products being negotiable and totally based on the quantity of order made as depicted in Figure 4.

Table 1. Features of e-commerce from technology and business implication

S.No	Features	Technology Implication	Business Implication
1	**Global reach**	E-Commerce technology to stretch across traditional culture and national boundaries.	E-Commerce technology providing worldwide services to the client. Also, having the ability to translate the multilingual websites.
2	**Ubiquity**	Internet technology is available everywhere (airports, coffee shop, hilly areas) and can be easily accessed using smart phones / tablets.	Virtual market is created with no geographical restrictions. Shopping can be carried out anywhere conveniently and lessens shopping costs.
3	**Universal standards**	The technical standards of the internet (Internet Standards) and for the conducting E-Commerce are shared by all of the nations in the world.	Reduced product search cost as a single repository is available that makes price of product detection easier, accurate and faster. Online E-Commerce store can be accessed any time and everywhere.
4	**Interactivity (Communication Improvement)**	Voice over Internet Protocol (VoIP) can be employed to track the communication record. Email can be used as communication mechanism to access all kind of mailing systems and tracking.	E-commerce technologies allow communication in a two-way fashion between the vendor and the consumer.
5	**Richness**	The audio, video, sent files, received files or data can be saved easily in the user account making it easier to track the details and further processing.	Information that is multifarious and content-rich can be conveyed without sacrificing reach. E-Commerce has changed the traditional trade-offs linking richness and reach.
6	**Information density**	The total amount and quality of information available to all market participants is vastly increased and is cheaper to deliver.	Online shopping allows a consumer or company to receive personal details, product shipping, billing and payment information from a customer all at once and sends the customer's information to the appropriate departments in a matter of seconds priority.
7	**Social technology**	Accelerate the client activity to share the information and content with one click.	It provides best source of sharing technology and e-Marketing that will enhance the business drastically.
8	**Personalization / Customization**	Enable vendors to target their marketing messages to a person's name, interests and past purchases.	It enables changing the product or service to suit the purchasing behavior and preferences of a consumer.

1.4.2 Business-to-Consumer (B2C)

In B2C E-Commerce environment, all electronic transaction of products or services is conducted directly between Business organization / manufacturer and customers. For instance, customer can select the product from the website of the business organization and order the same; the website in turn sends the notification to the organization that in turn will dispatch the products to the customer directly as depicted in Figure 5.

1.4.3 Consumer-to-Consumer (C2C)

In C2C E-Commerce environment, all electronic transaction of products or services is conducted directly between customers. For instance, if Customer-A wants to sell a product, he puts up an advertisement to be published in the website, Customer-B on having a look into the advertisement if wants to purchase the product. Customer-A provides the product to Customer-B who in turn provides money for the received items as depicted in Figure 6.

Table 2. Traditional commerce and e-commerce

S.No	Features for Comparison	Traditional Commerce	E-Commerce
1	**Information exchange**	Totally depends on intervention of humans for information exchange from one person to another.	Information sharing is done through electronic mechanism making it possible without human intervention.
2	**Transaction and Communication mechanisms**	Transactions and communication is carried out in a synchronous order. Human intervention is needed to perform communication and later to navigate to transaction.	Transactions and communication is carried out in an asynchronous fashion. Electronic system automatically handles and determines the exact interval to perform communication or to proceed with transaction.
3	**Platform**	Uniform platform is unavailable which makes it difficult for the vendors to flourish their business. It is possible only through personal communications and relation.	E-Commerce website provides the uniform platform where all the information is available at a single place. The growth of the business heavily relies on marketing, advertisement and other business activities across the globe through electronic medium.
4	**Cost effectiveness**	Cost has to be incurred for the role of middlemen to sell the company's product.	There is a direct link between the business and the customer, so total overhead cost is reduced.
5	**Time**	Lots of time is consumed to order the products and complete the transactions as it has to be done manually.	The products can be ordered online and the transaction can complete in few minutes through internet. Saves valuable time for both customer and business as a whole.
6	**Geographical accessibility**	Business organizations have to incur a lot of expenses on investment to enter international market.	By hosting a website, by placing advertisements on the internet and satisfying certain legal norms, a business can penetrate into global market.
7	**Introduction of new products**	It takes a lot of time and money to introduce a new product and analyze the response of the customers. Initially, cost has to be incurred to carry out pilot surveys to understand the taste of the customers.	It is easy to introduce a product on the website and get the immediate feedback of the customers. Based on the response, the products can be redefined and modified for a successful launch.
8	**Physical inspection**	Possible to physically inspect the products before the purchase.	While purchasing products, customers have to rely on electronic images available in the website.
9	**Product suitability**	Suitable for perishables and touch and feel items.	Not very suitable for perishable goods and high valuable items such as jewellery and antiques.
10	**Cyber crime**	Fraud is comparatively less as there is personal interaction between the buyer and the seller.	Lack of physical presence in markets and unclear legal issues give loopholes for frauds to take place in e-business transactions.
11	**Human resource**	Human resource in non- electronic environment is not a vital problem.	An organization requires technically qualified staff with an aptitude to update them in the ever changing world. E-business has difficulty in recruiting and retaining talented people.

1.4.4 Consumer-to-Business (C2B)

In C2B E-Commerce environment, all electronic transaction of services is conducted directly between Business organization and customers. For instance, customer approaches websites showing particular service offered by multiple business organizations. Customer reviews the multiple offers and chooses the organization service based that meet up his price expectations. The organization chosen by the customer deliver service to the customer as depicted in Figure 7.

Figure 3. Various e-commerce business models

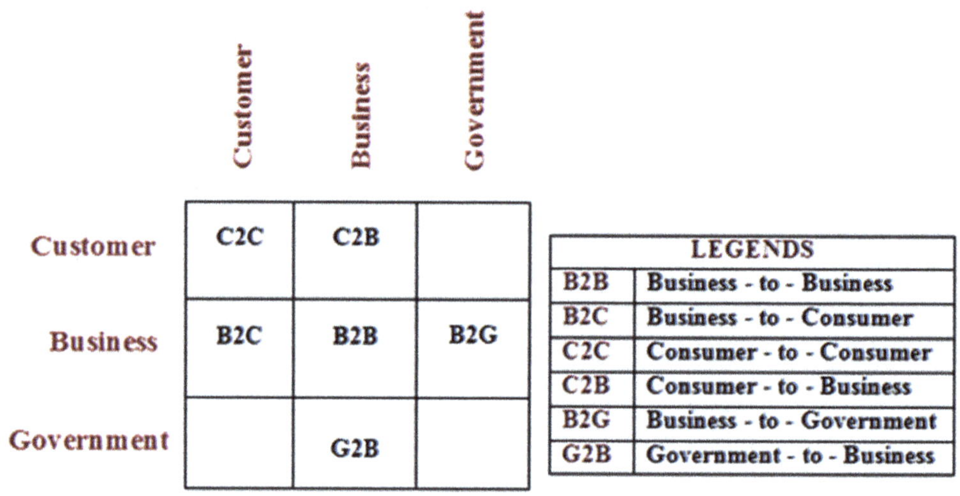

Figure 4. B2B e-commerce business models

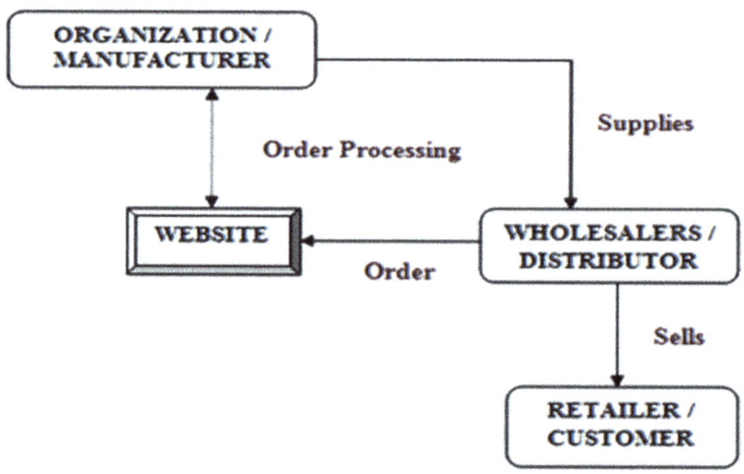

Figure 5. B2C e-commerce business models

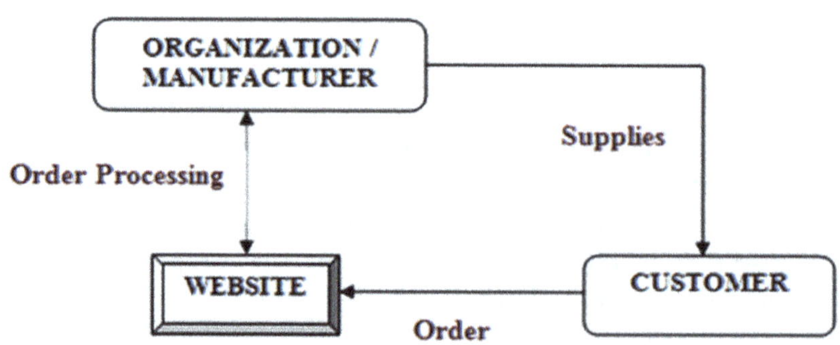

Figure 6. C2C e-commerce business models

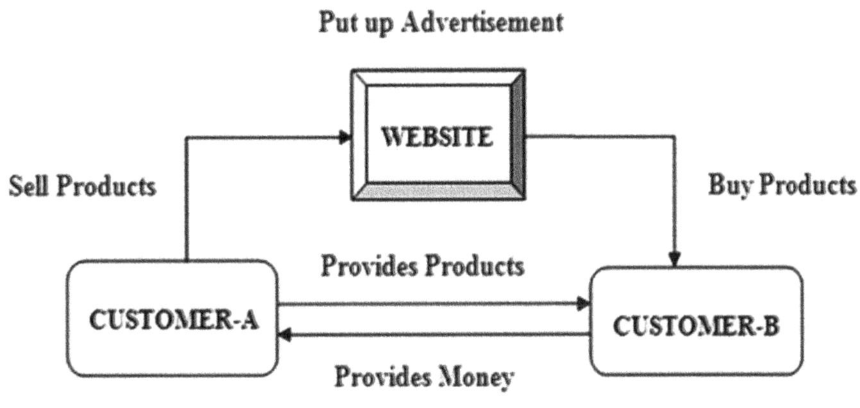

Figure 7. C2B e-commerce business models

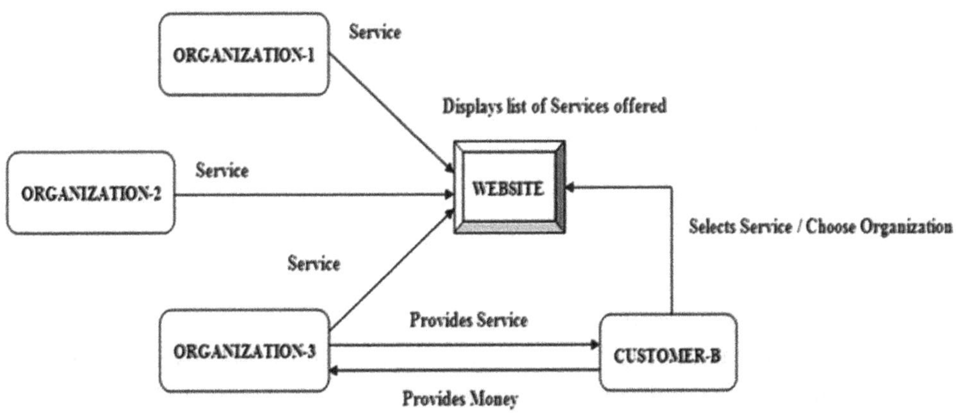

1.4.5 Business-to-Government (B2G)

In B2G E-Commerce environment, all electronic transaction of services is conducted directly between Business organizations and Government. It is the derivative of B2B E-Commerce business model. The website accredited by government to trade and exchange information with various organizations, For instance, here the organizations sells products, services or information to the Government or government agencies as depicted in Figure 8.

1.4.6 Government-to-Business (G2B)

In B2G E-Commerce environment, all electronic transaction of services is conducted directly between Government and Business organizations. Here, the initiative comes from a government organization and business organizations are the target group wherein government uses website to approach business organizations and such websites support auctions, tenders and application submission functionalities as depicted in Figure 9.

Figure 8. B2G e-commerce business models

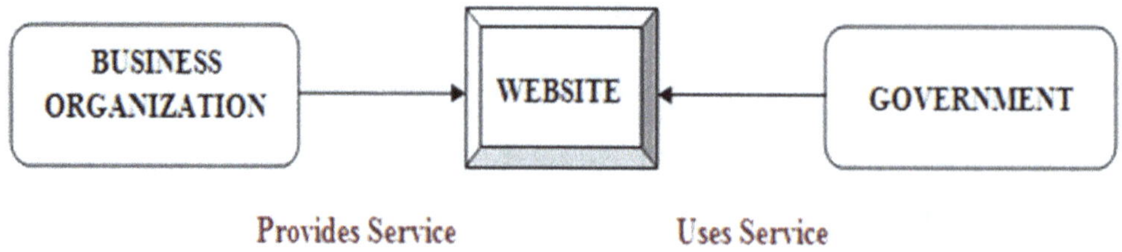

Figure 9. G2B e-commerce business models

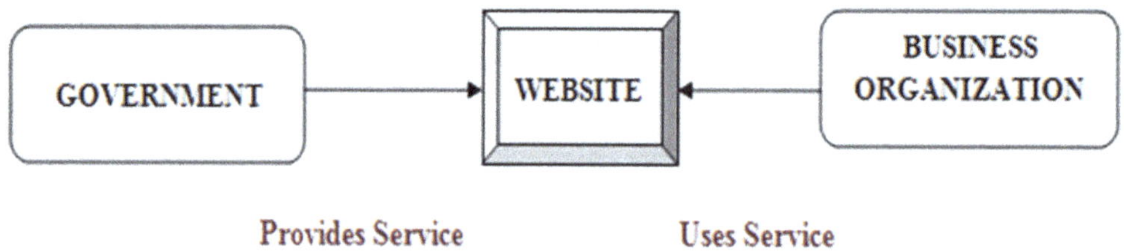

1.5 Applications of E-Commerce

There is several application of E-Commerce ranging from Procurement & Purchasing to marketing to e-banking to online publishing. Some of the applications have been listed below:

1. **Manufacturing:** E-Commerce platform provides the mechanism that covers the entire aspect of supply chain management. A supply chain is a set of connections between various organizations wherein one organization supplies products or services to other organization which, in turn, supply products or services to other companies, and process continues. The major areas to be considered in supply chain are production, distribution, inventory and location. Organizations uses an electronic exchange means by providing buy and sell products, trade market information and inventory information. This speeds up the flow of raw material and finished goods among the members of the business community.
2. **Finance:** Financial organizations use E-commerce to a huge extent wherein they provide the mechanism by which the customers can check the balances of their savings and loan accounts, transfer money to their other account and pay their bill through E-banking.
3. **Online Stock Trading:** E-Commerce is employed in online stock trading as many websites provide access to news, charts, information about company profile and analyst rating on the stocks.
4. **Online Marketing and Advertisement:** E-Commerce can be used to collect data about customer preferences for products, services, buying patterns that will help various marketing activities such as product feature enhancement to advertise the products among the customers.
5. **Auctions:** C2C E-commerce as discussed in the sub-section 1.4.3 basically involves the direct buying and selling of goods and services among customers using the concept of electronic bidding that enables the customer to receive the products and the services.

6. **E-Tailing / E-Retailing:** B2B E-Commerce as discussed in the sub-section 1.4.1 can be widely used in the field of E-Tailing wherein the retails goods can be sold in the internet using specified websites.
7. **Online Publishing:** E-Commerce concept such as global reach, universal standards, cost effectiveness, ubiquity and time can be used in the field of online publishing wherein the newsletters, magazine, databases, brochures, e-books and other promotional materials can be published online and accessed by variety of user irrespective of their geographical locations.

The various other applications of E-Commerce include but not restricted to online reservation, video on demand, online procurement etc.

1.6 Advantages of E-Commerce

The advantages of using E-Commerce vary from components to components. This section highlights the advantages from different perspectives i.e. to Organizations, to Customers, to Society as a whole.

1.6.1. Advantages to Organizations

Using E-Commerce, organizations can inflate their business market without the geographical constraint with minimum investment by identifying the customer buying pattern, suitable suppliers to supply the products and importantly consistent business partners.

It can help the organization to digitize the entire process that saves enormous amount of time, energy and resources providing faster and efficient product delivery to the customers.

In comparison to traditional commerce that involves lots of paper work, E-Commerce automates the entire procedures and reduces the effort required.

E-Commerce provides various ways to provide pre-sales and post sales assistance to provide better services to customers.

1.6.2. Advantages to Customers

E-Commerce provides customer with 24x7 supports by automating the business of enterprises and services are available anytime, anywhere. Here 24x7 refers to 24 hours of each seven days of a week. Using E-Banking facilities, customer can do transactions for the product or enquiry about any product/ services provided by a company any time irrespective of the locations and boundaries. It provides user with quicker delivery of products and the option of delivery.

The customers can compare products available and select the best and cheaper from the list available. The feedback adds a flavor to E-Commerce platform as customers can review the products and comment based on the services and product quality. The comment and review put forward by various customers for different products helps other customer to think before taking the final decision on purchasing the product.

There are several E-Commerce sites that provide the option of electronic auction and bidding. Also, the secondhand products can be purchased at much lesser price. The competitive environment created with the upcoming of different organizations provides substantial discounts on various products. The information about the product and the services can be generated in few seconds.

1.6.3. Advantages to Society

The competition among the various organizations selling products and providing services to customer has led to the decrease in the service and product price, this in turn permits even the less affluent people to avail the deal.

Irrespective of the geographical boundary, just with the click of the button, services of E-Commerce can be availed even by the people located at the remote corners of the society provided the internet connection is available. The various services in regard to healthcare, education can be delivered to people using E-Commerce.

The online publishing as discussed in section 1.5 helps in accessing newsletters, magazine, databases, brochures, e-books and other promotional materials either free or at minimal cost.

E-Commerce on the other hand promotes shopping and gaining services from anywhere without being physically present, that definitely helps the society in much aspect in terms of traffic, pollution, cleanliness etc.

1.7 Disadvantages of E-Commerce

Apart from the advantages there are several disadvantages of using E-Commerce which has been broadly classifies as technical and non-technical disadvantages in this section. Technical in terms of security, network bandwidth, software-hardware compatibility has been highlighted. Non-technical in terms of cybercrime, security, cost of building E-Commerce, maintenance, physical absence, and cost of internet has been discussed.

1.7.1. Technical Disadvantages

With the development of software development industry, there is no fix platform to build E-Commerce that results in the compatibility issues in regard to the hardware where it is deployed. The security issue is an important factor that acts as disadvantages as there are many cases of cyber crime and theft while performing online transaction.

Ecommerce can only be transacted with the help of an internet access device such as a computer or a smartphone which at times become difficult for the user to procure. Depending on the type of network bandwidth available at different location, accessibility to E-Commerce is an issue at times in many countries.

1.7.2. Non-Technical Disadvantages

Since the virtual environment is created during online shopping, physical absence of the customer does not allow them to touch and feel the product as done in traditional commerce.

The availability of several shopping search engines and comparison shopping websites which might help the customer to filter the best, sellers find it too restrictive as many of them get filtered out of the consumer's consideration set.

For an ecommerce business, its website is everything. Even a few minute of downtime can lead to a substantial loss of money, not to mention customer dissatisfaction.

The initial development and maintenance of E-Commerce is high. E-Commerce applications are still evolving and changing rapidly.

In addition, one also needs internet connectivity to participate in E-Commerce.

2. E-COMMERCE SOFTWARE

E-Commerce software also known as shopping cart software, E-Commerce website builder, online store builder or E-Commerce platform is the vital component behind the scenes of an online store, making it possible to easily manage inventory, add or remove products, calculate taxes etc. to manage a website and fulfill orders placed by customers. (Stone, 2016).

2.1 Importance of E-Commerce Software

The chief objective of developing E-Commerce software is to aid one imperative purpose i.e. to help the vendors or organizations sell products / services online. The core functions of E-Commerce are to manage three elements i.e. Products, Orders and Customers for running an efficacious online shop. In online business apart from software that manages the front end component faced by customer, additional software is required to accomplish back-end functionalities such as accounting, order management, inventory management and customer services. Merging together different available solutions to generate a complete module or platform is problematic and involve recurrent looking after. Providentially, a new variety of business software incorporates entire functionality into a sole E-Commerce platform using Software-as-a-Service (SaaS) model. With the setup that integrates applications and data, constructing pertinent online service is imaginable.

Small businesses organizations have numerous options when retailing online comes into picture. One mode is to sign up with marketplaces that permit the business organizations to list different products in a hosted storefront, such as eBay, Amazon and Etsy. However, if an organization wishes to govern and totally control the E-Commerce business, developing up its own website using E-Commerce software is the best thing to proceed with.

E-commerce is likely to have a gigantic influence on the way businesses are conducted by different organizations leading to progress in trade, growth in markets and renovating the way business are being conducted. There are various types of E-Commerce software available in the market, some software fulfills only the basic purpose of the system whereas other software's are more complex and considers innumerable payment mechanisms, offering an organization with the finest tracking system and in addition enabling the report generation for analyzing the products. However, the major concern is the choice of software to address the various issues of E-Commerce.

2.2 Features of E-Commerce Software

There are numerous E-Commerce software's available in the market stretching from open source to customized thereby leaving the vendors and organizations with massive choices to select the appropriate software as per their requirements and financial capabilities. E-Commerce software leverages the website, lessens operational costs and takes hold of the interest of the targeted customers. The following list describes some key E-Commerce software features that are generally used by vendors to relate the available options and select the best.

1. **Centralized Repository or Database:** One of the important feature E-Commerce software should provide is the centralized database that has the capability of storing and retrieving all appropriate data such as list of products, browsing history, order history, shipping status, payment status etc. This shall eradicate the difficulty of creating and maintaining multiple repositories for different types of data.
2. **Integration With:**
    a. **E-Commerce Website:** Another feature of E-Commerce software should be its capability to directly integrate with the E-Commerce website to facilitate and handle all procedures such as sale, finance, order fulfillment, advertisement, content management etc.
    b. **Finance:** The other feature of E-Commerce software is the ability to integrate with the accounting software packages like PeachTree, QuickBooks etc. to update information's in real time and for effective management of revenue, invoices, outstanding payments and other sales-related financial transactions.
    c. **Third Party:** Much E-Commerce software provides faultless integration with variety of other applications such as payment processing gateways like PayPal, shipping service providers etc. so that the customer is ensured with most efficient, convenient and flexible payment option and also the customer can customize their delivery options.
    d. **Social Media Integration:** Much E-Commerce software provides ideal integration with social media like Facebook, Twitter etc. that can lead to increase in followers, provide opportunity to spread the message, to connect to the target audiences and customer to advertise the product and services provided by the business organizations. As social media is not confined to number so hours of business, the communication and association can be done anytime from anywhere with the assistance of internet connectivity.
    e. **Advanced Promotion and Marketing:** E-Commerce software should incorporate the provision of freedom to customers and vendors by offering the amalgamation of multiple channels such as option for research, point of sales, advertisement, marketing etc. making advanced promotion and marketing possible. It provides variety of techniques to boost site promotion and marketing by supporting search engine optimization policies to make their site more noticeable, evident and reachable to prospective customers. In addition to this, some E-Commerce software examines customers browsing and viewing pattern and make use of it to get better sells by suggesting complementary products to the customer while they are shopping.
    f. **Reporting and Analysis:** E-Commerce software is capable of generating comprehensive statistical reports and also tracks, analyze important data such as keywords, referring sites, statistical data of customers browsing and viewing pattern to determine the most efficient way to improve sales or the products and services.
    g. **Easy-to-Use and Secure Shopping Cart:** E-Commerce software is cable of integrating a third party payment processing gateways that ensures a safe transactions to satisfy the enabling easy shopping, secure methods of payment, express checkout options, and customer accounts for research and making purchasing decisions.

h. **Global System Reporting:** E-Commerce software makes centralized data sourcing and reporting to be much effortless as it helps the organization to keep an account of the performance of various components like sales, marketing, customer service, stock, purchasing, and financials.
i. **Stock Control System:** E-Commerce software furthermore has the provision of stock control system along with warehouse management. A warehouse management system makes sales order processing easier as real time information can be used for packaging and delivery. The stock control system can assist the business organizations to maintain and update the stock inventory in real-time so that the organizations can based on the updates intimate the customer about the availability of products. This also helps the customer to view the availability of the products and the intimation regarding the product being out of stock.
j. **Consolidated Customer Relations:** E-Commerce software offers the mechanism of a Customer Relationship Management System (CRMS) that provides the customers an individual account to keep track of their activity history, track their shipment of products, payments etc. Customer relationship managers on the other hand can retrieve this account information to upsell, cross sell, and resolve customer issues and enquiries related to any products, services etc.

2.3 Types of E-Commerce Software

As already mentioned choosing the right E-Commerce software is the essential criterion of selling products / services online ideally suitable to establish a business. The various types of E-Commerce software's / platforms available have been depicted in Figure 10.

1. **Basic E-Commerce Software:** The simplest of all the E-Commerce software's available that is exceptionally affordable but lacks some features and capabilities, especially meant for small business organizations. This type of software's is very convenient to use and deploy, and are best for eLearning professionals who wishes to provide some eLearning courses on their site or blog. This kind of software does not provide a hosted E-Commerce site, so the business organization needs

Figure 10. Different types of e-commerce software's

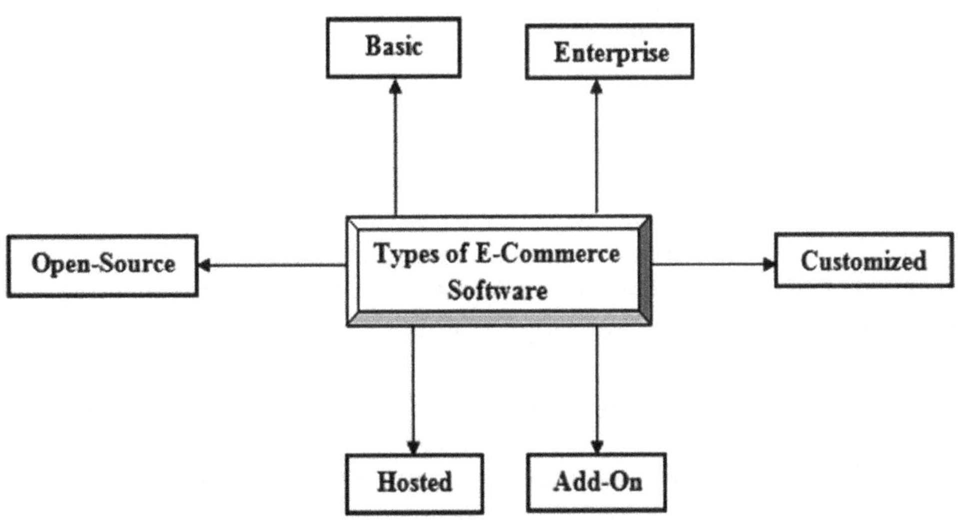

to pay separately for the website to be designed and hosted to start up with the selling of products or services. Example: SendOwl.

2. **Enterprise E-Commerce Software:** The kind of software especially meant for the diverse needs of large business organizations that can spend large amount to match up its requirements and is not at all meant for small organizations or E-Learning professionals. It provides numerous features such as personalized shopper experiences, custom site designs, cloud services, flexible Application Programming Interfaces (API's), local staging environment, premium web features (Secured Sockets Layers (SSL) certificates, Single Sign On (SSO) and Google Trusted Store tags), order and inventory management, payment gateways, multi-channel and multi-store, Customer Relationship Management (CRM), technical support, mobile capabilities and many more. Example: Magento, Shopifyplus, BigCommerce, Mozu, Volusion etc.
3. **Hosted E-Commerce Software:** The kind of software that provides the hosted platform that host the site for the business organization especially for eLearning professionals who wishes to focus on design and development of eLearning courses rather than building E-Commerce site from scratch. The organizations just need to pay monthly fee. Example: Wix, 3dcart, Highwire, Big Cartel, Squarespace, and LemonStand etc.
4. **Add-on E-Commerce Software:** The kind of software that provides add-ons or plugin and is suitable for eLearning professionals who already have any time blogging platform that allow access to plugins converting the blogging platform to an E-Commerce shop. While some plugins are completely free to install, however some plugins need to be purchased. Example: WooCommerce, Easy Digital Downloads etc.
5. **Customized E-Commerce Software:** The kind of software which includes all the features a business organization wishes to have. However, additional cost needs to be paid by the organization for all the extra features and personalization. It is the most expensive E-Commerce software, as it will seamlessly integrate the existing site of the business organization and include all of the branding required. Example: FoxyCart, Znode, E-Smart etc.
6. **Open Source E-Commerce Software:** The kind of software that are free and user friendly and is ideal for the business organization that is new to eLearning market. The major problem in this type of software is organization do not have access to professional customer support. The software need to be downloaded and installed in the system, which may be difficult for people not familiar with E-Commerce software. Example: osCommerce, SelfStartr, SimpleCart, PrestaShop etc.

3. E-COMMERCE SOFTWARE AND ITS COMPARISON

This section discusses about the various E-Commerce software available in the market. As discussed in Section 2.3 different types of E-Commerce software / platforms are available and under each category there are several software's available but to select the software based on the requirements of the business organization and the feasibility in terms of budget available is the major theme to work on.

3.1 Comparison of E-Commerce Software's Available in the Market

Out of hundreds of E-Commerce software available (Stone, 2016), this section few E-Commerce software and compares them based on some distinctive features considering few parameters such as general information, data storage system used, general features, features offered by shopping card and Checkout supported as highlighted in Table 3, Table 4, Table 5, Table 6 and Table 7.

3.2 Case Study on Shopify: An Enterprise E-Commerce Software Platform

Shopify is an enterprise E-Commerce software platform for online stores and a company headquartered in Ottawa, Ontario Canada founded in 2014 by Tobias Lutke, Daniel Weinand and Scott Lake that serves worldwide with a revenue of $ 151.7 Million (2016) as per the survey conducted "Shopify Expects Revenue to Surge in 2016". The official website is https://www.shopify.com.

3.2.1 Features of Shopify

Shopify provides several features in terms of its design, product management, interfaces, marketing etc. and few have been listed her under:

1. **Design:** Shopify provides a professional looking E-Commerce site that is fully customizable, flexible layout of dynamic content via the Liquid templating language, media assets being linked to individual product or entire shop as a whole and free to use with the developers accounts. It also provides forums where designers of Shopify discusses with the developers and provides tips and strategies to start up with the business using it.

Table 3. General information's of e-commerce software

E-Commerce Software	Creator	License	Language	Web Application framework
BigCommerce	BigCommerce Inc.	Proprietary	PHP	-
Drupal Commerce	Drupal Commerce	GPL	PHP	-
Magento	Varien	OSL 3.0	PHP	-
LemonStand	Limewheel Creative Inc.	Proprietary	PHP	-
Open Cart	OpenCart Ltd.	GPL	PHP	-
osCommerce	osCommerce	GNU GPL	PHP	-
Presta Shop	PrestaShop SA	OSL 3.0	PHP	Model-View-Controller
Shopify	Shopify	Proprietary	Ruby	Ruby on Rails
Supa Dupa	SupaDupa	Proprietary	Ruby	Ruby on Rails
Storehippo	Hippo Innovations P Ltd	Proprietary	Node.js	MEAN_(software_bundle)
WooCommerce	WooThemes	GPL	PHP	-
Zen Cart	Zen Ventures	GPL	PHP	-
Flick Rocket	ACE GmbH	Proprietary	C#	ASP.NET MVC
Nop Commerce	Nop Solutions Ltd	GPL	C#	ASP.NET MVC
Abante Cart	Belavier Commerce	OSL 3.0	PHP	-

Table 4. Data storage system used in various e-commerce software's

E-Commerce Software	MySQL	Oracle	MySQLi	MongoDB	SQLite
BigCommerce	√	X	X	X	X
Drupal Commerce	√	X	√	-	√
Magento	√	X	√	X	X
LemonStand	√	X	X	X	X
Open Cart	√	X	√	X	X
osCommerce	√	X	X	X	X
Presta Shop	√	X	√	X	X
Shopify	√	X	√	X	X
Supa Dupa	√	X	√	X	X
Storehippo	X	X	X	√	X
WooCommerce	√	X	√	X	X
Zen Cart	√	X	√	X	X
Flick Rocket	X	X	X	X	X
Nop Commerce	√	X	X	X	X
Abante Cart	√	X	√	X	√

√: Yes; X: No

Table 5. General features of e-commerce software

E-Commerce Software	Product Rating	Product Review	Reordering	Return	Searching	Social Bookmarking	Guest Account	Customer Testimonial	Featured Products
BigCommerce	Third Party	Third Party	√	√	√	√	√	Add on	√
Drupal Commerce	√	√	√	√	√	√	√	√	√
Magento	√	√	√	√	√	√	√	√	√
LemonStand	√	√	X	√	√	√	-	√	√
Open Cart	√	√	√	√	√	√	√	√	√
osCommerce	√	√	X	X	√	√	Add on	Add on	Add on
Presta Shop	√	√	√	√	√	√	√	√	√
Shopify	√	√	√	√	√	√	-	√	√
Supa Dupa	X	X	√	X	√	X	-	X	√
Storehippo	√	√	√	√	√	√	√	√	√
WooCommerce	√	√	√	√	√	√	√	√	√
Zen Cart	√	√	X	Add on	√	Add on	Add on	Add on	√
Flick Rocket	√	√	√	√	√	√	-	√	√
Nop Commerce	√	√	√	√	√	√	√	√	√
Abante Cart	√	√	√	√	√	√	√	√	√

√: Yes; X: No

Table 6. Features offered by e-commerce shopping site

E-Commerce Software	Source Code	Digital downloads	eBay listing integration	Taxation	Multiple Skins
BigCommerce	√	√	√	√	√
Drupal Commerce	√	√	X	√	√
Magento	√	√	√	√	√
LemonStand	√	√	X	√	√
Open Cart	√	√	Add on	√	√
osCommerce	√	√	-	√	NA
Presta Shop	√	√	√	√	√
Shopify	X	√	√	√	√
Supa Dupa	X	X	X	√	√
Storehippo	√	√	√	√	√
WooCommerce	√	√	√	√	√
Zen Cart	√	√	X	√	√
Flick Rocket	X	√	X	√	√
Nop Commerce	√	√	√	√	√
Abante Cart	√	√	X	√	√

√: Yes; X: No; NA: Not Applicable

2. **Product Management:** Shopify provides Easy to add, list, edit, and organize products using streamlined CMS interface; Inventory tracking for all products as per requirement of users; drag-and-drop ordering of product images; multiple variants for each product allow options with unique inventory tracking, prices, weights; Keyword tags to aid in searching and browsing within the ecommerce shop etc.
3. **Orders:** Shopify enables new order notifications via email, RSS, and on mobile phone with SMS messaging; Email customers from within Shopify; Track payment and shipping status on orders with detailed reports; Customizable views of your orders filtered by their current status; Orders can be exported in CSV format to use in your spreadsheets; Real-time notifications for orders using WebHooks; Order cancellation with automated chargeback option etc.
4. **Interfaces:** Shopify provides uncluttered interface; streamlined dashboard showing vital shop information each time user log in; interactive real-time statistics panel; inventory warnings placed in the sidebar to let user know when products are out of stock; blogs, pages, and site navigation all

Table 7. Checkout supported by e-commerce shopping site

E-Commerce Software	Checkout by Amazon	Google Checkout	PayPal Express	Amazon FPS
BigCommerce	X	X	√	X
Drupal Commerce	√	√	√	√
Magento	√	√	√	√
LemonStand	X	√	√	X
Open Cart	X	√	√	X
osCommerce	X	X	√	X
Presta Shop	√	√	√	√
Shopify	X	√	√	X
Supa Dupa	X	√	√	X
Storehippo	X	√	√	X
WooCommerce	X	√	√	X
Zen Cart	X	**Add on**	√	X
Flick Rocket	X	X	√	X
Nop Commerce	X	√	√	X
Abante Cart	X	X	√	X

√: Yes; X: No

managed through intuitive administration screens; full featured Asset system which lets use and re-use your stock photography, logos or product pdf's wherever user need them.

5. **Marketing:** Shopify's CMS was designed by SEO experts so the store created using Shopify store will rank in Google, Yahoo and Bing; Ability to create coupon codes for percentage or fixed amount off, free shipping, etc.; XML Sitemap automatically generated for search engine indexing; Shopify's blog and "Guru" coaches help with tips and tricks to get more sales.

Other features include:

- Certified Level 1 PCI compliant to ensure the security of your customer data.
- Built on a foundation of open source technology that is constantly being tuned and improved.
- Developed with the powerfully agile and expressive Ruby on Rails web framework.
- Hosted on our secure and expertly maintained Debian Linux servers, guarded by ultra-secure OpenBSD firewalls.
- Backed by the reliability and speed of MySQL databases.
- Operating from a World class data center.
- Compatible with many direct payment processors.

3.2.2 Creating Online Store Using Shopify

The user can create own online store using Shopify and start up with the business. This section highlights the different steps to create the online store using the free trial version of Shopify available on https://www.shopify.in/signup.

1. Firstly enter the email id and click on "Get started" button as depicted in Figure 11.
2. To create the store an appropriate store name needs to be provides along with the other relevant details such as email address and password which shall be later used to log into the online store created as depicted in Figure 12.
3. After clicking the "create your store" button, it takes few seconds to create the store and user needs to fill in certain details about the store created as depicted in Figures 13, 14, 15 and 16.
4. On clicking "Enter my store" button, this will divert the user to their page as depicted in Figure 16 wherein the user can perform certain operations just with the click of the button as depicted in Figures 17.

4. E-COMMERCE CHALLENGES AND SOLUTIONS

In an era of internet revolution, E-Commerce industries have exponentially increased year after year. The figure stated by Statista.com highlights that the retail E-Commerce sales amounted to 342.96 billion US dollars in the year 2015 and is projected to exceed 600 billion US dollars by 2019, which clearly indicates the escalation and progression of E-Commerce industry. However, the small and big company practicing E-Commerce faces numerous challenges and intends to overcome the same using several means and measures. This section highlights the challenges faced by E-Commerce industries and probable solution to cater to the challenges.

Figure 11. Getting started with Shopify

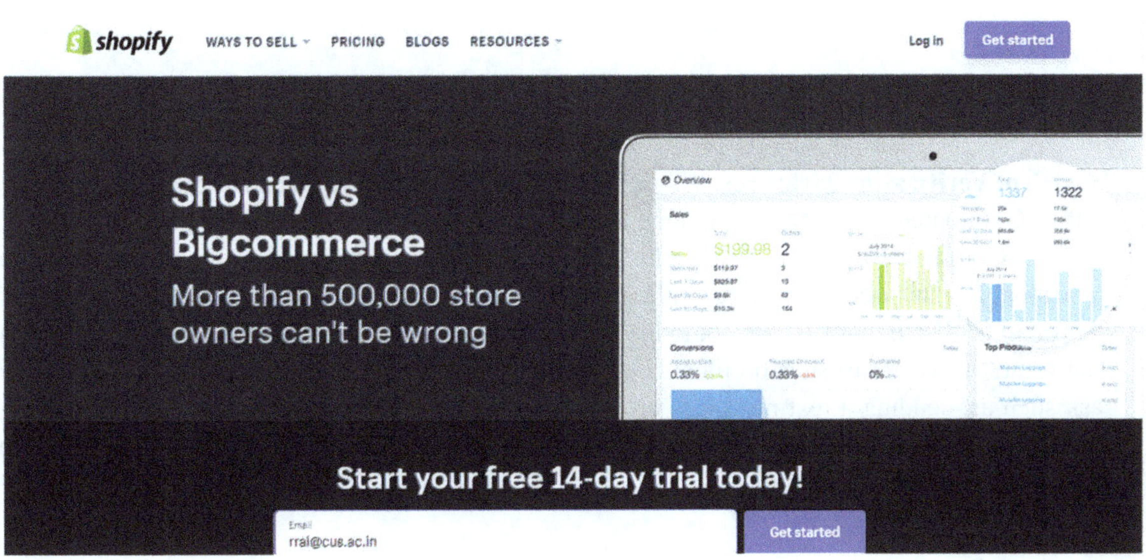

Figure 12. Creating the online store using Shopify

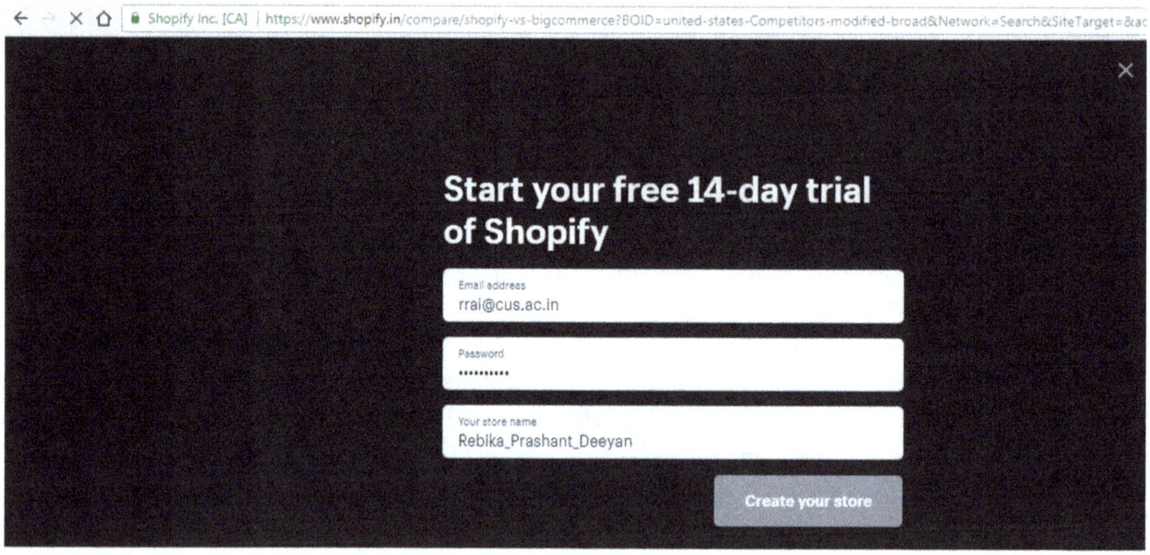

Figure 13. Processing the request for creation of the online store using Shopify

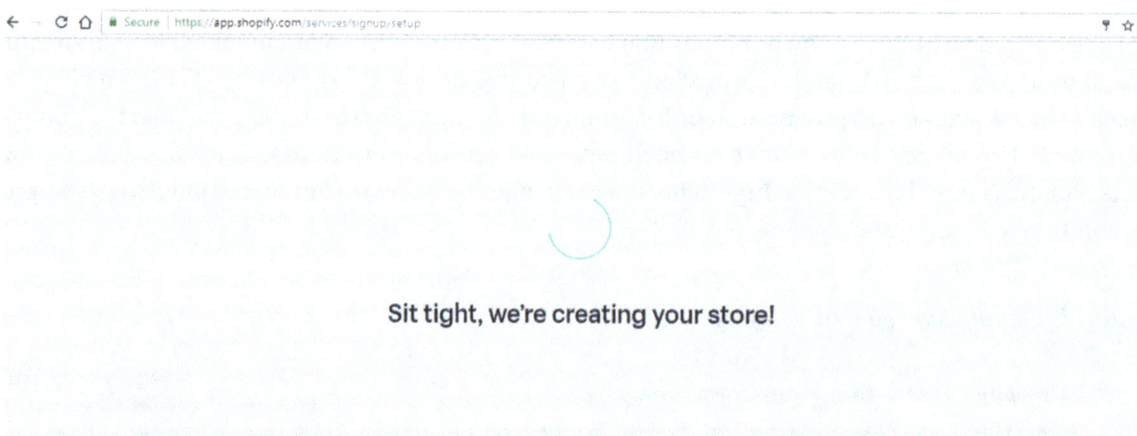

1. **Dearth of Verification Measures:** This is one of the major challenges faced by companies involved with E-Commerce which has led to huge loss in terms of revenues. Whenever the customer signs in the E-Commerce portal and enters his / her credentials, the credibility of customer is highly questionable. This becomes more challenging, when the customer further selects on (Cash On Delivery) COD purchase. These could lead to severe loss if the customer information is incorrect. The solution to cater to such problem could be to come up with the modules that could perform task such as: sending a text messages or email to the customer to confirm his/ her identity; For COD issue, a preset call can be triggered seeking the customer to authenticate the delivery address as provided earlier.

Figure 14. Filling up the details for creation of the online store using Shopify

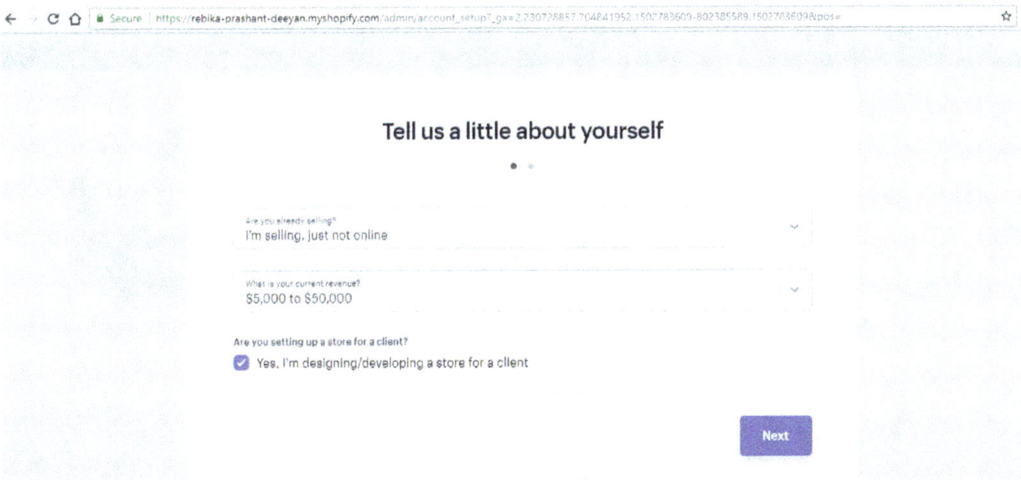

Figure 15. Adding the address for creation of the online store using Shopify

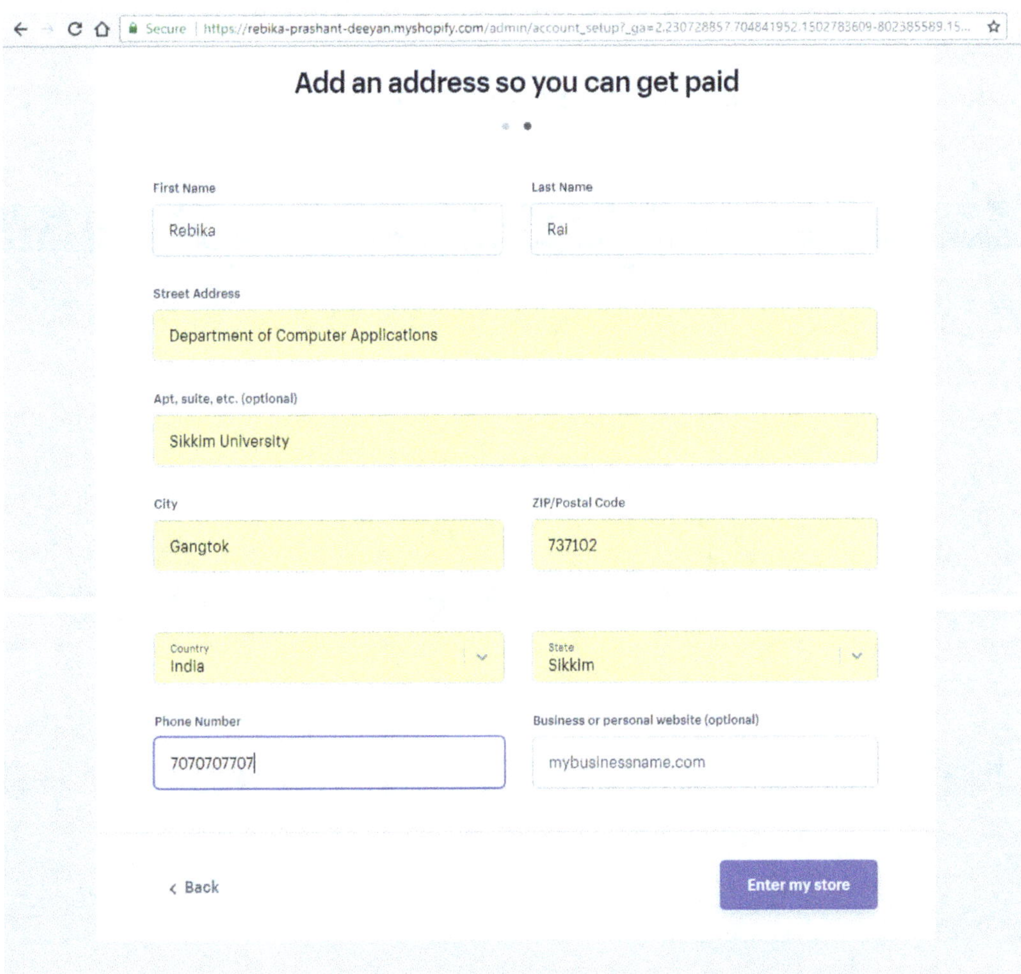

Figure 16. Home page of user store created

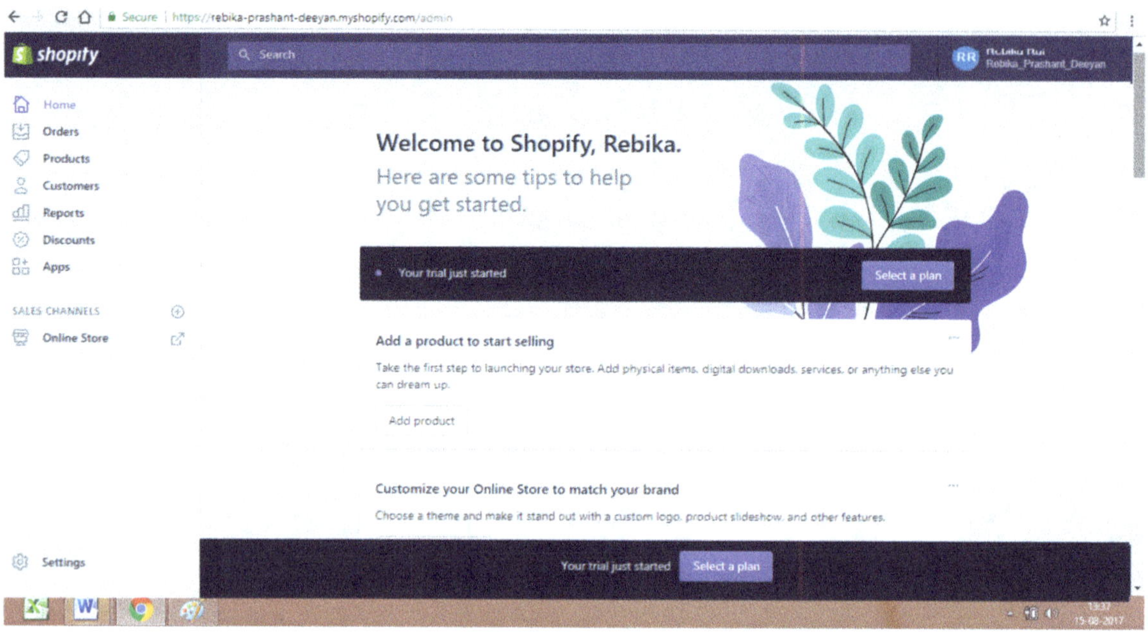

Figure 17. Several plans available once 14 days free trial is over

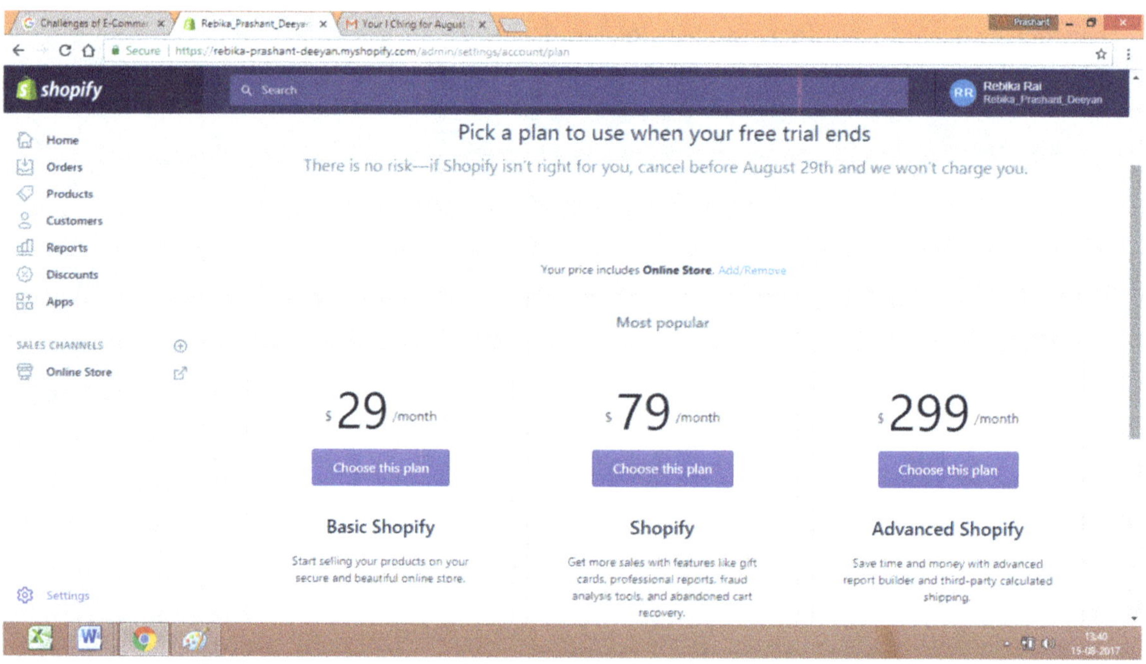

Figure 18. To add product to the online store using Shopify

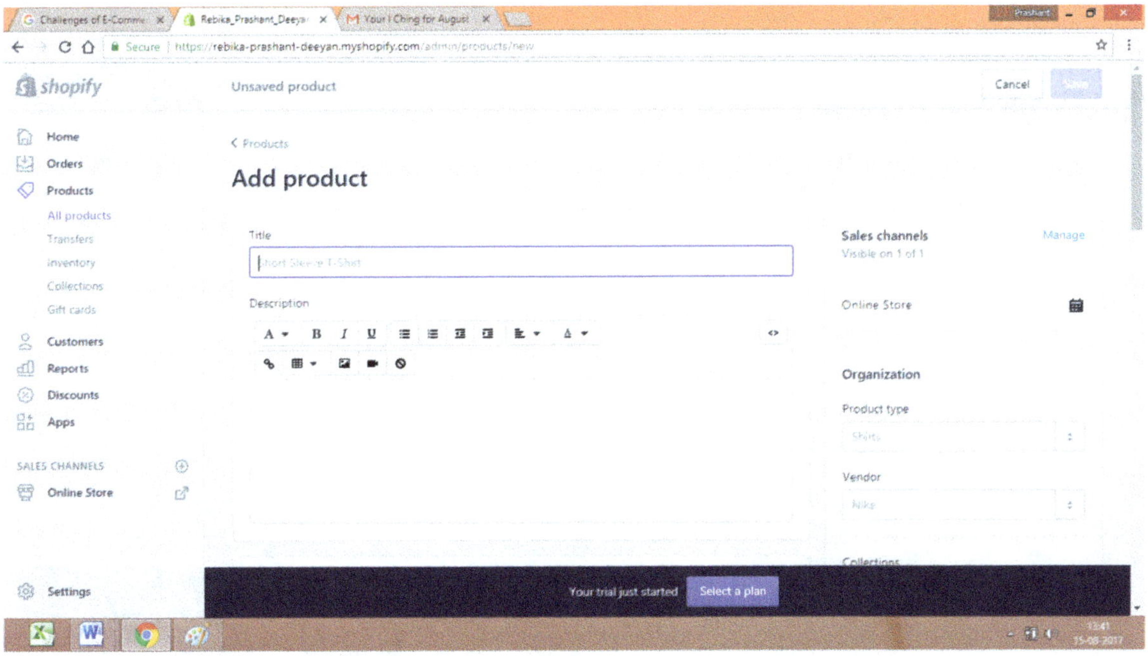

Figure 19. To add customer to the online store using Shopify

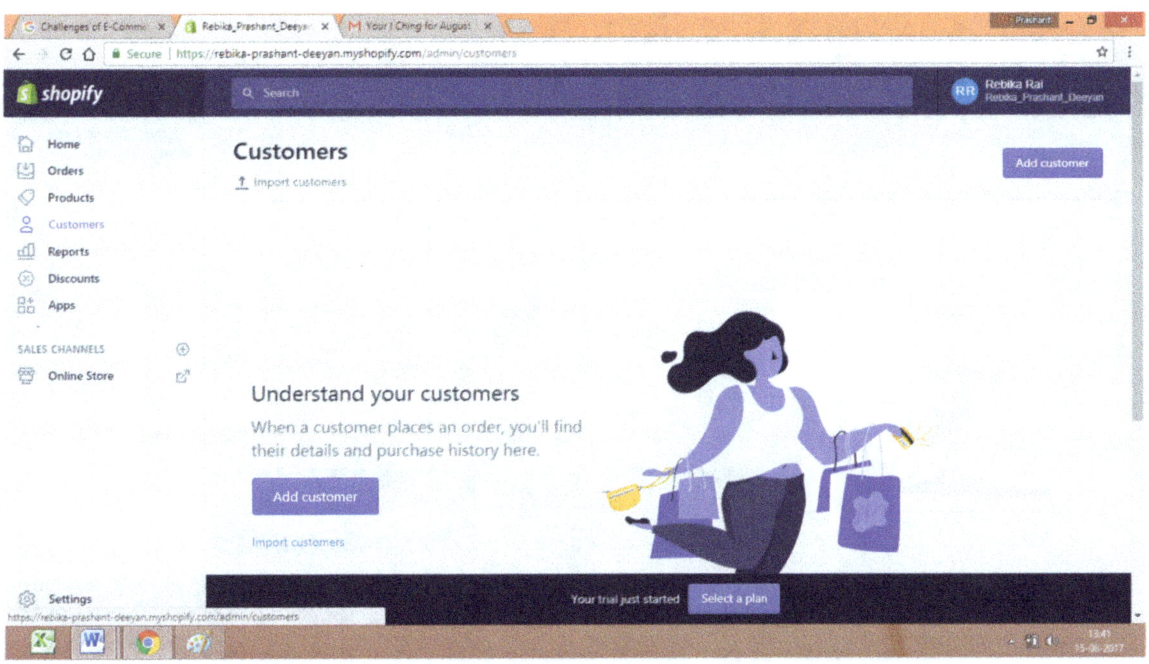

Figure 20. To add product to the online store using Shopify

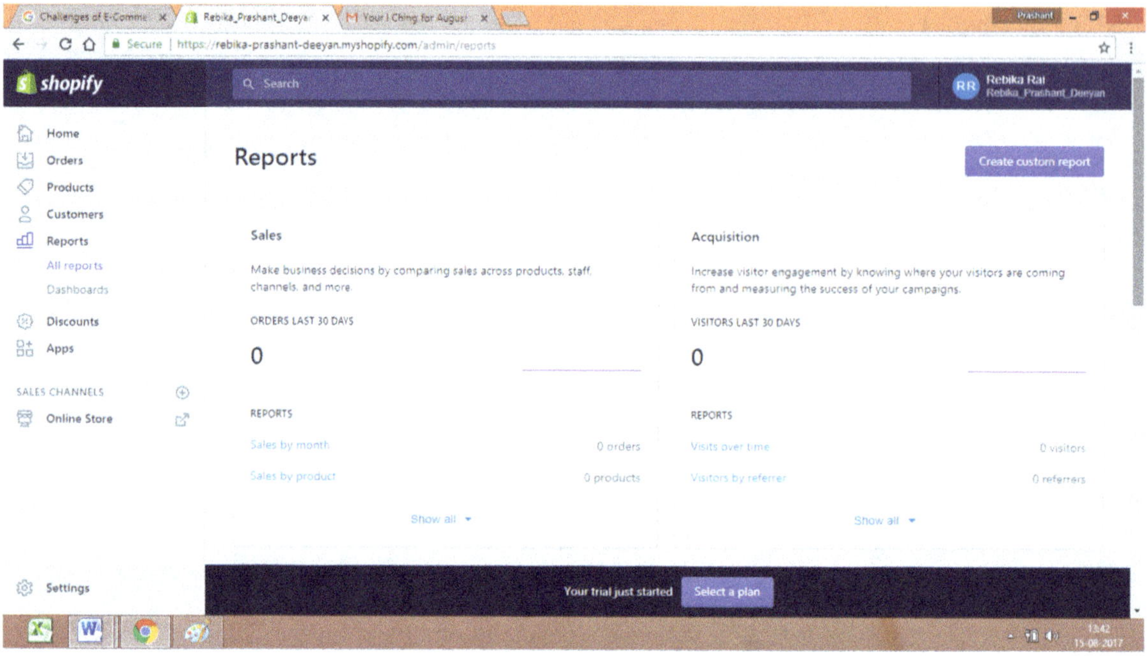

Figure 21. To get started with the app using Shopify

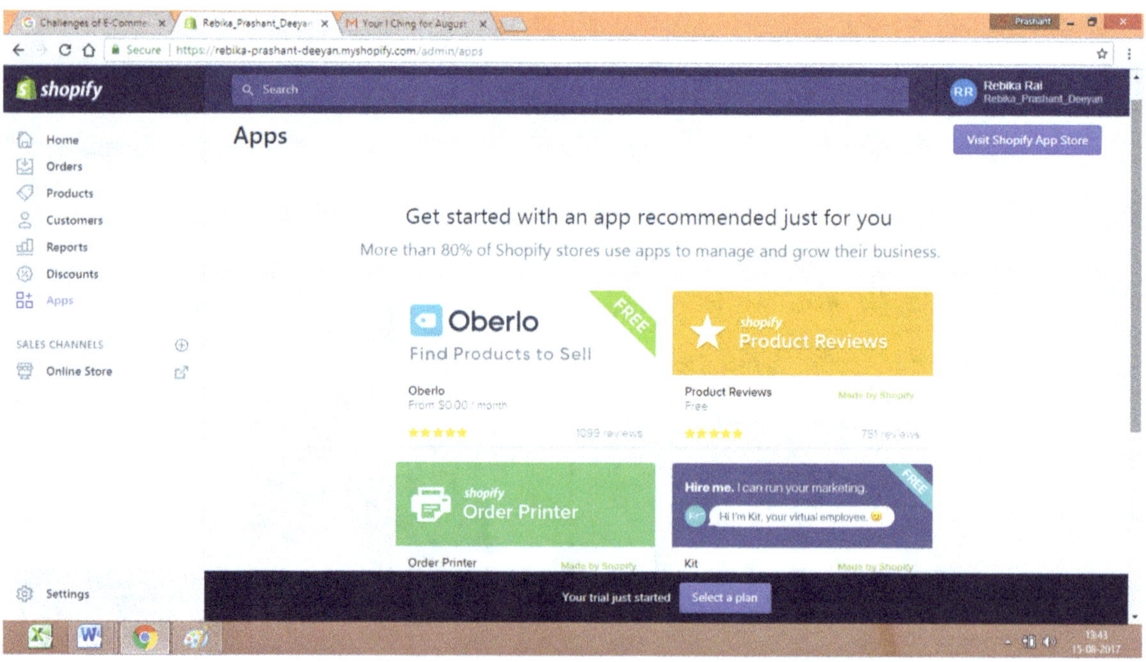

Figure 22. To create customized themes using Shopify

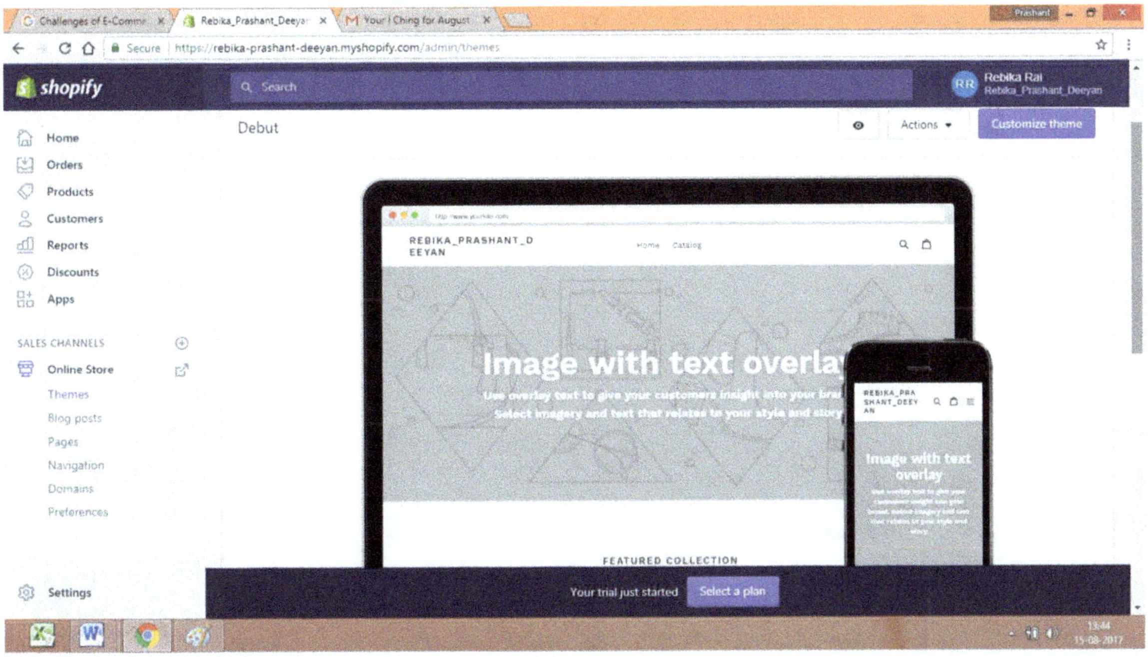

Figure 23. To write blog posts using Shopify

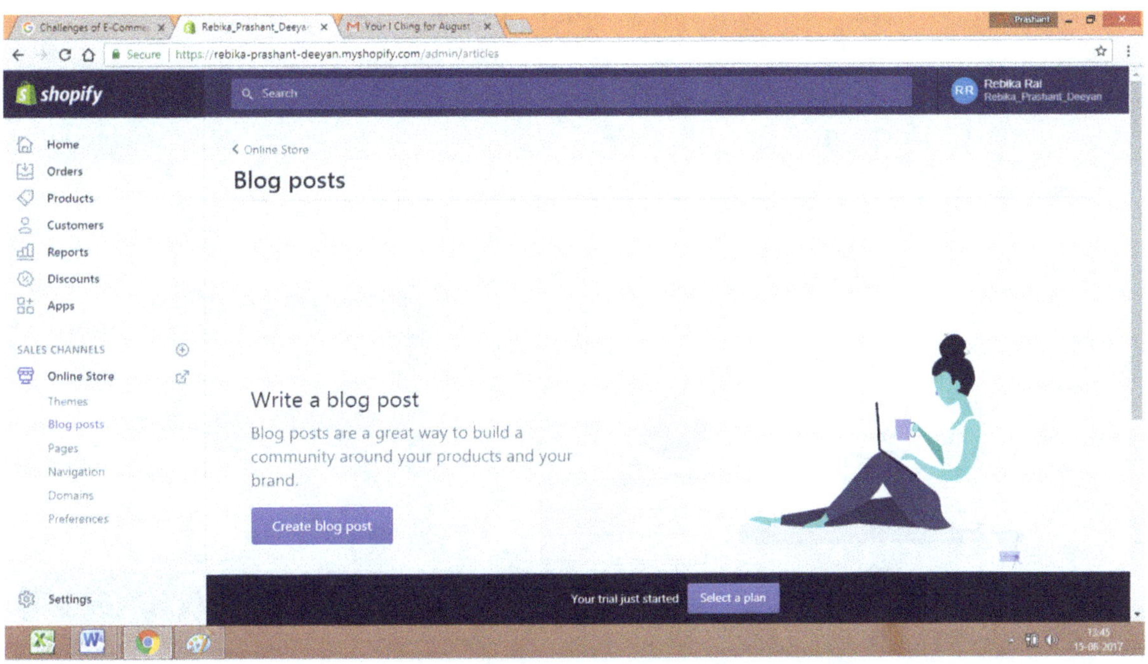

Figure 24. To add pages to the online store using Shopify

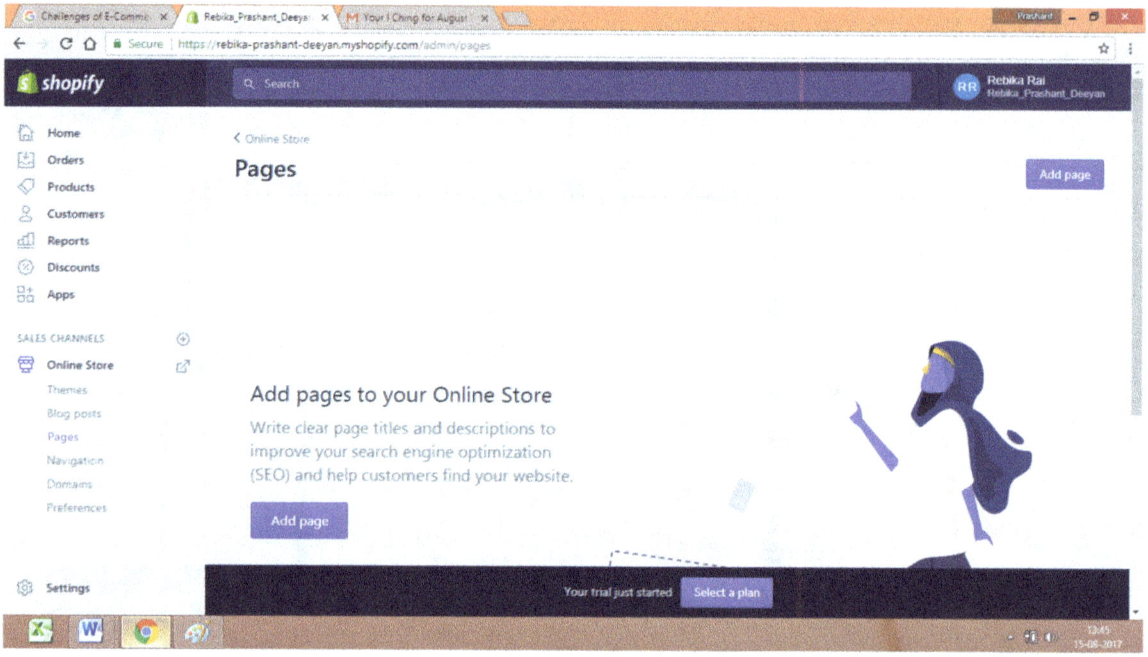

Figure 25. To connect to or but domain using Shopify

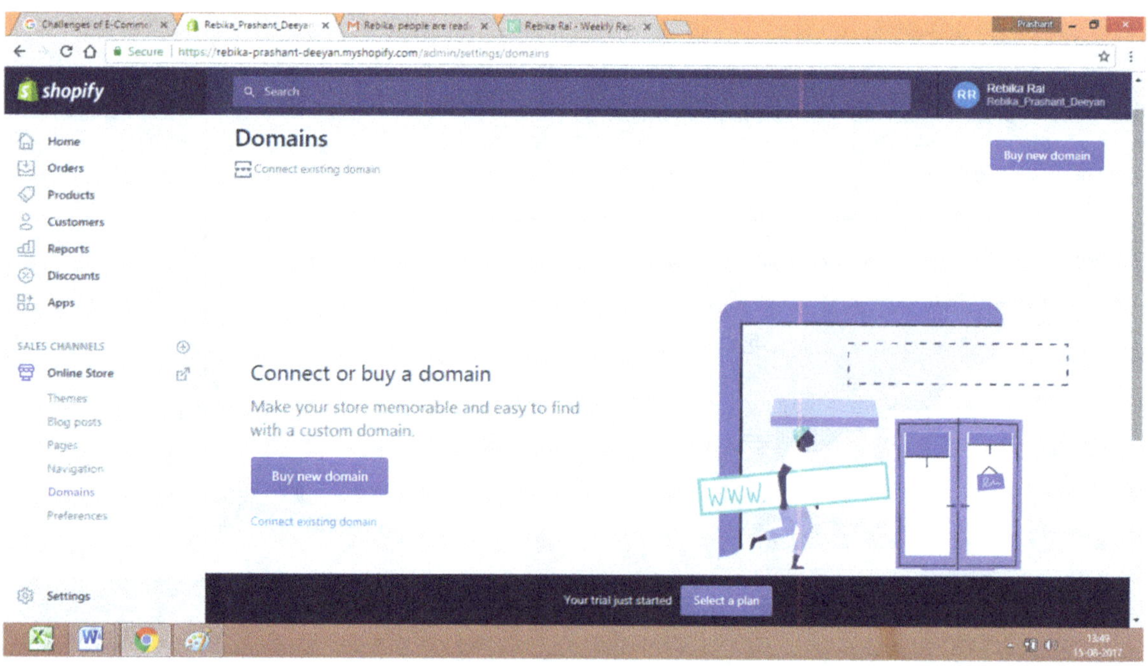

Figure 26. Several setting options using Shopify

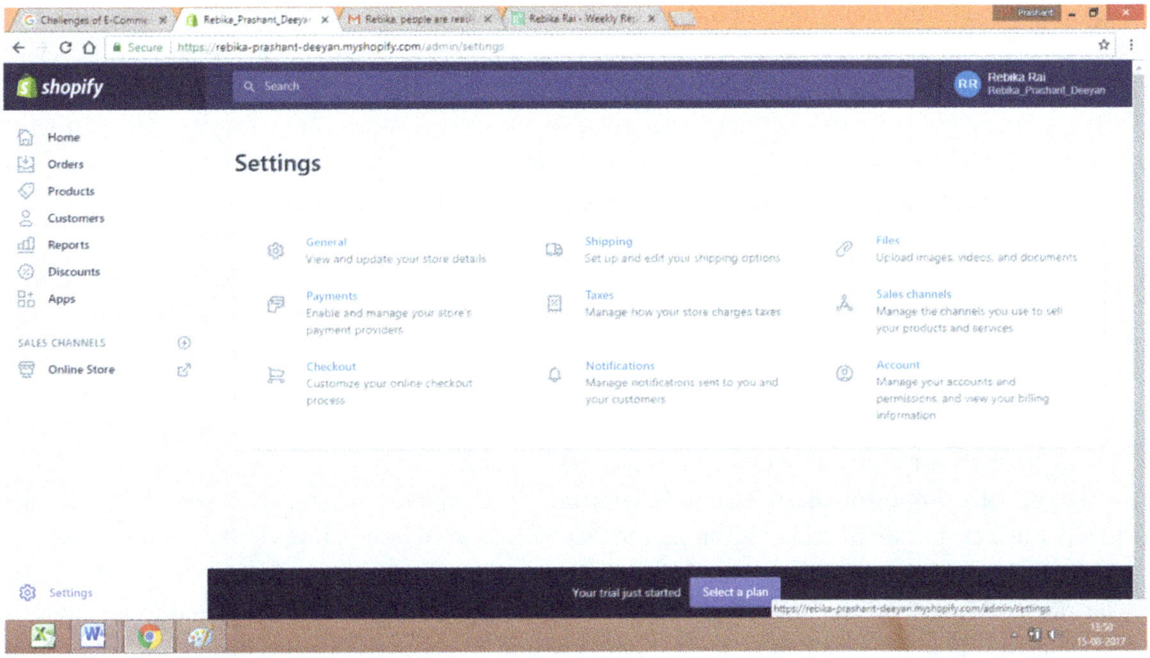

2. **Returning and Refunding of Products:** When the product reaches the customer and customer are unsatisfied if the specification laid by customer does not meet, in such scenario the product is returned. On the other hand, whenever the customer shops online, they always go for the retailers that offers hassle free returns which indicates that customer are conscious about return and refund policy. The company needs to bear the cost of returning of the shipment, which in turn would hamper in terms of reputation of the company. Cost of logistics and shipping has always been scary for those e-commerce sellers who deliver the product for free. Refund and return are part of customer service so in order to solve such problem and reduce the cost of operations, suitable returns management with smooth interaction platform with logistic partners and vendors need to be made available for the customer for stress free return and refund.
3. **Maintaining Customer Loyalty:** The business does not flourish, if the company fails to build and maintain the trust and loyalty of customer for long time. Many E-Commerce organization in spite of it appealing website and whopping sales in different products face the struggle with the customer is because the seller and a buyer doesn't know each other nor they can see each other while making a transaction unlike street-shopping. It takes few transactions, time and plenty of efforts by the company to build the customer trust and loyalty. The solution to such problem could be to provide an excellent service and ensuring the customer is satisfied from the time he / she places the order to shipping to receiving of the shipment. Providing loyalty points for every purchase that customer makes will enforce the customer to use the point in the next purchase. The company in turn can provide the online chat option in the website to cater to needs of the customer and solve the problem instantly enabling the customer to realize that customer satisfaction is more important than profit for the organization.

4. **Customer Problems Being Unnoticed and Unsolved:** As already specified, maintaining customer loyalty towards the company should be the foremost objective of any company especially in the set-up wherein multiple companies are competing and trying to attract customer by their services and offers. In such condition, when the company do not solve neither notice the problems and issues raised by the customer, the customer tends to select some other company for their further purchase. This raises a trust issue. The only solution to this problem is providing an easy interface and proper ticketing solutions; also the companies ensuring that it cater to ever ticket generated and solve the issues raised before anything else.
5. **Competing Against Retailers and Manufacturers:** The basic model for online stores requires buying products from manufacturers or distributors and sell that in retails from their online store. However, some retailers and manufacturers sell products directly to consumers. This leads to competition among retailers and manufacturers. The solution to such problem could be to restrict the manufacturers to sell products directly enforcing certain standard rules and policies; offer the products with some added benefits such as loyalty points.
6. **Struggle of Competing on Price and Shipping:** The competition in terms of price of the products deeply affects the small scale E-Commerce business as their competitors sell the same products at lesser price or huge discounts with free shipping on almost all orders or orders beyond a particular range. Almost, all the online customers gets attracted to higher discounts and free shipping in comparison to high price and some shipping amount to get the same product. To survive in such competitive market, ecommerce companies need to dispense their own inventory to fulfilment warehouses, become extremely resourceful shippers, or find some unique products to minimize this problem.
7. **Finding the Right Products to Sell:** As specified above, due to increase in the competition in the market, the small E-Commerce business is having hard time to compete with big E-Commerce Company to sell the same product wherein the larger company tends to sell the products with huge discount and free shipping. In such state, identifying the unique or right product is the need of an hour and has made it very difficult for retailers to source unique products unless they decide to manufacture on their own.
8. **Generating Targeted Traffic and Capturing Targeted Leads:** Marketing channels are increasing and manufacturers are considering multiple ways to drive the traffic towards their online store in order to make it popular among the different categories of customers. To mark it widely prevalent, the company needs to effectively leverage its existence through email, subscriber list, social media using tools such as Facebook custom audiences, display ads, mobile, shopping engines etc. Retailers must craft the correct message for the right audience in order to convert them into leads with hopes of turning them into customers.
9. **Retaining Customers and Personalization:** Attracting new customers using various means and measures as mentioned above is good for expanding the business and attracting customers however, retaining the current ones that is already in the list is more important. The retailers in turn can come up with offers for such customers to retain such customers by keeping track of such customers and providing them discounts, loyalty points, cashbacks, coupons, free shipping, displaying the list of customer with highest purchase and offering them some gifts etc. Since there are thousands and lacs of product options available on ecommerce websites, it is mandatory to know the buying trend

of a user and suggest better options on what they are looking for by sending personalized e-mails of products relevant to the consumer are important ways to explore and effective for adhering to these trends.

10. **Choosing the Right Technology and Partner:** Some online retailers may face growth challenges because their technology is limiting them or they've hired the wrong partners/agencies to help them manage their projects. Retailers wanting to achieve growth must be built on a good technology foundation. They must choose the right shopping cart solution, inventory management software, email software, CRM systems, analytics and so much more. In addition, hiring the wrong partners or agencies to help you implement projects or oversee marketing campaigns may also limit your growth. Online retailers must choose carefully who to work with.

REFERENCES

35 Key E-Commerce Platform Features. (2009). Retrieved April 4, 2017 from http://www.tokyowebdesigns.com/advice/1192/35-key-e-commerce-platform-features

Comparison of shopping cart software. (n.d.). Retrieved April 11, 2017 from https://en.wikipedia.org/wiki/Comparison_of_shopping_cart_software

History of Ecommerce: How Did It All Begin? (2011). Retrieved on April 4 from http://www.miva.com/blog/the-history-of-ecommerce-how-did-it-all-begin

Huang, Z., & Benyoucef, M. (2013). From e-commerce to social commerce: A close look at design features. *Electronic Commerce Research and Applications*, *12*(4), 246–259. doi:10.1016/j.elerap.2012.12.003

Kame, S. (2015). Electronic Commerce Challenges and Opportunities for Emerging Economies: Case of Egypt. *International Conference on Information Resources Management (CONF-IRM)*, 1-16.

Mitra, J. (2010). *E-Commerce*. Retrieved April 10 from https://www.slideshare.net/jsm268/e-commerce-3717853

Pappas, C. (2015). *Boost your eLearning Course Sales: 5 Tips to choose an eCommerce Platform*. Retrieved April 4, 2017 from https://elearningindustry.com/boost-elearning-course-sales-5-tips-choose-ecommerce-platform

Sarode, R. M. (2015). Future of E-Commerce in India Challenges & Opportunities. *International Journal of Applied Research*, *1*(12), 646–650.

Shopify ecommerce feature list. (n.d.). Retrieved August 12, 2017 from https://www.shopify.in/tour/ecommerce-cms

Stone, J. (2016). *The Best eCommerce Software of 2017*. Retrieved April 12, 2017 from http://www.toptenreviews.com/business/internet/best-ecommerce-software

Yin, L. X. (2008). *The history and evolution of e-commerce*. Retrieved April 6, 2017 form https://ecommerze.wordpress.com/2008/06/12/the-history-and-evoltion-of-e-commerce

KEY TERMS AND DEFINITIONS

Analytics: Involves studying past historical data to research potential trends, to analyze the effects of certain decisions or events, or to evaluate the performance of a given tool or scenario. The goal of analytics is to improve the business by gaining knowledge which can be used to make improvements or changes.

Business Model: A plan for the successful operation of a business, identifying sources of revenue, the intended customer base, products, and details of financing.

E-Commerce: A transaction of buying or selling online. Electronic commerce draws on technologies such as mobile commerce, electronic funds transfer, supply chain management, internet marketing, online transaction processing, electronic data interchange (EDI), inventory management systems, and automated data collection systems.

E-Commerce Software: The engine behind the scenes of an online store, making it possible to easily manage inventory, add or remove products, calculate taxes, and everything else required to manage a website and fulfill orders. It simplifies intricate processes in a friendly user interface that enables people with non-technical backgrounds to oversee an entire ecommerce operation. Despite the ease of use that ecommerce software brings to an online business, it is a multifaceted and complex machine.

Marketing: The action or business of promoting and selling products or services, including market research and advertising.

Open Source Software: Computer software with its source code made available with a license in which the copyright holder provides the rights to study, change, and distribute the software to anyone and for any purpose.

Order Management: The administration of business processes related to order of goods or services. An order management system (OMS) automates and streamlines order processing for businesses.

Payment Gateway: A payment gateway is an ecommerce service that processes credit card payments for online and traditional brick and mortar stores. Payment gateways facilitate these transactions by transferring key information between payment portals such as web-enabled mobile devices/websites and the front-end processor/bank.

Shopping Cart: A shopping cart is a piece of software that acts as an online store's catalog and ordering process. Typically, a shopping cart is the interface between a company's web site and its deeper infrastructure, allowing consumers to select merchandise; review what they have selected; make necessary modifications or additions; and purchase the merchandise.

Transaction: A transaction is an agreement between a buyer and a seller to exchange goods, services, or financial instruments. In simpler words, it is an agreement, contract, exchange, understanding, or transfer of cash or property that occurs between two or more parties and establishes a legal obligation.

Chapter 8
Security Issues in E-Commerce

Arram Sriram
Anurag Group of Institutions, India

Adiraju Prashanth Rao
Anurag Group of Institutions, India

ABSTRACT

E-commerce is selling and buying products in online shopping through the internet. When purchasing the products using internet, many security issues arise. These issues are to be addressed effectively and to be resolved. The security issue is an essential part of any transaction that takes place over the internet. Security becomes paramount not only for retailers but for any business that operates via the internet as the popularity of online shopping grows. This chapter focuses security protocols and their achievements in providing effective communication between end-users and business people.

1. INTRODUCTION

The term E-Commerce refers to the use of an electronic medium to carry out commercial transactions via internet. Now a day's E-Commerce is playing a very vital role in online retail marketing and the number of people using this technology is increasing in leaps and bounds all over the world. The security becomes a paramount as the popularity of online shopping grows exponentially in the present days, not only for retailers but for any business that operates via internet. This leads to numerous security risks for consumers. In present scenario, consumer needs to be very cautious while making any kind of online transactions or even surfing the internet. Common mistakes that leave people vulnerable include shopping on websites that aren't secure, giving out too much personal information, and leaving computers open to viruses. This chapter mainly focuses the e-commerce security issues, security threats and guidelines for safe and secure online shopping through shopping web sites. A consumer can very well secure his online shopping to some extend by religiously following the guidelines mentioned in (Niranjanamurthy & Chahar, 2013). Privacy is a state in which one is not observed or disturbed by other people whereas Security is the action of keeping something secret or the state of being kept secret. So e-commerce security is an essential part of the Information Security Framework which specifically applies to the components that affect e-commerce. These components are generally known as computer security, data security and other realms of the information security framework. The section defines e-commerce and its importance.

DOI: 10.4018/978-1-5225-3646-8.ch008

1.1 What Is Importance of E-Commerce?

E-commerce has shown enormous growth in the last few years. Sources say that the retail e-commerce sales around world will reach 12.8% in the year 2019 from 7.4% in 2015 (Kalakota & Whinston, 1996). E-commerce is rapidly increasing in the businesses all over the world. E-Commerce usage is moving towards uptrend direction and has received much attention from governments, businesses and regional bodies due to enormous increase of internet users.

The E-Commerce Applications are more popular due to the following reasons

- **Time Consuming Process:** It is very convenient for everyone to shop anytime, anywhere and in any device instead of visiting the shops in person. E-commerce proved its importance based on the fact where time is essence. In the commercial markets, time plays an important role to both the business and consumers. From the business perspective, with less time spent during each transaction, more transaction can be achieved on the same day. As for the consumer, they will save up more time during their transaction. Because of this, Ecommerce steps in and replaced the traditional commerce method where a single transaction can cost both parties a lot of valuable time. With just a few clicks in minutes, a transaction or an order can be placed and completed via the internet with ease. For instance, a banking transaction can be completed through the Internet within a few minutes compared to the traditional banking method which may take up to hours. This fact obviously proves that Ecommerce is beneficial to both business and consumer wise as payment and documentations can be completed with greater efficiency.
- **Product Comparisons:** View different products online is much simpler and more efficient than visiting different stores at different places. So researching the products is much easier by accessing different products online i.e. proper product comparison.
- **Reduction in Capital Investment:** Running an e-commerce business requires far less capital investments compared to owning physical shops. No need to invest on recruiting sales staff, rentals for high end retail stores and unwanted overheads. The only responsibility on you have in an online shop is to promote your website and deliver quality products on-time to the customers.
- **Tremendous Increase of Internet Users:** Electronic commerce, or Ecommerce, which literally means business trading through the Internet, has been around the globe since mid 90s. However, until the recent few years, Ecommerce is getting more and more attention from entrepreneur and consumers, both local and international. One of the main reasons is due to the highly successful operations of some well known names on the Internet, such as eBay, Yahoo and Dell. The sales revenue these companies shown in their annual reports are without doubt, one of the biggest factors why Ecommerce is important in the commercial market nowadays.
- **Business View:** Ecommerce is much more cost effective compared to traditional commerce method. This is due to the fact where through Ecommerce, the cost for the middleperson to sell their products can be saved and diverted to another aspect of their business. One example is the giant computer enterprise, Dell, which practice such a method by running most of their business through internet without involving any third parties. Aside from that, marketing for Ecommerce can achieve a better customer to cost ratio as putting an advertisement on the internet is comparably much cheaper than putting up a roadside banner or filming a television commercial. For Ecommerce, the total overheads needed to run the business is significantly much less compared to the traditional commerce method. The reason due to that is where most of the cost can be reduced

in Ecommerce. For example, in running an Ecommerce business, only a head office is needed rather than a head office with a few branches to run the business. In addition to that, most of the cost for staff, maintenance, communications and office rental can be substitute by a single cost, web hosting for the Ecommerce business.

To both the consumers and business, connectivity plays an important part as it is the key factor determining the whole business. From the business point of view, Ecommerce provides better connectivity for its potential customer as their respective website can be accessed virtually from anywhere through Internet. This way, more potential customers can get in touch with the company's business and thus, eliminating the limits of geographical location. From the customer standpoint, Ecommerce is much more convenient as they can browse through a whole directories of catalogues without any hassle, compare prices between products, buying from another country and on top of that, they can do it while at home or at work, without any necessity to move a single inch from their chair. Besides that, for both consumers and business, Ecommerce proves to be more convenient as online trading has less red tape compared to traditional commerce method.

In global market sense, the appearance of Ecommerce as a pioneer has opened up various windows of opportunities for a variety of other companies and investors. For instance, due to the booming of Ecommerce, more and more resources are being directed into electronic securities, internet facilities, business plans and new technologies. In result of this phenomenon, a variety of new markets have emerged from Ecommerce itself giving a boost to the global market. In short, if without any major obstacles, Ecommerce will certainly continue to mature in the global market and eventually, it will become an essential business plan for a company in order to survive and stay competitive in the ever changing market. The next section presents e-commerce applications and its usage.

1.2 E-Commerce Applications and Its Usages

Electronic commerce is the process of conducting commercial transactions electronically over the Internet (Kalakota & Whinston, 1996). This process is carried out primarily in five levels, and the main aspect of e-commerce is a merchant selling products or service to the consumers. There are five major segments under the broader category of e-business. However, the following are some popular e-commerce models used by companies engaged in e-commerce:

- Business to business e-commerce (B2B).
- Business to consumers e-commerce (B2C).
- Consumers to consumers e-commerce (C2C).
- Business to employees e-commerce (B2E).
- Consumer to business e-commerce (C2B).

1.2.1 Business to Business E-Commerce (B2B)

E-business is the process of conducting business on the Internet. Its scope includes not only buying and selling but also services, fulfilling the needs of customers and collaborating with business partners. Business to business e-commerce is smart business. The opportunity for business to business e-commerce is even greater. A wholesaler may sell products to the retailer. There is advanced e-commerce software which support multi-tier pricing. This helps to set up online stores to offer preferred pricing to some vendors and shared price to others. This includes internet-enabled initiatives of an enterprise to form commercial linkages with another enterprise, dealer, warehouse or manufacturer. In this form of e-commerce, e paperwork and time-to-market get vastly reduced. Throughout the world, this e-commerce mode is the biggest.

In a B2B transaction, the interaction is between businesses. For example, a website that is catching for the steel industry might have facility for buyers and sellers to list their requirements and post their products. It helps them in quickly closing the transactions and the buyer can get quality, material and can choose from different suppliers.

B2B commerce is a growing business in the e-commerce arena- with the increasing use of the internet, more and more business are realizing the commercial advantage of giving business clients a streamlined and easy manner to order products or service online. It facilitates access to the ordering process to only those with whom a concern has a commercial relationship.

Business to Business e-commerce provides small and medium enterprises (SMES) with an excellent opportunity to access new markets, improve customer service and reduce costs. And while hurdles exist, they should be viewed more as speed breakers rather than road barriers. As a medium of information storage and dissemination, the internet has and is emerging a clear winner. Its rate of penetration has far outpaced the growth of other popular media such as newspaper, radio and television. B2B transactions are however relatively high value in nature and organizations are slow to change their traditional systems for the supply chain management. The reasons for the growth in B2B e-commerce are many. In an increasing competitive scenario, e-commerce offers highly attractive cost saving options. The shift to this process is often driven by the needs of buyers. Innovative methods of enhancing B2B and B2C levels of e-commerce include:

- CD-ROM catalogues that are linked to the user's online catalogue, enabling him to browse offline and order online.
- Kiosks placed at physical store locations or in shopping malls to introduce users to the easy online ordering options.
- Extranets to link businesses together that conduct regular business to .business transactions and
- Affiliate programmes to drive business to your commerce site from other content related sites.

B2B e-commerce is expected to be the largest mode of transacting e-business and is a global phenomenon. It involves taking internet enabled initiatives to form commercial links with other enterprises, dealers or manufacturers. In this form of e-commerce, a business firm places orders for supplies with another business firms directly over the Internet. Paperwork and time required for processing the order and delivery of the goods are thus reduced to a great extent.

1.2.2 Business to Consumers E-Commerce (B2C)

It is for the customers to buy stores from the web. The problem to be recognized in this is to secure payment, using encryption, transaction integrity, quick response, time and reliability.B2C e-commerce involves selling of goods and services to consumers or end users. It allows them to browse the product catalogue, select products or services and complete the order online. In a B2C transaction, the interaction is between a consumer and the preferred business. For example, the most popular site is amazon.com, which is the first online bookseller who has proved a potential competitor to the traditional bricks and mortar booksellers such as Barrens and Noble. In this category of e-commerce, businesses use the internet to offer to consumers sales and services around the world 24 hours a day, seven days a week and 365 days a year, The sites Amazon, Rediff and Uphar are among those belonging to this category. These websites are meant for selling goods directly to consumers through the internet. The two-way accessibility of the internet enables operating companies to directly ascertain customer preference and buying trends. Businesses are using these consumer insights to formulate marketing strategies and offer to the customers what they want and when they want. E-business in this mode significantly reduces the costs associated with intermediaries, service centres and mass marketing campaigns. Since e-commerce makes just in time delivery possible, the supplier does not have to store the goods. He can procure them from the suppliers as and when he gets the order from the buyer through the internet.

B2C is the most popular form of e-commerce, wherein the individuals are directly involved in B2C e-commerce, and businesses use the internet for offering their products or services 24 hours a day through global access. The sites Amazon.com and Rediff are among these. These websites spell goods directly to consumers over the Internet. The two way accessibility feature of the internet enables operating companies to ascertain consumer preferences and buying trends directly.

1.2.3 Consumer to Consumer E-Commerce (C2C)

Here interaction is between consumers to consumer. For example, in sites like e-Buy Bid or Buy.com, Baazi.com which are auction sites, one can virtually sell and buy any goods (either used or new ones). This form of e-commerce is nothing but the cyber version of the good old auction houses. If anyone wants to sell anything, all one has to do is post a message on the site, giving details of the product and the expected price and wait for an interested customer to turn up and buy it. The buyer gets in touch with the seller through the Internet and the deal is crossed once the amount is finalized. Online message boards and barters are also examples of C2C e-commerce.

1.2.4 Consumer-to-Business E-Commerce (C2B)

E-commerce, by empowering the customer, has been strategically redefining business. An example of C2B model of e-commerce is the site Price line.Com, which allows prospective airline travelers, tourists in need of hotel reservations etc. to visit its websites and indicate their preferred price for travel between any two cities. If an airline is willing to issue a ticket on the customers offered price, the consumer can then travel to the mentioned destination at his terms.

1.2.5 Business to Employees E-Commerce (B2E)

This is concerned more with marketing a corporation's internal processes more efficiently. Customer care and support activities also hold ground. The requirement is that are all self-service with applications on the web that the employees can use themselves.

2. WHY SECURITY PLAY MAJOR ROLE IN E-COMMERCE APPLICATIONS

Security is an essential part of any transaction that takes place over the internet. Customer will lose his/her faith in e-business if its security is compromised. Following are the essential requirements for safe e-payments/transactions –

- **Confidential:** Information should not be accessible to unauthorized person. It should not be intercepted during transmission.
- **Integrity:** Information should not be altered during its transmission over the network.
- **Availability:** Information should be available wherever and whenever requirement within time limit specified.
- **Authenticity:** There should be a mechanism to authenticate user before giving him/her access to required information.
- **Non-Reputability:** It is protection against denial of order or denial of payment. Once a sender sends a message, the sender should not able to deny sending the message. Similarly the recipient of message should not be able to deny receipt.
- **Encryption:** Information should be encrypted and decrypted only by authorized user.
- **Auditability:** Data should be recorded in such a way that it can be audited for integrity requirements.
- Major security measures are following:
- **Encryption:** It is a very effective and practical way to safeguard the data being transmitted over the network. Sender of the information encrypt the data using a secret code and specified receiver only can decrypt the data using the same or different secret code.
- **Digital Signature:** Digital signature ensures the authenticity of the information. A digital signature is an e-signature authentic authenticated through encryption and password.
- **Security Certificates:** Security certificate is unique digital id used to verify identity of an individual website or user.

3. E-COMMERCE THREATS

Threats: Anyone with the capability, technology, opportunity, and intent to do harm.Potential threats can be foreign or domestic, internal or external, state-sponsored or a single rogue element. Terrorists, insiders, disgruntled employees, and hackers are included in this profile (President's Commission on Critical Infrastructure Protection).

Table 1.

Concern	2001	2000
Loss of Privacy/confidentiality, data misuse/abuse	28%	25%
Cracking, eavesdropping, spoofing, root kits	25%	20%
Viruses, Trojans, worms, hostile ActiveX and Java	21%	26%
System unavailability, denial of service, natural disasters, power interruptions	18%	20%

1. Intellectual property threats -- use existing materials found on the Internet without the owner's permission, e.g., music downloading, domain name (cyber squatting), software pirating
2. Client computer threats
    a. Trojan horse
    b. Active contents
    c. Viruses
3. Communication channel threats
    a. Sniffer program
    b. Backdoor
    c. Spoofing
    d. Denial-of-service
4. Server threats
    a. Privilege setting
    b. Server Side Include (SSI), Common Gateway Interface (CGI)
    c. File transfer
    d. Spamming

Countermeasure

A procedure that recognizes, reduces, or eliminates a threat:

1. Intellectual property protection
    a. Legislature
    b. Authentication
2. Client computer protection
    a. Privacy -- Cookie blockers; Anonymizer
    b. Digital certificate
    c. Browser protection
    d. Antivirus software
    e. Computer forensics expert
3. Communication channel protection
    a. Encryption
    b. Public-key encryption (asymmetric) vs Private-key encryption (symmetric).
    c. Encryption standard: Data Encryption Standard (DES), Advanced Encryption Standard (AES).
    d. Protocol
4. Secure Sockets Layer (SSL)
5. Secure Hyper Text Transfer Protocol (S-HTTP)
    a. Digital signature.
    b. Bind the message originator with the exact contents of the message.
    c. A hash function is used to transform messages into a 128-bit digest (message digest).
    d. The sender's private key is used to encrypt the message digest (digital signature).
    e. The message + signature are sent to the receiver.
    f. The recipient uses the hash function to recalculate the message digest.
    g. The sender's public key is used to decrypt the message digest.
    h. Check to see if the recalculated message digest = decrypted message digest.

6. Server protection
    a. Access control and authentication
    b. Digital signature from user
    c. Username and password
    d. Access control list
    e. Firewalls
    f. International Computer Security Association's classification:
7. Packet filter firewall: checks IP address of incoming packet and rejects anything that does not match the list of trusted addresses (prone to IP spoofing).
8. Application level proxy server: examines the application used for each individual IP packet (e.g., HTTP, FTP) to verify its authenticity.
9. Stateful packet inspection: examines all parts of the IP packet to determine whether or not to accept or reject the requested communication.

4. SECURITY ISSUES IN E-COMMERCE APPLICATION

4.1 E-Commerce Security Threats

The direct threats to e-commerce servers can be classified as malicious code threats and transmission threats. (Gautam, 2014). Malicious or rogue programming code is introduced into the server in order to gain access to the system resources. Very often, the intent of malicious code attacks is to cause large scale damage to the e-commerce server. With transmission threats, the threats and risks can be classified as either as active or passive. With passive threats, the main goal is to listen (or eavesdrop) to transmissions to the server. With active threats, the intent is to alter the flow of data transmission or to create a rogue transmission aimed directly at the e-commerce server.

1. **Malicious Code Attacks: Viruses and Worms:** A virus attaches itself to executable code and is executed when the software program begins to run or an infected file is opened. However, a worm does not need a host to replicate. Rather, the worm replicates itself through the internet, and can literally infect millions of computers on a global basis in just a matter of hours. Worms by themselves do not cause damage to a system like a virus does. However, worms can shut down parts of the internet or ecommerce servers, because they can use up valuable resources of the internet, as well as the memory and processing power of servers and other computers.
2. **Trojan Horses:** A Trojan horse is a piece of programming code that is layered behind another program, and can perform covert, malicious functions. For example, your e-commerce server can display a "cool-looking" screen saver, but behind that could be a piece of hidden code, causing damage to your system. One way to get a Trojan horse attack is by downloading software from the internet. Make sure that whatever software is downloaded comes from an authentic and verified source, and that all defense mechanisms are activated on your server.
3. **Logic Bombs:** A logic bomb is a version of a Trojan horse, however, it is event or time specific. For example, a logic bomb will release malicious or rogue code in an e-commerce server after some specific time has elapsed or a particular event in application or processing has occurred.

4. **Transmission Threats - Denial of Service Attacks:** With a denial of service attack, the main intention is to deny your customers the services provided on your e-commerce server. This happens when a massive amount of invalid data is sent to the server. Because the server can handle and process so much information at any given time, it is unable to keep with the information and data overflow. As a result, the server becomes "confused", and subsequently shuts down. Ping of death: With a ping of death attack, a massive data packet is sent to the server. As a result, the memory buffers of the e-commerce server are totally overloaded, thus causing it to crash. SYN flooding: A SYN flood is a form of denial-of-service attack in which an attacker sends a succession of SYN requests to a target's system in an attempt to consume enough server resources to make the system unresponsive to legitimate traffic Ip spoofing: The intent here is to change the source address of a data packet to give it the appearance that it originated from another computer. With ip spoofing, it is difficult to identify the real attacker, since all e-commerce server logs will show connections from a legitimate source.
5. **E-Commerce Security Tools Firewalls (For Software and Hardware):** A firewall is a system designed to prevent unauthorized access to or from a private network. Firewalls can be implemented in both hardware and software, or a combination of both. Firewalls are frequently used to prevent unauthorized internet users from accessing private networks connected to the internet, especially intranets. All messages entering or leaving the intranet pass through the firewall, which examines each message and blocks those that do not meet the specified security criteria. Public key infrastructure: A pki (public key infrastructure) enables users of a basically unsecure public network such as the internet to securely and privately exchange data and money through the use of a public and a private cryptographic key pair that is obtained and shared through a trusted authority. Encryption software: Encryption software is software whose main task is encryption and decryption of data, usually in the form of files on (or sectors of) hard drives and removable media, email messages, or in the form of packets sent over computer networks. It is a very effective and practical way to safeguard the data being transmitted over the network. Sender of the information encrypts the data using a secret code and specified receiver only can decrypt the data using the same or different secret code. Digital signature: Digital signature ensures the authenticity of the information. A digital signature is a e-signature authentic authenticated through encryption and password. Security certificates: Security certificate is unique digital id used to verify identity of an individual website or user.
6. **Guidelines to Shop Online Safely Shop at Secure Web Sites:** A secure web site uses encryption and authentication standards to protect the confidentiality of information sent during web transactions. A secure web page can be identified using following guidelines:
    a. The url of a secure webpage begins with the letters https.
    b. Ensure that the address bar has some element of green in it. Different browsers use different elements. Microsoft's internet explorer - background is shaded green. Apple's Safari and Google's Chrome - https is shaded green.
    c. Look for a closed padlock. If that lock is open, you should assume it is not a secure site. Most web browsers display the 'lock' icon somewhere in the window of the browser. Microsoft's internet explorer displays a lock in the lower-right of the browser window. Mozilla's Firefox displays the lock icon in the lower-left corner of the window. The lock is not just a picture. You can click or double click on it to see details of the site's security. This is important because some fraudulent sites are built with a bar at the bottom of the page to imitate the lock icon of your browser.

7. **Investigate About the Web Site Before You Order:** Avoid doing business with unknown web sites. If you are going to deal with a web site for the first time, do your homework before buying their products. Start business with an unknown website by ordering something inexpensive. This will help you judge the authenticity of the web site. Reliable web sites should advertise their physical business address and contact number, either customer service or an order line. Call the phone number and ask questions to determine if the business is legitimate.
8. **Read the Web Site's Privacy and Security Policies:** Every reputable online web site offers information about how it processes your order. It is usually listed in the section entitled ——privacy policy (Shopping Online, 2014). Reputable companies will be open about how they collect data from you and what they do with it. Many now also belong to web-seal approval or trust mark programs that set out guidelines on the treatment of your information.
9. **Use Safe Payment Options:** Credit cards are generally the safest option because they allow buyers to seek a credit from the issuer if the product isn't delivered or isn't what was ordered (StaySafeOnline, n.d.) Also, unlike debit cards, credit cards may have a limit on the monetary amount you will be responsible for paying if your information is stolen and used by someone else. Never send cash through the mail or use a money-wiring service because you'll have no recourse if something goes wrong. Don't forget to review return policies. You want a no-hassle ability to return items.
10. **Use Virtual Credit Cards as Needed:** Virtual credit cards are temporary payment cards, and come in the form of a physical plastic card, or as a generated credit card number, and they're separate from your bank information (ITProPortal, n.d.). This type of disposable credit card payment method contains a pre-set spending amount, has a shorter-than-usual expiration date, and is equivalent to a regular credit card for most payments purposes. Virtual credit card payments are usually charged to your credit or debit card, rather than directly to your bank account, essentially offering an additional layer of protection. When you pay with a virtual credit card, your banking information remains separate from your individual purchase, thus ensuring if the card number is stolen, hackers cannot access your accounts or re-use the card fraudulently.
11. **Disclose Only the Bare Facts When You Order:** When making a purchase online, there is certain information that you must provide to the web merchant such as your name and address. Often, a merchant will try to obtain more information about you. They may ask questions about your leisure lifestyle or annual income. Be alert to the kinds of information being collected to complete the transaction. Make sure you think it is necessary for the vendor to request that information. Remember, you only need to fill out required fields on a vendors checkout form. Before providing personal or financial information, make sure you understand how your information will be stored and used. The information you provide is used to target you for marketing purposes. It can lead to "spam" or even direct mail and telephone solicitations. Don't answer any question you feel is not require to process your order. Often, the web site will mark which questions need to be answered with an asterisk (*).
12. **Keep Your Password Private:** You will usually be asked for a password before you make an online payment. This is to help keep your personal details private. (BBC, 2013). Make sure you use a strong password - one that is a combination of letters (upper and lower case), numbers and symbols. Never reveal your password to anyone. When selecting a password, do not use commonly known information, such as your birthdate, mother's maiden name, or numbers from your driver's license or social security number. Do not reuse the same password for other sites, particularly sites associated with sensitive information.

13. **Don't Fall for "Phishing" Messages:** Phishing is the process whereby someone attempts to obtain your confidential information, such as your passwords, your credit card number, your bank account details or other information protected by the data protection act. A phishing attack can be in the form of an official looking email or instant message, maybe directing you to an official looking website, or it could be an official sounding phone call. Recognizing a phishing attack There are number of clues that may indicate an email or website is not genuine such as:
    a. Suspicious email links. Try hovering your mouse over a link without clicking on it. If the address that pops up does not match the link address as it is written in the email, it's a clear indication of a phishing email.
    b. A link to a genuine website which takes you somewhere else.
    c. Spelling or grammatical mistakes, inappropriate use of capitals or exclamation marks, formatting errors.
    d. A generic email greeting.
    e. Claims that you need to act immediately to prevent something bad from happening (for example, your account will be deleted or your email will be lost).
    f. Requests for personal information, such as your password or bank account number However, you should always be wary as some phishing attacks may be sophisticated and difficult to spot. You should refuse to disclose confidential information until you have checked to your own satisfaction that the request is justified and legitimate and has been made by a genuine person or organization. There are various phishing filters, like smart screen filter in internet explorer, which will help protect you from phishing sites by warning you when it detects a distrustful website.
14. **Always Print or Save Copies of Your Orders:** Print and save records of your online transactions, including the product description, price, online receipt, terms of the sale, and copies of any email exchange with the seller. (StaySafeOnline, n.d.). If you cannot print one off, take a screenshot as a form of proof of purchase. We recommend you print out or save a copy of the web page(s) describing the item you ordered as well as the page showing company name, postal address, phone number, and legal terms, including return policy. Read your credit card statements as soon as you get them to make sure there aren't any unauthorized charges. If there is a discrepancy, call your bank and report it immediately TURN YOUR COMPUTER OFF WHEN YOU'RE FINISHED SHOPPING Many people leave their computers running and connected to the internet all day and night. This gives scammers 24/7 access to your computer to install malware and commit cybercrimes. To be safe, turn off your computer when it's not in use.

FIND OUT ABOUT BILLING, GUARANTEES, CANCELLATION POLICIES, SHIPPING AND DELIVERY CHARGES BEFORE YOU BUY You can look for following information:

1. Packaging costs, delivery costs etc.
2. Whether you will be billed before or after delivery of the products.
3. Whether you can track the item from the moment of purchase to arrival at your door - this will help alert you of any hiccups in the delivery.
4. Whether the product comes with a guarantee or warranty for defects etc.
5. How you can return the product if it doesn't work or meet your expectations - look for information on the site about cancellations, returns and refunds. Print off a copy for future reference.

6. Who will bear the cost of returning the item (postage, fees etc.) KNOW HOW ONLINE AUCTIONS OPERATE Online auctions connect buyers and sellers, allowing them to communicate in a bidding process over items for sale (Privacy Rights Clearinghouse, 2000). For the most part, online auction sites are a safe way to exchange goods. But it makes sense to be cautious and aware. Online auctions can be a lot of fun and can also help you find good deals. They also attract scammers. Scammers will often try to get you to deal outside of online auction sites. They may claim the winner of an auction that you were bidding on has pulled out and offer the item to you. Once you have paid, you will never hear from them again and the auction site will not be able to help you. Following are the guidelines for participating safely in online auctions:
    a. Always conduct transactions within the auction website and avoid private contact with buyers or sellers-scammers will often use this ploy to 'offer a better deal'.
    b. Keep printed and/or electronic records of all bids, item descriptions, emails to and from the seller, and transaction records or receipts.
    c. If the website uses a feedback rating system, check all comments left by previous buyers and sellers.
    d. Use a secure payment method.
    e. Avoid money transfers and direct debit, because they can be open to abuse.
    f. Consider using the insurance offered by the auction facility.
    g. Check the information on auction websites to help potential buyers and sellers.
    h. Take the time to read the information about ways to reduce the risk on the auction site and the terms and conditions of contracts entered into by bidders and sellers.
    i. Learn a site's return policy, as it may be difficult to return merchandise bought at auction. It's critical to check the policy, because you may be required to follow the seller's refund policy, rather than that of the auction site.

BE AWARE OF DYNAMIC PRICING Dynamic pricing is a blanket term for any shopping experience where the price of an item fluctuates frequently based on complicated algorithms (CSMonitor, n.d.). Some online retailers use dynamic pricing to engage in price discrimination by charging different prices to different consumers for identical goods or services. While online shopping enables consumers to easily compare prices, it also allows businesses to collect detailed information about a customer's purchasing history and preferences. Online stores can use that information to customize the prices they charge you. Online merchants can easily implement dynamic pricing by placing cookies on a customer's computer which will track the user's past interactions with the site. By using this information, sites can customize their interactions based on your past activities. Online stores can read the cookies on your browser to determine what products or services you searched for and bought and how much you paid for them. This information helps them to predict how much you might they visit the issuer's site. As a rule of thumb, assume all shared wi-fi networks are unsafe for your sensitive data. Everything from an online bank statement to a gmail account can be compromised when surfing the web on a shared wi-fi network. It's nearly impossible to accurately gauge how secure a wi-fi network is, and thus it's best to err on the side of caution. (Kamanec, 2013).

PROTECT YOUR ONLINE IDENTITY ON THE SOCIAL FRONT Online purchasing is getting more and more social, with 50 per cent of web sales projected to occur via social media by 2015 (Kamanec, 2013). Each time you join a new site through the "login with face book" option, you're extending your online identity further. In fact, an abundance of sites will first prompt you to become a member not by email, but by connecting a social media account. Is it a direct connection? Technically, no. Will it be used to shape your online identity? Absolutely. Your social media presence defines your digital footprint to the point where companies are looking to use your social media identity to combat online payment fraud and your social signals to tackle identity fraud in the near future. Once you realize that the majority of your online activity is interconnected, you can better defend yourself from making thoughtless choices that may endanger your data. Just like you shouldn't post something you don't want your employer to see on face book, you also shouldn't post anything you don't want a hacker to see, like a picture of your driver's license or passport, anything with a home address and any snapshots that include a visible credit card or credit card number.

5. SECURITY PROTOCOLS IN INTERNET

Following are the popular protocols used over the internet which ensures security of transactions made over the internet.

5.1 Secure Socket Layer (SSL)

It is the most commonly used protocol and is widely used across the industry. It meets following security requirements –

- Authentication
- Encryption
- Integrity
- Non-reputability

"https://" is to be used for HTTP urls with SSL, where as "http:/" is to be used for HTTP urls without SSL.

5.2 Secure Hypertext Transfer Protocol (SHTTP)

SHTTP extends the HTTP internet protocol with public key encryption, authentication and digital signature over the internet. Secure HTTP supports multiple security mechanism providing security to end users. SHTTP works by negotiating encryption scheme types used between client and server.

5.3 Secure Electronic Transaction

It is a secure protocol developed by MasterCard and Visa in collaboration. Thereoritically, it is the best security protocol. It has following components:

- **Card Holder's Digital Wallet Software:** Digital Wallet allows card holder to make secure purchases online via point and click interface.

- **Merchant Software:** This software helps merchants to communicate with potential customers and financial institutions in secure manner.
- **Payment Gateway Server Software:** Payment gateway provides automatic and standard payment process. It supports the process for merchant's certificate request.
- **Certificate Authority Software:** This software is used by financial institutions to issue digital certificates to card holders and merchants and to enable them to register their account agreements for secure electronic commerce.

5.4 How to Minimize Security Threats

1. Perform a risk assessment ◇ a list of information assets and their value to the firm
2. Develop a security policy ◇ a written statement on:
3. what assets to protect from whom?
4. why these assets are being protected?
5. who is responsible for what protection?
6. which behaviors are acceptable and unacceptable?
7. Develop an implementation plan ◇ a set of action steps to achieve security goals
8. Create a security organization ◇ a unit to administer the security policy
9. Perform a security audit ◇ a routine review of access logs and evaluation of security procedures

5.5 Security Measures

1. **Secure Electronic Transaction (SET) Protocol:** Developed jointly by MasterCard and Visa with the goal of providing a secure payment environment for the transmission of credit card data.

SET payment transaction:

- A shopper makes a purchase and transmits encrypted billing information with his/her digital certificate to the merchant.
- The merchant transfers the SET-coded transaction to a payment card-processing center.
- The processing center decrypts the transaction.
- A certification authority certifies the digital certificate as belonging to the shopper.

Table 2.

Features	*SSL*	*SET*
Encryption of data during transmission	Yes	Yes
Confirmation of message integrity	Yes	Yes
Authentication of merchant	Yes	Yes
Authentication of consumer	No	Yes
Transmission of specific data only on a "need know" basis	No	Yes
Inclusion of bank or trusted third party in transaction	No	Yes
No need for merchant to secure credit card data internally	No	Yes

- The processing center routes the transaction to the shopper's bank for approval.
- The merchant receives notification from the shopper's bank that the transaction is approved.
- The shopper's payment card account is charged for the transaction amount.
- The merchant ships the merchandize and transmits the transaction amount to the merchant's bank for deposit.

2. **Disposable Credit Numbers:** One-time-use credit card numbers (private payment number) are transmitted to the merchant
    a. Register with American Express or Discover
    b. Download software (a Private Payment icon tray will be displayed on the screen)
    c. Shop online
    d. Click on the Private Payment icon
    e. Log-in
    f. Select the credit card to be used
    g. View unique, one-time-use credit card number and expiration date
    h. Enter the one-time-used credit card number and expiration date into merchant's standard form

6. ONLINE BANKING APPLICATION (E-COMMERCE AND BANKING INDUSTRY)

Structure:

1. Objectives
2. Introduction to Electronic Commerce and Banking
3. Changing Dynamics in the Banking Industry
4. Home Banking Implementation Approaches
5. Open versus Closed System
6. Management Issues in Online Banking

6.1 Objectives

The motive of this chapter is to present an introduction to Electronic Commerce and Banking Industry and within that framework the key e-banking concepts, changing dynamics, implementation approaches, and management issues in the banking industry are discussed.

After going through this lesson, you will be able to:

- Describe the concept of electronic banking.
- Explain the changing market structure and customer needs in banking industry.
- Differentiate between online banking and electronic banking.
- Discuss the management issues related to online banking.
- Describe some of the marketing and pricing related issues in online banking.

6.2 Introduction to Electronic Commerce and Banking

The decade of 90s has witnessed a sea change in the way of doing banking. The scenario has been improving at a very fast pace as electronic commerce (e-commerce) is receiving more and more attention in the banking industry. Technology has made a tremendous impact on this industry by reducing operating costs and also by providing adequate customer services. To some extent, the intense interest of bankers in electronic banking (e-banking) reflects a more general interest in the role of the internet as a vehicle for commercial activity. At its core, e-banking involves the collection, storage, transfer and processing of information assets and internet is an incredibly powerful and efficient tool for handling these information processes.

'Anywhere banking' and *'Anytime banking'* have become a reality. There is no specific online banking region to which the transactions are limited. Bookkeeping is simplified and automated and so is tax computation. Bills are paid with a minimum of effort. E-banking offers a wider outreach for banking institutions. E-banking is most useful when it saves the consumer time and money. It is particularly useful for those who have a lot of bills to pay and already use a personal financial program like Intuit's Quicken or Microsoft Money. The need for e-banking is continuously increasing as more and more consumers gain addiction to doing their banking transaction the quick and easy way. Moreover, since e-banking business is secure, many commercial concerns are also turning to doing their banking via the Internet.

E-banking makes use of electronic currency. Check cards or debit cards, smart cards or stored-value cards, digital cash and digital checks are the different types of electronic currency. If anyone uses a check card to make purchases, the funds are transferred immediately from his/her account to the company's account. Smart cards have a specific amount of credit embedded in it. The chip in the card contains both personal and financial information of the user. Digital cash is one way of allowing consumers make purchases over the Internet instead of using a credit card. Digital checks are used with electronic bill paying services. Consumers can use personal finance software packages or they can use software provided by a bank.

Loans are now marketed as products, with a number of value–added services attached to them. Banks are selling mutual funds, providing education loans, car loans, home loans, credit cards and debit cards. There have been associations with petroleum companies, airline companies, hospitality industry, and media houses to promote products and services.

Restructuring in the banking arena is already in progress. If banks are talking anytime, anywhere service for their customers, they are changing their organizations to fit in with the new reality of making them more productive and function driven. Public sector banks are also reorienting themselves to change their profile to be able to raise fresh capital from the market.

The Internet is an extremely efficient device for banks of all sizes to collect and to manage information in order to meet the various financial needs of individuals and businesses, in particular by integrating services or "bundling" them together. On one hand, the Internet allows financial firms of different sizes to enter markets and reach customers previously out of reach to them. On the other hand, there are substantial economies of scale and scope in data storage and data processing, and larger banks are better positioned to exploit these scales and scope economies than smaller banks.

6.3 What Is E-Commerce and E-Banking?

E-commerce may broadly be defined as all the transactional commerce conducted electronically between businesses and other businesses (B2B), between businesses and their end-customers (B2C) and within an enterprise, over the internet, extranets and intranets (Kalakota & Whinston, 1996). E-commerce or online commercial transactions has emerged as a major economic force. It is not just the purchase of goods online, but also the electronic exchange of services, including information and knowledge, such as legal advice, archival data, design and financial services. Information, its provision and access, is as critical an issue in e-commerce as it always has been in any sort of commerce. Online access is already a requirement for full social, economic and educational participation in the light of stated government and private sector goals of electronic service delivery.

Electronic banking is using electronic means to transfer funds directly from one account to another. Electronic banking is a system that enables bank customers to access accounts and general information on bank products and services through a personal computer or other intelligent device.

Some electronic banking services are ATMs, direct deposit and withdrawal services, pay by phone systems, point-of-sale transfer terminals, Web banking or PC banking services, even banking from mobile phone. Electronic banking offers consumers the convenience of accessing and transferring funds between their accounts, paying their bills and other purchases, twenty-four hours a day, seven days a week.

A fully-integrated bank e-commerce system combines a powerful and flexible enterprise server with software and services that can take full advantage of already accumulated information such as consumer demographics, credit records, risk profiles and account histories to help exploit customer preferences, accelerate speed to market and improve the bottom line. Forward-looking banks are focusing on the need for e-banking, personalized data and customer service, and the highest possible network security. E-banking has had a noticeable impact on bank performance.

6.4 E-Commerce Banking: Technological Benefits and Barriers

New technologies offer unprecedented levels of communication and expanding possibilities for equal information access and independent living. Digital technologies can reduce the expense and difficulty of providing information.

The barriers to e-banking may be security and privacy concerns, particularly with credit cards, shipping and delivery costs, time consuming, difficulty of finding websites/products, complexity of ordering process. Trust and accountability are the main requirements. E-banking cannot be expected to suit all users, and may present serious access barriers to some people with disabilities, but for other people it represents independence and equality.

6.5 Changing Dynamics in the Banking Industry

Globalization and liberalization of financial markets may have paved the way to increased access to cross-border banking, but the significant advances in electronic technology are what have accelerated access to anonymous and instantaneous cross-border banking. Even without the liberalization of financial markets, the new technologies have permitted this to occur.

With the development of technologies in the banking industry, there has been a major change in the banking system and in the way banks strive for increased profitability.

In the past, the banking industry was mainly concerned with asset quality and capitalization, but today performing well on asset quality and capitalization is not sufficient. A thorough understanding of competitive environment and the new ways to increase revenue are the basic desires of modern banks. and new competitors. E-banking can meet the customers' changing needs and a broad range of banking requirements by having:

- Available 24 hours a day, 7 days a week.
- Ability to access financial information.
- Query capability for finding particular payments or deposits.
- Customized account reporting options.
- Details of accrued interest and charges on individual accounts.
- Option to make payments directly from one's bank account to any other's account.
- Batch processing of credit card transactions.
- Transaction details in a file that can be interfaced with a variety of accounting packages.
- Capacity to group and process one-to many payments such as creditor payments, salaries etc.
- Ability to process direct debit transactions.
- Option to post-date payments for a future date.
- Features to create payments in external software packages, such as payroll and accounting packages, for processing by the bank.
- Provision of weekly market commentary and daily exchange rate information.

In addition, for international trading, e-banking may offer a full suite of international transactions including:

- Foreign Currency Account Transfers
- Telegraphic Transfers
- International Cheques (Bank Drafts)
- Letter of Credit Application and Amendment
- Guarantee and Shipping Company Guarantee
- Collections

6.6 E-Commerce and New Technology Based Banking Services

Imagine the convenience of everyday banking without having to leave the office. Imagine not having to write cheques, and post payments every month. With just a personal computer, a modem and bank of electronic banking, one can effectively

Following are the distinct factors contributing to the new competitive environment:

- E-commerce and changing consumer needs – Absolute essentials for competitive banking
- E-commerce and new technology-based banking services
- Optimization of branch networks in order to reduce cost
- Banking and bank regulation - Potential challenges for regulatory policy
- E-commerce and trends in banking industry

6.7 E-Commerce and Changing Consumer Needs: Absolute Essentials for Competitive Banking

In this changing environment, consumers' requirements are changing substantially. Now Customers want to access account related information, download account data for use with personal finance software products, transfer funds between accounts, and pay bills electronically. The bank must be able to safeguard customer information and personal privacy. Consolidation of the banking industry and the expanding scope of products offered by financial service firms means that the industry will be responsible for maintaining and safeguarding huge databases containing extensive information on individuals.

In such an intensely competitive networked banking marketplace, the demands of e-commerce go far beyond simple interconnection. Competitive demands have made clear the need for banks to stay at the cutting edge of e-commerce technology so that they can provide high levels of service all the time, anywhere, over any communications channel. Banks need e-commerce systems that are integrated with the entire chain of back office and business decision processes for optimum flexibility, responsiveness to changing market requirements, and profitability. Now is the time for advanced e-commerce as no one want to be left behind by its traditional manage all monthly bills including payments to creditors, rates, power and all other invoices. The ability to transfer money between accounts, obtain transaction details and instant access to all financial records is more simple and easier. In fact, nearly all regular banking such as transfers, reconciliations and payments, paying wages and salaries from own office is quite possible through electronic banking. PC connects directly to the bank's computer for simple and convenient access whenever needed.

6.8 Optimization of Branch Networks in Order to Reduce Cost

The main aim of e-banking through the optimization of the branch networks is to tighten internal financial controls, reduce compliance costs, improve operational efficiency and organizational effectiveness, better capital management for significant savings of cash reserves, reduce capital costs from better risk management, improve strategic decision making, enhance perception and reputation among investor and client communities, and provide more flexibility.

With the widespread growth of the internet, customers want to use technology anywhere in the world to access a bank's network. The Internet, as an enabling technology, has made banking products and services available to more customers and eliminated geographic and proprietary systems barriers. With an expanded market, banks also have opportunities to expand or change their product and service offerings. Harnessing enabling technology to provide convenience and quality service through multiple channels at value for money price points is the bank's mission from inception in this electronic age. To this end the banks invested in a scalable architecture that allowed them to ramp up easily and handle the rapidly growing volume of customers, apart from reducing costs. To achieve and maintain an edge on its competition, a bank needs an open e-commerce platform that can:

- Integrate new e-commerce applications with existing applications to optimize IT investments and save on reprogramming and management costs
- Provide the power and scalability to handle multiple workloads, shift resources to match changing workloads, handle unpredictable peaks, and grow with the business

- Provide rock-solid security and advanced services availability for transactions all the time, around the world
- Exploit the value of customer and market data by deploying business intelligence (BI) and customer relationship management (CRM) software to help better anticipate, understand and respond to customer wants and needs
- Unify enterprise management chain with an open server platform that integrates purchase and sales processes with information on customers and product offerings for more timely, targeted and personalized customer service
- Integrate future technologies and new ways of doing business with customers

6.8 Banking and Bank Regulations: Potential Challenges for Regulatory Policy

For redistributing capital from areas of excess to areas of scarcity, the most strategic option are the banks and this is the interest of governments of all the countries to watch closely and regulate the financial services in order to control redistribution of capital. Many regulatory reforms have come in to action in the recent years for removing the competitive protections that banks enjoyed for a long time. To survive in the increasing competition from mutual funds, brokerage firms, and insurance companies, banks have to provide complete financial services. Regulatory reforms are expected to allow investment banks to broaden their financial product lines. E-banking has also to accelerate the ongoing process of "financial deepening" i.e. the widening applicability of more formalized financial markets in the economy.

Globalization and increased competition are trends that have shaped the banking industry for decades. The expansion of e-banking contribute to these trends in the same way that previous advancements in telecommunications and data processing did; i.e., by reducing barriers associated with geography and national boundaries. Not only will competition be enhanced by the reduction of geographical barriers, but also by the increased ability of bank customers to search for and locate new suppliers electronically.

There are several ways in which the development of e-banking generates potential challenges for regulatory policy.

1. E-banking and developing technology, more generally are changing the structure and function of financial institutions. The existing regulatory structure has been developed based on traditional lines of demarcation among different types of financial institutions, but these lines of demarcation are becoming less relevant over time.
2. E-banking may raise either new concerns or, more likely, accentuate or lessen concern about existing public policy issues. The most prominent example of a public policy concern accentuated by e-banking has been the issue of privacy.
3. E-banking challenges traditional methods of safety and soundness supervision by changing the nature and scope of existing risks, and possibly by creating new risks.
4. Finally, the nature and scope of technological change may require authorities to rebalance their emphases on regulatory rules and industry discretion.

6.9 E-Commerce and the Trends in Banking Industry

With the entry of private banks, the competitive landscape changed significantly over the last few years. There has been one pervasive goal among the banks to increase market share. Banks are employing multiple ways such as increasing the number of branches, installing ATMs, and providing telephone and internet banking. Banks are also adopting new technology and offering new products and services which sometimes take banks beyond their traditional role as pure financial service providers. Banks have established e-shopping malls and portals for making business-to-commerce (B2C) transaction. Banks also are now providing advice on investments and mutual funds.

Financial matters are the most sensitive issue for the consumers all over the world and paid extremely careful attention about personal finances. The reduced level of job security and the need to plan for the future are major concerns over personal debt, saving, retirement planning, and tax planning for the consumers. These concerns can be seen in the trend of customer purchase of investment services like mutual funds, annuities, and trust services.

All over the world, bank's traditional business of taking deposits and lending out the proceeds is on a decline. With the spread of information technology, companies find it cheaper to raise money from capital market than from borrowing from banks and investors have other and often more attractive ways to invest their money than just putting into plain savings accounts offered by banks. These twin pressures compounded by the decline in interest rates have squeezed the net interest margins of the banking industry.

Along with the focus on new products and business opportunities, foreign banks are also developing the global processing centers by taking advantage of the infotech savvy staff and less expensive skilled labor.

7. HOME BANKING IMPLEMENTATION APPROACHES

Home banking services enable to perform banking tasks, pay bills and communicate with the creditors quickly and easily from any computer available which is equipped with internet access. Home Banking allows one to bank on his/her own time.

In the year of 1970s home banking was started via a telephone, which enabled customers to check their account balances, pay bills, transfer funds and general information etc. At that time, with telephone banking, customers use numeric password on telephone to access banking services and to check their account balances etc.

In the year of 1980s home banking was considered via two-way cable TV, which enabled customers to check their account balances, pay bills, transfer funds and general information etc.

In the last decades of the 20th century, computer technology transformed the banking industry. The wide distribution of automated teller machines (ATMs) by the mid-1980s gave customers 24-hour access to cash and account information. On-line banking through the internet and banking through automated phone systems now allow for electronic payment of bills, money transfers, and loan applications without entering a bank branch.

Home banking in historical order, can be broadly classified into four main categories:

- Proprietary bank dial-up services
- Off-the shelf home finance software
- Online services-based banking
- World Wide Web-based banking

7.1 Proprietary Bank Dial-Up Services

The home banking service along with a personal computer and modem enables the customers to transfer funds or pay bills directly from their accounts to the creditors' account and the bank acts as an electronic gateway. Individual customers can subscribe for the dial-up service to maintain electronic checkbook registers and personal budgets, see account balances, transfer funds among accounts, and make electronic payments to other merchants. This type of home banking was very easy to use.

7.2 Off-the Shelf Home Finance Software

This type of service is provided through the software which contributes in cementing relationship between current customers and helping banks to gain new customers. Intuit's Quicken, Microsoft Money, and Bank of America's MECA are some of the popular software which provide home banking services and small business financial services for PC users and allow to organize, understand, and manage personal finances. The information entered once can be seen and analyzed using a set of reports and graphs. This software also helps users to reconcile their bank accounts, and track credit card purchases, investments, cash, and other assets and liabilities.

Online banking services can also be availed through these software as these allow users to download and automatically categorize savings and loan account activity, brokerage activity, and charge account activity, thereby reducing data entry and providing an easily accessible view of their financial assortment.

7.3 Online Services-Based Banking

In this type of home banking service, banks set up their retail branches and subscribe their online services such as Prodigy, Compuserve, and America Online. Although Off-the shelf home finance software allow customers to manage their money, information regarding their financial transactions gets managed two times, once by the customer and once by the banks and the financial banking software cannot reduce this duplication of efforts. Now some home banking financial services systems are emerging that make the bank an electronic gateway and reduce the monthly paper chase of bills and checks.

7.4 World Wide Web-Based Banking

As internet use is growing explosively, World Wide Web-based banking is also gaining popularity with the same pace. This form of banking provides a convenient and superior customer service in a secure electronic environment. Banks are setting up their websites to float their financial products on the internet.

Online banking and internet banking are the two terms which have different meanings in terms of their operational processes. In case of internet banking, no additional software is to be purchased for storing data on customers' computers or no backup of any information is required, or no wait for new versions of software as all transactions occur on a secure server over the internet and banking can be done anywhere and anytime if the customer has a computer and a modem whereas for online banking, it requires a software such as Quicken, Microsoft Money, or AOL which has to be installed onto the computer which limits the customer to banking only from that computer. The first internet bank to provide banking services electronically to internet users was Security First Network Bank (SFNB) and is available on the internet with the website http://www.sfnb.com. This bank offers highest interest rate in

America for money market accounts. SFNB is offering joint accounts for multiple parties to access account information from various locations, full personal financial reports, and check imaging for internet banking customers to actually view scanned images of their checks online the day after they clear the bank.

8. OPEN VS. CLOSED SYSTEM

Open systems traditionally refer to a technology scheme that provides customers, external developers, or end-users to access the internal functions of a complex system via "public interfaces." In an open system, contents can be changed easily because of the use of standard technology and components. In simple words, a banking interface developed around the web is an open system that is easy to customize to a bank's changing needs. On the other hand, closed system cannot be changed since everything is proprietary. For example, Quicken cannot be modified unless a new version of this software is distributed by the vendor.

9. MANAGEMENT ISSUES IN ONLINE BANKING

Technology has thrown new challenges in the banking sector and new issues have started cropping up which are going to pose certain problems in the near future. The new entrants in the banking are with computer background. However, over a period of time they would acquire banking experience. Whereas the middle and senior level people have rich banking experience but their computer literacy is at a low level. Therefore, they feel handicapped in this regard since technology has become an indispensable tool in banking. Foreign banks and the new private sector banks have embraced technology right from the inception of their operations and therefore, they have adapted themselves to the changes in the technology easily.

The proliferation of technology-based systems offers tremendous opportunities for banks to communicate with and serve their customers. At the same time, the major challenge facing the banking industry is the optimum use of technology to provide customers with new financial products for satisfying their continually changing financial needs. Banks must deliver high quality products at the customers' convenience with high-tech, high-touch personal and affordable service taking into consideration the five key values: *simplicity, customized service, convenience, quality,* and *price*. In this competitive online banking environment, banks have to be willing to take risk and make strategic decisions about the products and services offered online, and about exploiting the service attributes that build customer retention for profitable customers.

The performance that customers believe is an excellent service, banks can and should deliver, is the true standard for assessing service quality. Therefore, gaining a good understanding of customers' service expectations, as well as variations in those expectations across different customer segments, are essential issues for the management of banks for improving service quality. Consistently delivering superior service quality is much more a matter of meeting and exceeding customers' expectations rather than simply conforming to banks defined specifications. One of the biggest shortcomings of service banks is a failure to understand accurately what is important to customers. Hence for the realization of the full potential of banking financial services following key points have to be considered:

- Attractive financial products and services have to be developed.
- Terminals at an affordable price are required for customers.
- Untapped needs of customers and new market segments have to be explored.
- Service quality on the part of banks has to be established for the customers.

9.1 Differentiation Between Financial Products and Services Strategies

The changing market structure requires the banks and software companies to take the strategic decisions to differentiate their products in the competitive online banking industry and exploit the service attributes that build customer retention for profitable customers.

The proliferation of internet web sites means there may be a substantial advantage for banks able to distinguish their products from those of other banks i.e. to engage in "branding". Doing so requires significant resources for advertising and marketing, a fact that is likely to work to the advantage of large firms. The internet provides a very effective searching device for consumers to choose the "best of breed" producers of specialized services. Intermediaries may play a role in helping users locate the "best" product given their individual preferences for quality, convenience, and price. These factors boost both the pace and scope of consolidation in the banking industry.

There are several significant strategic considerations that should be weighed in determining plans for developing an e-banking service and the type of services that should be offered.

1. Bank management must evaluate the degree to which current and future market demand for e-banking services warrant a change in their e-banking plans. The breakthrough in consumer usage of online banking may depend on developing new and better services rather than reducing the price of standard banking products. It also suggests that low demand for e-banking may be responsible for the "wait and see" posture of some banks toward offering e-banking.
2. Another consideration for banks in determining when, and how deep, to plunge into e-banking is the likely future competitive pressure generated by the development of the Internet. Banks face competition not only from their traditional rivals within the banking industry, but may increasingly find their market share threatened by banks from new, distant locations. In addition, non-bank firms (financial and non-financial) will increasingly contest banks for their most valuable customers.
3. A third strategic consideration in developing internet plans is the question of whether there are "early adopter" advantages. Some analysts point to the high market concentration of e-banking customers in a few large banks as evidence that there will be a few big winners and those laggards will have difficulty catching up. The early-adopter-advantage-view also argue that e-banking will increase the extent to which economies of scale and scope can be realized, and that early adopters will better position themselves to exploit them.

Further, because of the rapid pace and broad scope of technological change in banking and payments, today's early adopter advantage in capturing customers using the current set of e-banking options may suddenly be undermined by the introduction of a new technology.

9.2 Pricing Issues in Online Banking

One of the most crucial areas of decision making for banking is financial product pricing. E-banking is a significant non-interest expense at banks today. There are cases of many banks whose annual costs for e-banking are higher than those for their core systems. Many banks signed their original e-banking and bill-pay contracts several years ago when usage volumes were quite low and many vendors were still incurring high development costs. These contracts included some kind of per-account charge, activity-based pricing e.g. per bill paid, or a combination of the two.

Now, as products have matured and volumes have increased significantly, those same pricing schedules no longer make sense. In fact, many banks have been so successful that the earlier pricing structure is now punitive. Limited use of a cash management product for higher-end business customers can be included, with some limit on the number of customers.

As customer is not interested in paying per month subscription for a service that is already consumed by him at no price, it is much expensive to implement and operate online banking services. However, once a user confronts high connect charges, high subscription fees or both, shows interest in online banking services though customers are very price sensitive. Pricing affects online banking at three levels:

1. **Initial Software Pricing:** Banks have to design strategies through which they can occupy a bigger market share and gain masses of customers. One way of achieving can be through bundling of personal finance products and services in the form of software services with new PCs for the potential customers.
2. **Financial Product Pricing:** The development costs (associated with the design, implementation, and commercialization of a financial product), marketing costs (including costs of launching and maintaining financial products throughout its initial stage), and support costs (including the costs of providing and delivering the product, and maintaining it via back office systems) are the three major costs which have to be balanced.
3. **Usage Pricing:** The volume of transactions in the bank decides this form of pricing. Banks have to offer incentives to attract customers to the service. If the target customers find new products costly, they will resist adopting them.

Pricing is a complex issue that has both long-term implications in terms of cost recovery and profitability, and short-term implications in terms of market penetration. While designing the pricing strategies for the financial products and services, banks must have to consider the above-mentioned issues and make a balance between the costs incurred in providing, delivering, maintaining and promoting their financial products and services.

9.3 Marketing Issues: Attracting Customers and Keeping Customers

While winning customers may be hard, keeping them is even harder. Customers really want quick response, instant information, and solutions to their problems. They want exceptional customer service. No organization can afford to lose customers because of poor service, but many do. Customers remember how they have been treated and spread the news. In today's high tech and demanding consumer market, customer service is mission critical. When customers are pleased, they are likely to spend more on product or service and will call again.

Customer expectations are higher than ever, particularly when it comes to online banking services. Bank operations need to become highly customer-centric in the area of Internet banking to ensure that the services they are delivering are the ones their users will actually use. Customers want access to their accounts anytime, from anywhere, using their preferred device or channel. They expect data that is accurate, up-to-date, and consistent across all channels. They take for granted that they will receive informed and timely support whenever they need it. In short, they want online banking to make managing their accounts and satisfying their financial needs simple and easy. The applications that serve them must be visually appealing, easy to use and learn, and support user personalization that meets individual customer requirements. If an application is difficult to navigate or understand, customers simply would not use it, and may take their business elsewhere.

Additionally, as enterprise customer relationship management evolves, e-banking solutions need to complement and integrate with a banks' customer relationship management strategy. It is no longer acceptable for channels to be independent of one another. A system or solutions must integrate with back-end systems, scale to meet the needs of a growing user population, and contribute to a customer relationship management strategy that will increase customer retention, revenue per customer, and subsequently overall bank revenues.

While meeting demanding customer expectations, banks also need to nurture their own bottom line by building on the profitable relationships they have. They must be able to identify and serve their most profitable customers well, and take advantage of opportunities to offer additional products and services to targeted customers at the most appropriate time. To compete with aggressive competitors, banks and other financial institutions need to be able to:

- Provide services tailored to meet the needs of specific, high-profit market segments, such as businesses. Business customers are often a bank's most profitable customers. The need to attract and retain these customers is critical to a financial institution's healthy bottom line.
- Use the data that they have to identify customer segments and present targeted cross-sell messages when appropriate.
- Consolidate information about a customer so that a customer receives informed, timely, and relevant service regardless of the channel that they use.
- Quickly bring new services to market without disruption to existing services.
- Keep up with emerging technologies while maximizing return on investment.
- Minimize total cost of ownership.

9.4 Managing Financial Supply Chains in Online Banking

The financial supply chain parallels the physical supply chain and represents all transaction activities related to the flow of cash, from the buyer's initial order through reconciliation and payment to the seller. Until recently, the financial supply chain went virtually unnoticed. The amount of time required to process transactions was unthinkably long because the manufacturing supply chain itself was fraught with inefficiencies.

The supply chain financial flow is at a critical threshold of evolution. Current trends in supply chain and financial flow management clearly favor the use of automated payment solutions. Continued expansion in this area offers high potential for reducing significantly purchasing processing costs, accelerating payment and invoice reconciliation, reducing collections costs significantly, creating greater processing efficiencies in the procurement of goods, and enhancing visibility, which means less uncertainty in accounts receivable (A/R) and accounts payable (A/P) and a reduction in working capital needs. As the adoption of new automation solutions for financial flows becomes more widespread, the superior efficiencies gained from electronic payment technologies are becoming more measurable and substantial.

Today the typical financial supply chain remains somewhat fragmented, complex and not integrated with the physical supply chain. Goods move faster than money, and disparate parties are involved. Moreover, even in today's world, the financial supply chain is partially composed of paper-based processes. To stay competitive, "just-in-time" working capital management should be the goal. Financial supply chain solutions enable CFOs and treasury managers to accurately manage their receivables or payables, forecast their company's financial future, and reduce their working capital needs. By optimizing financial supply chains, banks can:

- Reduce their working capital needs by using better inventory control and cash flow management, potentially representing significant annual savings.
- Lower financing rates on required working capital through more effective management of their current asset position.
- Reduce the costs of risk management through greater cash flow predictability.
- Gain early warning into problems with any document in a commercial trade transaction that will likely cause payment to be delayed, then take corrective action to reconcile exceptions.
- Improve customers relations in this money-spinning market, to gain advantage, banks have to follow three strategies:
    - Powerful technology infrastructure, strong information architecture and lucrative online financial products and services have to be developed.
    - Form partnership to link customers, intermediaries, banks, and third-party service providers in the online financial supply chain.
    - Banks have to shift from mass production orientation to mass customization of financial products and services so as to capture the loyalty of the customers by providing simple, convenient, and customer-centered approach for services to the customers.

REFERENCES

Adam, N. R., & Yesha, Y. (1996). *Electronic Commerce*. Berlin: Springer-Verlag. doi:10.1007/3-540-60738-2

BankAmerica Corporation. (1998). *What is SET[tm] and How Does it Work?* Retrieved from http://www.bofa.com/spare_change/set_what_and_how.html

BBC. (2013). How to shop safely and securely online. *BBC*. Retrieved from: http://www.bbc.co.uk/webwise/0/22728224

Beware of Phishing. (n.d.). Retrieved from http://www2.le.ac.uk/offices/ias/topics/phishing

Blumenthal, H. (Ed.). (1998). *The OBI standard gains momentum*. Retrieved from http://www.netscapeworld.com/ned-12- 1997/ned-12-extranet.html

Christian Science Monitor. (n.d.). Everything you need to know about dynamic pricing. *Christian Science Monitor*. Retrieved from: http://www.csmonitor.com

Copeland & Hwang. (n.d.). *Electronic Data Interchange: Concepts and Effects*. Retrieved from http://www.isoc.org/isoc/whatis/conferences/inet/97/proceedings/C5/C5_1.HTM

Drummond, Janson, & Shih. (1998). *Requirements for Inter-operable Internet EDI*. EDIINT Working Group. Internet Draft.

E-Commerce (Electronic Commerce or EC). (n.d.). Retrieved from: http://searchcio.techtarget.com/definition/e-commerce

E-Commerce Security Systems. (n.d.). Retrieved from http://www.tutorialspoint.com/e_commerce/e_commerce_security.htm

EDICT Systems. (1999). Retrieved from http://www.edictsystems.com

ETHOS team. (1997). *Open Buying on the Internet (OBI) standard*. Retrieved from: http://www.tagish.co.uk/ethosub/lit5/c1aa.htm

Extensible Markup Language (XML). (1998). *W3C Recommendation*. Retrieved from: http://www.w3.org/TR/1998/REC-xml-19980210

Federal Supply Service (FSS). (n.d.). More About Electronic Data Interchange (EDI). *Federal Supply Service*. Retrieved from: http://www.fss.gsa.gov/edi_mae.html

Freibrun, E.S. (1993). *Electronic Data Interchange (EDI) and the Law*. Academic Press.

Gautam, R. (2014). Network Security Issues in e-Commerce. *International Journal of Advanced Research in Computer Science and Software Engineering*, *4*(3).

IT Pro Portal. (n.d.). E-commerce security tips: How to stay safe when shopping online. *IT Pro Portal*. Retrieved from: http://www.itproportal.com/2013/07/18/e-commerce-security-tips-how-to-stay-safewhen-shopping-online/

Kalakota, R., & Whinston, A. B. (1996). *Frontiers of electronic commerce*. Pearson Education.

Kamanec, K. (2013). E-commerce security tips. *IT Pro Portal*. Retrieved from: http://www.itproportal.com/2013/07/18/e-commerce-security-tips-how-to-stay-safe-when-shopping-online/

Mag, P. C. (n.d.). *E-Commerce Security Tips*. Retrieved from: http://www.pcmag.com/article2/0,2817,2421846,00.asp

Niranjanamurthy, M., & Chahar, D. D. R. (2013). The study of E-Commerce Security Issues and Solutions. *International Journal of Advanced Research in Computer and Communication Engineering*, *2*(7).

Privacy Rights Clearinghouse. (2000). Fact Sheet 23: Online Shopping Tips: E-Commerce and You. *Privacy Rights Clearinghouse*. Retrieved from: https://www.privacyrights.org/online-shopping-tips-e-commerce-and-you

Shopping Online. (2014). How to shop online without a credit card. *Shopping Online*. Retrieved from: http://shoppingonline-tips.blogspot.in/2014_07_01_archive.html

Stay Safe Online. (n.d.). Online shopping. *Stay Safe Online*. Retrieved from: http://www.staysafeonline.org/stay-safe-online/protect-your-personal-information/online-shopping

Threats to E-Commerce Servers-Part I. (n.d.). Retrieved from: http://www.technologyexecutivesclub.com/Articles/security/artThreatstoEcommerceServers.php

Chapter 9
Secure Payment Modes Technology for E-Commerce Applications

Niteesha Sharma
Anurag Group of Institutions, India

Adiraju Rao Prashanth
Anurag Group of Institutions, India

ABSTRACT

E-commerce refers to business and customers buying and selling products online. There are significant improvements in the areas of initiating sale of products, placing orders, making payments, and transfer of funds. This has led to a much better global economy and better living standards for all. While buying products online, it is essential to know the payment method that ensures authentication and also many other security issues. There are many payments modes available in market today. This chapter presents different protocols and its security issues that relate to a specific payment mode.

INTRODUCTION

Commerce is the most major aspect of any civilization. Improving Commerce can bring prosperity into all segments of society. In today's world there have been major changes to the commerce industry. The most important of it is the introduction of computers into the commerce industry. Computerization of commerce has taken the world by a storm. There are significant improvements in the areas of initiating sale of products, placing orders, making payments, and transfer of funds. This has led to a much better global economy and better living standards for all.

Payment started with the barter system centuries ago. Goods were exchanged directly between people in the barter system. The major drawback of barter system was that the buyer and the seller had to mutually like the goods that they had in surplus. This led to next generation of payment method called Commodity Money System. Here, the buyer would buy goods from the seller in exchange of some commodity in the form of gold, silver, corn etc. Commodity Money slowly evolved into standard of having paper notes

DOI: 10.4018/978-1-5225-3646-8.ch009

at the exchange parameter. The cash payment method does not require the seller to like the commodity that he/she is going to receive in exchange for the goods. About 80 percent of all the transactions in the world are done through cash payment. The process is simple and there is no bank involvement. There is however an overhead of printing notes.

The cash payment method is very insecure. There is no record of the transaction maintained. There is a possibility for generating counterfeit notes. Cash Payment is mostly used for low-value payments. Check Payment is employed for making medium to high value payment. A record of the transaction is maintained at the bank at the cost of the transaction fee. However, it is not a guaranteed form of payment since the checks do not represent real time cash. There is a possibility that the checks could be turned down by the buyer's bank due to various reasons. As the volume of check processing started increasing, banks had to think about ways of improving the turn-around time for payment processing.

Problems of traditional processing system (Raj Garg, 2016):

- **Lack of Security:** It is because the consumer has to send all the confidential data on paper, which is not secured and encrypted.
- **Lack of Convenience:** Traditional Processing system requires consumer to send paper cheques duly signed by them before performing any transaction. This may lead to in convenience by consumers.
- **Lack of Time and Eligibility:** Not all the buyers may have the bank accounts.

E-commerce (electronic commerce or EC) is the buying and selling of goods and services, or the transmitting of funds or data, over an electronic network, primarily the internet. These business transactions occur either as business-to-business, business-to-consumer, consumer-to-consumer or consumer-to-business. The terms e-commerce and e-business are often used interchangeably. The term e-tail is also sometimes used in reference to transactional processes for online shopping.

Advantages of E-Commerce

The advantages of E-Commerce are as follows:

- E-commerce helps organization to provide better customer services.
- E-Commerce reduces paper work a lot.
- E-Commerce increased the productivity of the organization.
- E-Commerce provides option of virtual auctions.
- Customers need not to travel to shop a product thus less traffic on road and low air pollution.
- E-Commerce application provides user more options to compare and select the cheaper and better option.

Applications of E-Commerce

The applications of E-commerce are used in various business areas such as retail and wholesale and manufacturing. The most common E-commerce applications are as follows:

Marketing

E-commerce marketing is a practice of redirecting and guiding online customers to an e-commerce website and convincing them to buy the products or the services online.

E-Commerce Marketing can be divided in to two major actions: maintaining and driving the website traffic and optimizing the user experience. Both the factors are essential and failure of one result in undetermined success of other. Big commerce is the leading e-commerce platform for growing mid-market retailers.

Finance

Most of the financial companies have been using E-commerce to a large extent. The customers can check their online account statements, balance, transfer money to other accounts and also pay their bill through online banking or e-banking systems. As the main developing trend of e-commerce in finance realm, the finance trends provide many advantages like the funds circulation can be delivered to whole world quickly, improving efficiency, improving security, can connect more number of users and have instantaneous access to information.

Manufacturing

Manufacturing can be defined as a process of collecting the raw materials and then converting them into finished qualitative goods or products for the consumers.

In order to raise the profitability and also to improve the customer's service many companies/ manufacturers move their supply chain operations on to internet using an electronic exchange which is a forum where all the manufacturers, suppliers, customers buy and sell goods and also trade the market information. Also effective e-commerce lies in the ability to deliver a buyer-centric and engaging online experience that enables customers to interact and transact with the brand and allows manufacturers to reduce administrative costs, increase sales and improve brand loyalty. This is achieved by reducing costs.

Different Payment Modes of E-Commerce

Electronic Commerce industry is exploding at a fast pace. One of the key aspects of electronic commerce is payments. There are different methods to pay electronically. These can be through Credit Cards, Electronic Checks, Electronic Cash, Debit Cards, or Charge Cards.

Figure 1. Typical scenario of e-commerce system involves three types of actors

- **Payer (P)/Consumer:** Payer transfers some money to his/her wallet.
- **Payee (R) / Merchant:** Payer transfers the withdrawn money to the payee's (R) wallet
- **Financial Institution:** A bank with whom both payer and payee have accounts.
- Main factors which help society to make use electronic payment systems are:
- **Decrease in Technology Cost:** Since the technology used in networks is being decreased day by day, the internet is becoming almost free everywhere.
- **E-Commerce is Secure:** The usage of secure electronic transaction ensures the security of financial transactions on internet.
- **Minimal Operational and Processing Cost, Time:** Due to reduced technology cost the processing cost of various commerce activities are becoming less with much more less usage of Paper and Time.
- **Increasing Online Commerce:** Considering the above two factors many Organizations are leading towards Online Commerce (Raj Garg, 2016).

E-Commerce involves trading using the latest electronic equipment and software between the sellers and the buyers. The trade in e-commerce is conducted in a slightly different way than the traditional trading. The first form of automated payments was to disburse salaries to employees from an employer's account. Gradually, the information revolution changed the outlook of the banking sector and computerized majority of the functions. This is achieved with the help of different E-commerce payment systems which is explained in detail in next section.

TYPES OF E-PAYMENT SYSTEMS

Bogdan-Alexandru URS (2015)presented the most used electronic payment systems are as following: Smart card-based e-payment system, online payment system, Mobile phone based payment system, E-Wallet Payment System and the E-Cheque Payment System. New payment types are continuously discovered and there are additional methods that exist or are being developed continuously each year.

Digital Cash

e-Cash or digital cash is purely software based, anonymous, untraceable, online token payment system, available on Unix, Windows as well as Macintosh platform (Rachna & Singh, 2013). Digital Cash entails the use of digital wallet where in it works as a system of purchasing cash credits in small amounts and storing them in the computer and using it for the electronic purchases. The digital cash numbers are unique and are issued by banks, money in your bank is converted into digital code. Also referred as e-currency, e- cash, e-money etc. Figure 2 represents e-cash processes in general:

Security in E-Cash

Any E-cash system to be accepted, security is one of the prime concerns that need to be considered. The originality of the message being transferred among consumers, merchants and banks need to be secured to avoid any unauthorized individual intercepting or changing the content of the messages. In order to protect E-cash from such illegal activity, E-cash system must possess quality such as integrity,

Figure 2. The usage of digital cash

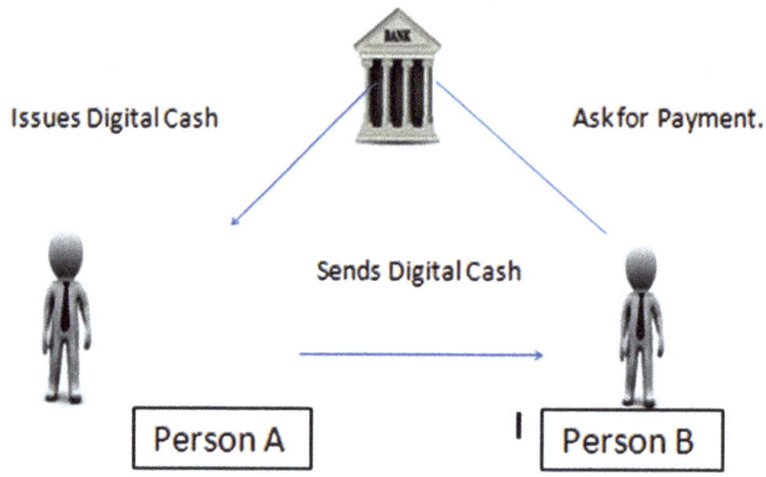

nonrepudiation and able to authenticate. All parties must know to whom they are dealing with, before engaging or committing in any transaction. Integrity comes in place where the message sent by consumers, merchants and banks must be intact when it reaches respective recipients. Razali (2002) discussed that once the integrity and authentication are achieved, consumers, merchants or banks could no longer deny the bank transactions.

Credit Cards

There are two major organizations issuing 80% of the credit cards in the market today. They are:

- Visa International and
- MasterCard.

An overview of the credit card processing is depicted in the Figure 3.

- Card Issuer
- Financial Network
- Acquirer
- Card Holder
- Merchant

There are four main partners in a Credit Card transaction.

1. The Issuing Bank is the bank that maintains the account of the buyer and issues a Credit Card to the buyer. The issuing bank also sets a limit on the amount of purchases that can be made using the card and the percentage of interest on the unpaid portion of the bill.
2. The cardholder is also known as the buyer in the transaction. The cardholder initiates a transaction.

Figure 3. Entities in conventional credit card processing system

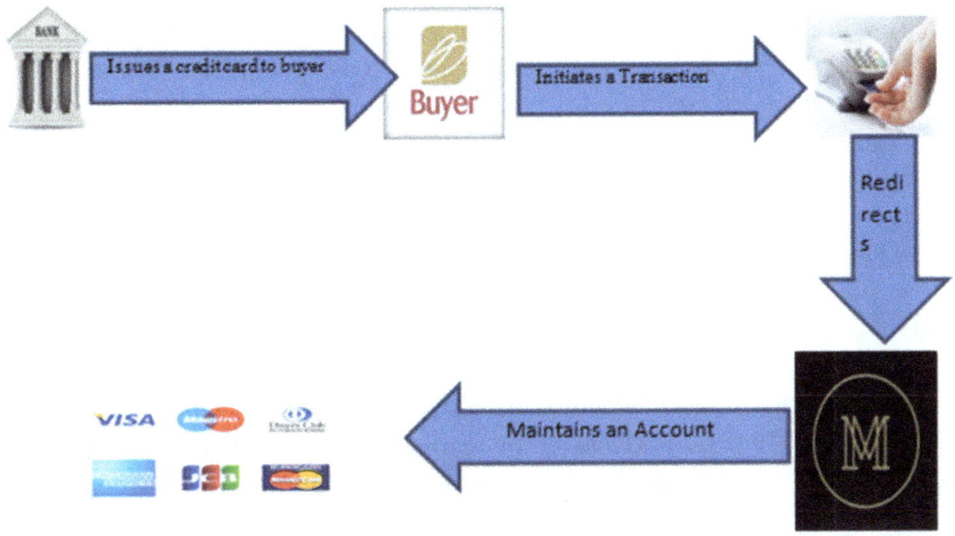

3. The merchant is the seller of goods and services.
4. The merchant maintains an account with a bank or a financial institution known as the acquirer. Acquiring institutions contracts with merchants to enable them to accept credit card transactions and charges a certain percentage of fees for the transaction.

Credit Card Payment Process

A Credit Card Payment is a two-step process:

1. Authorization
2. Capture/Settlement

Authorization is a process in which the merchant verifies the cardholder's identification and credit limit. The merchant sends the credit card information like the card number, expiration date, and amount to the acquirer. The acquirer will forward the card details to the issuing bank via the existing financial network. The credit card issuer will either return an approval, decline or referral for the authorization request. If the transaction was approved, then the merchant can deliver the goods purchased to the buyer. A transaction can be declined for various reasons like unavailable credit, bad credit history, wrong address, etc.

Capture/Settlement is the process of actual transfer of funds from the cardholder's account to the merchant's account. It collects the money for the merchant after the goods have been delivered.

Debit Cards

Debit card, like credit card is a small plastic card with a unique number mapped with the bank account number. It is required to have a bank account before getting a debit card from the bank. The major difference between debit card and credit card is that in case of payment through debit card, amount gets deducted from card's bank account immediately and there should be sufficient balance in bank account for the transaction to get completed. In case of credit card there is no such compulsion. Having restriction on amount being in bank account also helps customer to keep a check on his/her spending.

The Figure 4 demonstrates the usage of debit cards.

Smart Card

Smart card is again similar to credit card and debit card in appearance but it has a small microprocessor chip embedded in it, used to perform financial transactions. It has the capacity to store customer work related/personal information. Smart card is also used to store money which is reduced as per usage. Smart

Figure 4. Debit card payment processing cycle

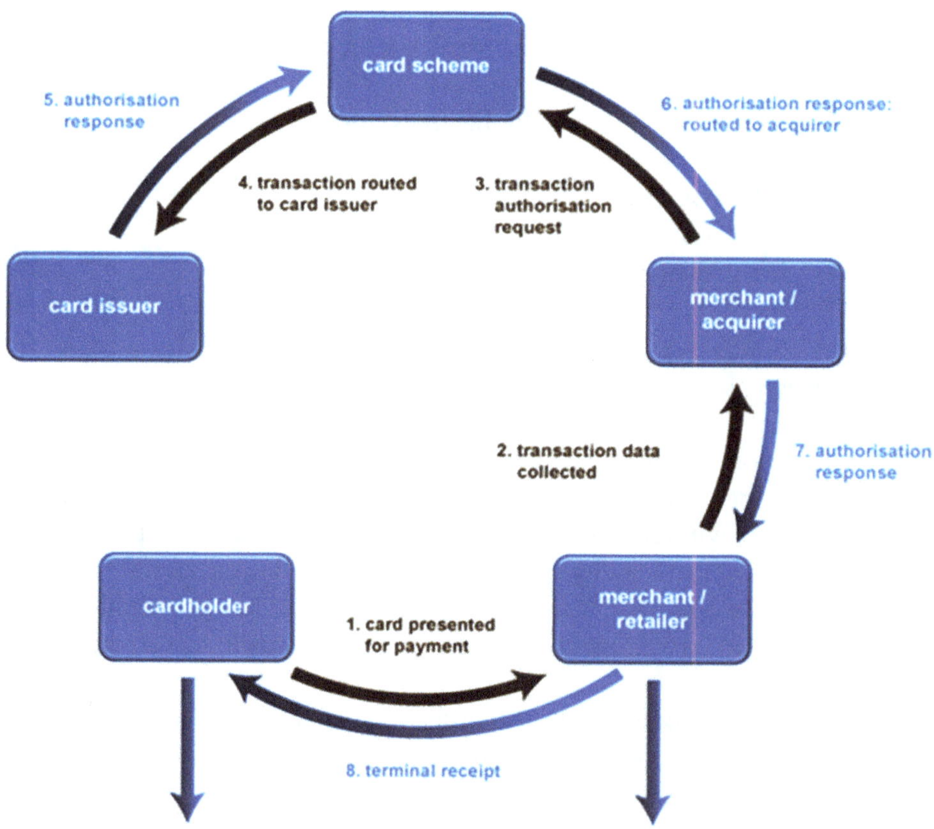

Figure 5. Smart card

card can be accessed only using a PIN of customer (Chakrabarti & Kardile, 2002, as cited in Sumanjeet, 2009). Smart cards are secure as they store information in encrypted format and are less expensive, provides faster processing. Mondex and Visa Cash cards are examples of smart cards.

Online Cheque or Electronic Fund Transfer

Electronic Fund transfer is a transaction that happens among the accounts of same bank or different bank without the intervention of bank staff members which share a common computerized network. EFT's are also called as online transactions or PIN-Debit transaction. In EFT's there is a financial house called as Automated Clearing House (ACH) responsible for transferring the money from Payer consumer) to Payee (Merchant) account on the completion of transaction.

Figure 6. The figure depicts the usage of Electronic Fund Transfer [EFT]

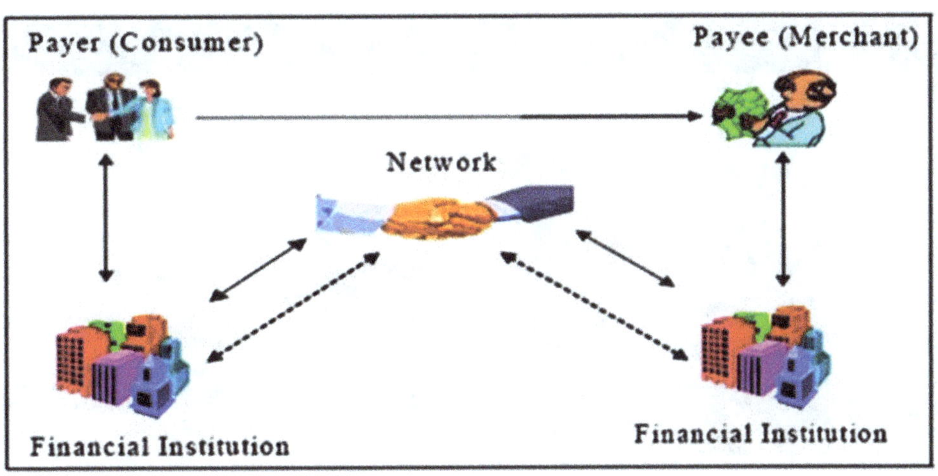

Electronic Wallets (E-Wallets)

E-wallet applications may reside on mobile devices, computers or on Web servers at a service that manages digital wallet information. These apps can make online purchasing faster populating order forms with billing, shipping and other information that you'd normally type manually. Some digital wallets may also store other important personal information, such as your driver's license and health care card data. If you lose a mobile device that has a digital wallet, people who find it won't be able to read its information because it's encrypted.

Electronic wallets being very useful for frequent online shoppers are commercially available for pocket, palm-sized, handheld, and desktop PCs as presented by the authors (Kaur & Pathak, 2015). They offer a secure, convenient, and portable tool for online shopping. They store personal and financial information such as credit cards, passwords, PINs, and much more. E-Wallets allow higher speed and much more efficiency for online shoppers.

METHODS OF ONLINE PAYMENT

Credit cards constitute a popular method of online payment but can be expensive for the merchant to accept because of transaction fees primarily. Debit cards constitute an excellent alternative with similar security but usually much cheaper charges. Besides card-based payments, other forms of payment have emerged and sometimes even claimed market leadership. Wallets like PayPal and Alipay are playing major roles in the ecosystem.

Net Banking

This is a system; well known that does not involve any sort of physical card. It is used by customers who have accounts enabled with Internet banking. Instead of entering card details on the purchaser's site, in this system the payment gateway allows one to specify which bank they wish to pay from. Then the user

Figure 7. The figure depicts the usages of E-wallet

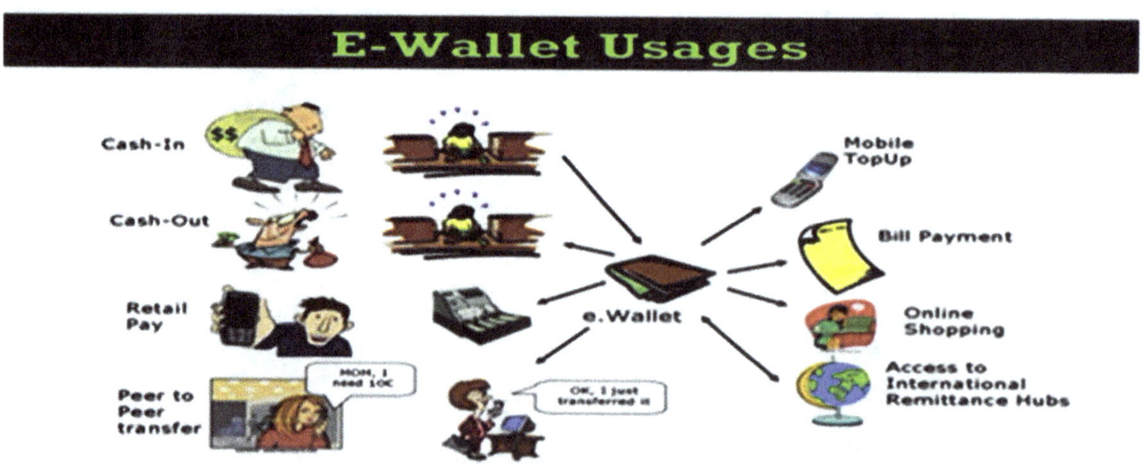

is redirected to the bank's website, where one can authenticate oneself and then approve the payment. Typically there will also be some form of two-factor authentication.

It is typically seen as being safer than using credit cards, with the result that nearly all merchant accounts in India offer it as an option.

PayPal

PayPal is a global e-commerce business allowing payments and money transfers to be made through the Internet. Online money transfers serve as electronic alternatives to paying with traditional paper methods, such as cheques and money orders. It is subject to the US economic sanction list and other rules and interventions required by US laws or government. PayPal is an acquirer, a performing payment processing for online vendors, auction sites, and other commercial users, for which it charges a fee. It may also charge a fee for receiving money, proportional to the amount received. The fees depend on the currency used, the payment option used, the country of the sender, the country of the recipient, the amount sent and the recipient's account type.

Paymentwall

Paymentwall an e-commerce solutions providing company launched in 2010, offers a wide range of online payment methods that its clients can integrate on their website.

Google Wallet

Google Wallet was launched in 2011, serving a similar function as PayPal to facilitate payments and transfer money online. It also features a security that has not been cracked to date and the ability to send payments as attachments via email.

Mobile Money Wallets

In developing countries the banked population is very less, especially in tier II and tier III cities. Taking the example of India, there are more mobile phone users than there are people with active bank accounts. Telecom operators, in such geographies, have started offering mobile money wallets which allows adding funds easily through their existing mobile subscription number, by visiting physical recharge points close to their homes and offices and converting their cash into mobile wallet currency. This can be used for online transaction and E-Commerce purchases. Many payment options such as Airtel Money and M-Pesa in Kenya, ATW are being accepted as alternate payment options on various E-Commerce websites.

Comparison of E-Payment Systems

The table below shows the comparison of various E-payment systems such as Digital cash, credit cards, debit cards, smart cards, EFT, E-wallets against various features like users, transaction, efficiency etc., as presented by Sumanjeet (2009).

Table 1. Statistics of online shoppers as a percentage of Internet users in India

S. No	Feature	Digital Cash	Credit Cards	Debit Cards	Smart Cards	Electronic Fund Transfer	E-Wallets
1	Users	Any User	Any Credit Card Holders	Any user with a bank or credit card account	Any user with a bank or credit card account	Any User with a bank account	Any User with a bank account
2	Payment Time	Prepaid	Paid later	Prepaid	Prepaid	Direct Debit	Quick Payments
3	Transaction	Online	Online	Offline	Offline	Online	Online
4	Transfer Limit	Depends on Prepaid limit	Depends on limit of credit card	Depends on amount of money in account	Depends on amount of money Saved	Depend on account limits	Depends on Merchant
5	Mobility	No	Yes	Yes	Yes	Yes	Yes

SECURITY MECHANISMS IN E-COMMERCE APPLICATIONS

E-commerce security is the protection of e-commerce assets from unauthorized access, use, alteration, or destruction. While security features do not guarantee a secure system, they are necessary to build a secure system. Online payment security protecting card details is the primary security risk with electronic transactions. Customers are very comfortable using cards in shops and over the phone despite the ever-present risk of details being copied or stolen. With payments over the Internet, there is more resistance towards disclosing card information.

Perception can get in the way of fact. Both software and hardware companies have invested a great deal to further protect online data and build up customer confidence. Be aware of the security issue and help customers to feel at ease by telling them about the precautions we have taken. In the current Internet climate it is vitally important that we are not only secure but are seen to be secure.

Security is an essential part of any transaction that takes place over the internet. Customer will lose his/her faith in e-business if its security is compromised (Tutorials Point, 2017).

Following are the essential requirements for safe e-payments/transactions:

- **Authentication:** Verifies who you say you are. It enforces that you are the only one allowed to logon to your Internet banking account.
- **Authorization:** Allows only you to manipulate your resources in specific ways. This prevents you from increasing the balance of your account or deleting a bill.
- **Encryption:** Deals with information hiding. It ensures you cannot spy on others during Internet banking transactions.
- **Auditing:** Keeps a record of operations. Merchants use auditing to prove that you bought specific merchandise.
- **Integrity:** prevention against unauthorized data modification.
- **Nonrepudiation:** prevention against any one party from reneging on an agreement after the fact.
- **Availability:** prevention against data delays.

Measures to Ensure Security

Major security measures are following:

- **Encryption:** It is a very effective and practical way to safeguard the data being transmitted over the network. Sender of the information encrypts the data using a secret code and specified receiver only can decrypt the data using the same or different secret code.
- **Digital Signature:** Digital signature ensures the authenticity of the information. A digital signature is an e-signature authentic authenticated through encryption and password.
- **Security Certificates:** Security certificate is unique digital id used to verify identity of an individual website or user.

Some of the best known options for the encryption and security of personal and card details are explained below. Almost every payment solution mentioned in this online payments tool includes this technology as standard. Online retailers will not need extra security measures if they use these market-tested and well-established products (Camenisch, Piveteau, Stadle, 1996).

Protocols for Securing E-Commerce Transaction

The security of E-Commerce transactions depends both on the network protocols and the payment framework used to perform the transaction.

Network Transport Security

Models such as Digi Cash, First Virtual, and Millicent provide a secure payment method. However, the transaction still depends on the privacy and authentication of the data stream. Basic TCP/IP networking protocols do not include encryption and strong authentication. Higher level protocols such as HTTP, FTP, and Telnet do little to provide advanced security measures beyond user id and password authentication. All information sent using these protocols is unencrypted, so the data stream lacks confidentiality.

Traditional networking protocols and applications are unable to enforce strong security measures for performing E-Commerce transactions securely. This lack of security led to the design and implementation of many new security protocols that strive to reach different security goals. There are some secure transport protocols that provide confidentiality and authentication between systems and applications by using encryption. The following section describes some of the more popular secure transport protocols.

Virtual Private Networking (VPN)

Virtual Private Networking technology provides the medium to use the public Internet backbone as an appropriate channel for private data communication. With encryption and encapsulation technology, a VPN essentially carves out a private passageway through the Internet. VPNs will allow remote offices, company road warriors, and even business partners or customers to use the Internet, rather than pricey private lines, to reach company networks. So the companies can save a lot of money.

Virtual private networks are flexible. They are point-to-multipoint connections, rather than point-to-point links. They can be set up or closed down at the network administrators will, making them ideal for short-term projects.

VPN has many advantages: It is much cheaper for connecting WANs than 800 numbers or dedicated T1 lines. It provides encryption and authentication services for a fairly good measure of privacy. Maintenance of the WAN-to-WAN connection is left to Internet Service Providers. It is highly flexible, and can be set up and taken down very easily.

IPSec (Ipv6)

IPsec is a framework of open standards developed by the Internet Engineering Task Force (IETF). IPsec provides security for transmission of sensitive information over unprotected networks such as the Internet. IPSec acts at the network layer, protecting and authenticating IP packets between participating IPSec devices ("peers"), such as Cisco routers. IPsec provides the following network security services.

1. **Data Confidentiality:** The IPsec sender can encrypt packets before transmitting them across a Network.
2. **Data Integrity:** The IPSec receiver can authenticate packets sent by the IPSec sender to ensure that the data has not been altered during transmission.
3. **Data Origin Authentication:** The IPSec receiver can authenticate the source of the IPSec packets sent.
4. **Anti-Replay:** The IPSec receiver can detect and reject replayed packets.

Secure Socket Layer (SSL)

SSL is the Secure Sockets Layer protocol. Version 2.0 originated by Netscape Development Corporation, and version 3.0 was designed with public review and input from industry.

SSL (Secure Sockets Layer) is a communication system that ensures privacy when communicating with other SSL-enabled products. Technically speaking, SSL is a protocol that runs above TCP/IP and below HTTP or other top-level protocols. It is symmetric encryption nested within public-key encryption, authenticated through the use of certificates. An SSL connection can only occur between an SSL-enabled client and an SSL-enabled server. In fact, when a server is running in SSL mode, it can only communicate through SSL.

SSL allows traffic to be scrambled (or encrypted). The standard SSL developed by Netscape provides a high level of protection. It meets the following security requirements like:Authentication, Encryption, Integrity, and Non-reputability.

Secure Electronic Transaction (SET)

SET encrypts payment card transaction data and verifies that both parties in the transaction are genuine. SET, originally developed by Mastercard and Visa in collaboration with leading technology providers, has a large corporate backing and is perceived to be more secure as a result of its validation from card companies.

Private Communications Technology

SSL, created by Netscape, provides users with authentication of the server they are attaching to, encryption of the data sent and received, and integrity of the data being sent and received. PCT, created by Microsoft, provides protection against eavesdropping on a network or altering a network packet.

The Private Communications Technology (PCT) protocol furnishes the following elements of transmission security for client/server relationships over the Internet:

- Provides symmetric session-encryption keys between servers and clients.
- Accommodates authentication of server to client via Certificate of Authority (CA) trusted public keys; optionally, it also authenticates client to server.
- Verifies message integrity with hash function message digests, as explained earlier for the SET protocol.

Secure Hypertext Transfer Protocol (SHTTP)

SHTTP extends the HTTP internet protocol with public key encryption, authentication and digital signature over the internet. Secure HTTP supports multiple security mechanism providing security to end users. SHTTP works by negotiating encryption scheme types used between client and server.

CONCLUSION

Technology has inarguably made our lives easier. It has cut across distance, space and even time. One of the technological innovations in banking, finance and commerce is the Electronic Payments. E-Commerce or Electronics Commerce sites use electronic payment where electronic payment refers to paperless monetary transactions. Electronic Payments provides greater freedom to individuals in paying their taxes, licenses, fees, fines and purchases at unconventional locations and at whichever time of the day, 365 days of the year. Electronic payment has revolutionized the business processing by reducing paper work, transaction costs, labor cost. Being user friendly and less time consuming than manual processing, it helps business organization to expand its market expansion.

FUTURE RESEARCH DIRECTIONS

On the basis of present study, the first remark is that despite the existence of variety of e-commerce payment systems, credit cards are the most dominant payment system. Second, alternative e-commerce payment systems are some countries are debit cards. In fact, like many other studies, the present study also reveals that the smart card based e-commerce payment system is best and it is expected that in the future smart cards will eventually replace the other electronic payment systems. Third, given the limited users bases, e-cash is not a feasible payment option. Thus, there are number of factors which affect the usage of e-commerce payment systems. Among all these user base is most important. Added to this, success of e-commerce payment systems also depends on consumer preferences, ease of use, cost, industry agreement, authorization, security, authentication, non-refutability, accessibility and reliability and anonymity and public policy.

REFERENCES

Bogdan-Alexandru, U. R. S. (2015). Security Issues and Solutions in E-payment Systems. *Fiat Iustitia,* (2), 172-179. Retrieved from http://oaji.net/articles/2016/2064-1452602042.pdf

Camenisch, J., Piveteau, J. M., & Stadler, M. (1996). An Efficient Fair Payment System. *ACM Conference on Computer and Communications Security*, 88–94.

Confederation of Indian Industry. (2016). *E-Commerce in India: A Game Changer for the Economy.* Retrieved from http://www.bing.com/cr?IG=6F0F7F2F91334641BE5B3DE4745E7E89&CID=2B68C210B2166BF20A09C91FB3106ADC&rd=1&h=CQvneHAH_csyTTkglzFhbQUkKBR5oc1HDUEEsVBxqtQ&v=1&r=http%3a%2f%2fwww.italiaindia.com%2fimages%2fuploads%2fpdf%2fapril-2016-e-commerce-in-india.pdf&p=DevEx,5065.1

Kaur, K., & Pathak, A. (2015). E-Payment System on E-Commerce in India. *International Journal of Engineering Research and Applications*, *5*(2), 79–87. Retrieved from http://www.ijera.com/papers/Vol5_issue2/Part%20-%201/M502017987.pdf

Rachna, & Singh, P. (2013). Issues and Challenges of Electronic Payment Systems. *International Journal for Research in Management and Pharmacy, 2*(9), 25-30. Retrieved from https://raijmronlineresearch.files.wordpress.com/2017/08/3_25-30-rachna-et-al.pdf

Raj Garg, C. A. (2016). Importance of E-Commerce Payment System in Less paper Work. *International Journal of Business Quantitative Economics and Applied Management Research*, *2*(11), 47–59. Retrieved from http://ijbemr.com/wp-content/uploads/2016/05/IMPORTANCE-OF-E-COMMERCE-PAYMENT-SYSTEM-IN-LESS-PAPER-WORK.pdf

Razali, R. (2002). *Global Information Assurance Certification Paper*. Retrieved from https://www.giac.org/paper/gsec/1799/overview-e-cash-implementation-security-issues/103204

Sumanjeet, S. (2009). Emergence of payment systems in the age of electronic commerce: The state of art. *2009 First Asian Himalayas International Conference on Internet, 3*(3), 18-40. Retrieved from https://globip.com/articles/asiapacific-vol3-article2.pdf

Tutorials Point. (2017, August 15). *E-Commerce Security Systems*. Retrieved from https://www.tutorialspoint.com/e_commerce/e_commerce_security.htm

Chapter 10
Design Methodology for Effective User Interface Design for E-Commerce Applications

Namratha Birudaraju
Anurag Group of Institutions, India

Adiraju Prasanth Rao
Anurag Group of Institutions, India

ABSTRACT

There are many customers who shop online. Many of these users interact with the system using well-defined user interfaces only. So, there is a need to develop effective user interfaces that are more user friendly, minimize the keyboard operations, and maximize effective interaction with the system. This chapter focuses on designing effective user interfaces by considering human parameters for e-commerce applications.

INTRODUCTION

Electronic commerce is the application of communication and information sharing technologies among trading partners to the pursuit of business objectives. E-Commerce can be defined as a modern business methodology that addresses the needs of organizations, merchants, and consumers to cut costs while improving the quality of goods and services and increasing the speed of service delivery. E-commerce is associated with the buying and selling of information, products and services via computer networks. The effects of e-commerce are already appearing in all areas of business, from customer service to new product design. It facilitates new types of information based business processes for reaching and interacting with customers – online advertising and marketing, online-order taking and on-line customer service etc. It can also reduce costs in managing orders and interacting with a wide range of suppliers and trading partners, areas that typically add significant overhead to the cost of products and services. Also, E-commerce enables the formation of new types of information-based products such as

DOI: 10.4018/978-1-5225-3646-8.ch010

interactive games, electronic books, and information-on demand that can be very profitable for content providers and useful for consumers. The explosion in the use of electronic commerce (e-commerce) by the business sector has been tremendous since its inception only a few years ago. From governments to multinational companies to one-person start-ups, e-commerce is increasingly viewed as a key business modality of the future. Ease of transaction, widening markets, and decreased overheads are factors that make e-commerce solutions more and more attractive, as evident with the growth of online sales. Virtual enterprises are business arrangements in which trading partners separated by geography and expertise are able to engage in complex joint business activities, as if they were a single enterprise. One example would be true supply chain integration, where planning and forecast data are transmitted quickly and accurately throughout a multi-tier supply chain. Another example would be non-competing suppliers with a common customer using E-commerce to allow that customer to do "one stop shopping" with the assurance that a single phone call will bring the right materials to the right location at the right time.

Development of E-Commerce (EC) applications started in the early 1970s with electronic funds transfer (EFT), which refers to the computer-based systems used to perform financial transactions electronically. However, the use of these applications was limited to financial institutes, large corporations, and some businesses. Electronic data interchange (EDI) was then developed in the late 1970s to improve the limitation of electronic funds transfer. Electronic data interchange enlarged the pool of participating company from manufacturers, retailers, services, and others. Such systems were called Interorganizational System (IOS). An Interorganizational System (IOS) allows the flow of information to be automated between organizations to reach a desired supply-chain management system, which enables the development of competitive organizations.

The user interface design of website plays a vital role in bringing high volume web traffic to it. Therefore, web designers should give due importance to the user interface of the site which is being designed by them. The use of effective and simple user interface design will be of immense help in achieving the objectives of a website. A good user interface not only increases the site usability but also leads to the smooth completion of any task at hand thereby making everything enjoyable and flexible as per the requirements of users. A fundamental reality of application development is that the user interface is the system to the users. What users want is for developers to build applications that meet their needs and that are easy to use. Constantine (1995) points out that the reality is that a good user interface allows people who understand the problem domain to work with the application without having to read the manuals or receive training. Interface design is important for several reasons. First of all the more intuitive the user interface the easier it is to use, and the easier it is to use the cheaper it is. The better the user interface the easier it is to train people to use it, reducing training costs. The better the user interface the less help people will need to use it, reducing support costs. The better the user interface the more users will like to use it, increasing their satisfaction with the work that have done.

The design of interfaces that attempt to encompass an extensive amount of merchandise has to employ methods where the product is either display successfully in a smaller scope while retaining its informational value. When it comes to e-commerce, User Interface design makes a difference between customers who abandon their carts and the ones that place an order. Elements like high quality product images are useful to persuade users to make a purchase. Clear call to action buttons and Seamless check-outs demonstrate that graphic and intuitive design must combine to make user navigation easy to use. Attention to user interface design details like the shopping cart, images, and call to actions will increase purchases and boost customer satisfaction.

The web interface becomes a major success factor since customers interface with sellers in cyberspace through the seller's website. There were many of consumer reports frustrations with the lack of interface standard features within e-commerce websites. This phenomenon makes e-commerce sites lose up to 50% of potential online sales because users cannot find what they want.

BACKGROUND

User interfaces are inputs and outputs that more directly involve a system user. Their design varies widely depending on such factors as interface purpose, user characteristics, and characteristics of a specific interface device (Hughes, Brusilovsky & Lewis, 2002).

As increasingly more products and services are sold over the Internet, it becomes all the more important to build up knowledge in e-commerce-specific user interface (UI) and user experience (UX) design. The entire user experience must therefore be designed to induce a positive affective state by strategically addressing consumers' concerns.

In order to explore issue of user interface, identify and analyze features of user interfaces and common location of e-commerce function on e-commerce web sites. In e-commerce, the website is the firm's interface with the customer, and its usability is crucial to the success of the venture (Turban & Gehrke 2000). The web is the primary infrastructure for e-commerce and offers some advantages.

E-commerce site should focus on being functional in navigation and interface, facilitate purchasing speed for both repeat customers and new purchases, be as direct as possible with minimal monetization through advertisements, and put a premium on data security to promote customer confidence in making a purchase through the software.

First, a web site enhances the corporation's image and improves communications with other corporations, thus improving efficiency in business process and reducing cost (Alper, 1999; Zona Research, Inc., 2000). Second, customer interface with sellers in cyberspace through the sellers' web site, therefore a well-constructed web site can determine the user's willingness to stay in a site, revisit it, and buy on the net.

Whereas a poorly constructed web site can lead to lost revenues and negative effect on corporate image (Zona Research, Inc., 2000).

Although there have been many studies focusing on the importance of web site design features (Huang et al., 2006; Kim et al., 2003; Tarafdar & Zhang, 2006; Turban & Gehrke, 2000), there have been few studies that have sought to identify the standard features of user interface in ecommerce web sites.

E-Commerce website design involves complex issues, including shopping carts, large catalogues, payment security issues, etc. Some authors suggest that certain features that make a website effective must be included. Coopee et al (2000) recommend that websites include easy payment processing and website security user tracking. Also: the company information must be easy to find online, customers must have reason to visit the website, the site must be visually appealing to users and navigation must be clear and simple (Cell 2000).

According to Najjar (2001), search, contact us, registration and shopping carts are major features of an e-commerce website. Cyr et al (2004) points out that users have differences in preferences of website design, access to product details, navigation and availability of products.

There are many individuals and organizations have published their own sets of guidelines. Entering the keywords "web design guidelines" into an internet search engine returns about 7,860,000 hits. The objective of these guidelines is to help designers make a better design decision that will result in a more usable or useful design. However, many of those guidelines are abstract and open to broad interpretation. Determining what kind of empirical support is available for web design guidelines is particularly challenging.

From 1990s onwards, electronic commerce would additionally include enterprise resource planning systems (ERP), data mining and data warehousing. The term 'electronic commerce' was coined in the early 1990s when Internet became commercialized and users began flocking to participate in the World Wide Web. The earliest example of many-to-many electronic commerce in physical goods was the Boston Computer Exchange, a marketplace for used computers launched in 1982. The first online information marketplace, including online consulting, was likely the American Information Exchange, another pre-Internet online system introduced in 1991.Since 1995, many innovative applications, ranging from direct online sales to e-learning experiences had been developed. Almost every organization in the world has a Web site. In 1999, the emphasis of e-commerce shifted from Business-to-Consumer (B2C) to Business-to-Business (B2B). In 2001, from B2B to B2E, e-government, e-learning, and m-commerce. In 2005, social networks started to rise and so did e-commerce and wireless applications-e-commerce will undoubtedly continue to shift and change in the future (ECommerze, 2008).

The Table 1 describes the evolution of e commerce.

E-Commerce Pioneers

Companies such as eBay and Amazon began to lead the way in e-commerce, both were among the first to establish prominent e-commerce brands. The most prominent e-commerce categories today are computers, books, office supplies, music, and a variety of electronics.

Amazon.com, Inc., founded by Jeff Bezos, was the original e-commerce pioneer and certainly the most recognizable. In the beginning, Amazon's business model required massive investment in warehousing, delivery and fulfillment capability and took years for Amazon to gain profitability.

Table 1. Evolution of e-commerce

Year	Event
1984	EDI, or electronic data interchange, was standardized through ASC X12. This guaranteed that companies would be able to complete transactions with one another reliably.
1992	CompuServe offers online retail products to its customers. This gives people the first chance to buy things off their computer.
1994	Netscape arrived. Providing users a simple browser to surf the Internet and a safe online transaction technology called Secure Sockets Layer.
1995	Two of the biggest names in e-commerce are launched: Amazon.com and eBay.com.
1998	DSL, or Digital Subscriber Line, provides fast, always-on Internet service to subscribers across California. This prompts people to spend more time, and money, online.
1999	Retail spending over the Internet reaches $20 billion, according to Business.com.
2000	The U.S government extended the moratorium on Internet taxes until at least 2005.

Amazon began as just an online bookstore but over the years has extended its offering to a wide variety of product categories, including electronics, software, music, DVD's, CD's, video games, MP3's, clothing, shoes, health and beauty products and even household goods. Today, Amazon generates anywhere between 30 to 40% of its total sales revenue from affiliates or third party merchants who list and sell their products on Amazon's web site.

User Interface and Its Principles

User Interface (UI) Design focuses on anticipating what users might need to do and ensuring that the interface has elements that are easy to access, understand, and use to facilitate those actions. UI brings together concepts from interaction design, visual design, and information architecture.

Understanding the User Interface

1. **User-Centered Design:** Design techniques that embody the view that the user interface is the entire system.
2. **Usability:** Degree to which a system is easy to learn and use.
3. **Metaphors:** Analogies between features of the user interface and aspects of physical reality that users are familiar with.
4. **Direct Manipulation Metaphor:** Metaphor in which objects on a display are manipulated to look like physical objects (pictures) or graphic symbols that represent them (icons).
5. **Desktop Metaphor:** Metaphor in which the visual display is organized into distinct regions, with a large empty workspace in the middle and a collection of tool icons around the perimeter.
6. **Document Metaphor:** Metaphor in which data is visually represented as paper pages or forms.
7. **Dialog Metaphor:** Metaphor in which user and computer accomplish a task by engaging in a conversation or dialog via text, voice, or tools such as labeled buttons.

User Interface Design Principles

User Interface needs to be streamlined and easy to use for novice users, it should also not be boring for experienced and educated ones. Constantine and Lockwood describe a collection of principles for improving the quality of your user interface design. These principles are:

1. **The Structure Principle:** Your design should organize the user interface purposefully, meaningfully, useful ways based on clear, consistent models that are apparent, and recognizable to users, putting related things together and separating unrelated things, differentiating dissimilar things and making similar things resemble one another.
2. **The Simplicity Principle:** Your design should make simple, common tasks simple to do, communicating clearly and simply in the user's own language, and providing good shortcuts that are related to longer procedures.
3. **The Visibility Principle:** Your design should keep all needed options and materials for a given task visible without distracting the user with extraneous or redundant information.

4. **The Feedback Principle:** Your design should keep users informed of actions or interpretations, changes of state or condition, and errors or exceptions that are relevant and of interest to the user through clear, concise, and unambiguous language familiar to users.
5. **The Tolerance Principle:** Your design should be flexible and tolerant, reducing the cost of mistakes and also preventing errors wherever possible by tolerating varied inputs.
6. **The Reuse Principle:** Your design should reuse internal and external components maintaining consistency with purpose rather than merely arbitrary consistency, thus reducing the need for users to rethink and remember.

Choosing Interface Elements

Interface elements include but are not limited to:

- **Input Controls:** These controls are used to select, sort or search particular items in. Examples are: buttons, text fields, checkboxes, radio buttons, dropdown lists, list boxes, toggles, date field
  - **Text Box:** A rectangular box that accepts text typed on a keyboard or recognized from speech input
  - **List Box:** A text box that contains a list of predefined data values
  - **Combo Box:** A text box that contains a predefined list of acceptable entries but permits the user to enter a new value when the list doesn't contain the desired value
  - **Radio Buttons:** A group of choices from which the user selects only one; the system then automatically turns off all other buttons in the group
  - **Check Boxes:** Similar to radio buttons, but the user can select multiple items within the group
  - **Cascading Style Sheets (CSS):** Web page encoding standard that enables a Web site designer to specify parts of a page that will always look the same and parts that will vary by task or audience
  - **Assistive Technologies:** Software (such as text-to-speech and voice-recognition utilities) that adapts user interfaces to the special needs of persons with disabilities
- **Navigational Components:** These are used to move or navigate from one page to other.
  - **Examples:** Slider, search field, pagination, tags, icons
- **Informational Components:** These are used to provide information to the user.
  - **Examples:** Tooltips, icons, progress bar, notifications, message boxes.
- **Containers:** There are times when multiple elements might be appropriate for displaying content. When this happens, it's important to consider the trade-offs.

Defining a User Experience

Here are some of the elements that impact the user experience of your online store.

- Visual appeal. Colors, branding, imagery, layout.
- Search and navigation. Ability to find what you are looking for quickly.
- Site map. How the site is categorized and grouped.

- Content. Quality and quantity of text, images, videos that are associated with products and product categories.
- Ease of use. Can users easily navigate across the site, in and out of the cart, create shopping lists, find shipping costs?
- Availability of help. Online chat, email help, self service accounts.
- Performance. Is the site fast?
- Payment options and process. Do you offer several payment methods, can users store credit card information, checkout with PayPal Express or other 3rd party payment systems?
- Shopping cart. Is it visually appealing? Is shipping info available?
- Image features. Zoom and pan, alternate images?
- Personalization. Is the store delivering personalized content?
- Merchandising. Are promotional items well displayed and available, using best-seller lists, cross-sells, and up-sells?
- Sale of goods
- Purchase of goods
- Financial assistance
- Advertising
- Sharing of products

The reality is the user experience is impacted by every single element of your website. You can have a well designed site with great navigation and performance, but if your shopping cart is lacking a shipping estimator, you may lose buyers to a poorly designed site that includes one.

Best Practices for Designing an Interface

Once you know about the user, make sure to consider the following when designing the interface:

- **Keep the Interface Simple:** The best interfaces are almost invisible to the user. They avoid unnecessary elements and are clear in the language they use on labels and in messaging.
- **Create Consistency and Use Common UI Elements:** By using common elements in your UI, users feel more comfortable and are able to get things done more quickly. It is also important to create patterns in language, layout and design throughout the site to help facilitate efficiency.
- **Be Purposeful in Page Layout:** Consider the spatial relationships between items on the page and structure the page based on importance. Careful placement of items can help scanning and readability.
- **Strategically Use Color and Texture:** You can direct attention toward or redirect attention away from items using color, light, contrast, and texture to your advantage.
- **Use Typography to Create Hierarchy and Clarity:** Different sizes, fonts, and arrangement of the text to help increase scanability, legibility and readability.
- **Make Sure That the System Communicates What's Happening:** Always inform your users of location, actions, changes in state, or errors. The use of various UI elements to communicate status and, if necessary, next steps can reduce frustration for your user.
- **Think About the Defaults:** By carefully thinking about and anticipating the goals people bring to site, you can create defaults that reduce the burden on the user.

Figure 1 explains user interface design process with an example.

Guidelines for Designing Windows and Forms

Interface Layout and Formatting

High-quality interfaces are well laid out, with the fields easily identified and understood. As you design your interfaces, you should think about these:

- **Consistency:** All the forms within a system need to have the same look and feel.
- **Labels and Headings:** Labels should also be easy to identify and read.
- **Distribution and Order:** Related fields are usually placed next to each other and can be grouped within a box.
- **Fonts and Colors:** Variations in font face and size can help users distinguish different parts of the form, but only a handful of font and size variations should be used for larger screens and as few as possible should be used for small screens.

Figure 1. User interface design process example

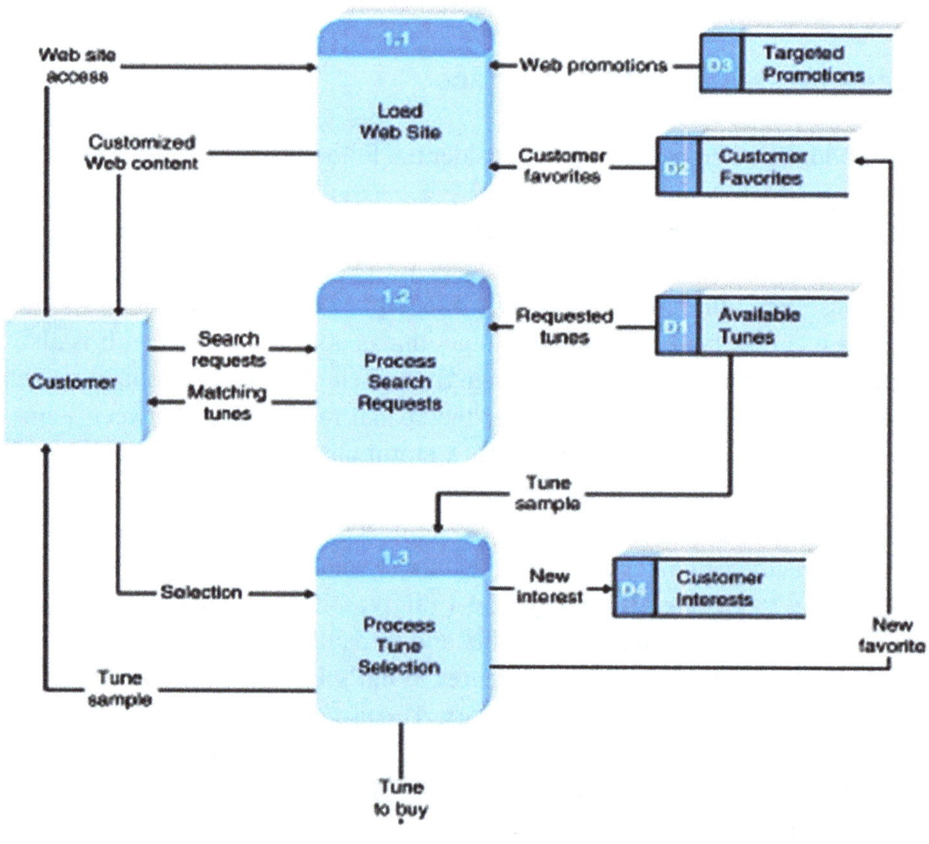

Data Entry

Several types of data-entry controls are widely used in user interfaces, including Text boxes, List boxes, Combo boxes, Radio buttons, and Check boxes.

Guidelines for Web Browser User Interfaces

Consistency

Consistency is especially critical within Web sites because most sites contain a large number of pages that serve many different purposes and audiences. Cascading style sheets (CSS) are a Web page encoding standard, and they enable a Web site designer to specify parts of the site's pages that will always look the same and parts that will vary by task or audience.

Performance Considerations

Performance considerations are also an important issue in Web applications. Web sites in general and browser-based forms in particular are sensitive to application design and to the quality of the network connections between the user's computing device and the servers that host the site. Designers of Web-based user interfaces must perform a careful balancing act, providing embedded programming code within a page to avoid refreshes but not overloading page content so as to avoid long delays when the user moves from page to page.

Pictures, Video, and Sound

Web-based interfaces are often preferred for their inherent ability to mix text, images, and sound. Powerful and compelling interfaces can be constructed, and they are especially important in customer-facing systems. However, heavy use of sound and images exacerbates the previously discussed performance issues and also creates issues of compatibility. Compatibility issues arise for sound and video because there are so many ways in which they can be encoded. Thus, Web site designers must carefully choose which formats and plug-ins will be used.

Users With Disabilities

Designers of all user interfaces must be sensitive to the special needs of persons with disabilities. Because the Web is such a fundamental resource in the modern world, standards have been developed to ensure maximal usability for those who are visually impaired or have limited dexterity. Providing this kind of support is part of the class of software called assistive technologies.

Guidelines for Handheld Devices

Designing Web and app-based user interfaces for handheld devices presents additional design challenges, including:

- Small screen size
- Small keyboards and touch screens
- Limited network capacity
- App design guidelines and toolkits

The small screen area provides relatively limited space in which to display content. Thus, designers must pare down the user-interface content to ensure readability and to avoid cluttering the screen. Mobile device user interfaces must avoid detailed textual input whenever possible and must provide touch controls that are well spaced and easy to locate.

User Interface Perspective

Being concentrated on not only logic and transitions but also looks and style, UI design stage also contributes much to the success of the e-commerce project. It is the aspect which creates visual performance and sets the solid ground for the desirability of the interface and positive emotional feedback from the buyer. At UI design stage for e-commerce, designers have to find the general stylistic concept which will support UX aspects mentioned before and will give the online point-of-sale the attractive looks. Some aspects, which designers have to take into account in this perspective, are:

- Choice of colors that correspond to the brand image and strengthen emotional feedback
- Setting the style corresponding to the nature of the commercial offer:
- Reaching the website, people should instantly understand if it sells household goods, fresh vegetables, trendy clothes, exclusive devices or anything else
- Visual hierarchy which makes the core zones of interaction instantly noticeable.
- General harmony of perception which sets the feeling of aesthetic satisfaction supporting positive user experience.
- Simple check-list for some essential aspects designers would rather consider working on e-commerce projects:
    - **Know the Buyers:** User research will help to get the needs and wishes of target audience.
    - **Have Users Informed:** Make the screens or pages filled with information and functionality users really need for making purchase.
    - **Keep Design Consistent:** Not only does the website or app itself need consistency of design for all the screens in terms of general branding, but also social networks, print materials and actual point-of-sales appearance if they exist.
    - **Refresh the Experience:** Minor changes or attractive details added to the interface from time to time without breaking general visual consistency can give the feeling of refreshment, like new looks of mannequins do in the window displays of the shop.
    - **Check Your Solutions:** User testing can have a great impact on understanding the factors that boost conversions. Ideally, it should be applied not only in the process of design but also after the launch of e-commerce platform on the basis of real user interactions and troubles which can arise.
    - **Be Careful About Revolutions and Wow-Effect:** The power of habit plays the big role in the products of this kind. Choosing layout, menus or icons, which stand too far from the ones users are generally accustomed to, can bring confusion and frustration. For example, usage

of any other image instead of the magnifying glass to mark the search field can result in bad user experience as buyers know that visual symbol and will look for it. So, making this sort of experiments, take time to test them well.

- **Respect the Buyers:** Remember, that they are not abstract metrics-every figure in conversion report is about real people. Look for the interface that will respect their time, effort and needs and it will bring positive experience of shopping for both sides.

To summarize designing e-commerce website or mobile app, designers should definitely consider the following aspects:

- Operational simplicity
- Strong branding
- Security of users' data
- Effective use of visual elements
- Clear data presentation via menus, catalogs etc.
- User's ability to leave feedback about goods and services
- Easily available general and contact information about the business providing goods or services
- Design that supports the offer not overshadowing it.

Challenges of Designing a User Interface

Designing the user interface for an e-commerce site is very challenging. Various researches investigating the major determinant features of an effective web site have been done before. Some of them are explained below.

Coopee et al. (2000) suggested that web site designers should include some essential features into any commercial web site they design, as follows: catalog development, users tracking, payment processing, online fulfillment, web site security, privacy, business-business sales models, and business-customer sales models.

Cell (2000) provided some guidelines for creating customer friendly web site: make company easy to find online, keep site navigation simple and clear, give customers a reason to visit the site, make site visually appealing, offer a menu of communications options, and answer e-mail promptly and professionally.

Najjar (2001) stated that designing the user interface for an e-commerce site is very challenging. The major sections to design include the overall page format, navigation, catalog, registration, personalization, checkout, and customer service. In page format, he considers download speed, the use of graphics, scrolling, and highlighted that a web designer should format the page to make it easy for users to interact with the web site by put user interface elements in familiar locations.

Cyr et al. (2004) addressed differences in preferences and perception of web site design across culture. They considered menu layout, access to product info, professional design, logical info presentation, screen design, navigation, sequencing, product attributes, and product availability as an important web site features.

Liu et al., (2003) studied about standard user interface in e-commerce site found that the lack of a standard user interface that can assist users to navigate different e-commerce sites would influence the individual's decision to accept site for online shopping purpose. The results also show a strong relationship between users' perceptions of usefulness and ease of use toward standard user interface.

Challenges of E-Commerce Applications

Five biggest challenges for launching an e-commerce marketplace are:

1. Seller and buyer retention: The issue of buyer retention can only be solved with the help of marketing efforts, wide ranges of sellers and providing the best shopping experience.
2. How to connect buyers with relevant sellers: To solve this issue different practices and methods are used like:
    a. Modern behavior driven on-site search systems
    b. Personalized matching algorithms and trigger based emails
    c. Auto filling sellers accounts (and tips for their rational filling)
    d. Handy navigation
3. How to make buyers trust sellers: To build trust in your business you should take into account the testimonials, rating, social proof.
4. A Good First Impression: The first impression is the longest lasting, it's very important to provide the best user experience on any device.
5. Shopping experience: The best shopping experience is the essence of all above, with amazingly beautiful multi-device design, intuitive UI and personalization.

Context-based personalization is one of the main trends of the e-commerce in 2016. It can help to map the customer's journey and anticipate their needs, providing shoppers with the information they need, when they need it.

Standardized User Interface

The need to standardize user interface is:

1. Easy access
2. Effective web design
3. Understand web

Standards in web developments are of increasing importance as programmers strive to make their components work across all browsers and accessible by the broadest set of customers (Clary,2003).

A standard ensures users can understand the individual interface elements in an e-commerce site and that customers know where to look for what features. [2]Jakob's law of the web user experience

Jacob Nielsen states:"Users expect 77% of the simpler Web design elements to behave in a certain way". Three different standardization levels according to him are:

1. **Standard:** 80% or more of websites use the same design approach. Users strongly expect standard elements to work a certain way when they visit a new site because that's how things always work.
2. **Convention:** 50-79% of websites use the same design approach. With a convention, users expect elements to work a certain way when they visit a new site because that's how things usually work.

3. **Confusion:** With these elements, no single design approach dominates, and even the most popular approach is used by at most 49% of websites. For such design elements, users don't know what to expect when they visit a new site.

Wireframe

A wireframe is a simple line drawing depicting the layout of a website before any decoration is added. It outlines size, placement and orientation of every part of your Web page.

Graphic Design

Graphic design of e commerce website should be visually pleasing as well as functional, usable, and "lightweight" (fast –loading)

Usability

The goal of ecommerce Usability is to fulfill the customer's purchasing needs as quickly and effortlessly as possible. Usability helps to make the site experience seamless for the consumer, which increases sales. Usability powers good user interface design through a user-centered design approach that analyzes the entire ecommerce transaction from the customer's perspective.

User Interface

User Interface (UI) Design focuses on anticipating what users might need to do and ensuring that the interface has elements that are easy to access, understand, and use to facilitate those actions. Website usability is delivered through the user interface design.

Figure 2. User interface design

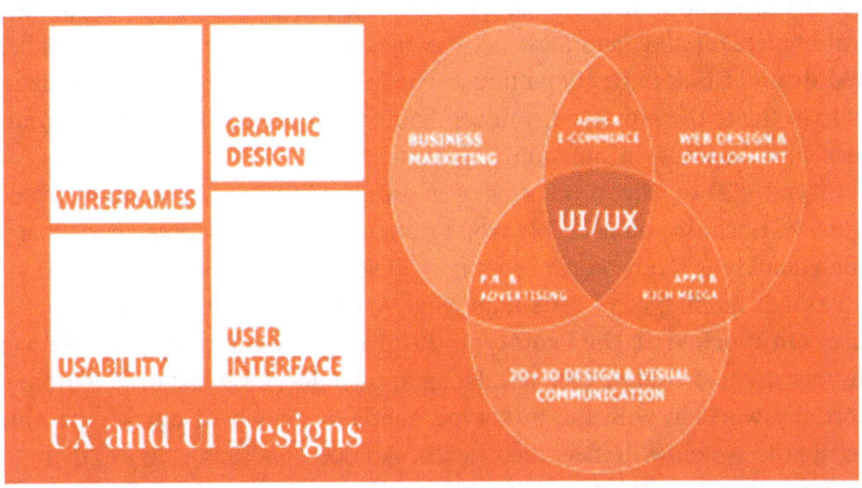

DESIGN OF USER INTERFACE

Prototyping

Prototyping (Ambler, 2001; Ambler, 1998a) is an iterative analysis technique in which users are actively involved in the mocking-up of screens and reports.

The purpose of a prototype is to show people the possible design(s) for the user interface of an application.

There are four steps to the prototyping process:

1. Determine the needs of your users. The requirements of your users drive the development of your prototype as they define the business objects that your system must support. You can gather these requirements in interviews, in CRC (class responsibility collaborator) modeling sessions, in use-case modeling sessions, and in class diagramming sessions (Ambler 2001; Ambler, 1998a; Ambler, 1998b).
2. Build the prototype. Using a prototyping tool or high-level language you develop the screens and reports needed by your users.
3. Evaluate the prototype. After a version of the prototype is built it needs to be evaluated. The main goal is that you need to verify that the prototype meets the needs of your users.
4. Determine if you're finished yet. You want to stop the prototyping process when you find the evaluation process is no longer generating any new requirements, or is generating a small number of not-so-important requirements.

Prototyping Tips and Techniques

1. **Look for Real-World Objects:** Good User Interfaces allow users to work with the real-world objects they are used to. Therefore you should start by looking for these kinds of objects and identify how people interact with them.
2. **Work With the Real Users:** The best people to get involved in prototyping are the ones who will actually use the application when it's done. These are the people who have the most to gain from a successful implementation, and these are the ones who know their own needs best.
3. **Set a Schedule and Stick to It:** By putting a schedule in place for when you will get together with your users to evaluate the prototype, you set their expectations and you force yourself to actually get the work done. A win-win situation.
4. **Use a Prototyping Tool:** Invest the money in a prototyping tool that allows you to put screens together quickly. Because you probably won't want to keep the prototype code that you write, code that's written quickly is rarely worth keeping, you shouldn't be too concerned if your prototyping tool generates a different type of code than what you intend to develop in.
5. **Get the Users to Work With the Prototype:** Just like you want to take a car for a test drive before you buy it your users should be able to take an application for a test drive before it is developed. Furthermore, by working with the prototype hands-on they will quickly be able to determine whether or not the system will meet their needs. A good approach is to ask them to work through some use-case scenarios using the prototype as if it is the real system.

6. **Understand the Underlying Business:** You need to understand the underlying business before you can develop a prototype that will support it. Perform interviews with key users, read internal documentation of how the business runs, and read documentation about how some of your competitors operate. The more you know about the business the more likely it is that you'll be able to build a prototype that supports it.
7. **There are Different Levels of Prototype:** I like to successively develop three different types of prototypes of a system: A hand-drawn prototype that shows its basic/rough functionality, an electronic prototype that shows the screens but not the data that will be displayed on them, and then finally the screens with data. By starting out simple in the beginning I avoid investing a lot of time in work that will most likely be thrown away. By successively increasing the complexity of the prototype as it gets closer to the final solution, my users get a better and better idea of how the application will actually work, providing the opportunity to provide greater and greater insight into improving it.
8. **Don't Spend a lot of Time Making the Code Good:** At the beginning of the prototyping process you will throw away a lot of your work as you learn more about the business. Therefore it doesn't make sense to invest a lot of effort in code that you probably aren't going to keep anyway.

General Guidelines

- Be consistent in a user interface, it's critical.
- Set user interface standards and stick to them.
- Choose industry standards so as to increase the chance that your applications
- will look and feel like other applications developed externally to your organization.
- Explain the rules of how your application works to your users. If it's consistent,
- then the rules should be simple and few in number.
- Support both novices and experts.
- Word text consistently, positively, and in full English.
- Look at other applications with a grain of salt because not everyone understands good user interface design.
- Display the objects that your users need to do their jobs on the desktop.
- Think in terms of clusters of business objects and their corresponding interface objects, not in terms of applications.
- Interface objects should look, feel, and behave exactly like the real-world objects that they represent.

Screen Design

- Navigation between screens and on screens are both important.
- Understand your widgets so that you know how to apply them properly.
- Use color sparingly and always have a secondary indicator.
- Follow the contrast rule – put dark text on light backgrounds and light text on dark backgrounds.
- Use fonts sparingly and consistently.
- When items are unavailable gray them out, don't remove them if you want your users to form accurate models.

- Use non-destructive default buttons.
- Left justify edit fields and right justify their labels.
- Right justify integers, decimal-align floating point numbers, and left justify strings.
- Don't create busy/crowded screens.
- Use group boxes and whitespace to group logically related items on the screen.
- Open windows in the center of the action.
- Pop-up menus shouldn't be the only source of functionality.

Experienced developers recognize the importance of all aspects of the user interface and recommend using several techniques that place the user at the center of the development process. These techniques are referred to collectively as user-centered design. User-centered design techniques emphasize three principles:

- Focus early on users and their work.
- Evaluate designs to ensure usability.
- Use iterative development.

The early focus on users and their work is consistent with the approach to systems analysis in this text. User-oriented analysis and design tasks are performed as early as possible and are often given higher priority than other tasks.

The goal of user-centered design is usability, the degree to which a system is easy to learn and use. Ease of learning and ease of use sometimes conflict. For example, a system can be easy to learn but be cumbersome to use all day. Usability is not always easy to achieve.

In general, the usability is a software quality attribute which measures the extent to which an application can be used by users to achieve effectiveness, efficiency and satisfaction in a specified context of use [3],[7]. Furthermore, the usability can be decomposed into five attributes:

1. Learnability, which measures the ease of learning the application functionality;
2. Efficiency, which measures the ease of use and the level of productivity attainable by the user;
3. Memorability, which measures the ease of remembering the application's functionality;
4. Low error rate, which measures how the application support users in making less errors; and
5. User's satisfaction, which measures how the users enjoy the application.

The third principle of user-centered design is iterative development-that is, doing some analysis, then some design, then some implementation, and then repeating the processes. After each iteration, the project team evaluates the work on the system to date. Iterative development keeps the focus on the user by continually returning to the user requirements during each iteration and by evaluating the system after each iteration.

There are many things that go into creating an optimal user interface design. Here's an overview:

- User Experience is the first and most strategic step to an optimized user interface design.
- User Experience conceptualization, planning, and design ensures the site will fulfill your business goals.
- The information architecture wireframes are the functional blueprints of the site.

- Information architecture also includes the careful planning and definition of the site's navigation, naming conventions and content organization.
- Usability helps to make the site experience as seamless as possible for the visitor to increase site engagement and sales.
- Usability powers good user interface design by promoting a user-centered design approach that analyzes the ecommerce transaction from the customer's perspective.

The design of web sites for effective performance is a complex and highly creative process that blends intuition, experience, and careful consideration of numerous technical issues and investigations (Nielsen, 2000; Sharma & Sharma, 2000; Sklar, 2000; Niererst, 1999).

Graphical features on the web are increasingly important to support information as well as interaction between consumers and business providers. Consumers are interested in information, representing style and interaction with web usage depending on the amount of graphical components. Graphical components support users' understanding and deter mination to purchase products from the web. In global markets, users are sensitive to interaction with product information on the web. Web designers provide information using text, colors, symbols and graphics on the web page.

Del Galdo and Nielson (1996) demonstrated that color and screen design directions have different psychological and social associations in different cultures. More importantly, different users have different concepts of screen usage. Because of the right-to left writing direction of the Arabic language, the common way to design the screen is to start reading from the top right-hand to the left-hand side (Del Galdo & Nielson, 1996). Designing screens normally needs to consider that Latin-based screen design starts from the top left and corner, and Chinese language can start from top right-hand to bottom left-hand or adopt the Latin-based style. However, it is very difficult to provide localized screen designs if they are not included in the original design of the application. As a result Graphic User Interface (GUI) applications need to be considered in localized interface design with globalized information on the web.

Although the cultural background of consumers is very important for interface design, current design practice takes minor account of cultural issues. Consumers' expectations are not taken into consideration in designing the functionality of web sites in Singapore. Singaporean designers emphasized that the graphics (pictures and animations) are important components and hence are heavily used to attract local customers. On the contrary, Australian web designers were less sensitive to the use of graphics on the web. However they preferred creating an image of the company on the web rather than using company's logo to reiterate company's image. Apparently Australian web designers are more customer-oriented in web design, in comparison to Singaporean web designers.

The web sites of leading IT companies did not have their interface to account for different user cultures. The web designers create graphic components on web sites lead to unique conventions leading to evolution of a new culture in expression of ideas on the web based e-market (WBEM).

CULTURAL ISSUES IN WEB DESIGNING

It helps to be able to quantify cultures. Importantly, this is not a way to make blanket statements about people from certain countries, but a way to clarify how groups interact with each other and the internet.

Designing an excellent user interface for one language in one country offers many challenges. Designing a user interface that can be successfully implemented for several language and several countries is even more difficult.

A company may wonder if it's even possible to design a single user interface that, when implemented, will provide an excellent user experience for the majority of the world's Internet users.

However, it remains an interesting questions to what extent web design should be complies with interface standards within different skill and cultural challenges. Following design standards simply ensures that users know what a company is talking about. User interface standards have become the object of increasingly intense activities in recent years [Abernethy 1988; Holdaway & Bevan 1989]. These activities are part of a general current interest in information processing standards [Berg & Schumny 1990].

Eliminate the confusing design elements and move as far as possible into the realm of design conventions will ensure users know what features to expect, know how these features will look in the interface, know where to find these features on the site and on the page, know how to operate each feature to achieve their goal, don't have to ponder the meaning of unknown design elements, don't miss important features because they overlook a non-standard design element. Cultural factors in information systems are likely to impact on effectiveness through user interface design.

Web interface design and user issues are significant factors in the measurement of systems implementation. Web implementation is not only concerned with developers' ideas but also with consumers' choices. Information on the web relies on both user groups.

In a global context, most interfaces do not promote effective usage due to use of inappropriate metaphors in a global context. Many of the icons, metaphors, shapes, colors of text and background, frame/text locations on screen, etc. employed in systems design are relevant to the culture of origin of the software. Most of these applications are directly translated into different languages at most and distributed to users internationally.

In an international context, the graphic features employed in interface development makes a somewhat lesser impact in the variety of contexts it is concerned with, although it will be very clear to a minor proportion of the population as a whole. This provides an indication that consideration of human factors in the design of user interface for an international user base is an important factor in promoting effective usage of information systems. (Johnston & Johal, 1999; Corbitt & Thanasankit,2001).

User Interface Design Tools

Here is a list of free online design tools for fonts, patterns, logos, images, website design, team collaboration, and design inspiration.

- **Adobe Color:** Adobe Color lets you create color palettes using a handy color wheel. Set the base color and get the four complementary hues. Save your five-color palettes, or explore and edit other popular themes. Use the mobile app to create color schemes from real life images.
- **Pictaculous:** Pictaculous is a color palette generator. Use it to create a color palette from an image. Upload an image with your primary colors, and quickly receive a palette of complementary colors for your theme.
- **Colordot:** Colordot is a handy tool to identify and save colors. Just move your mouse to change colors, click to save. Colordot also has useful mobile app to create and share color palettes.

- **Google Fonts:** Google Fonts makes it quick and easy for everyone to use web fonts, including professional designers and developers. All of the fonts are open source. Customize them for your own use, or collaborate with the original designer to improve them.
- **Font Squirrel:** Font Squirrel is a website for free, high-quality, designer-friendly, commercial-use fonts. View font lists that are recently added and most downloaded.
- **Fontello:** Fontello is a tool to pack vector images into web fonts. It builds everything necessary to include graphics into your web pages. Also, Fontello has a big built-in collection of open source artworks.
- **Typecast:** Typecast is a tool to design a working prototype using simple visual controls, then export production-ready HTML and CSS or share by URL. Build common HTML elements like headings, paragraph text, block quotes, and lists. Focus on the finer points: precise control over your typography.
- **Modular Scale:** Modular Scale is a tool to help web designers size their type in a more meaningful way. Use the base and ratio controls to adjust a spectrum of typography.
- **Patternizer:** Patternizer is a tool to design your own patterns or browse free featured patterns. Patterns can be saved and shared with anyone, allowing for collaboration and remixing. Patternizer generates code that can be used with patternizer.js to create these patterns on any canvas element.
- **Subtle Patterns:** Subtle Patterns is another free pattern resource. Access over 400 free patterns to download. Sketch and Photoshop formats are ready to export for the web.
- **Freepik:** Freepik is a search engine of free vector designs, icons, and images. Freepik illustrations and graphic resources are selected by its design team to provide users with content that can be used in both personal and commercial projects.
- **Logopond:** Logopond is a website for logo design inspiration. Get ideas on your own logo direction, or find designers to tap.
- **Spaces Logo Maker:** This is a handy tool to easily make your own logo. Just type your brand name into the logo generator, choose a font, choose an icon, and experiment with different options. Spaces also has a variety of other useful generator tools for slogans, QR codes, image resizing, and more.
- **Dribble:** Dribbble is a website to discover, explore, and promote design. Web designers, graphic designers, illustrators, icon artists, typographers, logo designers, and other creative types share small screenshots that show their work, process, and current projects.
- **VSCO:** VSCO is a photo editing app to create, edit, and publish images from your smartphone. VSCO also has a community platform to promote and discover images.
- **Paper:** Paper is a useful free tool to create designs. Create sharp drawings and diagrams with Paper's sketch tools. Draw on photos or quickly spotlight details. Easily create notes — swipe right to create checklists, left to create titles.
- **Niice:** Niice is a website to gather, share, and discuss visual elements. Niice's drag-and-drop interface makes it easy to create boards for design collaboration.
- **Marvel:** Marvel is an app for design, prototyping, and collaboration. Create screens directly in Marvel, add images from Sketch or Photoshop, or sync designs from your cloud storage. Link all your designs together, then add gestures and transitions to make your prototype feel just like a real app or website.

- **Foundation:** Foundation is a responsive, front-end framework, with a collection of HTML, CSS, and JavaScript design patterns to build upon. Peruse its design gallery to see big brand websites built using Foundation.
- **Evernote:** Evernote is a useful tool to store, access, and share your design content. Snap a picture of a sketch or create a list or note. Keep your design images and plans synced across devices. Share ideas by collaborating seamlessly with your team in a group notebook.

Sample Applications

Vendio: Automated Selling on Amazon, EBay, and Facebook

With a focus on automation, Vendio ecommerce software saves you time with tools to easily put products on eBay, Amazon, Facebook and your own online Web store. List products once and they'll be published simultaneously on the supported marketplaces.

Other Vendio features include inventory control, sales and order management, email marketing, the shopping cart with drag-and-drop features and analytics reporting. Vendio Online Stores provides business owners with marketing features, including Google Analytics and built-in options, while a Vendio-powered Web store is optimized for mobile Apple iOS devices.

The KG TRAINS websites, powered by Vendio, offers a customized layout and a drag-and-drop to shopping cart feature for customers.

Intuit Ecommerce: The Merchant Account

Intuit's ecommerce offering offers a simple point and click interface that makes it easy to create and publish a store that you can update at any time.

With Intuit Websites, you'll get everything needed to design and launch an online store, including the domain name, hosting, the Simple Store ecommerce software, a site builder tool and online payments via Intuit merchant accounts. The merchant account is a big feature, as it enables small businesses to move beyond offering basic PayPal payments at checkout. Another nice feature of Intuit websites is the Facebook extension with which you can create a store a Facebook Business Page that automatically syncs with current store inventory.

Shopify: Advanced SEO and Analytics

Shopify hosted ecommerce lets you pick a template, optimize the design, add a product catalog, organize your products and create blog posts from a single administration dashboard. Shopify feature built-in mobile commerce that includes an iPhone app and mobile storefront. Marketing tools for SEO and coupon codes to help sell items are also available.

Shopify integrates with Google Analytics; this lets you automatically track customer purchases and shopping cart transactions connected to Google Analytics data. It also features built-in analytics to benchmark your online store's performance to help you track ecommerce over time.

The Shopify ecommerce platform powers The Artisan, a Philippine clothing brand that focuses on cut and sewn pieces.

FINDINGS

E-commerce sector has huge growth potential and Internet is the back-bone of e-commerce. [2] mentioned All of total 120 sites sampled (100%) provided a set of global link to the site's first-level pages.

Global links to the first level were most positioned at the top of pages (78%), presented as navigation bar (40%), and tabs (23%), Global links were most commonly HTML no underlined (71%). Another common practice was text graphics (25%), which give designer greater control over the font type, size, and weight of the text. From 120 sites sample, one hundred and six sites (88%) provided return to home function. 93 sites (78%) provided an explicit link to home. This link mainly positioned at the top of the page (81 sites, 68%) and left side of the page (30 sites, 25%); including implicit home link Thirteen sites (11%) only provide company logo as a link to homepage. Nearly all company logo located in the top left corner of the page, only 3 sites that located its logo in the top right corner of the page. Whereas, 14 sites (12%) did not provide an explicit homepage View cart function provides information about items that have placed in the shopping cart by user. Only 25 sites from total sample that provide view cart function. The placement of this function varied, with the greatest number of sites placing it at the top right of main content area (13 sites, 46%) and on the left side (8 sites, 29%).

Manage account function enable user access information such as their email preferences, billing address, and shipping address. Nineteen sites (16%) provide manage account function. The placement of the page varied, but tended towards the top right area of the page (63%) or on the left side. Common labels used to represent this function were account and login. There were 13 sites used login (68%), whereas the rest sites used account as label.

Get help function provides answer to questions that frequently or may ask by user when they purchase items online. The objective is to help users without having to contact the merchant. This function (including contact us link) was most commonly located at the top of the page on the right side or on the left side.

The search function allows users to enter keyword into a test field and find information that matches the keyword entered. Forty-three sites (36%) provided a search function. Search function primarily found at the top of the page (51%) or on the left side of the page (37%). The rest sites positioned the search function at the main content area and on the right side. None of those sites presented this function with an icon.

Search function commonly presented as a text field labeled "Search" (68%), "Product search" (14%), "Product Find" (5%), and "Keyword Search" (12%). Most sites provided the search function as a text field and button (68%). Catalogue function makes it easy for users to see products. Seventy-two sites (60%) provided catalogue function. Catalogue function usually found at the top of main content area (72%) and on the left side (28%). This function most commonly labeled "Products"; other label includes catalogue, gallery, and collection. Personalization Function rarely provided by the 120 sites sample. Only 29 sites (24%) provided personalization function. Personalization function primarily found on the left side (59%). There were varied label used to representing this function.

Present Status

Many researchers have been using virtual reality (VR) in e-commerce to provide consumers with a new type of mediated experience—a virtual consumer experience. "A virtual consumer experience is a psychological and emotional state that consumers undergo when they interact with products in a 3D environment or within intelligent agents" (Hughes, Brusilovsky & Lewis, 2002). It has the potential to rich consumers' experience (Hughes, Brusilovsky & Lewis, 2002). Hughes, Brusilovsky, and Lewis (2002) presented an adaptive navigation support system for using a virtual environment for online shopping, to help ease the consumer's navigation and to help the consumer focus on important product features. They used some detailed technologies-such as direct guidance, hiding, sorting, and annotation-for the adaptive navigation. Cássia, and Fernando [6] presented an adaptive 3D virtual environment with structure and content that changed according to the user's interest and preference and according to its application in e-commerce. They integrated intelligent agents, user models, and automatic content categorizations together in their system. Chittaro and Ranon (2000) presented two design guidelines (massive and walking product) to improve the usability of VR stores. In Sanna, Zunino, and Lamberti [11]'s presented VR e-commerce system which base on 5 Virtual Reality Modeling Language (VRML), an animated virtual human was introduced.

The virtual human was to be used as a virtual shopping assistant for helping online shoppers navigate through an e-commerce environment. Although prior studies show that VR can enhance e-commerce by providing virtual experiences and product interactions, VR technology can still only provide a virtual, not a real, experience. It is important to provide consumers with "real experiences" and "real object interactions".

Limitations

Non-Standard GUI Controls

Basic GUI widgets- command links and buttons, radio buttons and checkboxes, scrollbars, close boxes, and so on - are the lexical units that form dialog design's vocabulary. If you change the appearance or behavior of these units, it's like suddenly injecting foreign words into a natural-language communication.

Inconsistency

Non-standard GUI controls are a special case of the general problem of inconsistent design.

Confusion results when applications use different words or commands for the same thing, or when they use the same word for multiple concepts in different parts of the application.

Asking for the Same Info Twice

Users shouldn't have to enter the same information more than once.

No Default Values

Defaults help users in many ways. Most importantly, defaults can:

- Speed up the interaction by freeing users from having to specify a value if the default is acceptable;
- Teach, by example, the type of answer that is appropriate for the question; and
- Direct novice users toward a safe or common outcome, by letting them accept the default if they don't know what else to do.

System-Centric Features

- Too many applications expose their dirty laundry, offering features that reflect the system's internal view of the data rather than users' understanding of the problem space.

Reset Button on Web Forms

- The reset button clears the user's entire input and returns the form to its pristine state. Users would want that only if they're repeatedly completing the same form with completely different data, which almost never happens on websites.

FUTURE ENHANCEMENTS

Future e-commerce technologies will definitely introduce more attractive and convenient tools for the customers, but some things remain constant – delivery times will improve, customer service will get increasingly better, and product selection will become ever greater. Graphical images are becoming more important in conveying meaning to a concept on the web sites rather than text. Moreover, graphical components are better suited to be used in certain ways to improve WBEC. Not surprisingly graphic images can also be used to attract customers and increase company's presence in the global e-market. Future - E Commerce have to be made very meaningful and smart, just displaying the product depending on category will not work, interface should be more interactive and need to ask relevant question on basis of their searching pattern or browsing pattern. Cross selling and up selling also need to be smarter.

Designers must start studying the trends of real people, the answers to real trends are those that must be implemented onto the user interface, the designer no longer have full control, the ball has turned and the users are the ones placing demands on how things are to be done. The future of e-commerce can be described simply by saying web mall, made possible by the use of portals. Although shopping on line by simply clicking a button is extreme convenience, users become more demanding as time passes and e-commerce becomes more and more popular. Virtual malls give the users the capability of searching for a wide range of products from a single location. This will eliminate the need to search with different search engines it will be much more like the popular phrase one-stop shopping.

Users are the driving forces of this technology as well as the largest impediment. Like all consumers the demands never seem to end. What seems to be yet another driving force of this technology is the way the users are expecting to view the products.

The success of e-commerce depends on the ability to attract non-computer-literate people to use them with ease. Much like driving a car or talking on the telephone, electronic commerce follows the same rules, the users do not care how the inner workings really work the end result is the important point. Electronic commerce will make significant advantages as long as the interface is kept simple and can be used in the same context a telephone is being used today.

Users Have Changed

For a long time, we've been using a traditional way of working with media. We have a desk, a computer and the keyboard and mouse as input-devices. We have accepted that the internet is an essential part of our lives and it has become nearly impossible to completely disconnect, even if we would like to.

In the past, in general we had a lot of control over our designs. There is a task and there is a consequence. Web design has become far more complex and it has become important to guide a user through one flow to optimize their user experience. We have to think of behaviour patterns, desired outcomes and potential mistakes the user can make. We're no longer developing a static experience; rather, we're creating living, interacting systems.

Users' behaviour online also has changed incredibly. Google, for example, has divided their users in three main categories:

1. The repetitive user: someone checking the same piece of information over and over again, such as e-mail or stock prices.
2. The bored user: someone who has time to kill.
3. The urgent user: a user with a request to find something specific and fast.

Your online habits make you a repetitive user on certain websites. Social media websites are great examples of this. The games you play online, or the news websites you check sometimes, are a result of you being a bored user. Finally, the urgent user is the target audience we often develop websites for during client work. They want information and they want it fast, such as the price of a product, a service they're specifically looking for, or the closest location of something they need now.

For designing the best user experience, it's always a good idea to keep these principles in mind. You should be able to tailor your website to make repetitive (predictable), bored and fast use as integrated as possible.

Graphical User Interface

The graphical user interface isn't exactly the future, rather it's a current way of designing interfaces. The idea of graphical user interfaces is that you complete visual tasks to receive results, such as clicking on a link to open a new page.

We guide our users through metaphors (such as the shopping cart icon) and standards we use in web design.

Natural User Interface

The natural user interface is the current Natural user interfaces focus more on doing. Users interact with the device or platform to achieve results, ideally enjoying the actual interaction as much as the accomplishment itself. Gestures especially (tools such as the Leap_Motion can play an important role in this) are important assets in natural user interfaces.

Existing examples include websites which have the functionality you can swipe (on tablets for example) to navigate through a gallery slider.

A key element in natural user interface design is direct manipulation. Users love to have the feeling that they're directly engaging with a screen (use of gestures).

Organic User Interface

While we're still slowly moving from graphical user interfaces to natural user interfaces, a third spectacular evolution is on its way. Although it may take a while before we see and use it, it's closer than might seem at first sight. An organic user interface means that we manipulate the actual physical shape or position of a device to control it.

I'm referring in this case to bendable screens, and although this technology is very much in its infancy, it offers so many incredible opportunities to interact and navigate through devices.

Naturally, an organic user interface offers way more possibilities for input (and even output) than the previous interface concepts. At the moment we're used to point and click, though we're getting more involved with gestures, touch and (thanks to gyroscopes in devices) tilting and rotating, although it's still limited on the web. Eventually, we'll be bending, deforming and manipulating actual physical objects.

The future of e commerce [23] may be Personalization & Experience

Nearly all retail growth in the US at present is driven by ecommerce, and this looks set to continue in the years ahead as more people spend more money online. Greater personalization and a better customer experience will be the holy grail for ecommerce businesses in the future, as it becomes increasingly difficult to secure customers against a backdrop of ever increasing competition. Customers will eventually flock to those offering as close to the in-store experience as possible, and major ecommerce retailers are already striving to make things more personal and more tangible on web.

Delivery Drones

Perhaps one of the most exciting developments in ecommerce is one we are already starting to see in testing – drone delivery. Drones will in the future allow companies to deliver packages much more efficiently and quickly, with delivery times of just 60 or even 30 minutes from order entirely plausible. Drones will be sent out from distribution centres and travel directly to the delivery addresses provided, at significantly lower cost and logistical hassle than at present.

Curation and Pay Monthly Models

Product curation and pay monthly models are likely to continue to form an increasing part of the future of ecommerce. People don't want to buy generic products from you – Amazon is cheaper and quicker. But they do want to buy curated products, lifestyle products, and ecommerce packages where your product knowledge and expertise can create an altogether more enjoyable, rounded experience. Tracking Into Stores

The boundaries between ecommerce and physical commerce, i.e. the retail store, will become less definite as time passes, and companies are already looking at ways of tying together online tracking and customer information with their real-world experience. This also complements the idea of greater customisation of the shopping experience, allowing retailers to use existing online data to personalise their entire relationship – both online and offline.

Pop Up Shops

Customers are already shopping in new, alternative ways to before. "Showrooming" and "webrooming", where customers visit a local shop then buy online for a cheaper price, or vice versa, present new challenges for retailers, in bridging the gap between the online and offline.

Pop up shops can provide the answer, and can serve as a low-cost way of reaching out to new customers and winning new long-term fans. Pop up shops give customers a chance to connect with your brand in a physical way, while helping you reach corners of your market that might otherwise have been impossible for you through your online channels.

The future of ecommerce is ofcourse still unclear. But any prudent ecommerce business owner should take stock of what analysts are saying about the future direction of their industry, so they can be sure to capitalise on these new opportunities as they arise.

Artificial Intelligence Systems

Ecommerce already enjoys a significant advantage over other types of business, in the sense that there are thousands of high quality apps, all readily integrated into each other so that even small-budget players can rapidly automate the entirety of the process. At the same time, technologies rapidly change and improve, thanks to the strong competitive drive across the industry – after all, another retailer is only a click away.

The next step for ecommerce will be the application of AI systems, running evolutionary algorithms designed to find the absolute optimum.

The upshot for those running ecommerce businesses is to embrace these processes as soon as viable. Where the major players go, smaller retailers follow, and it won't be long before a proliferation of AI driven systems improves the capabilities of the ecommerce industry even further.

Measurement Across All Devices

Not everyone sticks to a single device when buying from you. In fact, more people are moving between devices, from the web to mobile to apps, before turning into paying customers. Measuring analytics across devices is still in its infancy, but it is becoming a more significant field of interest for those in ecommerce.

Once tracking of usage across multiple devices becomes more sophisticated, the processes of testing, tweaking and optimising the user experience still further can be set in motion. This will unlock even more value for ecommerce retailers, through providing further detailed insights into how the same people respond to their offering across platforms.

CONCLUSION

This chapter mainly focuses on web designers and their function appears to be shifting more towards the job of interface designers and information architects. With devices and their interfaces changing, so too will websites and their functionality. One requirement for e-commerce sites is that the contact numbers and addresses should always be displayed. Trust is essential for any type of commerce; trust mechanisms must be developed to give buyers, sellers, and intermediaries an accepted level of confidence of the system. The last thing a business wants is the consumer to think that they have something to hide. This chapter demonstrated various ways to design the interface and its features.

In summary a site within the e-commerce environment must always take the user into consideration first. According to Ron Scheer, in "Make your web site easy to use" designers must organize and be ready to reorganize, focused on the purposes and intentions. Always remember your brand, make things easy to find, make content easily understood, anticipate user interactions, if technology makes it possible help users decide what action to perform. When considering the navigation aspects of the site, make it as flat as possible. Make options mutually exclusive make sure the user realizes where the links take them. Create patterns that are easily remembered and make sure that the road from beginning to end does not seem tedious to the users. Designers are not done when the site is implemented and published, tests must be made, regular maintenance should be done to assure up to date content and simplicity. Although these are requirements they do not ensure that the site will be successful, nevertheless they are essential for the opportunity to survive

E-commerce is a new way of conducting, managing and executing business transactions using computer and telecommunications networks. As awareness of the Internet throughout the commercial world and general public increases, competitiveness will force lower entry barriers, continued rapid innovation and expansion of markets. The real key to making electronic commerce over the Internet a normal, everyday business activity is the convergence of the telecommunications, content/media and software industries. E-Commerce is expected to improve the productivity and competitiveness of participating businesses by unprecedented access to an on-line global market place with millions of customers and thousands of products and services.

REFERENCES

Chittaro, L., & Ranon, R. (2000). Virtual Reality stores for 1-to-1 e-commerce. *Proc. Of the CHI2000 Workshop on Designing Interactive Systems for 1-to-1 E-Commerce.*

Costabile, M. (2001). *Usability in the Software Life Cycle. In Handbook of Software Engineering and Knowledge Eng* (Vol. 1). World Scientific Publishing.

Daugherty, T., Li, H., & Biocca, F. (2005). Experiential commerce: A summary of research investigating the impact of virtual experience on consumer learning. In *Society of Consumer Psychology: Online Advertising*. Mahwah, NJ: Lawrence Erlbaum Associates.

Ecommerce Guide. (n.d.). Retrieved from: https://ecommerceguide.com/guides/ecommerce-future/

ECommerze. (2008). *The history and evolution of e-commerce.* Retrieved from: https://ecommerze.wordpress.com/2008/06/12/the-history-and-evoltion-of-e-commerce/

Ess, D. L., & Sudweeks, F. (1998). *Proceedings International Cultural Attitudes Toward Technology and Communication-CaTac'98.* University of Sydney.

Fernandes, T. (1995). Introduction to Culture. Academic Press.

Hughes, S., Brusilovsky, P., & Lewis, M. (2002). Adaptive navigation support in 3D ecommerce activities. *Proc. of Workshop on Recommendation and Personalization in ECommerce at the 2nd International Conference on Adaptive Hypermedia and Adaptive Web-Based Systems (AH'2002)*, 132-139.

Kang, K.-S. (2001). Effectiveness of Graphical Components in Web Site E-commerce Application-A Cultural Perspective. EJISDC, 7(2), 1-6.

Nielsen, J. (2000). Designing Web Usability. New Riders Press.

Santos, C. T., & Osorio, F. S. (2004). AdapTIVE: An Intelligent Virtual Environment and Its Application in E-Commerce. *COMPSAC, 2004*, 468–473.

Shneiderman, B. (1997). Designing information-abundant web sites: Issues recommendations. *International Journal of Sociology*, *47*, 5–29.

Chapter 11
Electronic Commerce and Decision Support Systems:
Theories and Applications

Kijpokin Kasemsap
Suan Sunandha Rajabhat University, Thailand

ABSTRACT

Electronic Commerce (e-commerce) is an advanced online business tool that allows many companies to launch their websites and helps customers search their specific products shown on the websites. Decision Support Systems (DSSs) are computerized tools designed to facilitate strategic decision making. With the support of data mining and business intelligence methods, DSSs can effectively increase the performance of decision making and can present a sophisticated method of managerial thinking in a timely and effective manner toward gaining competitive advantage. The chapter argues that utilizing e-commerce and DSSs has the potential to enhance business performance and reach strategic goals in modern business.

INTRODUCTION

Electronic commerce (e-commerce) is the online business with the support of computers (Kasemsap, 2015a) and becomes one of the required ways of online shopping (Kasemsap, 2018a). E-commerce creates a paradigm shift in the way modern companies conduct business (Kuah & Wang, 2017), and can help enhance the digital economy (Kamel, 2010). E-commerce has a tangible impact on the way business is conducted (Strzębicki, 2015). E-commerce tools has been made available that are able to help customers by generating purposed recommendations (Palopoli, Rosaci, & Sarné, 2016).

The emergence of e-commerce has provided manufactures and vendors with more business opportunities (Acampora, Alghazzawi, Hagras, & Vitiello, 2016). Electronic retailers may enjoy early mover advantages because of the consumer demand inertia amplified by the nature of the Internet and the system design characteristics of e-commerce platforms (Wang, Cavusoglu, & Deng, 2016). E-commerce websites increasingly incorporate tracking technologies that can monitor consumer behavior on their websites (Currim, Mintz, & Siddarth, 2015). Evaluating usability issues allows improving the design of e-commerce websites (Díaz, Rusu, & Collazos, 2017).

DOI: 10.4018/978-1-5225-3646-8.ch011

Decision support systems (DSSs) are the computer systems designed to provide the assistance in evaluating alternative courses of action (Kasemsap, 2017a) and in enhancing decision-making processes (Kalina & Zvárová, 2013). Decision making is the cognitive process resulting in the selection of a course of action among several alternative scenarios (Kasemsap, 2016a) for solving complicated problems where multi-criteria objectives are involved (Tran, Abraham, & Jain, 2008). There is a growing trend to provide managers with information systems that can assist them in their decision-making processes (Averweg, 2010).

Because of the importance to individual, group, and organizational success (Forgionne, 2005), information systems research continues to examine the effective ways to improve the support for decision making (Forgionne, 2009). DSSs are a subset of information systems that support human decision making through computerized systems that offer contextual information (Bihl, Young II, & Weckman, 2014). The field of DSS development is reaching the end of its expansion stage, which is characterized by the proliferation of processes and methodologies in all areas of decision support (Gachet & Sprague, 2010).

The chapter is based on a literature review of e-commerce and DSSs. The extensive literature review provides a contribution to practitioners and researchers by indicating the theories and applications of e-commerce and DSSs in the digital age.

BACKGROUND

E-commerce represents one of the most promising directions for generating competitive advantage at the micro level of the organization and for increasing productivity at the macro level of the economy (Rahman & Raisinghani, 2000). Many companies have recognized the importance of developing an online platform with the objective of having a higher interaction with the client, and influence them in e-commerce, through the buying process (Ibarra, Partida, & Aguilar, 2015).

E-commerce has substantial potential to promote the growth of small and medium-sized enterprises (SMEs) in developed and developing countries (Kurnia, Choudrie, Mahbubur, & Alzougool, 2015). Due to the growth of e-commerce, more organizational resources are being directed into electronic securities, Internet facilities, business plans, and new technologies (Kasemsap, 2016b). E-commerce transforms the world into an information society (Kartiwi & MacGregor, 2008), and assists organizations in reducing the cost of entry and in expanding the market reach for a wide variety of business activities (Lin, Jalleh, & Huang, 2016).

Decisions are activities that individuals face and deal with every day (Abdou, Radaideh, & Lewis, 2010). The successes over the past 10 years in developing, implementing, and sustaining effective DSSs for decision making for both governments and businesses hold many beneficial lessons for the implementation of sophisticated systems under conditions of extreme difficulty (Kamel, 2006). Decision making is a crucial element of a manager's responsibility (Garrido, 2015) in both day-to-day operations and strategic planning (Abdelsalam, Dawoud, & ElKadi, 2013). Supporting decision taking by management in an integrated way means to support the global decision process of the organization and increase its efficiency and resilience (Garrido, 2015).

In recent years, DSSs have moved from a radical movement that changed the way information system was perceived in business, to a commercial information technology (IT) movement that all organizations engage (Wang & Radosevich, 2010). Nowadays, many DSSs are based on spatially distributed sensors (Dunkel, Bruns, & Pawlowski, 2010). Organizations continuously need to increase their business intelligence by monitoring systems that analyze information and develop significant indicators to decision makers toward handling both semi-structured and un-structured problems characterized by varying parameters in order to understand the problem and to help develop alternative solutions (Kamel & Zyada, 2005).

ASPECTS OF ELECTRONIC COMMERCE AND DECISION SUPPORT SYSTEMS

This section provides the overview of e-commerce; trust and privacy issues in e-commerce; e-commerce and logistics; the applications of e-commerce; the overview of DSSs; knowledge-based decision support systems (KBDSSs); DSSs, data mining, and business intelligence; and the importance of DSSs.

Overview of Electronic Commerce

E-commerce describes the process of buying, selling, transferring, or exchanging products, services, or information via computer networks including the Internet (Toland & Klepper, 2009). Through e-commerce, organizations can easily evaluate sales effectiveness, customer effectiveness, marketing campaigns, product mix, and customer engagement in global marketplace (Kasemsap, 2016c), and consumers can purchase the cheaper and better products via price comparison (Yıldız & Kurtuldu, 2014). E-commerce optimizes and enhances the relationship and communications among companies, producers, distributors, and customers (Choshin & Ghaffari, 2017).

An important driving force has been the parallel rise of social media, enabling pervasive interactions among consumers and between consumers and firms (Lee & Phang, 2015). The influence of user-generated content (UGC) on e-commerce websites and social media has been addressed in both practical and theoretical fields (Yan et al., 2016). E-commerce and research and development (R&D) have a positive impact on gross domestic product (GDP) per capita based on the purchasing power parity, with e-commerce having a stronger development-enhancing effect in comparison to R&D (Anvari & Norouzi, 2016).

Given the tremendous success of the Internet and e-commerce in developed countries, emerging economies are quickly embracing IT as well (Agarwal & Wu, 2015). The Internet has provided great convenience for online shoppers, and has presented unprecedented opportunities for online retailers to understand their customers (Wu, Li, & Xu, 2014). In the wake of the rapid emergence of e-commerce, its evaluation is of great theoretical and practical importance (Kang, Jang, & Park, 2016). It is important for policymakers to consider both Internet application and e-commerce as the social and technical perspectives (Papazafeiropoulou & Pouloudi, 2003).

The implications of e-commerce include the facilitation of trade transactions and the acceleration of capital movement through the new rules of the digital economy with the removal of time and distance barriers (Kamel & Ghoneim, 2004). However, the global enterprises face the challenges of e-commerce, such as adjusting to competition in electronic markets, addressing privacy issues, and applying strategic management to corporate alliance systems (Raisinghani, 2000). Buyer concern about website security is a critical issue when it comes to maximizing the potential for e-commerce transactions (Hartono, Holsapple, Kim, Na, & Simpson, 2014).

Multi-attribute value theory (MAVT)-based recommender systems are recognized for dealing with various issues of recommender systems, such as the cold-start problem and changing preferences (Scholz, Dorner, Schryen, & Benlian, 2017). Recommender systems are utilized by consumers who are not familiar with the available attributes and ranges and who wish to save time and effort. MAVT-based recommender systems can enhance consumers' decision processes in e-commerce shopping tasks.

Trust and Privacy Issues in Electronic Commerce

With the explosive growth of e-commerce worldwide, there are the growing concerns about fraudulent transaction attacks in e-commerce (Zhao et al., 2016). Consumers are concerned about the protection of their personal information and feel that privacy policies are important (Henderson, Snyder, & Byrd, 2003). In e-commerce environments, the reputation of sellers is a crucial issue to potential buyers in making decisions (Zhang, Wang, & Zhang, 2014). The inability to physically interact with an item, fear of risk security and privacy and lack of e-commerce infrastructure are the main barriers that prevent the consumers from online product shopping (Singh, Yadav, & Sahu, 2016).

A comprehensive conceptualization of trust in business-to-business (B2B) e-commerce should include trust in the infrastructure and the control mechanisms (Pavlou & Ratnasingam, 2003). Because mutual trust between buyers and sellers can enhance smoothness in communication and can increase buyers' confidence in online shopping, buyers are more willing to enjoy their transaction experiences with sellers (Huang, Chen, Ou, Davison, & Hua, 2017). Online exchanges often occur between strangers who cannot rely on past behavior or the prospect of future interactions to establish mutual trust (Bahbouhi & Moussa, 2017).

Online shopping as an alternative to in-store shopping can make much of traditional retail less attractive (Zhang, Zhu, & Ye, 2016). Ease of use has significant impact on usefulness, and trust has a significant impact on both ease of use and usefulness concerning online shopping (McCloskey, 2008). Consumer characteristics, company perspectives, website infrastructure, and interactions with consumers can affect the trust in e-commerce (Oliveira, Alhinho, Rita, & Dhillon, 2017). In addition, perception of website quality (PWSQ) and third party recognition (TPR) can influence the trust in e-commerce (Yoon & Occeña, 2015).

The rise of e-commerce forces IT personnel to move beyond infrastructure design and maintenance and consider numerous customer-facing aspects such as consumer data privacy and security. When developing IT systems and applications to accommodate e-commerce activities, data governance related regulatory compliance mandates, personally identifiable information privacy rules, and information protection protocols must be considered. To ensure the security, privacy, and effectiveness of e-commerce, businesses should authenticate business transactions, control access to resources (e.g., web pages for registered or selected users), encrypt communications, and implement security technologies

Electronic Commerce and Logistics

With large number of enterprises executing e-commerce (Masmoudi, Benaissa, & Chabchoub, 2014), logistics has been largely influenced (Yu, Wang, Zhong, & Huang, 2016). The goal of collaborative execution in global supply chain is to establish the smooth flow of information up the supply chain from customers to suppliers and the smooth flow of products and services down the supply chain from suppliers to customers (Kasemsap, 2016d). There are many retail and logistics companies utilizing e-commerce as the important business tool, such as Home Depot (U.S.), Amazon (U.S.), IKEA (Sweden), JingDong (China), and GuoMei (China). Carriers and logistics intermediary perform more roles than what people think they do, because network connection and the ambition to remain competitive make them to take up value-added services (Kasemsap, 2017b).

Home Depot is an American retailer company that sells home improvement products and construction products. In the traditional model, each retailer store of Home Depot has a logistics management department, and this department is in charge of the store's replenishment, storage management, in/out products flow control, and other related issues. When suppliers receive the stores' replenishment orders, they have two ways to deliver orders to retailers, of which one is directly sending products to the store, the other is using Home Depot's distribution center to ensure cost-effective transportation.

For the Line-Haul phase, the Home Depot sets the centralized inventory and replenishment (I&R) department in the headquarters, and develops a new network of distribution centers for store replenishment. The new I&R department of Home Depot takes place of the individual stores' replenishment teams, and is responsible for all the stores' inventory management. Regarding e-commerce logistics, the centralized replenishment of Home Depot improves the demand forecast accuracy and gains more power for Home Depot while negotiating with suppliers as the single order is much larger than before (Yu et al., 2016).

Amazon is an e-commerce and cloud computing company (Yu et al., 2016). It is the biggest Internet retailer in the U.S. It began as an online bookstore, but its current business scope covers DVD, blue ray, CD, video game, electronic, furniture, food, toys, and jewelry. Amazon has independent sales website facing different countries across the globe. Amazon saves a lot of storage costs by integrating the inventories in distribution center and the warehouses of partners. Thus, there is no need for Amazon to keep a high level of inventory as physical retail stores. The determinants for locating distribution centers consist of distance from customer-intensive places and level of taxes.

Within the distribution center, Amazon has different processing procedure and equipment while dealing with various product groups. Those products, which are easily classified and transported, are stored in highly automated equipment, whereas those irregularly shaped products are handled by the equipment of low-level automation. While dealing with intercity transportation, Amazon sets many injection points, such as transportation hubs. Transportation hubs are located in the districts where customers are highly concentrated to save cost. Orders are integrated in the distribution centers first. After that, the less than truckload (LTL) shippers or truckload shippers will supply the long-haul shipment service, carrying them from distribution centers to the injection points (Yu et al., 2016).

Applications of Electronic Commerce

E-commerce typically utilizes electronic communications technology of the World Wide Web, at some point in the transaction's life cycle, although e-commerce frequently depends on computer technologies other than the World Wide Web, such as databases, and e-mail, and on other non-computer technologies, such as transportation for physical products sold via e-commerce (Drougas, 2009). It will be very useful for customers if e-commerce is capable of being more automated and secure than is the case, since the time and energy they spend will be reduced (Yi, Siew, & Syed, 2000). For small transaction sizes, invoices are the most cost-efficient payment method, while prepayments dominate for large transaction sizes (Grüschow, Kemper, & Brettel, 2016).

In the business environment, e-commerce has made considerable business development in modern business (Kartiwi & MacGregor, 2008). In societies where commercial competition is accepted as an economic system, there is a positive relationship between the good operation of the system and the power of SMEs within the system (Zerenler & Gözlü, 2012). B2B e-commerce adoption enables SMEs to gain and sustain competitive advantage in a dynamic competitive environment (Hamad, Elbeltagi, Jones, & El-Gohary, 2015). Getting the pricing right has emerged as one of the most important keys to the success of e-commerce (Wu et al., 2014).

When problems occur in B2C e-commerce transactions, consumers require and expect an immediate redress procedure from merchants (Ong & Teh, 2016). Redress is concerned with internal complaint-handling procedures through which consumers seek compensation or to rectify the problems that occur during e-commerce transactions. Redress serves as an important determinant of consumer confidence and trust in e-commerce (Ong & Teh, 2016).

Overview of Decision Support Systems

Nowadays, information is a crucial element of an economic development of a society (Sobieska-Karpinska & Hernes, 2010). The important attributes of information are its urgency and actuality because a correct decision may be only made when the system is able to get the up-to-date information, which is needed to effectively make this decision (Sobieska-Karpinska & Hernes, 2010). The process of decision making in any organization is the resource-consuming system (Baruti, 2016). The manual and mechanical methods are associated with heavy cost of processing, low efficiency, inconsistency, lack of integrity, and long period of time in its processing so that institutions incur heavy bills in their decision-making processes (Baruti, 2016). DSSs in the domain of Industrial Engineering and Management can be the powerful tools, but more knowledge about the way users utilize these systems is required (Yuviler-Gavish & Naseraldin, 2016).

Traditional DSSs provide strong data management, modeling, and visualization capabilities for the decision maker but they do not explicitly support scenario management (Ahmed & Sundaram, 2010). The intelligent systems have extended the scope of traditional DSSs to assist users with real-time decision making, multiple information flows, dynamic data, information overload, time-pressured decisions, inaccurate data, difficult-to-access data, distributed decision making, and highly uncertain decision environments (Phillips-Wren, 2010). Regarding business perspectives, consumer decision support systems (CDSSs) help online users make effective purchasing decisions in e-commerce websites (Zhang & Pu, 2010).

Many businesses have made or are making significant investments in data warehouses that promote a myriad of DSSs (Wells & Hess, 2008). DSSs consist of three parts: database, model base, and user interface (Eom & Lee, 1990). Database involves the input data used in decision making. Model base includes many analytic or simulation models that utilize input data in order to produce strategic methods. The decision maker often interacts with data and models through the user interface (Tynjala, 2012). In addition, the factors of compliance, complementarity, and conformity can measure the performance of DSSs (Lebraty & Godé, 2015).

Knowledge-Based Decision Support Systems

Knowledge-based decision support systems (KBDSSs) are the systems designed to ensure more precise decision making by using appropriate data, information, and knowledge management (Chung, Boutaba, & Hariri, 2016). KBDSSs refer to decision making based on relevant knowledge, which is based on artificial intelligence, and on the application of information and communication technology (Chung et al., 2016). Artificial intelligence is the area of computer science that emphasizes the creation of intelligent machines that work and react like humans (Kasemsap, 2017c).

Based on the knowledge used for deduction, data is classified into knowledge-based systems using dictionary-defined knowledge, and non-knowledge–based systems using machine learning and multi-dimensional statistical pattern recognition techniques (Kim & Ryu, 2013). Park and Han (2016) presented efficient decision support for detecting content polluters on social networks with an approach based on automatic knowledge acquisition from behavioral patterns. This study is an efficient method for detecting content polluters on Twitter. Park and Han (2016) proposed a set of KBDSSs-related features that can be easily extracted from the messages and behaviors of Twitter users, and established a new breed of classifiers based on these features.

Decision Support Systems, Data Mining, and Business Intelligence

Data mining and business intelligence techniques can be integrated in order to develop more advanced DSSs (Domingues, Jorge, Soares, & Rezende, 2015). Data mining is the process of applying the computational methods in showing unknown data formats in large data sets (Kasemsap, 2015b). Data mining is profitably utilized to discover patterns and relationships in the data in order to help make better business decisions (Kasemsap, 2016e).

Business intelligence is an emerging technology that helps executives and managers manage information and data in an efficient way (Kasemsap, 2015c). Business intelligence involves creating any type of data visualization that provides the insight into a business for the purpose of making a decision or taking an action (Kasemsap, 2016f). Business intelligence provides the quick notification of business exceptions, advanced reporting, and the ability to compare data to improve the strategic management in global business (Kasemsap, 2017d).

Importance of Decision Support Systems

Effective decision making across organizations is of strategic importance as the global business environment becomes more complex (Setzekorn, Sugumaran, & Patnayakuni, 2004). DSSs can enhance various operations, financial management, and strategic decision making (Wang & Yao, 2010). DSSs include allowing and motivating participation in decision-making conversations of individuals who may contribute to decision-making processes and to the quality of their positive outcomes (Garrido, 2011). DSSs need to be designed and developed with extra functionality to meet the challenges, such as collaborative working (Liu, Duffy, Whitfield, Boyle, & McKenna, 2009).

DSSs can be considered as the integrated entities that provide individuals with both tools and information to assist their decision making (Sharma & Vyas, 2010). DSS research is often blended with many expansions experienced by various information system fields, such as organizational computing, e-commerce, and pervasive computing (Burstein & Holsapple, 2008). DSS development methodologies must be described at a meta-level (El-Gayar, Deokar, & Tao, 2011). Thus, maturity models (MM) can provide the necessary framework and benchmarks needed to evaluate DSS development methodologies (El-Gayar et al., 2011).

Regarding DSSs, many decision makers begin to seek cooperators on the Internet to help them solve complex decision problems (Xie & Wang, 2014). The data must be obtainable, preferably via common protocols shared with the operational infrastructure (Tolk, 2010). The benefits of agent technology are highlighted in relation to the desired features of DSS (Vahidov, 2004). Intelligent agents regarding agent technology have a high degree of self-determination capabilities, and they can decide for themselves when, where, and under what condition their decision-making action should be performed (Adla, 2013).

To achieve the effective DSSs, intelligent agents and automated forces must produce adequate behavior. If these requirements for simulation systems and their annotations are fulfilled, decision support simulation can significantly contribute to the situational awareness up to the cognitive levels of the decision makers (Tolk, 2010). Thus, DSSs can enhance human cognitive deficiencies by integrating various sources of information, providing intelligent access to relevant knowledge, and facilitating the process of making suitable decisions (Sodiya, Akinwale, Okeleye, & Emmanuel, 2012). Service efficiency, improved effectiveness, and increased stakeholder value are the expected benefits of DSSs exploitation (Ngwenya, 2013). Awareness of organizational resources-related online presence and availability can affect the decision-making process in pervasive computing environments (Russell & Forgionne, 2009).

FUTURE RESEARCH DIRECTIONS

The classification of the extensive literature in the domains of e-commerce and DSSs will provide the potential opportunities for future research. Social media marketing programs usually center on efforts to create the content that attracts attention and encourages readers to share it across their social networks toward competition in the global marketplace (Kasemsap, 2016g). The Internet of Things (IoT) relates to the utilization of advanced sensors, actuators, and various devices, and allows individuals to effectively control the important tasks (Kasemsap, 2018b). Customer relationship management (CRM) is the significant method that deals with exploring both customer needs and customer behaviors (Kasemsap, 2018c). Exploring the relationships among e-commerce, DSSs, social media marketing, the IoT, and CRM should be further studied.

CONCLUSION

This chapter indicated the overview of e-commerce; trust and privacy issues in e-commerce; e-commerce and logistics; the applications of e-commerce; the overview of DSSs; KBDSSs; DSSs, data mining, and business intelligence; and the importance of DSSs. E-commerce is the advanced online business tool that can allow many companies to launch their websites conformed to their customers' requirements and can help customers search their specific products shown on the websites. DSSs are the computerized tools designed to facilitate the strategic decision making. With the support of data mining and business intelligence methods, DSSs can effectively increase the performance of decision making and can present the sophisticated method of managerial thinking in the timely and effective manner toward gaining competitive advantage. Utilizing e-commerce and DSSs has the potential to enhance business performance and reach strategic goals in modern business.

REFERENCES

Abdelsalam, H. M., Dawoud, R. H., & ElKadi, H. A. (2013). An examination of the decision making styles of Egyptian managers. In S. Saeed, M. Khan, & R. Ahmad (Eds.), *Business strategies and approaches for effective engineering management* (pp. 219–236). Hershey, PA: IGI Global. doi:10.4018/978-1-4666-3658-3.ch013

Abdou, A., Radaideh, M., & Lewis, J. (2010). Decision support systems and their application in construction. In *Business information systems: Concepts, methodologies, tools and applications* (pp. 1024–1042). Hershey, PA: IGI Global. doi:10.4018/978-1-61520-969-9.ch061

Acampora, G., Alghazzawi, D., Hagras, H., & Vitiello, A. (2016). An interval type-2 fuzzy logic based framework for reputation management in peer-to-peer e-commerce. *Information Sciences*, *333*, 88–107. doi:10.1016/j.ins.2015.11.015

Adla, A. (2013). Modeling cooperative decision support systems with hybrid agents. *International Journal of Decision Support System Technology*, *5*(3), 31–48. doi:10.4018/jdsst.2013070103

Agarwal, J., & Wu, T. (2015). Factors influencing growth potential of e-commerce in emerging economies: An institution-based N-OLI framework and research propositions. *Thunderbird International Business Review*, *57*(3), 197–215. doi:10.1002/tie.21694

Ahmed, M. D., & Sundaram, D. (2010). A framework for a scenario driven decision support systems generator. In M. Hunter (Ed.), *Strategic information systems: Concepts, methodologies, tools, and applications* (pp. 662–679). Hershey, PA: IGI Global. doi:10.4018/978-1-60566-677-8.ch044

Anvari, R. D., & Norouzi, D. (2016). The impact of e-commerce and R&D on economic development in some selected countries. *Procedia: Social and Behavioral Sciences*, *229*, 354–362. doi:10.1016/j.sbspro.2016.07.146

Averweg, U. R. (2010). Decision support systems and decision-making processes. In M. Hunter (Ed.), *Strategic information systems: Concepts, methodologies, tools, and applications* (pp. 122–130). Hershey, PA: IGI Global. doi:10.4018/978-1-60566-677-8.ch010

Bahbouhi, J. E., & Moussa, N. (2017). Prisoner's dilemma game model for e-commerce. *Applied Mathematics and Computation*, *292*, 128–144. doi:10.1016/j.amc.2016.07.018

Baruti, S. S. (2016). Proposed framework for mobile decision support systems for higher learning institutions: Mobile decision support systems. *International Journal of Handheld Computing Research*, *7*(3), 24–37. doi:10.4018/IJHCR.2016070103

Bihl, T. J., Young, W. A. II, & Weckman, G. R. (2014). Decision support systems in business. In J. Wang (Ed.), *Encyclopedia of business analytics and optimization* (pp. 696–707). Hershey, PA: IGI Global. doi:10.4018/978-1-4666-5202-6.ch065

Burstein, F., & Holsapple, C. W. (2008). New horizons at the core of information systems: Decision support system advances. *Information Systems and e-Business Management*, *6*(2), 109–115. doi:10.1007/s10257-007-0076-7

Choshin, M., & Ghaffari, A. (2017). An investigation of the impact of effective factors on the success of e-commerce in small- and medium-sized companies. *Computers in Human Behavior*, *66*, 67–74. doi:10.1016/j.chb.2016.09.026

Chung, K., Boutaba, R., & Hariri, S. (2016). Knowledge based decision support system. *Information Technology & Management*, *17*(1), 1–3. doi:10.1007/s10799-015-0251-3

Currim, I. S., Mintz, O., & Siddarth, S. (2015). Information accessed or information available? The impact on consumer preferences inferred at a durable product e-commerce website. *Journal of Interactive Marketing*, *29*, 11–25. doi:10.1016/j.intmar.2014.09.003

Díaz, J., Rusu, C., & Collazos, C. A. (2017). Experimental validation of a set of cultural-oriented usability heuristics: E-commerce websites evaluation. *Computer Standards & Interfaces*, *50*, 160–178. doi:10.1016/j.csi.2016.09.013

Domingues, M. A., Jorge, A. M., Soares, C., & Rezende, S. O. (2015). Web mining for the integration of data mining with business intelligence in web-based decision support systems. In A. Azevedo & M. Santos (Eds.), *Integration of data mining in business intelligence systems* (pp. 120–142). Hershey, PA: IGI Global. doi:10.4018/978-1-4666-6477-7.ch007

Drougas, B. A. (2009). Electronic commerce for health products services-problems-quality and future. In A. Lazakidou & K. Siassiakos (Eds.), *Handbook of research on distributed medical informatics and e-health* (pp. 190–197). Hershey, PA: IGI Global. doi:10.4018/978-1-60566-002-8.ch013

Dunkel, J., Bruns, R., & Pawlowski, O. (2010). Complex event processing in sensor-based decision support systems. In B. Nag (Ed.), *Intelligent systems in operations: Methods, models and applications in the supply chain* (pp. 64–79). Hershey, PA: IGI Global. doi:10.4018/978-1-61520-605-6.ch004

El-Gayar, O. F., Deokar, A. V., & Tao, J. (2011). DSS-CMM: A capability maturity model for DSS development processes. *International Journal of Decision Support System Technology*, *3*(4), 14–34. doi:10.4018/jdsst.2011100102

Eom, H. B., & Lee, S. M. (1990). Decision support systems applications research: A bibliography (1971-1988). *European Journal of Operational Research*, *46*(3), 333–342. doi:10.1016/0377-2217(90)90008-Y

Forgionne, G. A. (2005). Functional integration of decision making support. In M. Khosrow-Pour (Ed.), *Encyclopedia of information science and technology* (pp. 1236–1242). Hershey, PA: IGI Global. doi:10.4018/978-1-59140-553-5.ch218

Forgionne, G. A. (2009). Updated architectures for the integration of decision making support functionalities. In M. Khosrow-Pour (Ed.), *Encyclopedia of information science and technology* (2nd ed., pp. 3884–3889). Hershey, PA: IGI Global. doi:10.4018/978-1-60566-026-4.ch619

Gachet, A., & Sprague, R. (2010). Context in decision support systems development. In M. Hunter (Ed.), *Strategic information systems: Concepts, methodologies, tools, and applications* (pp. 604–613). Hershey, PA: IGI Global. doi:10.4018/978-1-60566-677-8.ch040

Garrido, P. (2011). Conversation-oriented decision support systems for organizations. In M. Cruz-Cunha & J. Varajao (Eds.), *Enterprise information systems design, implementation and management: Organizational applications* (pp. 118–131). Hershey, PA: IGI Global. doi:10.4018/978-1-61692-020-3.ch008

Garrido, P. (2015). Concepts for the design of a manager-centric global decision support system for organizations. In J. Varajão, M. Cruz-Cunha, & R. Martinho (Eds.), *Improving organizational effectiveness with enterprise information systems* (pp. 173–187). Hershey, PA: IGI Global. doi:10.4018/978-1-4666-8368-6.ch011

Grüschow, R. M., Kemper, J., & Brettel, M. (2016). How do different payment methods deliver cost and credit efficiency in electronic commerce? *Electronic Commerce Research and Applications*, *18*, 27–36. doi:10.1016/j.elerap.2016.06.001

Hamad, H., Elbeltagi, I., Jones, P., & El-Gohary, H. (2015). Antecedents of B2B e-commerce adoption and its effect on competitive advantage in manufacturing SMEs. *Strategic Change*, *24*(5), 405–428. doi:10.1002/jsc.2019

Hartono, E., Holsapple, C. W., Kim, K. Y., Na, K. S., & Simpson, J. T. (2014). Measuring perceived security in B2C electronic commerce website usage: A respecification and validation. *Decision Support Systems*, *62*, 11–21. doi:10.1016/j.dss.2014.02.006

Henderson, S. C., Snyder, C. A., & Byrd, T. A. (2003). Electronic commerce and data privacy: The impact of privacy concerns on electronic commerce use and regulatory preferences. In S. Lubbe (Ed.), *The economic and social impacts of e-commerce* (pp. 213–238). Hershey, PA: IGI Global. doi:10.4018/978-1-59140-043-1.ch012

Huang, Q., Chen, X., Ou, C. X., Davison, R. M., & Hua, Z. (2017). Understanding buyers' loyalty to a C2C platform: The roles of social capital, satisfaction and perceived effectiveness of e-commerce institutional mechanisms. *Information Systems Journal*, *27*(1), 91–119. doi:10.1111/isj.12079

Ibarra, L., Partida, A., & Aguilar, D. (2015). Electronic commerce as a business strategy: Impact in consumption habits in Hermosillo, Sonora's inhabitants. *Procedia: Social and Behavioral Sciences*, *175*, 275–282. doi:10.1016/j.sbspro.2015.01.1201

Kalina, J., & Zvárová, J. (2013). Decision support systems in the process of improving patient safety. In A. Moumtzoglou & A. Kastania (Eds.), *E-health technologies and improving patient safety: Exploring organizational factors* (pp. 71–83). Hershey, PA: IGI Global. doi:10.4018/978-1-4666-2657-7.ch005

Kamel, S. (2006). DSS for strategic decision making. In M. Khosrow-Pour (Ed.), *Cases on information technology and organizational politics & culture* (pp. 230–246). Hershey, PA: IGI Global. doi:10.4018/978-1-59904-411-8.ch015

Kamel, S. (2010). Electronic commerce prospects in emerging economies: Lessons from Egypt. In I. Lee (Ed.), *Encyclopedia of e-business development and management in the global economy* (pp. 1086–1097). Hershey, PA: IGI Global. doi:10.4018/978-1-61520-611-7.ch109

Kamel, S., & Ghoneim, S. (2004). The impact of the role of the government of Egypt on electronic commerce development and growth. In M. Khosrow-Pour (Ed.), *The social and cognitive impacts of e-commerce on modern organizations* (pp. 253–276). Hershey, PA: IGI Global. doi:10.4018/978-1-59140-249-7.ch012

Kamel, S., & Zyada, A. (2005). Using DSS for global competitiveness: An effective information-based decision making process in public administration. In Y. Lan (Ed.), *Global information society: Operating information systems in a dynamic global business environment* (pp. 113–129). Hershey, PA: IGI Global. doi:10.4018/978-1-59140-306-7.ch006

Kang, D., Jang, W., & Park, Y. (2016). Evaluation of e-commerce websites using fuzzy hierarchical TOPSIS based on E-S-QUAL. *Applied Soft Computing*, *42*, 53–65. doi:10.1016/j.asoc.2016.01.017

Kartiwi, M., & MacGregor, R. C. (2008). Electronic commerce adoption barriers in small to medium-sized enterprises (SMEs) in developed and developing countries: A cross-country comparison. In A. Becker (Ed.), *Electronic commerce: Concepts, methodologies, tools, and applications* (pp. 1441–1457). Hershey, PA: IGI Global. doi:10.4018/978-1-59904-943-4.ch115

Kasemsap, K. (2015a). The role of electronic commerce in the global business environments. In F. Cipolla-Ficarra (Ed.), *Handbook of research on interactive information quality in expanding social network communications* (pp. 304–324). Hershey, PA: IGI Global. doi:10.4018/978-1-4666-7377-9.ch019

Kasemsap, K. (2015b). The role of data mining for business intelligence in knowledge management. In A. Azevedo & M. Santos (Eds.), *Integration of data mining in business intelligence systems* (pp. 12–33). Hershey, PA: IGI Global. doi:10.4018/978-1-4666-6477-7.ch002

Kasemsap, K. (2015c). Implementing business intelligence in contemporary organizations. In A. Haider (Ed.), *Business technologies in contemporary organizations: Adoption, assimilation, and institutionalization* (pp. 177–192). Hershey, PA: IGI Global. doi:10.4018/978-1-4666-6623-8.ch008

Kasemsap, K. (2016a). The fundamentals of neuroeconomics. In B. Christiansen & E. Lechman (Eds.), *Neuroeconomics and the decision-making process* (pp. 1–32). Hershey, PA: IGI Global. doi:10.4018/978-1-4666-9989-2.ch001

Kasemsap, K. (2016b). Advocating electronic business and electronic commerce in the global marketplace. In S. Dixit & A. Sinha (Eds.), *E-retailing challenges and opportunities in the global marketplace* (pp. 1–24). Hershey, PA: IGI Global. doi:10.4018/978-1-4666-9921-2.ch001

Kasemsap, K. (2016c). Implementing electronic commerce in global marketing. In I. Lee (Ed.), *Encyclopedia of e-commerce development, implementation, and management* (pp. 591–602). Hershey, PA: IGI Global. doi:10.4018/978-1-4666-9787-4.ch043

Kasemsap, K. (2016d). Encouraging supply chain networks and customer loyalty in global supply chain. In N. Kamath & S. Saurav (Eds.), *Handbook of research on strategic supply chain management in the retail industry* (pp. 87–112). Hershey, PA: IGI Global. doi:10.4018/978-1-4666-9894-9.ch006

Kasemsap, K. (2016e). Multifaceted applications of data mining, business intelligence, and knowledge management. *International Journal of Social and Organizational Dynamics in IT, 5*(1), 57–69. doi:10.4018/IJSODIT.2016010104

Kasemsap, K. (2016f). The fundamentals of business intelligence. *International Journal of Organizational and Collective Intelligence, 6*(2), 12–25. doi:10.4018/IJOCI.2016040102

Kasemsap, K. (2016g). The roles of social media marketing and brand management in global marketing. In W. Ozuem & G. Bowen (Eds.), *Competitive social media marketing strategies* (pp. 173–200). Hershey, PA: IGI Global. doi:10.4018/978-1-4666-9776-8.ch009

Kasemsap, K. (2017a). Mastering intelligent decision support systems in enterprise information management. In G. Sreedhar (Ed.), *Web data mining and the development of knowledge-based decision support systems* (pp. 35–56). Hershey, PA: IGI Global. doi:10.4018/978-1-5225-1877-8.ch004

Kasemsap, K. (2017b). The roles of logistics service providers and supply chain integration in global supply chain. In L. Saglietto & C. Cezanne (Eds.), *Global intermediation and logistics service providers* (pp. 265–285). Hershey, PA: IGI Global. doi:10.4018/978-1-5225-2133-4.ch014

Kasemsap, K. (2017c). Text mining: Current trends and applications. In G. Sreedhar (Ed.), *Web data mining and the development of knowledge-based decision support systems* (pp. 338–358). Hershey, PA: IGI Global. doi:10.4018/978-1-5225-1877-8.ch017

Kasemsap, K. (2017d). Mastering business process management and business intelligence in global business. In M. Tavana, K. Szabat, & K. Puranam (Eds.), *Organizational productivity and performance measurements using predictive modeling and analytics* (pp. 192–212). Hershey, PA: IGI Global. doi:10.4018/978-1-5225-0654-6.ch010

Kasemsap, K. (2018a). The importance of electronic commerce in modern business. In M. Khosrow-Pour (Ed.), *Encyclopedia of information science and technology* (4th ed.; pp. 2791–2801). Hershey, PA: IGI Global. doi:10.4018/978-1-5225-2255-3.ch243

Kasemsap, K. (2018b). Multifaceted applications of the Internet of Things. In M. Khosrow-Pour (Ed.), *Encyclopedia of information science and technology* (4th ed.; pp. 7775–7784). Hershey, PA: IGI Global. doi:10.4018/978-1-5225-2255-3.ch676

Kasemsap, K. (2018c). Facilitating customer relationship management in modern business. In M. Khosrow-Pour (Ed.), *Encyclopedia of information science and technology* (4th ed.; pp. 1594–1604). Hershey, PA: IGI Global. doi:10.4018/978-1-5225-2255-3.ch138

Kim, J. H., & Ryu, J. K. (2013). Recent trends on high-performance computing and security. *Cluster Computing, 16*(2), 207–208. doi:10.1007/s10586-013-0271-x

Kuah, A. T. H., & Wang, P. (2017). Fast-expanding "online" markets in South Korea and China: Are they worth pursuing? *Thunderbird International Business Review, 59*(1), 63–77. doi:10.1002/tie.21779

Kurnia, S., Choudrie, J., Mahbubur, R. M., & Alzougool, B. (2015). E-commerce technology adoption: A Malaysian grocery SME retail sector study. *Journal of Business Research, 68*(9), 1906–1918. doi:10.1016/j.jbusres.2014.12.010

Lebraty, J., & Godé, C. (2015). Assessing the performance of decision support systems in military environment: The 3C method. In A. Mesquita & C. Tsai (Eds.), *Human behavior, psychology, and social interaction in the digital era* (pp. 45–70). Hershey, PA: IGI Global. doi:10.4018/978-1-4666-8450-8.ch003

Lee, S. Y. T., & Phang, C. W. (2015). Leveraging social media for electronic commerce in Asia: Research areas and opportunities. *Electronic Commerce Research and Applications*, *14*(3), 145–149. doi:10.1016/j.elerap.2015.02.001

Lin, C., Jalleh, G., & Huang, Y. (2016). Evaluating and managing electronic commerce and outsourcing projects in hospitals. In A. Dwivedi (Ed.), *Reshaping medical practice and care with health information systems* (pp. 132–172). Hershey, PA: IGI Global. doi:10.4018/978-1-4666-9870-3.ch005

Liu, S., Duffy, A. H., Whitfield, R. I., Boyle, I. M., & McKenna, I. (2009). Towards the realization of an integrated decision support environment for organizational decision making. *International Journal of Decision Support System Technology*, *1*(4), 38–58. doi:10.4018/jdsst.2009062603

Masmoudi, M., Benaissa, M., & Chabchoub, H. (2014). Optimisation of e-commerce logistics distribution system: Problem modelling and exact resolution. *International Journal of Business Performance and Supply Chain Modelling*, *6*(3/4), 358–375. doi:10.1504/IJBPSCM.2014.065275

McCloskey, D. W. (2008). The importance of ease of use, usefulness, and trust to online consumers: An examination of the technology acceptance model with older consumers. In A. Becker (Ed.), *Electronic commerce: Concepts, methodologies, tools, and applications* (pp. 1400–1417). Hershey, PA: IGI Global. doi:10.4018/978-1-59904-943-4.ch112

Ngwenya, B. (2013). Decision support systems: An e-government strategy to enhance human resources output in public sector organisations. In Z. Mahmood (Ed.), *Developing e-government projects: Frameworks and methodologies* (pp. 44–62). Hershey, PA: IGI Global. doi:10.4018/978-1-4666-4245-4.ch003

Oliveira, T., Alhinho, M., Rita, P., & Dhillon, G. (2017). Modelling and testing consumer trust dimensions in e-commerce. *Computers in Human Behavior*, *71*, 153–164. doi:10.1016/j.chb.2017.01.050

Ong, C. E., & Teh, D. (2016). Redress procedures expected by consumers during a business-to-consumer e-commerce dispute. *Electronic Commerce Research and Applications*, *17*, 150–160. doi:10.1016/j.elerap.2016.04.006

Palopoli, L., Rosaci, D., & Sarné, G. M. L. (2016). A distributed and multi-tiered software architecture for assessing e-commerce recommendations. *Concurrency and Computation*, *28*(18), 4507–4531. doi:10.1002/cpe.3798

Papazafeiropoulou, A., & Pouloudi, A. (2003). Social issues in electronic commerce: Implications for policy makers. In M. Khosrow-Pour (Ed.), *Advanced topics in information resources management* (Vol. 2, pp. 173–191). Hershey, PA: IGI Global. doi:10.4018/978-1-59140-062-2.ch009

Park, B. J., & Han, J. S. (2016). Efficient decision support for detecting content polluters on social networks: An approach based on automatic knowledge acquisition from behavioral patterns. *Information Technology & Management*, *17*(1), 95–105. doi:10.1007/s10799-015-0250-4

Pavlou, P. A., & Ratnasingam, P. (2003). Technology trust in B2B electronic commerce: Conceptual foundations. In K. Kangas (Ed.), *Business strategies for information technology management* (pp. 200–215). Hershey, PA: IGI Global. doi:10.4018/978-1-93177-745-2.ch014

Phillips-Wren, G. E. (2010). Intelligent agents in decision support systems. In M. Hunter (Ed.), *Strategic information systems: Concepts, methodologies, tools, and applications* (pp. 857–866). Hershey, PA: IGI Global. doi:10.4018/978-1-60566-677-8.ch055

Rahman, S. M., & Raisinghani, M. S. (2000). *Electronic commerce: Opportunity and challenges*. Hershey, PA: IGI Global. doi:10.4018/978-1-87828-976-6

Raisinghani, M. S. (2000). Electronic commerce at the dawn of the third millennium. In S. Rahman & M. Raisinghani (Eds.), *Electronic commerce: Opportunity and challenges* (pp. 1–20). Hershey, PA: IGI Global. doi:10.4018/978-1-878289-76-6.ch001

Russell, S., & Forgionne, G. (2009). Decision support-related resource presence and availability awareness for DSS in pervasive computing environments. *International Journal of Decision Support System Technology*, *1*(1), 15–34. doi:10.4018/jdsst.2009010102

Scholz, M., Dorner, V., Schryen, G., & Benlian, A. (2017). A configuration-based recommender system for supporting e-commerce decisions. *European Journal of Operational Research*, *259*(1), 205–215. doi:10.1016/j.ejor.2016.09.057

Setzekorn, K., Sugumaran, V., & Patnayakuni, N. (2004). A comparison of implementation resistance factors for DMSS versus other information systems. In M. Khosrow-Pour (Ed.), Advanced topics in information resources management (Vol. 3, pp. 315–332). Hershey, PA: IGI Global. doi:10.4018/978-1-59140-253-4.ch015

Sharma, A., & Vyas, P. (2010). Decision support systems in Indian organized retail sector. In *Business information systems: Concepts, methodologies, tools and applications* (pp. 1043–1055). Hershey, PA: IGI Global. doi:10.4018/978-1-61520-969-9.ch062

Singh, N., Yadav, M., & Sahu, O. (2016). Consumer acceptance of apparel e-commerce: Ethiopia. *Intellectual Economics*, *10*(1), 55–62. doi:10.1016/j.intele.2016.06.001

Sobieska-Karpinska, J., & Hernes, M. (2010). Value of information in distributed decision support systems. In M. Pankowska (Ed.), *Infonomics for distributed business and decision-making environments: Creating information system ecology* (pp. 153–176). Hershey, PA: IGI Global. doi:10.4018/978-1-60566-890-1.ch009

Sodiya, A. S., Akinwale, A. T., Okeleye, K. A., & Emmanuel, J. A. (2012). An integrated decision support system for intercropping. In P. Zaraté (Ed.), *Integrated and strategic advancements in decision making support systems* (pp. 199–216). Hershey, PA: IGI Global. doi:10.4018/978-1-4666-1746-9.ch015

Strzębicki, D. (2015). The development of electronic commerce in agribusiness: The Polish example. *Procedia Economics and Finance*, *23*, 1314–1320. doi:10.1016/S2212-5671(15)00573-0

Toland, J., & Klepper, R. (2009). Business-to-consumer electronic commerce in developing countries. In M. Khosrow-Pour (Ed.), *Encyclopedia of information science and technology* (2nd ed.; pp. 489–494). Hershey, PA: IGI Global. doi:10.4018/978-1-60566-026-4.ch081

Tolk, A. (2010). Using simulation systems for decision support. In *Business information systems: Concepts, methodologies, tools and applications* (pp. 2163–2182). Hershey, PA: IGI Global. doi:10.4018/978-1-61520-969-9.ch131

Tran, C., Abraham, A., & Jain, L. (2008). Soft computing paradigms and regression trees in decision support systems. In V. Sugumaran (Ed.), *Intelligent information technologies: Concepts, methodologies, tools, and applications* (pp. 1011–1035). Hershey, PA: IGI Global. doi:10.4018/978-1-59904-941-0.ch058

Tynjala, T. (2012). Validation in supply chain decision support systems. *International Journal of Information Systems and Supply Chain Management, 5*(2), 39–58. doi:10.4018/jisscm.2012040103

Vahidov, R. (2004). Empowering modern managers: Towards an agent-based decision support system. In H. Nemati & C. Barko (Eds.), *Organizational data mining: Leveraging enterprise data resources for optimal performance* (pp. 170–187). Hershey, PA: IGI Global. doi:10.4018/978-1-59140-134-6.ch012

Wang, J., & Radosevich, D. (2010). Decision support systems. In M. Hunter (Ed.), *Strategic information systems: Concepts, methodologies, tools, and applications* (pp. 114–121). Hershey, PA: IGI Global. doi:10.4018/978-1-60566-677-8.ch009

Wang, J., & Yao, J. (2010). Group decision support systems. In M. Hunter (Ed.), *Strategic information systems: Concepts, methodologies, tools, and applications* (pp. 1543–1550). Hershey, PA: IGI Global. doi:10.4018/978-1-60566-677-8.ch099

Wang, S., Cavusoglu, H., & Deng, Z. (2016). Early mover advantage in e-commerce platforms with low entry barriers: The role of customer relationship management capabilities. *Information & Management, 53*(2), 197–206. doi:10.1016/j.im.2015.09.011

Wells, J. D., & Hess, T. J. (2008). Understanding decision-making in data warehousing and related decision support systems: An explanatory study of a customer relationship management application. In J. Wang (Ed.), *Data warehousing and mining: Concepts, methodologies, tools, and applications* (pp. 2185–2200). Hershey, PA: IGI Global. doi:10.4018/978-1-59904-951-9.ch129

Wu, J., Li, L., & Xu, L. D. (2014). A randomized pricing decision support system in electronic commerce. *Decision Support Systems, 58*, 43–52. doi:10.1016/j.dss.2013.01.015

Xie, Y., & Wang, H. (2014). A group cooperative decision support system based on extended contract net. *Group Decision and Negotiation, 23*(5), 1191–1217. doi:10.1007/s10726-013-9369-z

Yan, Q., Wu, S., Wang, L., Wu, P., Chen, H., & Wei, G. (2016). E-WOM from e-commerce websites and social media: Which will consumers adopt? *Electronic Commerce Research and Applications, 17*, 62–73. doi:10.1016/j.elerap.2016.03.004

Yi, X., Siew, C. K., & Syed, M. R. (2000). Electronic commerce based on software agent. In S. Rahman & M. Raisinghani (Eds.), *Electronic commerce: Opportunity and challenges* (pp. 279–302). Hershey, PA: IGI Global. doi:10.4018/978-1-878289-76-6.ch018

Yıldız, S., & Kurtuldu, H. S. (2014). Factors affecting electronic service brand equity. In B. Christiansen, S. Yıldız, & E. Yıldız (Eds.), *Transcultural marketing for incremental and radical innovation* (pp. 434–492). Hershey, PA: IGI Global. doi:10.4018/978-1-4666-4749-7.ch022

Yoon, H. S., & Occeña, L. G. (2015). Influencing factors of trust in consumer-to-consumer electronic commerce with gender and age. *International Journal of Information Management*, *35*(3), 352–363. doi:10.1016/j.ijinfomgt.2015.02.003

Yu, Y., Wang, X., Zhong, R. Y., & Huang, G. Q. (2016). E-commerce logistics in supply chain management: Practice perspective. *Procedia CIRP*, *52*, 179–185. doi:10.1016/j.procir.2016.08.002

Yuviler-Gavish, N., & Naseraldin, H. (2016). The effect of previous experience when introducing a decision aid in a decision support system for supply chain management. *Cognition Technology and Work*, *18*(2), 439–447. doi:10.1007/s10111-016-0369-z

Zerenler, M., & Gözlü, S. (2012). Issues influencing electronic commerce activities of SMEs: A study of the Turkish automotive supplier industry. In *Human resources management: Concepts, methodologies, tools, and applications* (pp. 1035–1055). Hershey, PA: IGI Global. doi:10.4018/978-1-4666-1601-1.ch064

Zhang, D., Zhu, P., & Ye, Y. (2016). The effects of e-commerce on the demand for commercial real estate. *Cities (London, England)*, *51*, 106–120. doi:10.1016/j.cities.2015.11.012

Zhang, H., Wang, Y., & Zhang, X. (2014). The approaches to contextual transaction trust computation in e-commerce environments. *Security and Communication Networks*, *7*(9), 1331–1351. doi:10.1002/sec.839

Zhang, J., & Pu, P. (2010). Performance evaluation of consumer decision support systems. In M. Hunter (Ed.), *Strategic information systems: Concepts, methodologies, tools, and applications* (pp. 1465–1482). Hershey, PA: IGI Global. doi:10.4018/978-1-60566-677-8.ch094

Zhao, J., Lau, R. Y. K., Zhang, W., Zhang, K., Chen, X., & Tang, D. (2016). Extracting and reasoning about implicit behavioral evidences for detecting fraudulent online transactions in e-commerce. *Decision Support Systems*, *86*, 109–121. doi:10.1016/j.dss.2016.04.003

ADDITIONAL READING

Agudo-Peregrina, A. F., Pascual-Miguel, F. J., & Chaparro-Peláez, J. (2014). It's never the same: The role of homogeneity in online services. *Service Business*, *8*(3), 453–464. doi:10.1007/s11628-014-0249-7

Bhattacharya, A., Tiwari, M. K., & Harding, J. A. (2012). A framework for ontology based decision support system for e-learning modules, business modeling and manufacturing systems. *Journal of Intelligent Manufacturing*, *23*(5), 1763–1781. doi:10.1007/s10845-010-0480-6

Blasco-Arcas, L., Hernandez-Ortega, B., & Jimenez-Martinez, J. (2013). Adopting television as a new channel for e-commerce. The influence of interactive technologies on consumer behavior. *Electronic Commerce Research*, *13*(4), 457–475. doi:10.1007/s10660-013-9132-1

Chiu, C. M., Wang, E. T. G., Fang, Y. H., & Huang, H. Y. (2014). Understanding customers' repeat purchase intentions in B2C e-commerce: The roles of utilitarian value, hedonic value and perceived risk. *Information Systems Journal*, *24*(1), 85–114. doi:10.1111/j.1365-2575.2012.00407.x

Dakhlia, S., & Strauss, R. P. (2013). Should sales taxes be imposed on e-commerce? *Journal of Public Economic Theory*, *15*(6), 803–828. doi:10.1111/jpet.12055

Damos, P. (2015). Modular structure of web-based decision support systems for integrated pest management. A review. *Agronomy for Sustainable Development*, *35*(4), 1347–1372. doi:10.1007/s13593-015-0319-9

Dowie, J., Kjer Kaltoft, M., Salkeld, G., & Cunich, M. (2015). Towards generic online multicriteria decision support in patient-centred health care. *Health Expectations*, *18*(5), 689–702. doi:10.1111/hex.12111 PMID:23910715

Fauska, P., Kryvinska, N., & Strauss, C. (2014). Agile management of complex goods & services bundles for B2B e-commerce by global narrow-specialized companies. *Global Journal of Flexible Systems Management*, *15*(1), 5–23. doi:10.1007/s40171-013-0054-5

Hernes, M., & Sobieska-Karpińska, J. (2016). Application of the consensus method in a multiagent financial decision support system. *Information Systems and e-Business Management*, *14*(1), 167–185. doi:10.1007/s10257-015-0280-9

Islam, M. S., Sadiq, R., Rodriguez, M. J., Najjaran, H., & Hoorfar, M. (2016). Integrated decision support system for prognostic and diagnostic analyses of water distribution system failures. *Water Resources Management*, *30*(8), 2831–2850. doi:10.1007/s11269-016-1326-6

Little, R. G., Manzanares, T., & Wallace, W. A. (2015). Factors influencing the selection of decision support systems for emergency management: An empirical analysis of current use and user preferences. *Journal of Contingencies and Crisis Management*, *23*(4), 266–274. doi:10.1111/1468-5973.12097

Nam, W. H., Choi, J. Y., Yoo, S. H., & Jang, M. W. (2012). A decision support system for agricultural drought management using risk assessment. *Paddy and Water Environment*, *10*(3), 197–207. doi:10.1007/s10333-012-0329-z

Peng, L., & Lai, L. (2014). A service innovation evaluation framework for tourism e-commerce in China based on BP neural network. *Electronic Markets*, *24*(1), 37–46. doi:10.1007/s12525-013-0148-0

Piva, F., & Dahab, R. (2013). E-commerce of digital items and the problem of item validation: Introducing the concept of reversible degradation. *Applicable Algebra in Engineering, Communication and Computing*, *24*(3/4), 277–308. doi:10.1007/s00200-013-0197-9

Rezaei, R., Chiew, T. K., & Lee, S. P. (2014). A review on e-business interoperability frameworks. *Journal of Systems and Software*, *93*, 199–216. doi:10.1016/j.jss.2014.02.004

Rousta, B. A., & Araghinejad, S. (2015). Development of a multi criteria decision making tool for a water resources decision support system. *Water Resources Management*, *29*(15), 5713–5727. doi:10.1007/s11269-015-1142-4

Sadeghian, R., & Sadeghian, M. R. (2016). A decision support system based on artificial neural network and fuzzy analytic network process for selection of machine tools in a flexible manufacturing system. *International Journal of Advanced Manufacturing Technology*, *82*(9), 1795–1803. doi:10.1007/s00170-015-7440-4

Shan, S., Wang, L., Li, L., & Chen, Y. (2012). An emergency response decision support system framework for application in e-government. *Information Technology & Management*, *13*(4), 411–427. doi:10.1007/s10799-012-0130-0

Shiau, W. L., & Dwivedi, Y. K. (2013). Citation and co-citation analysis to identify core and emerging knowledge in electronic commerce research. *Scientometrics*, *94*(3), 1317–1337. doi:10.1007/s11192-012-0807-5

Shojaiemehr, B., & Rafsanjani, M. K. (2014). A fuzzy system approach to multilateral automated negotiation in B2C e-commerce. *Neural Computing & Applications*, *25*(2), 367–377. doi:10.1007/s00521-013-1491-y

Sigman, B. P., & Boston, B. J. (2013). Digital discernment: An e-commerce web site evaluation tool. *Decision Sciences Journal of Innovative Education*, *11*(1), 29–46. doi:10.1111/j.1540-4609.2012.00367.x

Sila, I. (2013). Factors affecting the adoption of B2B e-commerce technologies. *Electronic Commerce Research*, *13*(2), 199–236. doi:10.1007/s10660-013-9110-7

Taha, Z., & Rostam, S. J. (2012). A hybrid fuzzy AHP-PROMETHEE decision support system for machine tool selection in flexible manufacturing cell. *Journal of Intelligent Manufacturing*, *23*(6), 2137–2149. doi:10.1007/s10845-011-0560-2

Tehrani, F. T., & Abbasi, S. (2012). A model-based decision support system for critiquing mechanical ventilation treatments. *Journal of Clinical Monitoring and Computing*, *26*(3), 207–215. doi:10.1007/s10877-012-9362-0 PMID:22532227

Tian, Z., Zhang, Z., & Guan, X. (2013). A new evolution model for B2C e-commerce market. *Information Technology and Management*, *14*(3), 205–215. doi:10.1007/s10799-013-0159-8

Wang, Q., Liu, S., Liu, W., Kapelan, Z., & Savic, D. (2013). Decision support system for emergency scheduling of raw water supply systems with multiple sources. *Frontiers of Environmental Science & Engineering*, *7*(5), 777–786. doi:10.1007/s11783-013-0537-9

Wimmer, H., Forgionne, G., Rada, R., & Yoon, V. (2012). A conceptual model for knowledge marts for decision making support systems. *International Journal of Decision Support System Technology*, *4*(4), 24–38. doi:10.4018/jdsst.2012100102

KEY TERMS AND DEFINITIONS

Business Intelligence: The advanced business method concerning strategic planning procedure.

Data Mining: The extraction of latent information from massive databases.

Decision Support Systems: The computer-related utilization that can help evaluate various business details toward achieving effective decision making.

Electronic Commerce: The online business approach that allows both individuals and companies to effectively conduct businesses.

Logistics: The procedure that relates to the transportation and storage of products and services.

Privacy: The term of concealing any issue from other people.

Trust: The expectation that someone or something is reliable.

Chapter 12
Application of Opinion Mining in E-Commerce

Brojo Kishore Mishra
C. V. Raman College of Engineering, India

Rekhanjali Sahoo
BPUT Rourkela, India

ABSTRACT

Social media has become an increasingly important part of our daily lives in the last few years. An area of substantial research is that of predicting product sales, such as books, video games, and movie tickets. Customer opinions play a very crucial role in daily life. When we have to make decisions, opinions of other individuals are also considered. Business organizations and corporate organizations are always eager to find consumer or individual views regarding their products, support, and service. In e-commerce, online shopping, and online tourism, it is very crucial to analyze the social data present on the web automatically; therefore, it is very important to create methods that automatically classify them. In this chapter, the authors do future prediction of financial market by taking past observations so that they can maximize their profit and orders can be placed on time.

INTRODUCTION

Opinion Mining or sentiment classification involves building a system to make use of reviews posted by the users and opinions that are expressed in blogs and forums as comments and reviews and sometimes may be as tweets about the product (Mining Hu & Bing Liu, 2004). Opinions are written on many things example a product, a topic, an individual, etc. In opinion mining task we identify the orientation of opinion by the holder towards any object which may be a collection of features or components or attributes. Opinion Mining sometimes called as Sentiment Classification is defined as mining and analyzing of reviews, views, emotions and opinions automatically from text, big data and speech by means of various methods (Andrea Esuli, 2008). Generally, data mining (sometimes called data or knowledge discovery) is the process of analyzing data from different perspectives and summarizing it into useful information-information that can be used to increase revenue, cuts costs, or both. (Mining Hu & Bing Liu, 2004).

DOI: 10.4018/978-1-5225-3646-8.ch012

In our proposed object Opinion mining helps in e-commerce for taking decision to buy any product. In e-commerce, online shopping and online tourism, it's very crucial to analyze the good amount of social data present on the Web automatically therefore, it's very important to create methods that automatically classify them. Opinion Mining sometimes called as Sentiment Classification is defined as mining and analyzing of reviews, views, emotions and opinions automatically from text, big data and speech by means of various methods (Mining Hu & Bing Liu, 2004). Our main theme is to create a system for analyzing opinions which implies judgment of different consumer products. In our proposed project for sales prediction we will take into consideration the present date for future prediction.

To increase the buyers know more about the credit of E-commerce product sellers and the purchase rate of the E-commerce users, E-commerce credit evaluation model based on the opinion mining algorithm was put forward (Alexander Pak and Patrick Paroubek, 2010). Extract the feature words and views from the products and user reviews, and then make use of statistical and quantitative way to analyze them. In the mean time, a credit evaluation model with transaction time-frequency can be set up, which can be used to analyze the seller's credit of E-commerce users.

Opinion Mining

Given a set of evaluative text documents D that contain opinions (or sentiments) about an object, opinion mining aims to extract attributes and components of the object that have been commented on in each document d ∈D and to determine whether the comments are positive, negative or neutral (Antweiler & Frank, 2004).

E-Commerce

While some use E-commerce and E-business interchangeably, they are distinct concepts. Electronic business, commonly referred to as "e-Business" or "e-business", may be defined as the application of information and communication technologies (ICT) in support of all the activities of business (Au, W.H., Chan K. C. C. & Yao, 2003). Commerce constitutes the exchange of products and services between businesses, groups and individuals and can be seen as one of the essential activities of any business. Electronic commerce focuses on the use of ICT to enable the external activities and relationships of the business with individuals, groups and other businesses.

E-Commerce is a particular form of e-Business. Electronic business methods enable companies to link their internal and external data processing systems more efficiently and flexibly, to work more closely with suppliers and partners, and to better satisfy the needs and expectations of their customers. Compared to e-Commerce, e-Business is a more generic term because it refers not only to information exchanges related to buying and selling but also servicing customers and collaborating with business partners, distributors and suppliers.

How Opinion Mining Possible for E-Commerce

The powerful functions of the Internet have promoted the development of E-commerce. In recent years, the product view comments have been an important evaluation when customers choose the goods and the sellers (Pak & Paroubek, 2010). It is mainly because the comments are based on the experience of buying goods, and the credibility is higher. The current E-commerce shopping websites have products and user reviews, after E-commerce transactions, the users can publish their own views and opinions of one's own accord within a period of time. However, the users are limited by cognitive ability and the immature information search behaviour in the face of the complicated comments. It doesn't necessarily for them to retrieve the information, for this reason, many products, users comments and sellers credit are used by the main basis of the credit evaluation of busying E-commerce products (Pak & Paroubek, 2010). How to effective use of E-commercecredit evaluation, and get the approval of the buyers, which are the only way to improve the purchase rate of E-commerce. Consequently, completing the E- commerce credit evaluation is the only way to solve this problem. How to quantitatively extract the effective point-view from the comments on the products and to help consumers better decisions. (Pak & Paroubek, 2010). The process that quantitative extract the opinion of product reviews is named opinion mining in which there are mainly include three basic elements: view the holder, the individuals or organizations who hold certain view of the particular objects; the object, the role of evaluation view; the view it is a perception, attitude or evaluation that the view holders make comments on the objects. Opinion mining is to understand the relationship among three basic elements. At present domestic opinion mining research are mainly focus on the comments of the car, bank, movie, electronic products and so on, and there are also some practical opinion mining system mostly by means of the characteristics, and the part of the comments to implement (Pak & Paroubek, 2010).

The opinion mining about E-commerce product review opinion is typically included:

1. Establish product reviews feature library and comments view feature library;
2. Extract feature evaluation; judge the point polarity of comment and strength;
3. Evaluate the characteristics of products and quantify the comments;
4. Summarize view mining and statistics;
5. Establish the credit evaluation application. To describe the role and effect of the process in the electronic commerce credit evaluation, this paper designs the model of the E-commerce credit evaluation system based on the opinion mining.

HISTORICAL BACKGROUND

Textual information in the world can be broadly classified into two main categories, facts and opinions (Wilson, Wiebe, & Hoffmann, 2005). Facts are objective statements about entities and events in the world. Opinions are subjective statements that reflect people's sentiments or perceptions about the entities and events. Much of the existing research on text information processing has been (almost exclusively) focused on mining and retrieval of factual information, e.g., information retrieval, Web search, and many other text mining and natural language processing tasks. Little work has been done on the processing of opinions until only recently. Yet, opinions are so important that whenever one needs to make a decision one wants to hear others' opinions. This is not only true for individuals but also true for organizations.

One of the main reasons for the lack of study on opinions is that there was little opinionated text before the World Wide Web. Before the Web, when an individual needs to make a decision, he/she typically asks for opinions from friends and families (Wilson, Wiebe, & Hoffmann, 2005). When an organization needs to find opinions of the general public about its products and services, it conducts surveys and focused groups. With the Web, especially with the explosive growth of the user generated content on the Web, the world has changed. One can post reviews of products at merchant sites and express views on almost anything in Internet forums, discussion groups, and blogs, which are collectively called the user generated content. Now if one wants to buy a product, it is no longer necessary to ask one's friends and families because there are plentiful of product reviews on the web which give the opinions of the existing users of the product. For a company, it may no longer need to conduct surveys, to organize focused groups or to employ external consultants in order to find consumer opinions or sentiments about its products and those of its competitors.

Finding opinion sources and monitoring them on the Web, however, can still be a formidable task because a large number of diverse sources exist on the Web and each source also contains a huge volume of information. In many cases, opinions are hidden in long forum posts and blogs (Wilson, Wiebe, & Hoffmann, 2005). It is very difficult for a human reader to find relevant sources, extract pertinent sentences, read them, summarize them and organize them into usable forms. An automated opinion mining and summarization system is thus needed. Opinion mining, also known as sentiment analysis, grows out of this need. In particular, it discusses the following topics: (1) the abstract model of opinion mining, (2) sentiment classification, (3) feature-based opinion mining and summarization, and (4) opinion mining from comparative sentences.

STEPS IN OPINION MINING APPROCH

We group the significant issues of Opinion mining into three classes (Minqing Hu & Bing Liu, 2004).

- Sentiment polarity identification,
- Subjectivity detection, and
- Joint topic-sentiment analysis.

There is one more interesting study in the opinion mining tasks classification called feature level. We discuss about feature level opinion mining in brief in this section.

- Document level opinion mining.
- Sentence level opinion mining.
- Phrase Level opinion mining.
- Feature Level opinion mining.

Document-Level Opinion Mining

It is about classifying the overall opinionated text presented by the authors in whole document as positive, negative or neutral about a certain subject or object (John Krum, Nigel Davies, and Chandra Narayanaswami, 2008). Therefore subjectivity / objectivity classification is important in this type of Sentiment Classification. The main challenge in this classification is to extract informative text for deducing sentiment of the entire document.

Sentence-Level Opinion Mining

The problem at this measure everything refers to sentences. In opinion data extraction and recovery and opinion question answering, sentences are generally placed and positioned focused around some criteria (Krum, Davies, & Narayanaswami, 2008). Opinion rundown intends to select a set of sentences which outline the opinion all the more exactly. At long last, opinion mining in relative sentences incorporates recognizing similar sentences and concentrating data from them.

Phrase-Level Opinion Mining

Phrase level mining came into picture because document level mining and sentence level mining approaches can't find accurately what actually users likes and they does not like. Phrase level opinion mining looks for sentiments on features of products (Krum, Davies, & Narayanaswami, 2008).

Feature Level Opinion Mining

Feature level opinion mining comes into picture when a customer or user looking for feedback of certain feature or attribute of a product rather than total feedback of the product. We see many customers interested in only certain features of some products rather than the whole product like some people look for a mobile that has excellent battery life and they are not concerned with other features like camera clarity, music clarity and so on (Krum, Davies, & Narayanaswami, 2008). In situations like mentioned in this section feature level opinion mining helps a lot for extracting polarity information for a particular feature or attribute from a product.

MODEL OF OPINION MINING

In general, opinions can be expressed on anything, e.g., a product, a service, a topic, an individual, an organization, or an event. The general term object is used to denote the entity that has been commented on (Wilson, Wiebe, & Hoffmann, 2005). An object has a set of components (or parts) and a set of at-

Figure 1. Process of opinion mining and sentiment analysis

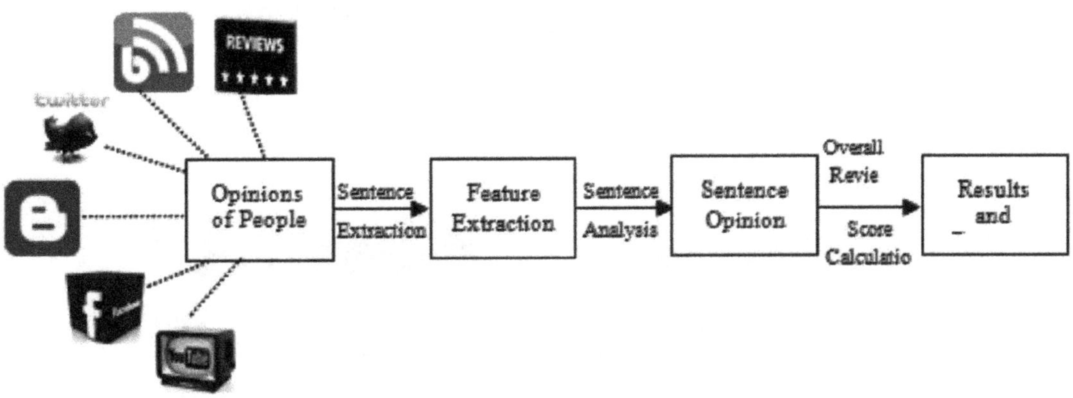

tributes. Each component may also haveits sub-components and its set of attributes and so on. Thus, the object can be hierarchically decomposed based on the part-of relationship.An object O is an entity which can be a product, topic, person, event, orOrganization. It is associated with a pair, O: (T, A), where T is a hierarchy or taxonomy of components (or parts) and sub-components of O, and A is a set of attributes of O. Each component has its own set of sub-components and attributes.

In this hierarchy or tree, the root is the object itself. Each non-root node is a component or subcomponent of the object. Each link is a part-of relationship. Each node is associated with a set of attributes. An opinion can be expressed on any node and any attribute of the node. However, for an ordinary user, it is probably too complex to use a hierarchical representation (Pak & Paroubek, 2010). To simplify it, the tree is flattened. The word "features" is used to represent both components and attributes.

Let an evaluative document be d, which can be a product review, a forum post or a blog that evaluates a particular object O. In the most general case, d consists of a sequence of sentences d = (s1, s2… sm). The opinion passage on a feature f of the object O evaluated in d is a group of consecutive sentences in d that expresses a positive or negative opinion on f. This means that it is possible that a sequence of sentences (at least one) together expresses an opinion on an object or a feature of the object (Abbasi, Chen & Salem, 2007). It is also possible that a single sentence expresses opinions on more than one feature, e.g., "The picture quality of this camera is good, but the battery life is short". The holder of a particular opinion is a person or an organization that holds the opinion. In the case of product reviews, forum postings and blogs, opinion holders are usually the authors of the posts. Opinion holders are important in news articles because they often explicitly state the person or organization that holds a

Figure 2. Model of opinion mining

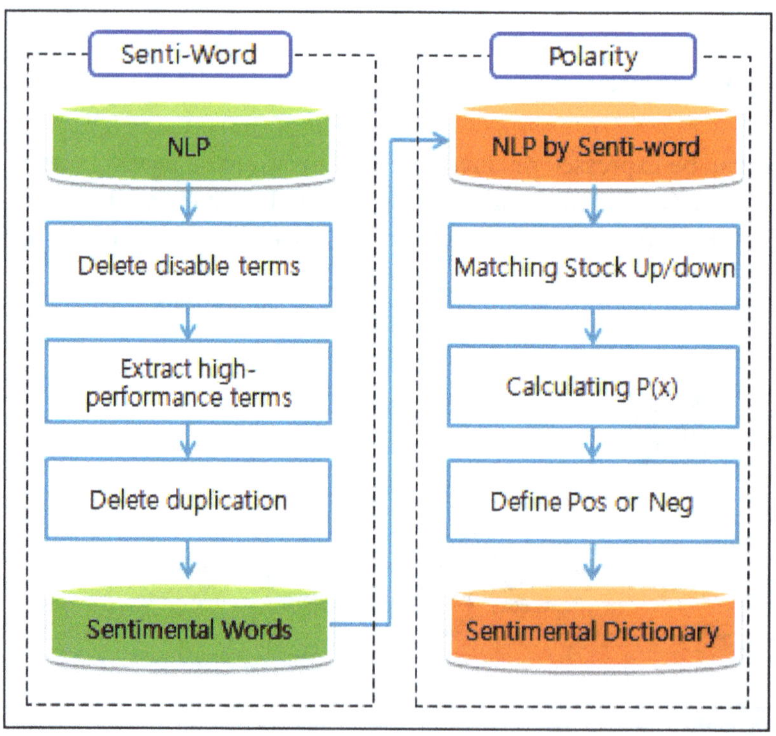

particular opinion. For example, the opinion holder in the sentence "John expressed his disagreement on the treaty" is "John". The semantic orientation of an opinion on a feature f states whether the opinion is positive, negative or neutral.

PROBLEM DESCRIPTION AND OBJECTIVES

Stock trading system is the specific domain used to illustrate these problems is that of automatic stock trading systems. We will address the task of building a stock trading system based on prediction models obtained with daily stock quotes data (Sarmento, Carvalho, Silva, & de Oliveira, 2009). Several models will be tried with the goal of predicting the future returns of the S&P 500 market index. These predictions will be used together with a trading strategy to reach a decision regarding the market orders to generate. Stock market trading is an application domain with a large potential for data mining. In effect, the existence of an enormous amount of historical data suggests that data mining can provide a competitive advantage over human inspection of these data. On the other hand, there are researchers claiming that the markets adapt so rapidly in terms of price adjustments that there is no space to obtain profits in a consistent way (Sarmento, Carvalho, Silva, & de Oliveira, 2009). This is usually known as the efficient markets hypothesis.

The general goal of stock trading is to maintain a portfolio of assets based on buy and sell orders (Sarmento, Carvalho, Silva, & de Oliveira, 2009). The long-term objective is to achieve as much profit as possible from these trading actions. Here, we will try to maximize our profit over a future testing period by means of trading actions (Buy, Sell, and Hold).(Richa Sharma, Shweta Nigam, and Rekha Jain.Supervised opinion mining techniques: A survey)

Our trading strategy will use as a basis for decision making the indications provided by the result of a data mining process. This process will consist of trying to predict the future evolution of the index based on a model obtained with historical quotes data. Thus our prediction model will be incorporated in a trading system that generates its decisions based on the predictions of the model. Our overall evaluation criteria will be the performance of this trading system, that is, the profit/loss resulting from the actions of the system as well as some other statistics that are of interest to investors. This means that our main evaluation criteria will be the operational results of applying the knowledge discovered by our data mining process and not the predictive accuracy of the models developed during this process.

IMPLIMENTATION AND RESULT ANALYSIS

The Available Data

Here, we will concentrate on trading the S&P 500 market index for sales prediction. Daily data concerning the quotes of this security is freely available in many places, for example, the Yahoo finance site (Sarmento, Carvalho, Silva, & de Oliveira, 2009). We have done our implementation part in R language.

An Introduction to R Language

R is an integrated suite of software facilities for data manipulation, calculation and graphical display (Moghaddam & Ester, 2012). Among other things it has an effective data handling and storage facility, a suite of operators for calculations on arrays, in particular matrices large, coherent, integrated collection of intermediate tools for data analysis, graphical facilities for data analysis and display either directly at the computer or on hardcopy, and well developed, simple and effective programming language (called 'S') which includes conditionals, loops, user defined recursive functions and input and output facilities. (Indeed most of the system supplied functions are themselves written in the S language.) The term "environment" is intended to characterize it as a fully planned and coherent system, rather than an incremental accretion of very specific and inflexible tools, as is frequently the case with other data analysis software.R is very much a vehicle for newly developing methods of interactive data analysis. It has developed rapidly, and has been extended by a large collection of packages (Samaneh Moghaddam and Martin Ester, 2012).However; most programs written in R are essentially ephemeral, written for a single piece of data analysis.

Advantages of R

R Is a Free, Open Source Language

To begin with, R is freely available! This means, anyone can download R from the internet (through a large network of mirror servers) and start working on it (Krum, Davies, & Narayanaswami,2008). What more? You can even modify the code and add your own innovations to it. R language has no license restrictions as it is issued under the GNU (General Public License) and is an open source programming language. R can run anywhere and anytime and can also be sold adhering to the conditions of the License.

R Is Cross-Platform Compatible

One of the biggest advantages of R is that you can run R on several operating systems and varied Software/Hardware. It is quite often used on Microsoft Windows (32-bit as well as 64-bit), Macintosh, GNU/Linux, UNIX and its derivatives such as Mac OS X, Darwin, FreeBSD, Solaris, etc. It also runs on some operating systems of Mainframes (Krum, Davies, & Narayanaswami, 2008). Thanks to the efforts put in by the R Development Core Team to make it cross-platform compatible!

Most Advanced Statistical Programming Language

As R is developed by top computational statisticians and computer language designers, R programming is looked upon as a product of "International collaboration". Undoubtedly, R is one of the most advanced statistical programming languages used world-wide by several statisticians to make their lives much easier and much more productive. R programmers can work on large complex objects (not limited to a small group of problems), exchange data in MS-Excel, ensure the accuracy of the code, keep a track of every computational step, preserve the history for later reference, work on advanced statistical analysis, do intricate visualizations and so on (Krum, Davies, & Narayanaswami, 2008). R is backed by very elaborate technical documentation and tutorials contributed by many users. The overall structure and syntax of R is exclusively developed for statistical computation.

Outstanding Graphical Outputs

R programming language has splendid Hi-Tech graphical capabilities that are incomparable with any other statistical language. That's why programmers love R! Look at the graphs created in R, whether they are box plots, histograms, polygons, scatter plots, bar plots, arrows, trees, mathematical symbols, ggplots, all these are very impressive and self-explanatory (Krum, Davies, & Narayanaswami, 2008). The graphs generated with R are high in quality and as good as publication graphs! You can create static or even dynamic graphs based on the packages you opt for! Thus, R is a fully programmable graphical language with outstanding features!

R Is Flexible 'n' Fun

Do you think there are some bugs in existing R language that need to be addressed? You are most welcome to do that! Or do you want to invent a new analysis? Then learn R programming and get a strong hold of the Analytics world! R being fully programmable, you can even do code enhancements, develop dynamic packages, computerize repetitive procedures, develop your own apps and Info Maps in R, create tables in Latex or Lynx and the list just goes on! (Krum, Davies, & Narayanaswami, 2008). It is easy and fun to write your own functions in R and distribute your own R software as an add-on package! The situation is such, that many new statistical methods are being developed attaching an R package to these.

R Is Extremely Comprehensive

Imagine a programming language offering over 4,800 packages from various repositories relating to Data mining, Bio-informatics, Econometrics, and Spatial analysis! R programming language consists of several standard statistical tests, analyses and models! R can work on objects of infinite size and intricacy with ease. The R programmers are not confined to a single method of achieving a desired graphical model

Figure 3. Graphical output using R

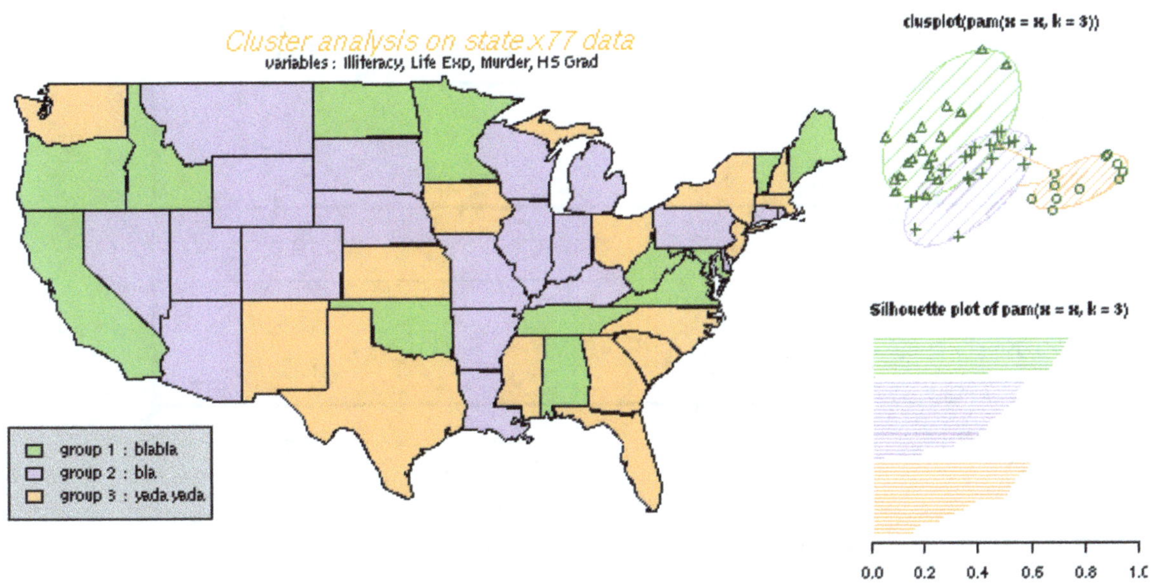

or statistical computation Krum, Davies, & Narayanaswami, 2008). Instead, R performs a wide variety of functions, such as data manipulation, classical statistical tests, statistical modeling (whether linear or nonlinear), and graphical techniques, classification, clustering, and so on.

R Supports Extensions

R is not only a very comprehensive language but also very extensible in its structure. Data structures in R consist of vectors, scalars, data frames, time series, matrices, lists, etc. R also supports matrix arithmetic as well as extensible object-system such as regression models and geo-spatial coordinates. R also supports procedural programming along with functions (Krum, Davies, & Narayanaswami, 2008) and also OOP (Object-Oriented Programming) for certain functions. R programming language also has the facility to extract data from Google using RCurl package, join the vectors or data frames of different length into a single data frame, zip fastener to join rows or columns of two data frames in a different manner and also get hold of the Normalized Google Distance (NGD) with R!

R Has a Vast Community

With more and more people and companies adopting R as the "Statistical Language", R has created a vast community for itself! These like-minded people with their own experiences bring in a lot of value-addition to the discussion forums, social media, R conferences and other networking channels. Through these

Figure 4. Extension diagram

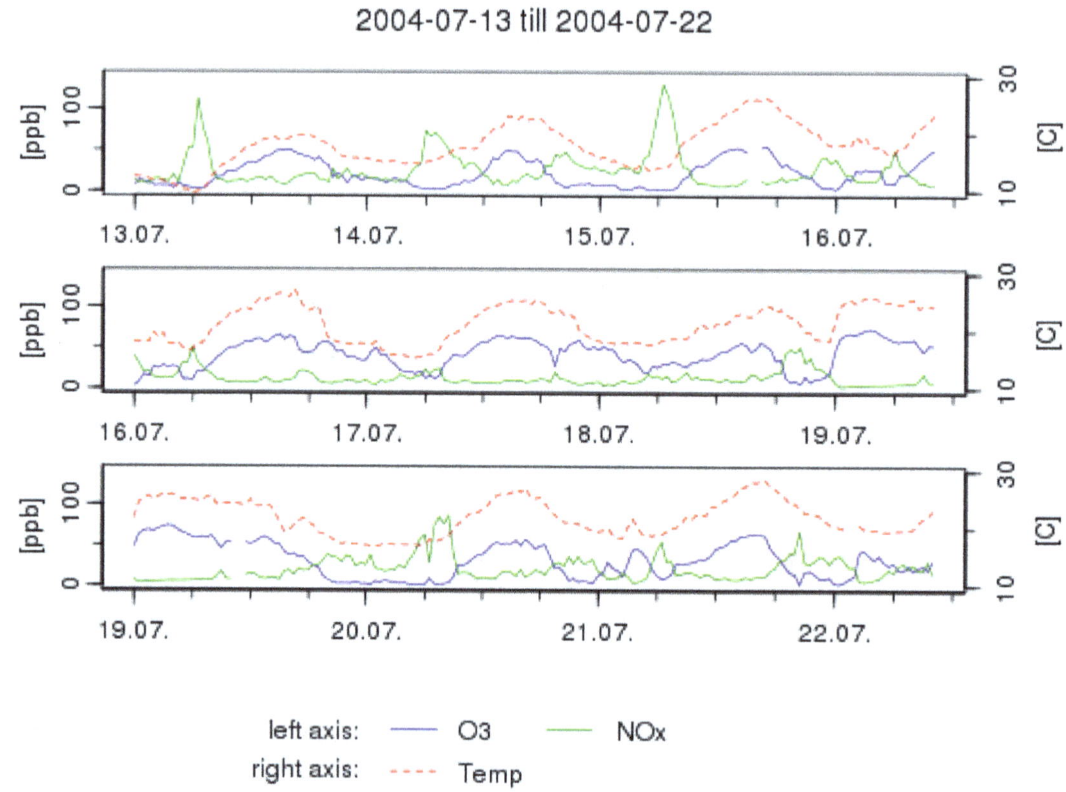

active groups using R, students and professionals can get a clear view what R is all about, advantages of R and how to use the striking features of R in their professional lives (Krum, Davies, & Narayanaswami, 2008). Get support from the R professionals and get your queries solved within a short period of time. Become a part of the vast community of 2 million people and get started with R!

R Easily Relates to Other Programming Languages

After realizing what R can do in business analysis, a new trend has become where existing software as well as emerging software are integrated with various R packages to make them more productive. Now R is getting attached to many file systems, applications and databases (Krum, Davies, & Narayanaswami, 2008). Thus, R relates to other programming languages easily. R is also quite friendly while importing data not only from Microsoft Excel, but also, Microsoft Access, MySQL, SQLite, Oracle, and so on. R can also beeasily connected to various databases using ODBC (Open Database Connectivity Protocol) and the ROracle package.

Disadvantages of R

R has a steep learning curve it does take a while to get used to the power of R but no steeper than for other statistical languages. R is not so easy to use for the novice (Akshat Bakliwal, 2013). There are several simple-to use graphical user interfaces (GUIs) for R that encompass point and-click interactions, but they generally do not have the polish of the commercial offerings.

Documentation is sometimes patchy and terse, and impenetrable to the non-statistician. However, some very high-standard books are increasingly plugging the documentation gaps.

The quality of some packages is less than perfect, although if a package is useful to many people, it will quickly evolve into a very robust product through collaborative efforts.

There is, in general, no one to complain to if something doesn't work. R is a software application that many people freely devote their own time to developing. Problems are usually dealt with quickly on the open mailing lists, and bugs disappear with lightning speed. Users who do require it can purchase support from a number of vendors internationally.

Many R commands give little thought to memory management, and so R can very quickly consume all available memory. This can be a restriction when doing data mining. There are various solutions, including using 64 bit operating systems that can access much more memory than 32 bit ones.

In order to get the data through the book R package, it is enough to issue (Sarmento, Carvalho, J Silva, & de Oliveira, 2009)

- Library(DMwR)
- Data(GSPC)

The first statement is only required if we have not issued it before in our R session. The second instruction will load an object, GSPC, of class xts. At the book Web site, we can find these data in two alternative formats. The first is a comma separated values (CSV) file that can be read into R in the same way as the data used (Sarmento, Carvalho, J Silva, & de Oliveira, 2009). The other format is a MySQL database file that we can use to create a database with the S&P 500 quotes in MySQL. For the sake of completeness we will also mention another way of getting this data into R, which consists of downloading it directly from the Web.

Whichever source we choose to use, the daily stock quotes data includes information regarding the following properties:

- Date of the stock exchange session
- Open price at the beginning of the session
- Highest price during the session
- Lowest price
- Closing price of the session
- Volume of transactions
- Adjusted close price

In our project work, we will do many experiments on future prediction by taking past observations. So we will do experiments on handling time dependent data.

Handling Time-Dependent Data

The data available for this depends on time. This means that each observation of our dataset has a time tag attached to it (Sarmento, Carvalho, J Silva, & de Oliveira, 2009). This type of data is frequently known as time series data. A time series is a set of ordered observations of a Variable Y (Esuli, 2008):

y1,y2,…,yt-1,yt,yt+1,……...yn

where yt is the value of the series variable Y at time t.

The main goal of time series analysis is to obtain a model based on past observations of the variable, y1,y2,…,yt-1,yt, which allows us to make predictions regarding future observations of the variable, yt+1,……...yn (Esuli, 2008).

In the case of our stocks data, we have what is usually known as a multivariate time series, because we measure several variables at the same time tags, namely the Open, High, Low, Close, Volume, and AdjClose.

Among the most flexible R packages for handling time-dependent data are zoo and xts (Sarmento, Carvalho, J Silva, & de Oliveira, 2009).

R has several packages devoted to the analysis of this type of data, and in effect it has special classes of objects that are used to store type-dependent data. Among the most flexible R packages for handling time-dependent data are zoo and xts.

Xts provides a set of extra facilities to handle this type of data. In technical terms the class xts extends the class zoo, which means that any xts object is also a zoo object, and thus we can apply any method designed for zoo objects to xts objects.

The following examples illustrate how to create objects of class xts (Sarmento, Carvalho, J Silva, & de Oliveira, 2009).

```
> Library (base)
> Library (zoo)
> Library (xts)
> X1 <- xts (norm (100), seq (as.POSIXct ("2000-01-01"), len = 100,
```

```
+      by = "day"))
> X1[1:5]
                  [, 1]
2000-01-01 0.2165208
2000-01-02 -1.4699709
2000-01-03 -1.2893820
2000-01-04 -0.2883122
2000-01-05 -1.2706681
```

In the above example, we have created x1 object [1] of class xts. Here, sequence is generated by sequence function.

```
• x2 <- xts(rnorm(100), seq(as.POSIXct("2000-01-01 13:00"),+      len = 100, by
= "min"))> X2[1:4]                  [, 1]
2000-01-01 13:00:00   0.1613590
2000-01-01 13:01:00 -0.3493827
2000-01-01 13:02:00 -0.6000655
2000-01-01 13:03:00   0.5198814
> X3 <- xts (rnorm (3), as. Date(c ("2005-01-01", "2005-01-10",+      "2005-01-
12")))
• x3
                  [, 1]
2005-01-01   0.8533171
2005-01-10 -0.3912313
2005-01-12   0.1352078
The function xts () receives the time series data in the first argument (Lu´ıs
Sarmento, Paula Carvalho, M´ario J Silva, and Eug´enio de Oliveira, 2009).
```

This can either be a vector or a matrix if we have a multivariate time series. Each column often matrix is interpreted as a variable being sampled at each time tag. Here, we have used most common class to represent time information in R: POSIXct class.

- Multiple time series can be created in a similar fashion. library(base)
- library(zoo)
- library(xts)
- mts.vals<- matrix(round(norms(25),2),5,5)
- colnames(mts.vals) <- paste('ts', 1:5, sep='')
- mts<- xts(mts.vals, as.POSIXct(c('2003-01-01','2003-01-04', + '2003-01-05','2003-01-06','2003-02-16')))
- mts

```
           ts1   ts2   ts3   ts4   ts5
2003-01-01 0.28 -0.86 0.36 -0.11 -1.31
2003-01-04 -0.62 0.62 0.17 -0.01 0.40
```

```
2003-01-05 -1.95 0.44 1.77 -0.13 0.46
2003-01-06 -0.67 -0.39 0.26 0.08 -0.39
2003-02-16 -1.69 0.06 -0.72 -0.53 -0.02
```

- mts["2003-01",c("ts2","ts5")] ts2 ts5

```
2003-01-01 -0.86 -1.31
2003-01-04 0.62 0.40
2003-01-05 0.44 0.46
2003-01-06 -0.39 -0.39
```

The functions index () and time () can be used to "extract" the time tags information of any xts object, while the core data () function obtains the data values of time series:

```
> index (mts)
[1] "2003-01-01 IST" "2003-01-04 IST" "2003-01-05 IST" "2003-01-06 IST"
[5] "2003-02-16 IST"
```

- core data(mts)

```
 ts1     ts2      ts3         ts4      ts5
[1,] 0.28 -0.86 0.36 -0.11 -1.31
[2,] -0.62 0.62 0.17 -0.01 0.40
[3,]-1.95    0.44 1.77 -0.13 0.46
[4,]-0.67 -0.39 0.26 0.08 -0.39
[5,]-1.69 0.06 -0.72 -0.53 -0.02
```

Xts objects are adequate to store stock quotes data, (Esuli, 2008) as they allow storing multiple time series with irregular time tags, and providing powerful indexing schemes.

How We Will Get Data for Sales Prediction

It has various formats for obtaining the quotes but we have chosen to get the data directly from the Web. The way of getting the S&P 500 quotes is to use the free service provided by Yahoo finance, (Andrea Esuli,2008) which allows downloading a CSV file with the quotes we want. The t series R package includes the functionget.hist.quote () that can be used to download the quotes into a zoo object.

The following is an example of the use of this function to get the quotes of S&P 500(coded in R): (Sarmento, Carvalho, J Silva, & de Oliveira, 2009).

```
>library (base)
>library (zoo)
>library (xts)
>library (t series)
> GSPC <- as.xts(get.hist.quote("^GSPC",start="1970-01-02", quote=c("Open",
```

Table 1. S & P 500 quotes

	Open	High	Low	Close	Volume	AdjClose
1970-01-02	92.06	93.54	91.79	93.00	8050000	93.00
1970-01-05	93.00	94.25	92.53	93.46	11490000	93.46
1970-01-06	93.46	93.81	92.13	92.82	11460000	92.82
1970-01-07	92.82	93.38	91.93	92.63	10010000	92.63
1970-01-08	92.63	93.47	91.99	92.68	10670000	92.68
1970-01-09	92.68	93.25	91.82	92.40	9380000	92.40

```
"High", "Low", "Close", "Volume", "AdjClose")))
>head (GSPC)
```

As the function get.hist.quote () returns an object of class zoo, we have again used the function as.xts () to coerce it to xts. We should remark that if we issue these commands, we will get more data than what is provided with the object in the book package(Statistical Horizons Haverford. Handling missing Data by Maximum Likelihood. USA).

Now we are trying to obtain the S&P 500 quotes by using quantmod package. As example data, the time series of the S&P 500 index is used.quantmod provides a very suitable function for downloading financial date from the web. This function is called get Symbols. The first argument of this function is a character vector specifying the names of the symbols to be downloaded and the second one specifies the environment where the object is created. The help page of this function (? get Symbols) provides more information. Here, we are using quantmod package in various aspects to know how it is helpful for obtaining daily quotes.

By default, objects are created in the workspace. Here, we use a separate environment which we call sp500 to store the downloaded data. We first create the environment:

```
>library (base)
> library (zoo)
> library (xts)
> library (quantmod)
> sp500 <- new.env()
```

We can then download the S&P 500 time series (symbol: ^GSPC) from 1960-01-04 to 2009-01-01 from yahoo finance via:

```
> get Symbols ("^GSPC", env = sp500, src = "yahoo",
+                    from = as.Date ("1960-01-04"), to = as.Date ("2009-01-
01"))
```

There are several possibilities, to load the variable GSPC from the environment sp500 to a variable in the global environment (also known as the workspace), e.g., via: (Bo Pang and Lillian Lee,2008)

```
R> GSPC <- sp500$GSPC
R> GSPC1 <- get ("GSPC", envir = sp500)
R> GSPC2 <- with (sp500, GSPC)
The object GSPC1 and GSPC2 are identical to GSPC so we can remove them from
the workspace with:
R> rm (GSPC1)
R> rm (GSPC2)
```

The function head shows the first six rows of the data.

- head(GSPC)

This is on OHLC time series with at least the (daily) Open, Hi, Lo and Close prices for the symbol; (Pang & Lee, 2008) here, it also contains the traded volume and the closing price adjusted for splits and dividends.

The function get Symbols () receives on the first argument a set of symbol names and will fetch the quotes of these symbols from different web sources or even local databases (Sarmento, Carvalho, Silva, & de Oliveira, 2009).

- head(GSPC$GSPC.Volume)

```
GSPC.Volume
```

As well as very confidently selecting observations according to their time stamp by using a character \row" index in the ISO 8601 date/time format `CCYY-MM-DD HH:MM:SS', where more granular elements may be left out in which case all observations with time stamp \matching" the given one will be used (Bo Pang and Lillian Lee, 2008).

E.g., to get all observations in March 1970:

```
>GSPC ["1970-03"]
```

Table 2. S&P 500 data using quantmod package

	GSPC.Open	GSPC.High	GSPC.Low	GSPC.Close	GSPC.Volume	GSPC.AdjClose
1960-01-04	59.91	59.91	59.91	59.91	3990000	59.91
1960-01-05	60.39	60.39	60.39	60.39	3710000	60.39
1960-01-06	60.13	60.13	60.13	60.13	3730000	60.13
1960-01-07	59.69	59.69	59.69	59.69	3310000	59.69
1960-01-08	59.50	59.50	59.50	59.50	3290000	59.50
1960-01-11	58.77	58.77	58.77	58.77	3470000	58.77

Table 3. S&P 500 volume

	GSPC.Volume
1960-01-04	3990000
1960-01-05	3710000
1960-01-06	3730000
1960-01-07	3310000
1960-01-08	3290000
1960-01-11	3470000

Table 4. S&P 500 quotes on 1970

	Open	High	Low	Close	Volume	AdjClose
1970-03-02	89.50	90.80	88.92	89.71	12270000	89.71
1970-03-03	89.71	90.67	88.96	90.23	11700000	90.23
1970-03-04	90.23	91.05	89.32	90.04	11850000	90.04
1970-03-05	90.04	90.99	89.38	90.00	11370000	90.00
1970-03-06	90.00	90.36	88.84	89.44	10980000	89.44
1970-03-09	89.43	89.43	87.94	88.51	9760000	88.51
1970-03-10	88.51	89.41	87.89	88.75	9450000	88.75
1970-03-11	88.75	89.58	88.11	88.69	9180000	88.69
1970-03-12	88.69	89.09	87.68	88.33	9140000	88.33
1970-03-13	88.33	89.43	87.29	87.86	9560000	87.86
1970-03-16	87.86	87.97	86.39	86.91	8910000	86.91
1970-03-17	86.91	87.86	86.36	87.29	9090000	87.29
1970-03-18	87.29	88.28	86.93	87.54	9790000	87.54
1970-03-19	87.54	88.20	86.88	87.42	8930000	87.42
1970-03-20	87.42	87.77	86.43	87.06	7910000	87.06
1970-03-23	87.06	87.64	86.19	86.99	7330000	86.99
1970-03-24	86.99	88.43	86.90	87.98	8840000	87.98
1970-03-25	88.11	91.07	88.11	89.77	17500000	89.77
1970-03-26	89.77	90.65	89.18	89.92	11350000	89.92
1970-03-30	89.92	90.41	88.91	89.63	9600000	89.63
1970-03-31	89.63	90.17	88.85	89.63	8370000	89.63
1970-03-19	87.54	88.20	86.88	87.42	8930000	87.42

For OHLC time series objects, quantmod also provides convenience (column) extractors and transformers, such as Cl () for extracting the closing price, OpCl () for the transformation from opening to closing prices, and ClCl () for the changes in closing prices (Bo Pang and Lillian Lee,2008).

- head (Cl (GSPC))
  GSPC.Close

Table 5. Closing value 1960

	GSPC.Close
1960-01-04	59.91
1960-01-05	60.39
1960-01-06	60.13
1960-01-07	59.69
1960-01-08	59.50
1960-01-11	58.77

>head (OpCl(GSPC))

Table 6. Open to closing 1960

	OpC1.Close
1960-01-04	0
1960-01-05	0
1960-01-06	0
1960-01-07	0
1960-01-08	0
1960-01-11	0

> head (ClCl(GSPC))

Table 7. Changes in closing price

	C1C1.GSPC
1960-01-04	NA
1960-01-05	0.008012001
1960-01-06	-0.004305316
1960-01-07	-0.00731512
1960-01-08	-0.003183096
1960-01-11	-0.012268908

Their convenience function nextfri computes for each “Date” the next Friday.

```
R> nextfri <- function(x) 7 * ceiling (as. numeric(x - 5 + 4)/7) + as. Date (5 - 4)
```

We get the aggregated data then via

```
R> SP.we <- aggregate (GSPC, nextfri, tail, 1)
```

The function aggregate splits the data into subsets here according to the function nextfri (Bo Pang and Lillian Lee, 2008). l and computes statistics for each, i.e., takes the last value, which is done by tail.

This works because the data object is also a Z's ordered observations" (zoo) object which knows to apply nextfri () to the index (timestamps). However, this loses the xts class: if this is not desired, one can use

```
R>SP.we<- xts (aggregate (GSPC, nextfri, tail, 1))
```

Instead.

(Alternatively, package quantmod provides apply. Weekly (), which uses a slightly different end-pointstrategy.)

We can now extract the closing prices for the last trading day in every week:

```
R> SPC.we <- Cl(SP.we)
```

and create a plot of this time series via

```
R>plot(SPC.we)
```

Finally, we can create log-returns by hand" and visualize these as well

```
> lr <- diff (log (SPC.we))

>plot (lr)
```

Defining the Prediction Tasks

Generally speaking, our goal is to have good forecasts of the future price of the S&P 500 index so that profitable orders can be placed on time (Sarmento, Carvalho, Silva, & Oliveira, 2009). This general goal should allow us to easily define what to predict with our models- it should resort to forecast the future values of the price time series. If we will do good future prediction, then sales will be increased in our e-commerce site and orders will be easily placed on time. This increases our sales and somehow maximizes our profit. Let, we assume that if the prices vary more than p%, we consider this worth-while in terms

Of trading. In this context, we want our prediction models to forecast whether this margin is attainable in the next k days. Within these k days we will observe prices both above and below this percentage. This means that predicting a particular quote for a specific future time t+k might not be the best idea. In effect we want is to have a prediction of the overall dynamics of the price in the next k days, and this is not captured by a particular price at a specific time. For instance, the closing price at time t+k may represent a variation much lower than p%, but it could have been preceded by a period of prices representing variations much higher than p% within the window t…..t+k. We will describe a variable, calculated with the quotes data that can be seen as an indicator of the tendency in the next k days.

The value of this indicator should be related to the confidence we have that the target margin p will be attainable in the next k days. The idea is that positive variations will lead us to buy, while negative

Figure 5. Plot of the weekly S&P 500 index closing values from 1960-01-04 to 2009-01-01(Pang & Lee, 2008)

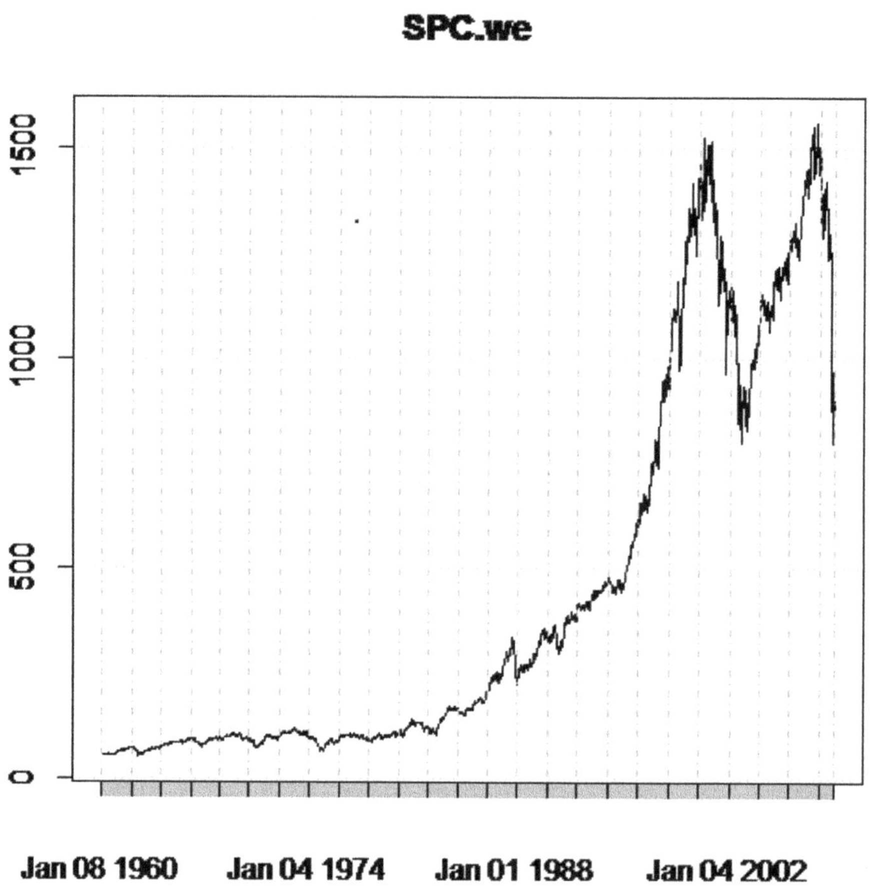

variations will trigger sell actions. The indicator we are proposing resumes the tendency as a single value, positive for upward tendencies, and negative for downward for downward price tendencies.

Let the daily average price be approximated by

$$\overline{P}_i = \frac{C_i + H_i + L_i}{3}$$

where these are the close, high, and low quotes for day i respectively.

Let, VI is the set of k percentage variations of today's close to the following k day's average prices (Esuli, 2008).

$$V_i = \left\{ \frac{\overline{P}_{i+j} - C_i}{C_i} \right\}_{j=1}^{k}$$

Figure 6. Plot of the weekly S&P 500 index log-returns values from 1960-01-04 to 2009-01-01(Pang & Lee, 2008)

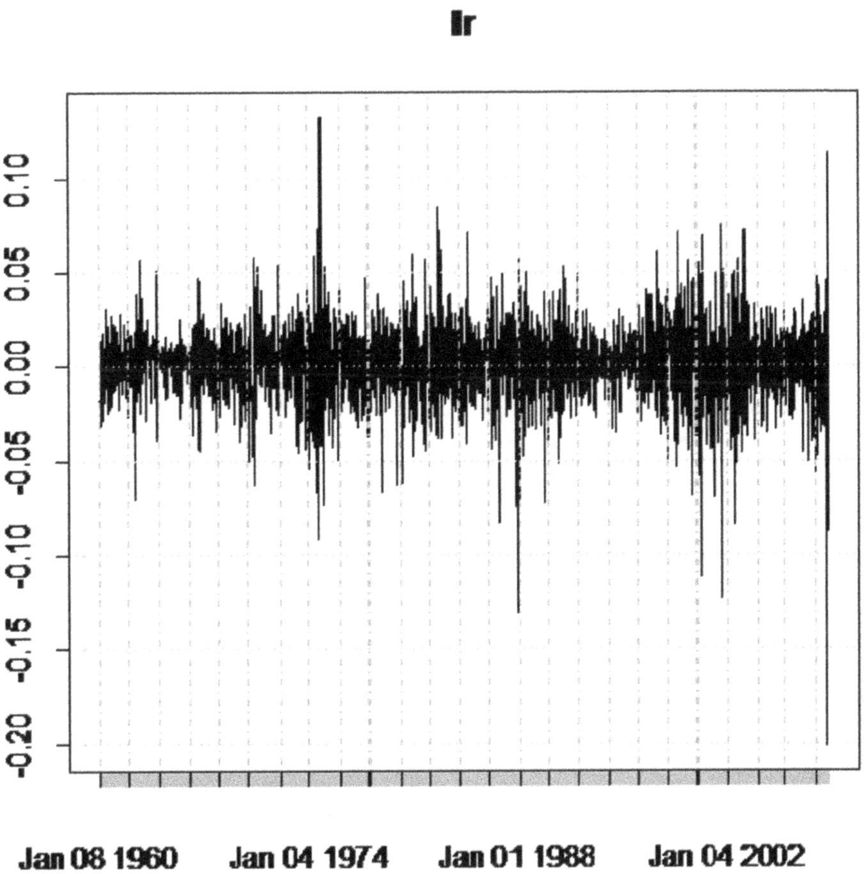

Our indicator variable is the total sum of the variations whose absolute value is above our target margin p% (Sarmento, Carvalho, Silva, & Oliveira, 2009):

$$T_i = \sum \left\{ v \in V_i : v > p\% \lor v < -p\% \right\}$$

The general idea of the variable T is to signal k-days periods that have several days with average daily prices clearly above the target variation. High positive values of T mean that there are several average daily prices that are p% higher than today's close. On the other hand, highly negative values of T suggest sell actions, given the prices will probably decline. Values around zero can be caused by periods with "flat" prices or by conflicting positive and negative variations that cancel each other.

The following function implements this simple indicator:

- T.ind <- function(quotes, tgt.margin = 0.025, n.days = 10) {

+ v <- apply (HLC (quotes), 1, mean)

```
+ r <- matrix (NA, ncol = n.days, nrow = NROW (quotes))

+ For (x in 1:n.days) r [, x] <- Next (Delt (v, k = x), x)

+ x <- apply(r, 1, function(x) sum(x[x > tgt.margin | x <

+ -tgt.margin]))

+ If (is.xts (quotes))

+ Xts(x, time (quotes))

+ else x

+ }
```

The function HLC () extracts the High,Low, and Close quotes from a quotes object(Richa Sharma, Shweta Nigam, and Rekha Jain).Supervised opinion mining techniques: A survey. We then obtain the returns of the next n.days days with respect to the current close price. The Next () function allows one to shift the values of a time series in time.

Delt () function can be used to calculate percentage or log returns of a series of prices (Sarmento, Carvalho, Silva, & Oliveira, 2009). Finally, the T.ind () function sums up the large absolutereturn that is, returns above the target variation margin, which we have set by default to 2.5%.

- Now we are focusing on the following code to get a better idea of the behaviour of this indicator: library(base)
- library(zoo)
- library(xts)
- library(quantmod)
- getSymbols(GSPC)
- head(GSPC)
- candleChart(last(GSPC, “3 months”), theme = “white”, TA = NULL)
- avgPrice <- function(p) apply(HLC(p), 1, mean)
- addAvgPrice <- newTA(FUN = avgPrice, col = 1, legend = “AvgPrice”)
- addT.ind <- newTA(FUN = T.ind, col = “red”, legend = “tgtret”)
- addAvgPrice(on = 1)
- addT.ind()

The function candle Chart () draws candlestick graphs of stock quotes (Sarmento, Carvalho, Silva, & Oliveira, 2009). These graphs represent the daily quotes by a colored box and a vertical bar. The bar represents the High and Low prices of the day, while the box represents the Open-Close amplitude. The color of the box indicates if the top of the box is the Open or the Close price, that is, if the prices declined or rose across the daily session. We have added two indicators to the candlesticks graph: the average price and our T indicator. The functionnewTA () can be used to create new plotting functions for indicators that we wish to include in candlestick graphs (Asur & Huberman,2010).

The return value of this function is a plotting function. This means that the objects addT.ind and addAvgPrice can be called like any other R function. Each of them adds an indicator to the initial graph produced by the candle Chart () function (Sarmento, Carvalho, Silva, & Oliveira, 2009). The function addAvgPrice () was called with the parameter set to 1, which means that the indicator will be plotted on the first graph window. The function addT.ind () was not called with this argument, leading to a new graph below the candlesticks. The T indicator achieves the highest values when there is a subsequent period of positive variations.

In our approach to this problem we will assume that the correct trading action at time t is related to what our expectations are concerning the evolution of prices in the next k days (Richa Sharma, Shweta Nigam, and Rekha Jain.Supervised opinion mining techniques: A survey).

The correct trading signal a time t will be "buy" if the T score is higher than a certain threshold, and will be "sell" if the score is below another threshold (Andrea Esuli,2008).In all other cases, the correct signal will be do nothing. We want to be able to predict the correct signal for time t. Its goal is to summarize the observed future behavior of the prices into a single value and not to predict this behavior

Figure 7. S&P 500 on the last three months and our indicator

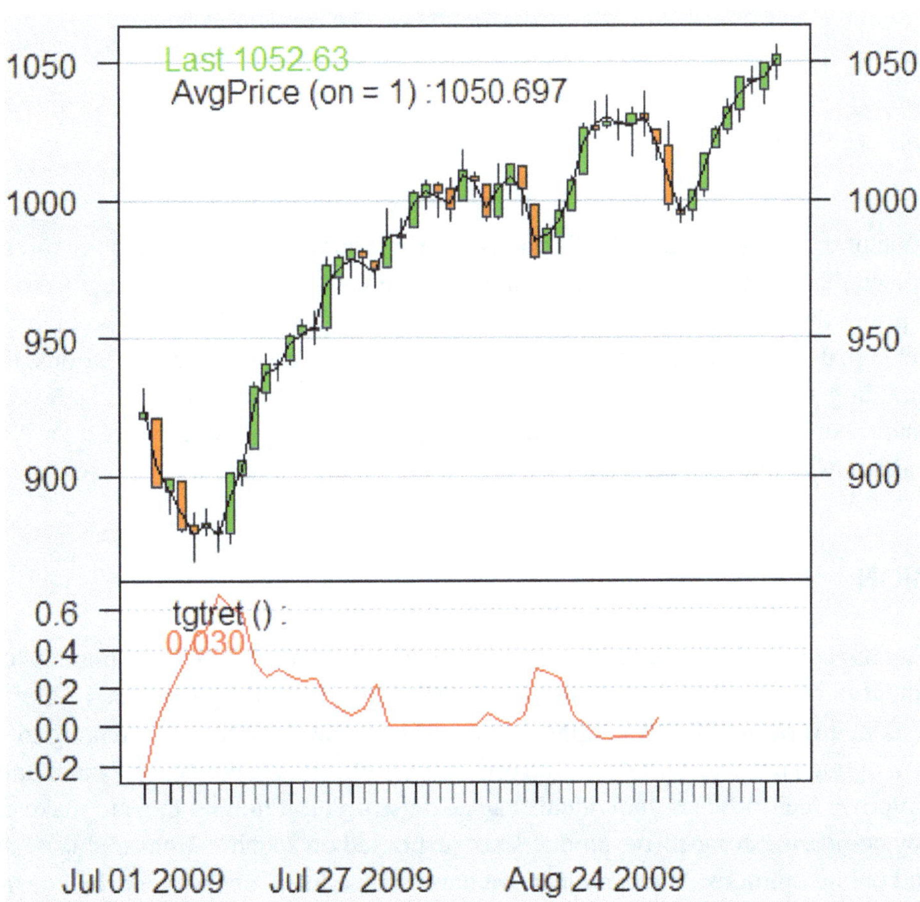

(Sarmento, Carvalho, Silva, & Oliveira, 2009). We have defined an indicator (T) that summarizes the behavior of the price time series in the next k days. Our data mining goal will be to predict this behavior. By observing the past behavior it is possible to predict the future behavior of the financial markets. More precisely, we are assuming that if in the past a certain behavior p was followed by another behavior f, and if that causal claim happened frequently, then it is plausible to assume that this will occur again in the future; and thus if we observe p now, we predict that we will observe f next. We are approximating the future behavior (f) by our indicator (T).

We will center our analysis on the Close quote, as our buy/sell decisions will be made at the end of each daily session (Bakliwal, 2013).The initial set of features will be formed by several past returns on the Close price. The h-days returns, or percentage variations, can be calculated as

$$R_{i-h} = \frac{C_i - C_{i-h}}{C_{i-h}}$$

where, Ci is the Close price at session i. We have included in the set of candidate features ten of these returns by varying h from 1 to 10 (Esuli, 2008). Here we have used T value as the target variable and try to obtain models that forecast this value using the predictor's information (Sarmento, Carvalho, Silva, & Oliveira, 2009). From the predicted T values we have to lead three possible trading actions.

$$Signal = \begin{cases} sell & if\ T < -0.1 \\ hold & if\ -0.1 \le T \le 0.1 \\ buy & if\ T > 0.1 \end{cases}$$

The selection of the values 0.1 and -0.1 is purely heuristic and we can also use other thresholds. Still, these values mean that during the 10-day period used to generate the T values, there were at least four average daily prices that are above 2.5% above the current close (4*0.025=0.1). Too high absolute will originate fewer signals, while too small values may lead us to trade on too small variations of the market, thus incurring a larger risk. Function trading .signals (), available in the book package, can carry out this transformation of the numeric T values into a factor with three possible values: "s","h", and "b", for sell, hold and buy actions respectively.

CONCLUSION

Opinion mining has become a fascinating research area due to the availability of a huge volume of user-generated content in review sites, forums and blogs (Minqing Hu & Bing Liu, 2004). Opinion mining has applications in a variety of fields ranging from market research to decision making to advertising. With the help of opinion mining, companies can estimate the extent of product acceptance and can devise strategies to improve their product. Individuals can also use opinion mining tools to make decisions on their buying by comparing competitive products not just based on specifications but also based on user experience and public opinions. In our project, we have done a lot of experiments by considering time series. We have used two most flexible packages in R: zoo and xts. Also we have used quantmod package for obtaining stock quotes of any market index. In our project, we have taken S&P 500 quotes for sales prediction. Here, we have done future predictions on the basis of past and present observations. In our future work, we will do more analysis by taking various prediction models like ArtificialNeuralNetworks (ANN), SupportVectorMachine (SVM) etc. for further evaluation

REFERENCES

Abbasi, A., Chen, H., & Salem, A. (2007). *Sentiment Analysis in Multiple Languages: Feature Selection for Opinion Classification in Web Forums*. Retrieved from:http://ai.arizona.edu/intranet/papers/ahmedabbasi_sentimenttois.pdf

Allison, P. D. (2012). Statistical Horizons Haverford. In *Handling missing Data by Maximum Likelihood*. Academic Press.

Antweiler, W., & Frank, M. Z. (2004). The Information Content of Internet Stock Message Boards. *The Journal of Finance*, *59*(3), 1259–1294. doi:10.1111/j.1540-6261.2004.00662.x

Asur, S., & Huberman. (2010). Predicting the future with social media. In *Proceedings of IEEE/WIC/ACM International Conference on Web Intelligence and Intelligent Agent Technology (WI IAT)*. IEEE.

Au, W. H., Chan, K. C. C., & Yao, X. (2003). A novel evolutionary data mining algorithm with applications to churn prediction. *IEEE Transactions on Evolutionary Computation*, *7*(6), 532–545. doi:10.1109/TEVC.2003.819264

Bakliwal, A. (2013). *Fine-grained opinion mining from different genre of social media content*. Academic Press.

Esuli, A. (2008). Automatic generation of lexical resources for opinion mining: models, algorithms and applications. *ACM SIGIR Forum, 42*, 105–106.

Hu, M., & Liu, B. (2004). Mining and summarizing customer reviews In *Proceedings of the tenth. ACM SIGKDD international conference on Knowledge discovery and data mining* (pp. 168–177). ACM.

Krum, J., Davies, N., & Narayanaswami, C. (2008). *Pervasive Computing User-generated content*. IEEE.

Moghaddam, S., & Ester, M. (2012). Aspect-based opinion mining from online reviews. In *Tutorial at SIGIR Conference*. Academic Press.

Pak, A., & Paroubek, P. (2010). *Twitter as a corpus for sentiment analysis and opinion mining*. LREC.

Pang, B., & Lee, L. (2008). Opinion mining and sentiment analysis. *Foundations and Trends in Information Retrieval, 2*(1-2), 1–135.

Sarmento, L., Carvalho, P., Silva, M. J., & de Oliveira, E. (2009). Automatic creation of a reference corpusfor political opinion mining in user-generated content. In *Proceedings of the 1st international CIKM workshopon Topic-sentiment analysis for mass opinion* (pp. 29–36). ACM. doi:10.1145/1651461.1651468

Sharma, R., Nigam, S., & Jain, R. (2013). *Supervised opinion mining techniques: A survey*. Academic Press.

Wilson, T., Wiebe, J., & Hoffmann, P. (2005). Recognizing contextual polarity in phrase-level sentiment analysis. In *Proceedings of the conference on human language technology and empirical methods in natural language processing*. Association for Computational Linguistics.

Chapter 13
Applications of Social Graphs:
Author, Email, Telephone Using Graph Mining Techniques

Bapuji Rao
Indira Gandhi Institute of Technology, India

Sasmita Mishra
Indira Gandhi Institute of Technology, India

Sarojananda Mishra
Indira Gandhi Institute of Technology, India

ABSTRACT

The chapter focuses on the applications of three social graphs, namely author, email, and telephone. The important application of author graph is the real network communications among the authors publishing research papers. The authors have proposed an algorithm to extract sub-graphs of authors. Individual email sending is more frequently within a group rather than group sending. Such group entities can be detected and analyzed further for knowledge discovery. For this, the authors have proposed an algorithm for extraction of strong and weak communicator's sub-graph. The telephone graph with multiple distinct types of connectivity information can be derived as layers and considered an important application. Therefore, the information retrieval can be represented as multi-layer graphs. Each layer has its own set of edges over the same underlying nodes of base-layer. Therefore, the edges of different layers typically are related but unique in behavior. For this, the authors have proposed an algorithm for representation of telephone graph as a multi-layer graph.

INTRODUCTION

Social networks are generally modeled as graphs, which sometimes referred as a social graph. The entities are the nodes or vertices, and an edge or arc connects two nodes if they are related. Social graphs are undirected or directed depending on the kind of relationships. The degree of the relationship is represented by labeling the edges. There are some examples of social networks. They are Friends

DOI: 10.4018/978-1-5225-3646-8.ch013

Network, Authors Networks, Collaboration Networks of Authors and Papers, Collaboration Networks of Teachers, Students, and Text Books, Facebook, Twitter, Google+, Email Networks, Telephone Networks, Collaboration Networks of Authors and Papers, Information Networks, Infrastructure Networks, Biological Networks and so on by Cook et al (2007) and Rajaraman et al (2011). In case of Facebook social network's friends' graph is considered as undirected graph by Cook et al (2007). Sometimes social graphs can also be directed graphs. In this case the graph of followers on Twitter or Google+ is considered as directed graph by Cook et al (2007). So "Social Network" is a network which represents the broader class of networks by Cook et al (2007). This chapter is meant for some applications of social graphs such as Authors graph, Email graph, and Telephone graph. From these graphs, the authors have retrieved successfully information using graph mining techniques. For these applications the authors have proposed three algorithms. To implement those algorithms, the authors have proposed three graphs namely Authors, Email, and Telephone.

LITERATURE REVIEW

Data Mining is the process of discovering interesting, non-trivial, implicit, previously unknown and potentially important information and patterns from data by Cook et al (2007). A graph can represent any complex relationships between data objects in pictorial way. The entities are mapped to vertices and the relationship is represented as an edge between the related pair of vertices. Hence graph based data mining is called as graph mining which aims at discovering the interesting sub-structures within a structural data. The authors have proposed an algorithm for discovering sub-graphs such as individual authors published papers, authors associated with individually published papers and authors associated with others having no individual published papers from authors graph using graph mining techniques.

Email mining includes spam detection, email categorization, contact analysis, email network property analysis and email visualization proposed by Tang et al (2014). Graph based ranking algorithms for email correspondents according to their degree of expertise on subjects of interests proposed by Dom et al (2003). A graph based mining approach for email and document classification proposed by Aery et al (2014). Hence the authors have proposed an algorithm for discovering sub-graphs such as weak connected and strong connected from email graphs using graph mining techniques.

The fundamental study of networks in the study of complex network systems in biological, social, information, engineering, and physical sciences can be seen in Boccaletti et al (2006), Newman (2010) and Estrada (2011). In traditional studies of networks, generally the nodes are connected to each other by a single type of static edge that forms all connections between them. It is overall a gross over simplification. This kind of static connection leads to misleading results and lack of addressing certain problems. So the inter-layer connections have the ability to generate new structure in the form of dynamic correlations between components of a system. Hence it is necessary to develop a framework that solves all the common problems related to the network by De Domenico et al (2013).

For example, a social network user may currently be logged into Facebook but not logged into some other social networking site such as Google+, Twitter etc. The presence of nodes in multi-layer systems of social network guarantees the possibility of self-interactions in a particular social network. This feature is not similar to the functions in interdependent networks, which were the ideas in interconnected communities within a single and larger network by Buldyrev et al (2010) and Dickison et al (2012).

When the source of connectivity information for a group of users is more than one, then there is a possibility of existence of multi-layer networks. The direct communication link in a social network is the knowledge, considered as relational information. From this the authors have derived a behavioural relationships based on user interests by Oselio et al (2011).

The layer which has "relational" information between users is an extrinsic layer which is considered as the base layer and the layer which has "behavioral" information between users is considered as the sub-layer of the social network by Oselio et al (2011) [1]. An Email network has been used by Oselio et al (2011) which is an example of social network. In this network, two layers can be created. The 1st layer is considered as relational network is created from the headers of emails by identifying the sender and receiver(s) of each message, which includes CC and BCC recipients and the 2nd layer, is considered as behavioral network is recovered from using the contents of email messages.

A multi-layer network is a quadruplet $M = (V_M, E_M, V, L)$. The first two elements V_M and E_M in M form a graph $G_M = (V_M, E_M)$. So, one can interpret a multi-layer network as a graph whose nodes are labeled can be seen in Kivelä et al (2014). A weighted multi-layer network M can be defined as its edges by weights in the underlying graph G_M (i.e. mapping each edge with a real number by using a function $W: E \rightarrow R$). So, a multi-layer network M can be undirected or directed if the underlying graph GM is undirected or directed.

An example of the most general type of multi-layer network $M = (V_M, E_M, V, L)$ in Figure 2(a) can be seen in Kivelä et al (2014). Another example of Zachary Karate Club (ZKC) network is represented as a multi-layer network in Figure 3(a) can be seen in Kivelä et al (2014).

Generally an ordinary graph (i.e. monoplex network) can be represented using adjacency matrices. For a node-aligned multi-layer network, it can be represented using a order of 2X(d+1) adjacency tensor $\mathbf{A} \in \{0, 1\}^{|V| X |V| X |L_1| X |L_1| ... X |L_d| X |L_d|}$ can be seen in De Domenico et al (2013) and Wasserman et al (1994). In social networks, multi-dimensional arrays are sometimes called super-sociomatrices and adjacency matrices are called sociomatrices can be seen in Wasserman et al (1994).

The organization of this chapter is as follows. The authors have initiated the chapter with related definitions of Authors Graph, Email Graph, and Multi-Layer Graph on graph theory, and followed by literature surveys. The first section discussed on retrieval of sub-graphs from Authors Graph such as individual authors published papers, authors associated with individually published papers and authors associated with others having no individual published papers using proposed graph mining approach. Then the proposed algorithm using graph mining techniques is discussed with an example. Finally, the experimental results snapshots are included. The second section focuses on discovering of sub-graphs such as weak connected and strong connected from email graphs. Then the proposed algorithm is discussed with two examples. The first example is the proposed model's dataset creation and applied on the proposed algorithm. The second example is the benchmark dataset applied on the proposed algorithm. Finally, the experimental results snapshots are included. The third and final section focuses on representation of telephone graph as multi-layer using graph mining techniques. The proposed model is considered as example of representation of telephone graph as multi-layer graph. The proposed algorithm is on the proposed model's dataset to represent telephone graph with four layers of graph. Further, the experimental results snapshots are included followed by the conclusion.

MODELLING AUTHORS NETWORK

An Authors network can be modelled as a social network graph G = (V, E), where V is the set of Authors Id as nodes and E is the pair of authors participated for publication of research paper as edges. The edges are considered as undirected edge and having some weight which is considered as total number of research papers published between the pair of authors. Hence the authors graph is said to be a weighted undirected author's graph.

Nodes represent individual authors who can publish research papers. An edge is shown between two authors who can publish one or more research papers jointly. The communities in this network are authors working on a particular topic. So the Authors network can be represented as a graph having authors Id as nodes and nodes are connected with an edge if two authors are related to publish a paper is shown with weight i.e. number of research published papers jointly. In case of authors research published papers alone can be shown with a self edge known as self-loop. The authors propose a weighted authors graph having Ids {1, 2, 3, ..., 56} is depicted in Figure 1. The edge and self-loop with weights is considered as the number of published papers between the authors and the individual authors. Its weighted adjacency matrix only consists of zeros and non-zeros is depicted in Figure 2. The diagonal elements are the indication of individual authors research published papers.

From the authors graph, the authors can mine sub-graphs such as: (a) Sub-graph of authors having only individual published papers depicted in Figure 3, (b) Sub-graph of authors having only jointly published papers depicted in Figure 4, and (c) Sub-graph having jointly published papers with authors individual published papers depicted in Figure 5. It can be seen in Rao et al (2015), Rao et al (2015 ICATCCT), Rao et al (2016 Cha) and Rao et al (2016).

Figure 1. Weighted authors graph having vertices V = {1, 2, 3, 4, 5, 6,........, 56}

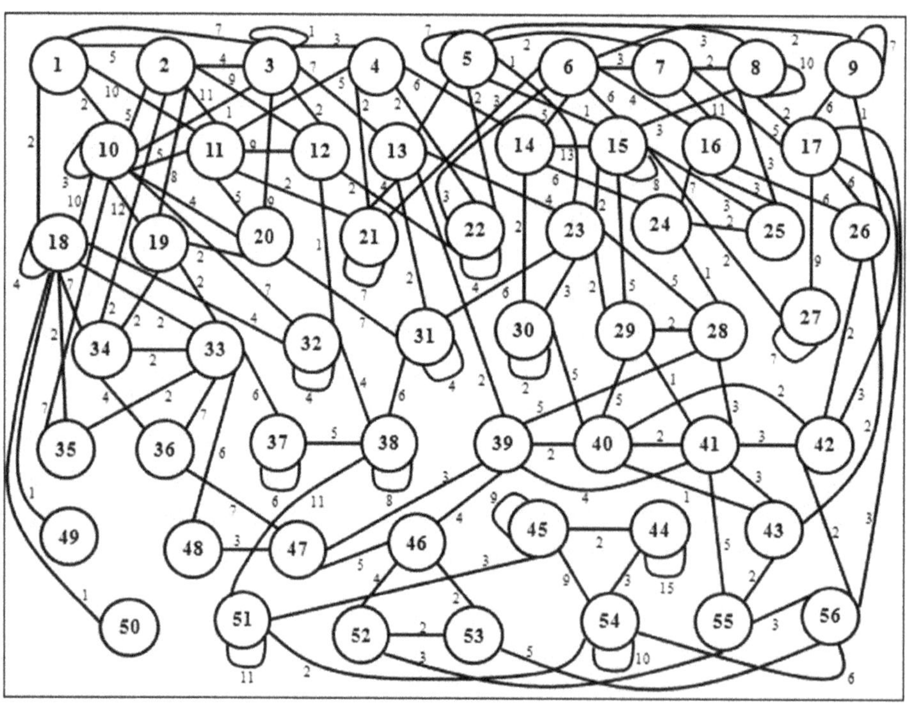

Figure 2. Adjacency matrix of Figure 1

AutId	1	2	3	4	5	6	7	8	9	10	11	12	13	14	15	16	17	18	19	20	21	22	23
1	0	5	7	0	0	0	0	0	0	2	10	0	0	0	0	0	0	2	0	0	0	0	0
2	5	0	4	0	0	0	0	0	0	5	11	9	0	0	0	0	0	0	8	0	0	0	0
3	7	4	1	3	0	0	0	0	0	1	0	2	7	0	0	0	0	0	0	9	0	0	0
4	0	0	3	0	0	0	0	0	0	0	5	0	0	6	0	0	0	0	0	0	2	2	0
5	0	0	0	0	7	0	2	3	0	0	0	0	0	0	1	0	0	0	0	0	0	2	1
6	0	0	0	0	0	0	3	0	2	0	0	0	0	5	6	4	0	0	0	0	3	3	0
7	0	0	0	0	0	3	0	2	0	0	0	0	0	0	0	11	5	0	0	0	0	0	0
8	0	0	0	0	0	0	2	10	0	0	0	0	0	0	3	0	2	0	0	0	0	0	0
9	0	0	0	0	0	0	0	0	7	0	0	0	0	0	0	0	6	0	0	0	0	0	0
10	2	5	1	0	0	0	0	0	0	3	5	0	0	0	0	0	0	10	12	4	0	0	0
11	10	11	0	5	0	0	0	0	0	5	0	9	0	0	0	0	0	0	0	5	2	0	0
12	0	9	2	0	0	0	0	0	0	0	9	0	0	0	0	0	0	0	0	0	0	2	0
13	0	0	7	7	6	0	0	0	0	0	0	0	0	0	0	0	0	0	0	0	4	0	4
14	0	0	0	6	0	0	0	0	0	0	0	0	0	0	13	0	0	0	0	0	0	0	0
15	0	0	0	0	1	6	0	3	0	0	0	0	0	13	8	0	0	0	0	0	0	0	2
16	0	0	0	0	0	4	11	0	0	0	0	0	0	0	0	0	0	0	0	0	0	0	0
17	0	0	0	0	0	0	5	2	6	0	0	0	0	0	0	0	0	0	0	0	0	0	0
18	2	0	0	0	0	0	0	0	0	10	0	0	0	0	0	0	0	4	0	0	0	0	0
19	0	8	0	0	0	0	0	0	0	12	0	0	0	0	0	0	0	0	0	2	0	0	0
20	0	0	9	0	0	0	0	0	0	4	5	0	0	0	0	0	0	0	2	0	0	0	0
21	0	0	0	2	0	3	0	0	0	0	2	0	4	0	0	0	0	0	0	0	7	0	0
22	0	0	0	2	2	3	0	0	0	0	0	2	0	0	0	0	0	0	0	0	0	4	0
23	0	0	0	0	1	0	0	0	0	0	0	0	4	0	2	0	0	0	0	0	0	0	0

Figure 3. Sub-graph of authors having only individual published papers

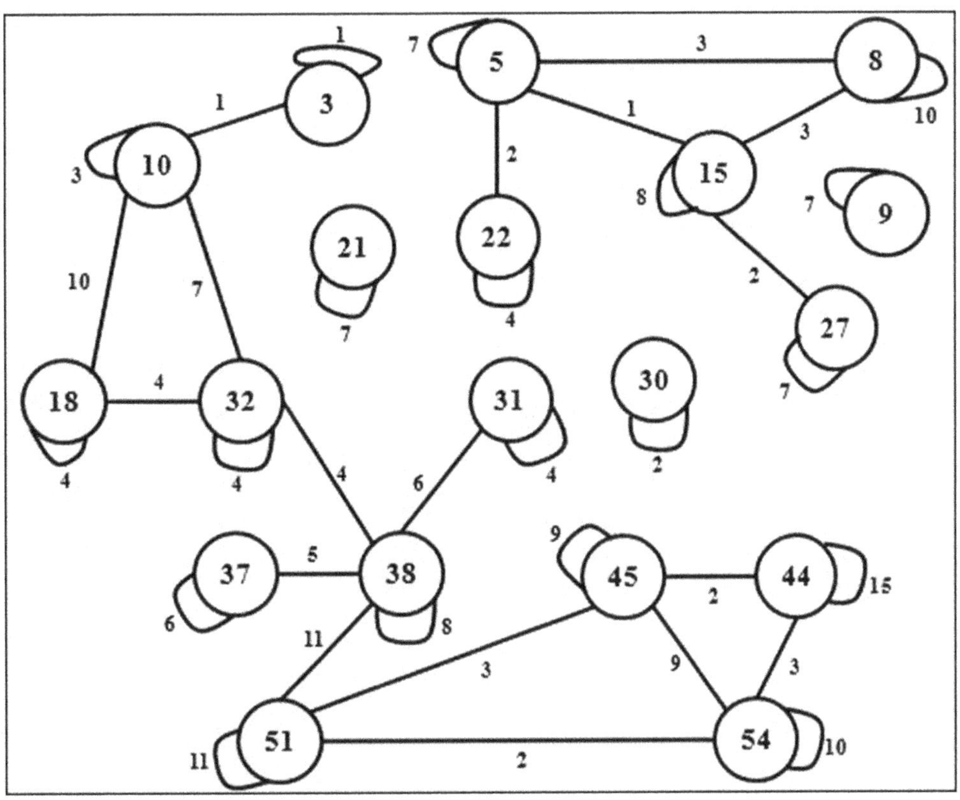

Figure 4. Sub-graph of authors having only jointly published papers

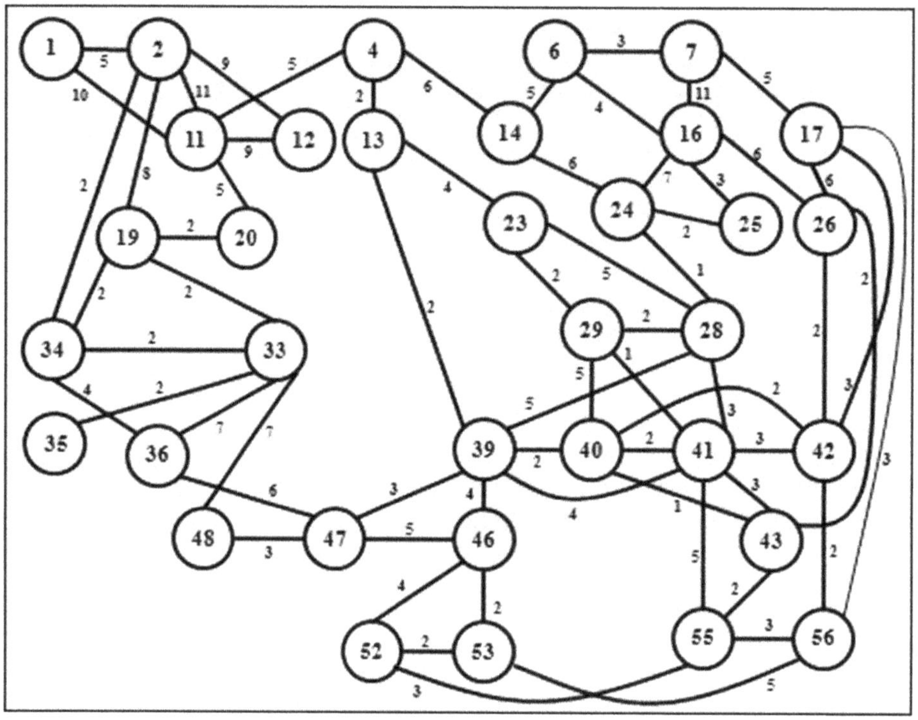

Figure 5. Sub-graph having jointly published papers with authors individual published papers

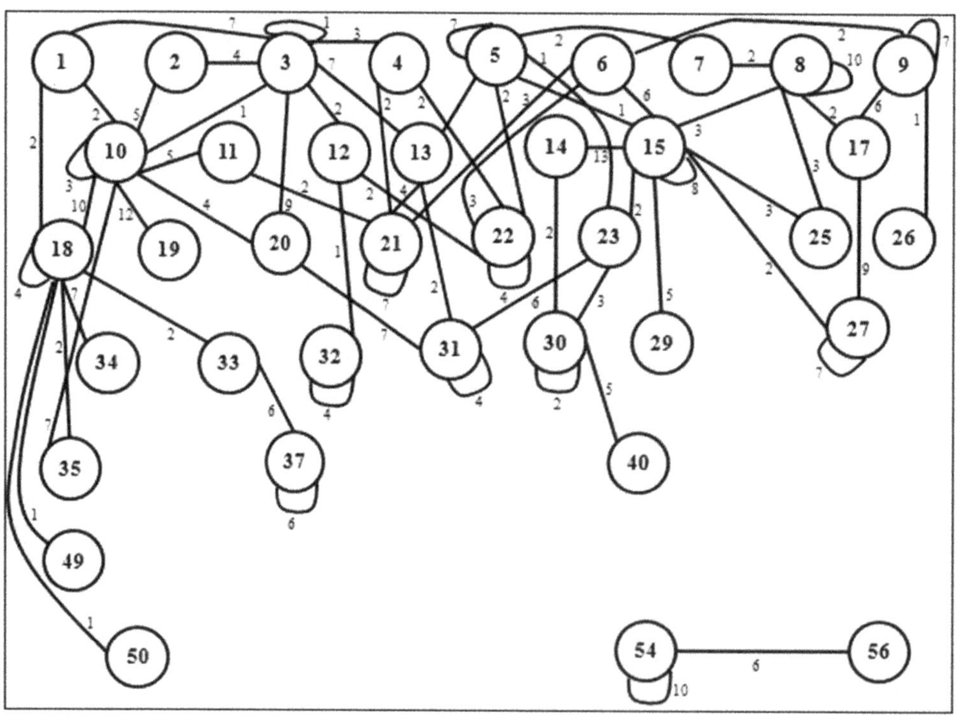

PROPOSED ALGORITHM

Algorithm For Extraction of Sub-Graphs From Authors Graph

Algorithm Authors_Paper_Sub_Graph_Extraction()
Algorithm conventions by Horowitz et al (1998) and Lipschutz (Tata McGraw-Hill)

```
// Global Declarations
na: Total number of authors, m: Total number of authors with individual published papers.
n: Total number of authors with no individual published papers.
AM[na+1][na+1]: Authors adjacency matrix.
IP[m+1][m+1]: Adjacency matrix of authors with individual published papers.
JP[n+1][n+1]: Adjacency matrix of authors with no individual published papers.
IJP[na+1][na+1]: Adjacency matrix of authors with no individual published papers and associated with authors with individual published papers.
IPV[m][2]: Matrix to hold authors ID with individual published papers and number of published papers.
JPV[n]: Array to hold authors ID with no individual published papers.
Authors.Txt: Text file contains total number of authors Id, from author Id, to author Id, and total number of published papers.
{
  // author adjacency matrix creation
     AAMC();
  // individual authors published papers adjacency matrix creation
     IAPP();
  // jointly associated authors published papers adjacency matrix creation
     JAAPP();
// jointly individual authors published papers adjacency matrix creation
    JIAPP();
}
```

PROCEDURE FOR AUTHORS ADJACENCY MATRIX CREATION

Procedure AAMC()

```
fa, ta, np: To assign from author Id, to author Id, and number of published papers.
{
   // assign authors Id at 1st row and 1st column of AM[ ][ ]
   for i:=1 to na do
```

```
        AM[1][i+1]:=AM[i+1][1]:=i;
    // open file which contains number of authors, from Author Id, and to Au-
thor Id details
        open("Authors.Txt");  //open file
        read(na);
    while (Not EOF)
    do
    {
       // read from author Id, to author Id, and number of published papers
from file
        read(fa, ta, np);
      // assign np at AM[fa+1][ta+1]
       AM[fa+1][ta+1]:=np;
}
    close("Authors.Txt");   // close the file
 }
```

PROCEDURE FOR INDIVIDUAL AUTHORS PUBLISHED PAPERS ADJACENCY MATRIX CREATION

Procedure IAPP()

```
{
  m:=0;
  // count and find the authors Id with individual published papers
  for i:=2 to (na+1) do
     if(AM[i][i]≠0) then
     {
      m:=m+1;  IPV[m][1]:=i-1;
      IPV[m][2]:=AM[i][i];
      }
  // assign author Ids from IPV[][1] to IP[ ][ ]
   for i:=1 to m do
   {
     IP[1][i+1]:=IP[i+1][1]:=IPV[i][1];
   }
  // traverse AM[][] for detection between authors with individual published
papers
   for i:=1 to (m-1) do
      for j:=i+1 to m do
        if(AM[IPV[i][1]+1][IPV[j][1]+1] ≠0) then
```

```
                    IP[i+1][j+1]:= AM[IPV[i][1]+1][IPV[j][1]+1];
            else IP[i+1][j+1]:=0;
    // assign no. of papers from IPV[][2] diagonally to IP[ ][ ]
        for i:=1 to m do
            IP[i+1][i+1]:=IPV[i][2];
    // assign lower diagonal with upper diagonal in IP[ ][ ]
        for i:=2 to m do
            for j:=i+1 to (m+1) do
                IP[j][i]:=IP[i][j];
}
```

PROCEDURE FOR JOINTLY ASSOCIATED AUTHORS PUBLISHED PAPERS ADJACENCY MATRIX

Procedure JAAPP()

```
{
    n:=0;
    // count and find the authors Id with no individual published papers
        for i:=2 to (na+1) do
        {  n:=n+1;    JPV[n]:=(i-1);    }
    // assign JPV[]'s Id to JP[ ][ ]
        for i:=1 to n do
        { JP[1][i+1]:=JP[i+1][1]:=JPV[i]; }
    // traverse AM[][] for detection between authors with no individual pub-
lished papers
        for i:=2 to (n-1) do
            for j:=i+1 to n do
                if(AM[JPV[i]+1][JPV[j]+1]≠0) then JP[i+1][j+1]:=AM[JPV[i]+1]
[JPV[j]+1];
            else JP[i+1][j+1]:=0;
    // assign 0s diagonally to JP[ ][ ]
        for i:=2 to (n+1) do
                JP[i][i]:=0;
    // assign lower diagonal with upper diagonal in JP[ ][ ]
        for i:=2 to n do
            for j:=i+1 to (n+1) do
                JP[j][i]:=JP[i][j];
}
```

PROCEDURE FOR JOINTLY INDIVIDUAL AUTHORS PUBLISHED PAPERS ADJACENCY MATRIX

Procedure JIAPP()

```
{
   // assign authors 'na' Ids and 0s to IJP[ ][ ]
    for i:=1 to na+1 do
    {
       IJP[1][i+1]:=IJP[i+1][1]:=i;
          for j:=1 to na+1 do
               IJP[i+1][j+1]:=0;
     }
// traverse AM[ ][ ] for detection between authors with no individual papers
and authors with // individual published papers
for i:=1 to n do  // for authors with no individual published papers
{
 if(AM[JPV[i]+1][IPV[1][1]+1]≠0) then
    IJP[JPV[i]+1][IPV[1][1]+1]:=AM[JPV[i]+1][IPV[1][1]+1];
 for j:=2 to m do  // for authors with individual published papers
   if(AM[JPV[i]+1][IPV[j][1]+1]≠0) then
     IJP[JPV[i]+1][IPV[j][1]+1]:=AM[JPV[i]+1][IPV[j][1]+1];
 }
// assign diagonally individual authors total number of published papers to
IJP[ ][ ]
for i:=1 to na do
      IJP[IPV[i][1]+1][IPV[i][1]+1]:=IPV[i][2];
// assign joint authors number of papers (by traversing IJP[ ][ ] row-wise and
assign by //column-wise)
  for i:=1 to na do
    for j:=1 to na do
      if(IJP[i+1][j+1]≠0) then  IJP[j+1][i+1]:=IJP[i+1][j+1];
}
```

The proposed algorithm has four procedures namely AAMC(), IAPP(), JAAPP(), and JIAPP(). The procedure AAMC() is to read dataset file "Authors.Txt" which contains total number of authors Id, from author Id, to author Id, and total number of published papers between those authors Id. These details are read and assign to the authors adjacency matrix AM[][]. So the author's adjacency matrix only contains zeros and non-zeros (i.e., number of published papers).

The procedure IAPP() is to detect the relationship between the individual authors published papers authors Id from authors adjacency matrix AM[][, and assign to the matrix IP[][].

The procedure JAAPP() is to detect the relationship between the jointly associated published papers authors Id from the authors adjacency matrix AM[][] and assign to the matrix JP[][].

The procedure JIAPP() is to detect the relationship between jointly associated published papers authors Id and individually published papers authors Id from authors adjacency matrix AM[][], and assign to the matrix IJP[][].

From the resultant matrices IP[][], JP[][] and IJP[][], it is able to draw three sub-graphs for individual authors published papers, jointly associated authors published papers, and jointly individual authors published papers respectively. These three sub-graphs are depicted from Figure 3 to Figure 5.

EXPERIMENTAL RESULTS

For the proposed Authors Graph, the authors have created a dataset file called "Authors.Txt", which contains details such as total number of authors Id, from authors Id, to authors Id, and total number of published paper(s) between those authors Id. The dataset text file is depicted in Figure 6. The 1st line indicates total number of authors Id (here it is 56) and from 2nd line onwards indicates "from authors Id", "to authors Id", and number of published papers (it is the weight of the edge between those authors Id. After input the dataset file "Authors.Txt" to the proposed algorithm, its weighted adjacency matrix was created and is depicted in Figure 2. Using this matrix, the desired three adjacency matrices were created. These adjacency matrices are depicted from Figure 7 to Figure 9.

The individual author's published papers adjacency matrix contains the following authors Id {3, 5, 8, 9, 10, 15, 18, 21, 22, 27, 30, 31, 32, 37, 38, 44, 45, 51, 54}. The jointly associated authors published papers adjacency matrix contains the following authors Id {1, 2, 4, 6, 7, 11, 12, 13, 14, 16, 17, 19, 20, 23, 24, 25, 26, 28, 29, 33, 34, 35, 36, 39, 40, 1, 42, 43, 45, 47, 48, 52, 53, 55, 56}. The adjacency matrix of jointly associated authors published papers contains all authors Id except the following Ids {16, 24, 36, 39, 41, 42, 43, 46, 47, 48, 52, 53, 55}. Finally using these three adjacency matrices the respective sub-graphs are drawn and these sub-graphs are depicted from Figure 3 to Figure 5. The algorithm was written in C++ and compiled with TurboC++. The example dataset was input to the algorithm and observed satisfactory results.

PROPOSED MODEL DATASET

See Figure 6.

RESULTS

See Figures 7, 8 and 9.

MODELLING EMAIL NETWORK

An email network can be modelled as a social network graph G = (V, E), where V is the set of email addresses (or Ids) as nodes and E is the email interactions between the Ids as edges. The edges are considered as directed edge. Hence the email graph is said to be a directed email graph. The out-degree of

Figure 6. Dataset of Figure 1

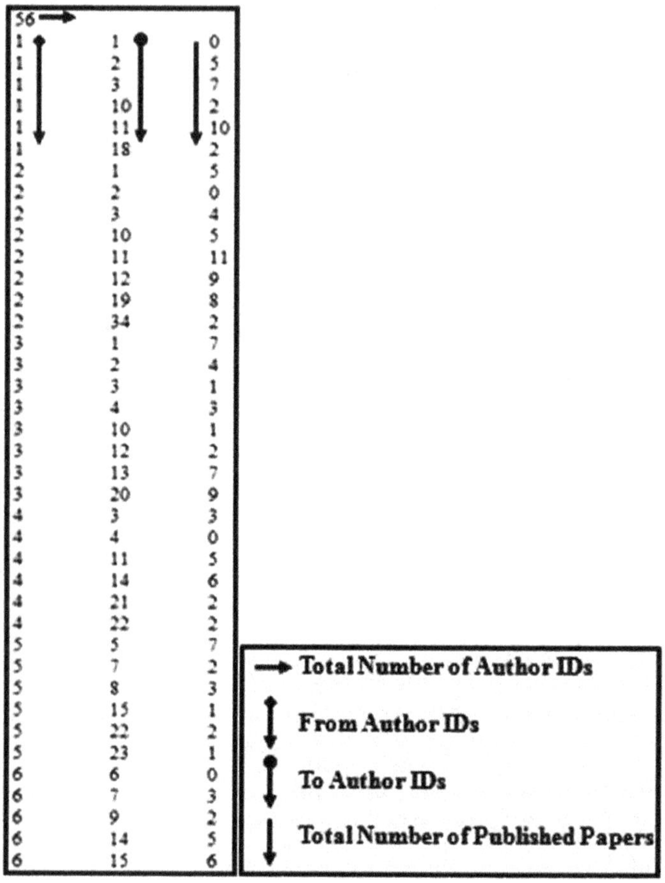

Figure 7. Individual authors published papers adjacency matrix

AutId	3	5	8	9	10	15	18	21	22	27	30	31	32	37	38	44	45	51	54
3	1	0	0	0	1	0	0	0	0	0	0	0	0	0	0	0	0	0	0
5	0	7	3	0	0	1	0	0	2	0	0	0	0	0	0	0	0	0	0
8	0	3	10	0	0	3	0	0	0	0	0	0	0	0	0	0	0	0	0
9	0	0	0	7	0	0	0	0	0	0	0	0	0	0	0	0	0	0	0
10	1	0	0	0	3	0	10	0	0	0	0	0	7	0	0	0	0	0	0
15	0	1	3	0	0	8	0	0	0	2	0	0	0	0	0	0	0	0	0
18	0	0	0	0	10	0	4	0	0	0	0	0	4	0	0	0	0	0	0
21	0	0	0	0	0	0	0	7	0	0	0	0	0	0	0	0	0	0	0
22	0	2	0	0	0	0	0	0	4	0	0	0	0	0	0	0	0	0	0
27	0	0	0	0	0	2	0	0	0	7	0	0	0	0	0	0	0	0	0
30	0	0	0	0	0	0	0	0	0	0	2	0	0	0	0	0	0	0	0
31	0	0	0	0	0	0	0	0	0	0	0	4	0	0	6	0	0	0	0
32	0	0	0	0	7	0	4	0	0	0	0	0	4	0	4	0	0	0	0
37	0	0	0	0	0	0	0	0	0	0	0	0	0	6	5	0	0	0	0
38	0	0	0	0	0	0	0	0	0	0	0	6	4	5	8	0	0	11	0
44	0	0	0	0	0	0	0	0	0	0	0	0	0	0	0	15	2	0	3
45	0	0	0	0	0	0	0	0	0	0	0	0	0	0	0	2	9	3	9
51	0	0	0	0	0	0	0	0	0	0	0	0	0	0	11	0	3	11	2
54	0	0	0	0	0	0	0	0	0	0	0	0	0	0	0	3	9	2	10

Figure 8. Jointly associated authors published papers adjacency matrix

AutId	1	2	4	6	7	11	12	13	14	16	17	19	20	23	24	25	26	28	29
1	0	5	0	0	0	10	0	0	0	0	0	0	0	0	0	0	0	0	0
2	5	0	0	0	0	11	9	0	0	0	0	8	0	0	0	0	0	0	0
4	0	0	0	0	0	5	0	0	6	0	0	0	0	0	0	0	0	0	0
6	0	0	0	0	3	0	0	0	5	4	0	0	0	0	0	0	0	0	0
7	0	0	0	3	0	0	0	0	0	11	5	0	0	0	0	0	0	0	0
11	10	11	5	0	0	0	9	0	0	0	0	0	5	0	0	0	0	0	0
12	0	9	0	0	0	9	0	0	0	0	0	0	0	0	0	0	0	0	0
13	0	0	0	0	0	0	0	0	0	0	0	0	0	4	0	0	0	0	0
14	0	0	6	5	0	0	0	0	0	0	0	0	0	0	6	0	0	0	0
16	0	0	0	4	11	0	0	0	0	0	0	0	0	0	7	3	6	0	0
17	0	0	0	0	5	0	0	0	0	0	0	0	0	0	0	0	6	0	0
19	0	8	0	0	0	0	0	0	0	0	0	0	2	0	0	0	0	0	0
20	0	0	0	0	0	5	0	0	0	0	0	2	0	0	0	0	0	0	0
23	0	0	0	0	0	0	0	4	0	0	0	0	0	0	0	0	0	5	2
24	0	0	0	0	0	0	0	0	6	7	0	0	0	0	0	2	0	1	0
25	0	0	0	0	0	0	0	0	0	3	0	0	0	0	2	0	0	0	0
26	0	0	0	0	0	0	0	0	0	6	6	0	0	0	0	0	0	0	0
28	0	0	0	0	0	0	0	0	0	0	0	0	0	5	1	0	0	0	0
29	0	0	0	0	0	0	0	0	0	0	0	0	0	2	0	0	0	0	0

Figure 9. Jointly individual authors published papers adjacency matrix

AutId	1	2	3	4	5	6	7	8	9	10	11	12	13	14	15	17	18	19	20
1	0	0	7	0	0	0	0	0	0	2	0	0	0	0	0	0	2	0	0
2	0	0	4	0	0	0	0	0	0	5	0	0	0	0	0	0	0	0	0
3	7	4	1	3	0	0	0	0	0	0	0	2	7	0	0	0	0	0	9
4	0	0	3	0	0	0	0	0	0	0	0	0	0	0	0	0	0	0	0
5	0	0	0	0	7	0	0	0	0	0	0	0	6	0	0	0	0	0	0
6	0	0	0	0	0	0	0	0	2	0	0	0	0	0	6	0	0	0	0
7	0	0	0	0	0	0	0	2	0	0	0	0	0	0	0	0	0	0	0
8	0	0	0	0	0	0	2	10	0	0	0	0	0	0	3	2	0	0	0
9	0	0	0	0	0	2	0	0	7	0	0	0	0	0	0	6	0	0	0
10	2	5	0	0	0	0	0	0	0	3	5	0	0	0	0	0	0	12	4
11	0	0	0	0	0	0	0	0	0	5	0	0	0	0	0	0	0	0	0
12	0	0	2	0	0	0	0	0	0	0	0	0	0	0	0	0	0	0	0
13	0	0	7	0	6	0	0	0	0	0	0	0	0	0	0	0	0	0	0
14	0	0	0	0	0	0	0	0	0	0	0	0	0	0	13	0	0	0	0
15	0	0	0	0	0	6	0	3	0	0	0	0	0	13	8	0	0	0	0
17	0	0	0	0	0	0	0	2	6	0	0	0	0	0	0	0	0	0	0
18	2	0	0	0	0	0	0	0	0	0	0	0	0	0	0	0	4	0	0
19	0	0	0	0	0	0	0	0	0	12	0	0	0	0	0	0	0	0	0
20	0	0	9	0	0	0	0	0	0	4	0	0	0	0	0	0	0	0	0

mail Id, V; Out-Degree(V) is the mails sent by V. Similarly the in-degree of mail Id, V; In-Degree(V) is the mails received by V.

In email graph, the nodes represent email Ids, which are again individuals. An edge between the Ids represents that there is at least one email sent in one direction. Hence the edge is shown in a directed arrow. Therefore the proposed email graph is a directed graph or digraph. So the edge can be considered as weak edge or strong edge. In a strong edge the communication always in both the directions, where as in a weak edge the communication always in one direction only. Similar kind of mail Ids can be grouped into one community. Sometimes the edges may be considered as weighted edge by labeling the edge with number of mails sent from one Id to another during a period of time such as weekly or monthly and can be seen in Cook et al (2007), Rao et al (2015), Rao et al (2015 ICATCCT) and Rao et al (2016 Chapter).

The email network can be represented as a graph having Ids (or nodes) and the nodes are connected with a directed edge which indicates its communication directions can be seen in Rao et al (2015) and Rao et al (2015 ICATCCT). So it can be represented as a directed graph or digraph. The authors propose an email graph which is depicted in Figure 10. It has 59 numbers of Ids, ID = {1, 2, 3, ..., 59 }. To represent this email graph, an adjacency matrix of order 59X59 is needed. It finally assigns with 0s and 1s, where 0 is the indication of no mail is sent and 1 is the indication of some mail is sent between the pair of Ids where the actual edge is created during period of time (i.e., weekly or monthly). The email graphs adjacency matrix is depicted in Figure 11.

In a directed email graph, it is easy to find in-degree and out-degree of all email Ids. Using out-degree of Ids, it is possible to retrieve the strong communicator sub-graph as well as weak communicator sub-graph. The strong communicator sub-graph consists of all email Ids with highest out-degree which is depicted in Figure 12. Similarly the weak communicator sub-graph consists of all the email Ids with zero out-degree which is depicted in Figure 13. The weak communicator and strong communicator sub-graph's adjacency matrices are depicted in Figure 14 and Figure 15 respectively. Hence from the above proposed email graph in Figure 10, one can extract the following knowledge: (i) Strong Communicator Sub-Graph, the Ids to send more mails to other Ids in email graph frequently and (ii) Weak Communicator Sub-Graph, the Ids never send mails to other Ids in email graph, is sometimes called a sink Id. Hence the sink Id's out-degree is always zero.

Figure 10. Email graph

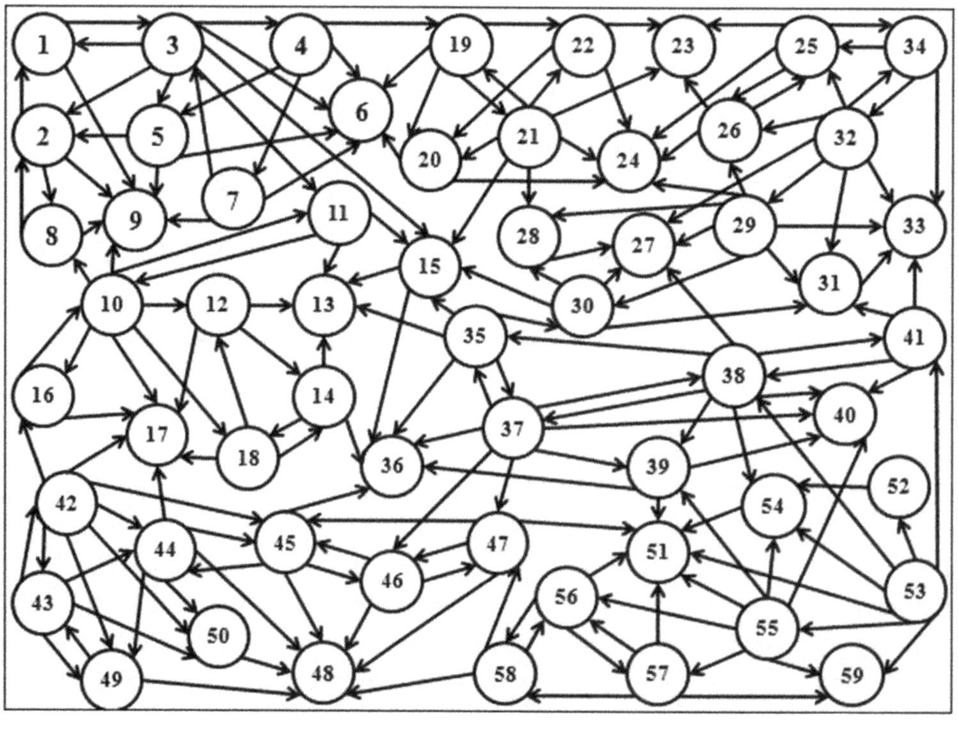

Figure 11. Adjacency matrix of Email graph

	1	2	3	4	5	6	7	8	9	10	11	12	13	14	15	16	17	18	19	20	21	22	23
1	0	0	1	0	0	0	0	0	1	0	0	0	0	0	0	0	0	0	0	0	0	0	0
2	1	0	0	0	0	0	0	1	1	0	0	0	0	0	0	0	0	0	0	0	0	0	0
3	1	1	0	1	1	1	0	0	0	0	1	0	0	0	1	0	0	0	0	0	0	0	0
4	0	0	0	0	1	1	1	0	0	0	0	0	0	0	0	0	0	0	1	0	0	0	0
5	0	1	0	0	0	1	0	0	1	0	0	0	0	0	0	0	0	0	0	0	0	0	0
6	0	0	0	0	0	0	0	0	0	0	0	0	0	0	0	0	0	0	0	0	0	0	0
7	0	0	1	0	0	1	0	0	1	0	0	0	0	0	0	0	0	0	0	0	0	0	0
8	0	1	0	0	0	0	0	0	1	0	0	0	0	0	0	0	0	0	0	0	0	0	0
9	0	0	0	0	0	0	0	0	0	0	0	0	0	0	0	0	0	0	0	0	0	0	0
10	0	0	0	0	0	0	0	1	1	0	1	1	0	0	0	1	1	1	0	0	0	0	0
11	0	0	0	0	0	0	0	0	0	1	0	0	1	0	1	0	0	0	0	0	0	0	0
12	0	0	0	0	0	0	0	0	0	0	0	0	1	1	0	0	1	0	0	0	0	0	0
13	0	0	0	0	0	0	0	0	0	0	0	0	0	0	0	0	0	0	0	0	0	0	0
14	0	0	0	0	0	0	0	0	0	0	0	0	1	0	0	0	0	1	0	0	0	0	0
15	0	0	0	0	0	0	0	0	0	0	0	0	1	0	0	0	0	0	0	0	0	0	0
16	0	0	0	0	0	0	0	0	0	1	0	0	0	0	0	0	1	0	0	0	0	0	0
17	0	0	0	0	0	0	0	0	0	0	0	0	0	0	0	0	0	0	0	0	0	0	0
18	0	0	0	0	0	0	0	0	0	0	0	1	0	1	0	0	1	0	0	0	0	0	0
19	0	0	0	0	0	1	0	0	0	0	0	0	0	0	0	0	0	0	0	1	1	1	0
20	0	0	0	0	0	1	0	0	0	0	0	0	0	0	0	0	0	0	0	0	0	0	0
21	0	0	0	0	0	0	0	0	0	0	0	0	0	0	1	0	0	0	1	1	0	1	1
22	0	0	0	0	0	0	0	0	0	0	0	0	0	0	0	0	0	0	0	1	0	0	0
23	0	0	0	0	0	0	0	0	0	0	0	0	0	0	0	0	0	0	0	0	0	0	0

Figure 12. Strong communicator sub-graph

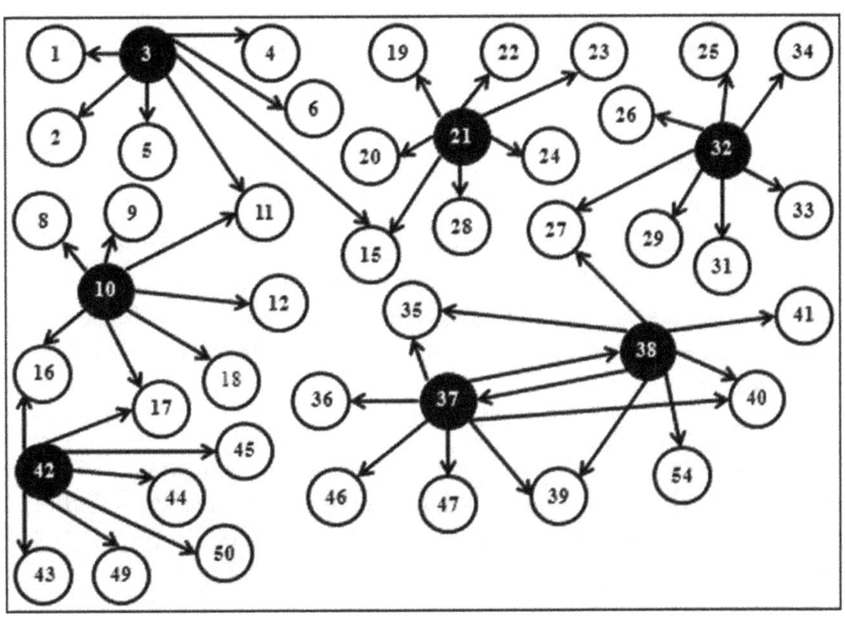

Figure 13. Weak communicator sub-graph

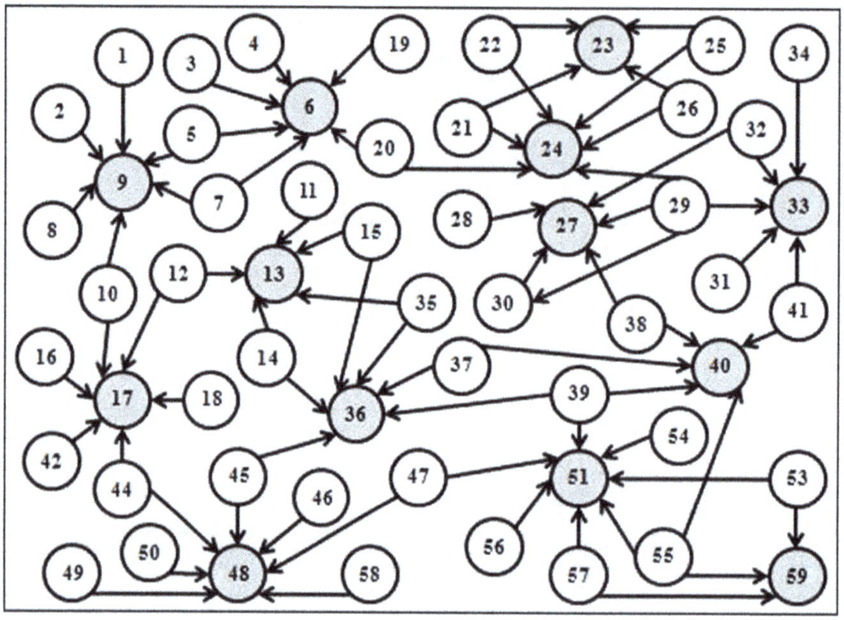

Strong communicator mail Ids which send mails to large number of mail Ids in a period of time (i.e., weekly or monthly). Such mail Ids out-degree is considered as the highest out-degree across the email graph. Such email Ids are grouped into a sub-graph, is said be strong communicator sub-graph. Similarly in contrast to strong communicator, the weak communicators are the mail Ids which receives mails from other Ids but never send mails to other ids for a particular period of time. Such Ids attain some in-degree but do not attain out-degree (i.e., zero out-degree). These mail Ids are grouped into a sub-graph, is said to be weak communicator sub-graph. Often these Ids are said to be sink Id since it has no out-degree.

PROPOSED ALGORITHM

The proposed algorithm has four phases. Phase-I reads email graph data from a text file called "*Data-Mail.Txt*" which contains total number of mail Ids, from mail Id, and to mail Id, where the actual edge is created. By using these details, an adjacency matrix Email[][] is created which only contains the edge data of all the mail Ids in the forms of 1s and 0s. Then the email adjacency matrix is written in a text file called "*MailEdge.Txt*".

Phase-II counts all the mail Ids out-degree and store in a matrix Outdeg[][]. Then it arranges the matrix Outdegree[][] in ascending order based on out-degree with respect to its email Ids.

Phase-III to gather all the email Ids with highest out-degree from the matrix Outdeg[][] and assign to the array Out_mail_no[]. Using the array Out_mail_no[] and email matrix Email[][], it writes the strong communicator adjacency matrix in a text file called "*Strong_Communicator.Txt*".

Figure 14. Weak communicator adjacency matrix

	6	9	13	17	23	24	27	33	36	40	48	51	59
1	0	1	0	0	0	0	0	0	0	0	0	0	0
2	0	1	0	0	0	0	0	0	0	0	0	0	0
3	1	0	0	0	0	0	0	0	0	0	0	0	0
4	1	0	0	0	0	0	0	0	0	0	0	0	0
5	1	1	0	0	0	0	0	0	0	0	0	0	0
7	1	1	0	0	0	0	0	0	0	0	0	0	0
8	0	1	0	0	0	0	0	0	0	0	0	0	0
10	0	1	0	1	0	0	0	0	0	0	0	0	0
11	0	0	1	0	0	0	0	0	0	0	0	0	0
12	0	0	1	1	0	0	0	0	0	0	0	0	0
14	0	0	1	0	0	0	0	0	1	0	0	0	0
15	0	0	1	0	0	0	0	0	1	0	0	0	0
16	0	0	0	1	0	0	0	0	0	0	0	0	0
18	0	0	0	1	0	0	0	0	0	0	0	0	0
19	1	0	0	0	0	0	0	0	0	0	0	0	0
20	1	0	0	0	0	1	0	0	0	0	0	0	0
21	0	0	0	0	1	1	0	0	0	0	0	0	0
22	0	0	0	0	0	1	0	0	0	0	0	0	0
25	0	0	0	0	1	0	0	0	0	0	0	0	0
26	0	0	0	0	1	1	0	0	0	0	0	0	0
28	0	0	0	0	0	0	1	0	0	0	0	0	0
29	0	0	0	0	0	0	1	1	0	0	0	0	0
30	0	0	0	0	0	0	1	0	0	0	0	0	0

Figure 15. Strong communicator adjacency matrix

	1	2	4	5	6	8	9	11	12	15	16	17	18	19	20	22	23	24	25	26	27	28	29	31	33	34	35	36	37	38	39	40	41	43	44	45	46	47	49	50	54
3	1	1	1	1	1	0	0	1	0	1	0	0	0	0	0	0	0	0	0	0	0	0	0	0	0	0	0	0	0	0	0	0	0	0	0	0	0	0	0	0	0
10	0	0	0	0	0	1	1	1	1	0	1	1	1	0	0	0	0	0	0	0	0	0	0	0	0	0	0	0	0	0	0	0	0	0	0	0	0	0	0	0	0
21	0	0	0	0	0	0	0	0	0	1	0	0	0	1	1	1	1	1	0	0	0	1	0	0	0	0	0	0	0	0	0	0	0	0	0	0	0	0	0	0	0
32	0	0	0	0	0	0	0	0	0	0	0	0	0	0	0	0	0	0	1	1	1	0	1	1	1	1	0	0	0	0	0	0	0	0	0	0	0	0	0	0	0
37	0	0	0	0	0	0	0	0	0	0	0	0	0	0	0	0	0	0	0	0	0	0	0	0	0	0	1	1	0	1	1	1	0	0	0	0	1	1	0	0	0
38	0	0	0	0	0	0	0	0	0	0	0	0	0	0	0	0	0	0	0	0	1	0	0	0	0	0	1	0	1	0	1	1	1	0	0	0	0	0	0	0	1
42	0	0	0	0	0	0	0	0	0	0	1	1	0	0	0	0	0	0	0	0	0	0	0	0	0	0	0	0	0	0	0	0	0	1	1	1	0	0	1	1	0

Finally, Phase-IV to gather all email Ids with zero out-degree from the matrix Outdeg[][] and assign to the array Zero_out_mail_no[]. Using array Zero_out_mail_no[] and email matrix Email[][], it writes the weak adjacency matrix in a file called "*Weak_Communicator.Txt*".

Using strong and weak communicator adjacency matrices, it is possible to draw the respective subgraphs (See Figure 12 and Figure 13).

ALGORITHM FOR EXTRACTION OF STRONG AND WEAK-COMMUNICATOR SUB-GRAPHS

Algorithm Strong_Weak_Communicator_Sub_Graph()

Algorithm conventions by Horowitz et al (1998) and Lipschutz (Tata McGraw-Hill)

```
n: To read number of mail Ids.
Id1, Id2: To assign from mail Id and to mail Id.
DataMail.Txt: Text file contains number of mail Ids, from mail Id, and to mail
Id.
MailEdge.Txt: Text file to write the email adjacency matrix.
Strong_Communicator.Txt, Weak_Communicator.Txt: Text files to write strong
communicator adjacency matrix and weak communicator adjacency matrix.
Email[n][n]: Double dimension array to store edge data (i.e., 0s and 1s) of n-
email Ids.
Outdeg[n][2]: Double dimension array to store n-email Ids and their total out-
degrees.
Out_mail_no[m]: To store m-email Id's highest out-degree.
Zero_out_mail_no[m]: To store m-email Id's zero out-degree.
{
// read email data
Read_Email_Data();
// to find out highest out-degree ID.
Detect_Highest_OutDegree_Id();
// to create strong communicator adjacency matrix
Strong_Communicator();
// to create weak communicator adjacency matrix
Call  Weak_Communicator();
}
```

PROCEDURE FOR READING EMAIL DATA AND CREATION OF EMAIL ADJACENCY MATRIX

Procedure Read_Email_Data()

```
{
open ("DataMail.Txt");
// read number of email Ids
    read (n);
// assign 0s to Email[][]
      repeat for i:=1 to n do
```

```
        repeat for j:=1 to  n do
            Email[i][j]:=0;
// read "from Id" and "to Id" from file
     while (Not EOF)
     do
     {
          read (Id1, Id2);
          // row-side email Id's index detection
          repeat for i:=1 to n do
          {   if (i=Id1) then break;  }
          // column-side email Id's index detection
          repeat for j:=1 to n do
          {   if (j=Id2) then break;  }
           // assign 1 to Email[i][j]'s position
           Email[i][j]:=1;
     }
close ("DataMail.Txt");
// write Email[][] in file MailEdge.Txt
open ("MailEdge.Txt");
repeat for i:=1 to n do
{
   repeat for j:=1 to n do
        write (Email[i][j]);
}
close ("MailEdge.Txt");
}
```

PROCEDURE FOR DETECTION OF EMAIL IDS WITH HIGHEST OUT-DEGREE

Procedure Detect_Highest_OutDegree_Id()

```
{
// count out-degree and assign to the matrix Outdeg[][].
repeat for i:=1 to n do
{
   // assign Ids and 0s to Outdeg[][].
   Outdeg[i][1]:=i;
   Outdeg[i][2]:=0;
   // to count ith Id's Out-degree.
  repeat for j:=1 to n do
     if (Email[i][j]=1) then Outdeg[i][2]:=Outdeg[i][2]+1;
}
```

```
// arrange Outdeg[][] in descending order on Out-degree.
    repeat for i:=1to (n-1) do
       repeat for j:=i+1 to n do
           if (Outdeg[i][2] < Outdeg[j][2]) then
           {
             swap (Outdeg[i][1], Outdeg[j][1]);
             swap (Outdeg[i][2], Outdeg[j][2]);
           }
}
```

PROCEDURE FOR WRITING STRONG COMMUNICATOR ADJACENCY MATRIX

Procedure Strong_Communicator()

```
{
   open ("Strong_Communicator.Txt");    // open the file
   // assign Outdeg[1][2] is the highest Out-degree
   Highest_Outdegree:=Outdeg[1][2];
   // index for Out_mail_no[] array for storing of Id with highest Out-degree
   j:=1;
  Out_mail_no[j]:=Outdeg[1][1];
  // find the index position of remaining highest Out-degree email Ids
  repeat for i:=2 to n do
    if (Outdeg[i][2]=Highest_Outdegree) then
    {
      j:=j+1;  Out_mail_no[j]:=Outdeg[i][1];
     }
  // extraction of Strong Communicator Adjacency Matrix from Email[][] by us-
ing
  // Out_mail_no[] and write in file
  repeat for k:=1 to j do
     repeat for i:=1 to  n do
         if (Out_mail_no[k]=i) then
         {
             write (i);  // write Strong Communicator Id
            // write the edge data from ith Id to nth Ids
            repeat for d:=1 to n do
                write (Email[i][d]);
          }
// close the file
close ("Strong_Communicator.Txt");
}
```

PROCEDURE FOR WRITING WEAK COMMUNICATOR ADJACENCY MATRIX

Procedure Weak_Communicator()

```
{
// open the file
open ("Weak_Communicator.Txt");
// index for Zero_out_mail_no[] array
j:=0;
// assign email Id's with zero out-degree in the array
   repeat for i:=1 to n do
      if (Outdeg[i][2]=0) then
      {
        j:=j+1;
       Zero_out_mail_no[j]:=Outdeg[i][1];
       }
   // arrange Zero_out_mail_no[] in ascending order
   repeat for i:=1 to (j-1) do
     repeat for k:=i+1to  j do
        if (Zero_out_mail_no[i]>Zero_out_mail_no[k]) then
                swap (Zero_out_mail_no[i], Zero_out_mail_no[k]);
  // write all in-degree Ids at the first row of file.
  repeat for i:=1 to j do
      write (Zero_out_mail_no[i]);
// extraction of Weak Communicator Adjacency Matrix from Email[][] by using
// Zero_out_mail_no[] and write in file
repeat for i:=1 to n do
{
    // write the edge data from ith Id to kth Id
    repeat for d:=1 to n do
       repeat for k:=1 to j do
          if (Zero_out_mail_no[k]=d) then write (Email[i][Zero_out_mail_
no[k]]);
}
// close the file
close ("Weak_Communicator.Txt");
}
```

EXPERIMENTAL RESULTS

Proposed Model Dataset

For the proposed email graph, the authors have created a dataset file called "*DataMail.Txt*", which contains details such as total number of email Ids, "from mail Ids", and "to mail Ids". The dataset text file

Figure 16. Mail dataset file

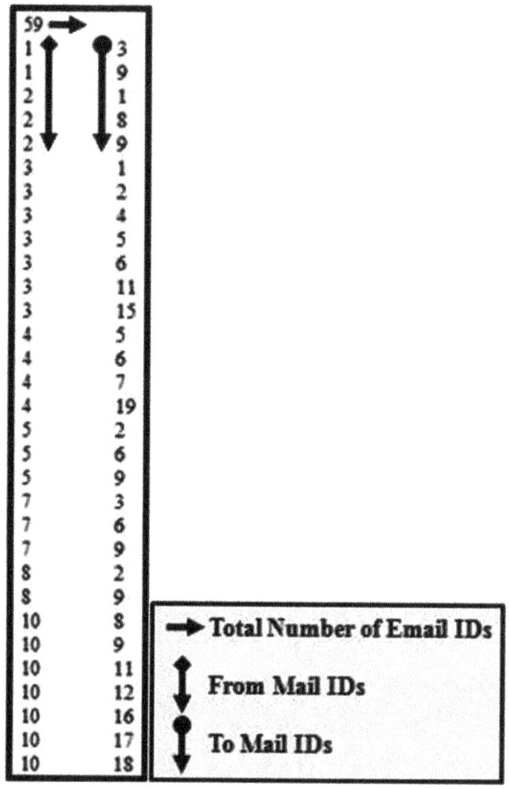

is shown in Figure 16. The 1st row indicates total number of email Ids (here it is 59) and from 2nd row onwards indicates "from email Ids" and "to email Ids" where the actual edge is created.

After input the dataset file "*DataMail.Txt*" to the proposed algorithm, its adjacency matrix as a file namely "*MailEdge.Txt*" was created. After that two more text files namely "*Strong_Communicator.Txt*" and "*Weak_Communicator.Txt*" were created. These text files are depicted in Figure 11, Figure 14, and Figure 15 respectively.

The strong communicator email Ids whose highest out-degree is 7, and the email Ids are 3, 10, 21, 32, 37, 38, and 42 (See Figure 12). Similarly the weak communicator email Ids whose out-degree is zero, and the email Ids are 6, 9, 13, 17, 23, 24, 27, 33, 36, 40, 48, 51, and 59 (See Figure 13).

Benchmark Dataset

The benchmark dataset file called "*DataMail.Txt*" has been taken from Guimera et al (2003), which contain total number of email Ids, from email Ids, and to email Ids. The 1st row indicates total number of email Ids (here it is 1133) and from 2nd row onwards contains "from email Ids" and "to email Ids" where the actual edge is created (See Figure 17).

After input the dataset file "*DataMail.Txt*" to the proposed algorithm, its adjacency matrix as a file namely "*MailEdge.Txt*" was created. After that two more text files namely "*Strong_Communicator.Txt*"

Figure 17. Mail dataset file

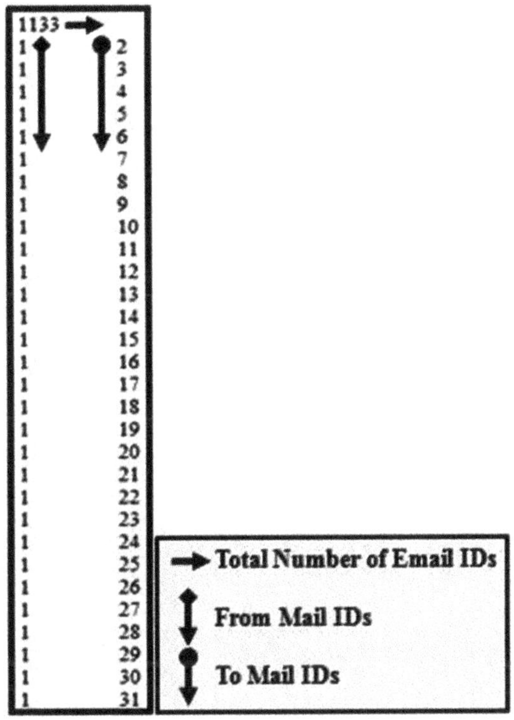

and "*Weak_Communicator.Txt*" were created. These text files are depicted in Figure 18, Figure 19, and Figure 20 respectively.

The algorithm was written in C++ and compiled with TurboC++. Both the examples dataset were input to the algorithm and observed satisfactory results.

MODELLING MULTI-LAYER TELEPHONE GRAPH

Based on Oselio et al (2011), the authors have proposed a telephone graph as another example of social network for representing as multi-layer graph. This telephone graph is considered as directed weighted graph. The edge between two phone numbers has a direction and a weight (i.e., total number of calls made). From this graph the authors try to create four numbers of layers. The first layer is the relational layer which is considered as the base layer where as the remaining three layers are behaviour layers which is considered as the sub-layers. The base layer holds the actual telephone graph. The sub-layers hold the behaviour of the telephone graph based on particular characteristics. These behaviour layers are formed with the characteristics of call duration of the user i.e., low-call durations, medium-call durations and high-call durations. Hence this proposed telephone graph has four numbers of layers.

Figure 21 shows the representation of proposed telephone graph in multi-layer graph form. The base layer is the actual telephone graph layer which has twenty numbers of users ID. The users ID are ranging from 1 to 20. Here the telephone graph is the directed weighted graph because the edges with a specific direction; assign with a weight (i.e., the total number of calls made by the user). The calls made by the

Figure 18. Adjacency mail matrix

	1	2	3	4	5	6	7	8	9	10	11	12	13	14	15	16	17	18	19	20	21	22	23	24	25	26	27	28	29	30	31
1	0	1	1	1	1	1	1	1	1	1	1	1	1	1	1	1	1	1	1	1	1	1	1	1	1	1	1	1	1	1	1
2	1	0	1	1	0	1	1	1	1	1	1	0	1	0	0	1	0	1	1	1	0	1	0	1	0	0	0	0	0	0	0
3	1	1	0	1	0	1	1	1	1	0	1	1	1	0	0	1	0	1	1	1	1	1	1	0	0	0	1	1	0	0	0
4	1	1	1	0	0	0	0	0	0	0	1	0	0	0	0	0	0	0	0	0	0	1	0	0	0	0	0	0	0	0	0
5	1	0	0	0	0	1	0	0	0	0	0	0	1	0	0	0	0	0	0	0	0	0	0	0	0	0	0	0	0	0	0
6	1	1	1	0	1	0	1	1	0	0	0	0	1	0	0	1	0	1	0	0	0	1	0	0	0	0	1	1	0	0	0
7	1	1	1	0	0	1	0	0	1	1	0	0	1	0	1	1	0	0	1	0	0	1	0	0	0	0	0	1	0	0	0
8	1	1	1	0	0	1	0	0	0	0	0	0	0	0	0	0	0	0	0	0	0	1	0	0	0	0	0	1	0	0	0
9	1	1	1	0	0	0	1	0	0	1	0	0	1	0	0	1	0	0	0	0	1	1	0	1	0	0	0	0	0	1	0
10	1	1	0	0	0	0	1	0	1	0	0	0	0	0	0	1	0	0	0	0	0	0	0	1	0	0	0	0	0	1	0
11	1	1	1	1	0	0	0	0	0	0	0	0	0	0	0	0	0	1	1	1	0	1	0	0	1	0	1	0	0	0	0
12	1	0	1	0	0	0	0	0	0	0	0	0	0	0	0	0	0	0	0	0	0	0	0	0	0	0	0	0	0	0	0
13	1	1	1	0	1	1	1	0	1	0	0	0	0	1	0	1	0	1	0	0	0	1	0	1	0	0	0	1	0	0	0
14	1	0	0	0	0	0	0	0	0	0	0	0	1	0	1	1	0	0	0	0	0	0	0	1	0	0	0	0	0	0	0
15	1	0	0	0	0	0	1	0	0	0	0	0	0	1	0	0	0	0	0	0	0	0	1	0	0	0	0	0	0	0	0
16	1	1	1	0	0	1	1	0	1	1	0	0	1	1	0	0	0	0	0	0	0	0	0	1	0	0	0	0	0	1	0

Figure 19. Strong communicator adjacency matrix

	1	2	3	5	6	7	9	10	12	13	14	15	16	18	19	20	21	22	23	24	25	28	29	30	31	33	34	38	39	40	41	42	43	44	45	46	47	48	49
16	1	1	1	0	1	1	1	1	0	1	1	0	0	0	0	0	0	0	0	1	0	0	0	1	0	1	1	0	0	0	0	0	0	0	0	0	0	0	0
21	1	0	1	0	0	0	1	1	0	0	0	0	0	1	0	0	0	0	1	0	1	0	0	0	0	0	0	0	1	1	1	0	0	0	0	1	1	0	0
23	1	0	1	0	0	0	0	0	0	0	0	1	0	1	0	0	1	0	0	0	1	0	0	0	0	0	0	1	1	0	0	1	1	1	1	1	0	0	0
41	1	0	1	0	0	0	1	0	0	0	0	0	0	0	1	1	1	0	0	0	0	0	0	0	0	0	0	0	1	0	0	0	0	0	0	1	1	1	0
42	0	0	1	0	0	0	0	0	0	0	0	0	0	0	0	0	0	0	1	0	0	0	0	0	0	0	0	0	1	1	0	0	0	1	1	0	0	0	0
76	0	0	0	1	0	1	0	1	0	1	0	1	0	0	0	0	0	0	0	0	0	0	0	0	0	0	0	0	0	0	0	0	0	0	0	0	0	0	1
105	0	0	0	0	0	0	0	0	0	0	0	0	1	0	0	0	1	0	0	0	0	0	0	0	0	0	0	0	1	1	0	1	0	0	0	0	0	0	1
196	0	0	0	0	0	0	0	1	0	0	0	0	1	0	0	0	0	0	1	0	0	0	0	1	0	0	0	0	0	0	0	0	0	0	0	0	0	0	0
233	0	1	0	0	0	0	0	0	0	0	0	0	0	0	1	1	0	0	0	0	0	1	0	0	0	0	0	1	0	1	0	0	0	0	0	0	0	0	0
333	0	0	0	0	0	0	0	0	0	0	0	0	0	0	0	0	0	0	0	0	0	0	0	0	1	0	0	0	0	0	0	1	0	0	1	0	0	0	0
354	0	0	0	0	0	0	0	0	0	0	0	0	0	0	0	0	0	1	0	0	0	0	1	1	0	0	0	0	1	1	1	1	0	0	0	1	0	0	0
355	0	0	1	0	1	0	1	0	1	0	0	0	0	0	0	0	0	0	0	0	0	0	0	0	0	0	0	0	1	1	1	1	0	0	1	0	0	0	0

Figure 20. Weak communicator adjacency matrix

	35	37	111	175	253	261	294	318	1111
2	1	1	0	0	0	0	0	0	0
6	1	0	0	0	0	0	0	0	0
10	0	0	1	0	0	0	0	0	0
14	1	0	0	1	0	0	0	0	0
19	0	1	0	0	0	0	0	0	0
21	0	0	1	0	1	1	0	0	0
22	0	1	0	0	0	0	0	0	0
24	0	0	0	0	0	0	1	0	0
30	0	0	0	0	0	0	0	1	0
1133	0	0	0	0	0	0	0	0	1

user can be characterized into three groups such as low-call durations, medium-call durations, and high-call durations respectively. Due to these characteristics of base layer graph, three sub-layers are formed. The 1st sub-layer is low-call durations graph, the 2nd sub-layer is medium-call durations graph, and the last one is high-call durations graph.

Each layer can be represented as weighted adjacency matrix. Based on the definition of multi-layer network, this telephone graph can be represented as a multi-dimensional array having the order 4X20X20, where 4 is the total number of layers and 20X20 is the order of each layer. It means the above telephone graph has four numbers of double dimension arrays of order 20X20. Its weighted adjacency matrix representations are depicted from Figure 22 to Figure 25.

PROPOSED ALGORITHM

Algorithm CDG()

```
// Global declarations
Structure Telephone
{
  Number id;
```

Figure 21. Multi-layer network of telephone graph

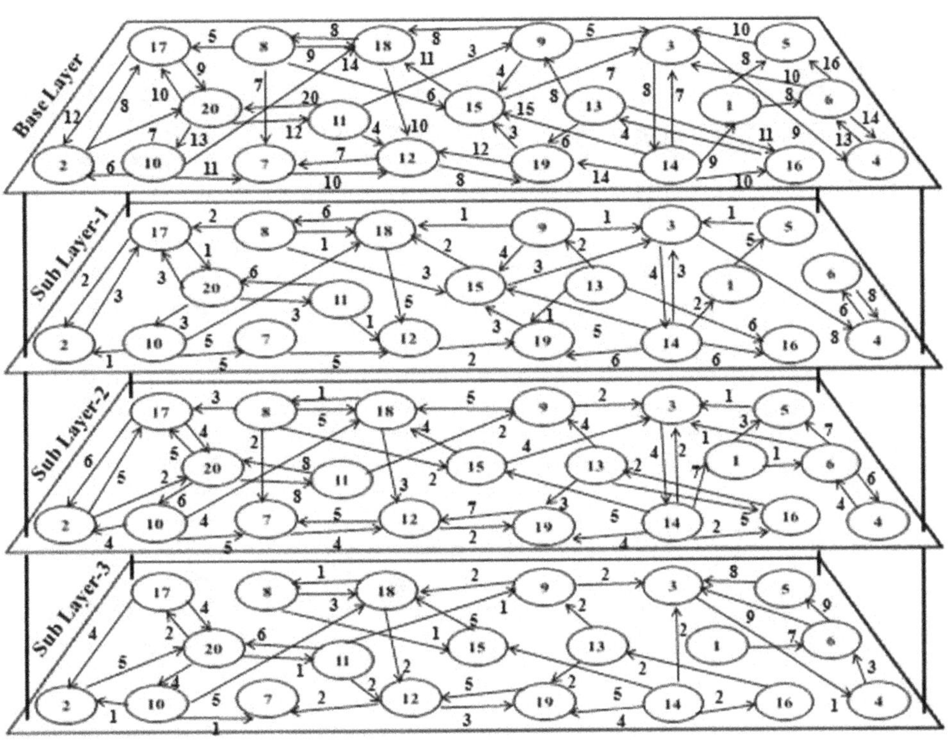

Figure 22. Base layer weighted adjacency matrix

Base Layer	17	8	18	9	3	5	20	11	15	13	1	6	2	10	7	12	19	14	16	4
17	0	0	0	0	0	0	9	0	0	0	0	0	12	0	0	0	0	0	0	0
8	5	0	9	0	0	0	0	0	6	0	0	0	0	0	7	0	0	0	0	0
18	0	8	0	0	0	0	0	0	0	0	0	0	0	0	0	10	0	0	0	0
9	0	0	8	0	5	0	0	0	4	0	0	0	0	0	0	0	0	0	0	0
3	0	0	0	0	0	0	0	0	0	0	0	0	0	0	0	0	0	8	0	9
5	0	0	0	0	10	0	0	0	0	0	0	0	0	0	0	0	0	0	0	0
20	10	0	0	0	0	0	0	12	0	0	0	0	0	13	0	0	0	0	0	0
11	0	0	0	3	0	0	20	0	0	0	0	0	0	0	0	4	0	0	0	0
15	0	0	11	0	7	0	0	0	0	0	0	0	0	0	0	0	0	0	0	0
13	0	0	0	8	0	0	0	0	0	0	0	0	0	0	0	0	6	0	11	0
1	0	0	0	0	0	8	0	0	0	0	0	8	0	0	0	0	0	0	0	0
6	0	0	0	0	10	16	0	0	0	0	0	0	0	0	0	0	0	0	0	14
2	8	0	0	0	0	0	7	0	0	0	0	0	0	0	0	0	0	0	0	0
10	0	0	14	0	0	0	0	0	0	0	0	0	6	0	11	0	0	0	0	0
7	0	0	0	0	0	0	0	0	0	0	0	0	0	0	0	10	0	0	0	0
12	0	0	0	0	0	0	0	0	0	0	0	0	0	0	7	0	8	0	0	0
19	0	0	0	0	0	0	0	0	3	0	0	0	0	0	0	12	0	0	0	0
14	0	0	0	0	7	0	0	0	15	0	9	0	0	0	0	0	14	0	10	0
16	0	0	0	0	0	0	0	0	0	4	0	0	0	0	0	0	0	0	0	0
4	0	0	0	0	0	0	0	0	0	0	0	13	0	0	0	0	0	0	0	0

Figure 23. Sub layer-1 weighted adjacency matrix

Low Call	17	8	18	9	3	5	20	11	15	13	1	6	2	10	7	12	19	14	16	4
17	0	0	0	0	0	0	1	0	0	0	0	0	2	0	0	0	0	0	0	0
8	2	0	1	0	0	0	0	0	3	0	0	0	0	0	0	0	0	0	0	0
18	0	6		0	0	0	0	0	0	0	0	0	0	0	0	5	0	0	0	0
9	0	0	1	0	1	0	0	0	4	0	0	0	0	0	0	0	0	0	0	0
3	0	0	0	0	0	0	0	0	0	0	0	0	0	0	0	0	0	4	0	8
5	0	0	0	0	1	0	0	0	0	0	0	0	0	0	0	0	0	0	0	0
20	3	0	0	0	0	0	0	3	0	0	0	0	0	3	0	0	0	0	0	0
11	0	0	0	0	0	0	6	0	0	0	0	0	0	0	0	1	0	0	0	0
15	0	0	2		3	0	0	0	0	0	0	0	0	0	0	0	0	0	0	0
13	0	0	0	2	0	0	0	0	0	0	0	0	0	0	0	0	1	0	6	0
1	0	0	0	0	0	5	0	0	0	0	0	0	0	0	0	0	0	0	0	0
6	0	0	0	0	0	0	0	0	0	0	0	0	0	0	0	0	0	0	0	8
2	3	0	0	0	0	0	0	0	0	0	0	0	0	0	0	0	0	0	0	0
10	0	0	5	0	0	0	0	0	0	0	0	0	1	0	5	0	0	0	0	0
7	0	0	0	0	0	0	0	0	0	0	0	0	0	0	0	5	0	0	0	0
12	0	0	0	0	0	0	0	0	0	0	0	0	0	0	0	0	2	0	0	0
19	0	0	0	0	0	0	0	0	3	0	0	0	0	0	0	0	0	0	0	0
14	0	0	0	0	3	0	0	0	5		2	0	0	0	0	0	6	0	6	0
16	0	0	0	0	0	0	0	0	0	0	0	0	0	0	0	0	0	0	0	0
4	0	0	0	0	0	0	0	0	0	0	0	6	0	0	0	0	0	0	0	0

Figure 24. Sub layer-2 weighted adjacency matrix

Medium Call	17	8	18	9	3	5	20	11	15	13	1	6	2	10	7	12	19	14	16	4
17	0	0	0	0	0	0	4	0	0	0	0	0	6	0	0	0	0	0	0	0
8	3	0	5	0	0	0	0	0	2	0	0	0	0	0	2	0	0	0	0	0
18	0	1	0	0	0	0	0	0	0	0	0	0	0	0	0	3	0	0	0	0
9	0	0	5	0	2	0	0	0	0	0	0	0	0	0	0	0	0	0	0	0
3	0	0	0	0	0	0	0	0	0	0	0	0	0	0	0	0	0	4	0	0
5	0	0	0	0	1	0	0	0	0	0	0	0	0	0	0	0	0	0	0	0
20	5	0	0	0	0	0	0	8	0	0	0	0	0	6	0	0	0	0	0	0
11	0	0	0	2	0	0	8	0	0	0	0	0	0	0	0	1	0	0	0	0
15	0	0	4		4	0	0	0	0	0	0	0	0	0	0	0	0	0	0	0
13	0	0	0	4	0	0	0	0	0	0	0	0	0	0	0	0	3	0	5	0
1	0	0	0	0	0	3	0	0	0	0	0	1	0	0	0	0	0	0	0	0
6	0	0	0	0	1	7	0	0	0	0	0	0	0	0	0	0	0	0	0	6
2	5	0	0	0	0	0	2	0	0	0	0	0	0	0	0	0	0	0	0	0
10	0	0	4	0	0	0	0	0	0	0	0	0	4	0	5	0	0	0	0	0
7	0	0	0	0	0	0	0	0	0	0	0	0	0	0	0	4	0	0	0	0
12	0	0	0	0	0	0	0	0	0	0	0	0	0	0	5	0	3	0	0	0
19	0	0	0	0	0	0	0	0	0	0	0	0	0	0	0	7	0	0	0	0
14	0	0	0	0	2	0	0	0	5	0	7	0	0	0	0	0	4	0	2	0
16	0	0	0	0	0	0	0	0	0	2	0	0	0	0	0	0	0	0	0	0
4	0	0	0	0	0	0	0	0	0	0	0	4	0	0	0	0	0	0	0	0

Figure 25. Sub layer-3 weighted adjacency matrix

High Call	17	8	18	9	3	5	20	11	15	13	1	6	2	10	7	12	19	14	16	4
17	0	0	0	0	0	0	4	0	0	0	0	0	4	0	0	0	0	0	0	0
8	0	0	3	0	0	0	0	0	1	0	0	0	0	0	0	0	0	0	0	0
18	0	1	0	0	0	0	0	0	0	0	0	0	0	0	0	2	0	0	0	0
9	0	0	2	0	2	0	0	0	0	0	0	0	0	0	0	0	0	0	0	0
3	0	0	0	0	0	0	0	0	0	0	0	0	0	0	0	0	0	0	0	1
5	0	0	0	0	8	0	0	0	0	0	0	0	0	0	0	0	0	0	0	0
20	2	0	0	0	0	0	0	1	0	0	0	0	0	4	0	0	0	0	0	0
11	0	0	0	1	0	0	6	0	0	0	0	0	0	0	0	2	0	0	0	0
15	0	0	5	0	0	0	0	0	0	0	0	0	0	0	0	0	0	0	0	0
13	0	0	0	2	0	0	0	0	0	0	0	0	0	0	0	0	2	0	0	0
1	0	0	0	0	0	0	0	0	0	0	0	7	0	0	0	0	0	0	0	0
6	0	0	0	0	9	9	0	0	0	0	0	0	0	0	0	0	0	0	0	0
2	0	0	0	0	0	0	5	0	0	0	0	0	0	0	0	0	0	0	0	0
10	0	0	5	0	0	0	0	0	0	0	0	0	1	0	1	0	0	0	0	0
7	0	0	0	0	0	0	0	0	0	0	0	0	0	0	0	0	0	0	0	0
12	0	0	0	0	0	0	0	0	0	0	0	0	0	0	2	0	3	0	0	0
19	0	0	0	0	0	0	0	0	0	0	0	0	0	0	0	5	0	0	0	0
14	0	0	0	0	2	0	0	0	5	0	0	0	0	0	0	0	4	0	2	0
16	0	0	0	0	0	0	0	0	0	2	0	0	0	0	0	0	0	0	0	0
4	0	0	0	0	0	0	0	0	0	0	0	3	0	0	0	0	0	0	0	0

```
  Structure CallerPhone
  {
   // Caller id, no. of calls, and call durations
      Number cid, nc;
      Real cd[100];
} CallerId[100];
};
nl: Number of layers.
tid: Number of users.
Id[tid]: Array to store all the users Id.
ANM[nl][tid][tid]: Mullti-dimension array to assign layer of network matrices.
Degree[tid]: Array to store out-going calls.
Phone[tid]: Array of Telephone structure kind.
PhoneId.Txt: Text file contains number of layers, total number of users and
their ids.
ANetData.Txt: Text file contains the telephone graph's edge (no. of calls)
data.
CallData.Txt: Text file contains the telephone graph details such as user id,
caller id, number of calls, and call durations of each call.
{ open ("PhoneId.Txt");  // open the file
   read (nl, tid);  // read number of layers, number of users, and ids
  repeat for i:=1 to tid do
      read (Id[i]);
  close ("PhoneId.Txt");     // close the file
  open ("ANetData.Txt");  // open the file
  // read data from file and assign to the 1st layer
  repeat for i:=1to tid do
     repeat for j:=1to tid do
         read (ANM[1][i][j]);
  close ("ANetData.Txt");     // close the file
  // assign 0s to Degree[]
  repeat for i:=1to tid do
       Degree[i]:=0;
  // to count outgoing calls of all users
  repeat for i:=1 to tid do
      repeat for j:=1 to tid do
         if (ANM[1][i][j]≠0) then Degree[i]:=Degree[i]+1;
  open ("CallData.Txt");  // open the file
  repeat for i:=1 to tid do
```

```
  {  read (Phone[i].id);  // read user id
      // read caller id, number of calls and calls duration
      repeat for j:=1 to Degree[i] do
      { read (Phone[i].CallerId[j].cd, nc);
         Phone[i].CallerId[j].nc:=nc;
         repeat for k:=1 to nc do
             read (Phone[i].CallerId[j].cd[k]);
       }
    }
Layers_Creation(ANM, Phone);  // procedure to creation of layers
Layers_Show(ANM);  // procedure to show layers
}
```

Procedure Layers_Show (ANM)

```
{
  repeat for i:=1 to nl do
     repeat for j:=1 to tid do
       repeat for k:=1 to tid do
            display (ANM[i][j][k]);
}
```

Procedure Layers_Creation (ANM, PHONE)

```
{ // assign 0s to ANM[][][] from 2nd to 'nl' layers.
  repeat for i:=2 to nl do
     repeat for j:=1 to tid do
        repeat for k:=1 to tid do
            ANM[i][j][k]:=0;
  repeat for i:=1 to tid do
  {   // to find the index position of user id
       repeat for rindex:=1 to tid do
          if (Id[rindex]=Phone[i].id) then break;
```

Figure 26. Dataset of phone Id details

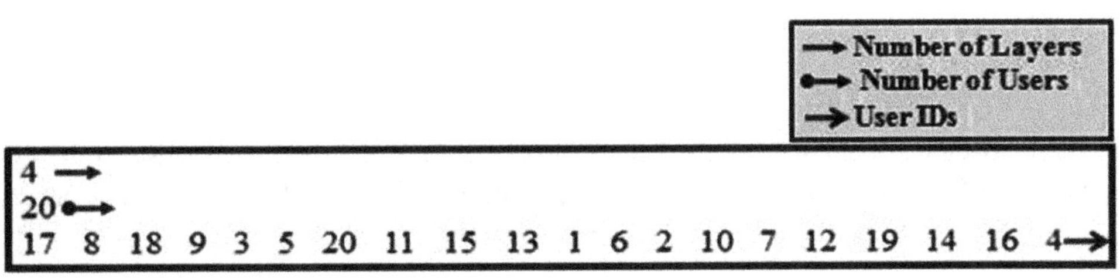

```
        // number of callers from Degree[i].
        repeat for j:=1 to Degree[i] do
        {   nc:=Phone[i].CallerId[j].nc;
             repeat for cindex:=1 to tid do   // to find the index position of
caller id
                 if (Id[cindex]=Phone[i].CallerId[j].cid) then break;
             repeat for k:=1to nc do            // to count call durations
             {
                Duration:=Phone[i].CallerId[j].cd[k];
                if (Duration>0 and Duration<=5) then  // to count in 2nd layer
                              ANM[2][rindex][cindex]:=ANM[2][rindex][cindex]+1;
                  if (Duration>5 and Duration<=10) then    // to count in 3rd
layer
                              ANM[3][rindex][cindex]:=ANM[3][rindex][cindex]+1;
                 if (Duration>10) then                              // to
count in 4th layer
                              ANM[4][rindex][cindex]:=ANM[4][rindex][cindex]+1;
                }
          }
     }
}
```

EXPERIMENTAL RESULTS

Three data files namely "*PhoneId.Txt* ", "*ANetData.Txt* ", and "*CallData.Txt*" are considered as datasets to the proposed algorithm and depicted in Figure 26, Figure 27 and Figure 28 respectively. The 1st data file contains total number of layers, number of ids, and the ids. The 2nd data file contains the actual number of calls between the users as edge weight. The 3rd data file contains the Ids, caller Ids, numbers of calls made, and the call durations. The algorithm has been implemented in C++ programming language and the output is satisfactory. The screen shots are depicted from Figure 29 to Figure 33.

Finally, the Phase-III of algorithm reads the details of user Id, caller Id, number of calls made, and calls durations of each call from text file "*CallData.Txt*" which is depicted in Figure 28. These details are assigned to array of structure Phone[]. Based on the details of Phone[], the layers of telephone graph are created by calling the procedure Layers_Creation().

CONCLUSION

The authors have studied the real world social network such as authors network, email network, and telephone network using the basic concepts of graph theory. So this chapter is all about applications

Figure 27. Dataset of edge details

0	0	0	0	0	0	9	0	0	0	0	0	12	0	0	0	0	0	0	0
5	0	9	0	0	0	0	0	6	0	0	0	0	0	7	0	0	0	0	0
0	8	0	0	0	0	0	0	0	0	0	0	0	0	0	10	0	0	0	0
0	0	8	0	5	0	0	0	4	0	0	0	0	0	0	0	0	0	0	0
0	0	0	0	0	0	0	0	0	0	0	0	0	0	0	0	0	8	0	9
0	0	0	0	10	0	0	0	0	0	0	0	0	0	0	0	0	0	0	0
10	0	0	0	0	0	0	12	0	0	0	0	0	13	0	0	0	0	0	0
0	0	0	3	0	0	20	0	0	0	0	0	0	0	0	4	0	0	0	0
0	0	11	0	7	0	0	0	0	0	0	0	0	0	0	0	0	0	0	0
0	0	0	8	0	0	0	0	0	0	0	0	0	0	0	0	6	0	11	0
0	0	0	0	0	8	0	0	0	0	0	8	0	0	0	0	0	0	0	0
0	0	0	0	10	16	0	0	0	0	0	0	0	0	0	0	0	0	0	14
8	0	0	0	0	0	7	0	0	0	0	0	0	0	0	0	0	0	0	0
0	0	14	0	0	0	0	0	0	0	0	0	6	0	11	0	0	0	0	0
0	0	0	0	0	0	0	0	0	0	0	0	0	0	0	10	0	0	0	0
0	0	0	0	0	0	0	0	0	0	0	0	0	0	7	0	8	0	0	0
0	0	0	0	0	0	0	0	3	0	0	0	0	0	0	12	0	0	0	0
0	0	0	0	7	0	0	0	15	0	9	0	0	0	0	0	14	0	10	0
0	0	0	0	0	0	0	0	0	4	0	0	0	0	0	0	0	0	0	0
0	0	0	0	0	0	0	0	0	0	0	13	0	0	0	0	0	0	0	0

Figure 28. Dataset of call details

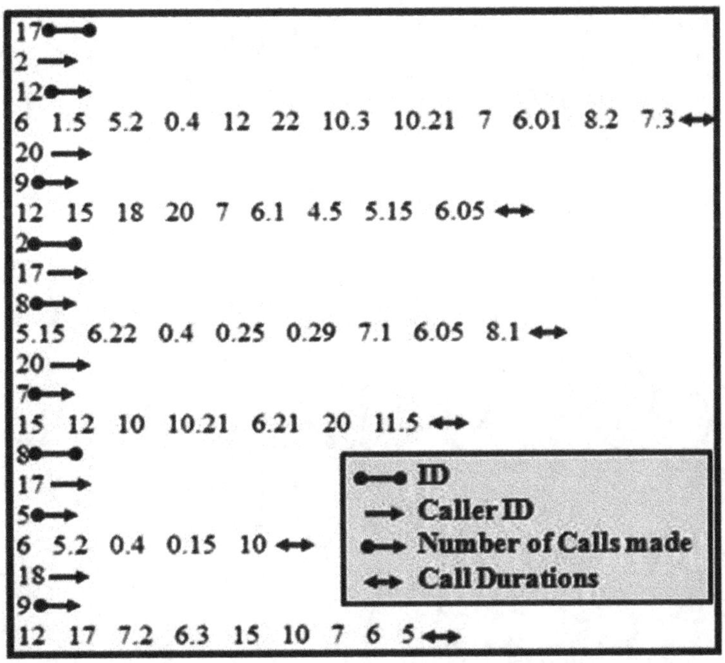

Figure 29. Dataset input

```
Enter File Name Contains No. of Layers, No. of Users and IDs:- PhoneId.txt

Enter File Name Contains Telephone Graph's Edge Data :- ANetData.txt

Enter File Name Contains ID, Caller ID,
Total Calls and Call Durations:- CallData.txt_
```

Figure 30. Actual telephone adjacency matrix

Actual Telephone Adjacency Matrix

	17	8	18	9	3	5	20	11	15	13	1	6	2	10	7	12	19	14	16	4
17	0	0	0	0	0	0	9	0	0	0	0	0	12	0	0	0	0	0	0	0
8	5	0	9	0	0	0	0	0	6	0	0	0	0	0	7	0	0	0	0	0
18	0	8	0	0	0	0	0	0	0	0	0	0	0	0	0	10	0	0	0	0
9	0	0	8	0	5	0	0	0	4	0	0	0	0	0	0	0	0	0	0	0
3	0	0	0	0	0	0	0	0	0	0	0	0	0	0	0	0	0	8	0	9
5	0	0	0	0	10	0	0	0	0	0	0	0	0	0	0	0	0	0	0	0
20	10	0	0	0	0	0	0	12	0	0	0	0	0	13	0	0	0	0	0	0
11	0	0	0	3	0	0	20	0	0	0	0	0	0	0	0	4	0	0	0	0
15	0	0	11	0	7	0	0	0	0	0	0	0	0	0	0	0	0	0	0	0
13	0	0	0	8	0	0	0	0	0	0	0	0	0	0	0	0	6	0	11	0
1	0	0	0	0	0	8	0	0	0	0	0	8	0	0	0	0	0	0	0	0
6	0	0	0	0	10	16	0	0	0	0	0	0	0	0	0	0	0	0	0	14
2	8	0	0	0	0	0	7	0	0	0	0	0	0	0	0	0	0	0	0	0
10	0	0	14	0	0	0	0	0	0	0	0	0	6	0	11	0	0	0	0	0
7	0	0	0	0	0	0	0	0	0	0	0	0	0	0	0	10	0	0	0	0
12	0	0	0	0	0	0	0	0	0	0	0	0	0	0	7	0	8	0	0	0
19	0	0	0	0	0	0	0	0	3	0	0	0	0	0	0	12	0	0	0	0
14	0	0	0	0	7	0	0	0	15	0	9	0	0	0	0	0	14	0	10	0
16	0	0	0	0	0	0	0	0	0	4	0	0	0	0	0	0	0	0	0	0
4	0	0	0	0	0	0	0	0	0	0	0	13	0	0	0	0	0	0	0	0

Press Any Key to See the Next Layer.....

Figure 31. Low-call duration adjacency matrix

Low-Call Duration Adjacency Matrix

	17	8	18	9	3	5	20	11	15	13	1	6	2	10	7	12	19	14	16	4
17	0	0	0	0	0	0	1	0	0	0	0	0	2	0	0	0	0	0	0	0
8	2	0	1	0	0	0	0	0	3	0	0	0	0	0	5	0	0	0	0	0
18	0	6	0	0	0	0	0	0	0	0	0	0	0	0	0	5	0	0	0	0
9	0	0	1	0	1	0	0	0	4	0	0	0	0	0	0	0	0	0	0	0
3	0	0	0	0	0	0	0	0	0	0	0	0	0	0	0	0	0	4	0	8
5	0	0	0	0	1	0	0	0	0	0	0	0	0	0	0	0	0	0	0	0
20	3	0	0	0	0	0	0	3	0	0	0	0	0	3	0	0	0	0	0	0
11	0	0	0	0	0	0	6	0	0	0	0	0	0	0	0	1	0	0	0	0
15	0	0	2	0	3	0	0	0	0	0	0	0	0	0	0	0	0	0	0	0
13	0	0	0	2	0	0	0	0	0	0	0	0	0	0	0	0	1	0	6	0
1	0	0	0	0	0	5	0	0	0	0	0	0	0	0	0	0	0	0	0	0
6	0	0	0	0	0	0	0	0	0	0	0	0	0	0	0	0	0	0	0	8
2	3	0	0	0	0	0	0	0	0	0	0	0	0	0	0	0	0	0	0	0
10	0	0	5	0	0	0	0	0	0	0	0	0	1	0	5	0	0	0	0	0
7	0	0	0	0	0	0	0	0	0	0	0	0	0	0	0	5	0	0	0	0
12	0	0	0	0	0	0	0	0	0	0	0	0	0	0	0	0	2	0	0	0
19	0	0	0	0	0	0	0	0	3	0	0	0	0	0	0	0	0	0	0	0
14	0	0	0	0	3	0	0	0	5	0	2	0	0	0	0	0	6	0	6	0
16	0	0	0	0	0	0	0	0	0	0	0	0	0	0	0	0	0	0	0	0
4	0	0	0	0	0	0	0	0	0	0	0	6	0	0	0	0	0	0	0	0

Press Any Key to See the Next Layer.....

of social graph related to three real worlds social graph i.e. authors graph, email graph, and telephone graph. The authors have proposed three algorithms for authors graph, email graph, and telephone graph using graph mining techniques.

The first proposed algorithm for authors graph for mining sub-graphs about authors research published papers such as authors having jointly published papers with author's individual published papers, authors having only jointly published papers, and authors having only individual published papers from authors

Figure 32. Medium-call adjacency matrix

Medium-Call Duration Adjacency Matrix

	17	8	18	9	3	5	20	11	15	13	1	6	2	10	7	12	19	14	16	4
17	0	0	0	0	0	0	4	0	0	0	0	0	6	0	0	0	0	0	0	0
8	3	0	5	0	0	0	0	0	2	0	0	0	0	0	2	0	0	0	0	0
18	0	1	0	0	0	0	0	0	0	0	0	0	0	0	0	3	0	0	0	0
9	0	0	5	0	2	0	0	0	0	0	0	0	0	0	0	0	0	0	0	0
3	0	0	0	0	0	0	0	0	0	0	0	0	0	0	0	0	0	4	0	0
5	0	0	0	0	1	0	0	0	0	0	0	0	0	0	0	0	0	0	0	0
20	5	0	0	0	0	0	0	8	0	0	0	0	0	6	0	0	0	0	0	0
11	0	0	0	2	0	0	8	0	0	0	0	0	0	0	0	1	0	0	0	0
15	0	0	4	0	4	0	0	0	0	0	0	0	0	0	0	0	0	0	0	0
13	0	0	0	4	0	0	0	0	0	0	0	0	0	0	0	0	3	0	5	0
1	0	0	0	0	0	3	0	0	0	0	0	1	0	0	0	0	0	0	0	0
6	0	0	0	0	1	7	0	0	0	0	0	0	0	0	0	0	0	0	0	6
2	5	0	0	0	0	0	2	0	0	0	0	0	0	0	0	0	0	0	0	0
10	0	0	4	0	0	0	0	0	0	0	0	4	0	5	0	0	0	0	0	0
7	0	0	0	0	0	0	0	0	0	0	0	0	0	0	0	4	0	0	0	0
12	0	0	0	0	0	0	0	0	0	0	0	0	0	0	5	0	3	0	0	0
19	0	0	0	0	0	0	0	0	0	0	0	0	0	0	0	7	0	0	0	0
14	0	0	0	0	2	0	0	0	5	0	7	0	0	0	0	0	4	0	2	0
16	0	0	0	0	0	0	0	0	0	2	0	0	0	0	0	0	0	0	0	0
4	0	0	0	0	0	0	0	0	0	0	0	4	0	0	0	0	0	0	0	0

Press Any Key to See the Next Layer.....

Figure 33. High-call adjacency matrix

High-Call Duration Adjacency Matrix

	17	8	18	9	3	5	20	11	15	13	1	6	2	10	7	12	19	14	16	4
17	0	0	0	0	0	0	4	0	0	0	0	0	4	0	0	0	0	0	0	0
8	0	0	3	0	0	0	0	0	1	0	0	0	0	0	0	0	0	0	0	0
18	0	1	0	0	0	0	0	0	0	0	0	0	0	0	0	2	0	0	0	0
9	0	0	2	0	2	0	0	0	0	0	0	0	0	0	0	0	0	0	0	0
3	0	0	0	0	0	0	0	0	0	0	0	0	0	0	0	0	0	0	0	1
5	0	0	0	0	8	0	0	0	0	0	0	0	0	0	0	0	0	0	0	0
20	2	0	0	0	0	0	0	1	0	0	0	0	0	4	0	0	0	0	0	0
11	0	0	0	1	0	0	6	0	0	0	0	0	0	0	0	2	0	0	0	0
15	0	0	5	0	0	0	0	0	0	0	0	0	0	0	0	0	0	0	0	0
13	0	0	0	2	0	0	0	0	0	0	0	0	0	0	0	0	2	0	0	0
1	0	0	0	0	0	0	0	0	0	0	0	7	0	0	0	0	0	0	0	0
6	0	0	0	0	9	9	0	0	0	0	0	0	0	0	0	0	0	0	0	0
2	0	0	0	0	0	0	5	0	0	0	0	0	0	0	0	0	0	0	0	0
10	0	0	5	0	0	0	0	0	0	0	0	0	1	0	1	0	0	0	0	0
7	0	0	0	0	0	0	0	0	0	0	0	0	0	0	0	1	0	0	0	0
12	0	0	0	0	0	0	0	0	0	0	0	0	0	0	2	0	3	0	0	0
19	0	0	0	0	0	0	0	0	0	0	0	0	0	0	0	5	0	0	0	0
14	0	0	0	0	2	0	0	0	5	0	0	0	0	0	0	0	4	0	2	0
16	0	0	0	0	0	0	0	0	0	2	0	0	0	0	0	0	0	0	0	0
4	0	0	0	0	0	0	0	0	0	0	0	3	0	0	0	0	0	0	0	0

Press Any Key to See the Next Layer.....

graph. The second proposed algorithm for mining strong communicator as well as weak communicator sub-graphs from email graph. Similarly the third proposed algorithm for representation of telephone graph as a multi-layer graph. Finally these three proposed algorithms were implemented using C++ programming language and observed satisfactory results.

REFERENCES

Aery, M., & Chakravarthy, S. (2014). eMailSift: Adapting Graph Mining Techniques for Email Classification. University of Texas.

Boccaletti, S., Latora, V., Moreno, Y., Chavez, M., & Hwang, D. U. (2006). Complex networks: Structure and dynamics. *Physics Reports*, *424*(4-5), 175–308. doi:10.1016/j.physrep.2005.10.009

Buldyrev, S. V., Parshani, R., Paul, G., Stanley, H. E., & Havlin, S. (2010). Catastrophic cascade of failures in interdependent networks. *Nature*, *464*(7291), 1025–1028. doi:10.1038/nature08932 PMID:20393559

Cook, D. J., & Holder, L. B. (2007). *Mining Graph Data*. John Wiley & Sons, Inc.

De Domenico, M., Solé-Ribalta, A., Cozzo, E., Kivelä, M., Moreno, Y., Porter, M. A., & Arenas, A. et al. (2013). Mathematical formulation of multilayer networks. *Physical Review X*, *3*(4), 041022. doi:10.1103/PhysRevX.3.041022

Dickison, M., Havlin, S., & Stanley, H. E. (2012). Epidemics on interconnected networks. *Phys. Rev. E*, *85*(6), 066109. doi:10.1103/PhysRevE.85.066109 PMID:23005164

Dom, B., Eiron, I., Cozzi, A., & Zhang, Y. (2003). Graph-Based Ranking Algorithms for E-mail Expertise. *Proceedings of DMKD'03: 8th ACM SIGMOD*. doi:10.1145/882082.882093

Estrada, E. (2011). *The Structure of Complex Networks: Theory and Applications*. Oxford, UK: Oxford University Press. doi:10.1093/acprof:oso/9780199591756.001.0001

Guimera, R., Danon, L., Diaz-Guilera, A., Giralt, F., & Arenas, A. (2003). Self-similar community structure in a network of human interactins. *Physical Review. E*, *68*(6), 065103. doi:10.1103/PhysRevE.68.065103 PMID:14754250

Horowitz, Sahani, & Rajasekaran. (1998). *Fundamentals of Computer Algorithms*. Galgotia Publications Pvt. Ltd.

Kivelä, M., Arenas, A., Barthelemy, M., Gleeson, J. P., Moreno, Y., & Porter, M. A. (2014). Multilayer networks. *Journal of Complex Networks*, *2*(3), 203–271. doi:10.1093/comnet/cnu016

Lipschutz, S. (n.d.). *Schaum's outline of Data Structures*. New Delhi. *Tata McGraw-Hill Publishing Company Limited.*

Newman, M. E. J. (2010). *Networks: An Introduction*. Oxford University Press. doi:10.1093/acprof:oso/9780199206650.001.0001

Oselio, B., Kulesza, A., & Hero, A. O. (2011). *Multi-layer graph analytics for social networks*. University of Michigan. Retrieved from http://www.cs.cmu.edu/~enron

Rajaraman, A., Leskovec, J., & Ullman, J. D. (2011). *Mining of Massive Datasets.* Cambridge University Press. doi:10.1017/CBO9781139058452

Rao, B., & Mishra, S. N. (2015). *An Approach to Mining Information from Telephone Graph Using Graph Mining Techniques. In Proceedings of iCATccT 2015* (pp. 424–429). Davangere, India: BIET.

Rao, B., Mishra, S. N., & Maharana, H. S. (2015). Algorithm for Representation of Call-Duration Graphs of Telephone Graph Using Multi-Layer Graph Techniques. *Proceedings of ICCI 2015 in Advances in Computational Intelligence*, 415-425.

Rao, B., Mishra, S. N., & Maharana, H. S. (2016). An Approach to Mining Strong and Weak Communicator Sub-Graphs from Email Graph Using Graph Mining Techniques. *Proceedings of ICCTICT, 2016*, 271–276.

Rao, B., & Mitra, A. (2016). *Graph Mining and Its Applications in Studying Community Based Graph under the Preview of Social Network. In Product Innovation through Knowledge Management and Social Media Strategies.* IGI Global. doi:10.4018/976-1-4666-9607-5

Tang, G., Pei, J., & Luk, W.-S. (2014). Email mining: Tasks, common techniques, and tools. *Knowledge and Information Systems, 41*(1), 1–31. doi:10.1007/s10115-013-0658-2

Wasserman, S., & Faust, K. (1994). *Social Network Analysis: Methods and Applications.* Cambridge, UK: Cambridge University Press. doi:10.1017/CBO9780511815478

Compilation of References

35 Key E-Commerce Platform Features. (2009). Retrieved April 4, 2017 from http://www.tokyowebdesigns.com/advice/1192/35-key-e-commerce-platform-features

Abbasi, A., Chen, H., & Salem, A. (2007). *Sentiment Analysis in Multiple Languages: Feature Selection for Opinion Classification in Web Forums*. Retrieved from:http://ai.arizona.edu/intranet/papers/ahmedabbasi_sentimenttois.pdf

Abbasi, F. H., & Harris, R. J. (2009, November). Experiences with a Generation III virtual Honeynet. In *Telecommunication Networks and Applications Conference (ATNAC), 2009 Australasian* (pp. 1-6). IEEE. doi:10.1109/ATNAC.2009.5464785

Abdallah, A., Maarof, M. A., & Zainal, A. (2016). Fraud detection system: A survey. *Journal of Network and Computer Applications*, *68*, 90–113. doi:10.1016/j.jnca.2016.04.007

Abdelsalam, H. M., Dawoud, R. H., & ElKadi, H. A. (2013). An examination of the decision making styles of Egyptian managers. In S. Saeed, M. Khan, & R. Ahmad (Eds.), *Business strategies and approaches for effective engineering management* (pp. 219–236). Hershey, PA: IGI Global. doi:10.4018/978-1-4666-3658-3.ch013

Abdou, A., Radaideh, M., & Lewis, J. (2010). Decision support systems and their application in construction. In *Business information systems: Concepts, methodologies, tools and applications* (pp. 1024–1042). Hershey, PA: IGI Global. doi:10.4018/978-1-61520-969-9.ch061

Acampora, G., Alghazzawi, D., Hagras, H., & Vitiello, A. (2016). An interval type-2 fuzzy logic based framework for reputation management in peer-to-peer e-commerce. *Information Sciences*, *333*, 88–107. doi:10.1016/j.ins.2015.11.015

Aciar, S., Avesani, P., De la Rosa, J. L., Hormazabal, N., & Serra, A. (2009, June). Adaptive business intelligence for an open negotiation environment. In *Digital Ecosystems and Technologies, 2009. DEST'09. 3rd IEEE International Conference on* (pp. 517-522). IEEE. doi:10.1109/DEST.2009.5276732

Adam, N. R., & Yesha, Y. (1996). *Electronic Commerce*. Berlin: Springer-Verlag. doi:10.1007/3-540-60738-2

Adla, A. (2013). Modeling cooperative decision support systems with hybrid agents. *International Journal of Decision Support System Technology*, *5*(3), 31–48. doi:10.4018/jdsst.2013070103

Aery, M., & Chakravarthy, S. (2014). eMailSift: Adapting Graph Mining Techniques for Email Classification. University of Texas.

Agarwal, J., & Wu, T. (2015). Factors influencing growth potential of e-commerce in emerging economies: An institution-based N-OLI framework and research propositions. *Thunderbird International Business Review*, *57*(3), 197–215. doi:10.1002/tie.21694

Ahmed, M. D., & Sundaram, D. (2010). A framework for a scenario driven decision support systems generator. In M. Hunter (Ed.), *Strategic information systems: Concepts, methodologies, tools, and applications* (pp. 662–679). Hershey, PA: IGI Global. doi:10.4018/978-1-60566-677-8.ch044

Al-Azmi & Abdul-Aziz. (2013). *Data, text and web mining for business intelligence: A survey.* arXiv preprint arXiv:1304.3563

Allison, P. D. (2012). Statistical Horizons Haverford. In *Handling missing Data by Maximum Likelihood.* Academic Press.

Amazon Web Services (AWS). (2017). Retrieved from https://aws.amazon.com/

Amazon Web Services. (n.d.). *Customer Success.* Reterieved from https://aws.amazon.com/solutions/case-studies/

Android Operating System. (2017). Retrieved from http://en.wikipedia.org/wiki/Android

Android. (2017). Retrieved in February, 2017, from www.developer.android.com

Antweiler, W., & Frank, M. Z. (2004). The Information Content of Internet Stock Message Boards. *The Journal of Finance*, *59*(3), 1259–1294. doi:10.1111/j.1540-6261.2004.00662.x

Anvari, R. D., & Norouzi, D. (2016). The impact of e-commerce and R&D on economic development in some selected countries. *Procedia: Social and Behavioral Sciences*, *229*, 354–362. doi:10.1016/j.sbspro.2016.07.146

API Amazon Document. (2017, 12 February), Retrieved from http://docs.2017.aws.amazon.com/apigateway/api-reference/

Ashley, P., Hinton, H., & Vandenwauver, M. (2001, December). Wired versus wireless security: The Internet, WAP and iMode for e-commerce. In *Computer Security Applications Conference, 2001. ACSAC 2001. Proceedings 17th Annual* (pp. 296-306). IEEE. doi:10.1109/ACSAC.2001.991545

Asur, S., & Huberman. (2010). Predicting the future with social media. In *Proceedings of IEEE/WIC/ACM International Conference on Web Intelligence and Intelligent Agent Technology (WI IAT)*. IEEE.

Au, W. H., Chan, K. C. C., & Yao, X. (2003). A novel evolutionary data mining algorithm with applications to churn prediction. *IEEE Transactions on Evolutionary Computation*, *7*(6), 532–545. doi:10.1109/TEVC.2003.819264

Averweg, U. R. (2010). Decision support systems and decision-making processes. In M. Hunter (Ed.), *Strategic information systems: Concepts, methodologies, tools, and applications* (pp. 122–130). Hershey, PA: IGI Global. doi:10.4018/978-1-60566-677-8.ch010

AWS. (2017). *AWS History and Benefits.* Retrieved January 29, 2017, from http://www.crestinfotech.com/aws-history-benefits/

Baesens, B. (2015). APATE: A novel approach for automated credit card transaction fraud detection using network-based extensions. *Decision Support Systems*, 38–48.

Baesens, B., Van Vlasslaer, V., & Verbeke, W. (2015). Fraud:Detection, Prevention and Analystics. In *Fraud Analytics using Discriptive, Predictive and Social Network Techniques, A Guide To Data Science for Fraud Detection* (pp. 1–25). Wiley & Sons.

Bahbouhi, J. E., & Moussa, N. (2017). Prisoner's dilemma game model for e-commerce. *Applied Mathematics and Computation*, *292*, 128–144. doi:10.1016/j.amc.2016.07.018

Bahrami, M., Arabzad, S. M., & Ghorbani, M. (2012). Innovation in market management by utilizing business intelligence: Introducing proposed framework. *Procedia: Social and Behavioral Sciences*, *41*, 160–167. doi:10.1016/j.sbspro.2012.04.020

Bajo, J., Borrajo, M. L., De Paz, J. F., Corchado, J. M., & Pellicer, M. A. (2012). A multi-agent system for web-based risk management in small and medium business. *Expert Systems with Applications*, *39*(8), 6921–6931. doi:10.1016/j.eswa.2012.01.001

Bakliwal, A. (2013). *Fine-grained opinion mining from different genre of social media content*. Academic Press.

Bandre, S. R., & Nandimath, J. N. (2015, January). Design consideration of network intrusion detection system using Hadoop and GPGPU. In *Pervasive Computing (ICPC), 2015 International Conference on* (pp. 1-6). IEEE. doi:10.1109/PERVASIVE.2015.7087201

BankAmerica Corporation. (1998). *What is SET[tm] and How Does it Work?* Retrieved from http://www.bofa.com/spare_change/set_what_and_how.html

Banrescu, A. (2015). Detecting and Preventing Fraud with Data Analytics. *Procedia Economics and Finance*, *32*, 1827–1836. doi:10.1016/S2212-5671(15)01485-9

Bariso, P. F., III. (2016). *No Need to Fear Robots: Online "Bot" Use under the Computer Fraud and Abuse Act*. Academic Press.

Baruti, S. S. (2016). Proposed framework for mobile decision support systems for higher learning institutions: Mobile decision support systems. *International Journal of Handheld Computing Research*, *7*(3), 24–37. doi:10.4018/IJHCR.2016070103

Bawany, N. Z., Shamsi, J. A., & Salah, K. (2017). DDoS Attack Detection and Mitigation Using SDN: Methods, Practices, and Solutions. *Arabian Journal for Science and Engineering*, *42*(2), 425–441. doi:10.1007/s13369-017-2414-5

BBC. (2013). How to shop safely and securely online. *BBC*. Retrieved from: http://www.bbc.co.uk/webwise/0/22728224

Behdad, M., Barone, L., Bennamoun, M., & French, T. (2012). Nature-Inspired Techniques in the Context of Fraud Detection. *IEEE Transactions on Systems, Man and Cybernetics. Part C, Applications and Reviews*, *42*(6), 1273–1290. doi:10.1109/TSMCC.2012.2215851

Beware of Phishing. (n.d.). Retrieved from http://www2.le.ac.uk/offices/ias/topics/phishing

Bhattacharyya, S., Jha, S., Tharakunnel, K., & Westland, J. Ch. (2011). Data mining for credit card fraud: A comparative study. *Decision Support Systems*, *3*(50), 602–613. doi:10.1016/j.dss.2010.08.008

Bherde, G. P., & Pund, M. A. (2016, September). Recent attack prevention techniques in web service applications. In *Automatic Control and Dynamic Optimization Techniques (ICACDOT), International Conference on* (pp. 1174-1180). IEEE. doi:10.1109/ICACDOT.2016.7877771

Bhuyan, M. H., Bhattacharyya, D. K., & Kalita, J. K. (2014). Network anomaly detection: Methods, systems and tools. *IEEE Communications Surveys and Tutorials*, *16*(1), 303–336. doi:10.1109/SURV.2013.052213.00046

Bihl, T. J., Young, W. A. II, & Weckman, G. R. (2014). Decision support systems in business. In J. Wang (Ed.), *Encyclopedia of business analytics and optimization* (pp. 696–707). Hershey, PA: IGI Global. doi:10.4018/978-1-4666-5202-6.ch065

Bitools.net. (n.d.). *Business Intelligence Tools and Software - Pentaho Analysis*. Retrieved October 03, 2016, from http://www.bitool.net/software/pentaho-analysis.html

Blumenthal, H. (Ed.). (1998). *The OBI standard gains momentum*. Retrieved from http://www.netscapeworld.com/ned-12- 1997/ned-12-extranet.html

Boccaletti, S., Latora, V., Moreno, Y., Chavez, M., & Hwang, D. U. (2006). Complex networks: Structure and dynamics. *Physics Reports*, *424*(4-5), 175–308. doi:10.1016/j.physrep.2005.10.009

Bogdan-Alexandru, U. R. S. (2015). Security Issues and Solutions in E-payment Systems. *Fiat Iustitia,* (2), 172-179. Retrieved from http://oaji.net/articles/2016/2064-1452602042.pdf

Bolton, R. J., & Hand, D. J. (2002). Statistical fraud detection: A review. *Statistical Science*, *28*(3), 235–255.

Booch, G., Jacobson, I., & Rumbaugh, J. (1999). *Unified Modeling Language User Guide* (2nd ed.). Addison-Wesley.

Buldyrev, S. V., Parshani, R., Paul, G., Stanley, H. E., & Havlin, S. (2010). Catastrophic cascade of failures in interdependent networks. *Nature*, *464*(7291), 1025–1028. doi:10.1038/nature08932 PMID:20393559

Burstein, F., & Holsapple, C. W. (2008). New horizons at the core of information systems: Decision support system advances. *Information Systems and e-Business Management*, *6*(2), 109–115. doi:10.1007/s10257-007-0076-7

Business Intelligent-Columo. (n.d.). *Business Intelligence for Finance People*. Retrieved December 23, 2016, from http://www.calumo.com/business-intelligence-for-finance/

Büyüközkan, G., & Güleryüz, S. (2016). Multi Criteria Group Decision Making Approach for Smart Phone Selection Using Intuitionistic Fuzzy TOPSIS. *International Journal of Computational Intelligence Systems*, *9*(4), 709–725. doi: 10.1080/18756891.2016.1204119

Camenisch, J., Piveteau, J. M., & Stadler, M. (1996). An Efficient Fair Payment System. *ACM Conference on Computer and Communications Security*, 88–94.

Chandola, V., Banerjee, A., & Kumar, V. (2009). Anomalydetection:a urveyrvey. *ACM Computing Surveys*, *41*(3), 1–58. doi:10.1145/1541880.1541882

Chan, H., Lee, R., Dillon, T., & Chang, E. (2008). *E-Commerce Fundamental and Applications*. New Delhi: WILEY.

Chan, K., & Leibowitz, J. (2006). The synergy of social network analysis and knowledge mapping: A case study. *Int. J. Management and Decision Making*, *7*(1), 19. doi:10.1504/IJMDM.2006.008169

Chen, W. S., & Du, Y. K. (2009). Using neural networks and data mining techniques for the financial distress prediction model. *Expert Systems with Applications*, *36*(2), 4075–4086. doi:10.1016/j.eswa.2008.03.020

Cheon, J., & Choe, T. Y. (2013). Distributed processing of snort alert log using hadoop. *IACSIT International Journal of Engineering and Technology*, *5*(3), 2685–2690.

Cheung, C. F., & Li, F. L. (2012). A quantitative correlation coefficient mining method for business intelligence in small and medium enterprises of trading business. *Expert Systems with Applications*, *39*(7), 6279–6291. doi:10.1016/j.eswa.2011.10.021

Chian Tan, F.T., Guo, Z., Cahalaneb, M., & Cheng, D. (n.d.). *Developing business analytic capabilities for combating e-commerce identity fraud: A study of Trustev's digital verification solution*. Academic Press.

Chittaro, L., & Ranon, R. (2000). Virtual Reality stores for 1-to-1 e-commerce. *Proc. Of the CHI2000 Workshop on Designing Interactive Systems for 1-to-1 E-Commerce*.

Chonka, A., Xiang, Y., Zhou, W., & Bonti, A. (2011). Cloud security defence to protect cloud computing against HTTP-DoS and XML-DoS attacks. *Journal of Network and Computer Applications*, *34*(4), 1097–1107. doi:10.1016/j.jnca.2010.06.004

Choshin, M., & Ghaffari, A. (2017). An investigation of the impact of effective factors on the success of e-commerce in small- and medium-sized companies. *Computers in Human Behavior*, *66*, 67–74. doi:10.1016/j.chb.2016.09.026

Christian Science Monitor. (n.d.). Everything you need to know about dynamic pricing. *Christian Science Monitor*. Retrieved from: http://www.csmonitor.com

Chung, K., Boutaba, R., & Hariri, S. (2016). Knowledge based decision support system. *Information Technology & Management*, *17*(1), 1–3. doi:10.1007/s10799-015-0251-3

Chung, W., & Tseng, T. L. B. (2012). Discovering business intelligence from online product reviews: A rule-induction framework. *Expert Systems with Applications*, *39*(15), 11870–11879. doi:10.1016/j.eswa.2012.02.059

Coderre, D. G. (2009). *Fraud Analysis Techniques Using ACL*. John Wiley & Sons.

Colin, J. (2001). *The Amazon Case Study Analysis*. Retrieved from http://www.ecommerce-digest.com/amazon-case-study.html

Combe, C. (2012). Introduction to *e*-business. Routledge. doi:10.1017/CBO9780511805936

Comparison of shopping cart software. (n.d.). Retrieved April 11, 2017 from https://en.wikipedia.org/wiki/Comparison_of_shopping_cart_software

Confederation of Indian Industry. (2016). *E-Commerce in India: A Game Changer for the Economy*. Retrieved from http://www.bing.com/cr?IG=6F0F7F2F91334641BE5B3DE4745E7E89&CID=2B68C210B2166BF20A09C91FB3106ADC&rd=1&h=CQvneHAH_csyTTkglzFhbQUkKBR5oc1HDUEEsVBxqtQ&v=1&r=http%3a%2f%2fwww.italiaindia.com%2fimages%2fuploads%2fpdf%2fapril-2016-e-commerce-in-india.pdf&p=DevEx,5065.1

Cook, D. J., & Holder, L. B. (2007). *Mining Graph Data*. John Wiley & Sons, Inc.

Copeland & Hwang. (n.d.). *Electronic Data Interchange: Concepts and Effects*. Retrieved from http://www.isoc.org/isoc/whatis/conferences/inet/97/proceedings/C5/C5_1.HTM

Costabile, M. (2001). *Usability in the Software Life Cycle. In Handbook of Software Engineering and Knowledge Eng* (Vol. 1). World Scientific Publishing.

Cox, B. L., & Jantti, M. (2012). Capturing business intelligence required for targeted marketing, demonstrating value, and driving process improvement. *Library & Information Science Research*, *34*(4), 308–316. doi:10.1016/j.lisr.2012.06.002

Currim, I. S., Mintz, O., & Siddarth, S. (2015). Information accessed or information available? The impact on consumer preferences inferred at a durable product e-commerce website. *Journal of Interactive Marketing*, *29*, 11–25. doi:10.1016/j.intmar.2014.09.003

Cvitaš, A. (2011, May). Relation extraction from text documents. In *MIPRO, 2011 Proceedings of the 34th International Convention* (pp. 1565-1570). IEEE.

Cybenko, G., & Landwehr, C. E. (2012). Security analytics and measurements. *IEEE Security and Privacy*, *3*(10), 5–8. doi:10.1109/MSP.2012.75

Dai, S. Y., & Kuo, S. Y. (2007, December). Mapmon: A host-based malware detection tool. In *Dependable Computing, 2007. PRDC 2007. 13th Pacific Rim International Symposium on* (pp. 349-356). IEEE. doi:10.1109/PRDC.2007.23

Dal Pozzolo, A., Caelen, O., Borgne, Y., Waterschoot, S., & Bontempi, G. (2014). Learned lessons in credit card fraud detection from a practitioner perspective. *Expert Systems with Applications*, *41*(10), 4915–4928. doi:10.1016/j.eswa.2014.02.026

Daugherty, T., Li, H., & Biocca, F. (2005). Experiential commerce: A summary of research investigating the impact of virtual experience on consumer learning. In *Society of Consumer Psychology: Online Advertising*. Mahwah, NJ: Lawrence Erlbaum Associates.

De Domenico, M., Solé-Ribalta, A., Cozzo, E., Kivelä, M., Moreno, Y., Porter, M. A., & Arenas, A. et al. (2013). Mathematical formulation of multilayer networks. *Physical Review X*, *3*(4), 041022. doi:10.1103/PhysRevX.3.041022

Delen, D., & Demirkan, H. (2013). Data, information and analytics as services. *Decision Support Systems*, *55*(1), 359–363. doi:10.1016/j.dss.2012.05.044

Dennis, P. (2004). *E-Commerce Principles and Introduction Technology*. New Delhi: Tata McGraw Hill Publication.

Díaz, J., Rusu, C., & Collazos, C. A. (2017). Experimental validation of a set of cultural-oriented usability heuristics: E-commerce websites evaluation. *Computer Standards & Interfaces*, *50*, 160–178. doi:10.1016/j.csi.2016.09.013

Dickison, M., Havlin, S., & Stanley, H. E. (2012). Epidemics on interconnected networks. *Phys. Rev. E*, *85*(6), 066109. doi:10.1103/PhysRevE.85.066109 PMID:23005164

Dom, B., Eiron, I., Cozzi, A., & Zhang, Y. (2003). Graph-Based Ranking Algorithms for E-mail Expertise. *Proceedings of DMKD'03: 8th ACM SIGMOD*. doi:10.1145/882082.882093

Domingues, M. A., Jorge, A. M., Soares, C., & Rezende, S. O. (2015). Web mining for the integration of data mining with business intelligence in web-based decision support systems. In A. Azevedo & M. Santos (Eds.), *Integration of data mining in business intelligence systems* (pp. 120–142). Hershey, PA: IGI Global. doi:10.4018/978-1-4666-6477-7.ch007

Douglas Crockford. (2017). In *Wikipedia*. Retrieved on February 21, 2017 from https://en.wikipedia.org/wiki/Douglas_Crockford

Drougas, B. A. (2009). Electronic commerce for health products services-problems-quality and future. In A. Lazakidou & K. Siassiakos (Eds.), *Handbook of research on distributed medical informatics and e-health* (pp. 190–197). Hershey, PA: IGI Global. doi:10.4018/978-1-60566-002-8.ch013

Drummond, Janson, & Shih. (1998). *Requirements for Inter-operable Internet EDI*. EDIINT Working Group. Internet Draft.

Dunham, K., & Melnick, J. (2008). *Malicious bots: an inside look into the cyber-criminal underground of the internet*. CRC Press. doi:10.1201/9781420069068

Dunkel, J., Bruns, R., & Pawlowski, O. (2010). Complex event processing in sensor-based decision support systems. In B. Nag (Ed.), *Intelligent systems in operations: Methods, models and applications in the supply chain* (pp. 64–79). Hershey, PA: IGI Global. doi:10.4018/978-1-61520-605-6.ch004

E-Commerce (Electronic Commerce or EC). (n.d.). Retrieved from: http://searchcio.techtarget.com/definition/e-commerce

Ecommerce Guide. (n.d.). Retrieved from: https://ecommerceguide.com/guides/ecommerce-future/

E-Commerce Security Systems. (n.d.). Retrieved from http://www.tutorialspoint.com/e_commerce/e_commerce_security.htm

ECommerze. (2008). *The history and evolution of e-commerce*. Retrieved from: https://ecommerze.wordpress.com/2008/06/12/the-history-and-evoltion-of-e-commerce/

EDICT Systems. (1999). Retrieved from http://www.edictsystems.com

El-Gayar, O. F., Deokar, A. V., & Tao, J. (2011). DSS-CMM: A capability maturity model for DSS development processes. *International Journal of Decision Support System Technology*, *3*(4), 14–34. doi:10.4018/jdsst.2011100102

ElliottTimo. (2014). *Digital Business & Business Analytics–Self-Service vs Traditional Business Intelligence*. Retrieved October 03, 2016, from http://timoelliott.com/blog/2014/04/qa-self-service-vs-traditional-business-intelligence.html

Eom, H. B., & Lee, S. M. (1990). Decision support systems applications research: A bibliography (1971-1988). *European Journal of Operational Research, 46*(3), 333–342. doi:10.1016/0377-2217(90)90008-Y

Erl, T. (2009).I ntroducing SOA. In Service Oriented Architecture Concept, Technologies and Design (pp. 1-42). Pearson Education Inc.

Esponda, F. (2009). *Immune System Inspired Digital Representations: Storing all but the valuable data*. VDM Verlag Saarbrucken.

Ess, D. L., & Sudweeks, F. (1998). *Proceedings International Cultural Attitudes Toward Technology and Communication-CaTac'98*. University of Sydney.

Estrada, E. (2011). *The Structure of Complex Networks: Theory and Applications*. Oxford, UK: Oxford University Press. doi:10.1093/acprof:oso/9780199591756.001.0001

Esuli, A. (2008). Automatic generation of lexical resources for opinion mining: models, algorithms and applications. *ACM SIGIR Forum, 42*, 105–106.

ETHOS team. (1997). *Open Buying on the Internet (OBI) standard.* Retrieved from: http://www.tagish.co.uk/ethosub/lit5/c1aa.htm

EtnoteamS. P. A. (2000). Retrieved from http://ww.etnoteam.it/webquality

Etzioni, O. (1996). The World Wide Web: Quagmire or Gold Mine. Communications of the ACM, 39(11), 65-68.

Extensible Markup Language (XML). (1998). *W3C Recommendation.* Retrieved from: http://www.w3.org/TR/1998/REC-xml-19980210

Fairwarning. (2016). *Salesforce Data Protection through User Activity Monitoring*. FairWarning, Inc.

Federal Supply Service (FSS). (n.d.). More About Electronic Data Interchange (EDI). *Federal Supply Service.* Retrieved from: http://www.fss.gsa.gov/edi_mae.html

Fernandes, T. (1995). Introduction to Culture. Academic Press.

Flipkart. (2015). *Product APIs Reference*. Retrieved from https://affiliate.flipkart.com/api-docs/af_prod_ref.html

Fonseca, J., Vieira, M., & Madeira, H. (2007, December). Testing and comparing web vulnerability scanning tools for SQL injection and XSS attacks. In *Dependable Computing, 2007. PRDC 2007. 13th Pacific Rim International Symposium on* (pp. 365-372). IEEE. doi:10.1109/PRDC.2007.55

Forgionne, G. A. (2005). Functional integration of decision making support. In M. Khosrow-Pour (Ed.), *Encyclopedia of information science and technology* (pp. 1236–1242). Hershey, PA: IGI Global. doi:10.4018/978-1-59140-553-5.ch218

Forgionne, G. A. (2009). Updated architectures for the integration of decision making support functionalities. In M. Khosrow-Pour (Ed.), *Encyclopedia of information science and technology* (2nd ed., pp. 3884–3889). Hershey, PA: IGI Global. doi:10.4018/978-1-60566-026-4.ch619

Foster, K., Smith, G., Ariyachandra, T., & Frolick, M. N. (2015). Business intelligence competency center: Improving data and decisions. *Information Systems Management, 32*(3), 229–233. doi:10.1080/10580530.2015.1044343

Francois, J., Wang, S., Bronzi, W., State, R., & Engel, T. (2014, November). Botcloud: Detecting botnets using mapreduce. In *2014 IEEE International Workshop on Information Forensics and Security* (pp. 1-6). IEEE.

Freibrun, E.S. (1993). *Electronic Data Interchange (EDI) and the Law*. Academic Press.

Furnell, S. (2006). E-commerce security. In Enterprise Information Systems Assurance and System Security: Managerial and Technical Issues (pp. 131-149). IGI Global. doi:10.4018/978-1-59140-911-3.ch009

Gachet, A., & Sprague, R. (2010). Context in decision support systems development. In M. Hunter (Ed.), *Strategic information systems: Concepts, methodologies, tools, and applications* (pp. 604–613). Hershey, PA: IGI Global. doi:10.4018/978-1-60566-677-8.ch040

Gadge, J. (2008, December). Comprehensive test mechanism to detect attack on Web Services. In *Networks, 2008. ICON 2008. 16th IEEE International Conference on* (pp. 1-6). IEEE.

Gao, H., Liu, H., Yao, D., Liu, X., & Aickelin, U. (2010, July). An audio CAPTCHA to distinguish humans from computers. In *Electronic Commerce and Security (ISECS), 2010 Third International Symposium on* (pp. 265-269). IEEE. doi:10.1109/ISECS.2010.65

Gao, H., Yao, D., Liu, H., Liu, X., & Wang, L. (2010, December). A novel image based CAPTCHA using jigsaw puzzle. In *Computational Science and Engineering (CSE), 2010 IEEE 13th International Conference on* (pp. 351-356). IEEE. doi:10.1109/CSE.2010.53

Garrido, P. (2011). Conversation-oriented decision support systems for organizations. In M. Cruz-Cunha & J. Varajao (Eds.), *Enterprise information systems design, implementation and management: Organizational applications* (pp. 118–131). Hershey, PA: IGI Global. doi:10.4018/978-1-61692-020-3.ch008

Garrido, P. (2015). Concepts for the design of a manager-centric global decision support system for organizations. In J. Varajão, M. Cruz-Cunha, & R. Martinho (Eds.), *Improving organizational effectiveness with enterprise information systems* (pp. 173–187). Hershey, PA: IGI Global. doi:10.4018/978-1-4666-8368-6.ch011

Gautam, R. (2014). Network Security Issues in e-Commerce. *International Journal of Advanced Research in Computer Science and Software Engineering*, *4*(3).

Geer, D. (2005). Malicious bots threaten network security. *Computer*, *38*(1), 18–20. doi:10.1109/MC.2005.26

Genc, Y., Mason, W., & Nickerson, J. V. (2013). *Semantic transforms using collaborative knowledge bases*. Academic Press.

George, J., Kumar, V., & Kumar, S. (2015). Data Warehouse Design Considerations for a Healthcare Business Intelligence System. *World Congress on Engineering*.

Ghosh, S., & Reilly, D. L. (1994). Credit card fraud detection with a neural network. *Proceedings of the 27th Hawaii International Conference on system Sciences*, 3. doi:10.1109/HICSS.1994.323314

Givens, Storey, & Sugumaran. (2013). A method for improving business intelligence interpretation through the use of semantic technology. In *International Conference on Application of Natural Language to Information Systems*. Springer.

Gordeychik, S. (2007). *Web Application Security Statistics*. Retrieved September 1, 2017, from http://projects.webappsec.org/w/page/13246989/webapplicationsecuritystatistics

Gordeychik, S., Grossman, J., Khera, M., Lantinga, M., Wysopal, C., Eng, C., & Evteev, D. (2010). *Web application security statistics*. The Web Application Security Consortium.

Gounder, M. S., Iyer, V. V., & Al Mazyad, A. (2016, March). A survey on business intelligence tools for university dashboard development. In *Big Data and Smart City (ICBDSC), 2016 3rd MEC International Conference on* (pp. 1-7). IEEE. doi:10.1109/ICBDSC.2016.7460347

Graphics, Visualization and Usability (GVU) Centre. (1998). *GVU's user surveys*. Georgia Tech Research Corporation. Retrieved from WWW.cc.gatech.edu/gvu/user_ surveys/

Grawemeyer, B., & Johnson, H. (2011). Using and managing multiple passwords: A week to a view. *Journal of Interacting with Computers*, *23*(3), 256–267. doi:10.1016/j.intcom.2011.03.007

Greenstein, M., Feinman, T., & Vasarhelyi, M. (2001). *Electronic Commerce: Security, Risk management, and Control with Powerweb Passcode Card (E-Commerce)*. New Delhi: Tata McGraw Hill Publications.

Grüschow, R. M., Kemper, J., & Brettel, M. (2016). How do different payment methods deliver cost and credit efficiency in electronic commerce? *Electronic Commerce Research and Applications*, *18*, 27–36. doi:10.1016/j.elerap.2016.06.001

Gu, G., Perdisci, R., Zhang, J., & Lee, W. (2008, July). BotMiner: Clustering Analysis of Network Traffic for Protocol-and Structure-Independent Botnet Detection. In *USENIX Security Symposium* (*Vol. 5*, No. 2, pp. 139-154). Academic Press.

Guimera, R., Danon, L., Diaz-Guilera, A., Giralt, F., & Arenas, A. (2003). Self-similar community structure in a network of human interactins. *Physical Review. E*, *68*(6), 065103. doi:10.1103/PhysRevE.68.065103 PMID:14754250

Guntuku, S. C., Narang, P., & Hota, C. (2013). *Real-time Peer-to-Peer Botnet Detection Framework based on Bayesian Regularized Neural Network*. Academic Press.

Gupta, B., Goul, M., & Dinter, B. (2015). Business Intelligence and Big Data in Higher Education: Status of a Multi-Year Model Curriculum Development Effort for Business School Undergraduates, MS Graduates, and MBAs. CAIS, 36, 23.

Gupta, A. N., & Thilagam, P. S. (2013). Attacks on web services need to secure xml on web. *Computing in Science & Engineering*, *3*(5), 1.

Hamad, H., Elbeltagi, I., Jones, P., & El-Gohary, H. (2015). Antecedents of B2B e-commerce adoption and its effect on competitive advantage in manufacturing SMEs. *Strategic Change*, *24*(5), 405–428. doi:10.1002/jsc.2019

Hanson, W., & Kalyanam, K. (2009). *E-Commerce Web Marketing*. New Delhi: Cengage Learning.

Hartono, E., Holsapple, C. W., Kim, K. Y., Na, K. S., & Simpson, J. T. (2014). Measuring perceived security in B2C electronic commerce website usage: A respecification and validation. *Decision Support Systems*, *62*, 11–21. doi:10.1016/j.dss.2014.02.006

Hayashi, Y., Hsieh, M. H., & Setiono, R. (2010). Understanding consumer heterogeneity: A business intelligence application of neural networks. *Knowledge-Based Systems*, *23*(8), 856–863. doi:10.1016/j.knosys.2010.05.010

Hemmati, S., Ebadian, M., & Nahvi, A. (2012). A new decision making structure for managing arriving orders in MTO environments. *Expert Systems with Applications*, *39*(3), 2669–2676. doi:10.1016/j.eswa.2011.08.122

Henderson, G., & Hammersburg, C. (2016). *An Enterprise Approach to Fraud Detection and Prevention in Government Programs*. White paper by SAS Institute Inc.

Henderson, S. C., Snyder, C. A., & Byrd, T. A. (2003). Electronic commerce and data privacy: The impact of privacy concerns on electronic commerce use and regulatory preferences. In S. Lubbe (Ed.), *The economic and social impacts of e-commerce* (pp. 213–238). Hershey, PA: IGI Global. doi:10.4018/978-1-59140-043-1.ch012

Herdley, J. (2017). *Jsoup Java HTML Parser, with best of DOM, CSS, and jquery*. Retrieved February 2017, from https://jsoup.org/

Hinley, C., O'Leary, R., & Samdarshi, S. (2015). *WhiteHat website security statistic report 2015*. Retrieved September 1, 2017 from https://www.whitehatsec.com

Hinze, A., Voisard, A., & Buchanan, G. (2009). Tip: Personalizing information delivery in a tourist information system. *Information Technology & Tourism*, *11*(3), 247–264. doi:10.3727/109830509X12596187864071

History of Ecommerce: How Did It All Begin? (2011). Retrieved on April 4 from http://www.miva.com/blog/the-history-of-ecommerce-how-did-it-all-begin

Hongyi, C., & Kocaoglu, D. F. (2008). A sensitivity analysis algorithm for hierarchical decision models. *European Journal of Operational Research*, *185*(1), 266–288. doi:10.1016/j.ejor.2006.12.029

Horowitz, Sahani, & Rajasekaran. (1998). *Fundamentals of Computer Algorithms*. Galgotia Publications Pvt. Ltd.

Hsieh, K. L. (2011). Employing a recommendation expert system based on mental accounting and artificial neural networks into mining business intelligence for study abroad's P/S recommendations. *Expert Systems with Applications*, *38*(12), 14376–14381. doi:10.1016/j.eswa.2011.03.078

Hu, M., & Liu, B. (2004). Mining and summarizing customer reviews In *Proceedings of the tenth. ACM SIGKDD international conference on Knowledge discovery and data mining* (pp. 168–177). ACM.

Huang, H., Zhong, S., & Tan, J. (2009, August). Browser-side countermeasures for deceptive phishing attack. In *Information Assurance and Security, 2009. IAS'09. Fifth International Conference on* (Vol. 1, pp. 352-355). IEEE. doi:10.1109/IAS.2009.12

Huang, Q., Chen, X., Ou, C. X., Davison, R. M., & Hua, Z. (2017). Understanding buyers' loyalty to a C2C platform: The roles of social capital, satisfaction and perceived effectiveness of e-commerce institutional mechanisms. *Information Systems Journal*, *27*(1), 91–119. doi:10.1111/isj.12079

Huang, Z., & Benyoucef, M. (2013). From e-commerce to social commerce: A close look at design features. *Electronic Commerce Research and Applications*, *12*(4), 246–259. doi:10.1016/j.elerap.2012.12.003

Hughes, S., Brusilovsky, P., & Lewis, M. (2002). Adaptive navigation support in 3D ecommerce activities. *Proc. of Workshop on Recommendation and Personalization in ECommerce at the 2nd International Conference on Adaptive Hypermedia and Adaptive Web-Based Systems (AH'2002)*, 132-139.

Hwang & Yoon. (1981). Multiple criteria decision making. *Lecture Notes in Economics and Mathematical Systems, 186*.

Ibarra, L., Partida, A., & Aguilar, D. (2015). Electronic commerce as a business strategy: Impact in consumption habits in Hermosillo, Sonora's inhabitants. *Procedia: Social and Behavioral Sciences*, *175*, 275–282. doi:10.1016/j.sbspro.2015.01.1201

Introducing, J. S. O. N. (2017). Retrieved February 2017, from http://www.json.org/

Ishaya, T., & Folarin, M. (2012). A service oriented approach to Business Intelligence in Telecoms industry. *Telematics and Informatics*, *29*(3), 273–285. doi:10.1016/j.tele.2012.01.004

Ishizaka, A., & Labib, A. (2009). Analytic hierarchy process and expert choice: Benefits and limitations. *Or Insight, 22*(4), 201-220.

IT Pro Portal. (n.d.). E-commerce security tips: How to stay safe when shopping online. *IT Pro Portal.* Retrieved from: http://www.itproportal.com/2013/07/18/e-commerce-security-tips-how-to-stay-safewhen-shopping-online/

Jang-Jaccard, J., & Nepal, S. (2014). A survey of emerging threats in cyber security. *Journal of Computer and System Sciences*, *80*(5), 973–993. doi:10.1016/j.jcss.2014.02.005

Java Virtual Machine. (2017). Retrieved February 15, 2017 from. from https://en.wikipedia.org/wiki/Java_virtual_machine

Jha, S., Guillen, M., & Westland, J. C. (2012). Employing transaction aggregation strategy to detect credit card fraud. *Expert Systems with Applications*, *16*(39), 12650–12657. doi:10.1016/j.eswa.2012.05.018

Joseph, P. T., & S. J. (2009). E-Commerce: An Indian Perspective. New Delhi: PHI.

Jungck, P., & Shim, S. S. Y. (2004). Issues in High Speed Internet Security. In Proceedings of Computing Practices. The IEEE Computer Society.

Kalakota, R., & Whinston, A. B. (1996). *Frontiers of electronic commerce.* Pearson Education.

Kalakota, R., & Whinston, A. B. (1997). *Electronic Commerce: A Manager's Guide.* Addison-Wesley.

Kalina, J., & Zvárová, J. (2013). Decision support systems in the process of improving patient safety. In A. Moumtzoglou & A. Kastania (Eds.), *E-health technologies and improving patient safety: Exploring organizational factors* (pp. 71–83). Hershey, PA: IGI Global. doi:10.4018/978-1-4666-2657-7.ch005

Kamanec, K. (2013). E-commerce security tips. *IT Pro Portal.* Retrieved from: http://www.itproportal.com/2013/07/18/e-commerce-security-tips-how-to-stay-safe-when-shopping-online/

Kamel, S. (2006). DSS for strategic decision making. In M. Khosrow-Pour (Ed.), *Cases on information technology and organizational politics & culture* (pp. 230–246). Hershey, PA: IGI Global. doi:10.4018/978-1-59904-411-8.ch015

Kamel, S. (2010). Electronic commerce prospects in emerging economies: Lessons from Egypt. In I. Lee (Ed.), *Encyclopedia of e-business development and management in the global economy* (pp. 1086–1097). Hershey, PA: IGI Global. doi:10.4018/978-1-61520-611-7.ch109

Kamel, S., & Ghoneim, S. (2004). The impact of the role of the government of Egypt on electronic commerce development and growth. In M. Khosrow-Pour (Ed.), *The social and cognitive impacts of e-commerce on modern organizations* (pp. 253–276). Hershey, PA: IGI Global. doi:10.4018/978-1-59140-249-7.ch012

Kamel, S., & Zyada, A. (2005). Using DSS for global competitiveness: An effective information-based decision making process in public administration. In Y. Lan (Ed.), *Global information society: Operating information systems in a dynamic global business environment* (pp. 113–129). Hershey, PA: IGI Global. doi:10.4018/978-1-59140-306-7.ch006

Kame, S. (2015). Electronic Commerce Challenges and Opportunities for Emerging Economies: Case of Egypt. *International Conference on Information Resources Management (CONF-IRM)*, 1-16.

Kang, K.-S. (2001). Effectiveness of Graphical Components in Web Site E-commerce Application-A Cultural Perspective. EJISDC, 7(2), 1-6.

Kang, D., Jang, W., & Park, Y. (2016). Evaluation of e-commerce websites using fuzzy hierarchical TOPSIS based on E-S-QUAL. *Applied Soft Computing*, *42*, 53–65. doi:10.1016/j.asoc.2016.01.017

Karlof, C., Shankar, U., Tygar, J. D., & Wagner, D. (2007, October). Dynamic pharming attacks and locked same-origin policies for web browsers. In *Proceedings of the 14th ACM conference on Computer and communications security* (pp. 58-71). ACM. doi:10.1145/1315245.1315254

Kartiwi, M., & MacGregor, R. C. (2008). Electronic commerce adoption barriers in small to medium-sized enterprises (SMEs) in developed and developing countries: A cross-country comparison. In A. Becker (Ed.), *Electronic commerce: Concepts, methodologies, tools, and applications* (pp. 1441–1457). Hershey, PA: IGI Global. doi:10.4018/978-1-59904-943-4.ch115

Kasemsap, K. (2015a). The role of electronic commerce in the global business environments. In F. Cipolla-Ficarra (Ed.), *Handbook of research on interactive information quality in expanding social network communications* (pp. 304–324). Hershey, PA: IGI Global. doi:10.4018/978-1-4666-7377-9.ch019

Kasemsap, K. (2015b). The role of data mining for business intelligence in knowledge management. In A. Azevedo & M. Santos (Eds.), *Integration of data mining in business intelligence systems* (pp. 12–33). Hershey, PA: IGI Global. doi:10.4018/978-1-4666-6477-7.ch002

Kasemsap, K. (2015c). Implementing business intelligence in contemporary organizations. In A. Haider (Ed.), *Business technologies in contemporary organizations: Adoption, assimilation, and institutionalization* (pp. 177–192). Hershey, PA: IGI Global. doi:10.4018/978-1-4666-6623-8.ch008

Kasemsap, K. (2016a). The fundamentals of neuroeconomics. In B. Christiansen & E. Lechman (Eds.), *Neuroeconomics and the decision-making process* (pp. 1–32). Hershey, PA: IGI Global. doi:10.4018/978-1-4666-9989-2.ch001

Kasemsap, K. (2016b). Advocating electronic business and electronic commerce in the global marketplace. In S. Dixit & A. Sinha (Eds.), *E-retailing challenges and opportunities in the global marketplace* (pp. 1–24). Hershey, PA: IGI Global. doi:10.4018/978-1-4666-9921-2.ch001

Kasemsap, K. (2016c). Implementing electronic commerce in global marketing. In I. Lee (Ed.), *Encyclopedia of e-commerce development, implementation, and management* (pp. 591–602). Hershey, PA: IGI Global. doi:10.4018/978-1-4666-9787-4.ch043

Kasemsap, K. (2016d). Encouraging supply chain networks and customer loyalty in global supply chain. In N. Kamath & S. Saurav (Eds.), *Handbook of research on strategic supply chain management in the retail industry* (pp. 87–112). Hershey, PA: IGI Global. doi:10.4018/978-1-4666-9894-9.ch006

Kasemsap, K. (2016e). Multifaceted applications of data mining, business intelligence, and knowledge management. *International Journal of Social and Organizational Dynamics in IT*, *5*(1), 57–69. doi:10.4018/IJSODIT.2016010104

Kasemsap, K. (2016f). The fundamentals of business intelligence. *International Journal of Organizational and Collective Intelligence*, *6*(2), 12–25. doi:10.4018/IJOCI.2016040102

Kasemsap, K. (2016g). The roles of social media marketing and brand management in global marketing. In W. Ozuem & G. Bowen (Eds.), *Competitive social media marketing strategies* (pp. 173–200). Hershey, PA: IGI Global. doi:10.4018/978-1-4666-9776-8.ch009

Kasemsap, K. (2017a). Mastering intelligent decision support systems in enterprise information management. In G. Sreedhar (Ed.), *Web data mining and the development of knowledge-based decision support systems* (pp. 35–56). Hershey, PA: IGI Global. doi:10.4018/978-1-5225-1877-8.ch004

Kasemsap, K. (2017b). The roles of logistics service providers and supply chain integration in global supply chain. In L. Saglietto & C. Cezanne (Eds.), *Global intermediation and logistics service providers* (pp. 265–285). Hershey, PA: IGI Global. doi:10.4018/978-1-5225-2133-4.ch014

Kasemsap, K. (2017c). Text mining: Current trends and applications. In G. Sreedhar (Ed.), *Web data mining and the development of knowledge-based decision support systems* (pp. 338–358). Hershey, PA: IGI Global. doi:10.4018/978-1-5225-1877-8.ch017

Kasemsap, K. (2017d). Mastering business process management and business intelligence in global business. In M. Tavana, K. Szabat, & K. Puranam (Eds.), *Organizational productivity and performance measurements using predictive modeling and analytics* (pp. 192–212). Hershey, PA: IGI Global. doi:10.4018/978-1-5225-0654-6.ch010

Kasemsap, K. (2018a). The importance of electronic commerce in modern business. In M. Khosrow-Pour (Ed.), *Encyclopedia of information science and technology* (4th ed.; pp. 2791–2801). Hershey, PA: IGI Global. doi:10.4018/978-1-5225-2255-3.ch243

Kasemsap, K. (2018b). Multifaceted applications of the Internet of Things. In M. Khosrow-Pour (Ed.), *Encyclopedia of information science and technology* (4th ed.; pp. 7775–7784). Hershey, PA: IGI Global. doi:10.4018/978-1-5225-2255-3.ch676

Kasemsap, K. (2018c). Facilitating customer relationship management in modern business. In M. Khosrow-Pour (Ed.), *Encyclopedia of information science and technology* (4th ed.; pp. 1594–1604). Hershey, PA: IGI Global. doi:10.4018/978-1-5225-2255-3.ch138

Kaur, K., & Pathak, A. (2015). E-Payment System on E-Commerce in India. *International Journal of Engineering Research and Applications*, *5*(2), 79–87. Retrieved from http://www.ijera.com/papers/Vol5_issue2/Part%20-%201/M502017987.pdf

Khan, A. A. (2013). *Preventing phishing attacks using one time password and user machine identification*. arXiv preprint arXiv:1305.2704

Khedr, A. (2013). Business intelligence framework to support chronic liver disease treatment. *International Journal of Computers & Technology, 4*(2), 307-312.

Kim, H. D., Lee, I., & Lee, C. K. (2013). Building Web 2.0 enterprises: A study of small and medium enterprises in the United States. *International Small Business Journal*, *31*(2), 156–174. doi:10.1177/0266242611409785

Kim, J. H., & Ryu, J. K. (2013). Recent trends on high-performance computing and security. *Cluster Computing*, *16*(2), 207–208. doi:10.1007/s10586-013-0271-x

Kirda, E., Kruegel, C., Banks, G., Vigna, G., & Kemmerer, R. (2006, August). Behavior-based Spyware Detection. *Usenix Security, 6*.

Kivelä, M., Arenas, A., Barthelemy, M., Gleeson, J. P., Moreno, Y., & Porter, M. A. (2014). Multilayer networks. *Journal of Complex Networks*, *2*(3), 203–271. doi:10.1093/comnet/cnu016

Kleesuwan, S., Mitatha, S., Yupapin, P. P., & Piyatamrong, B. (2010). Business intelligence in Thailand's higher educational resources management. *Procedia: Social and Behavioral Sciences*, *2*(1), 84–87. doi:10.1016/j.sbspro.2010.01.018

Korosec, M., Duhovnik, J., & Vukasinovic, N. (2010). Identification and optimization of key process parameters in noncontact laser scanning for reverse engineering. *Journal of Computer-Aided Design*, *42*(8), 744–748. doi:10.1016/j.cad.2010.02.003

Krum, J., Davies, N., & Narayanaswami, C. (2008). *Pervasive Computing User-generated content*. IEEE.

Kuah, A. T. H., & Wang, P. (2017). Fast-expanding "online" markets in South Korea and China: Are they worth pursuing? *Thunderbird International Business Review*, *59*(1), 63–77. doi:10.1002/tie.21779

Kumar, M., & Hanumanthappa, M. (2013, December). Scalable intrusion detection systems log analysis using cloud computing infrastructure. In *Computational Intelligence and Computing Research (ICCIC), 2013 IEEE International Conference on* (pp. 1-4). IEEE. doi:10.1109/ICCIC.2013.6724158

Kumar, S. (2007, July). Smurf-based distributed denial of service (ddos) attack amplification in internet. In *Internet Monitoring and Protection, 2007. ICIMP 2007. Second International Conference on* (pp. 25-25). IEEE.

Kurnia, S., Choudrie, J., Mahbubur, R. M., & Alzougool, B. (2015). E-commerce technology adoption: A Malaysian grocery SME retail sector study. *Journal of Business Research*, *68*(9), 1906–1918. doi:10.1016/j.jbusres.2014.12.010

Lampson. (2004). Computer Security Security in the real World. Proceedings of IEEE Computer, 37, 37-46.

Larson, D., & Chang, V. (2016). A review and future direction of agile, business intelligence, analytics and data science. *International Journal of Information Management*, *36*(5), 700–710. doi:10.1016/j.ijinfomgt.2016.04.013

Lau, F., Rubin, S. H., Smith, M. H., & Trajkovic, L. (2000). Distributed denial of service attacks. In *Systems, Man, and Cybernetics, 2000 IEEE International Conference on* (Vol. 3, pp. 2275-2280). IEEE. doi:10.1109/ICSMC.2000.886455

Lawrence, E. (2000). *Internet Commerce: Digital Models for Business*. New Delhi: Wiley.

Lebraty, J., & Godé, C. (2015). Assessing the performance of decision support systems in military environment: The 3C method. In A. Mesquita & C. Tsai (Eds.), *Human behavior, psychology, and social interaction in the digital era* (pp. 45–70). Hershey, PA: IGI Global. doi:10.4018/978-1-4666-8450-8.ch003

Lee, M.-W., & Kim, S. (2011), Integrating code search into the development session. *Proceedings of the 27th International Conference on Data Engineering*, 1336-1339. doi:10.1109/ICDE.2011.5767948

Lee, S. Y. T., & Phang, C. W. (2015). Leveraging social media for electronic commerce in Asia: Research areas and opportunities. *Electronic Commerce Research and Applications*, *14*(3), 145–149. doi:10.1016/j.elerap.2015.02.001

Lee, Y., & Lee, Y. (2013). Toward scalable internet traffic measurement and analysis with hadoop. *Computer Communication Review*, *43*(1), 5–13. doi:10.1145/2427036.2427038

Lei, J., & Ghorbani, A. (2012). Improved competitive learning neural networks for network intrusion and fraud detection. *Neurocomputing*, *1*(75), 135–145. doi:10.1016/j.neucom.2011.02.021

Leonard, K. J. (1993). Detecting credit card fraud using expert systems. *Computers & Industrial Engineering*, 25.

Levy, P. (2012). *Simple Strategies for Enhancing eCommerce Profitability*. First Data Corporation.

Lexis Nexis. (2014). *True cost of fraud study*. Retrieved from http://www.lexisnexis.com/risk/insights/true-cost-fraud.aspx

Li & Xue. (2011). *A Survey on Web Application Security (Technical report)*. Vanderbilt University.

Lin, C., Jalleh, G., & Huang, Y. (2016). Evaluating and managing electronic commerce and outsourcing projects in hospitals. In A. Dwivedi (Ed.), *Reshaping medical practice and care with health information systems* (pp. 132–172). Hershey, PA: IGI Global. doi:10.4018/978-1-4666-9870-3.ch005

Lipschutz, S. (n.d.). *Schaum's outline of Data Structures*. New Delhi. *Tata McGraw-Hill Publishing Company Limited.*

Li, S. T., Shue, L. Y., & Lee, S. F. (2008). Business intelligence approach to supporting strategy-making of ISP service management. *Expert Systems with Applications*, *35*(3), 739–754. doi:10.1016/j.eswa.2007.07.049

Liu, A. X. (2012, March). Firewall policy change-impact analysis. *Journal of ACM Transactions on Internet Technology*, *11*(4), 15.

Liu, S., Duffy, A. H., Whitfield, R. I., Boyle, I. M., & McKenna, I. (2009). Towards the realization of an integrated decision support environment for organizational decision making. *International Journal of Decision Support System Technology*, *1*(4), 38–58. doi:10.4018/jdsst.2009062603

M., R. V., & G., V. M. (2017). DSS for web mining using recommendation system. In G. Sreedhar (Ed.), *Web data mining and development of knowledge-based decision support systems* (pp. 22-34). Hershey, PA: IGI Global.

Mag, P. C. (n.d.). *E-Commerce Security Tips*. Retrieved from: http://www.pcmag.com/article2/0,2817,2421846,00.asp

Malekian, D., & Hashemi, M. R. (2013). *An Adaptive Profile based Fraud Detection Framework For Handling Concept Drift*. Academic Press.

Maleki, H., & Zahir, S. (2013). A comprehensive literature review of the rank reversal phenomenon in the analytic hierarchy process. *Journal of Multi-Criteria Decision Analysis*, *20*(3-4), 141–155. doi:10.1002/mcda.1479

Manadhata, P. K., Horne, W., & Rao, P. (Forthcoming). Big Data for Security: Processing Very Large Enterprise Event Datasets. In B. Furht & A. Escalante (Eds.), *Handbook of Big Data Analytics. s.l.* Springer. doi:10.1145/2382416.2382420

Mandic, K., Delibasic, B., Knezevic, S., & Benkovic, S. (2014). Analysis of the financial parameters of Serbian banks through the application of the fuzzy AHP and TOPSIS methods. *Economic Modelling, 43*, 30–37. doi:10.1016/j.econmod.2014.07.036

Mao, N., Song, M., & Deng, S. (2016). Application of TOPSIS method in evaluating the effects of supply vane angle of a task/ambient air conditioning system on energy utilization and thermal comfort. *Applied Energy, 180*, 536–545. doi:10.1016/j.apenergy.2016.08.011

Markov, Z., & Larose, D. T. (2007). *Data Mining the Web: Uncovering Patterns in Web Content*. Academic Press.

Martin, A., Lakshmi, T. M., & Venkatesan, V. P. (2014). An information delivery model for banking business. *International Journal of Information Management, 34*(2), 139–150. doi:10.1016/j.ijinfomgt.2013.12.003

Masmoudi, M., Benaissa, M., & Chabchoub, H. (2014). Optimisation of e-commerce logistics distribution system: Problem modelling and exact resolution. *International Journal of Business Performance and Supply Chain Modelling, 6*(3/4), 358–375. doi:10.1504/IJBPSCM.2014.065275

Masuda, T. (1990). Hierarchical sensitivity analysis of priority used in analytic hierarchy process. *International Journal of Systems Science, 21*(2), 415–427. doi:10.1080/00207729008910371

McCloskey, D. W. (2008). The importance of ease of use, usefulness, and trust to online consumers: An examination of the technology acceptance model with older consumers. In A. Becker (Ed.), *Electronic commerce: Concepts, methodologies, tools, and applications* (pp. 1400–1417). Hershey, PA: IGI Global. doi:10.4018/978-1-59904-943-4.ch112

Meirong, T., & Xuedong, C. (2010). Application of Agent-based Web Mining in E-business. *Second International Conference on Intelligent Human-Machine Systems and Cybernetics.*

Mell, P., & Grance, T. (2011). *The NIST definition of cloud.* Recommendations of the National Institute of Standards and Technology.

Mijatovic, V. (2004). Mechanisms for Detection and Prevention of Email Spamming. P*eer to Peer and SPAM in the Internet, 135.*

Miller, D., Harris, S., Harper, A., VanDyke, S., & Blask, C. (2010). *Security information and event management (SIEM) implementation.* McGraw Hill Professional.

Miller, S., McRobbie, G., & Begg, C. (2016, July). Business intelligence tools: Should they be 'gamified'? Project 'GamBIT': Evaluating user engagement. In *SAI Computing Conference (SAI)*, 2016 (pp. 758-763). IEEE. doi:10.1109/SAI.2016.7556065

Minegishi, T., & Niimi, A. (2011). Proposal of credit card fraudulent use detection by online- type decision tree construction and verification of generality. *Int. J. Inf. Secur. Res., 1*(4), 229–235.

Minoli, D., & Minoli, E. (1997). *Web Commerce Technology Handbook*. McGraw Hill.

Mitra, J. (2010). *E-Commerce*. Retrieved April 10 from https://www.slideshare.net/jsm268/e-commerce-3717853

Modi, T. (2011). *The cloud SOA ecosystem, ebiZ the insider's guide to next generation BPM, 2011.* Available at http://www.ebizq.net/topics/soa_management/features/11787.html?page=2

Moghaddam, S., & Ester, M. (2012). Aspect-based opinion mining from online reviews. In *Tutorial at SIGIR Conference*. Academic Press.

Morgan, J. P. (2015). *Payments Fraud and Control Survey report.* Retrieved from www.AFPonline.org

Moro, S., Cortez, P., & Rita, P. (2015). Business intelligence in banking: A literature analysis from 2002 to 2013 using text mining and latent Dirichlet allocation. *Expert Systems with Applications, 42*(3), 1314–1324. doi:10.1016/j.eswa.2014.09.024

Morris, L. V. (2016). The imperative for faculty: Understanding student success technologies and other analytics. *Innovative Higher Education, 41*(4), 269–271. doi:10.1007/s10755-016-9369-4

Nahorney, B. (2014). *Internet Security Threat Report 2014.* Retrived from www.threatmetrix.com

Netessine, S., & Rudi, N. (2006). Supply Chain Choice on the Internet. *Journal of Management Science, 52*(6), 844–864. doi:10.1287/mnsc.1060.0512

Newman, M. E. J. (2010). *Networks: An Introduction.* Oxford University Press. doi:10.1093/acprof:oso/9780199206650.001.0001

Ngai, E. W. T., Hu, Y., Wong, Y. H., Chen, Y., & Sun, X. (2011). The application of data mining techniques in financial fraud detection: A classification framework and an academic review of literature. *Decision Support Systems, 50*(3), 559–569. doi:10.1016/j.dss.2010.08.006

Ngwenya, B. (2013). Decision support systems: An e-government strategy to enhance human resources output in public sector organisations. In Z. Mahmood (Ed.), *Developing e-government projects: Frameworks and methodologies* (pp. 44–62). Hershey, PA: IGI Global. doi:10.4018/978-1-4666-4245-4.ch003

Nielsen, J. (2000). Designing Web Usability. New Riders Press.

Niranjanamurthy, M., & Chahar, D. D. R. (2013). The study of E-Commerce Security Issues and Solutions. *International Journal of Advanced Research in Computer and Communication Engineering, 2*(7).

Niu, L., Lu, J., Zhang, G., & Wu, D. (2013). FACETS: A cognitive business intelligence system. *Information Systems, 38*(6), 835–862. doi:10.1016/j.is.2013.02.002

O'Leary, D. E. (2000). *Enterprise resource planning systems: Systems, life cycle, electronic commerce, and risk.* Cambridge University Press.

Obayiuwana, E., & Falowo, O. (2015, September). A multimoora approach to access network selection process in heterogeneous wireless networks. In *AFRICON, 2015* (pp. 1–5). IEEE. doi:10.1109/AFRCON.2015.7331973

Oh, J., Im, C., & Jeong, H. (2010, March). A system for analyzing advance bot behavior. In *International Conference on Information Systems, Technology and Management* (pp. 56-63). Springer Berlin Heidelberg. doi:10.1007/978-3-642-12035-0_7

Oliveira, T., Alhinho, M., Rita, P., & Dhillon, G. (2017). Modelling and testing consumer trust dimensions in e-commerce. *Computers in Human Behavior, 71*, 153–164. doi:10.1016/j.chb.2017.01.050

Ong, C. E., & Teh, D. (2016). Redress procedures expected by consumers during a business-to-consumer e-commerce dispute. *Electronic Commerce Research and Applications, 17*, 150–160. doi:10.1016/j.elerap.2016.04.006

Oriyano. (2009). *Anatomy of a Web attack: Understanding the most common attack types.* IBM Corporation.

Orrin, S. (2007). The SOA/XML Threat Model and New XML/SOA/Web 2.0 Attacks & Threats. In Security conference DEFCON (Vol. 15). Academic Press.

Ortega, C. M., Lorences, C. P., & Marx-Gómez, H. J. (2014). Architecture for business intelligence design on the IT service management scope. In *Engineering and Management of IT-based Service Systems* (pp. 201–213). Springer Berlin Heidelberg. doi:10.1007/978-3-642-39928-2_10

Oselio, B., Kulesza, A., & Hero, A. O. (2011). *Multi-layer graph analytics for social networks*. University of Michigan. Retrieved from http://www.cs.cmu.edu/~enron

Oztaysi, B. (2014). A decision model for information technology selection using AHP integrated TOPSIS-Grey: The case of content management systems. *Knowledge-Based Systems*, *70*, 44–54. doi:10.1016/j.knosys.2014.02.010

Padma, V., Sanjana, B. L., & Rao, M. V. (2017). Comparative study for selection of an item based on multi-criteria DSS. *International Journal of Computer Science and Information Security*, *15*(2).

Pak, A., & Paroubek, P. (2010). *Twitter as a corpus for sentiment analysis and opinion mining*. LREC.

Palopoli, L., Rosaci, D., & Sarné, G. M. L. (2016). A distributed and multi-tiered software architecture for assessing e-commerce recommendations. *Concurrency and Computation*, *28*(18), 4507–4531. doi:10.1002/cpe.3798

Pang, B., & Lee, L. (2008). Opinion mining and sentiment analysis. *Foundations and Trends in Information Retrieval*, *2*(1-2), 1–135.

Papazafeiropoulou, A., & Pouloudi, A. (2003). Social issues in electronic commerce: Implications for policy makers. In M. Khosrow-Pour (Ed.), *Advanced topics in information resources management* (Vol. 2, pp. 173–191). Hershey, PA: IGI Global. doi:10.4018/978-1-59140-062-2.ch009

Pappas, C. (2015). *Boost your eLearning Course Sales: 5 Tips to choose an eCommerce Platform*. Retrieved April 4, 2017 from https://elearningindustry.com/boost-elearning-course-sales-5-tips-choose-ecommerce-platform

Park, B. J., & Han, J. S. (2016). Efficient decision support for detecting content polluters on social networks: An approach based on automatic knowledge acquisition from behavioral patterns. *Information Technology & Management*, *17*(1), 95–105. doi:10.1007/s10799-015-0250-4

Park, K. H., & Park, K.-W. (2011). ACCENT: Cognitive cryptography plugged compression for SSL/TLS-based cloud computing services. *Journal of ACM Transactions on Internet Technology*, *11*(2), 7.

Parmar, B. (2012). Protecting against spear-phishing. *Computer Fraud & Security*, *2012*(1), 8–11. doi:10.1016/S1361-3723(12)70007-6

Pavlou, P. A., & Ratnasingam, P. (2003). Technology trust in B2B electronic commerce: Conceptual foundations. In K. Kangas (Ed.), *Business strategies for information technology management* (pp. 200–215). Hershey, PA: IGI Global. doi:10.4018/978-1-93177-745-2.ch014

Petite, S. (2002). *Anatomy of a Web Application: Security Considerations*. White Paper. Sanctum Inc.

Phan, D. D., & Vogel, D. R. (2010). A model of customer relationship management and business intelligence systems for catalogue and online retailers. *Information & Management*, *47*(2), 69–77. doi:10.1016/j.im.2009.09.001

Phillips-Wren, G. E. (2010). Intelligent agents in decision support systems. In M. Hunter (Ed.), *Strategic information systems: Concepts, methodologies, tools, and applications* (pp. 857–866). Hershey, PA: IGI Global. doi:10.4018/978-1-60566-677-8.ch055

Piedade, M. B., & Santos, M. Y. (2009). *Business intelligence in higher education: managing the relationships with students*. Academic Press.

Pitkow, J. E., & Kehoe, C. M. (1996). Emerging trends in the WWW user population. *Communications of the ACM, 39*(6), 106–108. doi:10.1145/228503.228525

Pozzolo, A. D., Caelen, O., Waterschoot, S., & Bontempi, G. (2013).Racing for unbalanced methods selection. *Proceedings of the IEEE 14th International Conference on Intelligent Data Engineering and Automated Learning (IDEAL).* doi:10.1007/978-3-642-41278-3_4

Pozzolo, A. D., Caelen, O., & Bontempi, G. (2015). When is under sampling effective in unbalanced classification tasks. *European Conference on Machine Learning(ECML-KDD).*

Pozzolo, A. D., Caelen, O., Johnson, R. A., & Bontempi, G. (2015). Calibrating Probability with Undersampling for Unbalanced Classification. *IEEE Symposium on Computational Intelligence and Data Mining (CIDM).* doi:10.1109/SSCI.2015.33

Prathibha, P. G., & Dileesh, E. D. (2013). Design of a hybrid intrusion detection system using snort and hadoop. *International Journal of Computers and Applications, 73*(10).

Privacy Rights Clearinghouse. (2000). Fact Sheet 23: Online Shopping Tips: E-Commerce and You. *Privacy Rights Clearinghouse.* Retrieved from: https://www.privacyrights.org/online-shopping-tips-e-commerce-and-you

Rachna, & Singh, P. (2013). Issues and Challenges of Electronic Payment Systems. *International Journal for Research in Management and Pharmacy, 2*(9), 25-30. Retrieved from https://raijmronlineresearch.files.wordpress.com/2017/08/3_25-30-rachna-et-al.pdf

Rahimi, M. I. (2006). *Web application firewall.* University Technology, Mara.

Rahman, S. M., & Raisinghani, M. S. (2000). *Electronic commerce: Opportunity and challenges.* Hershey, PA: IGI Global. doi:10.4018/978-1-87828-976-6

Raisinghani, M. S. (2000). Electronic commerce at the dawn of the third millennium. In S. Rahman & M. Raisinghani (Eds.), *Electronic commerce: Opportunity and challenges* (pp. 1–20). Hershey, PA: IGI Global. doi:10.4018/978-1-878289-76-6.ch001

Raj Garg, C. A. (2016). Importance of E-Commerce Payment System in Less paper Work. *International Journal of Business Quantitative Economics and Applied Management Research, 2*(11), 47–59. Retrieved from http://ijbemr.com/wp-content/uploads/2016/05/IMPORTANCE-OF-E-COMMERCE-PAYMENT-SYSTEM-IN-LESS-PAPER-WORK.pdf

Rajaraman, A., Leskovec, J., & Ullman, J. D. (2011). *Mining of Massive Datasets.* Cambridge University Press. doi:10.1017/CBO9781139058452

Rajaraman, V. (2009). *Essentials of E-Commerce Techonology.* New Delhi: PHI.

Ramakrishnan, T., Jones, M. C., & Sidorova, A. (2012). Factors influencing business intelligence (BI) data collection strategies: An empirical investigation. *Decision Support Systems, 52*(2), 486–496. doi:10.1016/j.dss.2011.10.009

Ranjan, J. (2009). Business Intelligence: Concepts, components, techniques and benefits. *Journal of Theoretical and Applied Information Technology, 9*(1), 60–70.

Rao, B., & Mishra, S. N. (2015). *An Approach to Mining Information from Telephone Graph Using Graph Mining Techniques. In Proceedings of iCATccT 2015* (pp. 424–429). Davangere, India: BIET.

Rao, B., Mishra, S. N., & Maharana, H. S. (2015). Algorithm for Representation of Call-Duration Graphs of Telephone Graph Using Multi-Layer Graph Techniques. *Proceedings of ICCI 2015 in Advances in Computational Intelligence,* 415-425.

Rao, B., Mishra, S. N., & Maharana, H. S. (2016). An Approach to Mining Strong and Weak Communicator Sub-Graphs from Email Graph Using Graph Mining Techniques. *Proceedings of ICCTICT, 2016*, 271–276.

Rao, B., & Mitra, A. (2016). *Graph Mining and Its Applications in Studying Community Based Graph under the Preview of Social Network. In Product Innovation through Knowledge Management and Social Media Strategies*. IGI Global. doi:10.4018/976-1-4666-9607-5

Razali, R. (2002). *Global Information Assurance Certification Paper*. Retrieved from https://www.giac.org/paper/gsec/1799/overview-e-cash-implementation-security-issues/103204

Reaux, R. A., & Carroll, J. M. (1997). Human factors in information access of distributed systems. In G. Salvendy (Ed.), *Handbook of Human Factors and Ergonomics* (2nd ed.). New York: Wiley.

Richards, K. (1999). Network based intrusion detection: A review of technologies. *Computers & Security*, *18*(8), 671–682. doi:10.1016/S0167-4048(99)80131-X

Robinson, N., Graux, H., Parrilli, D., Klautzer, L., & Lorenzo, V. (2011). *Comparative study on legislative and non-legislative measures to combat identity theft and identity related crime*. Technical Report TR-982-EC, RAND Europe and Time-lex.

Rodríguez-Gómez, R. A., Maciá-Fernández, G., & García-Teodoro, P. (2013). Survey and taxonomy of botnet research through life-cycle. *ACM Computing Surveys*, *45*(4), 45. doi:10.1145/2501654.2501659

Rouhani, S., Ghazanfari, M., & Jafari, M. (2012). Evaluation model of business intelligence for enterprise systems using fuzzy TOPSIS. *Expert Systems with Applications*, *39*(3), 3764–3771. doi:10.1016/j.eswa.2011.09.074

Rubin, E., & Rubin, A. (2013). The impact of business intelligence systems on stock return volatility. *Information & Management*, *50*(2), 67–75. doi:10.1016/j.im.2013.01.002

Russell, S., & Forgionne, G. (2009). Decision support-related resource presence and availability awareness for DSS in pervasive computing environments. *International Journal of Decision Support System Technology*, *1*(1), 15–34. doi:10.4018/jdsst.2009010102

Ryman-Tubb, N., & Krause, P. (2011). Neural Network Rule Extraction to Detect Credit Card Fraud. In L. Iliadis & C. Jayne (Eds.), *Engineering Applications of Neural Networks, IFIP Advances in Information and Communication Technology 363* (pp. 101–110). Springer Berlin Heidelberg. doi:10.1007/978-3-642-23957-1_12

Sahin, Y., & Duman, E. (2011). Detecting Credit Card Fraud by Decision Trees and Support Vector Machines. *Proceeding of International MultiConference of Engineers and Computer Scientist*.

Sakthivel, G., Ilangkumaran, M., & Gaikwad, A. (2015). A hybrid multi-criteria decision modeling approach for the best biodiesel blend selection based on ANP-TOPSIS analysis. *Ain Shams Engineering Journal*, *6*(1), 239–256. doi:10.1016/j.asej.2014.08.003

Salerno, J. J., & Boulware, D. M. (2006). *U.S. Patent No. 7,072,890*. Washington, DC: U.S. Patent and Trademark Office.

Sangkatsanee, P., & Charnsripinyo, C. (2011). Practical real-time intrusion detection using machine learning approaches. *Journal of Computer Communications*, *34*(18), 2227–2235. doi:10.1016/j.comcom.2011.07.001

Santos, C. T., & Osorio, F. S. (2004). AdapTIVE: An Intelligent Virtual Environment and Its Application in E-Commerce. *COMPSAC, 2004*, 468–473.

Sarmento, L., Carvalho, P., Silva, M. J., & de Oliveira, E. (2009). Automatic creation of a reference corpusfor political opinion mining in user-generated content. In *Proceedings of the 1st international CIKM workshopon Topic-sentiment analysis for mass opinion* (pp. 29–36). ACM. doi:10.1145/1651461.1651468

Sarode, R. M. (2015). Future of E-Commerce in India Challenges & Opportunities. *International Journal of Applied Research, 1*(12), 646–650.

Schneide, P. G. (2007). *E-Commerce: Strategy, Technology and Implementation.* New Delhi: Cengage Learning.

Scholz, M., Dorner, V., Schryen, G., & Benlian, A. (2017). A configuration-based recommender system for supporting e-commerce decisions. *European Journal of Operational Research, 259*(1), 205–215. doi:10.1016/j.ejor.2016.09.057

Senthil, S., Srirangacharyulu, B., & Ramesh, A. (2014). A robust hybrid multi-criteria decision making methodology for contractor evaluation and selection in third-party reverse logistics. *Expert Systems with Applications, 41*(1), 50–58. doi:10.1016/j.eswa.2013.07.010

Setzekorn, K., Sugumaran, V., & Patnayakuni, N. (2004). A comparison of implementation resistance factors for DMSS versus other information systems. In M. Khosrow-Pour (Ed.), Advanced topics in information resources management (Vol. 3, pp. 315–332). Hershey, PA: IGI Global. doi:10.4018/978-1-59140-253-4.ch015

Sharma, A., & Vyas, P. (2010). Decision support systems in Indian organized retail sector. In *Business information systems: Concepts, methodologies, tools and applications* (pp. 1043–1055). Hershey, PA: IGI Global. doi:10.4018/978-1-61520-969-9.ch062

Sharma, M., Yadav, K., Yadav, N., & Ferdinand, K. C. (2017). Zika virus pandemic—analysis of Facebook as a social media health information platform. *American Journal of Infection Control, 45*(3), 301–302. doi:10.1016/j.ajic.2016.08.022 PMID:27776823

Sharma, R., Nigam, S., & Jain, R. (2013). *Supervised opinion mining techniques: A survey.* Academic Press.

Shawar, B. A., & Atwell, E. (2007). Chatbots: are they really useful? In *LDV Forum* (Vol. 22, No. 1, pp. 29-49). Academic Press.

Shawar, B. A., & Atwell, E. (2003). Using dialogue corpora to train a chatbot. *Proceedings of the Corpus Linguistics 2003 conference*, 681-690.

Sherly, K.K., & Nedunchezhian, R. (2010). *Boat adaptive credit card fraud detection system.* Academic Press.

Shih, H. S., Shyur, H. J., & Lee, E. S. (2007). An extension of TOPSIS for group decision making. *Mathematical and Computer Modelling, 45*(7), 801–813. doi:10.1016/j.mcm.2006.03.023

Shneiderman, B. (1997). Designing information-abundant web sites: Issues recommendations. *International Journal of Sociology, 47*, 5–29.

Shopify ecommerce feature list. (n.d.). Retrieved August 12, 2017 from https://www.shopify.in/tour/ecommerce-cms

Shopping Online. (2014). How to shop online without a credit card. *Shopping Online.* Retrieved from: http://shoppingonline-tips.blogspot.in/2014_07_01_archive.html

Shukla, A., & Dhir, S. (2016). Tools for Data Visualization in Business Intelligence: Case Study Using the Tool Qlikview. In *Information Systems Design and Intelligent Applications* (pp. 319–326). New Delhi: Springer. doi:10.1007/978-81-322-2752-6_31

Sima, C. (2004). *Security at Next Level. Whitepaper.* SPI Dynamic Inc.

Singh, K., Guntuku, S. C., Thakur, A., & Hota, C. (2014). Big data analytics framework for peer-to-peer botnet detection using random forests. *Information Sciences*, *278*, 488–497. doi:10.1016/j.ins.2014.03.066

Singh, M., & Huhns, M. (2004). *Service-Oriented Computing: Semantics, Processes, Agents*. Wiley. doi:10.1002/0470091509

Singh, N., Yadav, M., & Sahu, O. (2016). Consumer acceptance of apparel e-commerce: Ethiopia. *Intellectual Economics*, *10*(1), 55–62. doi:10.1016/j.intele.2016.06.001

Sobieska-Karpinska, J., & Hernes, M. (2010). Value of information in distributed decision support systems. In M. Pankowska (Ed.), *Infonomics for distributed business and decision-making environments: Creating information system ecology* (pp. 153–176). Hershey, PA: IGI Global. doi:10.4018/978-1-60566-890-1.ch009

Sodiya, A. S., Akinwale, A. T., Okeleye, K. A., & Emmanuel, J. A. (2012). An integrated decision support system for intercropping. In P. Zaraté (Ed.), *Integrated and strategic advancements in decision making support systems* (pp. 199–216). Hershey, PA: IGI Global. doi:10.4018/978-1-4666-1746-9.ch015

Sreedhar, G. (2017). Development of Efficient Decision Support Systems using Web Data Mining. In G. Sreedhar (Ed.), *Web Data Mining and the Development of Knowledge based Decision Support Systems* (pp. 1–11). Hershey, PA: Information Science Publishing. doi:10.4018/978-1-5225-1877-8.ch001

Sreedhar, G., & Anandaraja Chari, A. (2017). First Look on Web Mining Techniques to Improve Business Intelligence of E-Commerce Web Applications. In *Hand Book of Research on Advanced Data Mining Techniques and Applications of Business Intelligence* (pp. 298–314). Hershey, PA: Information Science Publishing. doi:10.4018/978-1-5225-2031-3.ch018

Sridevi, M., Rao, R. R., & Rao, M. V. (2016). A survey on Recommender Systems. *International Journal of Computer Science and Information Security*, *14*(5).

Stay Safe Online. (n.d.). Online shopping. *Stay Safe Online*. Retrieved from: http://www.staysafeonline.org/stay-safe-online/protect-your-personal-information/online-shopping

Stone, J. (2016). *The Best eCommerce Software of 2017*. Retrieved April 12, 2017 from http://www.toptenreviews.com/business/internet/best-ecommerce-software

Strzębicki, D. (2015). The development of electronic commerce in agribusiness: The Polish example. *Procedia Economics and Finance*, *23*, 1314–1320. doi:10.1016/S2212-5671(15)00573-0

Studer, R. (2011). Economic and technical analysis of botnets and denial-of-service attacks. *Communication Systems*, *4*, 19.

Sudjianto, A., Nair, S., Yuan, M., Zhang, A. J., Kern, D., & Cela-Diaz, F. (2010). Statistical Methods for Fighting Financial Crimes. *Technometrics*, *52*(1), 5–19. doi:10.1198/TECH.2010.07032

Sumanjeet, S. (2009). Emergence of payment systems in the age of electronic commerce: The state of art. *2009 First Asian Himalayas International Conference on Internet*, *3*(3), 18-40. Retrieved from https://globip.com/articles/asiapacific-vol3-article2.pdf

Sun, Z., Zou, H., & Strang, K. (2015). *Big Data Analytics as a service for Business Intelligence*. International Federation for Information Processing.

Suryawanshi, D. J., & Mande, U. A (2014). *Parallel Processing of Internet Traffic Measurement and Analysis Using Hadoop*. Academic Press.

Su, Z., & Wassermann, G. (2006, January). The essence of command injection attacks in web applications. *ACM SIGPLAN Notices*, *41*(1), 372–382. doi:10.1145/1111320.1111070

Tang, G., Pei, J., & Luk, W.-S. (2014). Email mining: Tasks, common techniques, and tools. *Knowledge and Information Systems*, *41*(1), 1–31. doi:10.1007/s10115-013-0658-2

Tan, Z., Jamdagni, A., He, X., Nanda, P., & Liu, R. P. (2014). A system for denial-of-service attack detection based on multivariate correlation analysis. *IEEE Transactions on Parallel and Distributed Systems*, *25*(2), 447–456. doi:10.1109/TPDS.2013.146

Tao, Z. (2013, August). Detection and service security mechanism of xml injection attacks. In *International Conference on Information Computing and Applications* (pp. 67-75). Springer. doi:10.1007/978-3-642-53703-5_8

Tavana, M., & Hatami-Marbini, A. (2011). A group AHP-TOPSIS framework for human spaceflight mission planning at NASA. *Expert Systems with Applications*, *38*(11), 13588–13603.

The New Boston. (n.d.). *Featured Tutorial - Android App Development for Beginners*. Retrieved in February 2017, from http://www.thenewboston.com/

Threats to E-Commerce Servers-Part I. (n.d.). Retrieved from: http://www.technologyexecutivesclub.com/Articles/security/artThreatstoEcommerceServers.php

Tobias, P. A., & Trindade, D. (2011). *Applied reliability*. CRC Press.

Toland, J., & Klepper, R. (2009). Business-to-consumer electronic commerce in developing countries. In M. Khosrow-Pour (Ed.), *Encyclopedia of information science and technology* (2nd ed.; pp. 489–494). Hershey, PA: IGI Global. doi:10.4018/978-1-60566-026-4.ch081

Tolk, A. (2010). Using simulation systems for decision support. In *Business information systems: Concepts, methodologies, tools and applications* (pp. 2163–2182). Hershey, PA: IGI Global. doi:10.4018/978-1-61520-969-9.ch131

Tran, C., Abraham, A., & Jain, L. (2008). Soft computing paradigms and regression trees in decision support systems. In V. Sugumaran (Ed.), *Intelligent information technologies: Concepts, methodologies, tools, and applications* (pp. 1011–1035). Hershey, PA: IGI Global. doi:10.4018/978-1-59904-941-0.ch058

Triantaphyllou, E., & Lin, C. T. (1996). Development and evaluation of five fuzzy multiattribute decision-making methods. *International Journal of Approximate Reasoning, 14*(4), 281-310.

Trumpy, E., Bertani, R., Manzella, A., & Sander, M. (2015). The web-oriented framework of the world geothermal production database: A business intelligence platform for wide data distribution and analysis. *Renewable Energy*, *74*, 379–389. doi:10.1016/j.renene.2014.08.036

Tsipenyuk, K., Chess, B., & McGraw, G. (2005). Seven pernicious kingdoms: A taxonomy of software security errors. *IEEE Security and Privacy*, *3*(6), 81–84. doi:10.1109/MSP.2005.159

Tutorials Point. (2017, August 15). *E-Commerce Security Systems*. Retrieved from https://www.tutorialspoint.com/e_commerce/e_commerce_security.htm

Tyagi, A. K., & Aghila, G. (2011). A wide scale survey on botnet. *International Journal of Computers and Applications*, *34*(9), 9–22.

Tynjala, T. (2012). Validation in supply chain decision support systems. *International Journal of Information Systems and Supply Chain Management*, *5*(2), 39–58. doi:10.4018/jisscm.2012040103

Types of software testing and definitions of testing terms. (2017, April 17). Retrieved from http://www.softwaretestinghelp.com/types-of-software-testing/

UNDP. (2011). *Invitation to Bid - Version Control Software*. United Nations Development Programme Procurement Support Office.

Unleash the Power of Predictive Analytics with the SAP HANA. (2016). Retrieved from www.sap.com/trypredictive

Vahidov, R. (2004). Empowering modern managers: Towards an agent-based decision support system. In H. Nemati & C. Barko (Eds.), *Organizational data mining: Leveraging enterprise data resources for optimal performance* (pp. 170–187). Hershey, PA: IGI Global. doi:10.4018/978-1-59140-134-6.ch012

Van Vlasselaer, V., Bravo, C., Caelen, O., Eliassi-Rad, T., Akoglu, L., Snoeck, M., & Baesens, B. (2015). APATE: a novel approach for automated credit card transaction fraud detection using network-based extensions. In Decis. Support Syst. (pp. 38– 48). Academic Press.

Vargiu, E., & Urru, M. (2012). Exploiting web scraping in a collaborative filtering-based approach to web advertising. *Artificial Intelligence Review*, *2*(1), 44.

Verizon Inc. (2010). *2010 Data Breach Investigation Report*. Retrieved July 15th, 2013, from http://www.verizonenterprise.com/resources/reports/rp_2010-data-breach-report_en_xg.pdf

Vieira, M., Antunes, N., & Madeira, H. (2009, June). Using web security scanners to detect vulnerabilities in web services. In *Dependable Systems & Networks, 2009. DSN'09. IEEE/IFIP International Conference on* (pp. 566-571). IEEE. doi:10.1109/DSN.2009.5270294

Vlasselaer, V., Eliassi-Rad, T., Akoglu, L., Snoeck, M., & Basens, B. (2015). Gotchal Network Based fraud Detection for Social Security Fraud. *Management Science*.

Von Ahn, L., Blum, M., Hopper, N. J., & Langford, J. (2003, May). CAPTCHA: Using hard AI problems for security. In *International Conference on the Theory and Applications of Cryptographic Techniques* (pp. 294-311). Springer Berlin Heidelberg. doi:10.1007/3-540-39200-9_18

Wang, J., & Radosevich, D. (2010). Decision support systems. In M. Hunter (Ed.), *Strategic information systems: Concepts, methodologies, tools, and applications* (pp. 114–121). Hershey, PA: IGI Global. doi:10.4018/978-1-60566-677-8.ch009

Wang, J., & Yao, J. (2010). Group decision support systems. In M. Hunter (Ed.), *Strategic information systems: Concepts, methodologies, tools, and applications* (pp. 1543–1550). Hershey, PA: IGI Global. doi:10.4018/978-1-60566-677-8.ch099

Wang, S., Cavusoglu, H., & Deng, Z. (2016). Early mover advantage in e-commerce platforms with low entry barriers: The role of customer relationship management capabilities. *Information & Management*, *53*(2), 197–206. doi:10.1016/j.im.2015.09.011

Wang, X. (2015). A comprehensive decision making model for the evaluation of green operations initiatives. *Technological Forecasting and Social Change*, *95*, 191–207. doi:10.1016/j.techfore.2015.02.004

Wang, X., Kohno, T., & Blakley, B. (2014, June). Polymorphism as a defense for automated attack of websites. In *International Conference on Applied Cryptography and Network Security* (pp. 513-530). Springer International Publishing. doi:10.1007/978-3-319-07536-5_30

Wasserman, S., & Faust, K. (1994). *Social Network Analysis: Methods and Applications*. Cambridge, UK: Cambridge University Press. doi:10.1017/CBO9780511815478

Watson, D., & Riden, J. (2008, April). The honeynet project: Data collection tools, infrastructure, archives and analysis. In *Information Security Threats Data Collection and Sharing, 2008. WISTDCS'08. WOMBAT Workshop on* (pp. 24-30). IEEE.

Weigold, T., Kramp, T., Hermann, R., Höring, F., Buhler, P., & Baentsch, M. (2008, March). The Zurich Trusted Information Channel–an efficient defence against man-in-the-middle and malicious software attacks. In *International Conference on Trusted Computing* (pp. 75-91). Springer Berlin Heidelberg. doi:10.1007/978-3-540-68979-9_6

Wells, J. D., & Hess, T. J. (2008). Understanding decision-making in data warehousing and related decision support systems: An explanatory study of a customer relationship management application. In J. Wang (Ed.), *Data warehousing and mining: Concepts, methodologies, tools, and applications* (pp. 2185–2200). Hershey, PA: IGI Global. doi:10.4018/978-1-59904-951-9.ch129

Whiteley, D. (2005). *E-Commerce: Strategy, Technologies and Application, Information System Series*. New Delhi: TMH.

Wilbur, K. C., & Zhu, Y. (2009). Click fraud. *Marketing Science*, *28*(2), 293–308. doi:10.1287/mksc.1080.0397

Wilson, T., Wiebe, J., & Hoffmann, P. (2005). Recognizing contextual polarity in phrase-level sentiment analysis. In *Proceedings of the conference on human language technology and empirical methods in natural language processing*. Association for Computational Linguistics.

Wokosin, L. (2002). Components of E-Commerce. *Annual Conference-Society for Technical Communication*, *49*, 172–175.

Wu, J., Li, L., & Xu, L. D. (2014). A randomized pricing decision support system in electronic commerce. *Decision Support Systems*, *58*, 43–52. doi:10.1016/j.dss.2013.01.015

Xie, Y., & Wang, H. (2014). A group cooperative decision support system based on extended contract net. *Group Decision and Negotiation*, *23*(5), 1191–1217. doi:10.1007/s10726-013-9369-z

Xu, K., Liao, S. S., Li, J., & Song, Y. (2011). Mining comparative opinions from customer reviews for Competitive Intelligence. *Decision Support Systems*, *50*(4), 743–754. doi:10.1016/j.dss.2010.08.021

Yan, Q., Wu, S., Wang, L., Wu, P., Chen, H., & Wei, G. (2016). E-WOM from e-commerce websites and social media: Which will consumers adopt? *Electronic Commerce Research and Applications*, *17*, 62–73. doi:10.1016/j.elerap.2016.03.004

Yee, C. G., Shin, W. H., & Rao, G. S. V. R. K. (2007, November). An adaptive intrusion detection and prevention (ID/IP) framework for web services. In *Convergence Information Technology, 2007. International Conference on* (pp. 528-534). IEEE.

Yen, T. F., & Reiter, M. K. (2010, June). Are your hosts trading or plotting? Telling P2P file-sharing and bots apart. In *Distributed Computing Systems (ICDCS), 2010 IEEE 30th International Conference on* (pp. 241-252). IEEE.

Yeoh, W., & Koronios, A. (2010). Critical success factors for business intelligence systems. *Journal of Computer Information Systems*, *50*(3), 23–32.

Yıldız, S., & Kurtuldu, H. S. (2014). Factors affecting electronic service brand equity. In B. Christiansen, S. Yıldız, & E. Yıldız (Eds.), *Transcultural marketing for incremental and radical innovation* (pp. 434–492). Hershey, PA: IGI Global. doi:10.4018/978-1-4666-4749-7.ch022

Yin, L. X. (2008). *The history and evolution of e-commerce*. Retrieved April 6, 2017 form https://ecommerze.wordpress.com/2008/06/12/the-history-and-evoltion-of-e-commerce

Yi, X., Siew, C. K., & Syed, M. R. (2000). Electronic commerce based on software agent. In S. Rahman & M. Raisinghani (Eds.), *Electronic commerce: Opportunity and challenges* (pp. 279–302). Hershey, PA: IGI Global. doi:10.4018/978-1-878289-76-6.ch018

Yoon, H. S., & Occeña, L. G. (2015). Influencing factors of trust in consumer-to-consumer electronic commerce with gender and age. *International Journal of Information Management*, *35*(3), 352–363. doi:10.1016/j.ijinfomgt.2015.02.003

Yuviler-Gavish, N., & Naseraldin, H. (2016). The effect of previous experience when introducing a decision aid in a decision support system for supply chain management. *Cognition Technology and Work*, *18*(2), 439–447. doi:10.1007/s10111-016-0369-z

Yu, Y., Wang, X., Zhong, R. Y., & Huang, G. Q. (2016). E-commerce logistics in supply chain management: Practice perspective. *Procedia CIRP*, *52*, 179–185. doi:10.1016/j.procir.2016.08.002

Zaliva, V. (2008). *Firewall policy modeling, analysis and simulation: a survey*. Source-Forge, Tech. Rep.

Zavadskas, E. K., Mardani, A., Turskis, Z., Jusoh, A., & Nor, K. M. (2016). Development of TOPSIS Method to Solve Complicated Decision-Making Problems—An Overview on Developments from 2000 to 2015. *International Journal of Information Technology & Decision Making*, *15*(03), 645–682. doi:10.1142/S0219622016300019

Zeidanloo, H. R., Shooshtari, M. J. Z., Amoli, P. V., Safari, M., & Zamani, M. (2010, July). A taxonomy of botnet detection techniques. In *Computer Science and Information Technology (ICCSIT), 2010 3rd IEEE International Conference on* (Vol. 2, pp. 158-162). IEEE. doi:10.1109/ICCSIT.2010.5563555

Zerenler, M., & Gözlü, S. (2012). Issues influencing electronic commerce activities of SMEs: A study of the Turkish automotive supplier industry. In *Human resources management: Concepts, methodologies, tools, and applications* (pp. 1035–1055). Hershey, PA: IGI Global. doi:10.4018/978-1-4666-1601-1.ch064

Zhang, F., Zhou, S., Qin, Z., & Liu, J. (2003, August). Honeypot: a supplemented active defense system for network security. In *Parallel and Distributed Computing, Applications and Technologies, 2003. PDCAT'2003. Proceedings of the Fourth International Conference on* (pp. 231-235). IEEE. doi:10.1109/PDCAT.2003.1236295

Zhang, D., Zhu, P., & Ye, Y. (2016). The effects of e-commerce on the demand for commercial real estate. *Cities (London, England)*, *51*, 106–120. doi:10.1016/j.cities.2015.11.012

Zhang, H., Wang, Y., & Zhang, X. (2014). The approaches to contextual transaction trust computation in e-commerce environments. *Security and Communication Networks*, *7*(9), 1331–1351. doi:10.1002/sec.839

Zhang, J., & Pu, P. (2010). Performance evaluation of consumer decision support systems. In M. Hunter (Ed.), *Strategic information systems: Concepts, methodologies, tools, and applications* (pp. 1465–1482). Hershey, PA: IGI Global. doi:10.4018/978-1-60566-677-8.ch094

Zhang, L., & Krintz, C. (2005). The design, implementation, and evaluation of adaptive code unloading for resource-constrained devices. *Journal of ACM Transactions on Architecture and Code Optimization*, *2*(2), 131–164. doi:10.1145/1071604.1071606

Zhao, L. W., & Zhang, W. (2008, October). A study on an integrative structure of business intelligence and ERP system based on multi-agent. In *Wireless Communications, Networking and Mobile Computing, 2008. WiCOM'08. 4th International Conference on* (pp. 1-4). IEEE. doi:10.1109/WiCom.2008.2828

Zhao, J., Lau, R. Y. K., Zhang, W., Zhang, K., Chen, X., & Tang, D. (2016). Extracting and reasoning about implicit behavioral evidences for detecting fraudulent online transactions in e-commerce. *Decision Support Systems*, *86*, 109–121. doi:10.1016/j.dss.2016.04.003

Zhao, L., Tian, P., & Li, X. (2012). Dynamic pricing in the presence of consumer inertia. *Omega*, *40*(2), 137–148. doi:10.1016/j.omega.2011.04.004

About the Contributors

G. Sreedhar is working as a Associate Professor in the Department of Computer Science, Rashtiya Sanskrit Vidyapeetha (Deemed University), Tirupati, India since 2001. G. Sreedhar received his Ph.D in Computer Science and Technology from Sri Krishnadevaraya University, Anantapur, India in the year 2011. He has over 16 years of Experience in Teaching and Research in the field of Computer Science. He published more than 20 research papers related to web engineering in reputed international journals. He published 4 books from reputed international publications and he presented more than 20 research papers in various national and international conferences. He handled research projects in computer science funded by University Grants Commission, Government of India. He is a member in various professional bodies like academic council, board of studies and editorial board member in various international journals in the field of computer science, Information Technology and other related fields. He has proven knowledge in the field of Computer Science and allied research areas.

* * *

Ratish Agarwal received his Bachelor's degree 2001, M. Tech in 2003 and Ph.D. in 2015 from RGPV, Bhopal, India. He is a member of IACSIT. He has published more than 20 papers in reputed International Journals and Conferences. At present, he is working as an Assistant Prof. in Department of Information Technology, UIT-RGPV, Bhopal. His area of Interest includes computer networks and communication.

Namratha Birudaraju is working as an Assistant Professor, Department of Information Technology, Anurag Group of Institutions, Hyderabad.

Lekhika Chettri is currently working as an Assistant Professor, Department of Computer Applications, Sikkim University, Government of India, Gangtok (Since May'2014). Prior to working with Sikkim University, she was working as Associate Network Management at Wipro InfoTech. Her Master's thesis versed on the implementation of "Recursive Visual Cryptography Scheme for Key Exchange". Her research interest includes areas such as Network Security, Mobile and Wireless Network and Internet of Things (IoT). She has published several research papers in various conferences, workshops and International Journals of repute.

Prashant Chettri is currently working as a Financial Consultant, HRDD, Government of Sikkim, Mangan, North Sikkim (Since July'2010). Prior to working with HRDD, Government of Sikkim, he was working as a teacher in Taktse International School (2006-2007). He completed his Bachelor of

Commerce (B.Com) from Pune University in the year 2006 and Master of Computer Applications (MCA) from Sikkim Manipal Institute of Technology in the year 2010. His Master's thesis versed on the implementation of "Proximity analysis uses Arc-GIS" in the field of Remote Sensing and Geographic Information System. Her research interest includes areas such as Remote Sensing and GIS, Database Management System, Big Data and Internet of Things (IoT). He has published several research papers in various conferences, workshops and International Journals of repute.

Sachin Goyal was born in India in March 1979. He has done his BE in Computer Science & Engg from ITM, RGPV, Bhopal, M. Tech in Artificial Intelligence from SATI, RGPV, Bhopal and pursuing PhD in IT from RGPV, Bhopal. His area of Interest includes Digital watermarking, Theoretical Computer science and computer network. He is presently working as a Assistant professor in Department of Information Technology, UIT, Rajiv Gandhi Proudyogiki Vishwavidyalaya, Bhopal.

Kijpokin Kasemsap received his BEng degree in Mechanical Engineering from King Mongkut's University of Technology, Thonburi, his MBA degree from Ramkhamhaeng University, and his DBA degree in Human Resource Management from Suan Sunandha Rajabhat University. Dr. Kasemsap is a Special Lecturer in the Faculty of Management Sciences, Suan Sunandha Rajabhat University, based in Bangkok, Thailand. Dr. Kasemsap is a Member of the International Economics Development and Research Center (IEDRC), the International Foundation for Research and Development (IFRD), and the International Innovative Scientific and Research Organization (IISRO). Dr. Kasemsap also serves on the International Advisory Committee (IAC) for the International Association of Academicians and Researchers (INAAR). Dr. Kasemsap is the sole author of over 250 peer-reviewed international publications and book chapters on business, education, and information technology. Dr. Kasemsap is included in the TOP 100 Professionals–2016 and in the 10th edition of 2000 Outstanding Intellectuals of the 21st Century by the International Biographical Centre, Cambridge, England.

Sridevi M. received her B.Tech degree in Computer Science and Engineering from JNTUH, Hyderabad in 2003, M.Tech in Computer Science and Engineering, JNTUH, Hyderabad, 2010 and pursuing Ph.D in Data Mining from JNTUH, Hyderabad, Telangana. She is an Associate Professor, in the department of Computer Science, Anurag Group of Institutions, Hyderabad, Telangana.

Varaprasad Rao M. obtained Doctorate in CSE. He has 16 years of teaching experience. He has published 16 papers in reputed/peer reviewed international journals. His area of research interest are Algorithms, Security, Mining, Recommended Systems, Cloud and Big Data.

Aruldoss Martin is an Assistant Professor with the Department of Computer Science, Central University of Tamil Nadu, India. He was a Research Scholar of Banking Technology, Pondicherry University, Puducherry, India. He has published research papers in world highly recognised Journals such IEEE transactions on evolutionary computation, Elsevier, Inderscience, Emerald and other top journals. He has received 319 citations indices for his publications. His h-index is 9 and i-10 index is 8. His research work on "Qualitative Bankruptcy data set" has been recognised by Bren School of Information and Computer Science, University of California, USA. Since its launching (Feb', 2014) more than 40000 researchers have visited the qualitative bankruptcy data set. His research interests include business intelligence, data analytics, multi-criteria reporting and information delivery techniques.

Brojo Kishore Mishra is an Associate Professor in the Department of IT and Institutional IQAC Coordinator, C. V. Raman College of Engineering (Autonomous), Bhubaneswar, Odisha, India. He is the Regional Student Coordinator (2016-17), CSI Region – IV, India. Also he is the State Captain for Smart India Hackathon 2017. He has received his Ph. D. (Computer Science) from Berhampur University in 2012 and has supervised more than 08 M. Tech. thesis and currently guiding 05 Ph.D research scholars in the area of Data Mining, Opinion Mining, Soft Computing and Security. Dr. Mishra has published more than 40 research papers in international journals and conference proceedings and 05 invited book chapters. He serves as Guest Editor in Recent Patents on Engineering, IJKDB, IJSE, and IJRSDA special issue journals and an editorial board member of many international journals. He was associated with a CSI funded research project as a Principal Investigator.

Saroja Nanda Mishra is currently working as Professor and Head of the Department of Computer Science, Engg. & Applications at Indira Gandhi Institute of Technology (IGIT), Sarang, Dhenkanal, Odisha, India. He has published more than 70 papers in International Journals and National Journals of repute. His research area focuses on fractal graphics, fractal geometry and internet data analysis. He has more than 25 years of teaching and research experiences. Many students obtained PhD degree and are continuing their PhD and M. Tech research work under his guidance.

Sasmita Mishra is currently working as Associate Professor in the Department of Computer Science, Engg. & Applications at Indira Gandhi Institute of Technology, Sarang, Dhenkanal, Odisha, India. She has published more than 80 papers in International Journals and National Journals of repute. Her research area focuses on multidimensional database, spatial data analysis and fractal & its applications. She has more than 25 years of teaching and research experiences. She is guiding many PhD and MTech scholars for their research work.

Durga Patel was born in India in September 1992. She has done her Diploma in Computer Science from Govt. Women's Polytechnic Collage, Jabilpur, BE in Information Technology from SATI, Vidisha, MTech In Information Technology from Banasthali University, Jaipur. Her area of interest includes Cloud Computing, Software Engineering. She is presently working as Assistant Professor, UIT, Rajiv Gandhi Proudyogiki Vishwavidyalaya, Bhopal.

R. K. Pateriya is an Associate Professor and Head of Computer Sc & Engineering Department at Maulana Azad National Institute of Technology Bhopal. He had 24 years of teaching experience in this institute of national importance. He has authored several papers in journals and conferences of international repute. His research interests are Information security, cloud computing, cyber forensics, information retrieval and image processing. He is a member of IEEE and Life Member of the Computer Society of India. He has supervised several B.Tech., M.Tech., and Ph.D. theses. He is also Reviewer of several reputed journals.

Rebika Rai is currently working as an Assistant Professor, Department of Computer Applications, Sikkim University, Government of India, Gangtok (Since July'2012). Prior to working with Sikkim University, she was working as an Assistant Professor-I in the Department of Computer Science & Engineering, Sikkim Manipal Institute of Technology (August 2006- June 2012). Her Master's thesis versed on the implementation of "A Hybrid framework for Robot Navigation and Path-Planning Using Swarm

Intelligence" and has submitted her Ph.D pre-synopsis on thesis entitled "Improved methodology for classifying different imagery using Swarm computing techniques". Her research interest includes areas such as Robotics, Swarm Intelligence, Database Management System, Image Processing and Internet of Things (IoT). She has published several research papers in various conferences, workshops and International Journals of repute. She is the co-author of a book "Introductory approach to Open-Source Hardware" and author of the chapter "Distributed Transaction Processing" of the book entitled "NoSQL: Database for Storage and Retrieval of data in Cloud" published by CRC Press, Taylor & Francis Group.

A. Prashanth Rao is a Professor in Anurag group of Institutions. Working from the last 6 years.

Bapuji Rao is currently working as Assistant Professor in the Department of Computer Science, Engg. & Applications at Indira Gandhi Institute of Technology, Sarang, Dhenkanal, Odisha, India. He received M.Tech (Computer Science) from Berhampur University, Berhampur, Odisha, India. He is pursuing PhD (CSE) from Biju Patnaik University of Technology (BPUT), Rourkela, Odisha, India. He has published 15 papers in International Conferences which includes IEEE-6, Springer-3, Elsevier-1, and McGraw-Hill-1. Two book chapters titled "Graph Mining and Its Applications in Studying Community Based Graph under the Preview of Social Network" in Product Innovation through Knowledge Management and Social Media Strategies, IGI Global, USA and titled "Some Other Applications in Community Graph under the Preview of Social Graph Using Graph-Mining Techniques" in Web Data Mining and the Development of Knowledge-Based Decision Support Systems, IGI Global, USA. His Current Research area focuses on Graph Mining, Social Network, Data Mining, Multi-Layer Graph, Opinion Mining, and Attributed Graph. He has 18 plus years of teaching and research experiences.

R. Rajeshwara Rao received his B.Tech from Nagarjuna University and M.Tech from JNT University degrees in Computer Science and in 1999 and 2003, respectively. He complete his Ph.D. from JNTUH His research areas of interest are speech processing, Neural Networks, Image processing and Pattern Recognition.

Niteesha Sharma is working at Anurag Group of Institutions, Assistant Professor, Department of IT.

Sonika Shrivastava is Ph.D. Research Scholar in Maulana Azad National Institute of Technology, with 10 years of teaching experience in various engineering colleges. Her M.tech is in Information Security . She has authored many research papers, her area of interest includes information security, cloud computing and data analysis.

Arram Sriram is an Asst. Prof, Working in Anurag Group of Institutions.

Deepak Singh Tomar obtained his B. E., M. Tech. and Ph. D. degrees in Computer Science and Engineering. He is currently Assistant Professor of CSE department at NIT- Bhopal, India. He is co-investigator of Information Security Education Awareness (ISEA) project under Govt. of India. Currently, he is chairman of cyber security center, MANIT, Bhopal. He has more than 21 years of teaching experience. He has guided 30 M Tech and 3 PhD Thesis. Besides this he guided 70 B Tech and 15 MCA projects. He has published more than 54 papers in national & international journals and conferences. He is holding positions in many world renowned professional bodies. His present research interests include web mining and cyber security.

Miranda Lakshmi Travis is working toward the Ph.D. degree in computer science with Bharathiar University, Coimbatore, India. She is an Assistant Professor with the PG and Research Department of Computer Science, St. Joseph's College (Autonomous), Cuddalore, India. She has published research papers in world highly recognised Journals such IEEE transactions on evolutionary computation, Elsevier, Inderscience, Emerald and other top journals. She has received 202 citations indices for his publications. His h-index is 7 and i-10 index is 4. Her research interests include multicriteria decision making, business intelligence, and software engineering.

Rizwan Ur Rahman obtained B.E and M.Tech in Computer Science from Maulana Azad National Institute of Technology (MANIT), Bhopal with Hons grade. His programming experience includes C/C++, C#, SQL, ASP, ASP.NET, VB, VB.NET; Win Forms, Web Forms and Java. He has worked on government projects and R&D department of CRISP. Currently he is an assistant professor in Maulana Azad National Institute of Technology. His area of research includes web programming and web security.

Venkatasamy Prasanna Venkatesan received the B.Sc. degree in physics from Madras University, Chennai, India, in 1986, the M.C.A degree from Pondicherry University, Puducherry, India, in 1990, and the M.Tech. and Ph.D. degrees from Pondicherry University, both in computer science and engineering, in 1995 and 2008, respectively. He is a Professor of Banking Technology with Pondicherry University, Puducherry, India. He has over 25 years of teaching and research experience in the field of computer science and engineering and banking technology. He has developed an architectural reference model for multilingual software. His research interests include Object Oriented Modelling and Design, Banking Technology, Service Oriented Architecture, Smart Banking and business intelligence. He has received 461 citations indices for his publications. His h-index is 12 and i-10 index is 12. He is a technical member of Harvard University, Cambridge, USA. His research work on "Qualitative Bankruptcy data set" has been recognised by University of California, USA.

Index

A

Amazon 95, 116, 118, 124-125, 128, 133-134, 139-140, 145, 150, 159, 183, 226-227, 242, 247, 254-255
Amazon Web Services 133, 139, 145
Analytics 3, 17, 50, 57, 74-76, 82-83, 89-93, 95, 101-106, 125, 139, 178, 242, 248, 279
Android 130-131, 136, 138-139, 141, 145
Author Graph 297

B

Banking Business 16, 23-24, 30
Base-Layer 297
Big Data Analysis 90
BOT 48-59, 61-62, 69-70, 72-74, 76
BOTNET 48-49, 57-60, 62, 68-69, 73-74, 92
Business Intelligence 1, 3-6, 12, 16-19, 83, 90-93, 96, 104, 106, 251-253, 257-258, 270
Business Model 3, 110, 116-119, 155, 178, 226

C

Cloud Computing 74, 83, 90, 93-94, 140, 255
Conflicting Criteria 22
Credit Card Fraud 82-83, 86, 89, 98-100, 106, 114

D

Data Mining 2-3, 6, 19, 50, 68, 73, 83, 86, 91-92, 95, 98, 104, 106, 150, 226, 251, 253, 257-258, 270-271, 277, 279, 281, 294, 298
Decision Making 1, 3, 16-17, 20-21, 52, 86, 88, 92, 101-102, 197, 203, 251-252, 256-258, 270, 277, 294
Decision Support Systems 3, 251-253, 256-257, 270
DoS 48-49, 61, 67, 73

E

e-banking systems 210
E-Commerce 1-3, 7, 9, 12-14, 48-52, 54-55, 76, 82-86, 92, 94-95, 101-103, 105-106, 110-116, 118, 121, 123-125, 128, 130-133, 143, 145, 148-163, 167, 178-184, 186, 193-198, 208-211, 217-219, 221-226, 232-234, 243-245, 248-249, 251-258, 271-273, 289
E-Commerce security 48-49, 76, 179, 186, 218
E-Commerce Software 148, 159-163, 178, 181
E-Commerce tools 251
e-commerce website 2, 12-14, 51, 55, 125, 159, 210, 225, 233
Efficiency 3, 7, 35, 74, 95, 103, 130, 197, 210, 216-217, 225, 238, 252, 256, 258
Electronic Commerce 1, 48, 110, 112-113, 121-123, 135, 148, 178, 181, 193-194, 209-210, 223-224, 226, 245, 249, 251, 253-255, 270, 272
Electronic Messaging 149-150
Electronic Publishing 149-150
Email Graph 298-299, 307, 309-312, 317, 328, 330

H

HTTP Compression 11

I

IBM 111
Identity Theft 82, 101, 106
Internet 2, 6, 8-9, 48, 50-51, 56-57, 72, 82-84, 89, 110, 112, 116-117, 123, 128, 139, 148-150, 158-159, 167, 178-184, 191, 194-195, 197, 199-202, 204, 209-210, 216-221, 225-226, 239-240, 243, 246, 249, 251-253, 255, 257-258, 272, 274, 278

Interoperability 130
IoT 6-7, 258

L

Logistics 7, 253-255, 258, 270
Lou Gerstner 111

M

Machine learning 6, 73-75, 82-83, 86-88, 100, 102, 104, 106, 257
Marketing 3, 18, 48, 92, 101, 111, 113, 121, 124-125, 150, 156, 163, 178-179, 183, 202-203, 210, 223, 242, 253, 258
Money Laundering 83, 91
Multi Criteria Decision Making (MCDM) 17
Multi Criteria Reporting 17, 24, 26, 39, 42

O

Online Marketing 121, 124
Online Shopping 3, 86, 135, 150, 158, 179, 190, 209, 216, 233, 244, 251, 254, 271-272
Open Source Software 178
Opinion Mining 271-277, 292-294
Order Management 159, 178, 242

P

Payment Gateway 49, 178, 216
Payment modes 208, 210
Paypal 150, 216-217, 242
Phishing 48-49, 56, 59, 63-64
Privacy 95, 179, 195, 197, 219-220, 233, 253-254, 258, 270
Product 3, 14, 20, 25, 30-32, 50-52, 54, 86, 93, 101, 104, 112-113, 116-117, 119-122, 125, 131-135, 142-143, 145, 151-152, 157-158, 163, 171-172, 182-183, 197-198, 202-203, 223-225, 227, 233, 239, 242-247, 253-255, 271-276, 278, 281, 294
Protocols 58, 83, 150, 179, 191, 208, 219-220, 254, 257

R

Recommendation System 90, 92

S

Search Engine Optimization 9, 54
Secure Electronic Transaction 191, 220
Secure Hypertext Transfer Protocol (SHTTP) 191, 221
Secure Socket Layer (SSL) 191, 220
Security 9, 26, 31, 33, 42, 48-50, 56-57, 64, 69, 71-76, 83, 86, 90-91, 95, 104-105, 114, 118, 122, 139, 151, 158, 179, 184, 186, 191-192, 195, 199-200, 208, 210-211, 216-222, 225, 233, 253-254, 277
SET 3, 6, 8, 16-17, 54, 58, 66, 72-75, 87, 91, 95, 98, 100, 102-104, 106, 128, 138, 158, 182, 192, 200, 202, 220, 234, 243, 247-248, 257, 272, 275-276, 282, 286, 290, 292-294, 297, 300, 307
Shopping Cart 133, 159, 178, 224, 229, 242-243, 246
Small and Medium Enterprises (SMES) 182
Social Security Fraud 83
SSL 138, 191, 220-221
Strong Communicator 310-313, 316, 318, 320, 330
Sub-Graph 297, 300-302, 310-312
Sub-Layer 299, 321
Supply Chain Management 178, 182
SURBL Database Check 11

T

Telephone Graph 297-299, 319, 321, 326, 328, 330
TOPSIS 16-18, 22-23, 26-28, 30, 33-35, 37-39, 42, 132
Transaction 48-49, 51, 83, 86, 89-90, 92, 95, 98, 100, 102-106, 111-112, 116-117, 119-121, 128, 130, 150-153, 155, 158, 178-179, 182-184, 191-192, 194, 197, 199, 204, 209, 212-221, 224, 235, 254-255, 272
Trust 25, 64, 195, 199, 248, 253-254, 256, 258, 270

U

User Interface 114, 136-137, 178, 223-225, 227, 230, 232-236, 238-240, 245-247, 256
User Preference 16-17, 22, 24, 26, 30, 33-34
User Specific Reporting 17, 21

W

W3C Validation 8
Weak Communicator 297, 310, 312-313, 317-318, 320, 330
Website 1-2, 8-9, 12-14, 51-55, 57, 64, 71, 73, 117, 125, 140, 148, 152, 155, 158, 160, 163, 178, 181-182, 200, 210, 217, 224-225, 229, 233, 235, 240, 246, 253-255

Z

Zwass 111

www.ingramcontent.com/pod-product-compliance
Lightning Source LLC
LaVergne TN
LVHW060303011026
849161LV00011B/2763